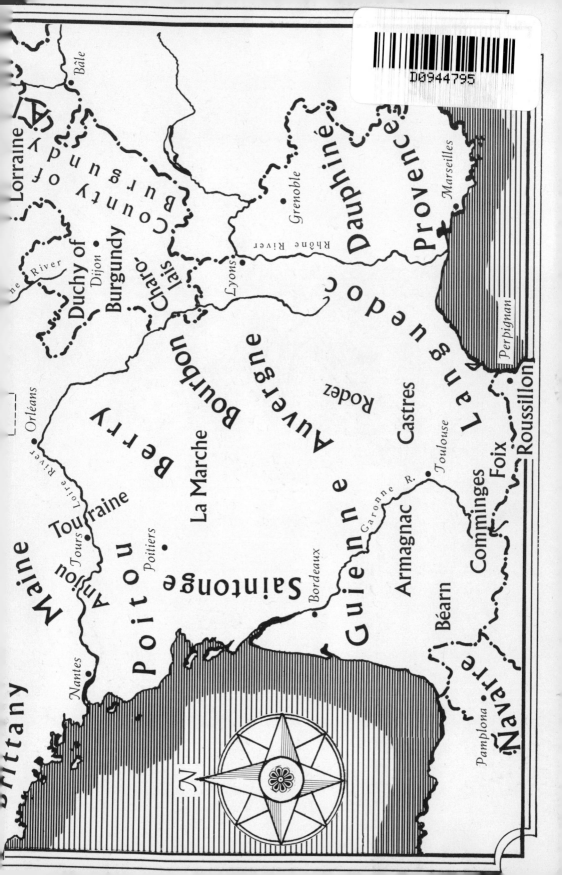

LOUIS XI

BY PAUL MURRAY KENDALL

RICHARD THE THIRD
WARWICK THE KINGMAKER
THE YORKIST AGE
THE ART OF BIOGRAPHY
LOUIS XI

(EDITOR)
RICHARD III: THE GREAT DEBATE

LOUIS XI

". . . the universal spider . . ."

PAUL MURRAY KENDALL

W · W · NORTON & COMPANY · INC ·
NEW YORK

To Edward Hodnett

CONTENTS

ILLUSTRATIONS

MAPS

Picardy and the Somme Towns 110
Grandson and Morat   299

ENDPAPER MAP

France, with fifteenth-century provinces, and the possessions of the Duke of Burgundy from 1467 to 1476 in heavy outline.

PREFACE

I VENTURE to recommend the notes. They are not "scholarly apparatus," which is relegated to a bibliography listing sources and other works most often employed throughout the biography and also indicating, for each section, material of special interest. The notes, in truth, are portions of the narrative which limitation of space forced me to retire from the biography proper but which I could not bear to part with.

A considerable part of this biography is based on Italian diplomatic documents, principally Milanese, most of which have not been published and almost none of which have been used by previous biographers of King Louis. Among these dispatches and instructions I have found some letters of Louis XI not included in the standard edition of his correspondence; and these documents have also filled out blanks in the "Itinerary" of the King published in that same edition. The Milanese diplomatic papers of the period are now in the course of publication: *Dispatches, with Related Documents, of Milanese Ambassadors in France and Burgundy, 1450-83*, edited by Paul Murray Kendall and Vincent Ilardi.

In any attempt to recapture the past, the matter of money values must be mentioned. Most modern historians agree, I believe, that it is impossible to translate with any worthwhile degree of accuracy or even significance, the money of distant times into contemporary terms. For example, a "fix" obtained by determining the relative prices of wheat will go awry when compared with the relative prices of clothing; what wages will buy is often misleading since in the past there were fewer goods competing for household expenditure; changing standards of living, not to mention more or less continuous inflation characteristic of the European economy since the discovery of precious metals in the New World, further distort and obscure the picture.

In the France of Louis XI a standard unit of money (to simplify) was the "livre tournois," i.e., the pound of Tours, equivalent of the "franc," which was divided into twenty "sols" (sous); and the gold coin most often mentioned, the "écu," crown, was worth about a livre and a half, or thirty sols. The yield of the royal domain, estimated at 100,000 livres, produced, then, an annual income of about 66,000 gold crowns. An English pound of the time would buy approximately five French crowns. The average artisan earned perhaps twenty to twenty-five crowns a year; a middling landed squire lived well on an annual income of 125 to 150 crowns; the great nobles enjoyed revenues of from 4,000 or 5,000 crowns to 20,000 a year, and more—but were perpetually hard up because rents and royal pensions came in slowly, coin was scarce, and these princes had enormous sums to pay out in wages to the swarms of household servants and adherents who exemplified their grandeur. Food, ordinary clothing, humble housing were, by our standards, very cheap; but really good cloth, first-rate horses, armor, imported goods, and what, in general, we today call "luxury items" could be very expensive indeed. I can but ruefully ask the reader to be satisfied with the relative values of the world of Louis XI which context will suggest.

Having labored on this biography for some thirteen years, I have accumulated so many debts to scholars, associates, friends, staffs of libraries and archives in the United States, Britain, France, and Italy, that I am forced to compress in one inadequate expression of gratitude my appreciation for invariably helpful and sometimes invaluable counsel. Parts of this book came into being during the tenure of two John Simon Guggenheim fellowships, 1957–58 and 1961–62, of a grant from the American Philosophical Society, 1959, and of a Regents Professorship at Ohio University, 1966– . I am happy to acknowledge a special indebtedness to Vernon Alden, former President of that University, to many colleagues there, and to my publisher and friend, George P. Brockway. Finally, to my wife, Carol, to my daughters, Carol and Gillian, and my son-in-law, Kerry Ahearn, I owe the kind of thanks that can never be expressed for the kind of understanding that can never be deserved.

PAUL MURRAY KENDALL

PROLOGUE

WHEN LOUIS XI BECAME KING on July 22, 1461, the France he inherited was farther removed in time, by a century and a half, from the eighth century of Charlemagne than the world of the 1970's is from Louis's France. Though Charlemagne would have found much to amaze him in the realm of King Louis—great cities, heavy commercial traffic on the roads, magnificent buildings ecclesiastical and lay, the wealth and importance of townsmen, a bewildering complexity of governmental offices, the art of printing and the subtlety of minds and manners—still, Charles the Great would undoubtedly have felt much more at home in the world of Louis XI than would we, though closer to it.

The general acceleration of change, the disappearance first of feudalism and then of monarchy, the power of the middle classes and the expectations of the lower ones, the speed of travel, materialism and technology and science, the confusing paradox of a tightly organized and orderly society shot through with organized violence of a unique intensity and efficiency—such developments and aspects of the present day, commonplaces of our milieu, shut us off from the simpler age of Louis XI.

The men of Louis's time (and of Charlemagne's before them) knew what was right, even though they did not always follow the right; they knew there was a fount of mercy, even though they themselves were not always merciful; they were tolerant of bastardy and unsurprised by sin; they knew that punishment and retribution are the wages of evil, even though the wages are not always paid in this world; they had no doubt of the existence of God and even less of the prevalence of sorcery and the power of Goddess Fortune and her wheel. They had only a primitive sense of people in the mass, of the function and force of institutions, but they probably appreciated more violently than we the marvelous-ab-surd-comic-tragic fabric of human existence. Entertainments were few but deeply savored; boredom was nonexistent or unrecognized; the pre-cariousness of life was acknowledged; suffering and poverty were wide-spread but not disgraceful. Man's inhumanity to man did not insult prog-ress but merely exemplified, and proved, the Expulsion from the Gar-den. Belief and custom and resignation gentled the rough career of man.

Human behavior in the times of Louis XI was stretched between ex-tremes of pleasure and pain, enjoyment and misery, rage and repent-ance, violence and passivity. Men of the fifteenth century liked life highly spiced and hot in the heart. Wealth and rank flaunted their splendor; poverty showed its sores in the marketplace; punishment dis-played on the scaffold its horrors, supposedly edifying; whores wore the badge of their shame at their shoulders; lords were extravagantly lordly. Everything was pitched high.

Desperate crimes were committed for a pittance or a slight, and ter-rible retribution was exacted. Afflicted by original sin, recalcitrant and brutish, man could be subdued only by fierce punishments, which fur-thermore served as example to his brethren. In the nineteenth century lurid historical novels and dramas depicted gothic tortures devised by Louis XI: this is fable. King Louis used the methods of his time in the spirit of his time, unremarkably; and indeed he showed more humanity than many another ruler, of his time and after.

Great lords, tried and condemned to death for *lèse-majesté*, treach-ery to the crown, were conducted, the same day as their sentencing, to a scaffold erected in town square or market and suitably adorned in black hangings. After final words with a priest, perhaps a pious statement to the throngs who might be gazing in pity or yelling execrations, and after forgiving the executioner and uttering a last prayer, the lord knelt and laid his neck upon the block. The axe came down; the executioner sloshed the bleeding head in a pail of water and held it by the hair to show the crowd. Lesser traitors, however, underwent the full ordeal: hanged, they were quickly cut down alive, disemboweled and castrated by the executioner's knife, and hewed into four pieces—"drawn and quartered"—the bleeding quarters then impaled in public places. And there was boiling in oil for "coiners," i.e., counterfeiters, and sometimes for those found guilty of sexual deviance, a loathed crime; and there was burning at the stake for witches and heretics; and there was hanging or drowning in the river for routine offenses. Criminals spared the death penalty might have their eyes put out or lose an ear or the nose or have a hand chopped off, or be whipped up and down a city so that they never walked again. In King Louis's prisons men were incarcerated in wooden or metal cages, their legs loaded with irons, though not infrequently they were caged only at night, when chance of escape was greatest. Men were sometimes "put to the question," tortured in order to extract confessions, by being burned with hot irons or stretched in agony upon the rack. Such methods of imprisonment and torture were known before Louis's day, and after, and in other lands besides France.

On the other side of the picture, Louis was much more accessible than an American president, was seen by a larger proportion of the people than ever today see the chiefs of their states, took a greater interest —sometimes admonitory, sometimes benevolent—in his individual subjects, and knew by name a higher percentage of them (townsmen and gentry) than the modern prime minister or president or secretary of the party has time or inclination to do.

If it was then more painful to be alive, it was less demanding—and richer of reward simply because few rewards were expected. Louis XI, like Charlemagne—and unlike modern governments—exercised the irrationalities of mercy, practiced a forgiveness of betrayal and treachery unknown to our impersonal justice. King Louis was a man and could therefore hope to benefit by gratitude and would himself one day need to be forgiven. What you, a traitor, got from Louis might, it is true, depend on Louis's mood; what you now get in court is twenty years, regardless.

We who have waged death and destruction far more efficiently, horribly, and indiscriminately than any other human generation, who ride in seatbelted fear upon blood-spattered highways, who at nightfall flee from the lurking terrors of our metropolises—we somehow take it for granted, such is the conditioning of "progress" and the comfort of the familiar, that the horrors of another time are worse than ours. We are used to the devil on our own backs; the devil on our ancestors' backs looms scary through the murk of the past.

When Louis XI ascended the throne in the middle of the fifteenth century the dominant political-social system of Europe, feudalism, had been in existence, in varying forms, for more than half a millennium. Pressures from the outside as much as conditions within had prompted its growth. In the eighth, ninth, and tenth centuries, the precarious societies of the West, evolving from the Germanic kingdoms that had been established in the ruins of the Roman empire, were assailed on all sides by fierce invaders—the Saracens from the southeast, Magyars from the east, Vikings from the north. Against domestic turbulence and foreign onslaught central authority proved to be powerless. Means of defense, social organization, economic existence were reduced to the local level, could be dealt with only by the local strong man. By the end of the tenth century the invaders had been beaten off, or absorbed, as in the case of the Vikings, the Northmen, who secured the French province of Normandy. And feudalism, the institution that had enabled Europe to survive, the force of localism, had produced a network of lords, higher and lower, who were bound together by a closely defined system of obligation called vassalage, based on land tenure.

The great lord held his land from the King; his duchy or county formed a part of a kingdom. In return, he was obligated to the King for certain services: military duty, usually forty days a year, for which he would supply such number of knights and squires as his lands supported; and money payments on special occasions like the marriage of the King's daughter and other feudal "incidents." Otherwise, the Duke or Count ruled as master of his dominions—coined money, collected tariffs, administered the High Justice, the Middle, and the Low, regulated his own laws and customs, provided ecclesiastical benefices for his bastards, was counseled by his council, sent and received ambassadors. The lords and knights who held land from him, his vassals, did him military and other services, and since they were closer to him than the King was to him, he was generally able to exact a good deal more feudal obedience than he in turn paid.

To the people of any region the central authority, the King, remained remote indeed—an awesome figure, for he had been anointed, at his crowning in Rheims Cathedral, with the chrism, the holy oil, but one quite unrelated to a man's daily life and concerns. Authority meant the Duke or the Count. Government meant the Duke's vassal, the local lord. Justice meant the court of the manor, the fief, on which and by which a man lived.

Just as the majesty of God, the love for mankind of the Virgin, the miracles of the saints were explained in images of stone and stained glass, so too the greatness of high feudal personalities was constantly exemplified—in rituals of behavior like hunting, parading the countryside, giving audience; in splendor of dress and ornamentation; in households swarming with attendants and adherents. The meanings of life were emblemized rather than analyzed. Power must be clad in the ostentation proper to it. The size of a lord's retinue was not determined by functions to be performed but by the degree of greatness to be expressed. Punishment, reward, ceremony—all harbored, or once had harbored, symbolic values.

No aspect of life was more impregnated with symbolism than religion, which permeated all life. The Church was everywhere. It owned perhaps a third of the land and its wealth could not be counted. The army of its servants—monks and nuns, friars, priests, bishops, a host of officials and attendants in minor orders—included something like a quarter or a fifth of the population. Some fifty religious festivals and holidays marked the passing of the seasons; church bells were constantly ringing in the towns, for burials and requiems and weddings and thanksgivings and rituals of intercessions and celebrations of saints' days, as well as for a diversity of regular services; churchmen and their flock paraded through cities, a forest of burning tapers and crosses and sacred banners, to welcome a great lord or to beg God's aid against plague. Archbishops were temporal as well as spiritual lords, part of the feudal hierarchy. High ecclesiastics managed much of the King's business.

The Knight, to fight and rule, and the Priest, to pray and study— such were the dominant figures of this picturesque medieval society. Europe enjoyed a unity which transcended the boundaries of states and languages and loyalties: it was Christendom, headed by the Pope and the Emperor. Its learned tongue was Latin; its polite tongue, French; its faith, Catholic. Knight and Priest belonged to Christendom before they belonged to anything else.

This society was supported by a faceless mass of serfs and peasants, who counted for nothing except to supply their masters with the surplus of agricultural products and with the furnishings which made possible the splendid picturesqueness. If the reader finds little about the rural worker and the city laborer in this biography, the reason is that almost nothing is recorded about them: their lot was monotonous; their existence simple and narrow; the interest they aroused in chroniclers, nil. They toiled from sunup till sundown, lived on a level, most of them, of mere subsistence, and remained almost invisible upon the social landscape.

Slow though medieval change was, by our standards, the fifteenth century of Louis XI reveals a large transformation from the High Middle Ages of the twelfth and thirteenth; and France exhibited a different development from that of the Holy Roman Empire—the heir of Charlemagne's domain—and of Italy and of England.

A long wasting struggle between Pope and Emperor for the dominance of Christendom had resulted in the exhaustion of both. As a result, the Emperor now exerted small control over his Empire, a feudal
jigsaw of "free" cities, archbishoprics, margravates, duchies, counties.
The Empire was already on its way to becoming a ramshackle anach-
ronism that would endure until Napoleon put it out of its misery. In
Italy, the impotence of Pope and Emperor had permitted independent
states to spring into being, republics like Venice and Florence, the Kingdom of Naples, tyrannies like that of the Visconti at Milan, the Gonzaga
at Mantua—political entities that possessed no authority, in the feudal
sense, save what they could assert by their wit and resources. In Italy
the feudal nobility had, for the most part, joined forces with the towns,
been absorbed into the merchant oligarchies, so that feudalism, as exemplified in the sprawling states beyond the Alps, had well-nigh ceased to
exist in the peninsula, save for the Kingdom of Naples. The Italians hu-
mored the Emperor and listened to the Pope, and then did as they
pleased, bickering vigorously among themselves.

The conquest of England in 1066 by the Bastard William, Duke of
Normandy, brought that island within the framework of Continental feudalism, but with differences and modifications. Perhaps the chief difference was that William's successors rarely allowed great vassals to hold
large territorial entities and thus to exercise quasi-regal prerogatives,
but scattered their manors and lordships through many counties.° An
Earl of Lancaster never became the all-but-independent potentate that a
Count of Armagnac or a Duke of Brittany could boast himself to be. In
England, furthermore, partly because of local conditions, partly because
of the Black Death and the conquests in France of the fourteenth century, the feudal system had, by the fifteenth century, all but disintegrated. Serfdom, except in the remoter parts, was almost unknown. The
society ruled by King Edward IV (1461–83) was seignorial, not feudal.
In place of land tenure and vassalage as the political nexus, there developed a system of association between stronger and weaker known at the
time as "livery and maintenance," since called "bastard feudalism." In
return for protection and favors, a member of the gentry signed indentures with a lord by which he promised various services, including mili-

---

° The Percies and Nevilles in the North, the Mortimers in the West, form something of an exception; but these "Marcher," i.e., border, families needed, and expended,
their territorial resources in order to defend their regions against Scottish and Welsh
incursions.

tary service. The great lords, in turn, led their contingents of troops to France, not in response to feudal obligations, but in accordance with indentures negotiated with the King that specified the pay and condition of service for them and their men.

The King of England exercised greater control over his lords than did the King of France, until the accession of Louis XI; but the King of England, in turn, was much more limited in his authority. That King's High Court of Parliament, once an assemblage of barons, now Lords and Commons, was established as the source of law and the master of taxation. Strong Kings like Edward IV and Henry VII dominated Parliament, but the very act of domination acknowledged the limitation of their prerogative. True, the English lords disposed of three Kings within 150 years—Edward II (1307–27), Richard II (1377–99), and, in Louis XI's time as we shall see, feeble Henry VI (1422–61). The barons of England, however, did not remove these monarchs as a feudal reaction against royal power; it was rather that a particular group of barons imposed their candidate in order to enjoy, as his backers, the benefits of that power. Louis XI's friend the famous kingmaking Earl of Warwick earned his name, not in an endeavor to weaken monarchy, but in order to wield its prerogative himself. Out of the Wars of the Roses—in which Warwick played a central role in the triumph of the House of York over the House of Lancaster—will emerge the new monarchy, the beginnings of modern nationalism, of the Yorkist kings Edward IV and Richard III, which the Tudor dynasty founded by Henry VII will consolidate. Queen Elizabeth I is the great-granddaughter of Edward IV.

In the fifteenth century this emergence from the feudal past, this same movement toward a strong central authority and the development of nationalism—tearing asunder the internationalism of Christendom—can be found in the Iberian Peninsula. There Ferdinand and Isabella will unite the kingdoms of Aragon and Castile and drive out the Moors to create the beginnings of modern Spain. This force is brilliantly dramatized in the struggle of the Dukes of Burgundy, culminating in the career of Louis XI's mighty enemy Charles the Rash, to forge a state from their disparate dominions.

Louis XI, by his temperament and by his youthful experience of life, was sensitively tuned to these currents of his time; and in his extraordinary capacities as a ruler he possessed the means to undertake the transformation of France into a national monarchy. How he finally succeeded is the story to be herein unfolded. He wrought solidly: the state which he left to his successors would reach its apogee, essentially unchanged, in the reign of the Sun King, Louis XIV (1643–1715) and endure until the French Revolution.

The Kingdom of France Louis XI inherited, unlike its ancient adversary the Kingdom of England, was still haunted by the feudal past. The Hundred Years' War with England, ending in the expulsion of the English from France (except for Calais) eight years before Louis came to the throne, had served to accelerate the decay of the feudal system but not the pretensions of the princes associated with it. As the result of depopulation caused by war and plague and the falling back of farmlands into waste, manpower was in such demand that great numbers of serfs easily secured their freedom and peasant tenant-proprietors held their acreages on advantageous terms. For the same reasons many nobles had become impoverished, their income fixed and their costs rising. The great lords, though also feeling the pinch, resumed the independent airs and ways of their ancestors, profiting from the revival of localism and the weakness of the crown produced by the English invasions.

Furthermore, the royal domain, the territory directly ruled by the King, hardly equaled in extent the holdings of the great feudatories, the "magnates," as they were called. Essentially, the King possessed a wide strip of northern France—Normandy, Île de France, and Champagne; Touraine, Poitou, and Saintonge in central France; and the great southern provinces of Guienne, Languedoc, and Dauphiné. This royal domain was everywhere outflanked and circumscribed: in the north by the Duke of Burgundy's province of Picardy, Counties of Artois and Flanders, and to the east by his Duchy of Burgundy; to the west by the Duke of Brittany's peninsula and the provinces of Maine and Anjou held by the House of Anjou; in the center by the lands of the Dukes of Berry and Bourbon and the Count of La Marche; and in the south by the territories of the Counts of Armagnac and Foix and Comminges. Most of these magnates cherished additional claims and resources: the southern lords enjoyed a long tradition of all-but-independence; Brittany, thrusting into the Channel, could always secure help from England; the Duke of Burgundy possessed great imperial territories—Holland and Zeeland and Brabant and Luxembourg, and the County of Burgundy (Franche-Comté) among others; and the House of Anjou, in the same way, held the imperial Duchy of Lorraine and the imperial County of Provence. The royal domain was thus restricted in its coasts on the Channel, the Atlantic, and the Mediterranean, and hemmed in to the east. The amount of royal prerogative Louis XI, at the opening of his reign, was able to exert in holdings of his feudatories—rights of taxation, exercise of justice—varied greatly, depending on the authority that over the centuries his royal ancestors had managed to win in each particular fief. The Duke of Brittany, for example, claiming virtual autonomy, yielded to the crown only "homage by courtesy"; whereas the Count of Maine, surrounded by royal domain, exercised far fewer privileges and powers.

One ally that Louis XI would use, in his struggle to reduce these proud princes to royal subjects, Louis's ancestors had not been able to command. Into the medieval world of Knight and Priest there had thrust a third power, towns and townsmen, the developing money power of Europe, the power to whom the future would belong. The cluster of huts within walls that huddled about a bishop's mill or a noble's river ford or a royal fortress or harbor had become, by the time of Louis XI, a town displaying handsome edifices, ceremonials of wealth, municipal pride in its government and privileges. Paris, the Queen City of the West— harboring the Louvre, the Hôtel de St. Pol and other royal residences, the chief offices of the monarchy, the most famous university in Europe and the most sophisticated satirists in the world ("There's no clever wisecracking outside of Paris," declared François Villon, the marvelous scoundrel-poet of the age)—numbered perhaps 200,000 people, at least four times as many as London or Venice. Rouen, the second city of the realm, and Lyons, the third, were municipalities such as the earlier Middle Ages had never known.

Towns had, generally, in their development become the natural allies of the monarchy, in which they found a protector able to defend them against the encroachments of the local lord or ecclesiastic and eager to make use of their strength in its own struggle with the feudality. Towns, like their sovereign, were anti-feudal, and they were intensely jealous of the privileges they had won. They were rigorously governed, however: if once there had existed something like equality in infant municipalities, it had long since disappeared. The "freedom" on which they prided themselves meant freedom from outside interference, not freedom within their walls in any democratic sense. Town life was controlled, in minute detail, by a merchant-manufacturing oligarchy— the "superiors," or "the Clothing," as they were called in England because of the furred scarlet gowns they wore. In northern and much of central France, though not in the South, a hierarchy of craft and trading guilds, as in many other European regions, determined the economic, political, and social activity of the municipality. The ruling powers of the wealthiest guilds—usually merchants, goldsmiths, victualers, drapers, grocers, and a few other guilds depending on the particular locality

—were also the ruling powers of the religious fraternities and the ruling powers of the city.

Like their rural counterparts, the laboring classes in the city earned no more than a bare existence, were crowded into hovels, held no rights of citizenship. The average artisans, the small shopholders—tailors or shoemakers with few or no workmen—lived above or behind their shops in dark, crowded quarters; they were at the bottom of the guild hierarchy and of the citizenry. The guild masters, however, the great merchants, the bankers, enjoyed spacious dwellings of wood and stone displaying expanses of glass and rich wall hangings; lords were happy to occupy such lodgings—often more comfortable than their castles—when they visited a city. In fifteenth-century France, the King took care to communicate to his "good towns" his plans and policies. Municipal delegations usually received a hearty welcome at court. Louis XI called them "my friends," treated them to flatteringly informal sessions of conversation.

Small chance that a laborer's son or a peasant's could rise in this world; yet social mobility was accelerating. The Church had long provided a ladder by which a poor boy, gifted with brains and vigor, might climb to high rank; and now, in this era of Louis XI, such boys no longer had to enter holy orders, though many continued to do so. Finding the means to study at a university, they could hope for a career in the law or in government service or as the counselor of a lord; or, if their talents were military, they could achieve fortune as an officer in the royal standing army, created by King Louis's father, Charles VII. Ambitious nobles, leaving their damp, drafty castles, sought to win wealth in trade or business; while wealthy townsmen had little difficulty securing ennoblement from Louis XI, which enabled them to purchase fiefs and found a landed family.

Atop this socio-political pyramid of gentry and townsmen and ecclesiastics and the feudal magnates sat the King of France. Except for the privileges his predecessors had granted or been unable to abolish—charters to towns, jurisdictional concessions to lords—and for limitations dictated by his own prudence or the recalcitrance of subjects, the royal prerogative remained virtually unlimited. By his decrees, the Ordonnances, the King made war and peace, regulated trade, altered taxation, created governmental organizations, policed the realm. He was aided by a royal council, which was staffed with career men, lawyers and financial experts, learned bishops, the Chancellor and the Treasurer, and great lords. The latter were regarded as the King's "natural" advisers and friends: they were, most of them, his kin, being descended from younger sons and from daughters of previous kings, and thus these "Princes of the Blood" were regarded as sharing that special aptitude for rule which God confers upon monarchs. In this belief Louis XI, as we shall see, took very little stock. A privy, or inner, council, consisting of the intimates the King most trusted, initiated the important policies and the secret decisions.

The chief organs of government, the Parlement and the Chamber of Accounts—the latter corresponding roughly to the English Exchequer —were permanently situated in Paris. The Parlement of Paris, the supreme court of the land, heard appeals from regional parlements and from jurisdictions of the princes, and, in general, decided cases, civil and criminal, that affected the crown. The institution nearest to the English Parliament, the Three Estates—Nobles, Clergy, and the Bourgeois—was summoned but rarely by the King and did what it was bidden, which was usually to approve some special financial exaction or provide the sovereign with a vote of confidence in his policy. There were likewise provincial estates, which met more or less regularly, under the eye of royal officials, according to regional custom.

The King drew his revenue from three main sources: the yield of his domain lands and customs dues and feudal "incidents"; the *taille,* a tax upon income and possessions; and the *aides,* or sales taxes, which varied from province to province. In Paris there were almost seventy "farms," or imposts, on the production, distribution, and sale of all manner of goods and victuals. In earlier days the King had been expected to "live on his own," i.e., on the income of the domain and feudal perquisites; and in the fifteenth century it was still thought that he should do so, though the increase in governmental functions now rendered such a hope illusory. The *aides,* once voted by provincial estates as extraordinary subsidies to meet the King's emergencies, like countering invasion, had long been regularly collected. In most of the great fiefs of the magnates, the King's officers gathered in royal taxes and the profits of the royal monopoly on salt, the *gabelle.* The Treasurer of France managed the funds of the domain; Generals of Finances, one for each province, and their deputies, the *élus,* supervised the *aides* and the *taille,* which were much more lucrative than the yield of the domain; "Treasurers for the War" saw to the payment and supply of the army.

The King's household, with the Queen's and subsidiary households of royal offspring, was numbered in the hundreds. His Majesty was served by chamberlains and ushers and grooms, by equerries of the kitchen and equerries of the stables, by physicians and astrologers and his confessor and his almoner, by huntsmen and falconers and castellans, by his smart Scots guard, varying from fifty to one hundred archers, by his household gentlemen, a force of mounted men of arms, by a Keeper of the Purse and a Keeper of the Wardrobe, by trumpeters and heralds, by his Carver and his Cupbearer, by cooks and wine purveyors. The household, or a portion of it, was often on the move. It was easier for the King to travel from royal manor to manor in order to consume their produce than it was to transport the produce to the King; castles had periodically to be cleaned, their latrine pits emptied and the chambers "sweetened" with herbs; location of game, the changing hunting seasons, trouble in a remote province, vows to be fulfilled by prayer at a saint's shrine, also prompted the peregrinations of royalty. When the King with his guard and his household took to the road in a long train of horsemen and baggage wagons, he brought along furnishings, wall hangings, his wine cellar, coffers of books, his dogs, his bathtub. Sometimes he brought his Queen.

Whatever the King did was important; what manner of ruler he was, all important. Today we choose to hope that our history is essentially determined by mass movements, trends of thought, economic imperatives, social illuminations, the people participating in its destiny. In the fifteenth century, a savage or weak or foolish King could be an international disaster; a great King brightened the lives of millions. Justice was the King's justice; war or peace was the King's cause; and the King's justice, the King's cause, was the King.

So appears in the fifteenth century the broad realm of France, the arena in which will take place the strange, complex, sometimes grotesque and sometimes amusing, often hazardous and always supercharged life struggle of a King, Louis XI, which it is the object of this biography to recreate.

This is the story of a man who could make up his mind—and other people's minds. He needed to keep all his wits about him, to bend time to his purposes, to be twice as shrewd and thrice as diligent as his fellows, and, all the while, to hide his sense of comedy behind gestures of conformity; for, though he was a prince of the feodality of France, neither his early rearing nor the grain of his mind prepared him to fit into princely attitudes and accept feudal assumptions. As a powerless youth he rebelled against the world, and as a powerful king he stirred the world to rebellion against him. Louis XI issued more edicts than any

French monarch since Charlemagne, and he created an elaborate web of international relations. Books and monographs deal only piecemeal with this mass of political activity; the records of Louis's diplomacy have, most of them, not been published or even adequately explored. Institutional historians, furthermore, have neglected him: he was a creator rather than an organizer, partly because he saw the art of government as a function of his own mind and partly because, struggling with a recalcitrant cast of players, he had barely the time to act out his new drama and no time at all to write down the script.

His life and character, however, are elaborately documented. Indeed, there exists perhaps a larger body of intimate information about Louis XI than about any other human being who lived up to his time—which speaks for the increased efficiency of record keeping in the fifteenth century as well as for the force of Louis's collision with his contemporaries.[*] Ten volumes of letters, the ruins of a huge edifice, preserve the accent of his personality, witty and impatient and simple and imperious by turns. The prefaces to his decrees disclose in more official guise the movement of his ideas. Equally revealing in a different way, the portrait of Louis XI by Philippe de Commynes recreates the King as seen by an intimate adviser. For almost a decade Commynes served Louis's enemy Charles, Duke of Burgundy, and then one night (August 7–8, 1472) stole from Charles's camp to become the counselor and the biographer of the King of France. Finally, foreign envoys at the court of France, writing their day-to-day accounts, take us behind the façade of kingship into the workroom of the King. Louis spent all his life at full stretch, concentrated his hours on the multitudinous enterprises of a daring, ambitious ruler; and in portraying the drama as well as recording the substance of these labors, a succession of Milanese ambassadors—sending home something like seven hundred dispatches over two decades—made themselves the journalists of Louis's court. Whereas chronicles and government documents preserve decisions, the dispatches often reveal the perplexed process of decision making, the electric storm of Louis's mind in action. They capture the opacity of the future as it confronted the King, and register the fog of rumor, the surcharged emotional atmosphere, the pressure of ambiguous loyalties and explosive personalities through which Louis steered his course. If these

[*] In Louis's own age, the life and character of Pope Pius II (Aeneas Sylvius Piccolomini), documented by hundreds of letters, speeches, literary works, and by an autobiography that has few superiors in world literature, are preserved in comparable fullness.

sharp-eyed Italian observers were inevitably subject to prejudices and viewed the King through the aperture of their own special preoccupations, they were all men trained in the new statecraft of Italy, and, aware of the importance of precise information, they packed their reports not only with the substance of what the King said but often with his very words and gestures.

This mass of evidence exhibits a man of extraordinary powers wrapped in a personality so agile and various as to encompass the range of a dozen ordinary temperaments. His enemies called him, not without cause, "the universal spider"—a metaphor illuminated by the wiliest of them, John II of Aragon, when he gave warning that the King of France was "the inevitable conqueror in all negotiations." The Milanese ambassadors, who considered themselves more sophisticated than the men beyond the mountains, found him "the subtlest man alive." To Commynes, his sagacity, his knowledge of men and things, his quenchless vitality, made him the nonpareil of rulers.

But less than a generation after his death, in a time of princely reaction against his reign, Louis was described as drinking infants' blood in his last illness, poisoning his brother, delighting in the screams of tortured victims. Sir Walter Scott, seizing on these tales, stamped on the world's imagination (in *Quentin Durward*) the image of a sinister gargoyle lit by the lurid flames of the declining Middle Ages. Throughout the nineteenth and twentieth centuries, while Louis's French biographers kept up a cross fire of more or less scholarly argument, this popular image has persisted. In recent times Louis has found a notable defender, Pierre Champion (*Louis XI*, 2 vols., 1927); but Champion's biography is marred by omissions and distortions, and his deliberately impressionistic approach to his subject blurs the bold landscape of Louis's character.

To move from the legends to the life is to discover the sheer exuberance of the man, the ability to charm, the bottomless curiosity, the capacity for loyalty. Scott's "gothick" figure bears small resemblance to the King who was usually ready to forgive past treason in the hope of winning future loyalty and who—as an enemy admitted—"always wishes to safeguard his men and would prefer by far to lose ten thousand crowns than the least archer of his company." Devious Louis could be, and yet smoke screens of dissimulation concealed an astonishing plainness. In his instructions for an effigy for his tomb in the Church of Our Lady at Cléry, he ordered himself to be shown in ordinary hunter's costume, horn slung behind his shoulder, hat in hand, booted and spurred, sword at his side. Whatever else might be artful and calculated, the simplicity that men found so disconcerting but that gave such persuasiveness to his negotiations was wrought from the essential stuff of his nature. In appearance, nobody was more shaken by perils, more nervously timorous, and yet nobody courted dangers and took risks more zealously than he —he fed on what he appeared to dread. His temperament expressed itself in a repertory of outbursts, extravagant gestures, and superflux of speech. He was a connoisseur of irony, an indomitable actor, a comedian on a grand scale. Indeed, his career can be seen as a long comic poem, of which he is both author and protagonist. Like many other great comedians, he thoroughly appreciated his art; and like many other great comedians, he sometimes betrayed himself by his cleverness. But he always took his mission more seriously than he took himself.

He brought off one of the greatest political coups that the world has ever seen; yet he first had to survive crushing failure and he had to overcome serious disabilities of temperament. He sometimes fell prey to suspicions that obscured his vision. He chose to work by persuasion; yet he was ugly, thick-tongued, and careless of dignity. He often talked too much, and indiscreetly. He spun a web of policy that covered all Europe, but insisted on "doing everything out of his own head." He could not conceal from the feudal nobles he needed to conciliate his scorn of their archaic attitudes; and he intensified their alarms by flouting in dress and manner and thought the conventions of an age committed to convention. Restless to the marrow, he picked away at his own achievement; and when his sense of comedy got the better of him, he indulged in rascally exploits that endangered the profound labors of his life.

Yet, if he sometimes betrayed himself, he never betrayed the people of France. He possessed the rare talent of being able to learn from experience and thus to profit from failure; and his will was strong enough to command his weaknesses. In his life can be descried, repeatedly, variations on one of the grandest patterns of human existence: withdrawal and return. A human organism, emerging from the shelter of untested hopes and dreams, collides with a worldly reality for which it is unprepared. Cruelly wounded in spirit, an object of mockery or a victim of indifference, the organism shrinks into withdrawal. In this darkness it recharges its confidence by achieving a durable faith, a truer sense of realities outside the self, and thus rearmed comes forth to measure its strength against the world. This pattern has been vividly demonstrated by Thomas Carlyle in *Sartor Resartus* and by Wordsworth in *The Prelude;* it is exemplified in individuals as diverse as St. Augustine, King

Alfred of England, V. I. Lenin. For Louis XI it was the reiterated rhythm of his existence—failure and withdrawal and the rebound from failure. Indeed he seemed rather to embrace than endure the pattern. Adversity but strengthened his belief that the game is worth the candle without dulling his sense that the style is sometimes worth the game; and in his withdrawals he was too busy learning his lesson to spend energy on blaming his fate. Prosperity tended to soften the edge of his wariness, but he was never so dangerous as when he was in danger. What Louis said of Francesco Sforza, a fellow political adventurer, applies equally to himself: "He was never better than when the water was up to his neck."

It was in a time of endings not yet guessed at and beginnings only obscurely perceived that Louis XI tried his dreams and exerted his talents. The enigmatic, violent fifteenth century, heaving in the throes of change between the broken patterns of medieval life and the yet unshaped stuff of the nationalist Europe to come, threw up a blaze of flamboyant princes and astute adventurers. He came to the throne of a feudal realm racked for a century by invasions, civil strife, popular upheavals, princely ineptitude, plague. He handed on to his successors a national monarchy. To the twentieth century, perhaps his most startling accomplishment is that, as a means of destroying the mortal enemy of his crown, he invented cold war.* Well worth knowing as one of the founders of modern Europe, he lays claim to our imagination because he represents a supercharged moment in the time stream of human vitality. The labors of his life create an allegory of his character, even as his character provides the commentary upon his labors. Thus I have had to deal at some length with the fashioning of his achievement; but I have pursued the ruler in order to try to surprise the man.

* It may perhaps be disputed that he was the *first* to invent it; but, if not the originator of the idea—and who would that be?—he brought it to a stage of development not hitherto known.

Book I

THE DAUPHIN

THE ALIEN

1. *The Child of Shame*

The being that would one day become Louis XI, Most Christian King of France, was born about three o'clock in the afternoon of July 3, 1423, in the episcopal palace of Bourges hard by the great cathedral of St. Étienne. He had come into the world at an inopportune moment for a royal heir: the fortunes of his father, of his house, and of his country had almost struck bottom. His grandfather—if really his grandfather—had been a mad king, Charles VI, first kicked into a corner by lords greedy for his power and then made to resign his daughter and his kingdom to an alien conqueror, Henry V of England. Louis's father was known, to some, as Charles VII, King of France. His numerous enemies derisively called him the "King of Bourges." His whorish mother had proclaimed him a bastard; he had not been crowned at Rheims; and far from being the master of the scattering of princes over whom he still reigned, he was not even master of himself. A puppet on strings, he was manipulated by a clique of brigands masquerading as royal councilors.

Two hours after Louis's birth, docile twenty-one-year-old Charles was dutifully indicting an announcement of this joyous news to be sent to a slender list of towns and lords and foreign powers. In the bedchamber of Charles's wife, equally docile Marie of Anjou, the baby who would turn out to be one of the least docile offspring on record was surrounded by a pomp of tapestries, hung to honor the queen's lying-in. They had been borrowed: the magnificent hangings of the House of Valois, one of the greatest collections in Europe, had been appropriated, like so much else, by the English. These tapestries on loan bore the arms of Charles of Orléans, a name that rang the sad changes of the times.

The poet-Duke, captured eight years before at the battle of Agincourt (1415), was still a prisoner in England.

The day after his birth, Louis was borne into the Cathedral of St. Étienne to be christened. One godfather was the Chancellor of France, so-called; the other was a fourteen-year-old boy, John, Duke of Alençon, who was to become the brave companion-in-arms of Joan of Arc and then, half-mad, would plunge into endless treacheries. Guillaume of Champeaux, Duke-Bishop of Laon, conducted the service, a smooth-tongued rascal notorious for his "shameful and dishonest life." The infant was held at the font by Catherine de l'Isle-Bouchard, Countess of Tonnère, a woman as remarkable for her ruthless greed as for her beauty. He was christened Louis—"in memory of St. Louis," it was said.

Some days later, Paris blazed with bonfires; there was dancing in the streets; and the clergy paraded with banners and candles—not, however, in honor of the royal heir, Louis, but to celebrate a crushing victory of the English over Charles's ragged forces at Cravant. Not long after, an Anglo-Burgundian war party threatened Bourges itself. By the time Louis was two years old, rival factions within his father's court as well as English victories so threatened his existence that he was removed from his parents and hidden behind the grim walls of the castle of Loches.

This fortress in Touraine, where Louis remained until he was ten, is surrounded by a pleasant countryside, undulating and heavily forested, and was then rich in game. The castle itself is another matter. On a great upthrust of rock, a clutter of village huts at its base, rises a vast, dark, damp pile of masonry—a donjon seemingly as impenetrable as a cliff, surrounded by massive towered walls. It was not built for living but for fighting, a place where men could resist and endure burrowed into stone, with only a snatch of sky in the arrow slits. This eleventh-century stronghold, constructed by a spectacularly savage Count of Anjou, Foulque Nerra, swallowed up little Louis of Valois. Afterward, when he became King, he would use the castle to incarcerate prisoners. So perhaps he saw himself as a child, prisoner of France's misery and his father's feebleness.

Nothing is known of the first years he passed, in a penurious household, behind the blank battlements of Loches. In 1429, in the first good days the House of Valois had known for almost a century, little Louis suddenly found himself in the presence of Joan of Arc. She came to Loches in the glow of her first great victory over the English at Orléans. Louis can be seen for an instant, through a letter written by one of the young knights thronging Loches to join Joan's banner. After André de Laval had paid his respects to the Maid—she gave him a cup of wine and said smiling, "We will drink again, in Paris!"—he "went to visit My Lord the Dauphin at the castle. He is a most attractive and gracious lord, very well formed, agile, and clever indeed, of an age of about seven years."

He was, in fact, a month short of six when his life was touched by the girl in armor who had the flame of saints upon her tongue. Come to manhood, he will not mention her in his Ordonnances, his extant letters, his conversations reported by foreign envoys; but the fire of faith which illumined France and stirred the wonder of all Europe can hardly have failed to light the mind of an unusually impressionable child. Perhaps the impact of the Maid can be traced in his exhaustless confidence in the destiny of his House and in his fervent worship of the Virgin, especially the Virgin of Cléry, to whom, he will announce in one of his Ordonnances, "we have been devoted since our earliest youth." The church of Cléry, seven miles southwest of Orléans, harbored (and still harbors) a wooden image of Our Lady, dark with age, which a peasant had found in a field—a relic perhaps of primitive Christianity in Gaul. It appears that Joan of Arc had worshiped at the smashed altar of this shrine, sacked by the English during the siege of Orléans; it may even be that Louis had accompanied her on the pilgrimage.*

In Joan's great year, 1429, Louis began his formal schooling under the direction of Jean Majoris, Master of Arts, Canon of Rheims, to whom he afterward showed himself grateful. Bent over books in one of the gloomy chambers of Loches, the boy studied Latin grammar, rhetoric, sacred and profane history, mathematics, music—conventional subjects but attacked by a far from conventional mind and taught by a decidedly unconventional method.

The famous humanist and theologian Jean Gerson, Chancellor of the University of Paris, had drawn up the program of instruction, which was addressed to the preceptor as well as the pupil. Gerson counseled Majoris to gain the good will of the Dauphin's servants so that they might help him maintain an atmosphere favorable to learning, especially by eschewing that bane of princely character, flattery. Schoolwork was to be made as attractive as possible; to this end, Majoris should use books written in the French language (i.e., rather than conduct instruction in

---

* He would have had the opportunity to see her again during the interval, September, 1429–March, 1430—between the unsuccessful attempt on Paris and her capture at Compiègne—when she was with the court on the Loire.

Latin). He should likewise nurture the Dauphin's particular interests and sense of initiative, and spur the boy's efforts by praise rather than coercion. When correction became necessary, reprimands were to be preferred to corporal punishment. Finally, as moral guidance for the future ruler of France, Gerson recommended that Majoris emphasize the virtues of clemency and humility, reminding his pupil that all men, kings and beggars, are equal in the sight of God.

But books and the battlements of Loches did not surround all Louis's life. In the afternoon, taking horse, he would clatter down the rocky slope through the village and into the countryside. He learned to draw the bow and, as he grew older, to manage sword and lance and handle armor. Jousting, however, the chief princely entertainment of the time, his unprincely rearing gave him no occasion to enjoy, and as he grew in years he came to despise it: jousting meant lords prancing in the lists while the English pillaged the realm.

In these early years isolated from courts and princes, he grew to feel at home among simple people. He got used to plain talk and cheap clothes and ordinary fare and unpretentious quarters. In a time flecked with disaster and miracle, he became imbued too with the religious attitude of the folk about him. The Virgin stood near the awful Throne, but she had been a mother; she understood the needs of children; and of his own parents Louis saw little. Under the tutelage of Jean Majoris, he read the lives of the great saints and heard more homely tales from his companions. Once human beings like himself, saints would respond to reasonable dealing; in return for suitable rewards—after all, they could not take care of everybody—they did useful things like curing colic and making journeys safe and forwarding affairs.

Louis's affections, untouched by parental love, found an outlet in the world of animals, dogs and birds and more exotic creatures—mark of a lonely childhood and mark also, no doubt, of an arcane adjustment of self to world. Perhaps in the uncomplicated devotion of dogs, in the mysterious grace of a leopard, he found relief from the shames of his father and from his own disturbing sense of alienation.

In 1433, when he had reached the age of ten, a revolution at his father's court brought his release from the dark stronghold of Loches. He went to live with his mother and sisters in the airy castle of Amboise, perched high above the Loire River a few miles from the city of Tours. Nobody, except perhaps Jean Majoris, was yet aware of the formidable power which nature and schooling had prepared in the somnolent backwater of Loches. That schooling reached farther than books and exercise. What Louis discovered about his father's character, his father's government, in the years before his removal to Amboise, would shape his conduct as Dauphin and his policy as King. He had learned how it was that a once mighty realm had fallen so low and why he, son of the House of Capet, found himself the heir of misery and shame.

The medieval Kingdom of France, the acknowledged heart of Christendom, had stretched from the Flemish towns of Ghent and Bruges to the waters of the Mediterranean, prodigally dowered with rivers and harbors, with fertile plains, vine-covered uplands, forest and mountain and valley. By the time of little Louis's namesake, St. Louis (Louis IX), middle of the thirteenth century, the dukes and counts of the French feodality, once virtually independent rulers, had come to recognize, at least nominally, the sovereignty of the House of Capet. Serfs and peasants, traders at the fairs of Champagne, artisans in the workshops of Bruges and Rouen were providing, for the consumption of bishop and lord, a material plenty never before achieved in the West. The populous and prospering Kingdom of France gave the law to the chivalry and learning of all Europe. "The King of France," wrote the English historian Matthew Paris, "is the king of earthly kings."

Before the middle of the fourteenth century, this realm was hideously transformed—battered, within a generation, into a bloody anarchy.

Edward III, claiming the Crown of France,* thrust into France with an army the like of which the Continent had never seen. The English battle line, composed of dismounted men of arms flanked by archers wielding the long-bow, had perfected its tactics in the Scots wars. Charging upon these iron ranks, the beplumed hosts of France, cumbersome and disciplineless, dreaming of knightly exploits and fat ransoms, were shattered like glass under a hammer. In 1346 at Crécy, Edward III destroyed the chivalry of Philip VI. Ten years later, at Poitiers, Edward's son the Black Prince destroyed the host of Philip's successor, King John, and haled John a captive back to London. English armies, unopposed, raided the length and breadth of France, tearing bloody weals of fire and pillage. Mercenary companies, savage hordes of adventurers drawn from half the countries of Europe, swept from province to province, raping, murdering, destroying what they could not consume or carry away. Maddened by the extravagant folly of their princes, French

* Through his mother, Isabel, daughter of Philip the Fair.

peasants and townsmen rose in revolt, to cut the throats and burn the castles of their masters, while the proletariat of Paris, driving the King from his capital, established a regime of mob rule. Then, in the midst of anarchy, the plague struck. Spreading from south to north in the years 1347–50, the Black Death carried off something between a third and a half of the suffering population of France.

There came, at last, a break in thronging horrors. The House of Valois produced an able ruler, Charles V, who assumed the tattered crown when his father, King John, died in London in 1364. Under his sage guidance the English were slowly driven from most of the realm; the mercenary companies were slowly reduced to impotence. But it was only a lull. In 1392 wise King Charles's frivolous successor, Charles VI, went mad. A fierce political struggle developed between the King's uncle, the Duke of Burgundy, and the King's younger brother, Louis, Duke of Orléans, each bent upon appropriating the resources and controlling the government of the realm. When, in 1407, the new Duke of Burgundy, John the Fearless, engineered the assassination of the Duke of Orléans, France fell into the pit of civil strife. First the Burgundians then the Armagnacs * seized Paris and mad Charles VI, massacring their enemies in the streets.

Meanwhile, an ambitious and iron-willed prince had ascended the English throne. Unlike his great-grandfather Edward III, who was content to seize provinces and booty, Henry V (1413–22) bent all the energies of his kingdom to the winning of the French Crown, now enfeebled by faction and treachery. In 1415, promised aid by the Duke of Burgundy, he hewed his way into Normandy, then crushed the Armagnac feodality of France at Agincourt. Two years later he returned, determined on a methodical campaign of conquest.

It is at this moment that the dolorous tale of France ceased to be history for young Louis and suddenly became the living matrix of his own existence. His father-to-be, Charles, a younger son of Charles VI, became Dauphin upon the demise of two elder brothers. While Henry V's war machine chewed through Normandy, fifteen-year-old Charles found himself nominally heading the Armagnac government in Paris. In the early morning of May 29, 1418, the Parisian mob threw open the gates to the Burgundians. Armagnacs were butchered by scores—"their bodies lying about the streets like heaps of swine." The bold Provost of

* The partisans of Orléans were so called because the son of the assassinated Duke, Charles of Orléans, had married the daughter of the Count of Armagnac, Constable of France.

Paris, Tanneguy du Chastel, wrapped the Dauphin in a sheet and, with the aid of a handful of royal officers, managed to spirit him out of the city.

A year and a half later, Duke John of Burgundy met the Dauphin Charles and his ministers on the bridge at Montereau in an attempt at reconciliation. There were angry words; men drew swords; in a sudden scuffle the Duke of Burgundy was hacked to death. The Dauphin's men insisted that the Duke had provoked the affray; but there is some reason to believe, as the Duke's vengeful heir Philip believed, that the crime had been plotted in advance. Holding the mad King, Charles VI, Philip dictated an alliance with Henry V.* By the Treaty of Troyes (1420) the Dauphin Charles was declared to be illegitimate and disinherited. Henry, taking Charles's sister to wife, became Regent and heir of France.

The men who controlled young Charles could not halt the Anglo-Burgundian armies; soon only the region south of the Loire (excluding English Guienne)—little more than half of France—could be counted as the Dauphin's territory. The Duke of Brittany joined the Duke of Burgundy in the English alliance; other lords declared themselves neutral; the great feudal magnates of the South, like the Counts of Foix and Armagnac, acted as independent potentates. Only one seaport on the Atlantic remained to the Dauphin, La Rochelle. In the early autumn of 1422 Charles was taken there by his ministers in their endless quest for money and friends. As notables of the region were packed close about the Dauphin in the great hall of the episcopal palace, the wooden floor gave way. The two lords standing nearest him were crushed to death in the cellar beneath. When Charles was extricated from the tangle of planks and bodies, he was found to have suffered no more than bruises. But his mind was scored by terror. Henceforth, the Dauphin, shrinking from towns and crowds, holed himself up in isolated castles and wept and prayed in little chambers. He could not sleep on a plank floor or cross a wooden bridge nor endure to dine with a strange face in the room.

Not many days after the accident at La Rochelle, the Dauphin learned that Charles VI had died on October 22 (1422), two months after Henry V had descended into the tomb. By order of his council, Charles was clad in the red robe of kingship when he went to Mass next day. A banner was raised in the chapel. A few officers of arms cried,

---

* A century later, pointing out to King Francis I a crack in the skull of the murdered Duke, a monk remarked, "Sire, this is the hole through which the English passed into France."

"Vive le Roy!" In his "chamber of retreat," Charles implored heaven's aid and wept abundantly. Now that he could call himself King, there were signs throughout France of a rallying to his cause. During the winter, the citizens of the town of Tournai, faithful to the House of Valois, tried to keep up their courage by making "Dolphins" in the snow.* But Charles had nothing to offer the realm, and the men who governed him found good pickings in the ruins of a cause. All they did was to move Charles and his pregnant young wife, Marie of Anjou, into Bourges; for the flooding tide of English victories was now threatening the province of Berry.

Soon after, Louis made his appearance in this precarious world.

While the heir of France grew into boyhood, seeing little of his parents and nothing of a royal court, the fortunes of French France and the spirits of his father continued to sink. Charles VII looked the feeble monarch that he was. He had an undersized, slight figure and a sallow complexion. His face drooped from two small round eyes down a long nose and slack cheeks. The short green tunics he favored revealed the knock knees and meager shanks that caused him to walk with an unsteady gait. He was by nature timid and affable and passive, lacking not in shrewdness or wit but in the will to put them to use. The terrible fright he had experienced at La Rochelle had driven his disabilities deep into the bone; the military disaster at Verneuil—a defeat bloodier than Agincourt—which occurred the year after Louis's birth, sank the "King of Bourges" into abject apathy. His subjects heard nothing of him, the great lords ignored him, his court held him in an ignominious tutelage. When war threatened their own territories, the Count of Foix, the Duke of Brittany, the Count of Armagnac hastily made separate truces. Villages and fields were laid waste by bands of marauding troops. Men fled from the vicious no-man's-land of the open country to huddle miserably within town walls. Only the earth within the vicinity of fortified places was cultivated. The very beasts were so infected with the terror of the times that when a watcher's horn sounded the danger signal they instantly galloped for safety. "So went the realm from worse to worse," a Parisian noted in his journal, "and it could better be called a desert than France." English spearheads were pushing into the province of Maine, aiming for the Loire.

In 1425 the palace revolution which led to Louis's being hidden at

* The name of the creature and the title of the heir of France were cheerfully confused by men of the time.

Loches brought to power a frog-faced, dour brother of the Duke of Brittany, who, as Constable of France, took over the conduct of the war. Deprived of the clique who had "governed" him since he was spirited out of Paris in 1418, King Charles supinely put himself in the hands of one grasping favorite after another. Finally the Constable turned Charles and his government over to Georges de La Trémoille, a hulking lord as avaricious as the others but with political talents.[1]* Soon La Trémoille and the Constable, heedless of the English peril, were locked in a civil war fought among the fortresses of Poitou and Touraine. At the age of four, little Louis was snatched away from the castle of Loches, when La Trémoille feared an attack by his rival. Efforts had already been made to find the boy a marriage which would bolster the tottering House of France. He was offered to the Duke of Savoy, the King of Castile, the King of Scotland; but none of these rulers cared to match with so stained and precarious a cause. As the summer of 1428 gave way to autumn, the columns of the English were headed for the city of Orléans on the great bend of the Loire, the key to the south of France. In desperation King Charles's subjects demanded that he summon the Three Estates. Meeting in September at Chinon, a gloomy and fearful assembly voted a tax of 500,000 francs, but much of it was never collected and much of what was collected never reached the ragged bands of soldiers. The Estates begged the King to unite his lords and princes; they begged lords and princes to serve their sovereign "in this extremity." But La Trémoille held the King and few were willing to fight for La Trémoille.

On October 12 the English laid siege to Orléans.

Charles sold the last of his jewels; he had to have sleeves patched into his old doublet; he could not get credit from a cordwainer for a pair of new shoes; at one moment he had only four crowns in his purse. In February (1429) an attack on an English convoy of food for the besiegers of Orléans was beaten off with heavy losses. Most of the King's lords abandoned him. What money and troops were available, La Trémoille and the Constable appropriated for their private war. Wild plans were made for Charles to take refuge somewhere in the South or even in Scotland. Sunk in passive misery, the little King tried by tears and prayers to appease the divine wrath. Only God, he knew, could help him now.

Suddenly, in early March of 1429, the King's prayers were answered.

---

* Numbers refer to a section of notes beginning on page 391.

A sturdy girl with dark straight hair like a helmet, wearing a black doublet, hose, and a short gown of gray-black, rode into Chinon to tell Charles that he was the true heir of the Lilies and must be crowned at Rheims and that God had sent her to boot out the English. Then followed the blazing successes that set the kingdom afire—the relief of Orléans, English defeats at Jargeau and Patay, and the triumphant expedition to Rheims, where on July 17 the King of Bourges was crowned Charles VII of France. La Trémoille, who saw his power mortally threatened, had resisted the Maid every step of the way, desperately maintaining his ascendancy over the vacillating King. Joan's cry was now "On to Paris!" La Trémoille, infecting Charles with fears, managed to ruin the attempt on the capital. The following spring (1430), Joan of Arc, renouncing the do-nothing court on the Loire, rode northward to the fighting, was captured at Compiègne by a Burgundian lord.

She might then have been ransomed. Even after she was sold to the English she could perhaps have been saved; for the French, with the famous Talbot, greatest of English commanders, their prisoner, held a potent bargaining counter. On May 31, 1431, Joan the Maid was burned at the stake in the marketplace of Rouen. King Charles, dutifully listening to La Trémoille, had done nothing, said nothing, made no sign.

Charles continued to hide himself in country castles and La Trémoille pursued his depredations and the war with the English went badly as usual. But the realm had not, like the court, forgotten Joan of Arc: the flames at Rouen lighted a fire of national resistance. Weak and stained though it was, the monarchy offered the only hope of recovery; and young lords, a new generation, joined the King's entourage, determined that things must go better. La Trémoille—a fungus that could batten only on a sick organism—was doomed. He was surprised in his bedchamber by a band of armed men (June, 1433), forced to disgorge some of his ill-gotten treasure, and then permitted to retire to his lands.

The humiliated King was made to summon the Three Estates, and "new governors were delivered to him." This time, there were men of consequence among them.

Such was the picture of France and such the image of a father printed on the mind of the strong-willed, talented boy, who, following the overthrow of La Trémoille, went to live with his mother in the white-towered castle of Amboise on the Loire.

Louis's fortunes and those of the realm rose together. In the Queen's household he found himself treated like the Prince of France. The neighboring city of Tours, in 1434, gave him a splendid reception. And now he was happily accepted as a prospective son-in-law by the King of Scots, a mark of the changing times. In September of 1435, that great ally of the English the Duke of Burgundy signed a peace pact with Charles VII (Treaty of Arras) which cost the province of Picardy and other humiliating concessions but forcast the eventual end of the enemy occupation. Six months later, the Constable of France entered Paris.

In the summer of 1436, thirteen-year-old Louis Dauphin formally made his entrance on the stage of history, as a bridegroom. He was far from handsome, but he had features not quickly forgotten—masterful eyes set deep; long sardonic nose; mobile heavy mouth, and cocked jaw. It was an agile face, an actor's face, to charm men or daunt them.

On St. John's Day (June 24), with the Queen presiding over a courtly assemblage in the great hall of the castle of Tours, Louis met for the first time the girl he was to marry on the morrow, eleven-year-old Margaret of Scotland. She was a snowdrop out of the North, delicate and pretty and wayward, daughter of the poet-King, James I. Louis dutifully embraced her; then, taking her hand, he led her to the Queen. That good lady, quickly dispensing with state, brought the boy and girl into her own chambers so that they might divert themselves for a little before supper.

The next afternoon, when Louis, in a robe of blue-gray velvet ornamented with gold, arrived at the chapel of the castle, he found Margaret waiting for him in a long mantle and wearing a crown in her hair. Chroniclers report that the French and Scots attendants were all dressed in their best and that Charles VII and his Queen walked behind the young couple into the chapel. Not long after, all but a handful of the Scots were sent back to their homes, grumbling at the meanness of the King of France. Since bride and groom were too young to consummate the marriage, Margaret entered the household of the Queen to polish her courtly education.

What Louis thought of his bride or she of him is not on record. It may well be that he had made up his mind to dislike her long before she set sail from Scotland. She was his father's choice.

The King for his part had provided no jousts for Louis's wedding, though the marriage of a viscount's son would have been considered a mean affair without the breaking of many lances. Charles had not even bothered to journey the few miles down the Loire from the castle of Amboise in order to dignify the arrival of his son's bride. On the day of the wedding he rode into Tours only a few minutes before noon. He paid his respects to the Scots princess, but it does not appear that he went to see the Dauphin. When he entered the chapel for the wedding service, he was still dressed in gray riding habit and leggings and did not trouble to remove his spurs.

Thus did a father pointedly snub a son to whom he had previously devoted, as far as the records show, almost no attention at all. Neither normal parental concern nor a king's duty to cherish the welfare and dignity of his heir had been able to penetrate the passivity of Charles VII. It had seemingly been penetrated by something else, however: by something like envy of a boldness and vigor and assurance that he himself did not possess. It appears likely that this small jealousy had been given an edge by the prickly presence of a son hitherto kept comfortably at a distance. Indifference, occasionally barbed, was sufficient engine, King Charles evidently concluded, to chasten a willful boy. Louis for his part had apparently not concealed what he thought of his father's dolorous kingship, what he felt about his father's weakness of will. He was old enough and intelligent enough to have judged for himself the King's history, but too young to dissimulate a scorn which paternal affection might have softened and too energized against submissiveness to accept the role of deference which convention prescribed. Between King and Dauphin there already stretched a morass of mistrust and ill-feeling.

2. The Unfilial Son

WITHIN THREE YEARS Louis, at the age of sixteen, was conspiring with malcontent princes to take over the reins of government.

After his marriage he had assumed his place as Dauphin in the royal court. His formal schooling finished, he was given a household of his own; his tutor, Jean Majoris, became his confessor; and he received a yearly allowance, notable only for its modesty. He and his establishment were governed by the most austerely pious lord of the day, Bernard, Count of Pardiac, younger brother of the turbulent Count of Armagnac. No peasant more humbly put himself on his knees at divine worship than Pardiac; at mealtimes he sat in the midst of his servants reading from the Bible. If young Louis was not inspired to imitate this Puritan rigor, he always evinced great respect for the character of his governor, and would one day raise Pardiac's son to a dukedom.

The court of Charles VII was assuming a kingly air. The overthrow of La Trémoille had established in power the House of Anjou in the person of the Queen's younger brother, Charles, Count of Maine, a man of brilliant address if commonplace mind; and now that the monarchy was beginning to rise in the world, other great lords, too, sought places in the royal council and competed for the royal favor.

In the autumn of 1436 Louis accompanied the King on an expedition to extract money from the loyal southern provinces. He listened to delegations complaining of extortion by royal officials and of disorders perpetrated by feuding nobles. He beheld lands ruined by the freebooting companies, now call *Écorcheurs*, Flayers. He heard the men who ruled the King promise much and do almost nothing. Ignored by his father and itching to have a hand in affairs, he made some connections among lords excluded from power, like the Duke of Bourbon, who were hoping to overthrow the regime of the Count of Maine. As a sop to public opinion, clamoring for action against the English, the royal govern-

ment in the summer of 1437 mounted a small campaign to dislodge enemy garrisons along the upper Seine. Fourteen-year-old Louis was
permitted "to make his first arms." In July he led an assault upon Châ-
teau-London that quickly won the town. Then he returned to court to
claim a man's prerogative: he consummated his marriage with the little
Scots princess, Margaret.

It was apparently the Dauphin's small triumph which stirred King
Charles to a burst of martial activity he had never displayed before and
would never display again. He enacted a captain's role in the main operation of the summer, the siege and capture of the important town of
Montereau. On November 12 (1437), the King and the Dauphin, clad in
full armor except for helmets, made a state entry into Paris. The Parisians were hoping that the King would lighten taxes, procure food for
the hungry populace, clear the region of English marauders. Instead,
sinking once again into a complacent lethargy, he slipped away from the
gaunt city for the pleasant valley of the Loire—"without having done
any good, and it seemed that he had come only to see the town."

Early the following year, Charles of Maine promised an even more
ambitious summer campaign, but the plan fell to nothing through the
nerveless fingers of the King. The autumn harvest had failed; famine and
epidemics were killing thousands. Driven to make a gesture of action,
Charles's councilors decided upon another expedition into Languedoc,
which was again suffering a plague of Écorcheurs.[1] In the late spring of
1439, the King and the Dauphin arrived at Puy for the opening of the
Estates of Languedoc. Considering the harshness of the times, the assembly voted a handsome sum, 100,000 livres; but, made desperate by
their miseries, they pressed on the King's government a host of demands
for action against Écorcheurs and piratical nobles. King Charles smiled
and expressed his sympathy and promised that all would be put right. He
himself, unfortunately, had to go north on urgent business, but here was
his son and heir, the Dauphin Louis. He would make the Dauphin his
lieutenant-general in Languedoc with full power to restore order.
Charles provided his son with neither money nor soldiers—he had an
excellent sense of humor.

Louis, however, had at last received a mission on which he could
test his powers. On May 25 he made his state entry into Toulouse. He
was only fifteen years old, and his governor, the Count of Pardiac,
headed a council of able officers; but the actions of the Dauphin's government are unmistakably stamped with the talents of the Dauphin himself. Bands of Écorcheurs had established a virtual blockade of Toulouse

and held towns and castles throughout the countryside. Without troops, Louis could only apply the force of money to move them on. He commanded where he could and flattered where he had to. Aware that little could be done in this region without the help of that all-but-independent prince the Count of Foix, the Dauphin sent him a fetching invitation; and when the Count condescended to come to Toulouse, Louis so lapped him in fêtes and demonstrations of affectionate admiration that Foix was soon providing genuine support. Patiently, urgently, the Dauphin explained the need for funds to municipal councils and provincial estates, and grants began to come in. Finally able to buy off the Écorcheurs, he kept a sharp eye on their companies to see that they held to their bargain and quitted the province. Then he turned his persuasions on the bellicose Counts of Armagnac and Comminges, who had been waging private war for a decade, and brought them to agree, at least on paper, to arbitration. Meanwhile, he investigated all sorts of complaints on the spot, listening to appeals, striving to correct abuses, punishing brigandage, checking the extortions of petty nobles.

Word of the Dauphin's success was not long in reaching the royal court. By early summer, King Charles was sending peremptory orders for his son to come home. In bitterness and frustration, Louis complied. King and court, he found, were enjoying their usual comfortable idleness and showed no interest in his return. Louis asked for the province of Dauphiné but was refused. He asked for the money to set up a proper household for himself and his wife; but Margaret of Scotland had become the pet of the King and Queen, and her husband got nothing. Shrewd beyond his years though Louis was, he would never understand that his father meant, consciously or unconsciously, to revenge himself for his weakness by thwarting a son who was anything but weak. The Dauphin could not fail to recognize within himself the stirring of uncommon powers, and his temperament pushed him to take up the challenge of a world he had not been taught to love. If France had begun to recover—too slowly—under a King who let himself be managed by others, what might not be accomplished by that King's heir who had energy and will to manage for himself, and for the realm?

Not long after the Dauphin returned from the South, he was conspiring with the Duke of Bourbon.

Charles of Bourbon was one of the half-dozen greatest princes of France. His domains hardly touched by the war, he possessed money and patronage with which to maintain what amounted to a private military force, including several famous companies of Écorcheurs. As flamboyant as he was powerful, he was called by a contemporary "The best athlete in France and the most persuasive man of his time . . . an Absalom, another Trojan Paris." Bourbon was joined in his discontents by Louis's unstable godfather, John, Duke of Alençon, who, his lands ravaged or occupied by the English, resented the indifference of the court to his fallen fortune.

Bourbon and Alençon had been parading demands for better government and a vigorous prosecution of the war, but the plot they unfolded to Louis had more personal aims. Charles, Count of Maine, and other royal favorites were to be sent packing; and the King would be placed under the "tutelage" of the Dauphin. Doubtless Louis perceived the conclusion which the conspirators left unsaid—the Dauphin, in turn, would be under their tutelage. Perhaps *he* left something unsaid, too. At sixteen, he would be optimistic enough to believe that he could transform the figurehead envisaged by the plotters into the real head of government envisaged by himself.

By February of 1440 all plans were laid. The King was to be trapped between forces raised by Alençon and the Dauphin in Poitou and the armed bands of the Duke of Bourbon in Berry and Touraine. Louis and his godfather, raising the standard of revolt in Alençon's town of Niort, set about trying to win the support of lords and municipalities. But, when news finally came from Touraine, it was bad. An attempt to capture the King had failed; a royal force had routed Bourbon's bands. It was not long before Charles VII and his troops appeared at the gates of Niort. Louis and the Duke of Alençon galloped eastward to join the Duke of Bourbon in his strongholds of Auvergne and the Bourbonnais. But the great lords had now shied off; townsmen showed little enthusiasm for the rebel cause; and the King's army was beginning to ravage Bourbon's territories.

Alençon and Bourbon sent word that they were willing to negotiate, and a parley was held at Clermont. The rebel Dukes haughtily proclaimed their good intentions for the realm and indicated a conditional willingness to resume their obedience to the King. They then put forward some requests of the Dauphin. He asked for the province of Dauphiné, rightfully his, and for the government of Languedoc and Île de France. He demanded that Margaret the Dauphine join her husband's household with a proper allowance for her expenses. He declared that he would never consent to betray his followers, but, on the other hand, wanted nothing more than to be in the King's good grace. The royal negotiators answered that, when the Dauphin had dutifully asked pardon, his father would make suitable provision for him and his wife and would treat all rebels in a way that would content him. Though the King's proclamations had emphasized that the Dauphin were merely a tool in the hands of the rebel Dukes, this rejoinder suggests that the King himself did not take his son so lightly.

In the next negotiating session, the Dukes expressed their willingness to yield to the royal demands. However, they added uncomfortably, the Dauphin insisted on proposing new terms: if the King was set on violent measures, let him cease inflicting misery on his poor subjects and send his army against the English, a campaign which the Dauphin and the Dauphin's friends would happily support. The rebels would then submit themselves for judgment to the Three Estates, provided that if others (i.e., the Count of Maine and his adherents) were found guilty, these others would be appropriately punished. Louis crowned his impudence by adding that, if the King preferred, he was willing to accept the arbitrament of the Duke of Burgundy—a procedure that would subject Charles VII to the judgment of his most dangerous vassal!

Suddenly the Dukes of Bourbon and Alençon slipped away from Clermont: ready to deal with the King, they had found themselves unable to deal with the Dauphin. It was the puppet who had the stiff back.

The royal army resumed its advance. The flickering Duke of Alençon soon made a separate peace with his sovereign; other rebels rapidly submitted. The Duke of Bourbon recognized a lost cause when he saw one and he knew the rules of the princely game: a decent show of humility would be sufficient to purchase the King's pardon.

Finally Bourbon talked young Louis round, but only by stretching the truth: it was understood, he said, that all the Dauphin's followers were to be received into grace. Louis, not altogether reassured, kept three of his chief lords with him when he and the Duke of Bourbon made their way to the royal headquarters at Cusset. Just before they reached the town, a messenger halted the Dauphin's lords with the announcement that the King had not offered them pardons and would not see them.

Louis realized that he had been duped. Furious, he turned on the Duke of Bourbon: "So, fine friend, you could not bring yourself to tell me how this business was managed, that the King in fact has not pardoned the members of my household!" * Then he swore a great oath that he would not submit under such conditions.

---

* Throughout this biography, all quoted dialogue is drawn, unaltered (except for translation) from reliable contemporary sources. Variations which the reader may hereafter sense in the tone of Louis's talk are probably due to the inevitable differences in mind among those who recorded it. Even the most conscientious reporter does not reproduce what was said, but what he hears.

The Duke of Bourbon replied easily, "My lord, all will come well. You cannot go back now, for the King's advance guard has cut the road."

Nevertheless, it took all the persuasive power of Louis's entourage to make the headstrong youth realize that further defiance was useless.

The Dauphin found his perpetually unruffled father waiting for him alone in a chamber.

"Louis," said the King, after the Dauphin and the Duke of Bourbon had knelt thrice in the prescribed style, "you are welcome. You have been away for a long time. Tomorrow we will speak to you."

After his son had stalked from the room, Charles treated Bourbon to a long, calm lecture on his misdeeds.

Next day, following Mass, the Dauphin and the Duke appeared before the King and his council. They humbly begged him to extend his pardon to the three lords whom he had sent away. Charles refused, but said that those lords might return to their homes.

At this, Louis's temper got the better of him: "In that case, my lord, I shall have to reconsider my position."

King Charles was never milder: "Louis, the gates are open and if they are not wide enough I will have a length of wall beaten down so that you can go where it seems best to you. If you wish to depart, then do so; for with God's pleasure we will find some of our blood who will help us better to maintain our honor and sovereignty than you have so far done."

Without waiting for an answer, Charles then addressed himself to the Duke of Bourbon, who readily swore an oath to obey and serve the King forever.

Louis stayed. In a few days he saw all the officers of his household dismissed except his confessor and his cook; and in his father's entourage he was paraded through towns that, for supporting his rebellion, had been crushed into submission by the royal army.

The people of France, having recently heard of civil upheavals in the capital of Bohemia, called this rebellion the *Praguerie*. It had found little support in the realm, but some of those who bore the brunt of fighting against the English bitterly noted the contrast between Charles VII's haste to bring his son to heel and his slackness in prosecuting the war. The Bishop of Beauvais wrote boldly to the King that his court was beset by vicious flatterers. "What comfort has this [the defeat of the Praguerie] been to us, your poor sheep, who are here on the frontier? This is not the way we want you to awake—pursuing my very redoubted lord your son and others of your blood who did what they did, it seems, from a desire to have a voice in your councils."

The men about the King persuaded Charles to grant his son partial control of Dauphiné and give him additional lands to increase his income.

3. The Prince of Cutthroats

LOUIS'S FIRST collision with the world harshly demonstrated the vulnerability of ambition untempered by experience and humiliatingly mocked the youthful image of self as irresistible force. Wasting no time parading hurt pride or empty defiance, he withdrew into his mind in order to study what had happened to him. Having decided to submit, he submitted entirely and disciplined himself to make the most of submission. His governor, the Count of Pardiac, he treated with warm respect. The Master of his Household, whom he had put under arrest because of the man's loyalty to the King, he welcomed back into his service. He set about conciliating Charles, Count of Maine, and the other royal favorites. One lesson of the Praguerie he grasped immediately: the realm had nothing to expect from, and he had nothing in common with, the great lords and their feudal pretensions. Determined to master the trade of war and the trade of politics, he quietly followed the court, like any young lord with his fortunes to make, and wooed opportunity.

He saw King Charles's officers make a hash of operations to relieve Harfleur, besieged by the English. The following summer, 1441, he served in the campaign to take Pontoise, gateway to Normandy, which finally fell by assault in September. Advances made to him by a circle of princes, jealous of the growing strength of the Crown, he calmly ignored. Early in 1442 he rode southward with the royal army on an expedition against English Guienne.[1] The chronicles show that Louis spent the rest of the year in the field as a subordinate commander. In Guienne a number of places were captured but in the end most of them were lost. It was another mismanaged campaign. By this time there was talk of a great effort to be made in Normandy, but the royal ministers somehow failed to get it going. In the six years since Charles VII had so strangely bestirred himself at the siege of Montereau, the army had won no victories and recaptured only three towns of any consequence. The

English forces, meanwhile, no longer receiving any pay from the increasingly quarrel-racked government of Henry VI, plundered so viciously that the region from the Seine to the Somme was well-nigh reduced to wilderness, while bands of Écorcheurs ravaged countrysides from the Meuse to the Mediterranean.

In the first weeks of 1443, all France was appealing to Charles VII to come to the relief of the Norman town of Dieppe, snatched from the English several years before. The preceding November, the great Talbot had set siege to this important seaport, which, doggedly holding out though pounded all winter by English artillery, had become a symbol of national resistance. Now, at last, Louis's submerged years of self-discipline, of playing the game of court, bore fruit: he was appointed the King's lieutenant in the region between the Seine and the Somme with the charge of going to the relief of Dieppe. On Wednesday, August 14, eve of the Assumption of the Virgin Mary, the Dauphin Louis marshaled his fifteen hundred men of arms and his siege train in battle array before the stout wooden fortress, protected by deep ditches and heavily gunned, which the English had built on the steep hill overlooking the port. He had enlisted the best commanders of the day, including the Bastard of Orléans, Count of Dunois, the famed companion-in-arms of Joan of Arc, and a valiant captain of Écorcheurs, Antoine de Chabannes, Count of Dammartin. His men were well paid, well provisioned, and eager to fight under the Delphinal banner of the Virgin. The first attack of the French was beaten back, with severe losses; Louis and his commanders reorganized their forces, then led a second assault. This time they swarmed up the scaling ladders and over the walls into the fort. After a bloody hand-to-hand struggle, some three hundred of the English lay dead; the rest were made prisoners; their French adherents were promptly hanged. Declaring that the Virgin Mary had bestowed the victory, the Dauphin walked barefoot in humble thanksgiving to the church of St. Jacques of Dieppe. He also liberally rewarded the soldiers who had distinguished themselves in the attack and humble folk who had risked their necks to extricate the wounded.

While the news passed from town to town, provoking joyous celebrations out of all proportion to the military dimensions of the victory, the Dauphin did not neglect the thankless aftermath of the lieutenantship. To prevent soldiers from pillaging for a livelihood, Louis rode up and down the province of Île de France, settling troops in cantonments and pursuing the unpopular business of raising money. Then, before the end of October, he was hastily summoned back to court. There was a

fresh mission requiring the Dauphin's service: something had to be done
about the unruly Count of Armagnac, who was racking southern provinces with the raiding of his armed bands.

In a few weeks, Louis was heading southward with several thousand
men at his back and a staff of first-rate captains, including Antoine de
Chabannes. He quickly forced the capitulation of Armagnac's stronghold
of Rodez. By mid-January (1444), he had planted his banners before the
Count's battlements at Isle-Jourdain, some eighteen miles west of Toulouse. The Count, playing the usual princely game, gracefully yielded—
but, instead of receiving the usual pardon, he and most of his family
were promptly imprisoned in the fortress of Carcassonne. Louis did not
neglect to take into his entourage Armagnac's two best soldiers, the
hard-bitten Écorcheur Jean of Salazar, and Jean, the young Bastard of
Armagnac, both of whom would earn brilliant honors serving him till
death.

As Louis headed north in the early spring (1444), Antoine de Chabannes led a column through Burgundian territory, where he was momentarily checked by the Marshal of Burgundy but accomplished a satisfactory amount of pillage. On his return to the Dauphin's
headquarters, Louis greeted him with a smile. "Well, Count of Dammartin, I hear that the Marshal of Burgundy has given you a trouncing.
Faith of my body, this marshal acts just the opposite of others. The
other marshals do up horses, and this one does down men." °

Dammartin answered cheerfully, "True, my lord, but my band and I
have done ourselves up again, for we've had ten thousand crowns from
the Marshal's territory and I have well warmed myself in his villages
and drunk good wine."

Early in life Louis found his style, a winning familiarity well laced
with humor. In his second extant letter, written when he was about fifteen, he addressed one of his officers as "mon compère," my crony.† On
the other hand, he was already demanding absolute obedience and efficient service. His earliest extant communication contains the injunction
"See that there is no slip-up!"

It was that ancient adversary of France the English who now
opened up for the Dauphin Louis a much greater opportunity to exer-

---

° Louis was playing on the earlier meaning of the word "marshal"—a shoer of
horses.

† There is no satisfactory modern translation for *compère*, literally, "godfather
to my child." The English had a parallel expression, "gossip." Crony, intimate, side-
kick, bosom friend, pal, are but approximations.

cise his talents. On rejoining his father's court at Tours toward the end of April, 1444, he found that the Earl of Suffolk, chief minister of Henry VI, had come seeking a treaty with the French and a marriage alliance.[*] A truce of two years was agreed upon, sealed by the betrothal to Henry VI of Margaret of Anjou, the beautiful daughter of the Count of Maine's elder brother, René, titular King of Naples, Duke of Anjou and Lorraine. A wave of wild rejoicing ran through France. In the towns along the Anglo-French border, men for a generation had hardly dared venture beyond the walls. Now, the chroniclers report, they strolled joyously in field and wood, discovering the sensation of peace.

But the truce, however welcome, created a grave problem for the King's council, in which the Dauphin now took his place. The Écorcheurs, tens of thousands of them, if no longer employed in war, would ravage France to the bone. There was no military force in the kingdom capable of subduing them or driving them out; besides, were the truce not renewed, the best of these companies would be needed for the royal army. Fortunately, the Emperor of the Germanies and his cousin, the Duke of Austria, linked by a treaty of friendship with the King of France, were at this moment appealing for aid against the hardy Swiss mountaineers, who, all too successfully as usual, were resisting the efforts of the Hapsburgs to reduce them to a long-vanished obedience. Charles VII's government agreed to send an army to help the Emperor and the Duke. Lured by the promise of booty, the Écorcheurs of the realm, in their bloodthirsty and disorderly thousands, would be marshaled under the best captains of the day and thrust eastward, out of the suffering Kingdom of France, against the Swiss—and whatever else stood in their way. Fervently the Germans promised to provision and lodge their allies.

The Pied Piper who had managed to get himself chosen to charm away the rats was the Dauphin Louis. Seldom in the course of history has the heir of a great kingdom undertaken a mission so bizarre, so ambiguous, and so perilous. Officially, he was directed simply to aid the Austrians and make a useful demonstration on the Rhine of the power of France.

The rendezvous of the Écorcheurs was set for July 28 at Langres, at the eastward tip of royal France. One hundred and thirty miles beyond

[*] Two factions in the English court struggled to control the feeble Henry VI; the great nobles, backed by hired bands of retainers, used fraud or force to flout the law; and neither men nor money could be found to maintain the conquered territories in France. As the French slowly recovered from anarchy, the English were moving toward the civil strife of the Wars of the Roses.

stood the city of Bâle, an imperial town but allied to the Swiss. Between Langres and Bâle stretched lands dominated by the Duke of Burgundy. The Dauphin of France, become the Prince of Cutthroats, entered Langres on July 20 at the head of one thousand horse. Not many days before, he had turned twenty-one. The royal council provided him with several advisers, headed by Jean de Bueil, who was made chief of the army, but Louis remained in firm command of the expedition. From all over France bands of Écorcheurs were making their dreadful way to Langres—Gascons, Bretons, Spaniards, Lombards, Germans, Walloons, even a stout detachment of English volunteers. In all, about 140 captains —the élite of the Anglo-French wars—answered the Dauphin's call: bastards of noble houses, famous freebooters like Blanchelain, Blanchefort, Dimanche de Court, Lestrac, whose very names crackled with the sound of burning villages. By the beginning of August, something like twenty-five thousand men were trampling the fields about Langres. Half of them were first-rate soldiers, well mounted and well armed; the rest were the dregs of a generation of war, dead to everything but the shine of gold and the joys of rape. Many bands had brought their women with them, a savage horde riding mangy beasts or jolting the roads in baggage carts. For his bodyguard the Dauphin chose, appropriately enough, a troop of four hundred Spaniards whose marauding had earned them a reputation as detestable as that of Blanchelain's Bretons.

On Wednesday, August 5, the Dauphin and his wild thousands began moving eastward on a front of twenty miles. A week later, the campfires of the Écorcheurs were blooming in the summer night in a great arc about Lure. Austrian envoys, one after the other, had arrived at the Dauphin's headquarters, promising the Duke of Austria's Alsatian towns for cantonments and urging the Dauphin to move with all speed since the Swiss were pressing the siege of Zurich and sending men toward Bâle. Louis dispatched word to the Austrian chiefs that he would not continue his advance until he received a written promise of lodgings for twenty-five thousand horsemen for ten months. The Austrians hastily listed an array of towns on both sides of the Rhine which they swore to deliver to their allies.

Within two weeks of Louis's departure from Langres, his advance guard of two thousand horse under the daring Blanchefort were already coursing the countryside around Bâle. The Dauphin's troops had cut a swath of terror. An eyewitness wrote on August 19—the day Louis entered Montbéliard—"I have seen and heard about cruelties and atrocities such as no one has ever heard tell of before. It would be impossible to imagine the kinds of torture to which the Écorcheurs submit the poor folk they hold in their hands. All my body shakes at the picture, each time that it comes back to my memory." The village that one band spared, at the price of whatever could be squeezed from the inhabitants, the next troop burned or pillaged. Crops were fired, livestock driven off, wine presses and mills and tools wantonly destroyed. The Écorcheurs roasted peasants over slow fires to make them reveal hidden valuables and frequently neglected to remove the victims from the flames. Sometimes they thrust a man into a rabbit hutch and took turns violating his wife on top of it.

Another deputation of Austrian nobles arrived with news that the Swiss, on August 12, had laid siege to Farnsbourg, only fifteen miles east of Bâle. Louis had no difficulty discerning that the Austrians hoped their savage allies and their mountain enemies would destroy each other. Already rumors were running over Europe that when the Dauphin of France had taken Bâle and crushed the Swiss he would then "rule in Germany."

After a council of war, Jean de Bueil with the bulk of the army advanced toward Bâle. Two days later, Sunday, August 23, the Dauphin followed with the remainder of his forces. Swinging his bands northward of Bueil's troops, who had occupied Austrian strong places south of Bâle, Louis established his headquarters at the castle of Waltighoffen. On the 25th he led a scouting party to inspect the fortifications of the city; they rode so close to the walls that a burst of arquebus fire stretched a number of the Dauphin's companions on the ground. Early in the morning of the 26th the Dauphin got word that a reconnaissance force dispatched eastward had been assailed by the Swiss and driven back across the river Birse to Bueil's army. The enemy turned out to be a company of some twenty-five hundred picked men, who had been detached from the army besieging Farnsbourg to attack the Écorcheurs. During this preliminary engagement, the Dauphin and Bueil had marshaled their forces so as to use the advancing Swiss as bait for a trap which might deliver the city of Bâle into their hands. Bueil's army of some fifteen thousand mounted men of arms and archers was drawn up on a plateau which overlooked the Birse three quarters of a mile south of Bâle. The Dauphin held his smaller force well to the west, ready to pounce if the citizens of Bâle issued from the gates to help their friends.

The Swiss phalanx and Bueil's massive squadrons were soon locked in desperate battle, French horsemen hewing their way into a fearsome hedge of pikes and halberds. At mid-morning several thousand men is-

sued from the southern gate of Bâle to assail the Écorcheurs on the plateau. As the tail of the column was leaving the city, the front of it suddenly halted: the leaders had caught sight of the Dauphin's army to the
west and realized their peril. The citizens fled pell-mell back to the city.
Another half hour and the Dauphin might well have brought off his
game of swooping upon Bâle. By evening the Swiss force had been
wiped out. But they had first taken the lives of something like four thousand Écorcheurs.[2]

The news shook all the West, both sides of the news. Such a defeat
enhanced the military reputation of the Swiss as much as their past victories. On the other hand, the Dauphin, standing at the Rhine with a
fearsome army, had suddenly become a European power. In a single
blow he had fulfilled his engagements to the Austrians. The Swiss immediately raised the sieges of Zurich and Farnsbourg to form a defense line
and would undoubtedly be willing now to come to some kind of terms
with the Emperor.

Louis lost little time in exploring the consequences of his victory. He
showed no astonishment when, on August 29, envoys from the Emperor,
saying nothing about the provisions and lodging that had been promised, declared that His Imperial Majesty was shaken "to the very bow-
els" by the hideous army of barbarians that the French had loosed on
the lands of the Empire. A few days later the Dauphin dispatched to
Frederick III an embassy armed with very plain instructions: they were
to remind the Emperor of the Dauphin's services and of Austrian promises; if the Alsatian towns were not delivered at once, they would be
seized.

By this time, the beginning of September, Louis had withdrawn
three reconnaissance columns dispatched eastward, and was directing
the movement of his army into Alsace. On September 5 he set up his
headquarters at Ensisheim in the heart of Haute-Alsace. Already he was
negotiating, through the city of Bâle, with yesterday's foes, the Swiss
cantons. He told the envoys of Bâle that he would happily give a treasure of gold to have alive again not only his own dead but the valiant
mountain men. Quick to assimilate experience, he sensed that the Swiss
were a rising European power—and one that shared his views of feudal
princes. Whatever other ideas were now darting through his restless
brain, he meant to secure for France an alliance with the cantons. Loyally he insisted that they negotiate with the Emperor as well as with
himself, but in word and action he made clear that he ardently desired
their friendship. Knowing that they were suspicious of foreign entangle-

ments, he readily agreed to a truce so that they could examine his sincerity.

By the time this truce was declared on September 20, the Dauphin was skillfully deploying his Écorcheurs band by band throughout the Alsatian hills and on the plain of Basse-Alsace. Strasbourg and other strong towns he made no attempt to take; they remained beleaguered islands in a sea of raiding bands. A few places immediately opened their gates; others were brought to submit by threats; still others were stormed. Early in October, Louis was operating to the west near the Vosges Mountains. After capturing St. Hippolyte, he laid siege to the stubborn town of Dambach. For three days bombards and field pieces battered the walls, but it took several assaults to force a capitulation. In one of these the Dauphin, urging on his men in the thick of the fight, had his knee nailed to the saddle by an arrow. The wound turned out not to be serious; by the third week in October, Louis was back at Ensisheim pursuing his negotiations. On October 28 he secured his prize: he ratified a treaty of amity and mercantile intercourse with the Swiss.

Across the hundred miles from Montbéliard to Marlenheim north of Strasbourg, the Écorcheurs were established in fifteen major cantonments between the Vosges and the Rhine. Under the winter rains this region has become a sinkhole of misery and violence. In Haute-Alsace the Écorcheurs had things all their own way, harrying the countryside and terrifying townsmen as they pleased. But in Basse-Alsace a savage guerrilla warfare was waged day and night. The great towns, particularly Strasbourg, mounted continual raids and ambushes, and their troops killed as pitilessly as the Écorcheurs. In this nightmare of burned fields and smashed villages, the fittest of the Dauphin's companies were the ones who best maintained themselves, while the jackals of war perished at the hands of enraged Alsatians.

The Dauphin would need powerful backing to hold Alsace longer than a few months. Across his rear stretched lands of the Duke of Burgundy, who was deeply alarmed by the consequences of the expedition; and though the Emperor sent increasingly conciliatory embassies, he was endeavoring to raise an army. Money and supplies were urgently needed to keep the Écorcheurs in being as an effective fighting force. As soon as he established himself at Ensisheim, the Dauphin sent for his wife in order to set up a court and solidify the occupation of Alsace. Revolving plans to exploit his opportunity—nobody knows what plans—he was attempting to enlist the support of his father's government for a spring campaign.

The Dauphin's headquarters at Ensisheim had become a focal point of European politics. He had extended French power to the Rhine, exposed the weakness of the faithless Emperor, and caused several of the German princes to look to France rather than to the Duke of Burgundy. The Pope bestowed upon him the title of Gonfalonier, or Captain-General, of the Church. Envoys arrived from Genoa—once a French possession—with an invitation for the Dauphin to become the sovereign of the city. The Duke of Milan, who had no male heir, sent a rival embassy which, according to report, suggested that Louis might be named the Duke's successor. The Duke of Savoy had already ceded two counties adjacent to Dauphiné in order to secure an alliance. Rumors were circulating among Louis's officers that in the spring he would march into Italy in order to help the House of Anjou regain the Realm of Naples.

Then, quite suddenly, the bright horizons shut down; at the same time the Dauphin momentarily disappears from recorded history.

Once the task of settling the Écorcheurs had been accomplished and the treaty with the Swiss signed, Charles VII's government abruptly canceled the Dauphine's preparations for joining her husband; and the King, using the wounding of his son as a motive, sent message on message demanding that Louis return to court. Not only was he refused permission to undertake further operations, he was denied the means even to maintain himself over the winter. It may be that the royal council, decided that France could not then afford to undertake more than the Dauphin had already accomplished. However, while the son was laboring in the field, the father, stirred once more to emulation, had headed an ostentatious military parade in the direction of Metz which cost much and did nothing; and it is quite likely that, in the face of his own failure, King Charles was determined to allow his son no further successes.

Louis's realization that the game was up is marked by an answer he made in early November to yet another Imperial embassy: if the Emperor offered recompense for his failure to fulfill his promises, the French might be willing to evacuate Alsace the following March. Sometime in November the Dauphin increased the size of the garrison of Ensisheim from one thousand to six thousand men; he was establishing a strong reserve in the center of the occupation. It was the signal for his departure. Before the end of the month, Louis of France, his great adventure played out, rode southward for Montbéliard.

Hidden from the light of history, Louis remained at Montbéliard until the last days of January, 1445; he then emerged at his father's court at Nancy, but only to remain a shadowy and alien figure. When he arrived at Nancy, or shortly thereafter, he was suffering a bout of illness perhaps engendered or exacerbated by profound frustration. It may be that he had lingered at Montbéliard simply because he knew that nothing awaited him at home but idleness. So began his second withdrawal —into isolation, enforced patience, a re-examination of himself and his world.

4. The Malcontent

RETURNING FROM the horrors of Alsace, Louis at Nancy found himself in the world of Camelot. Though winter bound the earth, lords and ladies had flocked to the capital of Lorraine, feeling the springtime of France's revival and eager to display themselves, to seek the sunlight of royal favor, to enjoy what had not been known in the realm for almost half a century—the life of court.

Over the jousts, the dancing, the banquets, walks in the fields on sunny mornings, there presided a rosy apple of a man, "good King René," the thirty-five-year-old head of the House of Anjou, brother of Charles, Count of Maine, and of Marie, the Queen of France. Prince of picturesque misfortunes, he called himself King of Naples, but had miserably failed to make that title good; and he still owed the Duke of Burgundy an enormous ransom as a result of his being taken captive by the Duke fifteen years before.[1] Lover of the bright surfaces of life, René was the master organizer of tournaments, festivals, and all the curious entertainments by which feudal lords expressed the grandeur of their station. His household included a troop of brilliantly costumed Moors and a dwarf, Triboulet, who had a head "no bigger than a large orange." He laid out gardens, worked in stained glass, wrote romantic allegories in prose and verse. Patron as well as artist, he supported an array of versifiers and painters and sculptors and musicians—"he had in his train only folk clever at devising pastimes." His fiery son John, Duke of Calabria, had all the qualities of leadership except good sense. His sixteen-year-old daughter Margaret, beautiful and accomplished, was even now about to begin her wild, tragic destiny as the wife of Henry VI. When, in February (1445) the Duke of Suffolk and a train of lords arrived to escort Margaret of Anjou to England, the court blazed with princely feasts and tournaments.

At the apex of this chivalresque society sat the King, now Charles the Well Served, and soon to be Charles the Victorious. After providing a Holy Maid to save his honor and his crown, God had now, the time for holiness being past, given him the most beautiful girl in France, Agnès Sorel, "la Dame de Beauté"—for Charles had reinforced her right by nature to bear this title in bestowing upon her the Manor of Beauté near Paris. Though she had become Charles's mistress in the later months of 1443 and had already borne him a child, it was now at the court of Nancy that she became what France had never known before, the Official Mistress. Bold and gay, she surrounded Charles with gay young people; and the King, discovering the joy of youth in his forties, showered lands and honors upon the new favorites and could not get enough of their company. Agnès Sorel was clever enough to ally herself with the Norman lord, Pierre de Brezé, who had brought her to the King's attention and had now displaced the Count of Maine as the King's first minister. While the Angevins dominated the life of court and la Belle Agnès ruled the King, Pierre de Brezé, a valiant soldier and an able administrator, maintained himself atop a heap of competing political interests. Brezé was not above adroit tricks of manipulation and intrigue—how else could he have risen in such a court?—but he was a man of fine grain, richly dowered with the graces of humanity. The Burgundian historiographer Georges Chastellain declares him the most eloquent and witty speaker of the age—"when his sword could not conquer, his tongue won the day."

Against the bright colors of this court, the Dauphin appeared a somber figure. The prince of camps and council chambers was not for that time or for that place. He took no part in the life of jousts and banquets. Devoted to his mother, he made way like the rest of the world for Agnès Sorel. And, with the habit of managing great enterprises still upon him, he found himself abruptly unemployed—a young man who is everything and nothing, an alien being. His wife, too, belonged to the others. That fey little Scot, Margaret, had turned out to be the most fairylike of princesses and she was married to the most workaday of princes. In this season when Louis, destitute in the King's services, received not a penny from his father to pay his debts, Charles gave Margaret two thousand livres in order to buy silks and furs. Like her father, James I of Scotland, Margaret was enamored of poetry, though it is doubtful— none of her compositions has survived—that she possessed her father's genius. Of an evening she would recline in her chambers, exchanging verses with her ladies and a circle of poetical courtiers. Creature of the dreaming dark, spinning half a dozen rondeaux in a night, she sometimes did not come to the conjugal bed until, so it was reported, her lord "had already slept a sleep or two." Louis did not hide his dislike of her butterfly existence; she was the less happy but could imagine no other way of living. Worst of all, she bore no children. Apparently she wanted none; for it was said that in order to preserve her figure she drank vinegar and ate green apples and laced herself tightly, thinking that such a regimen was likely to prevent childbearing.

In an acrid humor, drowning in Angevins and royal "mignons," Louis resumed his place in the council. To keep himself and his officers going, he had to borrow 5,500 livres, in his "very great need," from a member of his household. The most he could get from his father's government was permission to ask some of the towns of the realm to help him defray his expenses. He managed somehow to send convoys of supplies to his men in Alsace.

As a member of the council, he played a part in the formation of the professional military force which his expedition had made possible. In the early spring of 1445, as the bands of *Écorcheurs* began to make their way back to France, the best of them were incorporated into an army consisting of fifteen mounted companies of one hundred lances each (six men to a lance). But in the competition for the command of companies the King's fondness for René of Anjou outweighed the services of the heir of France. The Dauphin's man, Antoine de Chabannes, Count of Dammartin, one of the first soldiers of the realm, was cast aside. Chabannes appeared at court dressed all in black. When the King asked him why he was in mourning, the tough Écorcheur replied, "Sire, when you take away from me my command, you take away my life." Chabannes might also have been speaking for his master.

Grimly Louis continued to play the prescribed game of court, applying like everybody else to Pierre de Brezé for preferment. He finally received a commission to conduct negotiations with the Duchess of Burgundy, who had come on an embassy to settle Franco-Burgundian jurisdictional disputes. A month later, his commission was abruptly withdrawn: he had refused to press, at the expense of French demands, for the cancelation of King René's debt to the Duke of Burgundy. The King, arriving at Châlons (in Champagne) from a pleasure jaunt in Lorraine with his delightful brother-in-law, soon arranged that, in return for numerous French concessions, René would be let off his ransom.

Milanese ambassadors had reported in late May, "There are in the bosom of the House of France bitter jealousies and red-hot factional strife. There could not be more violent hostility than that which reigns between the illustrious Lord Dauphin and the King of Sicily [René of

Anjou]. This comes from the fact that the King of Sicily is the one who runs everything in the realm." Charles, Duke of Orléans, and his bastard brother, the Count of Dunois, resented this dominance of the House of Anjou. The Angevins, meanwhile, were stirring intrigues to get rid of Pierre de Brezé, who had superseded the Count of Maine in power. Louis had little use for any of these ornamental lords, who regarded the royal power and the royal treasury as their private preserve.

Pierre de Brezé, sensing that the House of Anjou had joined forces against him with a number of other discontented lords, enlisted Agnès Sorel in his cause. Though Charles was fond of the House of Anjou, he was much fonder of la Dame de Beauté and he appreciated Brezé's abilities. He intimated to King René and the Count of Maine that they and their followers would do well to withdraw from court for a little while. Something like a new regime, still headed by Pierre de Brezé, took over the government. A few great lords remained, but a group of able career men now appeared at the council table. Among them was Jacques Coeur, Keeper of the King's Purse, the most remarkable entrepreneur of his time, who owned trading Companies all over France and whose Mediterranean fleet, freighting oriental luxuries to the West, made its master a figure of importance in the Moslem world. In the city of Bourges, of which his son was already Archbishop, Jacques Coeur (James Heart) built himself a wonderful palace flaunting the motto *À vaillans coeurs rien impossible* (to valiant hearts, nothing is impossible). It was said that his yearly income equaled that of all the rest of the merchants of France together.

King Charles, it appears, had bid for the Dauphin's support of the change in government by authorizing Brezé to hold out the prospect of another mission, this time a great enterprise in Italy. Louis was encouraged to believe that he would be empowered to conduct an armed force to aid Milan against Venice, the Duke of Milan then helping the Dauphin to reassert French sovereignty over Genoa. Bitterly at odds with the Angevins, Louis was in any case inclined to support this shift in power. He admired Jacques Coeur—for in his way Louis was also an entrepreneur —and the two men soon became closely linked. Louis even went so far as to pay court to Agnès Sorel, presenting her with a handsome set of tapestries which he had appropriated two years before from the castle of the Count of Armagnac.

But once the new government was in fair way to being established, the Dauphin's hope of extending French power beyond the Alps was quickly extinguished. Whatever Louis's amiable gestures, Agnès Sorel

could not find in the restless son of her royal lover anything but an
enemy. As for King Charles himself, he was not disposed to offer the
Dauphin further opportunities for success; besides, the shadow of a son
falls never so cold as when a father discovers his youth.

In the heavy heat of early August, in this tindery political weather of
shifts and disillusions, the Dauphin and his wife prepared to leave Châlons with the King for the milder climate of the Loire. Suddenly plans
for departure were canceled. The frail Scots princess had fallen ill. On
Saturday, August 7, she and her ladies had joined the court on a brief
pilgrimage. The day was very hot. Upon her return, she carelessly threw
off most of her clothes, enjoying the cool of her stone chamber. The next
morning she was feverish and racked with coughing; the doctor diagnosed that she was suffering from an inflammation of the lungs. On August 16, between ten and eleven at night, the Dauphine died. In her last
days she was tortured by the memory of scandalous insinuations noised
against her by a courtier.

The next day, deeply troubled, the Dauphin together with the King
and Queen quitted Châlons. Doubtless Louis did not experience sharp
grief, for Margaret had hardly been a wife to him and they were beings
of different worlds. It appears that not until the Dauphine's illness had
Louis realized the extent or the consequences of the scandalmongering.
Soon afterward he sought to have the culprit punished for his malice.
But the effort proved vain: the man continued to bask in the King's
good graces. It was yet another evidence of the small favor that the heir
of France enjoyed at the court of his father.[2]

From August 7 (1445), when Louis rode out of Châlons, until the
end of the year, he is almost completely lost to view. For the whole of
1446 the record is not much more revealing: some household accounts,
fewer than half a dozen letters, casual mention by the chroniclers, a
scattering of documents—this is the sum of it, except for two depositions
which consist of damaging disclosures about the Dauphin made by certain of his former servants. Submerged in his father's empty affability,
withdrawn into his restless thoughts, the Dauphin, in the sunlight of
the court of France, was in full shadow. Yet, the wheels of his mind
must turn; if they were not given wheat, they would grind chaff.

In the new year of 1446, the Dauphin sent Pierre de Brezé twenty-
five hogsheads of wine, Rhine wine—a reminder of former services as
well as a gift to further new hopes. He was again looking to Italy to furnish him an occupation. This time he was negotiating a secret pact with
his ally the Duke of Savoy, aimed at creating a French dominion across

the Alps. The treaty with Savoy, concluded in February, was promptly rejected by Charles and his council. Caged and frustrated, Louis turned in the early spring to plotting a palace revolution, angling for the support of his stalwart captain Antoine de Chabannes. Perhaps he expected to gain no more than to stir the King into offering him employment as the price of peace. His quarters were soon giving off a conspiratorial buzz which he seemingly made little attempt to conceal. But nothing happened.[3] He turned to another project, equally unpromising. For his service against the Count of Armagnac (1443–44), the royal government had given him certain confiscated Armagnac jurisdictions. The Dauphin conceived the idea of enlarging his power in Languedoc by securing the Seneschausée of Agenais, adjacent to his new possessions. Secretly he sent agents into the territory with the mission of persuading the inhabitants to put themselves under the Dauphin's lordship, a move which was promptly reported to the King. This undertaking was so brash and clumsy it is hard not to believe that Louis merely wanted to annoy his father.

For a while he resumed his desultory plotting.[4] Then, as summer gave way to autumn, he embarked on still another scheme, more moderate this time. Linking himself with René's brother Charles, Count of Maine, still resentful at being superseded by Pierre de Brezé, Louis launched a political campaign aimed at persuading the King to dismiss Brezé and Brezé's chief supporters from the government. Suddenly, a number of things happened almost at once. Antoine de Chabannes revealed in full detail the Dauphin's plotting of the past spring. Pierre de Brezé, alarmed for his position, managed to procure further disclosures from a menial. At the same time, the nobles, sensing that the Dauphin was none of theirs, closed ranks against him. The Count of Maine was reconciled with Brezé while the King looked on benevolently.

Louis relieved his feelings by indulging himself in a violent outburst against Agnès Sorel. Varying versions of the scandal coursed through Europe. Aeneas Sylvius Piccolomini (later Pope Pius II) recorded that, moved by his mother's tears, the Dauphin berated la Belle Agnès and then, drawing his sword in a fury, chased her to the King's bed. More restrained accounts have it that he gave her a buffet in public. There was in any case a fine explosion, which left the Dauphin in solitary disgrace. He cut the tails of all his horses, saying that they might as well be cropped like their master. But if he had failed utterly to find a channel to power, he at least succeeded in making his position so untenable that the King and Brezé were forced to provide him with a mission, of sorts.

In November, the Duke of Milan again offered to help the French regain Genoa in return for aid against Venice. The Milanese ambassadors were instructed to seek particularly the intervention of the Dauphin. The royal government agreed, in mid-December, to accept the Duke's proposals; at the same time a French embassy, in which Louis had managed to include one of his men, was negotiating with malcontent Geonese exiles at Marseilles. Liberal gifts of wine to the Milanese ambassadors and to some members of the royal council suggest that the Dauphin, even now, had to struggle in order to pry himself loose from court. In the end, he secured permission to betake himself to Dauphiné in order to receive the homage of the province and from that vantage point to further French interests in northern Italy. He received no real power to act, however, and was ordered to return to his father in four months. But if Charles VII had shackled him with a pseudo-mission, Louis offered only a pseudo-acquiescence. He had probably already made up his mind never to submit again to a parental benignity which mocked his talents and poisoned his character.

On December 28 at Tours, the Queen gave birth to a baby boy who was named after his father. The ceremony of baptism was to prove rich in ironies. One of the godfathers, the Count of Maine, would betray Louis on a critical day of battle, while another, Pierre de Brezé, would fall in that battle fighting for Louis's throne and life; and one of the godmothers, Brezé's wife, would treacherously deliver the city of Rouen to the prince she now held in her arms.

On January 1, 1447, Louis Dauphin set out for Dauphiné. It was yet another withdrawal, and he was now twenty-three. He never saw his father more. The King had still fifteen years to reign.

THE EXILE

5. The Emperor of Dauphiné

A CENTURY BEFORE, the last of the Dauphins of Dauphiné, nominally a part of the Empire, had bequeathed his little state to the heir of the King of France, on condition that it was never to be united to France itself. It was a region of flat lands and mountains, broken by rivers, forests, high valleys. Roughly triangular in shape, the province stretched along the river Rhône some 125 miles from St. Symphorien to Carpentras. Eastward, it thrust into the Alps, where it was bordered by the Duchy of Savoy. Dominions of the Duke of Burgundy lay to the north; King René's county of Provence, to the south. Vienne on the Rhône and Grenoble, the capital, were the most considerable towns; it was mainly a province of villages and isolated castles and reaches of wild country.

Politically, too, the region was a backwater. A crazyquilt of land tenures and jurisdictions, Dauphiné represented feudal debris left by the disintegration, first of Charlemagne's Empire and then of the old Kingdom of Burgundy. Following these upheavals, ambitious bishops had managed to make themselves the temporal rulers of their dioceses; lay lords turned themselves into petty despots. Over the centuries, the Dauphins had succeeded in building up a state of sorts, but it was a state full of enclaves, a jumble of privileges, and for some of their lands the Dauphins themselves were vassals of powerful churchmen.

The moment Louis set foot on the soil of Dauphiné, at St. Symphorien (January 13, 1447), he plunged into ruling his little threadbare state as if it were an empire.[1] Early in February he presided over a meeting of his Three Estates at Romans. Then he moved on down the Rhône to Valence and Montélimar, investigating local complaints and feudal jurisdictions. By May, he had come to an agreement with a papal legate which enabled him to secure the portion of the town of Montélimar possessed by the Pope, in exchange for another lordship.[2] In July he abolished a hodgepodge of administrative subdivisions and organized the province into two *baillages* and a *seneschaussée*. He established a Parlement, reorganized the Delphinal council, speeded up the process of litigation, brought into being an official register of documents, and set up a government postal service, the first in Europe. In July of 1452—at a moment when he was anxiously embroiled with his father—he founded a university at Valence with faculties of theology, civil and canon law, medicine, and liberal arts.

Louis rode up and down the primitive highways of Dauphiné, listening to complaints and claims, curbing the feudal lords, lay and ecclesiastical, stimulating the growth of towns, wooing prosperity for his subjects by every means at his command. To encourage agriculture, he put a tax on wheat coming into Dauphiné from France. He offered financial inducements to enterprising merchants, ennobled them, took their sons into his service, encouraged skilled foreign artisans to settle in Dauphiné by offering them all kinds of concessions.[3]

Meanwhile, Louis had brought all his powers to bear to subdue to his authority the great feudatories, clinging fiercely to their ancient rights. The nobles enjoyed, by law, the privilege of waging private war, and exercised, by custom, the privileges of potentates. Bishops and archbishops possessed courts and prisons and lorded it in the chief towns as temporal princes; in the very capital, Grenoble, the Dauphin was the vassal of the bishop.

Louis abolished private warfare, demanded that all nobles do homage to him, required them to furnish military service at their own expense, and made them respect the laws of Dauphiné as enforced by Delphinal officers. He met the challenge of the spiritual lords by a steady pressure of commissions—commissions inquiring into jurisdictional claims, commissions investigating encroachments on Delphinal powers.[4] By 1450 the Dauphin had succeeded in establishing his authority over prelates as well as nobles. In a series of public ceremonies in the autumn of that year, the Archbishop of Vienne and the Bishops of Grenoble and Valence did homage to the Dauphin as their lord and ceded their pretensions to temporal jurisdiction over their cities. In 1453 the Dauphin got his own man elected Archbishop of Vienne, much to the chagrin of Charles VII, who had designated another.

Churchmen and nobles did not submit gracefully to this new world;

they sent tales of horrible novelties to the royal court, where they were readily listened to. The King easily persuaded himself to regard his son's great work as a regime of "follies," directed by "evil councilors." But the tenants of the feudatories, the townsmen, and the *petite noblesse* of Dauphiné—they were of another mind. On a hot July afternoon, when Louis's crown and life trembled in the balance of battle, it would be the hard-bitten gentlemen of Dauphiné who closed round their King and broke the assault of the chivalry of Burgundy.

Louis's regime in Dauphiné was an apprenticeship and a portent. Nothing quite like it had ever been seen before. He transfomed his backward province into a state, doubled the extent of its territory, gave it a cohesion it had never known, and organized an administration that was probably more efficient than any other in Europe. He enacted in all more than a thousand decrees, ranging from broad reforms to minute regulations for the welfare of individuals and towns. Word spread throughout Europe of what the Son of France was doing in Dauphiné. Adventurous knights, like the Burgundian Olivier de La Marche, journeyed there to see for themselves. In after years the Dauphin and his rule passed into the lore of the province. He lost a number of followers; some he dismissed because he discovered, or suspected, that they had sold out to his father. But he gained many more. Young Frenchmen, struck by the Dauphin's accomplishments and aware of the advancement to be won from him for good service, made their way to Dauphiné. They came secretly and in haste, for the King sent orders flying to have them pursued.

During his early years in Dauphiné, Louis was able, for the first time, to fashion a life for himself. He had a state to manage and the officers and companions of his choice; he indulged to the full his passion for the chase; he was free of his father's court. He acknowledged two mistresses, one of whom, Félise Renard, daughter of an equerry, gave him two daughters he later married to men of high position. If he was too ambitious to call himself contented and too saturated in his passion for statecraft to be satisfied with repose, he nonetheless possessed a talent for simple pleasures, he enjoyed exercising his enormous curiosity, and he found the texture of life infinitely interesting. He was already famous as a tireless horseman, wearing out his entourage in endless cavalcades. He ate and drank heartily; he loved to talk, and also knew how to listen. He questioned everybody about everything, and he remembered the names and faces and the answers. Even the sparse records of his youth show flashes of the comedian, enacting with relish a repertory of

roles that half hid and half disclosed the complex, nervous, amused creature behind. He pursued experience as a fire eats a dry forest; and he focused all that he learned, all his vitality and will, upon the management
of men and affairs.

6. The Unchastened Rebel

By 1450 Louis had firmly established his administration, and Dauphiné ceased to consume all his energies.

Restlessly he took a hand in the shifting political combinations of Italy. Tensely he watched from afar the intrigues of the French court and tried to penetrate the mind of the King. He had agents and friends in the royal entourage, as his father had his in Dauphiné. The King's government continued to be enmeshed in jealousies and intrigues, which apparently Charles enjoyed; none of the royal courtiers had any desire to see the Dauphin reconciled with his father. Stories that the Dauphin was conspiring against the King found ready circulation at court, and, even when publicly proved false, were never repudiated by Charles VII.[1] Louis ruled his province on sufferance and he knew it; and the sufferance of his father grew more enigmatic year by year. He had organized a little army, but what could he do against the fifteen companies that Charles VII possessed?

During these first years of his sojourn in Dauphiné (1447–51), the Dauphin marked intently the changes in the King's fortunes and in the King's court.

In the summer of 1449, after the English had foolishly broken the Anglo-French truce, Pierre de Brezé and Dunois, the Bastard of Orléans, loosed their crack professional army upon Normandy. The Duke of Somerset, surrendering Rouen without striking a blow, hastily retreated to the coast. In 1450 the last enemy army was crushed at Formigny and the rest of Normandy won. The French completed their great work the following year by driving the English from the province of Guienne. Feeble-witted Henry VI held only Calais, and England was now torn by factional quarrels which would soon lead to the Wars of the Roses. The King of France had become Charles the Victorious, the mightiest ruler of Christendom.

The King himself was pursuing ever more hotly the pleasures of youth. In February of 1450, Agnès Sorel had died at Jumièges in Normandy. She was soon succeeded by a cousin of hers named Antoinette de Maignelais, reputedly almost as beautiful as la Belle Agnès. Charles's appetites had become so fired that Antoinette was soon serving not only as the King's mistress but also as his procuress-in-chief, gathering for his pleasure a troop of beautiful young concubines, who were clothed like queens.

These years were also the great years of Jacques Coeur. Member of the council, diplomat, Keeper of the Royal Purse, he likewise continued his spectacular career as the prince of merchants. Most of the lords of court were in his debt, and his greatest debtor was the King. He had done much to make possible the conquest of Normandy, throwing open his coffers to his sovereign and declaring, "Sire, all that I have is yours." From afar, the Dauphin maintained his close relationship with Jacques Coeur. They kept their liaison secret, for at court to be the Dauphin's friend redoubled dangers; but Coeur managed to lend the Dauphin money, aided him in his negotiations with the Italian states, and put at his service the powers and the personnel of his vast mercantile organization.

Louis and his father, meanwhile, retained the outward forms of cordiality. King Charles continued to include the Dauphin in the circle of those to whom he sent New Year's gifts; Louis, in January of 1449, dispatched a leopard to the King. The father, apparently, did not remind his son that he had long overstayed his leave in Dauphiné, nor did the son complain of his poverty or his exclusion from power. Then, suddenly, in February of 1451, Louis received an ominous intimation of his father's hidden thoughts: he was accused of "meddling with the affairs" of Jacques Coeur.

The Dauphin himself had precipitated matters by seeking the King's permission to marry a daughter of his ally and neighbor, the Duke of Savoy. Now twenty-seven years old, he was wifeless and childless at an age when the heir to a great kingdom should long since have established a family. Throughout 1450, however, Charles VII ignored the request, repeated by his son's envoys. Still another embassy, dispatched by Louis in November, received no reply until the last week in February, 1451. It was a dry answer: the King regarded the Savoy marriage as unsuitable. After adding that the Dauphin had failed to return to court and that his treatment of the Church in Dauphiné was displeasing, Louis's father concluded his message with the menacing reference to the Dauphin's relations with Jacques Coeur.

But Louis, foreseeing this sort of reply, had already taken matters into his own hands. In mid-February his representatives at the Court of Savoy signed the marriage contract. When this unpleasant news reached King Charles, he sent Normandy Herald posting to Chambéry to halt the ceremony. The Herald arrived in time, March 9, to watch the Dauphin and twelve-year-old Charlotte of Savoy, clad in robes of crimson velvet, enter the chapel where they were wedded.[2]

King Charles took his time in securing revenge. The Keeper of the King's Purse was the first to pay. In his usual manner Charles continued to caress the man to whom he owed so much, even as the blow was about to fall. On July 30, 1451—five months after the Dauphin's marriage—Jacques Coeur wrote confidently to his wife, "Whatever people may say . . . I am as well with the King as ever I have been." A few days later he was thrown into prison, bereft of all his goods, and accused—of poisoning Agnès Sorel! This charge, frighteningly absurd, served notice on Jacques Coeur, and on the Dauphin, that the King and his favorites meant to have Coeur's skin. In May of 1453 he was adjudged guilty of *lèse-majesté*, fined 400,000 crowns, deprived of all his possessions, and remitted indefinitely to prison. A year later, he escaped and made his way to Rome, where he was heartily welcomed by the Pope. Put in command of a fleet operating against the Turks, he died on the Isle of Chios, November 25, 1456. By that time, the Dauphin, too, was a fugitive. He had been able to do nothing for his friend, but when he became King he would advance Coeur's sons, take a number of Coeur's agents into his service, and put on record his gratitude for "the good and praiseworthy services done us by the late Jacques Coeur."

After Coeur was imprisoned, King Charles moved, slowly, calmly, against the son who had dared to marry to suit himself. At the beginning of 1452 the Dauphin was deprived of his pension. When Louis protested against the "evil reports" which were being poured into his father's ear, the King's answer was to take away from his son the last lands he held in France.

At the same time the royal government was exerting increasing pressure on the Duke of Savoy to dissociate himself from the Dauphin. In the summer of 1452 French troops began to move southeastward; ostensibly they were beginning an advance on Savoy but they could as well attack Dauphiné. Whispers were running that the King meant to disinherit the Dauphin and name Louis's brother, Charles, heir to the throne. Louis mustered his small forces, ordering his country folk to remove themselves and their goods to strong towns. Throughout September and October he dispatched embassies to his father: he declared himself willing humbly to beg the King's pardon if the King felt himself somehow injured. Charles VII first answered that he was undertaking his expedition not against the Dauphin but to punish the Duke of Savoy. He was soon demanding, however, that his son deliver up certain "evil councilors" to the royal justice and promise to do whatever he was commanded. Louis fired back an iron-hard answer—his only desire was to obey his father, but on two conditions: he would not return to court; and he would not abandon any of his men.

On October 27 (1452), the frightened Duke of Savoy, having hastened to meet the King, signed a treaty putting himself under the protection of France and renouncing the Dauphin. Reports reached Louis that his father, now not far from Dauphiné, was being urged to march against his son. At this perilous moment, fortune served the Dauphin a good turn. News came that an English expeditionary force, landing in Guienne, had been welcomed at Bordeaux. Louis immediately wrote to his father offering his services. They were brusquely refused. But the royal army began to withdraw from the southeast, heading for Guienne. Charles VII issued a public proclamation denouncing his son's "foolish enterprises." The enemies of France did not think Louis so foolish as his father wished to. The English had been intriguing with the ever-unstable Duke of Alençon° to make an entry into Normandy, but their hopes were dashed by a report that the Dauphin was to be the governor of that province; for, admitted an agent of Alençon, "the Dauphin is the man in all France that the English fear most."

Over the winter, 1452–53, the Dauphin tried to keep open the door of negotiations but the King now demanded complete obedience, with strict sureties. Consequently, as the spring of 1453 came round, Louis was ardently seeking expedients by which he might stave off what was rapidly becoming the inevitable. The preoccupation of the royal government with the campaign to drive the English from Guienne, the ambitions of his uncle, King René, and the political situation in Italy provided him with an opportunity. The states of Milan and Florence, under attack from Venice and the Kingdom of Naples (ruled by the Aragonese Alfonso V), induced King René, titular claimant to Naples, to come to their aid by giving him a subsidy and the hope (but only the hope) that they would afterward help him win his kingdom. Louis promptly offered his services to his uncle, and, with Charles VII's approval, they were ac-

---

° Louis's godfather, who had joined him and the Duke of Bourbon in the Praguerie.

cepted. While King René sailed from Provence in a Genoese fleet, the Dauphin crossed the Alps with René's troops and his small force. Breathing the heady air of Italian politics, he was revolving plans of his own.

As soon as he had descended into the Piedmont, he dispatched an embassy to Genoa to announce that he was coming to place that city, once a French lordship, under his protection. When Louis met his uncle at Villanova, he cheerfully proposed that King René help him to secure Genoa; and he would then, with the Genoese fleet, support René's Naples enterprise. By this time the Genoese were sending frantic appeals to René to protect them from this would-be enterprise; all northern Italy was fermenting with rumors that the audacious Son of France was bent upon a career of conquest. René's Italian allies, wanting no such disturbing force in their midst, persuaded the bewildered René that the Dauphin's visions boded ill for the House of Anjou. Obediently, he requested the Dauphin to return at once across the Alps. In vain Louis sought to negotiate with the Venetians, then made overtures to Milan. It was known that he had no backing from the King of France. There was nothing for him but to take the road back to his little province. He soon had the satisfaction of seeing his uncle make a hash of things in typically Angevin fashion. Milan and Florence let René help them in their war and then, as he was becoming no longer necessary, treated him with increasing coldness. René weakly threw up the game and in January of 1454 returned to Provence, a retreat so inglorious that even Charles VII was irritated with him for damaging French prestige.

But, however much the Dauphin enjoyed his uncle's discomforts, he could hardly hide from himself that in Italy he had enacted yet another failure, another withdrawal. And by the beginning of 1454, with the English beaten out of Guienne, King Charles was once again free to deal with his son.

7. Man Near the End of His Rope

THROUGHOUT 1454 and 1455 Louis watched the coils slowly closing round him. He had sought to chasten his father-in-law, the Duke of Savoy, by attacking the Duke's province of Bresse, then tried to forge an alliance with Savoy and Milan. The King of France promptly forced these states to renounce all links with his son. The Dauphin, a Milanese ambassador reported unsympathetically, "is a man unquiet and avid for novelties and poor." In December, 1455, Charles VII moved down into the Bourbonnais at the head of an army, spending Christmas at St. Pourçain, less than one hundred miles from the frontier of Dauphiné. Time was growing short.

As he would all his life, Louis meant to keep on negotiating till the clock struck midnight, and even after if possible. He made a slight move during the winter: he let it be known that he was thinking of heeding the Pope's call for a crusade. Early in the spring (1456) Louis ventured to send a communication to his father by a monk. Neither a message nor the monk came back. In mid-April he tried again: this time he dispatched one of his chief officers, Guillaume de Courcillon, on a formal mission to seek a reconciliation with his father. When the King asked Courcillon what his errand was, he replied, "Sire, there has been endless tale-bearing on both sides and there have been some very strange tales, sufficient to give you great suspicions and the Dauphin great fears. Your son, however, most humbly seeks your pardon and wishes only to be able to obey you." Courcillon added that the Dauphin of course stood by his two conditions, namely, his remaining in Dauphiné and surrendering none of his servants.

Four days later, the Chancellor, in the presence of King and council, delivered Charles's answer. The Dauphin's conditions were unacceptable; the King was already taking steps to deal with his son's disobedience. "This affair has lasted too long," the Chancellor finished. "His Majesty means to see the end of it. Messire Guillaume, take your leave of the King. You are dispatched."

When Louis heard Courcillon's report, he knew that time was running out. He was to be hunted down by main force and delivered to his father. Prepared to run any risks rather than submit, he had already decided what course he would take. He continued, however, to send embassies to his father, all of them insisting upon his two conditions and each more plain-speaking than the last. King Charles, in turn, berated Louis's envoys for their master's presumption and began sending troops toward Dauphiné. Louis's final embassy in July complained that the King's answers were harsh and menacing. The Dauphin, they told Charles, wants to satisfy you, but he can get nowhere with the men who advise you—it would be a hundred years before he would find any support there. On August 20 the Chancellor read out a reply as meaningless as Louis's protestations of obedience: The King has always wanted to employ the Dauphin in public business and desires only his welfare. Unless he returns to court without reservations, his father will proceed against his evil councilors.

By the time the Dauphin received this answer from his envoys, a French army was about to cross the frontier of Dauphiné.

Louis moved first.

He had made trails in several directions. Having maintained friendly relations with the Swiss, he had sent his Carver, Gaston du Lyon, to Berne in April seeking aid in case of need. He had opened cordial communications to the north with the Prince of Orange, vassal of the Duke of Burgundy. Later, he declared—perhaps only to emphasize the lengths to which he would go in order to stay out of his father's hands—that he had made an "appointment" in England and would be welcomed there. He had also shown increasing interest in the Pope's call for a crusade. But in the end he rejected all these havens of refuge and decided to flee to a prince whom he had never met, a prince, in fact, who was the man in all the world his father and his father's friends most disliked and feared—Philip the Good, Duke of Burgundy, the richest ruler in Christendom, whose domains extended in a broken arc from the Low Countries to Dauphiné.

Casting himself upon this resplendent uncle * would likewise enable him to maintain the perhaps useful fiction that he was leaving Dauphiné

---

* Louis's aunt, Michelle of France, had been the Duke's first wife. In this age, relations-in-law were referred to in the same terms as blood kin. Dauphin and Duke were directly related too, for Louis was the great-grandson of Charles V, while Philip was the grandson of Charles V's younger brother, Philippe le Hardi.

not as a fugitive but as a prospective crusader: two years before (1454), at the Feast of the Pheasant, the most famous banquet of the century, the Duke of Burgundy and his chief lords had sworn to take the Cross. Louis had been careful to develop an amicable correspondence with Philip. As early as the spring of 1455 he was probably thinking of the dominions of Burgundy for a refuge, for at that time he sent the Duke an artillery piece and some gayer presents and showed "great signs of love." But, even during his waning moments in Dauphiné, he never gave his uncle Philip the slightest hint that he meant to throw himself upon his hospitality. Philip might balk at unchivalrous collusion; besides, Louis sensed that the Duke of Burgundy, devotee of the Table Round, would much prefer playing benevolent uncle to a nephew washed up unexpectedly on his shores.

By the end of August, 1456, as Antoine de Chabannes headed the French advance into Dauphiné, Louis's final dispositions were taken. He had garrisoned his chief strong places, exhorted his commanders to hold them at all costs, and ordered the Governor of Dauphiné, Louis de Laval, and his other officers to remain firm in their duties.

Very early in the morning of August 30 he went off with some half a hundred followers, as if to go hunting. But he was soon galloping northward along mountainous trails. He was thirty-three years old, a landless fugitive. It was complete withdrawal.

THE REFUGEE

8. The Grateful Nephew

Afterward Louis let it be known
—so the Burgundian chronicler Chastellain recounts—that he had been
driven by a "fierce terror" of what his father meant to do with him. In
"wild imaginings" he saw himself sewed in a sack and thrown into a
river. Whether or not he was exaggerating, he indubitably made few
halts in his northward flight until he reached the famous Abbey of St.
Claude in Philip the Good's County of Burgundy. Here he had three Masses chanted, took some refreshment, and dictated a letter to his father:

"My very redoubted lord . . . since, as you know, my good uncle of
Burgundy means shortly to march against the Turk for the defense of
the Catholic faith and since my desire is, with your permission, to join
this enterprise . . . I am going to my good uncle in order to learn his
plans . . . and also to beg him to find a means whereby I can remain in
your good grace, which is the thing I most desire in this world. . . ." To
fortify this role, Louis then drew up a circular letter to the bishops of
the realm, explaining that he was journeying to the Duke of Burgundy
to see about undertaking a crusade and requesting their prayers for this
holy mission.

Not long after, he was riding hard for the Low Countries under the
escort of the Marshal of Burgundy. At Louvain, safely within the Duke's
lands, the Dauphin paused to await the wishes of Philip the Good. Soon
the news was blown over Europe; men everywhere discussed the turbulent and bizarre destiny of the heir of France. The Duke of Burgundy,
then on campaign in Holland, sent hasty word to the King that he had
known nothing of the Dauphin's flight and ordered an array of lords to

inform the fugitive that the Duke would meet him at Brussels on October 15.

At Louvain, meanwhile, Louis hunted and hawked and furbished up his charms and felt his way into the high style of the Burgundian nobility. As lords and gentry thronged Louvain to pay their respects to the amazing apparition, the Dauphin greeted each one warmly, asked his name—committing name and face to memory—said that of course he had heard of him and his exploits, took the man familiarly by the hand and bade him welcome. In a few days Louis was ceremoniously conducted to Brussels, where the Duchess of Burgundy and her daughter-in-law, the Countess of Charolais, were waiting to do the honors of the House of Burgundy.

When Louis rode into the courtyard of the castle about eight o'clock in the evening, he found a bevy of ladies standing in a row to welcome him. By the time he had dismounted, they were all kneeling on the cobblestones. Louis embraced the Duchess and the Countess, went down the line kissing all the ladies, and returned to raise the Duchess to her feet, talking in his usual familiar style. When he took her by the arm to indicate that she should precede him up the stairs, she halted, rigid with horror. That she should walk before the heir of France, never! Louis used all his arts of persuasion, but the Duchess was adamant. "Monsieur, you must be making fun of me. Otherwise you would not urge such an impropriety!" Louis protested, said that he should indeed do her honor for he was but the poorest subject of the Realm of France. In vain. Burgundian etiquette was unshakable, even by the Dauphin of the Lilies. When they arrived within the castle, there was another tender altercation. Duke Philip had sent orders that the Dauphin was to occupy his own private chambers. But this Louis refused to do, and not all the pleas of the Duchess could change his mind.

When word came on the morning of October 15 that the Duke of Burgundy was approaching Brussels, the Dauphin dispatched the chief men of his household to pay honor to his uncle. Then he sent a message that he himself was coming too. The Duke of Burgundy was struck to the heart by this monstrous solecism. In a few moments Louis was bombarded by messages begging him not to visit such a terrible mortification upon his uncle. The prospect "crucified him with woe." Finally Philip sent word that if the Dauphin emerged from the castle, he, the Duke, would flee from him so far that in a year Louis would never find him! The Duchess added her pleas, and with great difficulty the Dauphin was finally persuaded to await his uncle's coming; but he insisted upon sending every last one of his entourage to greet the Duke in his name.

Wait inside the castle Louis would not. As he escorted the Duchess down into the courtyard, the ducal cavalcade arrived at the gate. Philip of Burgundy—costume flashing with jewels, surrounded by a pageant of great barons—dismounted from his horse and, alone, passed through the gate into the court. The moment he saw the Dauphin, he fell upon his knees to make the first of the three obligatory "honors." The moment Louis saw Philip, he started toward him. The Duchess, scandalized, seized his arm to hold him back. Hurriedly the Duke moved forward to make his second honor. Louis broke free from the Duchess. As Philip was trying to get down to his knees for the third honor, guest flung arms around host, almost tumbling both of them to the ground. Louis tried to haul Philip to his feet. The Duke resisted. "My lord," he panted, "you are as welcome to me as was the Angel Gabriel to the Virgin Mary, for such great joy and honor I have never had!"

"By my faith, good uncle," Louis cried, "if you do not get up I will go off and leave you! You have long been the man in the world I have most desired to see—as well appears, for I have come from far in great danger to see you. . . ." By this time he had succeeded in raising the Duke. "Dear uncle, if God pleases we will make good cheer together, and I will tell you my adventures and you, you will tell me yours."

The Duke had tears in his eyes. Louis's were no drier. The onlookers wept for joy at the sight. For all that he meant to be a good Burgundian, Louis clung to his own simple style. "Uncle, you must go take off your leggings and relax in your chambers. Let us go up." The Dauphin went first but he kept hold of the Duke's hand and drew him close after.

An hour later, nephew and uncle were closeted together. Louis plunged into a recital of the quarrel with his father which had turned him into a fugitive. The old Duke promised that he would do all he could to reconcile King and Dauphin. While they talked, Louis could take stock at last of this most famous of European potentates, to whom he had confided his destiny.

The Duke, then almost sixty, was of medium height, slender, with a back still as straight as a tree. He had a long bony face and sensual lips and a forehead corded with veins which swelled dangerously, even as his bushy eyebrows tufted like horns, when he fell into one of his renowned rages. But he became angry only when he was crossed, and he was seldom crossed; usually he was courteous to all, high and low, for he was tranquilly sure of his greatness. His amiable manner had earned him the sobriquet of Bon Duc. His walk, his look, his bearing "proclaimed 'I am a Prince.'"

The domains and lordships of the Duke of Burgundy stretched from the North Sea to the Jura Mountains and from the Somme River to the Moselle. As Count of Flanders and of Artois and Duke of Burgundy he was a Peer of France. In his own right he ruled the Low Countries, Luxembourg and the County of Burgundy (Franche-Comté). Choosing his moment, he had deserted the English alliance, in 1435, to make peace with France and gain for himself the province of Picardy and important towns along the Somme River like Amiens and Abbeville. Patiently he had worked to weld his jigsaw of dominions into a unified state. Maintaining no professional army, he taxed his people lightly; and long years of peace had nursed prosperity in his lands. In the great commercial and industrial towns of Flanders thousands of artisans turned English wool into cloth that was exported to all parts of Europe.

Lapped in golden plenty, the Duke of Burgundy sought to express his greatness in a rhetoric of attitudes and images which curiously mingled traditional medieval splendors with a heightened style of courtly existence that bespoke the Renaissance. In the marketplace of Bruges, his knights thundered against each other in the lists, wearing golden chains on their legs to show themselves bound by the love of a lady fair. Committees labored to produce spectacles befitting ducal pride; men whiled away days discussing disputed points of ceremonial and protocol. Monarchs were flattered to be elected to Philip's famous knightly order, the Toison d'Or (Golden Fleece), rivaled only by England's far older Order of the Garter. Burgundian etiquette, the most elaborate and rigid in Europe, passed through Philip's descendants to the Court of Spain and then to the Versailles of Louis XIV.

Of late years the Duke had increasingly left the business of state to his officers. Within the glittering edifice of chivalry that his wealth and his fancy had erected, Philip gave himself up to an ingenious variety of pleasures. He maintained a fine band of musicians; he had a library of rare manuscripts, richly illuminated and bound with jewel-encrusted covers. Within his country place at Hesdin, not far from Calais, he indulged all the whims of his humor: in the gardens, little bridges collapsed to dump the unwary visitor into the water; sudden spouts of air blew up the ladies' dresses; books puffed dust into the beholder's eye; and in the Jason Room thunder, lightning, and rain could be produced. Despite his age, the Duke still hawked and hunted and played tennis.

His chief delight, however, was the pursuit of girls. When he married his third wife, Isabella of Portugal, he took as his motto *Autre n'auray* (I will have no other), but it was immediately understood that he meant no other *wife*. From some thirty acknowledged mistresses he had received a fine crop of bastards, for whom he made handsome provision at court or in the Church.

There were other aspects of his character, however, which the fugitive Dauphin of France would not be long in perceiving. Beneath the bright surface of courtly gesture Philip nursed an enormous vanity and kept a hard accounting of what he considered his due. He had sworn to lead a crusade, but he had carefully hedged round his oath with conditions which would enable him to go or not as he pleased. If his devoted historian, Georges Chastellain, found him the mirror of all chivalry, the citizens of Ghent, whose revolt against his encroachments he had mortally crushed in 1452, would tell a somewhat different story. "He is a deep river with hidden currents," a Milanese ambassador reported. On another occasion the Milanese observed, "The Duke is not accustomed to give without receiving."

The Dauphin settled into the pomps of the court at Brussels. Though Duke Philip insisted upon being treated as a sovereign prince, he let nobody forget that he was the first Peer of France and he yielded to none in his sentimental reverence for the House of the Lilies. Despite Louis's protests, however cold or rainy the weather, the Duke doffed his hood in the Dauphin's presence. When they rode together, Philip would not let the nose of his horse come farther forward than the tail of the Dauphin's. Gingerly, Louis felt his way into the intricacies of the Burgundian court, studying his uncle and his uncle's heir, Charles, Count of Charolais, ten years his junior. Never for an instant, despite the Duke's limitless reverence for his wishes, did he lose sight of the fact that he was a refugee, perhaps a hostage, and that if he meant to thrive he must please his host.

Louis solemnly asked Philip to allow the Count of Charolais and himself to swear a pact as brothers-in-arms. The Duke replied that the request was unfitting since the Dauphin was to be, one day, his son's sovereign lord. He then commanded young Charles to serve the Dauphin on every occasion, except against the King. Louis topped this request by a demand still more flattering and unfitting: he wanted his uncle to bestow upon him the collar of that famous order, the Toison d'Or; Philip was delighted to point out that the heir of France must not receive the livery of a subject but bestow liveries himself. Louis made a final request, more realistic and heartfelt: would the Duke provide him with a place where he might lodge himself and his followers? Philip, all benevolent uncle, assigned his nephew a pension of thirty-six thousand livres a year and the charming castle of Genappe, situated a dozen miles south of Brussels in a countryside to delight a hunter.

In these first weeks as a refugee, the Dauphin sent message after message to his little mountain empire, exhorting his officers to remain loyal. By the end of October he and his uncle had dispatched a conciliatory embassy to Charles VII. But the Dauphin's hopes of retaining his hold upon Dauphiné were quickly destroyed by the King's adroit use of power. He had followed his army into the province, sending ahead soothing assurances. By a mixture of threats and promises he won over the chief administrators left by his son, and thus undermined the resistance of the commanders of garrisons. Soon he was able to announce blandly to the Estates of Dauphiné that he intended no important changes in their government. They could do nothing but accept the King's commands.

One November day, the Dauphin's captain, Robin Malortie, appeared in Brussels. Louis welcomed him warmly and began to question him about conditions in Dauphiné. Malortie stammered out his news— King Charles's men had so confused him by their persuasions that, thinking it best for his master, he had surrendered his fortress. To show his unchanged allegiance he had brought with him the treasure of jewels which he had saved from the King's men. This admission was too much for the Dauphin. He started to his feet, shouted for his guards, and in a fury ordered Malortie then and there to be sewed in a sack and cast into a river. Poor Robin had touched the fugitive's tenderest nerve: what was left from the wreck of his career except the loyalty of Dauphiné to prove that his father's talk of evil government was lies? Fortunately for Robin, the Dauphin's lords and the Duke of Burgundy succeeded in mitigating Louis's anger, but Malortie was to spend many a month in prison, and, in low moments, Louis again had thoughts of sewing him in a sack—or so said, according to Chastellain. However, valiant Robin would live to prop Louis's throne with his warrior's arm and, in reward, Louis would make him Count of Conches and one of the great men of the realm.

Not long after Malortie had come to Brussels, near the end of November, the ambassadors of the Duke of Burgundy were heard by the King at St. Symphorien, in Dauphiné. To their assurances of the Duke of Burgundy's good will and of the Dauphin's desire, his two conditions granted, to be received into his father's grace, the King made formal reply, six days later, that he would never agree to his son's foolish conditions and that he was holding the Duke responsible for the Dauphin's actions. To this answer, read out by the Chancellor, Charles himself added a sting: "Tell your master that if he does anything to displease me, I will not have him in favor and tell him that what he thinks to be to his profit may be greatly to his harm." Charles had already put it more picturesquely to his intimates: "The Duke of Burgundy has taken in a fox that will eat his chickens."

Most of the inhabitants of Dauphiné remained loyal, in their hearts, to their fugitive master. At the risk of their lives, young men made their way to the Dauphin's side. Louis kept in touch with his people by letters and messengers, refusing to recognize the seizure of his province. What he did recognize, however, on hearing the report of the Burgundian ambassadors, was the fragility of his position.

During the winter of 1456–57, Louis moved with wary circumspection at his uncle's court. Upon his followers high and low he enjoined, on pain of severe punishment, a regimen of impeccable conduct; and he kept himself on an equally tight rein. It was not only that the Duke and his courtiers were a touchy lot; Louis was fast learning that the Court of Burgundy harbored factions and hatreds that could be dangerous to so prickly a guest. For many years Nicolas Rolin, Philip the Good's Chancellor, had administered the Burgundian dominions. Now that Rolin was growing old and his rule slipshod, two shrewd, acquisitive brothers, Antoine and Jean de Croy, had made their way into the bosom of the Duke and fastened their authority upon the state. Nicolas Rolin, looking to the future, sought to place his children in the household of the Count of Charolais, a maneuver that Philip the Good perceived with rancor. The de Croys likewise pressed for offices about the heir. Charles of Charolais, in turn, developed a deep hatred of the de Croys, ambitious upstarts, which he had so far concealed out of fear of his father's wrath. For, however much the Duke encouraged the Dauphin's rebellion against the King, he expected the strictest obedience from *his* son. Louis carefully cultivated the friendship of the Count of Charolais, a rigid and humorless young man, who fortunately shared his passion for hunting. Of necessity the Dauphin also encouraged the good will of the brothers de Croy, the men who ruled the Duke. Charolais did not conceal his resentment of the connection.

Such were the political discords at the Burgundian court when, in January of 1457, a violent quarrel erupted between the Duke of Bur-

gundy and the Count of Charolais over the refusal by Charolais to take
Jean de Croy's son into his household. Louis found himself in the midst
of a whirlwind—a bizarre imbroglio of princely passions that Burgundians were quick to blame upon the unlucky guest. It taxed all of Louis's
tact and ingenuity, stretched over many days, to persuade the father to
forgive, the son to ask humbly for forgiveness, and to arrange a properly
elaborate scene of reconciliation.[1]

With the approach of spring (1457), Philip of Burgundy prepared to
take to the road to visit some of his "good towns." Proud of their prosperity, he wanted the Dauphin to accompany him, and Louis was happy
with the opportunity of surveying the financial and industrial resources
of the Burgundian state. Throughout most of April and May he sojourned at the great commercial center Bruges. He endured with good
grace the tournaments in the market place and the long Burgundian
banquets, where Philip and his lords talked of chivalric enterprises; but
he also spent much time studying the city and its entrepreneurs, and
knit up a close relationship with the Italian financier "Jean Arnoulfin"
(Giovanni Arnolfini), a money agent of the Duke of Burgundy. One day,
poking about a canal near Bruges, he fell into the water and almost
drowned—such were the penalties of an insatiable appetite to understand things-as-they-are.

One pressing aspect of things-as-they-are was the childlessness of
the heir of France, who, at thirty-four, was middle-aged by the standards of that time. He had never consummated his marriage with Charlotte of Savoy, now eighteen and still in Dauphiné. With the encouragement of the Duke of Burgundy, who would, after all, foot the bill, Louis
in the late spring (1457) sent a man to Grenoble with a message to
Charlotte to join him. Duke Philip dispatched his chief Officer of Arms,
Toison d'Or, to smooth the way for this enterprise, which, he pointed
out, was laudable for many reasons, among them that Louis would thus
be able to live "out of sin," a subject on which no man, not even King
Charles, could speak with larger authority than Philip the Good.

With the Duke of Burgundy and his son, Louis was at Louvain
hunting stags in the fine July weather when he got word that Charlotte
was drawing near. Bidding farewell to the Duke and the Count—no
doubt with relief, for he had been continually exposed to their surcharged personalities since his arrival in Brussels the previous October
—the Dauphin rode with a few intimates to Namur to greet his wife.
She arrived on a Sunday. Without any ceremony at all, like a bourgeois
couple, they went to bed together that night for the first time.

Charlotte was not physically attractive, but she was a girl whose only thought was to fit herself into her lord's life according to his will; and, coming from a prolific family, she was likely to bear children readily. Louis was well satisfied with her. For the first dozen years of their marriage, but no longer, he indulged in a few fleeting amours; by the general standard of his time and station he was continent. For their honeymoon they remained briefly at Namur, then made their way by easy stages to Genappe.

9. The Squire of Genappe

THE CASTLE OF GENAPPE was charmingly islanded in a wide moat fed by a stream and sat amidst rolling country abounding in game. Here Louis remained throughout his five-year sojourn in the Burgundian dominions, except when the mounting hostility between France and Burgundy gave him urgent reason to consult with his uncle. The farther he stayed from Philip's court, the better chance he had of keeping clear of the strife between the Count of Charolais and Jean and Antoine de Croy. Charles of Charolais he invited to Genappe for the hunting and a taste of the simple life. His officers and servants Louis kept close about him, giving them strict orders to be courteous to all but to hold themselves apart from the Burgundian lords. Without ostentation the Dauphin and the Dauphine—Louis called her simply "my wife"—entertained the gentry of the region and visited back and forth.

Louis began his day on his knees in prayer. Even by the standards of that age, he spent more time than most folk in religious exercises, looking especially to the Virgin for heavenly aid, cultivating the attention of numerous saints, going on pilgrimages to the shrines round about, and hearing special Masses. On occasion he would pass three days together in private meditation, and on that singularly unlucky day of the week—the day on which fell, the preceding December, the commemoration of the Holy Innocents—Louis sequestered himself from all affairs. He spent lavishly on alms, religious foundations, bequests to shrines. If, however, he buoyantly pursued heaven's blessing upon his affairs, there is no evidence that he experienced profound religious feeling. His mind, though tough and realistic, harbored impulses toward propitiation which were hardly Christian. In these dark strains can be perceived perhaps the precariousness and solitude of his childhood, the primitive superstitions of the humble folk among whom he was reared, perhaps too a manifestation of the taint in his blood from his mad grandfather, Charles VI. Louis also probably regarded it as mere prudence to neglect no possible resource, however intangible. Gamesters walk warily.

On emerging from his chamber in the morning, Louis went to chapel to hear Mass, usually booted and spurred for the hunt. Then he breakfasted, or if he was eager to take to the woods, he mounted horseback immediately and munched a bit of bread and meat, talking with his companions, before setting forth. Hawking he enjoyed too but not so much as coursing to the hounds. He could not resist spending money on jet-black steeds and hawks and greyhounds and all manner of exotic birds and beasts. Unlike most princes of his time, Louis believed that the way to get was to pay. It amazed Olivier de La Marche that, instead of suggesting to someone that a few animals would be appreciated, "he bought them with gold and coin." Louis exercised his mind as vigorously as his body. He maintained close watch upon the shifting currents at the court of Burgundy; he received reports of what was happening everywhere in Europe; he enrolled himself as a student at the University of Louvain; he employed astrologers to read the enigma of the stars; he studied history and kept up his Italian; he corresponded with scholars.

Not till after he became King, however, did he find thirty gold crowns to pay "Jehan de Templo, now enfeebled by gout," who had "by our order translated from Latin into French the book of Xenophon the philosopher . . . and sent it to us in the town of Genappe where we were then. . . ." Despite the handsome pension provided by the Duke of Burgundy, the Dauphin was poor.

In January of 1458 he was anxiously writing to one of his secretaries, charged with securing dowry payments still owed by his father-in-law, the Duke of Savoy: "We believed that by Christmas past we would have had money from there [Savoy] . . . but it has all come to nothing. This puts us in a bad way, for, trusting to have had the money, we have borrowed from a bank the sum of 1,000 francs. The repayment date has almost passed and we are in great dread of defaulting on the sum; for to do so would not only be dishonorable but also damaging, because as you know these banks will not lend again to anyone who defaults. . . ." Louis was driven to borrowing from his entourage sums as small as thirty crowns which he could not promise to repay in less than four months. Sometimes there came a small windfall, as when Louis secured the loan of four thousand crowns from his secretary, Charles Astars. At other times, though there was always a chicken in the pot, finances were so low that an envoy of his, coming back from Italy with a magnificent suit of armor presented to him by the Duke of Milan, was forced to pawn the gift at Geneva in order to get home at all. But Astars and smaller creditors were all repaid, though Astars had to wait till 1462 for his money. In these difficulties, the financier Jean Arnoulfin was of great assistance, lending funds readily and buying cloth for the Dauphin's wardrobe and handling the payments from the Duke of Burgundy and whatever negotiable paper came from other sources:

"Jean, my friend, I have received your letter in which you write me that you have no plain velours but only velours on velours which is dearer. Actually, I prefer that. And I thank you for never failing me, and by my faith, if God pleases, I'll pay you well for all. Please deliver the velvet to the Lord de La Barde. And, Jean my friend, may God give you joy. Written in my own hand." Louis's large promises to Jean Arnoulfin would be abundantly redeemed.

On himself the Dauphin spent very little—hence probably the legend of extreme parsimony that later grew up about a man who was a byword with his contemporaries for his liberalities. Passing much of his time in the saddle, consuming his nervous energy in ranging thoughts, Louis ate heartily and enjoyed his wine, but he kept a plain table, eking out lack of ceremony with copious conversation. His dress was scandalously simple—coarse gray gowns; broad-brimmed hat, with cheap lead images of Virgin and saints stuck in the brim; short, serviceable hunting jackets and countrymen's boots. For appearances at the court of Burgundy he owned some velvet gowns furred with marten. The meager sums spent on dress and household, the Dauphin's indulgences in buying beasts and birds, even his large expenditures on religion, cannot account for his chronic poverty. The money went, as it had gone and would always go, on rewarding good service.

The Dauphin's couriers and the men of arms of his little guard received a basic wage of 120 crowns a year, an income of a well-to-do country squire. His two chief intimates, Jean, Bastard of Armagnac, and the Breton Jean, Lord of Montauban; his Squire-Carver and diplomatic agent Gaston du Lyon; his indefatigable first secretary Jean Bourré received great sums, even in this period; and for all ranks there were numerous supplementary rewards. On behalf of the clerics in his service and other prelates scattered far and wide—part of his net of information —the Dauphin turned out numerous letters to the Pope, to chapters with vacant prebends, to nobles possessing advowsons, recommending his followers for fat benefices.

The Dauphin was not an easy master. While still in his twenties, he had been called "the most suspicious man alive." Here at Genappe he found no reason to relax his guard: a careless word, a gibe by one of his household could plunge him into Burgundian imbroglios; he knew that at least one or two of the men about him were secret agents of the King; the talk was running ever louder through the courts of Europe that his brother, Charles, was to succeed to the Crown of France. Louis furthermore maintained stringent standards of allegiance and of efficiency. His frequent injunctions to "see that there is no slip-up!" reflect the hard service demanded by a man who never spared himself.

But Louis paid in more than money. Demanding strict loyalty, he was himself loyal, sometimes with risk and loss, to the men who passed his test of service. He made them the companions of his enterprises and the familiars of his chamber, joked with them, listened to them, dosed them when they were ill, found them good marriages when they were marriageable, respected their capacities and encouraged their ambitions. Here in Flanders he found a barber—that Olivier le Daim made famous by romancers—who, Louis soon discovered, had a flair for household management; he was put in charge of all his master's journeyings. When Louis's poverty forced him to cut down on his household, he sought places for those whom he had to let go. On one occasion he appealed to an uncle of his, probably the Count of Maine, to take care of a servant he could no longer afford to keep and "to do the best for him that you are able, until such a time as our situation mends; for he has loyally served us and for nothing in the world would we be willing to lose him." Of course, it may be that Louis was planting the man as a spy in his uncle's household.

For, if the King of France had his agents around Louis, the Dauphin had even more agents and well-wishers at the French court; nor did he lack adherents within the establishments of great lords and in important towns. Indeed the nerve ends of Louis's espionage extended even into the King's bed: Madame de Villequier (Antoinette de Mangnelais), the royal mistress, was Louis's chief spy, being "utterly devoted" to the Dauphin. When, in 1458, she left the King's flagging service to become mistress to the Duke of Brittany, that Duke was so often at court that she continued to be almost as useful as before.

Thus Louis of Valois, the greatest and least of royal heirs, passed at Genappe the days of his prime. The Dauphin's little country court became legend. It was believed for a long time that the *Cent Nouvelles Nouvelles,* a collection of Boccaccio-like tales originating in the Low Countries at this period, represented the hearty household entertain-

ments of the Dauphin; but though some of Louis's companions are mentioned, the ruler presiding over the assemblage is clearly meant to
be Philip of Burgundy. There is a story, however—apocryphal but
suggestive—that Louis used to go to the cottage of a peasant named
Conan in order to eat his delicious vegetables. Afterward, when Conan's
friend had become King of France, the peasant, growing an especially
fine crop of turnips one summer, gathered the best of them into a basket
and set off on foot to provide a treat for his old neighbor. But as he
plodded along the road he could not resist sampling his present. The
supply of turnips shrank until there was only one left. This, not knowing
what else to do, he shamefully presented to the King. And Louis paid
him a thousand gold pieces for it in memory of his younger days.

As the months of Louis's exile lengthened into years, relations between the King of France and the Duke of Burgundy grew increasingly
tense. There were incidents on the frontiers, conflicts between ducal and
royal officers in disputed jurisdictions. At the French court it was said
that the Duke of Burgundy was flaunting the Dauphin in the King's face
to provoke hostilities; in the Burgundian dominions rumors ran of
French troop movements and military preparations. Embassies journeyed back and forth, bearing empty protests of good will from Duke
and Dauphin and complaints or menaces from the King. "Daily there
ran new wild rumors; everybody kept his ear to the wind and no one
knew whether to expect peace or war." [1]

During the summer of 1458 death flirted capriciously with the King
and the Duke. Louis learned that an illness incurred by his father the
previous winter had left him with an ulcerous leg and an enfeebled con-
stitution. Then Duke Philip, overheating himself in a game of tennis, fell
into a fever, and for a time his life was despaired of. During his illness
the Burgundian state drifted aimlessly. The Dauphin, alarmed at Philip's precarious health and his own precarious position, sought to establish closer relations with Philip's moody heir, Charles.

The Count of Charolais was stockier than his father, with a powerful
torso and heavy shoulders. He had a shock of black hair, clear blue
eyes, and his father's high sensual coloring. He had inherited the Duke's
temper, too, which he struggled fiercely to master or conceal, and as he
paced a chamber, shoulders hunched and eyes on the ground, he gave
the impression of smoldering within. From boyhood, he had thrown
himself into all violent games. His favorite residence was at Gorcum in
Holland, for he loved to take to the sea in a storm and defy the ele-

ments. He jousted fiercely, as if he were a landless squire with his way to make by the address of his arm. He rigorously chastened his blood— perhaps in reaction to his father's life—by enforcing a sexual continence which, some felt, hardly befitted a prince, and he drank little wine, and that watered. He was adept at chess, composed and played music, and made some use of his father's great library. No evidence survives that he experienced delight in being alive. Such was the man of rigor, veiled in a darkness of spirit, whom the Dauphin assiduously studied. Perhaps he already sensed that, when this explosive personality became the ruler of Burgundy, his own fate and that of France might depend on his reading of Charolais's character.

During the summer of 1459 Louis's horizons momentarily lightened. On the early morning of July 27, Charlotte of Savoy gave birth to a baby boy. Joyously the Dauphin galloped to Our Lady of Hal to offer thanks to his patroness, the Virgin. From Hal the same day he dictated letters —to his father, to lords and prelates, to the "good towns" of the realm, and also to his younger brother—announcing that the Dauphin of France now had an heir. Philip of Burgundy and Antoine de Croy served as godfathers, Louis balancing the factions at the Burgundian court by choosing the Countess of Charolais for godmother. The infant was welcomed into the world with lavish presents and with public re- joicing in all Burgundian towns. Little Joachim died, however, when he was only four months old.[2]

By this time, the winter of 1459–60, Louis was no longer the prized guest reposing in the bosom of his uncle. Though the Duke never flagged in outward courtesies and though the Dauphin still made efforts to suit his conduct to the Duke's humor, suspicion and irritations had eroded the links that united them. Duke Philip was put off by the simplic- ity of the Dauphin's manner and the complexity of his thinking. The household at Genappe, despite its modest mien, had become the seat of a European power. Philip's pride was pinched because Louis received and dispatched envoys without opening all matters to his uncle, and Philip's feelings were injured because, as relations between France and Burgundy worsened, Louis began an exchange of messages with King Charles. Then there was the matter of the Duke's stiff-necked son and that son's obstinate hatred of the de Croys. Though Louis listened sympa- thetically to his uncle's plaints and though he assiduously cultivated An- toine and Jean de Croy, Philip had come to resent the Dauphin's atten- tions to young Charolais on those hunting parties at Genappe. The Duke was further stimulated in his jealousies by the attitude of his court, indeed of many of his subjects. Louis was now regarded as a Jonah, a man accursed, who brought misfortunes with him wherever he went. "After the Dauphin's arrival," records a popular chronicler, "never among the nobles of Duke Philip's court was there peace. From the beginning it was widely said that his coming was an evil portent and so it proved to be. He was never quiet, and always did he know in secret from France the will of his father."

Louis, for his part, grew impatient with Burgundian sensibilities and his own helplessness, and he had become increasingly disquieted by the slipshod government of Philip the Good. Duke Philip contrived to neglect his affairs without abandoning them to his servants. The de Croys were energetic, but they had to work as best they could through their master, and they were harassed at every turn by the enmity of the Count of Charolais. This feud entangled all business. The Duke's bastard sons and most of his great lords supported Charolais; but Philip of Burgundy, out of loyalty, out of anger against his son's pretension to meddle in the government, out of fear that he was being thought too old to manage his affairs, clung obstinately to the de Croys. For all his narrow means, Louis had an information service and a chancery far more effective than the Duke's.

The Dauphin's occasional communications with his father accomplished nothing: the King continued to demand his return to court as a condition for restoring Dauphiné and ignored his adamantine insistence that any agreement must include a guarantee of peace for the Duke of Burgundy. The faction in the royal council most bitterly anti-Burgundian was headed by the Dauphin's one-time adherent who had gone over to the King, Antonine de Chabannes, Count of Dammartin. Louis was not above a little rascality in attempting to shake the credit of his enemy— if the chronicle composed by a servant of Dammartin is to be believed. He wrote a letter for Madame de Villequier, unnamed in it, to put to use: "My *demoyselle*, I have read the letter you have written me. And I appreciate the news you have given me in your letters, and be assured that, with the aid of God and of Our Lady, one day I will reward you. I have likewise had letters from the Count of Dammartin, whom I pretend to hate, which are like yours. I beg you, tell him that I hold him always in high favor, as I have informed him. I will think on the matters about which he has written, and he will soon hear from me. My *demoyselle*, throw these letters into the fire and let me know if it seems to you that I am long to remain in the state in which I am [i.e., awaiting the King's demise]." A monk managed to let the letter fall as if by accident into the hands of a royal *valet de chambre,* who gave it to the King. The Count of Dammartin was dismissed from court, for a short time. Charles VII soon discovered, from a secret agent of his at Genappe, one of the Dauphin's secretaries, that the letter was a sham. There were other royal agents, too, on Louis's trail. A French spy at the Burgundian court forwarded reports. Normandy King of Arms was caught ferreting out information in the guise of a merchant, and when his belongings yielded letters that betrayed his mission, he cooled his heels awhile in prison.

The year 1460, with rumors of war growing ever more insistent, looked to be more menacing than '58 and '59, even though King Charles's government, like King Charles himself, was running down. The King dressed now like a young dandy in short jackets, green and red, and, more than ever, sequestered himself from business with his troop of girls and "mignons." At his intrigue-ridden council table, policy was pulled this way and that by competing interests. Angevins and supporters of the Duke of Orléans glowered at each other and both were at odds with the Count of Dammartin. Dammartin and the Count of Maine exchanged bitter words even in the King's presence. The Angevins were urging massive support for Duke John, son of King René. Securing possession of Genoa in 1458, he had used it as a base to invade the Kingdom of Naples the following year. Pierre de Brezé wanted to send armed assistance to King René's daughter Margaret, Henry VI's queen, embroiled in civil war with the Yorkists. It was the fortunes of the House of Anjou in Italy and England that, as the refugee of Genappe clearly perceived, were now weaving the warp and woof of the Dauphin's fate.

The arrival in England in 1445 of Margaret of Anjou, who was as passionately aggressive as her consort, Henry VI, was feeble, had sharpened the animosities between the court party, the Lancastrians (Henry being of the House of Lancaster), and a faction led by Richard, Duke of York,* which advocated reform of Henry's incompetent government and vigorous prosecution of the war in France. The expulsion of the English from the French domains, 1449–53, Jack Cade's rebellion of 1450, and an attack of lunacy suffered by Henry VI in 1453 (his grandfather, on the side of his mother, Katherine of France, was the mad Charles VI) brought Yorkists and Lancastrians to armed conflict in 1455, the first battle of St. Albans, at which the victorious Yorkists captured the King.

---

* York himself possessed a strong title to the throne, though he had not yet put forward his claim: he was descended in the female line from the second son of Edward III, whereas Henry VI was the grandson of the third son, John of Gaunt, Duke of Lancaster.

Though Queen Margaret was able, not long afterward, to regain possession of her hapless consort and the government, the Duke of York's chief
adherent, Richard Neville, Earl of Warwick (soon to be known as the
Kingmaker), built the Yorkists a powerful outpost at Calais, of which he
was Captain. In 1458 the Dauphin and the Duke of Burgundy, to
counter Charles VII's support of Queen Margaret and the Lancastrians,
entered into a secret understanding with Warwick. The following autumn, 1459, as Duke John of Anjou was establishing a strong beachhead
in the Kingdom of Naples, Margaret of Anjou and the Lancastrians succeeded in driving the Duke of York into flight to Ireland while the Earl
of Warwick and York's eldest son Edward, Earl of March, made their
way to Warwick's stronghold on the Channel.

The Dauphin soon learned that these Angevin-Lancastrian successes had strengthened the persuasions of those at the French court ad-
vocating war with Burgundy. Yet he did not lose hope that enemies of
Anjou in England and in Italy might still prove useful to the Duke of
Burgundy, and to himself. By the spring of 1460 he was actively engaged with the two greatest political adventurers of the time, Richard
Neville, Earl of Warwick, and Francesco Sforza, Duke of Milan.

A stroke of fortune gave Louis the opportunity to aid the cause of
Warwick, now completing preparations to resume the struggle against
Lancaster, and also to establish a connection between the Earl and
Francesco Sforza. There arrived in Bruges a diminutive papal legate
named Francesco Coppini, fizzing with ambitions, who had just been re-
buffed by Queen Margaret's government. The Pope had sent him to end
the party strife in England so that the English could support a crusade,
but Coppini had secret instructions from his patron, the Duke of Milan,
to promote an English attack upon France in order to divert the Angevin advance in Italy. Louis quickly put Coppini in touch with Warwick whose forceful personality did the rest. When the Earl of Warwick
embarked from Calais, on June 26 (1460), for the "enterprise of England," he carried with him some two thousand fighting men, an apostolic
legate to bless his cause, and the good wishes of his all-but-allies, the
Dauphin and the Duke of Burgundy. Within three weeks he had routed
the Lancastrians at the Battle of Northampton, taken Henry VI into his
hands, and formed a Yorkist government in the King's name. Louis soon
got word from an Italian agent that "today everything is in Warwick's
power . . . and he has done marvelous things." The Dauphin and the
Duke of Burgundy at once dispatched an embassy to the triumphant
Earl; but Louis was careful to cultivate friendly relations with Warwick
on his own. While Duke Philip shied away from a matrimonial alliance

—perhaps at the Dauphin's suggestion—Louis dispatched as his personal representative in England a man he was sure would be to Warwick's taste, the valiant Jean d'Estuer, Lord de La Barde.

At the same time Louis had been pushing hard his diplomatic campaign to forge a link with Francesco Sforza, Duke of Milan. This bastard son of a *condottiere* had begun his career by selling his military services to whoever would buy. Then Sforza had carved out a little domain in the Papal States, surrounded himself with able councilors, and won the friendship of Cosimo de' Medici, *de facto* ruler of the Republic of Florence. The disappearance of the last Visconti Duke of Milan, Filippo-Maria, who died without male heir in 1447, offered Francesco Sforza, married to the Duke's bastard daughter Bianca, a magnificent but doubtful opportunity. Powerful aspirants to the Duchy were soon in the field, including Charles, Duke of Orléans, claiming from his Visconti mother. Finally, after brilliant political maneuvering backed by military victories, Sforza entered Milan in 1450 and proclaimed himself Duke. In the ensuing decade, 1450–59, he had become the covert but indefatigable foe of French intervention in Italy: an Angevin triumph at Naples might well persuade Charles VII to support by force of arms the claim of the House of Orléans to Milan.*

The Dauphin Louis, from early youth, had profoundly admired this master politician, had studied all his campaigns, and during these years at Genappe had kept in communication with him. In the first six months of 1460 Louis dispatched a series of envoys to Milan, first to probe the possibilities, and then to make definite proposals, for a treaty. Sforza hesitated: he had been receiving increasingly ominous warnings from Charles VII against meddling with the Dauphin's affairs and against continuing his veiled opposition to the Angevin cause in Italy. Then in early July, as Warwick was defeating the Lancastrians, Duke John routed, at Sarno on July 8, the army of King Ferrante and appeared to have the Realm of Naples in his grasp.† Hastily Sforza provided military aid for Ferrante; and by September he had dispatched an envoy to Genappe to conclude a treaty with the Dauphin.

The treaty made no mention of the Duke of Burgundy. The exile of Genappe meant to keep Sforza to himself, for the same reason that he sought to maintain with Warwick a strong personal tie. He had no in-

---

* It was Sforza, and Cosimo de' Medici, who had invited King René into Italy in 1453—but only to make brief use of him against Venice.

† Alfonso V, King of Naples and Aragon, dying in 1458, had left Naples to his bastard son Ferrante and Aragon to his brother, John II.

tention of saving the skin of Louis Dauphin at the cost of creating an Anglo-Burgundian-Milanese *entente* that would menace the France of Louis King. Yet he had no backing but his wits; and even at best the Yorkist control of England, as Sforza's position in Italy, remained uncertain. His unhappy relations with Philip the Good, meanwhile, had continued to deteriorate, and there was no bottom to the quicksands at the court of Burgundy. During the Christmas of 1460, his fifth Christmas in the Low Countries, the Dauphin, now in his thirty-eighth year, anxiously awaited events over which he had no power and walked his tightrope with increasing strain. Sforza's ambassador had summed up the Dauphin's position for his master: "He is a man without a place."

10. Creature of Circumstance

IF THE DAUPHIN remained quietly at Genappe for the Christmas holidays, he was soon thereafter riding up the Brussels road to confer with the Duke of Burgundy. The complexion of his world had suddenly altered.

Over the Channel had come flying the news—a disaster to the Yorkist cause. On December 30, 1460, the Duke of York and the Earl of Warwick's father had been killed and their army routed at Wakefield in Yorkshire by a surprise attack led by the Queen's favorite, Henry, Duke of Somerset. Queen Margaret herself, bringing men from Scotland, had joined her victorious lords; and the Lancastrian power was expected to move on London at any moment. Letters from the Earl of Warwick and little Coppini, the papal legate, attempted to minimize this defeat, but Louis and his uncle knew that on Warwick's ability to recover himself might hang the issue of war between France and Burgundy.

Reports continued to arrive, each more alarming than the last, of Lancastrian hosts swarming southward, devastating the towns in their path; Warwick was urging the dispatch of an impressive Burgundian embassy to bolster the Yorkist cause; Coppini, turning queasy, was frantically writing in sympathetic ink between the lines of his letters. Louis and his uncle decided that an embassy was a little too risky at the moment. The Duke, however, dispatched across the Channel a band of troops armed with a comparatively new weapon, handguns that discharged lead-tipped arrows and cartridges of wildfire. The Dauphin struck a more intimate note: he ordered the Lord de La Barde to take the field with Warwick and sent him a banner bearing the image of the Virgin to display in the Yorkist ranks.

Then the world rocked again. The Count of Charolais exploded a string of violent charges against his enemies Antoine and Jean de Croy, and demanded that his father take action upon these accusations. Irritable and weary, Duke Philip tried vainly to smother the quarrel. Ducal government was paralyzed; Philip the Good's frustrations sharpened his suspicions of his nephew; again the Burgundian court was muttering against the guest who brought nothing but trouble with him. This time Louis himself was caught in the crossfire: Charolais had declared the brothers de Croy guilty of spreading a rumor that the heir of Burgundy was planning to deliver the Dauphin by force into the hands of the King of France. Disgusted by the humors of his uncle and the muddle of his uncle's court, the Dauphin quickly made his way back to his country castle. There he found awaiting him Prospero da Camogli, envoy and councilor of the Duke of Milan.

It was Prospero who had arrived the preceding September with a draft treaty negotiated by Louis's ambassadors and Francesco Sforza—a pact of mutual assistance, each party agreeing to supply several thousand foot and horse if the other was attacked. The document did much for the Dauphin's morale, though not his immediate prospects, and would be really valuable to the Duke only after his ally became King of France.

Once Louis had scanned the articles, he had genially observed that the treaty gave him all he could ask for—up to a point—and promised that Prospero's master could expect much from him when he became King. But . . . There turned out to be a very important *but*.

The treaty made no mention of Louis's Savoyard follower, Iacomo di Valperga. This lack would have to be remedied, for the Dauphin had taken Valperga under his protection and Valperga's lands had been overrun by the Duke of Savoy. During the summer, he reminded Prospero, he had addressed plea upon plea to Sforza to take action against Savoy on Valperga's behalf.[1] He added flatly that he would risk his succession to the throne rather than abandon his servant. Sforza's envoy tried to explain that he had no instructions concerning Valperga, that it was unheard of to include a single individual in a treaty of such importance. In long sessions of talk Louis made use of a battery of persuasions— bonhomie, intricate arguments, historical analogues, ironic queries about Sforza's good will mingled with assurances of his own devotion— and remained adamant.

Prospero da Camogli, a shrewd and diligent envoy, though a little inclined to testiness, had been trained in the most advanced statecraft of the time; but he had been slightly rattled at being dispatched to "the extreme edge of this terrene world" (as he reported) and even more rattled to find himself negotiating with a prince whose way of doing business no training could have prepared him for. Despite himself, Prospero was swept beyond his instructions, agreed to the addition of a clause that would require Sforza to aid Iacomo di Valperga as an adherent of the Dauphin. Prospero reported, a bit nervously, to the Duke that, with the Dauphin so well disposed to the interests of Milan, he thought he had driven a good bargain. Louis had graciously agreed to a rider that the Valperga clause was subject to approval by Sforza, and on October 6 he had signed the secret treaty.

Now in these anxious days of early February, 1461, the Dauphin learned from Prospero that the Duke of Milan had loyally ratified the treaty of Genappe. However, the Duke of Savoy had already seized all of Valperga's estates. Milan could not risk open war against Savoy. Prospero had therefore been sent to request the removal of the now meaningless Valperga clause. Louis replied reasonably that, such being the case, it would probably be best to substitute a recompense in money for the treaty article. As he anticipated—he had excellent listening posts in Italy—Prospero disclosed that the Duke of Milan, purely out of the goodness of his heart, was willing to offer a recompense, twelve thousand florins. But that sum was not nearly good enough. Louis was willing to discuss the matter further; meantime, he added casually, Sforza's envoy should try to work things out with Valperga himself. Outraged, Prospero sputtered that to discuss such a business with the man who was the subject of discussion was unheard of! Louis replied amiably, but inexorably, that Prospero could hold back from Valperga anything he wished.

Over the next two months Prospero's dispatches unfold the first really intimate view of the Dauphin in the characteristic occupation of his life, negotiation—precise turns of phrase that suggest the inflections of Louis's voice; a display of personality that drove the Milanese ambassador to despair, and admiration. Louis was enacting a role for Prospero's benefit, but he also yielded glimpses of an inner self innocent of calculation. In these most critical months of his life, he played his diplomatic comedy with an intensity and energy out of all proportion to its object.

After a wrenching interview with Valperga, Prospero returned to argue at length that the Savoyard himself was to blame for his troubles, not the Dauphin or the Duke of Milan. Louis replied agreeably that if Iacomo were not cast down by fortune he would indeed "make him see that he is a terrible man." But a prince should not afflict the afflicted. Whatever one could argue, "Iacomo di Valperga has lost, and he has lost while under the Dauphin's protection." Come what may, he would do the best for his adherent that he could. Prospero, at the suggestion of the inflexible Dauphin, unhappily agreed to see Valperga again—and hastily wrote to his master for fresh instructions. On February 23 Louis told him gloomily, "Prospero, since you inform me that you are commissioned to offer only twelve thousand florins, the matter seems so far from being settled that the best and shortest way out, I think, is to abandon our treaty." Abruptly he added; "Indeed . . . when I compare the Duke of Milan's writings with his words, either because of the language difficulty or some other cause, I find it impossible to understand either the *yes* or the *no* of his will concerning the rehabilitation of Valperga. . . . In any case, since at present I cannot pay Iacomo in money nor by remaking his fortune, at least I will satisfy him in my own way by linking his fate with mine."

After Louis had subjected Prospero to further emotional interviews with Valperga and had himself alternately castigated the Duke of Milan's niggardliness and assured the envoy that "I would like Iacomo to content himself with a modest offer, but I can do no more though God knows I have the best will in the world," Prospero begged to be accorded a final answer.

"Very well, since you force me"—the Dauphin was now using the intimate *tu*—"I will give you my decision." If Valperga was offered a castle, a small monthly allowance, and eighteen thousand florins cash, "you can arrange our alliance as you please; and the better you do for the Duke of Milan, the happier I will be. . . ." Prospero dispatched another plea for fresh instructions, precise ones, "for we have to deal with a person who speaks clearly and so wishes to be spoken to the same way." Baffled and annoyed though he was by Louis's fierce concentration on the minutest details of the Valperga business, he reported that in his judgment "the Dauphin is extremely able in handling great affairs and makes marvelous observations." Louis now altered his attack, but not his will: opening direct communications with Sforza, he indicated that he would accept, for removal of the clause, a loan of eighteen thousand florins. The Duke of Milan promptly closed with this face-saving offer, and the treaty of Genappe finally became a reality.

That this diplomatic campaign had been impolitic, even irrational, the Dauphin must have been aware. It was an assertion of identity by a fugitive. Doubtless he saw in the outcast Valperga a mirror of his own helplessness, but his passionate tenacity in upholding Iacomo was rooted in his long conflict with his father—Valperga had been abandoned by Charles VII and attacked by the King's client the Duke of Savoy. Besides, demanding entire loyalty, he refused to offer less himself.* By this time it was about all he had to offer.

Once again, distant events were shaking the Dauphin's life. Couriers brought tidings of a great battle that had been fought in England (second battle of St. Albans, February 17). Warwick's army, issuing from London to oppose the Lancastrian host, had been smashed; the Queen had recaptured her feeble husband; Warwick himself had fled, none knew where. But on March 4 letters arrived from Antoine de Croy which offered a gleam of hope: Warwick and the debris of his army had joined with young Edward of March (eldest son of the Duke of York), and they were preparing to attack the Queen's host, now quartered near London. Several days and several messengers later, a gentleman of the Burgundian court brought missives from Warwick himself, "very reverent and affectionate," with news of another revolution of events so violent that Louis could hardly credit the first report of it. After Warwick and Edward had entered London, the people had joyfully proclaimed young Edward King of England (Edward IV). The Queen and her forces had retired to Lancastrian strongholds in the North; Warwick and the new King were about to lead a great army in pursuit. The fate of England—and perhaps the fortunes of the Dauphin—hung in the balance.

Despite the perils of this whirling world, the de Croy-Charolais quarrel continued to absorb the energies and trammel the business of the Duke of Burgundy's government. Louis told Prospero da Camogli that he regarded his situation as very close to desperate. The ill-feeling between Dauphin and Duke gave the Milanese envoy "baticore"— palpitations of the heart. Louis's envoy to his father, Houaste de Montespédon, had come back with the usual message: Charles VII invited his son to return to the French court, with such entourage as he wished; but there was no mention of a guarantee for the Duke of Burgundy. At the pressing request of the Count of Maine, Louis again dispatched Houaste, with blunt instructions: he must have genuine assurances, not the kind that could be removed the next morning. To Prospero he remarked bitterly, "Just as the Pope cannot be excommunicated, the King cannot act the traitor."

---

* The moment Dauphin became King, Valperga received, as a temporary and symbolical appointment, the Chancellorship of France. Not long after, Louis forced the Duke of Savoy not only to rehabilitate the outcast's fortunes but to make him Chancellor of the Duchy.

Louis now learned that the Yorkists were marching northward for a struggle to the death with the Queen and her lords. Despite his aversion to the Burgundian court, he came to Brussels to keep in closer touch with events. Early in April, messengers brought the news that he was hoping for. In a fierce all-day battle at Towton in Yorkshire (March 29), Warwick and King Edward had smashed the Lancastrian army and driven Queen Margaret, King Henry, and the Duke of Somerset into headlong flight toward Scotland. Many of the Lancastrian lords lay dead on the battlefield, along with thousands of their followers. Louis himself had had a share in the Yorkists' victory, for on the snowy field of Towton the Lord de La Barde had fought at the side of King Edward under the banner of the Dauphin.

And now, from the court of France, came the most arresting tidings of all: King Charles was in bad health, had been ill on and off since January. Astrologers predicted that only a miracle would keep the King alive beyond August.

The seesaw of news continued. Warwick and King Edward appeared to have clinched their hold on England. Houaste came back from the French court, empty-handed; but it was now known that King Charles was seriously ill. By this time, war between France and Burgundy was all but overt: the French government had called up the nobles of Normandy and Duke Philip was summoning his vassals to arms. There was another broil between the Duke of Burgundy and his son. Louis's relations with his uncle had almost reached the breaking point. "Every day," Camogli reported, "the danger grows that this hostility will uncover itself. On the side of the Dauphin, only his need holds it hidden; on the side of the Duke, only the opportunity offered by the Dauphin's presence if war with France should break out." By early July, Louis had returned to his little court to wait and watch.

And then the wheel of fortune turned again, this time decisively. About July 10 a courier galloped into Genappe, lashing his mount ("battant ferrant"), to bring news that the King of France had been stricken with a mortal disease. A stream of messengers followed. Prospero da Camogli saw them "riding at breakneck speed" as they dusted past him toward Genappe with the latest word of the King's worsening illness.

Louis ordered his goods to be packed and sent his men on pilgrimage to pray for the health of the King of France. He himself, however, refused to show for his father a grief he did not feel. By July 20 he had begun intimating to his chief followers the offices that they could look to have. A day or two later he received a communication from the royal council, officially informing him of his father's mortal illness and assuring him of their devotion. He sent word to his uncle Philip to make ready. To his followers in France went an urgent summons: on hearing news of the King's death, they were to take horse immediately with their men and meet him in the neighborhood of Rheims. If a desperate attempt should be made to seat Louis's brother Charles upon the throne, it would be of prime importance for Louis to get himself crowned as soon as possible.

About July 25 the Dauphin received the tidings that transformed him into the Most Christian King of France, Louis XI. Charles had died, from an infection of the jaw that closed his throat, early in the morning of Wednesday, July 22. Louis ordered a requiem Mass for his father; but that afternoon he dressed himself in a short red-and-white jacket, put on a red-and-white hat (the colors of the King of France) and went hunting. He forbade his household to wear mourning. The following day, or the day after, he took horse with all his train of exiles, and avoiding large towns, made his way to Avesnes on the border of France. Here he awaited the coming of the Duke of Burgundy, who, at Lille, was making immense preparations to escort the King to Rheims.

As delegations of all kinds began to appear in Avesnes, Louis at last found himself exercising the power of kingship. He had just turned thirty-eight. Prospero da Camogli felt that it was a portentous moment. After reporting the King's "clear and admirable answers, made without taking counsel with anybody," Prospero wrote honestly, "He who had reputed him *inepto Delfino* must now call him *Aptissimo Re de France.* All this shows that his most excellent mind and profound intellect could not lodge itself in so small a fortune as was his formerly."

Book II

THE KING

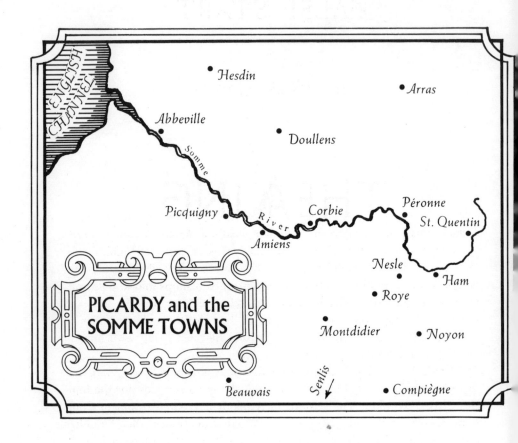

FALSE START

11. Hasty Heart

An army moved up the roads of France, dusty in the fine dry summer weather. As its advance guards reached Avesnes, Louis discovered that it was an army of humble subjects eager to draw profit from being the first to acknowledge their sovereign. Princes, nobles, gentlemen, adventurers, bishops and abbots, municipal delegations, office-holders and office-seekers pressed into the town. There was soon no lodging to be had within a dozen miles of Avesnes. Louis sent word to his uncle that he need bring with him no more than a ceremonial escort.

Louis XI quickly demonstrated that it was a new world, and that the King of France had forgotten neither the good services nor the injuries to the Dauphin. The bastard of Armagnac, created Count of Comminges, displaced André de Laval as Marshal of France; the Dauphin's other *compère,* Jean de Montauban, became Admiral in place of Jean de Bueil; Antoine de Croy was rewarded with the Grand Mastership of the Royal Household; Jean Arnoulfin became Receiver General of Normandy. The King would soon appoint as Chancellor a bold, ready-tongued official of the Parlement of Paris, who was even then being tried for accepting bribes. On the other hand, when Louis learned that Pierre de Brezé, representing the Estates of Normandy, dared to seek audience, he ordered him to return home forthwith and await the King's commands. Louis's capital enemy, Antoine de Chabannes, the Count of Dammartin, ventured to send a servant to Avesnes, but Admiral Montauban threatened to drown him in a river.

Toward the end of July, the Duke of Burgundy arrived, regretfully bringing with him only a modest escort of some four thousand lords and gentlemen, in a black cloud of cloaks. Louis and his household did not wear mourning until the funeral Mass for Charles VII, held on Sunday, August 3; and then after dinner the King donned scarlet and went hunting. The next morning he impatiently set out for Rheims. But he was not so impatient as to scant the politic task of removing the rancors between his uncle and himself. He publicly commanded the Bishop of Paris and the representatives of the Parlement and the University to pay the same reverence to the Duke of Burgundy that they would to him. On the road, Prospero da Camogli heard the King say that he wanted the Duke always to be near him, for the Duke had watched over the Dauphin a long time and now it was up to the King to watch over the Duke.

It was Philip the Good and his glittering chivalry who escorted the King into Rheims on the day before the coronation, which had been arranged for August 15, the Feast of the Assumption of Our Lady. And the following day, after Louis had been anointed in the age-old ceremony of the crowning of a King of France, it was the Duke of Burgundy who placed the crown upon Louis's head and shouted, "Vive le roy! Montjoye et St. Denis!"

In the afternoon, the King presided over his coronation banquet, plate and napery service all provided by the Duke of Burgundy. After a while, Louis took off his crown—it was a little too large—and set it casually on the table. As soon as he could, he extracted himself from the web of ceremony and withdrew to St. Thierry, outside Rheims, leaving to his uncle the happy task of entertaining the princes and prelates of the realm. In this day packed with ceremonies, one rite, overlooked by the chroniclers, meant more to Louis than all the others: he swore to cherish and augment his realm and to reunite to it those domains which had been separated, alienated, disjoined.

For the state entry into Paris, the King continued to indulge the Duke of Burgundy's love of display. On the early afternoon of Monday, August 31, the royal procession moved through the St. Denis gate and passed between tapestry-bedecked houses. All the windows along the route sprouted the heads of wealthy folk who had paid a fancy price to view the spectacle, and throngs jammed the roadway. Louis was not only the new sovereign of France; he was a curiosity, the prince of bizarre misfortunes, the formidable Dauphin who, everybody knew, had done and would undoubtedly continue to do amazing things. A thrill of expectancy had run through the realm—as vivid as the thrill of fear that coursed through the great lords.

The Burgundian nobles at the head of the parade showed themselves in cloth of gold and furred velvets and damask, the rue St. Denis ringing with the multitude of silver bells on their richly trapped horses. Four trumpeters sounded the approach of the King. Over a doublet of scarlet satin with large gold buttons embellished in rubies, he wore a gown of white damask fringed with gold. A canopy of blue satin spangled with fleurs-de-lys was held above his head by six citizens of Paris in scarlet satin. Then came an imperial figure, the lord of pageantry, mounted on a horse trapped in black satin crusted with gold and gems —the Duke of Burgundy, in a black velvet cloak winking with rubies and diamonds and pearls. The jaunty brim of his hat displayed an array of precious stones reported to be worth 400,000 crowns; and on a helmet borne ceremoniously after him flashed the Ruby of Flanders, "the marvel of Christianity" (which would one day lie in the dust of a battlefield).

The city of Paris had provided its traditional pageantry for a King who was outside all tradition. Soon after passing through the St. Denis gate, Louis beheld a fountain flowing with milk and wine and ypocras. On a scaffold nearby, male and female savages ("wodewoses" the English called these popular characters) "fought and made several countenances." Still more eye-catching, three pretty girls, completely naked, disported themselves as The Sirens in an artificial pond; a Parisian chronicler reported enthusiastically that each lovely breast, "droit, séparé, rond, et dure," provided a sight "bien plaisant." Perhaps as a corrective, the King was next treated to a pantomime of scenes from the Passion, staged before the Hospital of the Trinity. Farther along, the Parisians had arranged two shows to let their sovereign know that they understood his predilections and remembered his fame: they presented a scene of the chase, the hunters "making very great noise with dogs and horns"; and as the King passed the Châtelet, soldiers enacted the assault of the Dieppe bastille which Louis had stormed in 1443.

It was six o'clock by the time he reached the west front of Notre Dame, where the Bishop of Paris and his clergy and a delegation from the University awaited him. Here the King, weary of pageantry and no lover of the stiff-necked prelates ranged before him, put a brusque hand upon ceremony by interrupting the harangues of the Bishop and of the University orator. After the singing of the Te Deum in the cathedral, Louis rode to the Palace to preside over the inevitable banquet. He managed to endure the feast until midnight.

After dinner next day, Tuesday, September 1, the King left the Palace, now the home of the Parlement, and instead of taking up residence

in the royal mansion, the Hôtel de St. Pol, he withdrew to the more modest accommodation of the Hôtel des Tournelles. As often as possible he
avoided the festivities of the capital; however, he sometimes accompanied his uncle about the city, occasionally graced one of the Duke's entertainments. He was hoping to feed to the full his uncle's appetite for
glory. Philip the Good, at his Hôtel d'Artois, zealously displayed the
splendors of Burgundy. People of all ranks and conditions crowded into
the mansion to view the famous Gideon tapestries in gold and silk, and
to gape at the huge pavilion of black velvet erected in the courtyard.
Dances and feasts lasted until daylight. Before the King's Hôtel, Sunday,
September 13, the House of Burgundy staged a joust in which the Count
of Charolais and five other Burgundian lords challenged all comers. The
Duke, wearing a fortune in jewels upon his person, made his appearance
with the Duchess of Orléans perched before him on his horse. There
were so many prancing steeds and such a press of onlookers that four or
five people, mean folk, were trampled to death and a large number injured. Behind a screen of ladies at a window, King Louis watched for a
while. He was assiduously courting the Count of Charolais; he bestowed
gifts on Duke Philip's renowned bastard, Antoine; he succeeded, temporarily at least, in reconciling those sworn enemies within the Duke's entourage, Antoine de Croy, hated by Charolais, and the Count of St. Pol,
Charolais's crony.[1]

But it was not enough, not nearly enough for the Duke of Burgundy.
Philip's dream of establishing a Burgundian King of France had been
shattered. He was wounded to the heart of his pride because Louis did
not come seeking advice on every occasion, because he slighted his
princely entertainments, and because he injured the feelings and disap-
pointed the hopes of the Duke's friends. Unable to bridle his tongue,
Louis had made fun of the dandified clothes and pompous manners of
the Duke of Clèves, Philip's nephew. To importunate Burgundian office-
seekers who raked up past promises of favor Louis replied amiably, "My
friend, I am no longer the Dauphin as I was then; now I am King." He
had circumspectly established a council of lords and "wise men" to
make due provision for the "estates" and offices of the realm—i.e., to
give each prince his fitting share of the spoils—but the recommenda-
tions made by the council never came to anything; and though he invited
the Duke of Burgundy to nominate twenty-four of one hundred new
members of the Parlement, not one of the twenty-four received an appointment. Then Louis made a really dangerous misstep: intimating that
he had in mind breaking with his *quondam* friends the Yorkists, he sug-

gested that Philip the Good cancel his treaty of amity and mercantile intercourse with them. The moment Philip heard this cool proposition, he flew into one of his famous rages and threatened to quit Paris immediately—Chastellain says it would have taken only a turn of the hand to decide him. The too impetuous King, hastily disavowing his proposal, attempted to soothe the Duke by asking him to arrange negotiations between the Yorkists and his grateful nephew.

By this time Louis was weary of Paris; he was weary too of princely entertainments and princely sensibilities; and he was impatient to exercise his prerogative, without the Duke of Burgundy peering over his shoulder. Though the Duke was not to depart until the end of the month, Louis suddenly announced that he was leaving Paris on September 23. Making an effort to repair his relations with Philip, he rode to the Hôtel d'Artois on the 22nd—a flattering breach of etiquette for the King to come to the Duke—and before an assembly of royal councilors and city dignitaries whose presence he had commanded, he declared that he owed not only his crown but his life to his uncle. But Louis, who had waited decades to begin his life's work, could not wait any longer. Next morning he quitted—he fled—his uncle, his lords, his stifling capital; and he rode toward the Loire, heading down the last arc of his circle, to show his father, and the princes, and the ordinary folk whom the princes never saw that the exile of Genappe had his own ideas of how a kingdom should be ruled.

The Loire slides like a silvery, sinuous arrow across the midlands of France. Flowing out the Bourbonnais, it takes a broad serene course westward and, sweeping past Orléans and Blois in a great curve, rolls through Touraine and Anjou to meet the sea near the Breton port of Nantes. Under the mild skies of the Orléannais and Touraine the river, framed by a rocky scarp to the south and vineclad hills to the north, moves through long shimmering vistas and majestic bends. It is the heartland of the realm; it is also of the essence French—in climate, in charm of countryside, in its pleasant towns and airy castles, in the clear language of its inhabitants. Sky and water and reaches of forest weave long, tranquil days. Comfortable castles thrust into shining air offer seclusion to a worker-King, a secret, indefatigable being, who can survey his realm without being surveyed; and stag-haunted woods, stretches of wide, empty country stand ready to slake the passions of the ardent huntsman.

Louis XI will spend his kingship on the road, except when he is here. In many Ordonnances he will speak affectionately of the Duchy of Touraine "in which we have been nourished since our infancy." The castle of Amboise soaring high above the Loire, many-towered Orléans on the great bend of the river, Montargis in the wild country to the east, the town of Tours, home of that most French of saints, "My Lord St. Martin"—these formed the true capital of King Louis. He was drawn to the Loire perhaps by more than the memories of his boyhood and the predilections of his nature. It was here that Joan of Arc had announced her mission and won the victories which signaled the resurgence of France and the holy destiny of its kingship.

As Louis was approaching Tours, about ten days after he had left Paris, the citizens of the town sent to ask if he would like them to celebrate his entrance with "farces and moralities." He replied no, that he took no pleasure in them. He had come home to work.

Royal messengers and newly appointed officers were soon transmitting to all parts of France the will of the new King. During his years as Dauphin he had had plenty of leisure to study the weakness of royal government and the encroachments of the princes; to study the new statecraft of Italy; to develop his own style of managing men and affairs. That the realm he meant to dominate was ill prepared to accept, even to understand, that style troubled him not at all. He burned to speed up everything, transform everything, make his new world. He immediately instituted tax reforms, aimed at a more efficient tapping of resources. He took into service, along with other men of no rank but promising talents, several of the former associates of that great merchant Jacques Coeur. Since only nobles could acquire lordships, he embarked on a policy of ennobling his principal townsmen, in order to stimulate agriculture and signal his partnership with the middle orders; and he permitted enterprising nobles to engage in trade without losing the privileges of nobility. Rooting through the bureaucracy of the royal government, he cut down the number of offices and made increased demands on the rest.*
Louis himself set a stringent example of economy. He had announced that for a year he would maintain a household as simple as that of his modest court at Genappe, and, to the general amazement, he kept his word. Italian ambassadors were startled by the plainness of his establishment, where only the horseflesh was up to royal standard. The King, they wrote, "is very rich; but he aims at nothing else except to increase his income and decrease useless costs. . . ." If they reported "the ex-

---

* Like some of his more optimistic tax reforms, however, this shake-up in administration had to be modified a few years later.

tremely minute expenses of his household, it would seem a marvelous lie."

All the regions, all the institutions, of France quickly felt the force of Louis's will. The great organs of the Crown, like the Parlement of Paris and the Chamber of Accounts, had come into being in the early fourteenth century to carry out judicial and financial functions which in more primitive days had been administered, like everything else, by the *curia regis,* the group of officials and counselors about the King; and in inevitable bureaucratic evolution they had developed an elaborate officialdom, cumbersome procedures, and independent airs. Both the Parlement and the Chamber quickly learned that the new King meant them to exert their powers to the full but insisted on their acting as he directed and at an efficient pace. The army, too, was shaken up, receiving new captains and strict injunctions about billeting, duties, and discipline. Louis informed the "Master Generals of our Moneys" at Paris that he was sending a councilor to have the true value of the coinage investigated in detail; and he ordered them to "certify the matter to us immediately and also from hour to hour just as things go." Royal commands vibrated with the injunctions, "make no difficulty about the matter"; "accomplish the business immediately and without delay."

He quickly made the prelates and princes of the realm aware of his attitude toward feudal pretensions. Two months after reaching Tours, he abolished his father's Pragmatic Sanction (1438) which, in establishing a Gallican Church virtually free of papal control, had delivered an enormous patronage to ecclesiastics and nobles. He brusquely announced that he would not give a military command to any of the magnates. He kept at court none of the lords of his blood, the "natural" advisers of a king. Before he left Paris, he had deprived the Duke of Bourbon of the governorship of Guienne; he forced the Count of Foix to turn over a disputed lordship which had been adjudged to the Crown; he pared the pension list by which the lords had fattened themselves upon the Treasury. What hurt the feodality most, though the results were not immediately apparent: Louis galvanized into action the network of royal officers—*baillis* and *seneschals* who governed the chief administrative regions; their agents in the subdivisions, sergeants, judges, tax collectors —by ordering his men to enforce all royal rights, investigate all doubtful privileges, uphold the prerogatives and the justice of the crown against high and low. These officers, many of them Louis's appointees, enthusiastically set about applying the pressure of law upon the claims of the great feudatories.

The French princes had special connections abroad—Burgundy with the victorious Yorkists; Angevins with the refugee Lancastrians in Scotland and with Duke John's campaign in the Kingdom of Naples; the Count of Foix with Spain. The foreign policies King Louis adopted would profoundly affect his relations with his feodality at home. Furthermore, the European situation itself posed pressing dangers, and opportunities, for the French monarchy. Thus it was that during these autumn months (1461) at Tours, Louis XI was gazing intently beyond his borders. For the next two and a half years, most of the time spent on the road, the King would be preoccupied with international affairs—an enterprise in the Spanish peninsula, the perpetual threat represented by the ancient adversary across the Channel, French interests in Italy.

The Spanish opportunity had appeared suddenly, out of nowhere. It offered a new King the possibility of showing the world his mettle as well as magnificently augmenting his realm.

In the early morning of January 12, 1462, King Louis donned his traveling dress of coarse gray cloth, hung a crude wooden rosary about his neck, and rode out of Tours with some half a dozen companions. Coursing the woods along the road in pursuit of game, he was followed by his baggage train and discreetly shadowed by his Scots bodyguard. As he moved to La Rochelle and then turned southward for Bordeaux, he shot out before him diplomatic missives, admonitions, queries, commands, and he left in his wake startled officials and a trail of royal decrees. He investigated municipal governments, he established fairs and promoted trade regulations; he poked into religious establishments, confirming privileges and questioning relics and donating money for rebuilding. Through his five senses he was taking unto himself the countrysides, the institutions, the inhabitants of his realm. Years later he caused to be recorded in the *Rozier des Guerres*, written for the instruction of his son, "The Prince must think about the condition of his people and go among them often, as a good gardener cultivates his garden." As he journeyed southward to Guienne, he was sighting on the target of opportunity which had loomed beyond the Pyrenees.

ii

Louis XI had found his opportunity in the troubles of John II, King of Aragon, the smaller of the two realms, Aragon and Castile, into which Spain was then divided.

The chief province of the Aragonese crown, Catalonia with its prosperous seaport of Barcelona, having long enjoyed a semi-autonomy, had just revolted against its sovereign. That province included the Counties of Roussillon and Cerdagne (now French), which lie to the north of the Pyrenees and the possession of which by France would round out the southern borders of the realm. After attempts to woo the Catalans for himself had failed, Louis XI promptly turned to the hard-pressed King of Aragon with an offer that John II could not refuse. In return for giving military aid in subduing the Catalans, Louis secured, as pledge for the payment of 200,000 crowns—a sum John II would never raise —control of Roussillon and Cerdagne. Then, however, the intervention of the King of Castile, Henry IV, invited by the Catalans to become their ruler, threatened to put an end to Louis's acquisition and the King of Aragon's realm.[2] Unperturbed by this crisis, Louis XI, with the help of adroit agents and his own artistry, produced a *tour de force:* persuading the King of Castile to accept his arbitration, he bought off Henry IV with a few lands hitherto disputed between Castile and Aragon and thus left John II free to pursue his attempt to subdue the Catalans. At the same time he closed a firm grip upon Roussillon and Cerdagne. This diplomatic triumph, consummated in the early summer of 1463, sent a thrill of admiration and fear through the courts of Europe.[3]

In this same summer Louis XI secured an ally who, for statecraft and military skill, he prized above all other rulers, Francesco Sforza, Duke of Milan. On becoming King, he had found it expedient to support the Angevin invasion of the Kingdom of Naples—he could not afford to ruffle too many princely sensibilities, and the chivalric House of Anjou, though endowed with a permanently empty purse and a talent for political failure, was popular in France. In the winter and spring of 1462 he had sought to persuade Sforza to abandon King Ferrante of Naples and espouse the Angevin cause, even threatening Sforza's ambassadors with war. The Duke of Milan was not to be moved, however, and the King had no intention of carrying his display of hostility beyond diplomatic language. He probably foresaw that René's son, Duke John, would be driven from the Kingdom of Naples, an event that came about in the spring of 1463.[4] The following autumn, in response to Louis's invitation, there arrived at the French court Sforza's best ambassador, the mellow humanist Alberico Maletta, Doctor of Canon and Civil Law, a man entirely to the taste of the King, who immediately made him a confidant. In December, Louis confirmed the Alliance of Genappe, which as Dauphin he had negotiated with Sforza, and enfiefed the Duke of Milan

with the city-state of Genoa, crowning the Duke's ambitions.⁵ The
Duchy of Milan, though hardly as large as the average French province,
enjoyed a prosperous trade and industry, especially in fancy armor and
luxury goods, and the Duke, efficiently managing his resources, possessed the best army in Italy. It was Sforza's sagacity and intelligent
self-interest, however, that Louis most valued: on the Milanese alliance
he confidently based a long-range policy of making himself the benevolent overlord of the Italian peninsula.⁶

Meanwhile, during his Spanish adventures and his Italian negotiations, Louis XI was constantly preoccupied with Burgundy and with
England. It was the alliance of his uncle Philip of Burgundy with the
victor of Agincourt, Henry V, which had unleashed almost half a century of misery and ruin upon France.° With England, Louis had inherited a state of war; and his *quondam* Yorkist friends, Edward IV and
the Earl of Warwick, had promised their people, as part of their propaganda campaign against Henry VI and the Lancastrians, to rekindle the
military glories of the past. In 1462, Louis XI, to keep the Yorkists busy
at home and display Angevin sympathies, had provided a small expeditionary force for the indomitable Queen of Henry VI, Duke John's sister
Margaret of Anjou, come to France to seek aid. As leader of the venture
Louis chose his old enemy Pierre de Brezé, whom for a time he had imprisoned and then—appreciating Brezé's valor and abilities—restored to
favor. The expedition temporarily occupied a few castles in the north of
England, but, failing to stir a Lancastrian uprising, was forced to withdraw precipitately to Scotland, where Henry VI had taken refuge.

During this year 1462, Louis XI had managed, however, to keep
in touch informally with the kingmaking Earl of Warwick, who, as
young Edward IV's mentor, apparently controlled England. Lóuis
sensed that Warwick, an ambitious political adventurer whose power
rested on his services and his legend, might be open to personal inducements; and he had demonstrated to both King Edward and the
Earl that as long as he supported the Lancastrian cause there would be
trouble in England. He was now ready to deal with the Yorkists from
a position of strength. Realizing that he needed the good offices of
that friend of the Yorkists the Duke of Burgundy, he persuaded his
uncle Philip to postpone his projected crusade until the Duke had ac-

---

° In the year of 1463, more than a decade after the English had been driven
from the realm, a Milanese ambassador had difficulty finding lodgings at Pontoise
because so many of the houses in that war-torn city were still in ruins. Louis XI
frankly informed the Pope that the ravages of the Anglo-French war could not be
wholly repaired for a hundred years.

complished the great work of making peace between England and France. Under Philip's happy auspices, Louis XI in October of 1463 negotiated a year's truce with a Yorkist embassy, which, though not led by the Earl of Warwick himself as Louis hoped, had as chief the Earl's younger brother George, Bishop of Exeter and Chancellor of England. Arrangements were made for an Anglo-French peace conference, at which Warwick promised to be present.[7]

During these negotiations the King of France, seizing the opportunity of his uncle Philip's good humor which had been generated by his high role of peacemaker, produced another *tour de force*.

In the Treaty of Arras of 1435, Charles VII had separated Duke Philip of Burgundy from his English allies at the cost of an enormous concession: he yielded to the Duke the great northern province of Picardy and the principal towns along the Somme River. True, a clause in the treaty allowed for the repurchase of the territory for the sum of 400,000 gold crowns, but both Philip the Good and Charles VII knew that the King of France could never raise such a sum. From the moment Louis became King, he had intended to raise it. Now he set his Burgundian friends the brothers de Croy, chief favorites of the Duke, to preparing Philip's mind for the transaction; and he set his financial officers to combing the kingdom for the money.[8] The campaign soon cost him the friendship of the somber Count of Charolais, heir of Burgundy, who, after violently protesting against the repurchase to the King and violently quarreling with his father, flung away from the Burgundian court.

On September 28 (1463) the King of France was riding the road to his uncle's castle of Hesdin, to pursue, among other things, the negotiations with the English already begun at nearby St. Omer. Astride a scrubby little horse and clad in hunter's garb with horn slung behind his back, he was met a mile out of Hesdin village by his uncle Philip. As the splendid Duke of Burgundy and his meanly dressed companion passed through the village street lined with onlookers, bewildered queries rose on the air. "Where's the King? Which one is he? *That* one?" When the villagers realized that "*that* one" was indeed the King, they could not conceal their astonishment. Benedicité! Is *that* the King of France, the greatest monarch in the world? He seems more like a menial than a knight! The whole outfit is not worth more than twenty francs, his horse, and his dress. Now our Duke, our Prince, there is a man among men, an image of what a true prince should look like!"

The menial, who had brought with him a second, final, installment of 200,000 crowns for the repurchase of Picardy, promptly concluded the marvelous bargain he had engineered. For the rest of the year he explored, hunting from village to village, the great domain that he had reunited to the crown.

Thus, riding the Picard plains, he closed out 1463, an *annus mirabilis* of triumphs. He had secured Roussillon and Cerdagne; allied himself to the redoubtable adventurer after his own heart, Francesco Sforza; laid the foundations for a profitable intimacy with that other adventurer the Earl of Warwick, and for a settlement with the English; and regained northern France and the Somme towns for the realm.

By this whirlwind of diplomacy and regal assertion he had also aroused the fears and resentments of his feodality.

iii

FOR ALMOST TWO YEARS, Louis XI had been on the road, pursuing enterprises domestic and foreign with the same fierce concentration that drove him through wild countryside on the trail of stag and boar. As he made his restless way across the provinces of France, he was accompanied by only a few intimates and followed by a train of pack horses and carts bearing his bedding, bathtub, wine cellar, food, furniture, cages of birds, dogs, while the Scots guard hovered in the distance. Rain or shine, he would plunge off the road, or country track, to hunt along the way, clad in nondescript jacket and boots, sword on thigh and horn slung across his back. A Catalan embassy following the King of France northward in June of 1463 expected to overtake him in a few days. When they caught up with him, it was August 2 and they had had to journey all the way to Chartres. They were more fortunate, however, than a cleric of Évreux, who, departing from the King to take a message to his chapter and immediately setting forth with a reply, did not find his hard-riding sovereign till sixty days had passed. The middle-aged Milanese ambassador Alberico Maletta declared that he could no longer endure the labors of keeping up with the King. His life in France was lived either on horseback or in vile lodgings, and he was so exhausted that he "had had to have a carriage built for him in order to get about."

When Louis XI paused in a village or at a peasant's lonely cot for a meal, he dictated letters, consulted with advisers, and sometimes summoned an ambassador for a talk. An Italian envoy, shuddering at the "unpleasant, savage ways" he was forced to follow, found the King "dwelling in the open air in a sort of camp," and when His Majesty emerged "from a rude lodging after dinner," he took the envoy into another hut—"his bedroom"—for a chat. Reaching a town, Louis usually avoided the official welcome by turning down a side street, and he lodged with a merchant or a royal official or a cleric. His hosts frequently had a hard time of it. The dogs dirtied the floors, bird droppings spoiled the beds, and animal noises turned the lodgings into a zoo.

Neither the King's preoccupation with affairs nor his hardy peregrinations left much room in his life for his Queen. Patient, submissive Charlotte—a woman much like Louis's mother, Marie—and her infant daughter, Anne (born in 1461), and her numerous sisters and her household of ladies remained for the most part in that pleasantest of royal castles, Amboise, on the Loire. After King Louis left Touraine in the Christmas season of 1461, he rejoined Charlotte briefly in June of 1462, again that autumn, and spent a few days with her in mid-1463. He enjoyed the rustic seclusion and the hunting at Amboise, and he well understood the importance of begetting a male heir. Queen Charlotte, in the discreet words of Philippe de Commynes, "was not one of those women in whom a man would take great pleasure but in all a very good lady." Louis treated her with kindness, was more faithful to the conjugal bed than most princes; but it was not in his nature to share with her his heart or mind. She and her ladies led a secluded, monotonous existence. Alberico Maletta reported that Bona of Savoy and the Queen's other sisters were "scarcely seen even by the birds." In this humdrum court, stripped for action and always on the move, the younger generation sighed in vain for traditional royal splendors. "All gaiety is dead," lamented the poet Martial d'Auvergne—

> Farewell ladies and *demoiselles*
> Feasts and jousts and stately measures;
> Farewell balls and courtly *belles*,
> All our joys and worldly pleasures!

Louis severely organized his days around working, hunting, traveling—and not infrequently was he doing all three at the same time, clad in his pilgrim's gown of coarse gray cloth or in a nondescript hunting jacket, with a wool hood (his "bonnet") for frosty mornings and, atop that, a broad-brimmed hat which shed rain "like a tent." He had an eye for clothing only if it was practical and ingenious. When he greeted the Milanese ambassador, Alberico Maletta, early one rainy winter day —in his bedchamber, after saying his prayers on his knees by the fire— he touched the envoy's cloak to see how wet it was, and upon Alberico's showing him the hood, double-lined with wool, "he was very much im-

pressed and said that we Lombards are knowing in all our affairs." A little later, he told Alberico that he would be ashamed to wear a fur
undergown and that he understood the Duke of Milan did not wear
one. On Alberico's assuring him that Francesco Sforza wore little more
in winter than in summer, the King said yes, that was the way of war-
rior-lords, "and he insisted that I touch him so that I could see that he
was wearing only an undergown of thin satin lined with very light cloth.
And I had to touch him all the way to his shirt." Louis expected his men
to conform to royal ideas about dress. One day when a dandified squire
entered the royal chamber arrayed in a brilliant velvet doublet, the
King inquired of some of his household who the young man was.

He was told, "Sire, he is yours, one of your gentlemen of arms."

"Mine!" exclaimed Louis. "By the Pasques-Dieu! He is not mine!
Mine he will never be. Look at him! He is all in silk. He is too pretty
for me!" The King ordered the squire summarily discharged from the
army, saying that he wanted no such pompous asses about him.

But if Louis scorned the niceties of dress and princely graces, there
was one aristocratic entertainment of which he considered himself a
master—the chase. "You are aware," he reminded Alberico Maletta on
one occasion, "that I delight in hunting, and also that I know a great
deal about it." Louis prided himself particularly on his collection of
horses, dogs, and birds, constantly seeking the finest and rarest speci-
mens. After Alberico relayed to his master a request from the King for a
certain type of hounds "with big heads and hanging ears," the Duke of
Milan dispatched him a quantity of these dogs. Francesco Sforza had
not quite understood, however, that he had to do with a connoisseur.
Though the King courteously praised the hounds, he let Alberico know
that, next time, the Duke "need not offer so many but should send me
one or two pairs which are in every way perfect."

At times the King took pleasure in a mode of life that his age had no
name for but that would one day be called bourgeois comfort. When he
paused a few days in Paris, he liked to dine out in the homes of royal
officers and merchant aristocracy, where he enjoyed teasing the pretty
wives of citizens with gross sallies against women and accompanying copious talk with copious drafts of wine and plenty of good solid food.
Among intimates, or with strangers, he was always letting his tongue
wag—to quiz a visiting Italian about the differences between the
French and the Lombard countryside, to discuss the intricacies of Italian politics or large historical issues with Alberico Maletta, to expatiate
on the finer points of venery, to indulge in indiscreet railleries about

people, sometimes in their presence, whose good will be needed. He made fun of the pomposities of priests, he gibed at ambassadorial suavities, he stamped his feet and waved his arms in zestful imitation of the Count of Charolais having a fit of anger.

King Louis's government was an unconventional as himself—was, in fact, himself. He carried on his complex operations by simple, even primitive means. Ordinarily, a fifteenth-century King wielded his power mainly through a great council composed of lords, bishops, doctors of law, officers like the Chancellor, and humbler career men. High policy was initiated and confidential business dispatched by a more or less formally recognized circle of trusted advisers, the privy or secret or chamber council. The great council of Louis XI, headed by the Chancellor, contained few lords and none of the great feudatories, except for an occasional prince sojourning briefly at court. Louis kept this council at a distance, directing its labors by curt memoranda. The royal councilors, trailing the hard-riding King into remote countryside, were often forced to scatter themselves among several villages in order to find food and shelter. Ambassadors, like the Bohemians of 1464, sometimes discovered that the council chamber was no more than the Chancellor's bedroom in a rustic inn; and if the Chancellor was lodged in one hamlet and the secretary who kept the Great Seal in another, the final paperwork connected with a treaty took longer than the previous negotiations. Louis, however, provided a solution to this difficulty—he persuaded envoys to draw up treaties themselves, not only their own instruments but the copies to be deposited in the archives of France. This procedure occasioned a certain amount of grumbling but wonderfully dramatized Louis's trust in his allies.

The King's chamber council had no official existence—the chamber, anywhere; the council, his chief intimates who happened to be at hand. Louis carried on consultations as he was dressing in the morning. After he had heard Mass, he casually beckoned two or three of his men to join him for work in a small chamber. He discussed affairs while he was dining, while he was taking a late-afternoon stroll in a garden, while he was riding the roads. This circle of intimates drew up memoranda to be turned into official documents by the corps of secretaries and notaries, roughed out instructions to ambassadors, kept an eye on the Masters of Requests, who heard complaints and petitions from the King's subjects, listened to delegations from towns, conferred with foreign envoys. When serious trouble of any kind developed, one of them was sent to the spot to make inquiry and settle the matter. They were richly rewarded for their services but had no other life than service, Louis demanding of them the same intensity of labors he enjoyed inflicting on himself. Though the King discussed with them his designs, and, when they were at a distance, expected them to use their own initiative, he kept all the threads of power in his own hands. He had no ministers, only devoted agents of his will. But they were also his *compères;* he shared with them whatever leisure he had time for.

Louis depended chiefly upon his "old faithfuls" who had followed him from Dauphiné to Genappe. The Bastard of Armagnac, now Count of Comminges and Marshal of France, admired by all for his unfailing good will and courtesy, and the hard-fisted Admiral Jean de Montauban were the king's chief confidants, as foreign envoys were quick to note. Louis de Crussol, now Seneschal of Poitou, and Houaste de Montespédon, Bailli of Rouen, and Jean Bourré, first secretary and financial expert, came next in influence. A flamboyant prelate, and dextrous role player, Jean Jouffroy, Cardinal of Arras, for a time enjoyed great favor. A magnificent figure of a man—"tall, broad-chested, with ruddy face and hairy limbs"—the Cardinal amply represented the sensuality and the scholarship of the sophisticated Renaissance ecclesiastic. After an important foreign envoy had delivered the prescribed oration of greeting to the King, Jouffroy answered extemporaneously in fluent Latin adorned with classical allusions and philosophic sentiments. Not proving to be as useful as ornamental, however, he would shortly be given his *congé.*

The King judged his men only by their loyalty and their service. That Jean de Montauban had left Brittany under a cloud, that Jouffroy, a Prince of the Church, was anything but a prince of piety, that a new man now showing mettle, Charles de Melun, had sybaritic tastes and lecherous inclinations, mattered little to the ruler who had set himself, in whatever lifetime was left to him, to transform his world. Besides, as a comedian Louis XI, not unlike Geoffrey Chaucer, too zestfully appreciated the spectacle of human nature to pass judgment on it; judgment he left to the appropriate authority, Heaven. Among his lesser servants there could be found men tarnished in the eyes of society whose capacities he put to the service of France—like the cleric, Ambroise de Cambrai, notorious for forging a papal bull to allow the incestuous marriage of the Count of Armagnac and his sister, who became one of the Masters of Requests of the royal household.

Such was the shabby, toilsome, efficient, saddle-hardened court maintained by Louis XI. It knew nothing of repose, except during the cold months generally spent in the mild valley of the Loire. This winter of 1463–64, however, Louis could take no respite there. Riding the frozen plains of Picardy, he stayed close to the dominions of his uncle and English Calais. Louis still needed the good offices of Duke Philip for his coming negotiations with England; and the winning of the Earl of Warwick had now become the first imperative of his existence. The princes of his realm were beginning to show their teeth.

In January of 1464 he entered the Burgundian town of Arras with a small escort, poorly dressed and meanly mounted. He insisted on plain quarters, "though the Bishop's dwelling was the finest episcopal palace one could find and there were other handsome lodgings in the canons' cloister." Tiring of the town in a few days, he suddenly left his lodgings at seven o'clock in the morning with but half a dozen attendants, and in consequence his Scots guard frantically hauled themselves on their horses and galloped after him "and the rest of his household likewise, princes and others." His restlessness was provoked by bad news. The government of Philip the Good, he learned, had been reduced to a panicky muddle. The old Duke had terrified his courtiers by disclosing a solemn promise to the Pope to go crusading in the spring, and at the same time he hurled himself into a violent quarrel with his son. At Lille in mid-February, Louis XI was once again able to persuade his distracted uncle that before Philip went off to fight the Infidel he must first conclude the great work of reconciling England and France. A month later, the King dispatched his agent Jean de Lannoy to London with a fresh proposal for peace: a treaty sealed by a marriage alliance. To young Edward IV Louis offered his sister-in-law Bona of Savoy, who would, of course, bring with her a suitable dowry, to be supplied by the King of France.

Edward IV assured Lannoy that he would give serious consideration to the marriage. Warwick warmly committed himself to meet at an early date with the King of France in order to work out final terms. On Louis's orders, Lannoy had intimated to the Earl that if, once the Anglo-French treaty was signed, he was willing to lend his genius to King Louis, that King would be happy to reward him suitably, perhaps with a Continental lordship.

But, as spring advanced, Louis received letters from Warwick twice postponing their conference, King Edward's mentor explaining that he was delayed by important negotiations with the Scots. Hanging upon these messages from across the Channel, Louis alternated moods of exuberance and gloom. "The King is so eager for peace with the English," the Milanese ambassador recorded, "that it seems to him a thousand years until he can mount horse and go to Picardy. His Majesty has told me in secret that every day he prays to God and Holy Mary to grant him this boon. . . ." In early June, word finally came that the English embassy was on its way. Louis, who had been lingering in the neighborhood of Paris, rode northward to meet the Duke of Burgundy at Hesdin. Shortly after uncle and nephew had celebrated St. John's Day (June 24) together, Louis's hopes were abruptly deceived: the English embassy which arrived at Calais was not headed by the Earl of Warwick. It turned out, furthermore, when the two Englishmen reached Hesdin, that they had powers only to prolong the truce for another year, till October of 1465. However, the envoys, Lord Wenlock and Richard Whetehill, were both Warwick's men; and they assured the King of France that their master, delayed by the task of stamping out the last Lancastrian embers in the North, would surely cross the Channel by October 1.

Seeking to cover his acute disappointment, King Louis set about persuading his uncle to remain at Hesdin until October so that he would be ready to receive the Earl of Warwick. The old Duke—now so feeble, one onlooker thought, that he seemed to be "a lord bewitched" —agreed, grudgingly.[9]

These early July days at Hesdin mark a turning point in Louis XI's first years as King. Triumphs had been replaced by frustration. Ominous rumblings sounded in the world of the princes. Louis had conjured with time, but at a price. And he knew it. In secret he confided to his friend Alberico Maletta that he needed peace with England so that, he hoped, "he could keep himself from being put in subjection by the barons of his realm." With the Duke of Milan on one side "and Warwick on the other," he could then "manage the princes as he pleases. . . ."

The King rode southward from Hesdin on the morning of July 9 (1464). Though the Duke of Burgundy had still three years to live, Louis never saw his uncle again.

12. A Pride of Princes

As KING LOUIS and Alberico Maletta were preparing the infeudation of Genoa, in December of 1463, that wise old statesman Cosimo de' Medici, friend of France, was prophesying to a Milanese ambassador, "Before the end of 1464, His Majesty will have great trouble and more than he would like, because he rules his realm to suit his own ideas." Even from Florence, Cosimo could hear the conspiratorial buzz of discontented French prelates and princes. Louis did not fail to hear it; month by month the menacing sound had been growing louder in his ears. But he had been too busy, too confident, too much caught up in his own whirlwind, to do much about it—besides, he was always fighting the slipperiness of time. Hastening to reorganize his realm, to win Roussillon, to acquire Picardy, to find a means of containing the English, he had shouldered his way through princely sensibilities; he had underestimated or ignored the tenacity of seignorial pretensions.

He had let himself slide into a quarrel with Pius II, over papal assertions of power and financial exactions, which did not, however, win him the loyalty of his Gallican prelates. Pope Pius exacerbated the dispute by dispatching to the royal court two arrogant legates. Louis promptly packed them off when they went so far as to declare that "even Charlemagne had been no more than the Master of the Pope's Household." By a series of decrees in 1463–64 the King virtually restored the Pragmatic Sanction of his father, but established the monarchy, rather than the French ecclesiastical hierarchy, as master of the Church in France. Pius announced that the French were a parcel of fools governed by a fool and threatened to excommunicate Louis XI. In May of 1464, when Alberico Maletta informed the King that the Pope, about to set forth on his much publicized crusade, had fallen seriously ill, Louis quickly reassured him: "Never fear, Messire Alberico, that he will die, because he is a bad Pope!" Whipping off his hat, he added, "God pardon me." [1] On learning, at the end of August, of the death of Pius II, the King made known to his clergy that the change of popes would not change his will. This declaration but served to deepen the apprehensions of ambitious Gallican prelates—most of them allied by blood or interest to the great seignorial houses who had also once enjoyed the spoils of Gallicanism.

What was much more serious, however, the quarrel with the Pope had involved Louis XI in a rancorous dispute with the Duke of Brittany concerning feudal authority. When Francis II, in 1462, refused to accept the appointments of two prelates, a bishop and an abbot, who had intimate connections at the French court, the King of France hastily took up the challenge by claiming jurisdiction, as sovereign lord, over ecclesiastical benefices in Brittany. Duke Francis responded by repudiating all royal claims. Next to the Burgundian power, the Dukes of Brittany were the most independent and among the least tractable of the French princes. The Bretons, retaining a fierce separatist pride nursed by Celtic blood and language, maintained their own governmental institutions, customs, Church. Francis II was a pleasure-loving flighty young man— Louis Dauphin had remarked dryly to Sforza's envoy Camogli that the Duke suffered from a fistula in the head—but he was surrounded by a group of former royal officials who, on the accession of Louis XI, had thought it prudent to withdraw to the Breton court and who, for reasons of their own, encouraged Duke Francis to assert his independence.

King Louis's attempt to end the quarrel by appointing a commission of arbitration came to nothing. By the time he parted from his uncle at Hesdin in early July of 1464, Francis II was openly assembling troops and secretly putting himself in touch with the English. Louis XI soon received the unpleasant tidings, perhaps from the Earl of Warwick, that Francis's Vice-Chancellor Rouville, slipping across the Channel disguised as a friar, had negotiated a year's truce with Edward IV. Louis also learned that Francis himself had promised the English King, in writing, to aid him whenever Edward decided to reconquer Normandy. Arriving in that province, the King of France limited himself to calling out the feudal levy, as a measure of defense, and to making public the Duke of Brittany's treasonable dealings with the English.

The Duke's advisers promptly engineered a classic political retaliation—they returned the charge upon the accuser. In early August, Francis II dispatched letters to the princes of France in which he asserted that the King had offered Normandy or Guienne to the English in return for their help in crushing the French nobility. Pointedly included in the circle of those so addressed was the King's seventeen-year-old brother, Charles, Duke of Berry, heir to the throne, a weak and shallow young man. Louis hastened to circularize the princes with a denial of Brittany's absurd charge; but the accusation, he soon realized, had provided a handy excuse for the magnates to draw their ranks closer and troubled the minds of those who shared the seignorial outlook, men like Pierre de Brezé. In August, Louis spent several days with Brezé, and on September 1 restored him to his offices of Great Seneschal of Normandy and Captain of Rouen. Brezé told the King that he would gladly bring Francis II to him—hauling the Duke by his thumb if necessary—but he added earnestly, "Sire, if you wish to be loved by the French . . . seek no friendship with the English. . . ."

The King's failure to settle the Breton quarrel had created a rallying standard for malcontent princes. As a result of his regaining Picardy, Philip the Good had become a disillusioned uncle and Charles, Count of Charolais, a deadly enemy. The Duke of Orléans and his bastard half brother Jean, the redoubtable Count of Dunois, were angered by the alliance with Francesco Sforza, who ruled the Duchy they claimed for themselves. The Duke of Bourbon, nephew of Philip the Good, still smarted over his loss of the governorship of Guienne and, like the others, resented his exclusion from the King's counsels. The Angevins were sorely affronted that the King had not expended troops and treasure to support Duke John in the Kingdom of Naples and to reseat René's daughter Margaret on the throne of England. The King, Alberico Maletta reported, was well aware of an "understanding among the princes of the realm."

By the end of August (1464), Louis XI had made his way back to Picardy.[2] As he moved nervously about the countryside near Abbeville, some twenty miles south of Hesdin, he was listening for the hoofbeats of couriers from English Calais. All the hopes of his ardent being were fastened upon one man, Richard Neville, Earl of Warwick.

As the early days of September slipped by, English messengers crossed the Channel; Louis sent men to London. Two Genoese, returning to Bruges from England, dispatched word that the Earl of Warwick was preparing to come to the King of France at the end of September. Louis hastened to inform Maletta that these Genoese had scotched an odd rumor which had drifted across the Channel, a rumor that King Edward had taken a wife. Then the Duke of Burgundy sent impatient word that, according to information he had from London, an English embassy was not on the way, and it did not sort with his honor to wait any longer than the end of the month. But Louis, to the embarrassment of his court, continued to caress every courier and to hang upon anyone who had report or rumor to dispense. "I never saw a lord so ardently desire anything," Maletta reported, "as the King desires this peace with the English. I believe that if the Earl of Warwick came he would obtain anything from the King to make this peace." And still Louis waited, peering seaward. And his courtiers muttered. And the Duke of Burgundy fumed.

Then report and rumor swelled into a remorseless certainty: the Earl of Warwick was not coming.

Everybody at the French court from lords to kitchen boys knew that Edward IV had secretly wedded, "for love," an English lady. In mid-September he had brusquely announced to a meeting of his Great Council this humiliating rejection of Warwick's French policy. Edward's romantic marriage to Elizabeth Woodville, the widowed daughter of a mere lord, outraged both the commons and the nobles of England. Already news was seeping across the Channel that Warwick had quarreled furiously with the monarch who thus dared to defy him. King Louis refused to admit the truth, still spoke of the Earl of Warwick's coming.

At this raw-nerved moment of failure, as he hunted in the countryside only a few miles from Hesdin, where the Duke of Burgundy was working himself into a rage against his nephew, there exploded a sensational scandal.

The Count of Charolais's servant Olivier de La Marche came riding at breakneck speed to Hesdin with inflammatory news. A suspicious character, dressed as a merchant, had been caught climbing the wall of Gorcum castle, the favorite seat of the Count of Charolais in Holland. Cast into prison by the Count, he turned out to be the Bastard of Rubempré, an adventurer as rakish as the armed vessel he had berthed sixty miles down the coast—and what was much worse, he was the nephew of Antoine and Jean de Croy, the bitterest enemies of the Duke of Burgundy's son. By the time Olivier de La Marche reached Hesdin with Charolais's tidings, rumor was spreading through the Low Countries that the King of France had attempted to murder the heir of their dominions, and the lurid news was soon flying all over the West. La Marche's arrival threw the Burgundian court into a panic: might not the King, who had sought the life of the son, be also meditating a descent upon Hesdin to force his bidding upon the father?

Louis at first said nothing or contemptuously dismissed the story.

Grimly he told Maletta that he had sent no word to the Duke of Burgundy on the subject of the Bastard nor had the Duke of Burgundy sent any word to him. He added—with more optimism than truth—that Charolais had freed Rubempré. But the King soon realized that silence not only damaged his prestige but gave the Duke of Burgundy an excellent motive to be reconciled with the Count of Charolais. Louis then announced that he had dispatched the Bastard to intercept the Duke of Brittany's Vice-Chancellor Rouville, who, the King understood, was returning from England by way of Gorcum in order to inform Charolais of Breton intrigues with Edward IV. He had intended, he explained, to extract from Rouville the truth of what the Vice-Chancellor had been doing in England.[3]

Realizing that it was now imperative for him to have a talk with his uncle, Louis sent one of his best diplomats, Georges Havart, to Hesdin on Saturday, October 6, to announce that he would arrive on the following Monday. Very early Sunday morning, Havart reported to the King that the Duke of Burgundy had returned a noncommittal answer the afternoon before and that night had indulged himself before his court in a violent outburst against his nephew. As Louis and Havart were talking, an unpleasant piece of news reached the French court. That very morning the Duke of Burgundy had abruptly left Hesdin with a small escort. His courtiers, taken by surprise, had had to scramble their baggage together and set off on horseback in a disorderly stream to overtake their master. And that master was headed in the last direction in the world Louis wanted to see him take—toward his son.

On October 10 the King finally let it be announced that Edward IV had married and that no embassy would cross the Channel. Casually he remarked to Maletta that the Duke of Burgundy had left Hesdin because he had grown tired of waiting for the English. He added that his uncle "was so old that he does not know what he is doing."

But Louis knew that he had suffered a dangerously humiliating defeat that could become a disaster. Edward IV had unceremoniously broken the painfully knit threads of Anglo-French amity. The Duke of Brittany was successfully defying—and now the Duke of Burgundy had publicly flouted—the King of France. The other princes could not fail to be stimulated by the example.

ii

THE TROUBLED KING OF FRANCE rode for Normandy to see to its defenses: the Duke of Brittany had put his forces on a war footing. Wherever

Louis XI looked, he could descry menacing consequences of his overexu-
berant kingship. In quickly reaching for substantial ends, he had disre-
garded intangible costs. It was time—if there was time—for him to pull
in his horns, to adopt circumspection as his watchword and tradition as
his guide. Abruptly he set about transforming himself into the image of
a king as the seignorial world understood it. Even before leaving Hesdin, he had begun giving ear to his nobles, as his father had done. With
a straight face he remarked to Maletta, "It is not suitable for me to remain here any longer, since English affairs are in such a state of confusion. I have asked all the lords of my blood who are here to meet with
my council in two or three hours in order to decide if it is well that I
depart."

At Rouen, a secretary and kinsman of the Earl of Warwick, one
Robert Neville—who had arrived with hot assurances from Warwick that
ungrateful Edward IV had only temporarily got out of hand—was so
skillfully imposed upon by the King and royal agents that he sent home
a roseate view of Louis's situation. The rumored disaffection of the
French princes was false, he reported; the southern magnates were so
held in awe by that accomplished knight the Bastard of Armagnac, that
"the Count of Armagnac would not dare do anything without his permission, not even piss." The royal court was thronged with loyal lords.[4]

The last observation was at least partly true: Louis had summoned
dukes and counts, gravely consulted with them—and received an ava-
lanche of advice crackling with seignorial discontents. The lords disap-
proved of his unseemly conflict with the papacy; they wanted him to
support the Angevins by breaking with the King of Aragon, uncle of the
usurper Ferrante at Naples; they proposed that embassies be sent to
poll the princes on the subject of treating with England and urged him
to choose seignorial envoys, i.e., not those fellows of no station with
whom he surrounded himself. Louis XI listened to it all with due so-
lemnity, and acted on almost none of it. He diligently pursued, however,
the style of duly feudal kingship. To deal with Francis II, he ordered a
convocation of his great lords, at Tours in December, to pass judgment
on his charges against the Duke. He named a formal embassy to the
Duke of Burgundy, and one impressive enough to please his uncle's
amour-propre: the Chancellor of France, energetic but brusque Pierre
de Morvillier; Charles, Count of Eu, Peer of the realm; and Pierre de
Brezé's brother-in-law, the Archbishop of Narbonne. They were charged
to bear the King's complaints against the flagrant hostility of the Count

of Charolais and against the unseemly conduct of his father in vanishing from Hesdin.

The days of November began to wear away. An unusually harsh and bleak autumn settled over the land. Louis left Rouen for Nogent-le-Roi to visit Pierre de Brezé and hunt in the wild country about Nogent. He gave a hearty welcome one morning, in the usual "savage and unpleasant place," to Alberico Maletta, who had come to beg the King to let him return to Italy. Louis, however, needed somebody to talk to and kept the ambassador with him for two days, lodging Alberico in a neighboring village. He spoke with his usual animation, but dark thoughts showed through. In the course of discussing Italian affairs, he pointed out to Maletta that when the famous condottiere Niccolò Piccinino took the field, he immediately unleashed all his power in an offensive, and if the attack failed he then withdrew; whereas Francesco Sforza did the contrary: the Duke of Milan was at his best when the water was up to his neck. At the end of the conversation Alberico again begged to be given his *congé*, but Louis asked him to remain until the embassy to the Duke of Burgundy returned. The King added, with a laugh, "that he wanted to make his will with me. . . ."

On November 22, an ambassadorial cavalcade clattered into the courtyard of Nogent-le-Roi—the King's envoys returned from the court of Burgundy. Louis sent for them at once, conferred with them in private a long time, then, calling for his horse, rode off into the woods to digest their unpleasant report. The Duke of Burgundy had rejected the charges against his son and himself, but promised to send the King an embassy. As the Archbishop of Narbonne was bidding the heir of Burgundy a courteous farewell, Charolais had said fiercely into the Archbishop's ear, "Recommend me very humbly to the good grace of the King and tell him—he has had me well worked over by his Chancellor, but before a year passes he will be sorry for it!" [5]

Louis XI held tenaciously to his circumspect role. The assembly of the princes at Tours was announced for December 18. On November 20, Louis moved from Nogent-le-Roi to Chartres, his court swollen by officers and counselors and lords whom he had summoned to advise with him. "Multitudes" waited in the hall to see the King, while he was "continually consulting" with Marshal Armagnac, the Admiral, the Chancellor, and numerous nobles.

As the magnates of the realm began arriving in Tours, some coming by boat on the Loire, the weather turned bitter cold and men had to fight their way through heavy snow. The Seine and the Oise were covered with ice; it was said that on some days bread and wine froze on the table. Crowded with "many great lords and infinite other folk," the city seemed to Maletta "a hell." Louis XI arrived on the evening of December 16. King René came by land and the Duke of Orléans by water the next day. Maletta had tactfully asked if he should make himself inconspicuous since the King was trying to conciliate the princes and both René and Orléans were enemies of the Duke of Milan. Louis replied that he did not care about King René, who was a "grosso homo," but thought that, because of the Duke of Orléans, Maletta had perhaps better stay away from the assembly.

In the opening session, at which the King was not present, the President of the Parlement of Toulouse, who had participated in most of the negotiations with Brittany, traced the whole course of the dispute and presented the evidences on which the King based his claim to the ecclesiastical jurisdictions of the Duchy. Two days later, on December 20, the Chancellor delivered a savage attack upon the Duke of Brittany, charging him with denying the King's rights, insulting the King, and entering into treacherous relations with the English.

Louis himself then rose to address the assembly. Speaking far more moderately than the Chancellor, he declared that never had the Duke's predecessors put forward the pretensions which Francis exhibited and never had they so defied the lawful authority of the King. Louis had no desire to ruin the Duke of Brittany but only to uphold the prerogatives of the Crown. "I tell you that if I had conquered his province and got into my hands everything but one castle . . . and he wished to come to grace and mercy, I would accord it to him in such a manner that everyone would know I had no desire for his destruction. . . ." Well aware, however, that in some minds at least it was he rather than the Duke of Brittany who was on trial, Louis embarked on a defense of his record. In order to dispense justice and to investigate the needs of the realm, he had gone up and down the land as had none of his predecessors. He had acquired Roussillon and Cerdagne; he had redeemed the Somme towns from the Duke of Burgundy; he had labored night and day to reinvigorate France. Finally, Louis brought himself to deliver a panegyric of the Princes—without whom, he declared, he would be powerless, "for the lords are the pillars which sustain the Crown." Resting his case, he appealed for loyalty from all his vassals.

"The common opinion is that never did one see a man speak in

French better or more winningly. . . ." The King had said "so many fine and persuasive words that among the onlookers there was not one who did not weep." The response of the princes, after they had deliberated among themselves, was as enthusiastic as that of the spectators. King René, their spokesman, declared to his sovereign that they were all convinced of the guilt of Francis II, they were all determined to live and die in the King's service, and indeed they were ready to go in a body to the Duke of Brittany in order to engage him to submit to the royal will. Louis thanked them heartily for their fidelity but hastily declined their last proposition. Despite René's fervent pledge of loyalty, the last thing in the world Louis wanted was to offer an opportunity for the princes to forgather with Francis II.

In the intense cold the lords and their trains of followers rode away from Tours. Louis took the Duke of Orléans with him to ·Amboise. On the night of January 4–5 that princely poet, who fifty ·years before had been captured by the English at the battle of Agincourt, passed from the world of princes. About this same time there died a prince of poets— perhaps in prison, perhaps on the gallows, nobody knows where—who was anything but princely, François Villon. Louis and Villon would have understood each other very well. They rarely confused shadow and substance; their irreverent senses of humor got them into endless trouble; they were enormously fascinated by the pageant of human life; and each in his own way did what he felt he was fashioned to do rather than what the forms and powers of the world decreed.

iii

As Louis moved by wintry roads among his favorite castles in the Loire Valley, an enormous silence descended upon the realm—the silence of the princes.

There survives no record of what the King had read in their faces as they solemnly swore fidelity to him at Tours. He could claim to have treated most of them with consideration and a number of them handsomely, and to have forwarded their interests as best he could, when they did not conflict with the interests of the Kingdom. He had rehabilitated the Duke of Alençon, condemned by Charles VII. He had shown high favor to the southern magnates—the Count of Foix, the Count of Armagnac, the Count's cousin Jacques, son of his old governor the Count of Pardiac, whom he had created Duke of Nemours. He had paid public honors to the House of Orléans. He had supported the pretensions and tried to soothe the delicate feelings of the House of Anjou. Charles

VII had done no more for any of them. Yet the nobles of the realm were now regarding the reign of Louis's father as a golden age, and Louis's as a nightmare.

For one thing, under Charles VII the princes had aimed their discontents at each other as they jockeyed to dominate the royal government; whereas under Louis XI they were thwarted not by princely rivals for power but by the King himself. For another, all the great lords, from the powerful Duke of Burgundy to the least noble, had been subjected to a pressure of crown claims they had never felt before. Royal officers everywhere formed a zealous army who pushed to the limit the prerogatives of the sovereign. When the servants of the princes used force to get their way or flouted royal jurisdiction, they instantly found themselves faced with a suit. If they won a case here and there, a dozen other cases immediately popped up. Against this pressure, remorseless but legal, the princes could not make a very convincing protest and were the more frustrated. They feared too the efficient police network of the King, which had the embarrassing habit of intercepting secret communications; and they knew that their sovereign employed shadowy figures, like, for example, the Dutchman Étienne de Loup, who, "very private with the King," was charged with informing him if any lord was in secret contact with enemies of the Crown.

But the causes of discontent went deeper. Louis had accomplished too much; he had violated too many prejudices, shaken too many established attitudes, moved too quickly in too many directions. The fears aroused by the Dauphin's violently unconventional career had been confirmed by the doings of the King.

In sum, he was not kingly. He did not dress like a king; he did not talk like a king; he did not think like a king; he did not possess that natural affection for his princes and his lords with which all true kings are endowed. He surrounded himself with fearfully hardworking and fearfully intelligent and disgustingly lowborn fellows. He took all kinds of foreigners into his service and even preferred their company to that of honest Frenchmen. He paid annoying honors to the ambassador of that upstart adventurer Francesco Sforza, and called the Duke of Milan his friend; and he openly exhibited a desire for the friendship of the Earl of Warwick, who was not only an adventurer but an Englishman. Instead of consulting the princes, he did everything out of his own head, taking advice only from a small circle of intimates like the Bastard of Armagnac and the Admiral, Montauban, who had been with him most of his life. He was disturbingly unpredictable, thinking nothing of visiting great lords without advance notice, a mode of conduct that injured their dignities and made them exceedingly nervous. He and his court were painfully lacking in decorum and in a love of splendor that was the essence of kingship. What was to be made of a monarch who, visiting the Count of Maine, let Maine have his castle to himself and camped in the woods nearby?

And the King had let his tongue wag. He was heard to observe that the Duke of Bourbon did not have much brain power. On one occasion he called the Count of Maine and the Count of Dunois the Elders of Susannah. He enjoyed telling Alberico Maletta that the old Duke of Orléans claimed that Sforza had had him poisoned. The King added, laughing, "Poisoned and old as he is, he has made his wife pregnant." He enjoyed mimicking the rages of the Count of Charolais, showed his impatience with his uncle Philip's senile antics, and did not scruple to comment on the shortcomings of the Pope. Furthermore, though the princes complained of the King's dissimulations, which were so much more successful than their own, they were no better pleased on being treated to some home truths—as when Louis bluntly informed an adherent of the Duke of Orléans that the French had no business in Italy at all.

In the view of the great lords, the King failed to qualify for membership in the princely circle. He was a changeling, a man from nowhere, a rank outsider.

Louis XI was but too well aware of this feudal indictment, and of the secret league of the discontented which had sprung from it. Yet, if he now sensed the enormous silence of the princes, he gave no sign.

The King of France appeared to be an untroubled ruler: prosperous in his affairs, relaxed of mind, casual about future undertakings. In mid-February King Louis left the valley of the Loire for Poitiers, capital of the great southwestern province of Poitou. There he gave out that he planned to move farther south, to Bordeaux and Perpignan: he wanted to see the heir of the recently deceased Count of Foix securely settled in Navarre. At his side, for but a few more days, was Alberico Maletta. Louis had at last agreed, unhappily, to send home this Italian ambassador in whom he had found a counselor and friend. The times being so unsettled, the prudent Milanese had secured a successor.[6] For Alberico, Louis painted a picture of a king without care. England offered no threat to security; Louis thought that by foolishly rejecting the French marriage and breaking with the Earl of Warwick, King Edward IV might well have begun his own undoing. A Burgundian embassy, affirming the loyalty of Philip the Good and his son, had departed well content with the answers they had received. Louis had even intimated that he might restore the Count of Charolais's pension. As for the Duke of Brittany, now eager for peace, his envoys were arriving at any moment to clear the last lingering clouds from that horizon.

One small, but unexpected, domestic difficulty had developed. The King's heir and young brother, Charles, Duke of Berry, with whom he had been assiduously sharing his counsels and his company, had become moody and withdrawn, strange conduct for so slack and timid a young man. While the royal brothers were lodged at the castle of Razilly on their way to Poitiers, the King had been advised by Marshal Armagnac that the Duke of Berry was discontented with his lot and that it would be wise to propitiate him. Charles himself had then petulantly complained to his sovereign that his pension and the Duchy of Berry were too meager for his dignity. Louis had promptly increased his brother's pension by six thousand crowns and promised that, once the quarrel with the Duke of Brittany was settled, he would see about providing Charles with a larger *apanage*.

On February 20, two Breton ambassadors, the Chancellor of Brittany and the master spirit of Brittany, Odet d'Aydie, the Duke's chief councilor, rode into Poitiers to announce that Francis II had no other desire than to yield himself to the will of his sovereign lord. The Duke was eager to perform his submission in person and therefore asked to have Marshal Armagnac and the Admiral sent to escort him. The King and Odet d'Aydie indulged in a duel of compliments, Louis trying to persuade the Duke of Brittany's dangerous adviser to take service with him, and the clever Gascon, all charm, holding out hopes but promising nothing. On Sunday, March 3, Odet d'Aydie and the Chancellor of Brittany quitted Poitiers on most cordial terms with the King. Next morning the Marshal and the Admiral set out to meet Francis II. At the same time, King Louis with a small entourage left Poitiers to go on pilgrimage to Notre Dame du Pont at nearby St. Julien in the Limousin. The Duke of Berry was not in the King's party: he had said that he preferred to hunt. A few minutes after Louis departed, the King's brother left his quarters—he was lodging with one of the aldermen—and with a few friends galloped into the countryside.

Early on the morning of March 5, the pilgrim-King received a frantic message from Poitiers. Under cover of going hunting, the Duke of

Berry had stolen away, nobody knew where.

Instantly Louis divined whither his brother had fled and what his brother's departure signified. The princes had risen against their sovereign.

Louis rode hard for Poitiers.

13. The League of the Public Weal

THOUGH LOUIS XI had set off on pilgrimage with fewer than forty horse, by the time he reentered Poitiers he reportedly had mustered a thousand men. In a day or two he gathered round him the Count of Maine, both Marshals of France, Pierre de Brezé, veteran advisers Jean Bourré and Georges Havart, his diligent treasurer Étienne Chevalier, his expert on trade and finance Guillaume de Varye, and other captains and counselors. Ready to hand in the fortress of Thouars, only a few miles to the north, lay the royal treasure—said by the King's men to run to more than two million crowns.

Louis soon learned the circumstances of his brother's flight. After Odet d'Aydie and the Chancellor of Brittany left Poitiers on Sunday (March 3), they rode only four leagues from the city. Following the King's departure the next morning, the Duke of Berry and his "hunting party" hastily joined Odet and the Chancellor, and they all then galloped hard for Nantes, where the Duke of Brittany awaited them. Louis also discovered—if indeed he had not already known it—that the Count of Dunois had loaded his most valuable movables on a barge and floated down the Loire to become the leading spirit of the Breton revolt. The "terrible news" coursed through the kingdom. The bad old days when the strife of Armagnac and Burgundian had let the English into France were still painfully vivid in people's minds. "Please God he [King Louis] remedies matters quickly," wrote 'Frannequin' Nori, the Medici agent at Lyons. "While this lasts, the realm will be a forest of thieves, as formerly it was."

The King of France swiftly transformed his household into a military headquarters and stretched every nerve to probe the dimensions of rebellion, to assemble an army, to bind the realm to his cause. By March 7 royal messengers were bearing to the "good towns" exhortations to keep strict watch and to reject any propositions from the rebel lords who had suborned his naïve young brother; the King promised that he would move at once "to scotch this evil enterprise. . . ." On March 8, Louis made Charles de Melun Lieutenant-General of Paris; and four days later Melun and an energetic young prelate, Jean Balue, were reading out to the Parisians the King's orders to guard gates and walls, make ready the street chains, and stand staunch against treason. Louis was also sending appeals to some of the princes. "I beg you, my uncle," he addressed the all-important Duke of Burgundy, "that you will not allow [the Count of Charolais] nor any others to do anything against me . . . for I have my trust in you." He wrote in his own hand to the Duke of Bourbon requesting that "the moment you have read this letter, you mount horse and come to me. . . ."

On March 13, the King suddenly wheeled northward to Thouars, his fortress-treasury—a move which also put him on the road to King René's domain of Anjou. René had written vaguely that he was hoping to make an accord between the Dukes of Berry and Brittany and the King, but he said nothing about his own allegiance. At this moment the rebellion of the princes was publicly affirmed. The Duke of Bourbon issued a manifesto proclaiming that he and his fellow magnates, hearkening to the clamorous griefs of nobles, churchmen, the poor, had united on behalf of the *bien publique* (general welfare) to remedy injustices and to sweep away taxes which were driving the realm to perdition. Bourbon named as his collaborators in this public-spirited enterprise the head of the House of Anjou, King René; the Dukes of Berry, Brittany, Nemours, Calabria (Duke John); the Counts of Charolais, Armagnac, St. Pol, Dunois; and numerous barons. Followers of the Duke of Bourbon were appropriating royal tax moneys and seizing all royal officers, great and small, that they could get their hands on. Bourbon, furthermore, soon gained a notable adherent: on the night of March 9–10, that old Écorcheur and enemy of the Dauphin Antoine de Chabannes, Count of Dammartin, who had been condemned for *lèse-majesté* in 1463 by the Parlement of Paris and imprisoned in the Bastille, made a daring escape and betook himself to Moulins, Bourbon's capital.

From Thouars, on March 16, the King countered the rebel propaganda emanating from the Bourbonnais and Brittany by issuing his first manifesto. He reminded his subjects that until the princes had risen in arms for their own selfish ends, his realm had enjoyed "great tranquillity, trade was carried on freely everywhere, each one lived peacefully in his own house. . . ." If the rebels persisted in their intentions, the bad old days of civil strife would return and then "our ancient enemies the English . . . could invade the realm. . . ." All those who out of ignorance had dabbled in treason but would now swear to be loyal were offered full pardon for any offenses committed. Companies of lances and other troops were already poised on the borders of Brittany.

Had the rebellion of the princes, then, taken him unawares?

The *Mémoires* of Commynes, ambassadorial dispatches, the chronicles, the King's letters, all maintain silence. Perhaps the answer is to be taken for granted—the King must have had no inkling of trouble, else he would have behaved very differently in the weeks preceding the outbreak. Though he had known for at least a year that the princes of the realm were conspiring, it may be that, like Alberico Maletta, he estimated that they would not dare come to open war against him; or he may have been taken in by the effusive protestations of fidelity which the princes had expressed at Tours in their December assembly and by the humble requests for reconciliation which emanated from Francis II in January and February of 1465. By announcing that he considered his troubles with the Duke of Brittany ended and that he meant to go to Bordeaux and Perpignan in order to help the Count of Foix in Navarre, he had unquestionably given the princes the impression of a king lulled into complacency; and in leaving his brother at Poitiers while he went off on pilgrimage—an arrangement that must have been published at least a few days in advance or the conspirators could not have contrived with such perfect timing the Duke of Berry's flight—he had played directly into the hands of his enemies.

On the other hand, nothing in Louis's life before or after the rebellion, nothing in his character, nothing in the way he conducted his affairs gives much support for this picture of a monarch taken by surprise.

Olivier de La Marche declares that at Christmastime some five hundred squires, gentlemen, and ladies, each identifying himself by a bit of white silk in his belt, gathered at Notre Dame in Paris to concert plans for the rebellion of their lords. For months, the lords themselves had been exchanging conspiratorial messages. It is hard to believe that the conspicuous group described by La Marche could have escaped the notice of royal functionaries in Paris, that the constant coming-and-going of the princes' couriers did not result in the interception of incriminating communications by the King's officers. One such interception is on record, but it occurred only a few days before the Duke of Berry's flight: the Marshal of Lodgings, Josselin du Bois, arrested a courier bearing a message to Francis II that the Count of Charolais had disavowed his father's peaceful embassy to the King; and the missive probably contained other indications that trouble was at hand. "The secret" was, in fact, so loose that, in the Burgundian town of Macon, the news of the Duke of Berry's flight was taken to mean that the King's brother was proclaimed Regent. Louis himself had instantly understood the significance of his brother's disappearance; and he had dispatched a particularly pressing summons to the Duke of Bourbon, the prince who was to be the first to commence hostilities.

It is possible that, to avoid the charge of aggression, Louis had adopted his attitude of King-without-cares in order to encourage the revolt to come into the open, and the sooner the better. The quarrel between Edward IV and Warwick assured him that, at least for the moment, he had nothing to fear from England. The Duke of Burgundy's growing senility, the ominous implication of his reconciliation with his son likewise emphasized the urgency of time: Philip the Good, however annoyed at his nephew, would not, Louis believed, take arms against the King of France, whereas once the inflammatory Count of Charolais gained control of the Burgundian government, there was bound to be trouble.

It is most unlikely that Louis was rash enough to plant his brother at Poitiers so that Odet d'Aydie could pluck him as the prize apple of discord; yet, if he did not arrange this knowingly, his nerves may have arranged it for him. Perhaps a hidden feeling of guilt for his participation in the Praguerie forced him, unconsciously assuming his father's place, to allow his brother, malcontent heir to the throne, to play the Dauphin's role of figurehead for a parcel of self-seeking princes. And then, as Commynes well knew, "he could hardly endure repose"; and for months he had been fretted by manifestations of princely resentment which he could neither master by peaceful means nor assuage without wrecking his government.

In any case, if Louis was taken by surprise, he was not caught ill-prepared. At the moment the rebellion broke out, he was but fifty miles from his treasure vaults at Thouars, and within a few hours' ride of Poitiers were stationed several thousand soldiers of the standing army.

"This realm is topsy-turvy," the Duke of Milan was informed. "Nothing is seen or talked of but arms. . . . The whole country remains with ear cocked, and people do not know which side to take. Things cannot remain as they are." The news flowing in to the King was mostly good.

All the great towns sent solemn promises to stand by their allegiance—Amiens, Rheims, Rouen, Paris, Orléans, Poitiers, Montpellier. Bordeaux offered to dispatch two hundred crossbowmen paid for three months. "Those of Lyons" swore to live and die with the King—"they will be for him no matter what happens." The actions of the princes, however, grew daily more ominous. While armed men of the Duke of Bourbon took over towns in the Bourbonnais and Auvergne, and the southern lords and the Angevins waited in varying degrees of ambiguity, the Dukes of Berry and Brittany, at Nantes, launched a barrage of propaganda directed by the nimble-minded Odet d'Aydie and the Count of Dunois. The King's brother was put forward as cause and head of the rebellion —"in all these transactions no one is named except the Duke of Berry, he appearing as chief of the whole affair." His complaints of ill-treatment by the King, his appeal for the reform of the government, his demand for an *apanage* suitable to his station, it was proclaimed, had moved the princes to band together in a League of the Public Weal. The poor were to be relieved, taxes abolished, "disorders" repressed. It was, indeed, the Praguerie all over again, with a vengeance.

As the days of March passed, Louis continued lavishing honors on his Angevin uncle the Count of Maine, who was showing himself the loyalest of the loyal, but he grew increasingly suspicious of his Angevin uncle King René. Louis had presented him with the town of Gap in Provence to stimulate his fidelity and commissioned him to negotiate with the Dukes of Berry and Brittany. That lover of tournaments and poets, exhorted by his fellow princes and pushed by his bellicose son Duke John, probably wished himself well out of the whole business, but he had the wit to perceive that if the Angevins distributed themselves on both sides of the fence they could hardly lose. He was preserving so equivocal an attitude it was not clear whether he was treating or conspiring with Berry and Brittany.

On March 26 Louis suddenly marched from Thouars and took possession of King René's town of Saumur on the Loire, "a fine strong place with hills and waters." It was enough to bring René hurrying in—after the King, in response to his plea of poverty, had dispatched him twelve thousand crowns in cash and eighteen thousand more in assignments on crown revenue. On the evening of April 10 the head of the House of Anjou swore "in the King's hands" to serve him faithfully "for and against all." But Louis wryly informed Maletta that René had taken the oath "in the manner of Italy [i.e., out of mere opportunism]."

The southern lords—Foix, Armagnac, Nemours—sent the King fervent promises of support, but there were "divers reports" of their attitude. From the north came positive news; it was bad. At the beginning of March, the Duke of Burgundy had become ill, then recovered; but now, unmistakably senile, he was persuaded to turn over the government to the Count of Charolais, Louis's bitterest foe. At the worst possible moment, time had outrun the King of France. Picardy was immediately endangered. Louis had prudently remitted twenty thousand crowns' worth of taxes owed by the Picards and suspended the impost on wine produced by private growers. He had ordered his chief officers there to concert measures for defense. Word arriving, however, that Picardy was exhibiting a wavering allegiance, the King dispatched Marshal Roualt with one hundred lances to stiffen the loyalties of the province.

At Saumur, meanwhile, Louis XI was driving on his military preparations with every appearance of confidence. He paid out a quarter's wages to his troops, honored deserving warriors with presents of horses and armor, feasted his captains. Alberico Maletta, now on his way back to Milan, had left in his place a youthful envoy, Giovanni Pietro (or Jean Pierre, as the French called him) Panigarola,[1] who quickly took fire in the blaze of the King's vitality. "His Majesty uses the greatest diligence in mustering men and in deploying them. . . . He is in high spirits, makes good cheer, and provides for his affairs without losing a second."

The day King René appeared at Saumur, Wednesday, April 10, Louis dispatched eastward an advance guard of two hundred lances under three of his best captains. On April 17, six weeks after the flight of his brother, he rode out of Saumur to take the field. He was leaving about thirteen thousand men under the command of the Count of Maine to keep Charles of Berry and Francis II penned up in the Breton peninsula. He himself with an army of about eleven thousand, including eight hundred crack lances of the standing army, would attack the Duke of Bourbon, while another force from Dauphiné and Languedoc advanced on the Bourbonnais from the south. He was aiming to knock Bourbon out of the war before the other rebels could unite. Halting briefly at Tours, he got word that Francesco Sforza was preparing to send him four thousand horse and one thousand foot, all veteran troops.

ii

ON ST. GEORGE'S DAY, April 23, Louis XI left Tours with his army and his artillery train—the latter "stretching out more than six leagues on the road with twelve hundred horses required to pull it." The subtle, mercurial King of France had had a long experience in the not-so-subtle trade of war. He knew that men fight best for a sovereign who takes the field with them and understands the business better than most. Swiftly he pushed his forces westward toward the province of Berry, gateway to the Bourbonnais. On learning that its capital, his natal city of Bourges, had been seized by the Bastard of Bourbon, he dispatched forces to occupy the rest of the province and pressed onward to Montluçon, second city of the Bourbonnais, which blocked the road to Moulins, Bourbon's capital. After a single assault, he accepted the submission of the city on gentle terms. Jean Pierre Panigarola was amazed by the discipline of the royal troops—"In such a tumult of men of arms there is not a man who dares rob or take anything without paying"—and by the speed of the King's campaigning, "so astonishing that I must emphasize it."

Louis now turned his forces east and northeast toward the string of castles which guarded the roads from Montluçon to Moulins, some forty miles away, where lay the Duke of Bourbon and the Count of Dammartin. He learned that his men from Dauphiné, fighting their way northward under Robin Malortie, [*] had routed the enemy forces facing them. Towns in the Bourbonnais and in Auvergne were daily submitting. King René's renewed negotiations with the Dukes of Brittany and Berry, however, had produced nothing more than a declaration that the princes were content for Louis to reign provided that they took over the business of ruling. Word had come that Duke John, in Lorraine, had openly declared for the League of the Public Weal and was recruiting forces in Germany and among the Swiss. The Count of Armagnac was coming up from the south at last, but his several thousand hungry Gascons were devastating the country and Armagnac had ceased his protestations of loyalty. On the other hand, Jean Pierre Panigarola appeared in the King's chamber one morning with a letter from the Duke of Milan in his fingers and the news that Franceso Sforza "as a sign of adamant loyalty" had commissioned his son and heir, Count Galeazzo, to lead the five thousand foot and horse, which would soon be descending the Alpine passes to aid the King of France.

Louis pressed on his campaign. Detachments of the royal army were fanning out from Montluçon to garrison towns in all directions, while the main body, moving on Moulins despite downpours and

---

[*] Who had languished for a time in prison after incurring the Dauphin's wrath in 1456 (see page 86) but whom Louis had long since recognized for the valiant and faithful captain that he was.

flooded roads, closed a ring of bombards and men of arms around Heris-
son. The town had surrendered by the time the King, bringing Panigarola with him, appeared before the walls with five thousand horse—"all
well mounted and equipped and a goodly sight to see." [2]

Suddenly, at the beginning of the last week in May, there came a
change. The army advanced no further toward Moulins; King Louis remained at Montluçon. From the north had come fateful tidings. The
Count of Charolais had secured a money grant from his Three Estates in
order to muster an army for "the welfare of France." Each message
reaching royal headquarters made it clearer that Charolais did not aim
merely at conquering Picardy but would move on Paris to join his fellow princes in arms. Louis therefore ordered Marshal Roualt and his
other captains to unite their forces in the field. The King's next decision
showed, however, that he had little hope of blocking the advance of the
Burgundian army. He sent word to Robin Malortie, driving up from the
south, to abandon the pincers movement and join him at once. The
Bourbonnais campaign had become a trap. Under the pressure of time
he now chose to put his faith in his arts of negotiation. At forty-two, he
was still optimistic enough to undertake bargaining from weakness with
princes he knew he could not trust.

The King sent word to Moulins that he was ready to listen to the
peace overtures which the Duke of Bourbon had been trying to make for
some days. He also redoubled his efforts to bring into camp the coy and
ambiguous Duke of Nemours, who still remained, not many miles away,
at his castle of Montaigut. Louis kept a cheerful face to the world, but
before Sforza's ambassador, Jean Pierre Panigarola, he let down his
guard for a moment: "His Majesty says that if he should lose, he would
rather Your Highness have Dauphiné and Lyons than anyone else." The
Duke of Nemours, on receiving a surety for his safety, allowed himself to
be escorted to Montluçon. To the King who had made him a duke and
showered him with honors, Jacques d'Armagnac was all boyish charm
and avowals of devotion. He would never have sent his seal to the
princes, he explained easily, except that he had been told that his sovereign was planning to give Normandy or Guienne to the English. But
now that he understood the truth he had no other desire than to play
honest broker between the King and the rebel lords in order to bring
about a felicitous pacification of the realm. Louis was now committed to
working with whatever materials lay to hand. He assured Panigarola
that he knew his adversaries were playing for time; he counted, how-

ever, on making time work for him. Under Nemours' deft management, an eight-day truce was arranged in order to permit negotiations.

On May 28, the King and his forces entered St. Pourçain, some eighteen miles due south of Moulins. Next day he sent word to Georges Havart, who was on his way to Calais to negotiate with the Earl of Warwick, that envoys had "gone to Moulins . . . and we believe that to-morrow they will bring the Duke of Bourbon to Varennes [four miles distant, on the other side of the river Allier]; and we expect that we shall not part from one another until we have assured our business here. That done, we will draw into the Marches there [i.e., Picardy] to resist the enterprises and menaces of those who, against their honor and their oath of fealty, seek to put us in submission." On the 29th, or thereabouts, the Duke of Nemours duly brought the Duke of Bourbon to Varennes. Enthusiastically Nemours plied back and forth between Varennes and St. Pouçain, trailing Bourbon's envoys and the King's negotiators with him. With the arrival of each new day Louis expected to meet with the Duke of Bourbon; but the Duke, it turned out, did not want to come into his sovereign's presence until all arrangements had been made, and somehow there were always new points to be discussed.

The days of June were slipping by. Couriers arrived, dusty, with dusty tidings. Duke John had allied himself with the Count of Charolais, a linking of the two princely houses once most bitterly at odds. Each sweating messenger brought worse news from Picardy. The Burgundian army was now rolling southward, toward Paris. Louis sent word to Pierre de Brezé, commanding under the Count of Maine, to dispatch three hundred lances to Picardy, and ordered all the men of arms and archers of Île de France to reinforce the defenses of Paris.

Dangers much closer to him he now sensed for the first time. One of his chief councilors, of high Norman lineage, Louis d'Harcourt, Bishop of Bayeux and Patriarch of Jerusalem, found the opportunity at St. Pourçain to renew secret talks he had been holding with the Duke of Nemours on the subject of capturing the King. The Patriarch also thought it would be a fine stroke to burn the King's gunpowder stored at St. Pourçain. The King's favorite, Antoine du Lau, joined the plotters. Nemours, however, still considered the odds too great. Probably getting a whiff of this miasma of treachery, Louis added to his body archers on night duty an extra guard of 160 men; and Marshal Armagnac estab-lished a night watch of archers in his lodging. The Duke of Bourbon still evaded meeting the King. Louis desperately continued negotiations, mired in a predicament of his own making.

Early in the morning of June 14 he learned that, the night before, the Duke of Bourbon and the Duke of Nemours had ridden hard to Moulins. They had got word that two hundred lances from the Duchy of Burgundy, which, contrary to the truce, the Duke of Bourbon had summoned to his aid, had reached Bourbon's capital. The moment he received the news, Louis crossed the Allier to occupy Varennes, throwing out a screen of lances to block further reinforcements from the Duchy of Burgundy. The King had hardly reached the town when envoys from Nemours and Bourbon appeared. They announced blandly that, though the Dukes had thought it best to retire to Moulins, Bourbon was still eager to come to terms with his sovereign.

"We have lost twenty-two or twenty-three days we could not spare," a royal councilor wrote bleakly to the Chancellor. But Louis resumed negotiations—it was either that or abandon the campaign with nothing to show for it and rebel forces on his back. Two days later, June 16, as he was "expecting to complete an agreement," he learned that Bourbon and Nemours had slipped out of Moulins to the west and were riding southward to join the Count of Armagnac, who had cut his way through mountainous Auvergne with five thousand Gascons. These disasters were matched by news from the north. The Count of Charolais had crossed the Somme on June 6. Though the chief Picard towns held for the King, and Marshal Roualt was hanging on the Burgundian flank, the royal officers had failed to put an army in the field, and the way to Paris lay open.

At one o'clock in the morning of June 20 royal scouts brought word that Bourbon and Nemours, joined with Armagnac and his force, had tricked the city of Riom into opening its gates the morning before. By evening of the same day, Louis had moved his army and artillery within three miles of Gannat, a fortified town halfway between St. Pourçain and Riom. On the road the King was joined by the stout contingent from Dauphiné commanded by Robin Malortie. To Robin he promised a county in Normandy with an income of twenty thousand crowns. The men of Dauphiné, many of whom he must have known by name, he constituted his battle guard. Next morning, Friday, June 21, Louis delivered an assault on Gannat that drove the defenders pell-mell into the citadel. As soon as the King entered the town, a royal councilor wrote to the Chancellor, "he ranged his artillery against the citadel, broke the walls which held water in the moat, and began an attack on the fort, which at once yielded to him . . . at his will. This done, when he had eaten an egg—for there was nothing else—he mounted horse, and with all our troops and artillery we came to lodge at Aigueperse, five miles down the road and less than ten miles from Riom. . . ." The princes sent a herald with a proposed treaty, "bien étrange" in its insolence, which was curtly rejected. By evening of the next day, Saturday, Louis had thrust his army through driving rain to within sight of Riom.

The Duke of Bourbon, disguising himself as an archer, spurred out of Riom, made his way through the marshes to the southeast and so got back to Moulins. Next morning, Sunday, June 23, as Louis was oversee-ing the encirclement of the town and the placement of bombards, a her-ald issued from the gate, requested a parley. The King assented. Trot-ting across the fields with an escort came the Duke of Nemours, debonair as June itself. Louis, drinking the bitter dregs of time-run-out, greeted him cordially and listened to his proposals. By the end of the day a treaty had been agreed upon, a poor huddled-up thing which be-trays in every line the King's desperate necessity. A truce was arranged, to last until mid-August. Nemours and Armagnac and, according to their promise, Bourbon undertook to try to pacify the other princes, the King agreeing to bestow on the three lords fat pensions, offices, military com-mands. On this same Sunday (June 23) Louis dispatched word of this truce to the Parisians, asserting that he intended to arrive in his capital with all his army within fifteen days.

Riom lay 230 miles southwest of Paris.

Already his forces were dismantling their siege positions and start-ing up the long road to Île de France. Couriers were galloping the roads with orders to royal garrisons in the Bourbonnais to prepare their with-drawal. Louis spent the night of the 23rd and the 24th in the village of Marsat, outside Riom, working to get his army on the march. He also founded a perpetual Mass to be celebrated every day in the village church, where he had "several times in great devotion prayed to the adored image of the glorious Mary." On the 24th a councilor sent word to the Chancellor that thanks to the King's "tremendous energy" he "has got out of the imbroglio to his honor." But Louis was not out of it yet. He moved northward only ten miles to Aigueperse—and there the last precious days of June sped by on the wings of further "negotiations." Bourbon, ignoring the treaty, demanded control of more than half the standing army for the two southern lords and himself, a proposition the King rejected out of hand. There was nothing for it but to patch to-gether, hugger-mugger, an agreement with Nemours and Armagnac. Signed on June 30, it confirmed Louis's previous grants to them, they promising to join their sovereign at Montluçon.

And June was gone, thirty days of broken oaths, down which Louis XI had slid ever deeper into the pit of time, clawing at the slippery sides of faithlessness. He did not yet know, though he appears to have sensed, that the shadows of treason danced ever more boldly in his very lodgings. During this week at Aigueperse, the indefatigable Patriarch of Jerusalem and Antoine du Lau resumed their plotting with the Duke of Nemours. In the hall where the King was holding audience, even in the royal chamber, the Patriarch whispered his propositions. After they had captured their sovereign at Montluçon or in the open country—he rode with a very small escort—there would follow a pacification in which the princes would divide the government of France, the standing army, and the receipts of the treasury among themselves; and the Patriarch would head a council strait-jacketing the King. The scheme seemed "assez agréable" to the Duke of Nemours, but after a close call one evening, when the King's confidential secretary Jean Bourré appeared at Nemours' door and the Patriarch had to be popped into a closet, the Duke again nervously shied off.

The royal army was now strung along all the roads leading northward to Orléans; garrisons were pulling out of towns; crack cavalry units and mounted archers and light artillery led the way while foot soldiers slogged along behind. When Louis reached Montluçon, about July 3, there was no sign of Armagnac or Nemours: the treaty was a dead letter. He had already established a screen of rear guards, to the south against Armagnac, to the southeast against an attack from the Duchy of Burgundy, to the east against forces of the Duke of Bourbon. "The army," a veteran servant of the crown wrote to the Chancellor, "is not very large, but for its size, some twelve thousand troops, I never saw soldiers the equal of them, both in battle and on the march. . . ."

They had never been able to come to grips with the foe; now, retracing weary miles at top speed with the princes of France gathered against them, they realized that maybe the luck was out. But they were professionals, they were led by a king who knew the trade of war, and they drove themselves up the dusty summer roads with undiminished morale. The Duke of Bourbon's men sallied from Bourges to take the royal army in the flank, only to be severely beaten and driven back to the city. Forces of Marshal of Burgundy were so badly trounced by other rear guards that long after the King's legions had crossed the Loire the Marshal dared not make another move.

By the time Louis paused at Culan on July 7–8—165 miles south of Paris—he knew that the great Burgundian army had crossed the Oise at

Pont-Ste.-Maxence and was sweeping upon his capital. The Bretons had now begun to move eastward, the Count of Maine offering no resistance; and Duke John was about to march westward from Lorraine. The good towns all favored the royal cause; Paris appeared to be standing firm; most of the *petite noblesse* who were not dependent upon the magnates remained loyal, or indifferent. But, except for the Counts of Eu and Vendôme, who had small power, all the princes of France had taken arms to crush the monarch they regarded as an interloper.

From Culan, Louis wrote to his Chancellor, "We are marching with all diligence to Paris, and, God willing, we will reach Orléans on Saturday next [July 13]." He made it to Orléans on the 11th. The Burgundians, he learned, were already attacking Paris.

14. Montlhéry

On Thursday, July 11, the King of France heard Mass at Notre Dame de Cléry, eight miles southwest of Orléans, the representation of Our Lady that he most venerated. The fact of his presence there is preserved in an express message sent by the widowed Duchess of Orléans, niece to the Duke of Burgundy, to give warning to the Count of Charolais. The King had ridden "night and day," Panigarola reported.

Louis XI spent Friday and Saturday, July 12 and 13, marshaling his forces. Heavy cavalry and mounted archers were streaming across the Loire bridges at Orléans and Beaugency. Thousands of foot soldiers and most of the artillery units were still toiling up the roads from the Bourbonnais, followed by the rear guards and reinforcements coming from Languedoc. Louis could not wait for them, could not rest the men he had. He sent word to the capital that the royal army would arrive on Tuesday, July 16. Couriers now brought only worse and worse news, except for the tidings of Paris. The mass of Parisians were "all united in loyalty to the King." Marshal Roualt, who entered the city on June 30 with one hundred lances, and the King's Lieutenant-General, Charles de Melun, and Jean Balue, a coarse, tough, energetic, lecherous cleric, now Bishop-elect of Évreux, had organized a stout defense.

On the afternoon of July 5—the King still far away at Montluçon—the host of the Count of Charolais, perhaps twenty-five thousand strong and supported by the best artillery in Europe, appeared beneath the northern and western walls. Parleys failed to intimidate or suborn the loyalty of the capital; assaults upon two of the gates were easily beaten off, July 7 and 8; many of the Burgundians, excoriating the Duke of Brittany for failing his rendezvous with them, * were muttering that they would go no farther. But the Count of Charolais clamped down on discontents by declaring that he would press on even if he was accompa-

* Charolais and Francis II had agreed to join forces at St. Denis, outside Paris, on June 24.

nied only by a page. On the night of July 10 the Burgundians captured
the Seine bridge at St. Cloud, west of Paris. The way south toward the
Bretons, toward the King, lay open.

By the early-morning hours of Sunday, July 14, King Louis, assembling his forces at Beaugency on the north bank of the Loire, got word
that the Burgundian host had crossed the Seine and were advancing
down the Paris-Orléans road. He learned that the Bretons, too, were fast
closing in on him. Neither the Duke of Brittany nor the Duke of Berry
was in the least martial, but their captains included the Count of Dunois, suffering from gout but directing operations from a litter, a former
Marshal of France (Lohéac), the former Admiral of France (Jean de
Bueil), and the clever Gascon Odet d'Aydie. On hearing that the King
had been drawn off to Riom, the Breton army of some twelve thousand
men began moving eastward. The Count of Maine, with an army almost
as large as theirs, carefully retired before them. The Bretons crossed the
Loire at Ponts-de-Cé, close by the great walls of Angers, but King René
and his adherents made no move to stay their passage. They made their
way unopposed through Vendôme, Maine falling back to Tours; and at
midday on July 13—as Louis learned a few hours later—they entered
Châteaudun, twenty-five miles due north of Beaugency. They were now
poised to fall on the King's flank, if he moved toward Paris, or to join
the oncoming Burgundians before Louis could interpose his forces. To
close the iron ring about the royal army, Armagnac and Nemours and
Bourbon were advancing from the south, the Marshal of Burgundy from
the southeast, and Duke John, with a force of mercenary Swiss and
mounted men of arms, from the east.

Jean Pierre Panigarola, his dispatches crackling with excitement,
stayed close beside the King "in order to know how things stand from
hour to hour. Matters are rapidly drawing to a climax. There will have
to be an agreement very quickly or there is bound to be fighting, which
will be bloody and deadly because hate between the parties is flaming
high." The royal entourage exuded gloom and fear; some openly asserted
that the King would be forced to yield to all the demands of the princes,
for if he fought a pitched battle and lost he would be ruined. The King
himself preserved a stalwart countenance to the world, but Panigarola
felt that he was "afflicted in his mind."

A rumor reached Beaugency in the night of July 13–14 that the Bretons were pulling out of Châteaudun to join the Burgundian army. If it
was true, before the next nightfall an enemy host of thirty-five thousand

men would stand between the King and his capital. Early in the morning of Sunday, July 14, the King and his troops took to the road once more, driving at top speed through a dry, hot July countryside. Sometime during the evening of the 14th, the dusty squadrons pounded into Étampes. They had made almost fifty miles. The Bretons, quite content to linger at Châteaudun, were now well behind. Not many miles ahead, the Burgundians blocked the road to Paris.[1] Sometime during that night, the Count of Maine, Admiral Montauban, and Pierre de Brezé arrived at Étampes with the force which had allowed the Bretons to advance as they pleased. The bulk of the King's artillery and thousands of his troops were still strung out on the roads to the south.

Early the following morning, Monday, July 15, Louis assembled his army in open fields. Surrounded by his soldiers, he solemnly invoked the succor of heaven. Priests "sang nine Masses, at which the King was continually present in a white gown, kneeling with knees bare. . . ." When the Masses were finished and the King had uttered "most earnest prayers," he convoked a war council of all his lords and captains. Louis opened the sessions with a terse statement. The House of Burgundy had had the effrontery, he declared, to drive a rift between him and the lords of his blood, including his brother. Since this division threatened ruin to the realm, the King had no intention of permitting the Burgundians to do just as they pleased. He believed that "the omnipotent God and the most glorious Virgin, Mother Mary," supported his cause. Therefore, if the royal army attacked the Burgundians, "we will break them all and put them to total rout." However, he concluded, before he announced his final decision, he wanted the opinion of all his lords and captains because he desired reason and not emotion to conquer.

As Prince of the Blood, the Count of Maine spoke first. Painting all the perils of a pitched battle, he declared that the King should not put himself in such danger. The proper road to victory was by delay and negotiation, "not by rushing into things hastily." At all costs his royal nephew should avoid moving against the Burgundians. Jean de Montauban, Louis's Admiral and *compère*, solemnly endorsed the strategy urged by Maine, "being entirely unwilling that the King should attack his enemies."

According to an eyewitness, "While these things were being said, the King almost lost patience." *

The Great Seneschal of Normandy, the "beau parleur" of the world,

---

* Louis was probably unaware that Montauban had secretly reconciled himself with the Duke of Brittany.

now addressed the assembly. Pierre de Brezé, as the event would show, had had a bitter struggle with himself. In sympathies and attitude belonging to the era of Charles VII, he did not care for the new world of Louis XI, though Louis had shown him the warmest favor. Instinctively he had responded to the appeal of the princes, had given them his allegiance pledged with his seal. But, at the end of the road where ultimate decisions lie, the minister of the crown could not betray the monarchy he had done so much to strengthen; and the gallant gentleman could not desert, in the face of overwhelming numbers, the King's lean army. The Seneschal "summed up what had previously been said in the council so wisely that everyone was stupefied with amazement to hear him. Then he turned to the Count of Maine and in eloquent and moving speech showed him that the King should, without fail, deliver battle against the Burgundians, who, he declared, could not escape being utterly defeated." Most of the remaining captains enthusiastically endorsed Brezé.

Louis announced that he would continue his advance. He wanted to avoid, however, any subsequent charges that he had sought or opened war. He therefore added—and repeated to Panigarola and much later told Commynes—that he was thus holding to his original intention of entering Paris in order to rally the population of the capital to his banners. But, if the Count of Charolais blocked his road, he would fight. The King deposited his jewels and other treasure in the fortified tower of Étampes. Finally he sent an urgent message to his commanders in the capital: if on the morrow the Burgundians barred his march, he would engage them in battle; in which case, if all was well in Paris, Marshal Rouault should issue from the city to fall upon Charolais's rear.

In the late afternoon the royal army resumed its advance toward Paris, twenty-four miles away. The force of the Count of Maine, which had remained a few miles to the west, would join the King on the morrow. Scouts brought word that a Burgundian advance guard under the Count of St. Pol, thousands strong, had occupied the hill village of Montlhéry, about halfway between Paris and Étampes, though the castle there still held for the King; and that the main body of Charolais's army was drawn up at Longjumeau, three and a half miles behind. Louis halted his men for the night in the village of Étrechy, ten miles south of Montlhéry.

ii

In the soft darkness of a summer morning—Tuesday, July 16—the King and his army were already stirring. They marched before dawn. As they reached Arpajon, three and a half miles south of Montlhéry, they were joined by the forces of the Count of Maine. By this time, scouts had brought King Louis word that the forces of the Count of Charolais had joined St. Pol's advance guard and the Burgundians were forming a bat- tle line in the fields to the north of the ridge of Montlhéry.[2]

The King summoned a final war council. As the captains were as- sembling, Pierre de Brezé sought word alone with him. He had surveyed the royal army, Brezé said, and found the troops "overlabored" from their heroic march. Therefore, he urged the King not to fight that day. If they waited at least until the morrow, the men would have a chance to refresh themselves, troops still on the road could come up, and the garri- son at Paris would be better prepared to attack the Burgundian rear. The Count of Charolais, on the other hand, could look for no reinforce- ments.

Louis, stung by Brezé's sudden change of mind, asked him point- blank if he had not delivered his seal to the princes.

The Great Seneschal of Normandy smiled. Yes, it was true, he an- swered, the princes had his seal. But Louis had both his heart and his body. He would live or die for the King and with the King. "And he said it lightly, as if in jest, for thus was he accustomed to speak."

Louis studied him, and read his man. He gave Brezé the place of trust and honor: the Great Seneschal would command the advance guard of the royal army.

Brezé told one of his intimates, "I will put them [the opposing ar- mies] so close today to one another that he is a clever man who can part them"—these words the King himself years afterward recounted to Philippe de Commynes. Louis probably divined, as the motive for the Seneschal's counsel, that Brezé had reason to suspect treachery on the part of the Count of Maine, who made no secret of not wanting battle and who had in the early-morning hours apparently received a herald of the Count of St. Pol.

It was now nearing mid-morning, an airless July day of brutal sun. The council of war was brief. Louis announced that Pierre de Brezé would lead the advance guard, which, on the ridge of Montlhéry, would take up its position as the right wing. He himself would command the "center battle." His uncle, the Count of Maine, was to move up as rear guard and bring his force into a line on the left wing. Candidly the King disclosed the news which the scouts had brought. The host of the Count of Charolais were fortifying themselves in the Montlhéry plain with ditches and embankments, the laager of baggage wagons, and a great array of artillery. They far outnumbered the royal army. But they have few men of worth, the King went on. For his part, he counted them all as lost because they had put themselves in prison. It was the short, no-nonsense talk that professional military men on the eve of battle want to hear.

The Great Seneschal marshaled his troops and set forth. Then followed the royal banners. It was between ten and eleven o'clock in the morning when the King of France turned his horse's head to the right and, leaving the Paris road, ascended the ridge of Montlhéry to the castle which crowned it. His men of arms moved past him to take up their positions on the northern slope to the left of Brezé's advance guard.

A great sweep of country was spread out to the north before the King's eyes. From olden time the plain had been called "The Field of Tears." Almost a mile away, on a slight rise of uneven ground, the close-packed host of the Count of Charolais stretched from high ground to the west of the Paris road, on the King's left, almost to the village of Longpont, a little more than a mile to the east. To the King's right, a banner of red and gray dominated by a silver unicorn with horns and hoofs of gold marked the post of the Count of St. Pol, commanding the Burgundian left, a force of about eight thousand men. Pennons flaunted the heraldic insignia of St. Pol's two sons, Charolais's first Chamberlain the Lord of Hemeries,° and some of the proudest chivalry of Artois, Flanders, Hainault, and Picardy. Grouped about their master, St. Pol's body archers were clad in red-and-gray jackets ornamented with flashing metal. In the center of the field rose the standard of the Bastard of Burgundy, a blue barbican on a yellow background, surrounded by his body archers in red jackets bearing the white cross of St. Andrew. The red banner of the Lord of Ravenstein appeared close by. To Louis's left, near the Paris-Orléans road, a great flag, half black and half violet, surrounded by archers in the same colors, signaled the presence of the Count of Charolais.

Screening the Burgundian host, a rank of archers stood behind sharpened stakes, protection against a cavalry charge. In the middle were stationed a band of five hundred English bowmen, considered by Commynes to be "the flower of the Burgundian army." They had taken off their shoes and broached casks of wine and in the fighting fashion of their island were making themselves heartily comfortable. Back of the archers, the men of arms were haphazardly massed, some mounted, some dismounted. A rough semicircle of carts formed the Burgundian

---

° Antoine de Rolin, over whom Charolais had quarreled with his father in 1457; see note 1, p. 400.

laager in the center rear. Behind stretched the green wall of the forest of Séguiny. An expanse of wheat and oats and beans shimmered between the two armies. "It was bitterly hot." The sun burned on steel armor; the fields, "deeply furrowed," were powdery with July drought.

The Count of Charolais had left the King a magnificent defensive position. The ridge of Montlhéry, running roughly west-east, rose steeply from the Paris road, came to a peak where stood the castle, and then declined eastward into the plain. A little to the west of the castle, on the northern versant, huddled the village of Montlhéry. Pierre de Brezé had marshaled his Norman gentry and squadrons of lances, all mounted, behind "a great ditch and hedge" at the bottom of the slope, facing the much superior numbers of the Count of St. Pol. The King's "main battle," consisting of his Scots guard, his household regiment from Dauphiné, and units of the professional men of arms, were drawn up, backs to the castle, between Brezé's position and the village. The chief captains of this force, Marshal Armagnac and the old Écorcheur Salazar and Robin Malortie, had served Louis for more than two decades. The Count of Maine's left wing extended along the ridge above the village and westward down to the road.

However commanding his position on the ridge, however suspect some elements in the royal army, however inferior his numbers, the King of France, this torrid July morning, had no intention of standing on the defensive. He had come as sovereign lord, to sweep aside rebels who would deny him entry to his capital. Besides, he had few foot soldiers [*] and his men of arms were not trained to fight dismounted. That heavy cavalry of his had but one function, one thought: attack. And then . . . never more a risk taker than when all was at stake, Louis had the will to pit his army of about fourteen thousand men against some twenty-two thousand Burgundians in order to try for the knockout blow that would smash the League of the Public Weal and put paid forever to the menacing aspirations of the Dukes of Burgundy.

But the King was in no hurry. Between Étrechy and Montlhéry he had dispatched, one after another, three heralds to Paris with urgent orders for Marshal Roualt to issue from the city with all the men of arms he could muster and fall upon the Burgundian rear. Though making a roundabout journey, these messengers could reach the capital well be-

---

[*] Lack of foot soldiers would likewise hamper attack. Archers and grooms armed with long knives or leaden mauls had the mission, when the men of arms had clashed with an opposing force, of dashing forward to dispatch enemies who had been knocked from their horses in the *mélée*.

fore midday. With dispatch, Roualt should be bearing down on Charolais's army by the middle of the afternoon.

Now there was movement up and down the Burgundian line. Ser-
pentines and culverines and other field pieces were dragged forward
and planted in front of the archers. The boom and crackle of Charolais's
vaunted ordnance shook the July heat. Girault de Samien, royal cannon-
eer, worked to emplace the King's artillery, a meager array of pieces.
Here and there along the French line a cannonball struck the massed
cavalry; but men quickly closed up each bloody furrow. Samien's artillery, placed on the slope, at first fired over the heads of the enemy, but
when the pieces were repositioned, they began to take their toll also.
Noon passed. Over the thick yellow wheat gunsmoke hung heavy in the
brassy air. Since seven in the morning, the Burgundians had been standing in the glare of the sun without food or water. Some of the men of
arms made archers stand in front of them in order to create a little
shade. As the King's army had begun appearing on the ridge, Charolais's
captains anxiously awaited the word to attack, but no word came from
the Count of Charolais, inexperienced in war and, for all his hardihood,
uneasy and hesitant. The burning afternoon was beginning to wear
away. Here and there on both sides an impatient knight rode into the
wheat to engage an adversary in combat, and many "fine feats of arms"
entertained the armies.

About two o'clock Louis XI prepared to engage the enemy. Marshal
Roualt should be soon approaching. The King thinned his line a little to
provide Brezé with additional squadrons. Along the ridge he then made
his way from commander to commander. He himself ordered the final
disposition of squadrons, shifting detachments, explaining his battle
plans, heartening the men. To his captains he offered large rewards for
good service on this day.

He had decided on a rolling attack. Pierre de Brezé and the right
wing would make the first assault. Louis himself with the "main battle"
would then engage the Burgundian center. He did not expect men to
fight to the death for a king who commanded from the rear. Riding up
to the Count of Maine, he urged his uncle to display the well-known
valor of the House of Anjou. The Count replied that he would act as a
loyal servant of the crown. Maine was to attack last, Louis told him,
after Brezé and the King had delivered their blows. Louis probably
hoped that if Maine saw the day going for the royal army, he would,
whatever his sentiments, fight for the winning side.

The King rode back to the center of the line, dismounted. Falling upon his knees, he prayed to the God of Battles to bring victory to his cause. When he remounted his horse, he saw that the whole Burgundian host had begun a disorderly advance. Louis ordered Pierre de Brezé to hold his attack until the Burgundians were committed.

In a clamorous war council the Count of Charolais and his captains had finally decided to take up a position nearer the royal army, after which the Count of St. Pol, commanding the most powerful division and facing the gentlest slope, would lead an assault. The Burgundians slogged forward through deep crumbling furrows and thick wheat. About seven hundred yards from the ridge they straggled to a halt in a tangle of grain and beans and vines.

A brief pause: then, from his command post by the castle, Louis saw the men of arms and archers of St. Pol forming up for the attack. Squadrons of mounted crossbowmen trotted into the wheat, converging on the hedge that fronted Brezé's forces. The Burgundian foot archers now began to move forward. Behind them, the Count of St. Pol and a wave of men of arms, all mounted, got under way. The crossbowmen, moving "at a great trot and all in a mass"—as the lord of Haynin, close beside St. Pol, saw them—"advanced in such a grand manner toward the French that it seemed nobody could withstand them." As they neared the hedge, they began to "hover," i.e., ride up and down, discharging arrows.

Pierre de Brezé waited until St. Pol's red-and-gray banner had reached mid-plain. Then he signaled his captains. The squadrons turned, began to move up the slope, away from the hedge. The Count of St. Pol leaped to the conclusion that they were breaking in flight, sent messengers galloping to the Burgundian "main battle" with the great news. In response, numbers of men of arms urged their mounts diagonally across the field toward St. Pol.

But Brezé's trumpets had rung out. His cavalry wheeled on the slope to right and to left. In two disciplined bodies they swung round both flanks of the hedge, brushing aside the mounted crossbowmen as if they were gnats. Again the trumpets: a forest of lances swung down to make a wall of points. With the outnumbered French suddenly turning to attack them, St. Pol's men of arms excitedly spurred forward, flattening their unfortunate foot archers. Not to be outdone, the Burgundians streaming toward the fray from the center battle blindly rode down the English mercenaries—"and so they themselves broke the flower of their hope."

The two spears of heavy cavalry thrusting from each side of the hedge converged on the center of St. Pol's advancing thousands. The Great Seneschal of Normandy, first in the field, thundered through the wheat, setting a fearful pace. His ranks quickened their stride in an unbroken front.

The waves of horsemen crashed together. Contemptuously Pierre de Brezé ploughed far into the enemy mass. He hacked his way forward until he fought alone in a press of Burgundians. He was thrust through. He rolled dead on the ground.

He had not thrown away his life. His charge had ripped a ragged hole in St. Pol's line, thrown the Burgundian cavalry into confusion. Brezé's Norman compatriots, fired by the loss of their beloved Seneschal, drove savagely into the gap. The squadrons of the standing army— "flower of warriors," the Burgundian chronicler Du Clercq called them —thrust remorselessly forward, laying about with spear or sword or axe.

The chivalry of Burgundy, nursed on gay tournaments in the marketplace of Bruges, could not stand against this kind of fighting. Their ranks fell apart. Knights and squires wrenched their mounts around. The Lord of Hemeries, the Lord of Incey, surrounded by their followers, galloped full tilt from the field, plunged through the forest of Séguiny, and fled up the road toward Paris. St. Pol's massive wing disintegrated into fragments, some borne helpless backward, some turning in flight, the rear ranks leading the scramble for the safety of the forest or the laager or the Paris road. The Count of St. Pol and his household men were swept up in the rout.

The on-charging French split into arrows of pursuit, spurring hotly into the forest after their enemies, or turning to assail the Burgundian flank. Fleeing Burgundians from St. Pol's wing collided with advancing clumps of horsemen from the center, and the French drove into the *mêlée*. Clouds of dust and wheat particles were churned up, powdering the armor of men of arms lying crushed in the furrows.

It was mid-afternoon. Marshal Roualt's lances must be close at hand. King Louis, surveying the wild flight of the Burgundian left, the confusion in the Burgundian center, perceived that his moment had come.

The royal trumpets sounded. Closed about by his Scots guard and flanked by his Dauphiné regiment, the King of France led forward the tough men of arms who had fought the Bourbonnais campaign. Ahead of them, the Bastard of Burgundy and the lord of Ravenstein and St. Pol's brother Jacques were urging the disordered "middle battle" into movement. Some lances on the King's right peeled off to assail the tangle of

Burgundians in mid-plain. The King with the rest of his cavalry pounded straight for the enemy center.

Louis and his men, heading the charge, struck the Burgundians without slackening speed. In the first shock, one clash of arms, the enemy ranks were broken "à platte cousture"—knocked flat. The royal men of arms drove onward into the strugging mass. Soon the Burgundians were split into ribbons of horsemen galloping for the laager. Robin Malortie kept the men of Dauphiné together as they pushed forward, but many of the French, their thoughts on booty, headed pell-mell for the Burgundian baggage wagons. The King shouted to his captains to re-form their ranks. The rear of the field, the laager, the woods, still swarmed with Burgundians, shattered or demoralized though their squadrons were. Then Louis quickly made his way back to the ridge. It remained only for the Count of Maine to engage the Count of Charolais's wing while his own "center battle" closed on Charolais's flank—and the House of Burgundy would trouble France no more.

Louis spurred up to Maine—"Advance, my dearest uncle! Show me the Angevin valor in your attack!" The Count of Maine dutifully signaled his trumpeters. His squadrons began to move down the slope on either side of the village and through the village itself. The King rejoined his guards by the castle: down on the vast dust-obscured confusion of the plain, the forces of Charolais were at last getting themselves into motion. The men of Dauphiné and other royal troops had pulled back from the pursuit and were forming for the flank attack, but hundreds of the King's "center battle" were plundering the laager or conveying prisoners back to the ridge or still ransom hunting.

As Louis watched from the ridge, Maine's men of arms lowered their spears to "attack" position. But, as they reached the bottom of the village, the Count and his chief captains slowed, then halted the advance. Commands were shouted. The hedge of spears was raised. In the face of Charolais's oncoming Burgundians, the squadrons of the Count of Maine suddenly wheeled toward the road, turned their backs to the enemy, and broke into a gallop, sweeping the rest of the men of arms along with them. In a moment, a third of the King's forces was streaming southward from the field "in villainous flight."

The Count of Charolais, forgetting that he commanded an army, spurred into blind pursuit with hundreds of his followers, including young Philippe de Commynes.° But the remainder of the Burgundian

---

° Concerning the rout of St. Pol's wing and the flight of Maine's squadrons, Commynes indulged himself in sarcasms that became famous: "On both sides there

right wing—headed by captains who saw the real opportunity—
wheeled to their left and charged upon the ranks, just reforming, of the
King's "center battle."

Louis with his Scots guard galloped down into the plain: in an instant, his crushing victory had been transformed into a wild, doubtful
combat. Back at the laager, Burgundian grooms and archers were beating French pillagers to death with leaden mauls. The Bastard of Burgundy, rallying the remnants of his troops and fugitives from St. Pol's
wing, now drove forward against the royal squadrons. The Burgundians
from the right struck the King's small, ragged "center battle" in the flank
even as the Bastard of Burgundy's force engaged their front.

As the King headed across the plain for the *mêlée,* he met fugitives
from his crumbling lines. Rallying them to his standard, Louis and his
Scots thrust themselves into the forefront of the fighting. While Maine's
warriors galloped for the Loire and the Count of Charolais was gaily
"chassant" and French men of arms from the right and center continued
to pursue their fleeing enemies, the King of France and his band began
"a battle cruel and horrible." The subtle monarch who despised war was
all thrust and slash now. His crown, his life depended on his presence in
the thickest of the fight. The artillerymen on both sides had recklessly
trained their pieces on the field. Cannonballs cut bloody weals through
the packed struggling ranks. Suddenly the King and his mount were
rolling in the dust—the horse pierced by a lance, perhaps that of the
Bastard of Burgundy. The Bastard's men surged forward, crying, "The
King is dead!" The French, bewildered, began to give ground. With the
King gone . . .

But the Scots closed an iron ring around their master. They got him
to his feet. A fresh horse was led up. In the saddle once more, Louis
heard the cries, and saw his men faltering. He pushed up his face guard.
"See, my sons!" he shouted. "I am not taken! Turn back!" Clouds of dust
obscured the writhing lines. Agonized neighing of gashed horses, harsh
commands, the exultant yells of the Burgundians, boom of cannon and
clash of steel—trying to make himself heard above this hellish din,
Louis spurred through his ranks. "Have no fear!" he was yelling. "Today
the victory is ours!"

Enough men heard and saw to steady the rest. The royal squadrons

---

were men who showed their mettle and men who showed their heels. . . . On the
side of the King, an important man fled as far as Lusignan without pausing for
breath, and, on the side of the Count of Charolais, a man equally important fled as
far as Quesnoy-le-Comte [in Hainault]. These two had no desire to murder each
other."

tightened, held. In the heat and the terrible dust, horse-to-horse, breast-to-breast, men hewed and thrust savagely. From the slope Jean Pierre Panigarola, straining to see, was appalled. He would report, "They fought like rabid raging dogs."

The King spurred forward with his Scots to blunt a Burgundian surge. Then he pushed to the rear in order to survey the field, to rally stragglers. There was still no sign from Roualt. The weight of the enemy numbers pressed terribly upon front and flank of his squadrons. Louis plunged back into the *mêlée*. The hard-bitten gentlemen of Dauphiné were going down—they could be killed but not budged. In these instants some fifty of them perished, a much larger number suffered wounds. The Bastard of Armagnac, Marshal of France, and Robin Malortie fought like men unaware of mere mortality. Louis was shouting on the battle line, "If there were but six of us against these Burgundians we would conquer!" Everywhere the French stood solid for a long moment. . . . The pressure slackened. The front ranks of the Bastard were giving way; those in the rear began to turn their backs. Then the Burgundians were withdrawing into the fog of dust and smoke, retiring to the laager.

Louis and his commanders worked to check their squadrons, keep the men in battle order. Pursuit could be deadly: somewhere in his rear, Louis knew, the Count of Charolais was loose; it was impossible to see how many Burgundians had rallied to the laager or on the skirts of the forest; there was no knowing whether Maine's treachery might embolden another wavering heart.

Malortie, bleeding from severe face wounds, and the other royal captains succeeded in pulling back the bulk of their squadrons. The remnant of the King's "center battle," the only organized force on the field, moved slowly toward the ridge. Bloody horses, bright-jacketed Burgundian archers, men of arms stripped of their armor, were strewn across the trampled wheat. Parties of French horsemen returning from the pursuit joined the royal banners. Louis commanded the artillery to be brought forward and lay down a covering fire. He sent squadrons southward to cut the Étampes road in the hope of trapping Charolais. The King's haggard army began to take up positions, rank by rank, along the ridge. It was nearing seven o'clock. If Roualt had struck the Burgundian rear with only a hundred lances . . . But the highway from Paris stood empty. The Scots accompanied Louis, near exhaustion, to the castle. There for the first time that day he touched food and drink, before going back to his men.

Meanwhile the Count of Charolais was returning from the pursuit

—reluctantly, at the urgent bidding of a veteran captain. Accompanied only by about forty horse, he was unpleasantly astonished, as he swung around the village, to see the Scots guard up at the gate of the castle, which he was sure had been captured, and to behold on the plain no victorious banner of St. Andrew but a desolate scene of dust and death, with the royal army solidly drawn up on the slope.

At that instant a band of French men of arms—among the last of those pulling back to the ridge—charged upon Charolais's banner. Though outnumbered, they drove through the Burgundians, cutting down Charolais's pennon bearer. A sword slash hewed away the Count's faulty gorget, scored his neck. Streaming blood, he desperately defended himself. One of the French seized him by the shoulders—"My Lord, surrender! I know you well! Don't let yourself be killed!" But the burly Charolais struggled fiercely against his would-be captor, and at this moment one or two of his men managed to interpose themselves between their master and his assailant. As more Burgundians galloped up, the French men of arms made off toward the ridge.

Doggedly Charolais set up his standard in the plain. From the laager appeared the Bastard of Burgundy and a small force, his banner "so shredded that it was not a foot long." Commynes recalled, "I then saw such a half hour!—those of us with him [the Count of Charolais] would have had an eye only for flight if a hundred men had marched against us." ° After St. Pol had issued from the forest with a goodly band of men of arms, Charolais called up his artillery and summoned his plundered baggage wagons to enclose his now sizable force.

From the ridge, King Louis watched the summer twilight thicken over the field where the Burgundians, in larger numbers than his own force, huddled within their laager. Rouault was not coming. Rouault had sent no word. Behind him, the Breton army could be marching toward the field.

The two weary, blood-stained and dust-choked armies faced each other, motionless, at short range, as the rival artillery still boomed, until darkness fell upon "The Field of Tears."

King Louis commanded fires to be lit along the ridge, in the village. Then he gave orders to his captains to bestow the wounded in the baggage wagons and marshal their exhausted troops into marching order. Men of arms who had lost their mounts must go on foot or ride with the

---

° Writing a quarter of a century later, Commynes could still see in his mind's eye the steed he had ridden that day. He was "extremely weary, an old horse. By chance he thrust his muzzle into a pail of wine. I let him drink it up. Never had I found him so lively. . . ."

wounded. In the confusion some of the dead were left behind. The body of the Great Seneschal of Normandy, shrouded in night, lay disposed upon straw in the village street. As fires blazed on the slope, giving the Burgundians glum thoughts about the morrow, the King of France and his men moved away through the dark and took the road to Corbeil, ten miles eastward on the Seine. The eight thousand troopers of his right and center had so badly mauled thrice their number of Burgundians that he need fear no pursuit: he was able to march on toward Paris, as he had announced he would.

What thoughts Louis disclosed to Marshal Armagnac or others of his household, as he rode in the midst of his battered warriors, were apparently never recorded. Probably he had no heart to talk, even with his admiring friend Jean Pierre Panigarola, jogging somewhere along the line of march. Terrible might-have-beens hung in the night air. "I twice saw the enemy standards driven into flight and overthrown," Jean Pierre informed his master. If the Count of Maine had proved true, "the whole enemy army would inevitably have been put to the sword or taken prisoner. . . ." Even with Maine's defection, if Roualt had brought but three or four hundred men of arms to the field before sundown . . .

Whatever his bitter disappointment and his uncertainties about the future, Louis XI did not forget the men who had died for him. "For the Great Seneschal of Normandy . . . the King does not cease to grieve," noted Panigarola a little later, "and he ever more bitterly mourns his great losses. . . ."

A little before midnight, Louis entered Corbeil and disposed his army to rest.

15. The Siege of Paris

SOMETIME during the following day, at Corbeil, Louis learned that Marshal Roualt and Charles de Melun still commanded in Paris and that the capital held firm for the King. For a man who had failed the King's bitterest need, Roualt had done very well. When Louis's urgent commands had reached the capital about mid-day, the Marshal, Charles de Melun, and their energetic assistant, Jean Balue, Bishop-elect of Évreux, along with one or two Parisian nobles, had held a council of war. Balue urged the Marshal to ride immediately to Montlhéry with the strongest force of men of arms he could assemble. But Melun, having lost his nerve, argued that the King's messages had emphasized the defending of the capital. Roualt weakly accepted this excuse for doing nothing. At mid-afternoon word reached him that Burgundian lords fleeing from Montlhéry had crossed the bridge at St. Cloud and were in headlong flight for the Oise. Even this vigorous evidence of the royal army's success in battle could not move him to close the trap on the Burgundians. But he quickly rounded up five hundred men of arms, sallied forth from the city, and seized the bridge at St. Cloud. The fugitives who followed on the heels of Hemeries and Incey were all taken captive.[1]

About five o'clock on Thursday afternoon, July 18, the King of France entered his capital, to receive as hearty a welcome as he could have hoped. Numerous citizens had won themselves ransoms and spoils from Burgundian fugitives, and the Parisians had learned of their sovereign's valor in the battle—his troops were saying, "The man who saved the King's crown that day was the King.° The clergy of Paris with tapers and banners and a procession of notables came out to meet him.

° Commynes, not given to effusiveness, records, "I believe truly that if it had not been for him alone, all would have fled." Panigarola summed up for his master, one of the greatest soldiers of the age: "It can be affirmed that His Majesty bore himself as bravely as anyone ever read of Alexander or Caesar."

He passed through crowded streets ringing with cries of "Noël! Noël!" Louis took his evening meal with his equivocal Lieutenant-General, Charles de Melun. "And with him there supped also several lords, and daughters and wives of citizens. At table he recited the whole story of what had happened to him at Montlhéry, and he used such eloquent and moving words that both men and women wept copiously. He said further that, with God's pleasure, the Monday following he would once more go against his enemies. . . ."

In letters he dictated some hours later to his good towns he likewise announced that "once our troops have rested a little, we intend to take the field in pursuit of [the enemy]." The King worked to reorganize his squadrons, gather reinforcements, keep in fighting trim the city militia of some thirty thousand men. He could not afford to be choosy about adherents, whatever their motives. Of those who had fled with the Count of Maine, Panigarola reported, "the greater part have returned and more are returning every day—to whom His Majesty gives a very good welcome." Even the Count of Maine had sent word that he was coming back, with two hundred lances. Louis merely ordered him to include in his company the levy of Poitou. The only captain disgraced was Jean de Garguesalle, Master of the Horse, cashiered for desertion. The King strengthened his hold on Parisian hearts by a prudent decrease of taxation. Everyone that Panigarola talked to assured him that the city had never been better disposed to its sovereign than it was at present, "and there are no Burgundian partisans." He concluded his dispatch of July 26, "His Majesty has decided to follow up the enterprise."

On July 31, the Burgundians and Bretons left Étampes, where they had united after Montlhéry, and moved eastward toward the Seine. Louis dispatched Roualt and Salazar down the right bank to break bridges and harry the enemy, but he knew that ne could not hold the line of the river. After being halted for three days by the French, Charolais and the Dukes of Berry and Brittany got their men across the Seine on an improvised bridge. Louis also learned that Bourbon, Armagnac, and Nemours, with their ragged thousands, and the forces of Duke John and the Marshal of Burgundy were about to join the Burgundian-Breton army. Paris would soon be under siege.[2]

By this time the climate of the King's affairs was undergoing a bleak change. His hope of taking the field against the princes had been withered by counsels of fear and revelations of duplicity. Some of his captains declared that they did not trust their men, particularly those officers and troops who had returned after "playing the chicken at

Montlhéry"; gloomy advisers whispered their doubts in his ear; members of the Parlement urged peace at any cost, alleging that important elements in the capital were not to be trusted. It was among such officials and in the world of priests that disaffection was breeding. Ambitious bureaucrats hoped to climb through the favor of patrons among the magnates. Led by the Bishop of Paris, the clergy and the University looked, most of them, to the princes to make good the Church's pretensions at the expense of the Crown. There was uncovered a conspiracy initiated by a small group of bureaucrats, which was apparently aimed at seizing the royal palace. The King's agents kept turning up fresh instances of treachery.

Jean Pierre Panigarola, a daily observer of what passed in the King's chambers, got off a panicky dispatch to the Duke of Milan. "My Lord, as duty-bound, with tears in my eyes, I must inform you that His Majesty's affairs turn awry and every day go from bad to worse. He finds himself without counsel, because his councilors are dying of fear, especially the Admiral; and the Bastard of Armagnac is very ill. The King has nobody in whom he can trust. Now the Count of Boulogne has gone over to the princes. The royal men of arms, split up into bands for the defense of Paris, are very ill content with the King because he gives them no money. . . . During the past fifteen days men have deserted, a few at a time, to a total of more than a hundred lances." Royal agents had intercepted letters to certain Parisians, letters which revealed conspiracies to deliver the city and "which have given him a mistrust of Paris. . . ." Down at Lyons, one of the bulwarks of the kingdom, a trusted officer had been discovered in a plot to surrender that city to representatives of the Duke of Berry. "All these things have instilled so much apprehension in the King . . . that he . . . is confused and deeply troubled. His chamberlains and principal officers stand all with eyes on the ground."

Louis was exuberant in expressions of despair as of optimism; these vivid manifestations seemed to stimulate, rather than harass, the operations of his brain. By the time Panigarola wrote the dispatch, the King had determined upon a bold move—one which was designed to hearten his subjects but which could lose him his capital and his throne. When he announced that he was going into Normandy to gather men, money, and stocks of food for Paris, citizens wailed that he should not leave them at such a moment and councilors pelted him with warnings of disaster. On August 10, staunch to his vision, the King of France rode westward out of his capital at the head of a small force, leaving his trusted captains and troops to stiffen the militia of the city. He also discharged Charles de Melun from the lieutenant-generalship of Paris, appointing faithful old Charles, Count of Eu.[3]

While Louis XI halted for three days at Rouen, gentry by the hundreds rallied to his banners. On August 17 he set off again to garner the resources of France's richest province. Armed men continued to join his column; royal officers gathered in supplies of food, carts for transport, military equipment. The King forwarded to Paris a number of élite companies. On August 14 there had arrived in the capital a band of two hundred mounted men, led by a veteran captain, Jean Mignon, and armed with the very latest combination of weapons, crossbows, pikes, and hand guns—a formation which did not come into general use until the sixteenth century. Mignon's men were cheered by both earthly and heavenly consolation, for "in the rear of the company there rode eight 'ribauldes' and a black monk, their confessor."

When the King reached Évreux, on August 21, he learned that the standards of the rebel lords had at last appeared before the walls of his capital. He immediately dispatched the Admiral with a strong force to stiffen the Paris garrison.

Capturing bridges over the Marne, the army of the princes, on August 19, had swarmed along the right (north) bank of the Seine to the capital's eastern approaches.[4] The Count of Charolais and Duke John occupied the most advanced headquarters, at Conflans between Charenton and Paris, where the Duke of Burgundy possessed a manor house. The Duke of Brittany lodged to the east of them at St. Maur-des-Fossés on a great bend of the Marne; while a Breton contingent pushed on northward to occupy St. Denis. The Duke of Berry lodged by himself at the royal manor of Beauté-sur-Marne, once the property of Agnès Sorel.

By the time the King of France swung round, on August 24, to Chartres, where he was making a final muster of his forces, he had received alarming news from his capital.

Six heralds had arrived in Paris on the morning of Thursday, August 22, to request that the chief governing bodies of the capital send representatives to hear the just complaints of the princes. Next morning, a council of the "Estates" of Paris having decided to comply, Guillaume Chartier, Bishop of Paris, led the city's envoys to the castle of Beauté. Before the Duke of Berry, occupying a chair of state in the midst of his mighty lords, the gout-ridden Count of Dunois presented the demands

of the Leaguers to the delegation. The princes must be given control of
the finances of the realm, the distribution of offices, the entire standing
army, and "the person and government of the King." In short, they required the dismemberment of France. Dunois said nothing about the
sufferings of the poor or the abolition of taxes. He concluded fiercely—if
Paris did not open its gates by Sunday the 25th, on Monday the princes
would hurl their entire army against the walls. Then the representatives
of the city were led aside by great lords and plied with sweet reasona-
bleness, and doubtless other inducements as well. For the moment, it
was explained, the princes would be content to leave their army outside
the gates and enter the capital only with modest escorts. Several of the
delegates were quite persuaded by this gentle proposition—which, if it
had taken effect, as Commynes points out, would not only have meant
"Paris won!" but the entire enterprise gained; for once the capital
yielded, the rest of the realm would follow suit.

Next morning, Saturday, August 24, at eight o'clock the deputies reported to a gathering of notables in the town hall the demands made by
Dunois. The bold and astute Provost-Merchant, Henri de Livres, presiding over the assembly, soon realized from the tone of the discussion that
numerous delegates as well as some others in the hall favored admitting
the princes. He therefore abruptly adjourned the meeting, announcing
that a second session would be held in the afternoon. Then, alerting the
Count of Eu and his captains, Henri and other royal officers spread the
word among the Parisians that the envoys sent to Beauté were working
to have the Bretons and Burgundians introduced into the city.

By the time Henri de Livres convoked the afternoon session, the
people of Paris, roaring their anger and waving weapons, were moving
on the town hall, while the Count of Eu paraded archers and men of
arms through the streets. The unhappy delegates quickly agreed with
the majority of the notables that the question of admitting the princes
must be referred to the King's Lieutenant. Eu and his advisers then provided the envoys with an answer to deliver to the Leaguers: no reply to
their demands would be given until the King's good pleasure had been
consulted.

King Louis, kept in close touch with the situation, got off a dispatch
from Chartres which reached the city that evening: he and his uncle, the
Count of Maine, with a great force of troops would arrive in Paris the
following Tuesday. That same evening the Admiral reached the capital
with his reinforcements; and word came that the Milanese army under
Count Galeazzo had begun its campaign in the Bourbonnais.

All that night and the next day a "great watch of armed men" guarded streets and walls; the aroused populace were threatening death to the envoys and the notables who had supported them; the clergy in all the churches prayed for peace. At one o'clock on Sunday afternoon, the delegates set out for the castle of Beauté, "weeping and trembling in terror." When Dunois heard their uncompromising answer, he furiously shouted that on the morrow the princes would deliver a mortal assault if it cost the lives of 100,000 men. That night all Paris stood to arms, ready for the attack, but the morning did not make good Dunois's threat. The princes merely assembled their host in tight-packed ranks between the Seine and the park of Bois de Vincennes and remained for several hours on view.

About five o'clock in the afternoon of Wednesday, August 28, the King of France reentered his capital at the head of twelve thousand troops, a powerful artillery train, and wagons bearing seven hundred hogshead of flour. With him came the Count of Maine, the Count of Penthièvre and other lords. He rode through wildly cheering streets. "God gave sage counsel to the King, and he knew how to carry it out. . . . He arrived in the town the way a leader must come in order to hearten his people. . . ."

ii

THE KING maintained his role of aggressive confidence. The motley host of the besiegers pressing on the southeastern defenses of the capital made bellicose gestures as if preparing an assault. Louis XI zealously answered these with gestures of his own.

He himself led forces forth to skirmish, jabbing the enemy here and there. Bands of mounted men of arms from both sides took to the fields, clashed in a flurry of lance thrusts, drew off; sometimes there were individual exploits. Louis crossed the Seine in a ferry, "remaining on horseback," to superintend the digging of artillery emplacements on the south bank facing the Burgundian positions at Conflans and Charenton. Between the river and the St. Antoine Gate he was constructing bulwarks "in the Italian manner," i.e., according to the latest in military architecture. "The bombards from both sides are booming day and night, and no other sound can be heard," Panigarola reported. "Heedless of cannon fire, the King all day remains outside the walls, bearing himself valiantly." The princes found it impossible to block the rivers; and Paris was situated in a countryside rich in vines and grain and market produce. Henri de Livres, the Provost-Merchant, managed his business so efficiently that at no time did the capital feel the pinch of food shortages or even high prices. The Parisians were cheered by the seven hundred hogsheads of flour delivered to the bakers—"not though, at Paris, God be praised, there was any scarcity of bread, wine, or any other provisions. Only wood was a little dear." [5] If the King was besieged within his capital, the Leaguers would soon find themselves besieged by time. The rains of autumn were drawing near.

Louis had not long to wait for the princes to make the first move. On Tuesday, September 3—less than a week after the King had returned to Paris—the besiegers proposed a two-day truce to permit negotiations.[6] Graciously accepting, Louis chose as his chief emissary the Count of Maine, who was, at least, well qualified to understand the viewpoint of the Leaguers. Duke John, the Count of St. Pol, and Dunois spoke for the princes. While both sides continued to fortify positions, the Count of Maine made his way, daily and oftener, to a pavilion erected at Grange aux Merciers, a country house between the lines, for the convenience of representatives from both sides. Louis was well aware that the Count was playing a double game. To Charles de Melun he remarked dryly that his uncle was "a man of strange character and one to be handled very carefully." To Panigarola he permitted himself more pungent remarks about the web of intrigues that his uncle was weaving around the negotiations.* But Louis was forced to play his game with whatever counters lay to hand. Maine had to be used because the magnates expected to negotiate with no one of lesser rank than themselves and because it was important, for the morale of the realm, to display as an adherent a Prince of the Blood.

On Monday, September 9, King Louis himself issued from his capital, crossed the defensive ditches, and, before the great Bastille with its eight towers which guarded the St. Antoine Gate, met with the Count of St. Pol—the Count of Maine having entered the Burgundian lines as a hostage. While Louis and St. Pol talked amiably for more than an hour, thirsty Burgundians and Bretons were raiding the Parisian vineyards, "though the grapes were not even half ripe"; so that in self-defense the citizens had to sally forth and harvest what grapes they could find. It was, furthermore, the poorest vintage for a long time. The Parisians

---

* Two months later, he told the Milanese ambassador that if he had not returned to Paris when he did, he might have lost his capital because, through the agency of the Count of Maine, one of the gates was secretly left open to admit the Burgundians.

called the stuff "the wine of the year of the Burgundians." When Louis rode back from his conference with St. Pol, he remarked to those standing about the St. Antoine Gate that their enemies would not henceforth give them so much trouble—he would see to it. A bold officer called out, "But look, Sire, they are harvesting our vines and eating our grapes and we can't do anything about it!" The King retorted that it was better for the Burgundians to harvest their vines and eat their grapes than to break into Paris and seize the plate and valuables that the citizens had hidden in their cellars.

When Louis returned to his palace, he told Panigarola that St. Pol had acted remarkably humble and amenable to reason, perhaps because the Burgundians were depressed by the strength of the Paris fortifications and envisioned themselves caught before the walls by the arrival of winter. Matters were still up in the air; the lords changed their claims from hour to hour.

A few days later—the truce having been prolonged to September 13—the King received a formal set of demands. The princes claimed "recompense" for all the damages they had suffered in the war, which meant huge pensions and privileges galore, including control of the army. The Duke of Berry declared that a third of the realm was the proper share for a king's brother. The Count of Charolais insisted on the King's restoring Picardy and the Somme towns, the 400,000 crowns Louis had paid for repurchase serving as Burgundian indemnity. Duke John wanted sufficient troops and treasure to recover the Kingdom of Naples, Louis to abandon Francesco Sforza.

On Friday the thirteenth, the last day of truce, the King returned a cold reply: the pretensions of the princes were both exorbitant and confused; the League would be wise to negotiate more realistically. This answer the princes loftily disdained, but they proposed extending the truce until sunset on September 17. Louis now applied a little pressure: in sending back word of his acceptance, he added that from then on he would concede no more truces.

The princes resubmitted demands as overblown as ever, except that the Duke of Berry indicated he might consider Normandy for his *apanage*. Louis held off answering; at the expiration of the truce the Leaguers made no move to resume hostilities. The King then proposed terms of his own. To the Duke of Berry he offered the provinces of Brie and Champagne, declaring that he would never yield Normandy. To the other princes he suggested cash settlements, amounts unspecified, to meet their demands for "recompense." The money offer was refused, but the Duke of Berry's advisers began seriously to consider Brie and Champagne. In fact, the unnatural unanimity of the princes was beginning to crack, as pretension jostled pretension and mutual suspicions stirred to life. Not without reason, they already distrusted each other's appetites and feared the King's uncanny arts of persuasion. They had felt compelled to assemble formally at Charolais's dwelling and swear a solemn oath to sign no separate appointments with the King. Their captains and troops were also growing restive: food was running short, wages becoming uncertain, and the walls and bulwarks of Paris did not encourage thoughts of a headlong assault. King Louis's ally, time, was doing its work well.

On Saturday, September 21, at dawn, Louis XI was abruptly informed that his garrison at Pontoise had opened the gates of the town to an enemy force. The King did not conceal from his Milanese friend Panigarola his anguish at this "bitter loss." Pontoise, eighteen miles west of Paris, was the key to the great province of Normandy. If the princes gained control of Normandy, no offer but abject surrender could appease them. The siege of Paris was beginning to go the way of the battle of Montlhéry. Betrayal had suddenly turned time against the King.

iii

IF THE LEAGUERS were racing against want and winter, Louis was now forced to outrun treason. Well aware of the pressures straining the unity of the princes, he realized that he must find the means to divide them. Since they now scented power and spoils, it looked to be a bleak task— that of amply fulfilling the expectations of one member of the League in order to separate him from the others. There were only two princes with authority to serve his turn, the Duke of Brittany and the Count of Charolais. The former, however, was set upon the Duke of Berry's having Normandy, for reasons of his own; the latter, after chewing the cud of his bitterness against the King for two years, had just fought him in bloody battle. Since Normandy was the jewel of the French crown, the choice must then be Charolais—whose mind and character Louis had studied for a decade, with some of whose intimates he had maintained friendly links.

One morning, not many days after the loss of Pontoise, the King of France was rowed up river in humble style: there was but one boat and in that craft were but half a dozen attendants. On the right bank of the Seine in full pomp stood the Count of Charolais and the Count of St.

Pol, with a great force of cavalry at their backs. As Louis neared them, he was remembering what the Count of Charolais had fiercely whispered to the Archbishop of Narbonne the previous November—"Tell the King that he has had me well worked over by his Chancellor, but before a year passes he will regret it."

The array of troops was not reassuring. As the boat put in to the bank Louis called out, "My brother, do you guarantee my safety?"

Charolais replied, "My Lord, yes."

Commynes recounts the interview: "After the King disembarked with his party, the two Counts did him full honor, as was right; and he, not in the least formal, began to speak.

" 'My brother, I know that you are a gentleman and of the House of France.' "

Suspiciously Charolais inquired, " 'Why, my Lord?'

" 'Because when I dispatched my ambassadors to Lille to my uncle, your father, and to you, some time ago, and that fool Morvilliers spoke so well to you, you sent me a message by the Archbishop of Narbonne . . . that before the end of a year I would repent the words Morvilliers had said to you. Well, you have kept your promise to me—and indeed much before the end of a year!'

"The King said these words with a laughing countenance, knowing that the character of him to whom he was speaking was such that he would take pleasure in this speech; and surely it did please him.

" 'No doubt about it,' the King added, 'it is a great pleasure to deal with people who keep the promises they make!' "

In a stroke Louis had broken the ice and now he pressed on to heat the water. Disavowing the harsh language of Morvilliers, he used all the resources of his familiar-amiable style to make St. Pol and Charolais feel that, past hostility brushed aside, the King heartily appreciated their martial capacities and well understood that they must be given "indemnities" suitable to their greatness. For a long time Louis walked up and down the bank of the river between the two Counts, talking . . . talking. Charolais then told over the standard demands of the princes: Normandy for the Duke of Berry; Picardy for himself; this, that and the other for the rest; and he also touched on the welfare of the realm—"but that was the least of the question," Commynes remarks, "for the *Bien Publique* had been converted into the *Bien Particulière*."

The King stood immovable on his refusal to yield Normandy to his brother Charles. However, to the Count of Charolais, he indicated, nothing reasonable would be refused. As an additional demonstration of affection, he suggested that the Count of St. Pol receive the office of High Constable, the military chieftainship of France. When finally Louis climbed back into the boat, the farewells of the two Counts, Commynes notes, "were very gracious."

Behind the scenes Louis went intensively to work on those who had the ear of Charolais, including a wily archdeacon, who, Louis himself said—one craftsman appreciating another—"was so clever that, if necessary, he can manage two negotiations exactly contrary to each other." The Count of Charolais began to think that it would be well for the League to come to some kind of compromise terms with the King—i.e., the other members of the League. There was no question of compromising his own demands, the justice of which Louis XI now recognized so gratifyingly.

In Paris, meanwhile, nerves had grown edgy; the betrayal of Pontoise infected the city. Louis was aroused in the night of Monday, September 23, to receive a panicky report that the Burgundians were burning the capital. Ordering out the militia, he galloped to one of the city gates—only to learn that the rumor had been generated by the brilliant light of a comet. Two nights later the city was shaken by another commotion when it was learned that the gate of the Bastille had been left open and some guns spiked.[7] People's minds were further disturbed by a barrage of enemy "ballades, rondeaux, declamatory libels, and other things," aimed against the King's chief officers in order to create doubts of their loyalty. Still, the people of the capital stood firm in the King's cause.

Louis's campaign to divide the princes by winning over the Count of Charolais continued to prosper. His private Burgundian dealings had stirred deep suspicions among the other lords. They went so far as to insult Charolais by muttering among themselves in his own chamber when they were supposed to be holding council; and Commynes reveals that they grew so mistrustful and weary of the whole business that "had it not been for what happened a few days later, they would have all shamefully trailed away home." Under Louis's ministrations the Count of Charolais had perceived that since he was indispensable to his confederates, they must expect his own demands to be satisfied first and be willing to be guided by his wishes regarding peace. October, with its sharp promise of winter, had almost arrived. The King's brother no longer insisted on Normandy. On Saturday, September 28, a cart heaped with tax rolls and account books of the provinces of Brie and Champagne made its way to Grange aux Merciers so that the advisers of the

Duke of Berry could examine the revenues of the *apanage* proffered by the King. Agreement was in the air. Louis told Panigarola that matters were almost settled.

In the early-morning hours of Sunday, September 29, news reached the King of France that Rouen had yielded to the rebels. Pierre de Brezé's widow, worked upon by the cunning Patriarch of Jerusalem—who persuaded her that the King had betrayed her husband in battle—opened the gates to a force led by the Duke of Bourbon.

The fall of Rouen, capital of the Duchy of Normandy, meant that the whole province was now at the disposal of the League. It appeared that treachery had entirely subdued time to the will of the princes. In the richest Duchy of France, lying west of Paris, they could winter at their ease and wait for additional erosions of loyalty and mounting fears to deliver to them a sovereign penned in his capital. The King, within his private chamber, gave way to despairing outbursts. Panigarola found him "grieved to death" and "fearing even greater betrayals because he cannot put much trust in his troops." All the while, however, the mind of the King of France was racing over alternatives and coolly weighing possibilities. No question now of keeping Normandy—but how much could be saved from the wreck of the campaign he had almost won? Everything, he immediately perceived, depended upon his capacity to bend time once more to his purposes. If he moved fast enough . . . If the Count of Charolais was sufficiently indoctrinated . . . When the King emerged into his outer chamber, crowded with courtiers, he was all *sang-froid.* "Very prudently and cheerfully" he announced that "he was willing to give Normandy to the Duke of Berry—before it had been entirely won by force." He commanded a meeting of his great council. Already a royal emissary was galloping for Charolais's headquarters to invite the Count to an immediate colloquy with the King between the lines. It was hardly mid-morning.

iv

LOUIS moved so fast that when he met with the Count of Charolais that morning he was able to make Charolais the gift of the news of the fall of Rouen. He came to the point immediately and frankly: he would never have consented to give up the province, but since the Normans themselves had altered the situation, he was content to create his brother Duke of Normandy and to satisfy all the desires the Count had expressed in the past several days. Having determined to yield, Louis, as was his custom, yielded with grace, celerity, and lavish generosity. The heir of Burgundy would receive not only the Picard lands and towns the King had repurchased from Philip the Good but all royal territories north of the Somme, and Montdidier and Roye as well, an acquisition that pushed the Burgundian frontier to not much more than fifty miles from Paris. The Count of Charolais, desperately short of supplies, made no attempt to conceal his relief at the King's news, his interest in the King's offer. Louis had also devised for the occasion a new means of persuasion. . . .

The two men, each accompanied by only a handful of followers, fell into such an engrossing conversation as they walked that without realizing it they moved steadily closer to the walls of Paris, and suddenly Charolais found that they had entered one of the great outworks which the King had constructed. He managed to keep his countenance; but the Count of St. Pol and the lord of Contay and other Burgundian nobles who had witnessed his disappearance stewed in fear and anger until he emerged, unharmed, to return to his lines. According to a report that the lord of Haynin heard, wine was brought to the King while he and Charolais were within the bulwark. After Louis drank, a cup was offered to the Count. But the King said quickly, "Do not bring any wine to my fair brother; he does not drink between meals." The King spoke thus, Haynin notes approvingly, so that Charolais would have no cause for suspicion of poison. Apparently the subject of conversation which the two men had found so absorbing was a suggestion made by Louis that Charolais marry his daughter, Anne—the Count being then thirty-two and Anne, four. Louis seems to have thrown out a hint that in case he had no male heir the throne of France might go, not to his brother, Charles, but to his son-in-law, the Count of Charolais.

With this glittering vista hanging in the air, the Count not only accepted the King's terms on the spot but promised to secure the adherence of his confederates.

Not wasting a moment, Louis, that same Sunday, had his great council approve the bestowal of Normandy upon the King's brother, the grants to Charolais, and the appointment of St. Pol as Constable of France with annual wages of twenty-four thousand livres. On his side, the Count of Charolais persuaded the other princes to acquiesce, but they did so only after laying down the condition that he insist upon the fulfillment of their own reasonable demands. The Count was hardly listening. Having received all he could possibly ask for and being artfully primed by the King and the King's adroit helpers at Burgundian headquarters, Charolais was now impatient to bid farewell to his wearisome confederates (who did, after all, expect rather a lot for what they had done), and hence he was the readier to identify "reasonable demands" according to the King's, rather than the princes', interpretation.

On the following Tuesday (October 1) criers published in the streets of Paris a "truce forever" between the King and the princes. Graciously, Louis then sent merchants from the city with stocks of food and clothing. Thronging to the piles of goods stacked between the lines at the convent of St. Antoine des Champs, the Burgundians and Bretons presented a miserable appearance—"in tatters, unshod, and so bearded they looked like savages. . . ." The Parisian Chronicler Jean de Roye found them "full of sores and ordure." Some of Duke John's Swiss were so hungry that they seized great cheeses and without waiting to remove the rind "tore them with their teeth and then drank marvelous huge drafts of wine. . . ." All the world then perceived, like Panigarola, that they "could not have lasted much longer." On Saturday (October 5) was published the Treaty of Conflans, embodying the King's grants to his brother, to the Count of Charolais, and to the Count of Charolais's friend, the Count of St. Pol. Assiduously Louis entertained the cunning archdeacon and other influential Burgundians, paid flatteringly informal visits to their master. With every passing hour the Count of Charolais realized more clearly that his confederates would be well advised to accept what the King offered and betake themselves home.

These princes, greed now sharpened by anxiety, once more put their expectations in writing. Duke John still demanded that Louis break his league with the Duke of Milan and furnish an immediate expedition to recover Naples for the House of Anjou; the Duke of Brittany wanted a substantial recognition of his independence; the Duke of Nemours would be content with the governorship of Paris and of Île de France; the Count of Armagnac claimed the restoration of all his lands and a share of the taxes gathered in his territories. The princes must likewise be given huge pensions and control of the standing army. But Louis was now able to deal with them singly, a strategy which heightened their mutual suspicions and lowered their individual resistance.

On October 10 the King brought the Duke of Brittany to terms. Francis II was granted the ecclesiastical jurisdiction of his Duchy, over which he and the King had first quarreled, and some lands which had long been in dispute; and Louis promised to pardon the Count of Dunois and Antoine de Chabannes, Count of Dammartin. The Duke of Brittany meant to secure his main reward in another quarter: he saw himself as the lord of the new lord of Normandy, with all the rich offices of that great province at his disposal. Louis did not discourage this vision.

By this time the Count of Armagnac and the Duke of Nemours were harboring bitter thoughts against their more fortunate allies, and even Duke John was beginning to wonder whether his martial comrade the Count of Charolais was really such a good friend after all. On October 13 Louis suggested to Armagnac that he might be offered a pension of twelve thousand crowns and one hundred lances of the standing army. In a violent rage Armagnac returned to the princes, asserted that they were deceiving him and breaking their faith, and that "under the pretense of assembling for the public weal of the realm, each had come, it seemed to him now, for his own interest only." Charolais and St. Pol replied unsympathetically that "he should be content with the offer that had been made him, which was more than he deserved; and if he did not like it, he should take the shortest way home. . . ." The Duke of Nemours, growing frightened, was happy to receive from the King a few crumbs of privilege like the right to nominate certain royal officers in his Duchy. The King bluntly informed Duke John that under no circumstances would he break with his faithful ally the Duke of Milan—and when King René's son appealed to Charolais, the Count indicated uncomfortably that he felt obliged to remain neutral in the matter. As for Duke John's insistence on mounting an expedition to reconquer Naples, the King would offer no more than a subsidy, payments to be spread over several years. The final decision in this matter, and in all other princely claims at issue, "the King has submitted to the Count of Charolais," one of Charolais's secretaries recorded. "And His Majesty says 'Par la Pasques Dieu!' if all the world attacked him he would put himself into my Lord's hands." [8]

For other projects stirring in his mind, Louis would need somebody besides the Count of Charolais. On Thursday, October 24, he issued from Paris in a costume that amazed everybody, for he was clad like a king in a robe of royal purple richly furred with ermine. Somewhere outside the walls he had a very cordial conversation with his brother-in-law Jean, Duke of Bourbon. The Duke of Bourbon was one of the Discontented. While he was winning Normandy for the King's brother, the princes before Paris had been avidly dividing up the spoils, at least in their minds, without paying any attention to his claims. If not at this first meeting, then soon afterward, Louis sympathetically pointed out that since the other princes had selfishly inserted their demands first, little or nothing would be left for the Duke of Bourbon. On the other hand, if he wished to serve the King—and nobody appreciated his abilities as the King did—he might receive a great deal indeed from a sovereign who knew how to reward merit. Bourbon began thinking long thoughts.

Before the end of October the Burgundians were breaking camp and taking the roads to the north; the Bretons were moving out of St. Denis for Normandy. The right moment had come for the King to make his final offer to the lords of the Public Weal not included in the Pact of Conflans. On Monday evening, October 28, Louis issued from Paris, bringing with him a treaty—not a draft of proposals but a formal instrument in the shape of royal letters-patents. It was take-it-or-leave-it. What occurred at his conference with the princes was not reported, except for the result: the unhappy magnates accepted the letters-patents as Louis had drawn them up. On the morrow, the agreement was promulgated as the Treaty of St. Maur-des-Fossés. Peace was declared; the past was forgotten; neither party would punish adherents of the other for participation in the recent events; any lord who broke the appointment by attacking the King would be opposed by the rest of the confederates, and if the King undertook anything against one of the lords the others would come to his aid. The princes had plumed up their dignity by means of two articles in which the King agreed that they could not be forced to answer his summons, except for military service, and that he would not visit any of their dwellings without three days' advance notice. Louis readily accepted a feeble gesture made by the Leaguers in the direction of the public welfare: a Council of the Thirty-six was established to hear complaints and institute reforms. When this commission met some weeks later, the King had no difficulty transforming it into an instrument of his own will.

By the time the princes signed the agreement, the Duke of Bourbon had entered the service of the King, in return for receiving, at high wages, the governorship of eastern France from the Loire to Lyons, almost a quarter of the realm. But the King saw the possibility of getting a good deal for his money. As for the lords still empty-handed—Nemours, Armagnac, Duke John—Louis now needed to dole out to them no more than what a prudent regard for Charolais's humor indicated. In the end, the Count of Armagnac got very little except his pardon. The Duke of Nemours accepted the governorship of Roussillon and a pension. Duke John, fiercely demanding armies, was forced to settle for a sum of money. After the King had given the fiery Angevin a cool dressing-down, he confirmed his offer of 17,000 crowns by Christmas, a small gift of lands, and the promise of a subsidy of 300,000 crowns, the payments to be spread over three years.[9]

The King graciously insisted on a ceremonious farewell to the departing princes.[10] He and the Count of Charolais and Duke John escorted the new Duke of Normandy and his tutor, the Duke of Brittany, a few miles on their way to Pontoise and then turned off to "make" together the feast of All Saints Day (November 1) at the village of Villiers-le-Bel. The King took the occasion to offer, in writing, his daughter Anne of France to the heir of Burgundy. With the understanding that Charolais would fulfill the contract by the following Easter, he proposed for Anne's dowry 1,200,000 gold crowns, the sum to be secured by the delivery to Charolais of the County of Champagne, the right of collecting *aides* and taxes being reserved to the King.

About noon on November 3, Louis parted, very affectionately, from the Count of Charolais, and headed for Paris, probably in the company of Duke John. In bidding his sovereign farewell, Charolais remarked, vaguely, that he had no doubt the King would do what Duke John wanted. The League of the Public Weal was no more.

At the cost of satisfying the appetite of the Count of Charolais, Louis had succeeded in imposing, on princes sworn to have his skin, a treaty which dismissed their armies by concessions that mocked their demands. For all Panigarola's intimacy with the King and his intelligent curiosity, he never quite understood how this legerdemain had been managed. Nor did anyone else, in or out of Paris—except Louis.

But nobody knew better than Louis that the revolt of the feodality had been a disaster. The increase in princely pensions alone would cost his treasury 200,000 livres a year. He had lost Picardy and the Somme towns. He had lost the Duchy of Normandy, the prize of the realm. Before the eyes of his subjects he had been driven to make a humiliating composition with the high-flying princes of France. That treachery had deprived him of a crushing victory at Montlhéry, that treachery had prevented him from watching the armies of the League ignominiously melt away in the cold October rains did not obscure for Louis that the conduct of great affairs must be judged by results.

Still, the King, as time would show, had learned a great deal from his mistakes. Furthermore he could take comfort that the realm had learned something too—a satirist dated one of his works "The year that everyone tended to his own profit."

And the genie was out of the jar.

16. "A Snapper-Up of Unconsidered Trifles"

THE LOSS OF NORMANDY burned in Louis's blood. All that showed at the moment, however, was intense nervous energy.

Once more he made a withdrawal. Heading southward from Paris past the field of Montlhéry, he arrived in the city of Orléans about November 18. He told Jean Pierre Panigarola that he had decided to spend most of the winter there "because he is in the middle of his realm and lord of the Loire River" and can thus "discover if his enemies are plotting anything against him." The last half of the statement was at best a half-truth: he was preoccupied with visions of his own. The King lodged in the town and established his council in an adjoining dwelling; he had a connecting gallery built to screen his comings and goings. Closeted with captains and councilors for long hours, receiving reports of messengers and dictating replies, Louis now exhibited a kind of smoldering expectancy.

Veiled hints dropped to Panigarola of changes which he anticipated "before too many months had passed," bizarre suggestions planted in the breast of the Count of Charolais, the King's wooing of the Duke of Bourbon, shadowy liaisons developed with certain adherents of certain lords —these seemingly unrelated maneuvers now began to reveal a pattern. It spelled "Normandy." Any thought of regaining the Duchy appeared to be a fantasy—though the conditions necessary to create the opportunity were quite clear, if seemingly remote: Burgundian inertia and turmoil in Normandy. The nurturing of these conditions the King of France had not left to Goddess Fortune.

When Louis and Charolais had drawn up the marriage contract for Princess Anne at Villiers-le-Bel, a curious clause appeared. The County of Champagne, its taxes and other royal rights reserved for the King, was to serve as a pledge for the huge dowry that went with Louis's daughter; but if it happened "that the Duchy of Normandy, by death *or otherwise* [italics added], returned to the King," Charolais was to have Champagne without any reservation save simple homage. The clause thus posed an enticing question: since Charolais's only interest in securing Louis' brother his new Duchy had been to deprive the Crown of a great province, why should not the Count himself, instead, have such a province—and thus for his own good allow Louis to regain Normandy? As for that Duchy, when Louis bade farewell to his brother and the Duke of Brittany, he had given them some good advice—which he counted on their not taking. "Watch out for yourselves," he told them solicitously. He well knew that the relations between the two Dukes had become an explosive mixture which needed only a little artful shaking: even Normandy was not rich enough to accommodate the expectations fermenting in the ducal entourages.

Strange figures appeared at Orléans, were closeted with the King, and then disappeared—figures like Pierre Doriole, once a royal officer but now supposedly an adherent of the Duke of Normandy, and Tanneguy du Chastel, one of those who had fled from France at Louis's accession in order to take service with the Duke of Brittany. And there were other men, at the side of the two Dukes, who were in secret communication with the King of France. Intently Louis listened for the first signs of trouble in Normandy. He had tracked his brother and Francis II every mile of their journey.

It was some time after the middle of November when the two Dukes arrived at Mont-Sainte-Catherine, a monastery on the hilly outskirts of Rouen, where they paused until the citizens of Charles's new capital finished preparations for a triumphal entry. The Duke of Brittany, alarmed to find that his influence over his protégé was fading, had delayed the journey in an attempt to regain his ascendancy. Young Charles, for his part, had become frightened by a cacophony of demands for rewards . . . recompense . . . offices. . . . In the jostling throng about the two Dukes, feelings were running very high by the time the cavalcade reached Mont-Sainte-Catherine. The greed of the Bretons, claims by Norman nobles, the expectations of Charles's own household grew daily more insistent. Scattered among these embittered factions, the King's secret agents had no need to create trouble, needed only to exploit it.

The King's brother, cruelly entangled in his leading strings, felt himself sinking into a bog of violent passions. Then someone at his elbow, someone who knew how to choose the moment and to speak with soothing assurance, reminded him that the one man—fearsome though he might be—to help him at this juncture was the King. The distracted youth played the part which Louis had foreseen and for which he had provided a supporting cast. In his fright and bewilderment, the Duke of Normandy was induced to send a message to his brother. . . .

At six o'clock on the evening of Monday, November 25, the King of France rode gaily into the city of Orléans with the Duke of Bourbon at his side and the youthful Duchess of Orléans perched on his horse. He was a new man. That morning he had made his way to the Church of Our Lady at Cléry in order to perform his Montlhéry vow. The Virgin Mary, or the Destiny of France, had answered his prayers. There appeared before him the messenger from his brother, who turned out to be no less than the Master of the Duke of Normandy's Household. He had a letter in his hand.

Reading, the King discovered Charles's missive to be a feckless complaint about the overwhelming burdens thrust upon him. The messenger, queried by Louis, gave it the interpretation the King was waiting for.

Louis passed the letter to the Duke of Bourbon. "I will have to succor my brother," he observed casually. "I believe that I will have to take back my Duchy of Normandy."

ii

ON THE AFTERNOON OF November 29 Louis XI got word that four days before, on the very day his brother's emissary reached him at Cléry, an explosion had finally occurred at Mont-Sainte-Catherine. The King, upon issuing from his chamber to take a little exercise and order his thoughts, caught sight of a special Milanese envoy he knew well, Emanuel de Iacoppo, and vigorously beckoned to him. "Manuel . . . I have just now had news that in Normandy they tried to kill the Duke of Brittany and that the whole province is in confusion." Louis added that he was hourly expecting ambassadors from each of the warring factions.

It turned out that the Norman lords and the citizens of Rouen had become increasingly disturbed by rumors that Francis II meant to carry the new Duke of Normandy off to Brittany or, worse yet, was planning to deliver Charles to the King. On the evening of November 25, the Count of Harcourt and a party of armed nobles appeared at the gates of Mont-Sainte-Catherine, shouldered their way to the King's brother, insisted that he enter Rouen immediately, and coldly invited Francis II to accompany them. When Francis angrily refused, the Normans swept

Charles away in the plain velvet gown he was wearing, put him on a horse and escorted him to the city. In a great fright the Duke of Brittany called his followers and immediately headed for the safety of Caen —dispatching a letter to the King in which he accused the Normans of trying to ambush him and declared that he was entirely at his sovereign's service. Messages now streamed into Orléans from the Duke of Brittany and from the Duke of Normandy. To retaliate against Charles, Francis II was ready to turn over to Louis the town of Caen and the other Norman places he held. Charles's communications were so chaotic that the King had no difficulty interpreting them to mean that his brother was willing to resign his Duchy.

Royal squadrons were beginning to move on Normandy by December 1. The Admiral was dispatched with *carte-blanche* to deal with the Duke of Brittany. On December 3 the Duke of Bourbon left Orléans with his half brother Louis the Bastard to take command of the main army. Charles de Melun was leading a force westward from Paris.

Emanuel de Iacoppo feared that the Dukes of Brittany and Normandy might have concocted this elaborate stratagem in order to capture the King, but Louis assured him cheerfully "that his affairs were not that dangerous because the French do not have such vigor in managing that sort of thing as have the Italians." When Manuel wondered about the attitude of the Count of Charolais, who might be up to something, the King declared that there was no danger there either because of the marriage contract between them and because he was keeping the Count so fully informed that he had no reason to suspect anything.

"It is a pity," Iacoppo reported, "to see how tremendously occupied the King is. He rises very early, says his prayers, goes to Mass, and returns to his dwelling. He then follows a carefully arranged program. He holds council, which takes place in a house contiguous to the King's, and he remains there as long as is necessary. Then he comes to the chamber where he eats, and, continually dispatching business, he is usually at dinner till past two o'clock in the afternoon. Dinner finished, he withdraws into another chamber and without any intermission returns to his affairs. At the bottom of the day, either on foot or a-horse, he takes a little exercise in making a turn about the city. On coming back to his quarters, he consults with some of his men until the supper hour. He sups early and goes to bed late."

By December 11 the King had ridden out of Orléans to direct his campaign. He was aiming to move across lower Normandy and join the Duke of Brittany at Caen. The Duke of Bourbon, sweeping through middle Normandy, had already taken possession of Évreux. Charles de Melun was driving down the north bank of the Seine to win upper Normandy. The three-pronged attack would converge upon the capital of the province, Rouen.

While Louis halted briefly at Chartres, there rode in to yield himself that old Écorcheur Antoine de Chabannes, Count of Dammartin, the best soldier of the League, now disillusioned by the fecklessness of the princes he had served. The King welcomed him with honor, gave him a magnificent set of bards and armor worked in gold, and immediately drew him into the inner circle of his advisers. "Not losing an hour and continually in the saddle," Louis XI pounded across lower Normandy to enter Caen on December 19. He established his quarters in a house next to the lodging of the Duke of Brittany and immediately set to work to complete what Francis's quarrel with Charles had begun. The following day the Duke performed a ceremony of obedience to the King. That evening Louis supped with Francis and afterward they played cards; during the day they met without ceremony three or four times, putting their heads together like old cronies. It was a miracle to see it, Panigarola thought.

On December 23, Louis and Francis promulgated the Treaty of Caen, in which, the past being forgotten, each party agreed not to support the rebels of the other, and Francis II engaged himself to aid the King against his enemies, reserving, however, his allies, Duke John and the Count of Charolais. The treaty cost Louis the verbal promise of 120,000 crowns, which he duly paid; as a special mark of favor to the Duke, he accepted into his grace the Count of Dammartin, the former Marshal Lohéac, Odet d'Aydie, the Count of Dunois, and some others, and agreed not to pardon six men about the King's brother whom Francis regarded as chiefly responsible for the quarrel.

Louis was thus gaining valuable servants—and repairing past errors—rather than pleasing the Duke of Brittany. He restored Lohéac to his marshalship, kept Dunois and Dammartin close by his side; and it would not be long before, persuading the Duke of Brittany to yield, he took into his service the six whom Francis had excepted from pardon. These men all received better appointments, Commynes notes, than ever they held under Charles VII: Louis did not believe in retrieving his mistakes half-heartedly.

By the time the King ratified the Treaty of Caen, all Normandy had fallen into his hands save for the towns of Louviers, Pont de l'Arche, and Rouen, and royal forces were beginning to close in on the Norman capital. "Night and day," Panigarola reported, "the King acts with the greatest vigilance. . . . Daily these Normans come to ask pardons for the wrongs they have committed, bearing the keys of cities in their hands . . . and His Majesty benignly receives everybody and forgets past things. . . . Now the King is establishing new officials for all of Normandy . . . so Your Highness can judge with what consummate prudence and astuteness His Majesty has crushed the rebellion of his enemies. . . ."

The Duke of Bourbon, having forced Vernon to yield, was setting siege to Louviers. Louis's chief fear now was that his brother might flee to the dominions of the Duke of Burgundy or even into England. Therefore, on Christmas Day, after consultation with the Duke of Brittany, he dispatched two Bretons to Charles, offering to receive his brother into his grace and provide him with a worthy *apanage* to be decided by the Dukes of Brittany and of Bourbon. "For many days," wrote Panigarola, faithfully staying at Louis's heels, "His Majesty has ridden armed and works tirelessly, as is his custom; and it is every day more clearly to be seen that he is a man who loves and can endure toils and travails." By the end of December, the King was approaching Louviers, still besieged by the Duke of Bourbon.

As Louis moved across Normandy, he was continually looking over his shoulder to survey the lords of the realm. Word had reached him that the Duke of Nemours was plotting to deliver Roussillon to his cousin the Count of Armagnac. One threatening message from the King, however, punctured the plot and produced from Nemours a sworn reaffirmation of his fidelity. To the Count of Foix, Louis gave permission to embroil himself in the perpetual troubles of Navarre "so that he will spend his money and have no reason to injure the King nor to intrigue against him." Louis had already dismissed Foix's son from court "because when he was here he secretly informed the King's brother of what was being done. . . ." Duke John and King René kept sending representatives, demanding money and protesting loyalty; Duke John was eagerly proposing that he come to court. Louis remarked to Panigarola that before he received the Duke into his household, "he would rather take four Turks," but in dealing with Duke John he had to emulate "the brothers of St. Francis, namely use hypocrisy as they do." The Count of Charolais, after a considerable silence, replied to the news of the King's advance into Normandy with "pleasant words" and the announcement that he was sending an embassy.

Louviers having yielded on New Year's Day (1466), Louis rode to

Pont de l'Arche on the evening of January 5 to supervise the establishment of the siege. "Vigorously he directed the planting of the springardes, the bringing up of the bombards, the digging of defensive ditches, and the placement of his troops." Then he ordered his artillery to begin firing, and the next morning he proceeded methodically to "close his siege sector by sector. . . ." °

The King's network of roadblocks garnered a remorseless harvest, as men high and low attempted to flee the hopeless cause of the King's brother. Charles's General of Finances, disguised as a cordelier and accompanied by a monk, was caught attempting to make his way to Picardy. Quickly tried by the Provost-Marshal, he and the monk were drowned in the Eure. "Almost every morning," Panigarola recorded, "one finds bodies in the river." Young Charles was despatching a confusion of messages which alternated fretful complaints and vague offers to do what the King wanted.

Meanwhile Louis pressed Pont de l'Arche closely, "remaining armed at the siege day and night. Standing in the ditches to order the approach work of his troops and to determine where best to give the assault, he saw to everything from point to point, according to what was happening. . . ." When the city, gateway to Rouen, was delivered to him on January 9, Louis granted pardon to the inhabitants and allowed the soldiers of his brother to join his army if they wished. That evening Charles sent word that he was willing to negotiate for an *apanage* through the Dukes of Brittany and Bourbon, as the King had proposed, and asked for a truce. From Honfleur the following day, the Duke of Brittany dispatched to his whilom protégé a guarantee of safety so that he could leave Rouen. Louis then proclaimed a truce of ten days between himself and his brother.

On January 14 he received a delegation of citizens from Rouen, demanded that the city return to its allegiance, promised pardon to all and the maintenance of the city's privileges. He warned the delegation, however, that he was not to be put off by words: he wanted an answer from them by the 16th or "on the following day they could expect to be besieged at home."

By this time the men of Rouen had no desire except to be rid of a

---

° Panigarola had a taste of the risks the King ran in insisting upon doing everything. Wishing to study French military methods, he and a friend of his, a Milanese knight, were standing in the front lines watching when "a missile from an enemy springarde passed close beside me and gave me a great fright. . . ." His friend laughed, "because he was farther away from the shot than I. We decided then not to go too close."

Duke who brought them only trouble. After the envoys returned to the city, the citizens drove out the councilors of the King's brother; and Charles himself with a tattered following fearfully made his way to Honfleur. On the 16th a delegation from the Norman capital humbly yielded their city to the King.[1] Next morning Louis sent representatives to take possession of Rouen.

He had won back Normandy.

There remained the question of winning back his brother Charles, now discussing terms with the Duke of Brittany at Honfleur. The trouble was, almost any sizable *apanage* could be dangerous. Dauphiné bordered Burgundian lands, Savoy, and Angevin Provence. Champagne would put young Charles cheek by jowl with the Count of Charolais. The Duchy of Guienne offered the temptation to intrigue with the Yorkists in a province that had known English rule for hundreds of years. On the other hand, if Charles fled into Brittany or to the Duke of Burgundy, he could always be used by the princes as the figurehead of a new Bien Publique. As Louis anxiously weighed the alternatives, he received a skittish notice from Francis II that the Duke thought it time to return to Brittany.

Louis replied that he himself would come to Honfleur to conclude the agreement with his brother, and by the beginning of February he had moved westward from Rouen to Pont-Audemer. His outriders had already set out for the coast when he received news that halted him in his tracks. On hearing a rumor that the King was approaching with an army, brother Charles and the Duke of Brittany had ridden in hot haste for Caen.[2] Louis dispatched streams of envoys—to assure the fugitives that the rumor was false, to offer his brother as *apanage* the County of Roussillon, and, after that was abruptly refused, a portion of Dauphiné, likewise refused by a now terrified Charles. On February 9, Louis's final envoys returned with the news that the King's brother had withdrawn to Brittany with his friend Francis.

The King's campaign for Normandy, the first step to recover himself, had concluded with but one loose end. That one, however, was dangerous; and as Louis prepared to leave his newly regained province, he was listening intently for ominous signals from the court of Burgundy. The Count of Charolais, however, had made no move—except to order to the Norman seaport of Dieppe a Burgundian troop, which arrived too late, and to send a secret invitation to Charles to join him, which was intercepted by the King's alert officers. Louis shortly received the embassy Charolais had promised: it bore assurances of the Count's devotion.

His work in Normandy finished, the King of France took the road back to Orléans. His officials were firmly settled in their posts; the province was as tranquil as if the interlude of the King's brother had never existed; there was not a prince stirring. In two months he had regained, almost without bloodshed, the greatest Duchy of France—more than half the territory relinquished to the League. He had forced ignominy and loss to yield him a startling increment. To the realm and the princes he had served notice that he would never accept the submission of his monarchy to the feudal past. For himself he had brilliantly tested his style, withdrawal as prelude to return. Even before he finally brought the Leaguers to terms, and his throne and neck were yet in hazard, he had begun exploring the means of retrieval and recovery.

When the betrayal of Rouen, the previous September, had forced Louis, on the verge of victory, to come to terms with the princes, he had said something to Jean Pierre Panigarola that not only clenched in a few words the force of his character but also partly disclosed the moral basis of his ministry. His decision to yield, he told Jean Pierre, resulted entirely from his own considered judgment of the situation—"it was the best thing to do, seeing the dangers and the treasons that were daily being discovered. . . ." His watchword, Louis went on, would always be "*Sapiens nihil invitus facit*"—the wise man does only what he has deliberately willed. Perhaps it was not the holy oil of coronation or the fortuitous genealogy of the royal succession, but his readiness to assume total responsibility for the destiny of France, that, in his mind, made him true King.

THE SPINNING OF
THE STRANDS

17. Péronne

FOR A YEAR, from the spring of 1466 to the spring of 1467, Louis XI remained in the region of the Loire. It was another withdrawal, this one self-imposed. He was taking stock—of his losses, of his mistakes, of quickly revived conspiracies among his intransigent princes, and of his own resources. He made few moves, endless calculations. He renewed his touch with the countryside of France. Long days of hunting relieved the hidden hours during which he pondered the patchwork of information and rumor received from his agents and sought to penetrate the minds of his enemies. Evidently he blamed no one for his errors but himself, perhaps because it never occurred to him that they could not be retrieved.

At moments in the first weeks of this withdrawal he enjoyed, or enjoyed giving the impression of, indulging himself in gallantries. A Milanese envoy was treated to a charming afternoon in a castle garden by a lovely girl, called only "Mademoiselle," who was evidently a friend of the King's. After accompanying the King into wild country, he reported that His Majesty went hunting almost every day, "and mostly with some lady on his saddle." In the late spring of 1466 a Bohemian embassy returning from England paid a call on King René at Angers and then made their way to King Louis's "hunting court." After the cultivated hospitality of René ("a comely merry old man") they found the King's residence "mean," though they were impressed by the "sixty doorkeepers and guards" who kept strict watch on all comings and goings. The diarist among the Bohemians recorded that the King was "a man of no great height and with black hair, brownish countenance, eyes deep in his head, a long nose, and small legs." They were also accorded an audience with the Queen—"verily it was a pity that she was but a middling handsome woman." Louis was now forty-three years old, and rapidly balding. He had lost none of his ebullience, though he was becoming more difficult of access and jealous of his privacy. Neither long hours in the saddle nor thinking tired him.

Changing times wove fresh motifs in the patterns of living and ruling.

The House of Anjou, always a prickly element of existence, Louis XI found an opportunity to favor and thus, temporarily, to anesthetize. In the spring of 1466 he finally permitted Duke John to come to court. Before his violent cousin arrived at Meung-sur-Loire, Louis "inspected the castle minutely, room by room," reports Panigarola, "and, finding a secret entry he had not known about, had it blocked up." The King was rapidly wearying of John's Neapolitan fantasies and his attempts to dominate the royal council, when events in Spain opened up new Angevin prospects. The still rebellious Catalans chose King René and René's son as their defenders against John II of Aragon. It required little urging for Louis XI to promise his support: he duly broke diplomatic ties with John II and found a little money and a few troops for Duke John. He did not scruple to tell Panigarola that he was sending his cousin to Spain so that "he will not give trouble to this court but only to the Catalans." As the Duke was departing on his mission, Louis succeeded in bringing off an ironic *coup*. He managed to worm out of Duke John the seal of John's uncle, Charles, Count of Maine. The seal represented Maine's oath of allegiance, in return for a guarantee of his status, to the League of the Public Weal; and Maine had refused to deliver it to any of the Leaguers except his trusty nephew. With this proof of Maine's treachery, Louis promptly deprived him of the governorship of Languedoc, forced him to undergo a humiliating interrogatory, and only pardoned him on condition that he stay at home and cease to meddle in public affairs.

As usual, King Louis was arranging marriages great and small—and expressing himself freely on the sexes. After he had reviewed (in 1467) a drill by the Paris militia, the less martial members of which had some difficulty with their mounts, his *compère* Louis de Crussol remarked to him "Sire, do you not see that in this muster there are more than ten thousand who would not be able to make ten leagues on horseback?" Louis replied, "By the faith of my body, my lord of Crussol, I believe indeed that their wives ride better than they do!"

The King did not like his matchmaking efforts to go unappreciated. When Galeazzo-Maria, the Duke of Milan's heir, proved slow to accept the Queen's sister Bona of Savoy (once proposed for Edward IV), Louis snapped to the Milanese ambassadors—well, was it "yes" or "no"? Bona was a lovely, clean girl. If they had any doubts about it, he would conduct her to the Queen and have her inspected nude! He was somewhat mollified after the Milanese assured him that Galeazzo-Maria would not dream of making any other marriage, not even with God!

Personal misfortune, too, lent its somber·tone to the dappled patterns of daily life. On an evening in mid-March (1466), as Louis XI was speaking with Jean Pierre Panigarola, a message arrived that Francesco Sforza, Duke of Milan, was dead. Louis was so overcome by emotion that he had to withdraw. For weeks afterward the mention of Sforza's name caused him to change color. He perhaps felt closer in spirit to this fellow adventurer whom he never met than to any other human being. The King immediately confirmed his alliance with Sforza's heir, Galeazzo-Maria, and sent word to all powers that the Duchy of Milan was under his benevolent protection. Months later, on the evening of December 4, 1466, the Queen gave birth to a premature baby boy. Louis named him François in honor of a dear friend. The infant's life flickered, he was hastily baptized; four hours later he was dead. The King, Queen, and all the court were reduced to bitter tears, "seemingly unable to raise eyes from the ground so much do they grieve." This son would have replaced Louis's rebellious brother Charles as heir to the throne, thus depriving his enemies of a potent weapon, and, as Panigarola sympathetically recorded, "helped stabilize the King's rule and realm." Louis sustained the blow with fortitude, "not waiting to be consoled but rather consoling others." Though the loss was hard to bear, "the King says that he holds his kingdom through the omnipotent God, and when it pleases God he will give up to Him son and every other thing, thinking all for the best." Perhaps Louis's willingness to assume full responsibility for the realm of France made it easier for him to accept the supreme responsibility of the deity.*

Daily, meanwhile, his corps of secretaries translated his rapid dicta-

---

* His veneration for the faith did not, however, extend to the deity's earthly servants. In forwarding, through Panigarola, some advice to the new Duke of Milan regarding a diplomatic mission, he remarked that "he thought it necessary that in this project there should be included some priests, friars, or prelates because without them, it appears, there may never be treachery among the lords nor deceit, nor indeed can frauds be perpetrated without their intervention."

tion into the sealed orders that administered a kingdom. In response to petitions, reports, dispatches brought by his hard-worked couriers, the impulses of his will sped to the length and breadth of France along the network of royal officials and to his envoys in foreign parts. He continually prodded the Chancery and the Chamber of Accounts in dry, blunt notes: "Don't let anything go wrong"—"Make an end of the matter, Chancellor, I beg you, so that it never again has to be spoken of"—"Expedite the business at once without creating any difficulties." He kept in close touch with his good towns, their local politics, the state of their defenses, their trade. Perceiving an opportunity to stimulate industry in Lyons and improve the kingdom's balance of payments, he established in that city the manufacture of silk cloth.[1] He enlarged his standing army from seventeen to twenty companies of heavy cavalry. He established a great artillery park between Montargis and Orléans—"a stupendous thing," the Milanese ambassador thought it—and "almost daily" when he was at Montargis he visited the workshops making cannon and siege weapons. He took care to consult with his great council, "well furnished with doctors and prelates." The Council of the Thirty-Six—completely loyal, like its head, the aged Count of Dunois—he established in Paris as a kind of supreme court of inquiry and public policy.

In September (1466) he confided to a Milanese envoy that "although in the past he found himself in such extremity that he had both his feet almost entirely outside his realm, nevertheless at present he has one foot very firm and the other becomes more stable daily; and he hopes with the grace of God he will, from day to day, still better knit up his affairs."

Earlier, to Panigarola, he had expressed himself even more succinctly: "it was necessary for him to make a new world."

The King's new world was reflected in the changes of its personnel. Antoine du Lau, once the King's favorite, had been cast into prison. Charles de Melun, the eloquent "Charlot," was dismissed from all his posts, and, in 1468, tried and executed for treason—the King allowing Melun's enemies full scope to bring about his death. He was no more guilty than others who regained royal favor; apparently Louis could not forget what Melun's timidity had cost him on the day of Montlhéry. The Bastard of Armagnac, Count of Comminges, had left the court to become Governor of Guienne and hold in check the southern lords. Familiar figures remained, like Louis de Crussol and Gaston du Lyon. Two comparative newcomers were fast rising in favor: Louis de Beaumont, lord of La Forêt, a sagacious counselor, and the diligent Bishop of Évreux, Jean Balue. The King had also retrieved the costly error he had committed at the beginning of his reign in dismissing some of his father's best officers. Guillaume Juvenel des Ursins, who had faithfully served the King after being deprived of the chancellorship, and Robert d'Estouteville, discharged from the provostship of Paris, who had played the stalwart at Montlhéry, were restored to the offices they had held under Charles VII. Most of Louis's intimates were now men whose loyalties he had newly regained: Antoine de Chabannes, Count of Dammartin, who would shortly become Grand Master of the Royal Household; Marshal Lohéac; the brilliant Tanneguy du Chastel, now Governor of Roussillon; the Duke of Bourbon, who had proved himself in the Normandy campaign and was "in more authority with the King every day"; and Louis, Bastard of Bourbon, able and valiant (and worth two of his ducal brother), whom the King married to his natural daughter Jeanne and appointed Admiral of France on the demise of Jean de Montauban (May, 1466). Before the end of 1466 Louis XI had even managed to draw into his service the new Constable of France, Louis of Luxembourg, Count of St. Pol, pattern of chivalric attitudes and crony of the Count of Charolais. St. Pol, owning broad estates in France as well as in the Burgundian dominions and seeing himself as arbiter of the two powers, considered it indispensable to his greatness to keep one from dominating the other. A coolness had recently fallen between him and Charolais, two imperious personalities; perhaps also St. Pol estimated that Burgundy was growing too strong. After intricate anglings and persuasions the King bagged the game. He bestowed upon the Count of St. Pol a bride, the Queen's sister Maria, with a dowry of forty thousand crowns, the County of Eu, and the governorship of Normandy. Louis had no illusions about the precariousness of such a loyalty; but St. Pol was a prime catch to display to the realm and might so entangle himself in his own ambiguities, with Louis's help, as to become the prisoner instead of the master of his double role.

To make his new world Louis XI was forced to maneuver within political dimensions which the War of the Public Weal had narrowed and hardened. Brittany and Burgundy now acted as an alliance of foreign powers, threatening the western and northern borders of the realm. At the same time, the Duke and Count could still pose as lords of the

Lilies in order to attract the support of disaffected feudatories. The indicated strategy of statecraft—to separate the princes in order to deal with them singly—was sufficiently obvious, and had already been so successfully employed by the King, that Charolais and Francis II were bound to be on their guard against it. Still, such a policy was the only game Louis had confidence in; and he possessed the wiriness of intellect, the patience, and the optimism to play it. The government of Edward IV—in a state of war with France since the expiration of the truce in 1465—had remained the dominant factor of Louis's political mathematics. Unless he secured a settlement with England, the princes could always use against him the weapon of an English invasion to dismember France. In the spring of 1466, before Francis II and Charolais quite understood what was happening, Louis XI managed to negotiate a truce with England to last until March of 1468. Thus he won almost two years in which to pursue, through his friend the Earl of Warwick, a durable treaty with the Yorkists and to employ his arts in sundering the bond between Brittany and Burgundy.

What called him forth, toward the end of April, 1467, from his year's withdrawal was the prospect of meeting at last Richard Neville, the kingmaking Earl.

ii

SUDDENLY, in the countryside south of Chartres, the King fell ill. He was brought to a small dwelling, the only one in the vicinity. The royal court and guard had to encamp in the surrounding fields. The Duke of Bourbon, finding lodging three miles away, became so fatigued with riding back and forth, tending to affairs and keeping vigil by the King, that he himself became ill. Louis had been stricken with a violent attack of hemorrhoids, combined with a raging fever; he had bloody flux, vomited blood, and was assaulted by intense headaches. For days he lay in helpless pain, refusing to see a doctor, making many vows to heaven. Finally he summoned the royal physician and, with or without his aid, he slowly began to recover. By May 25 he was just strong enough to ride to Chartres in order to give thanks to the Virgin in her magnificent cathedral and to show himself to the people—rumors had flown through the kingdom that he was dead. In a brief conversation, for he was still very weak, he told the Milanese ambassadors he had been so prostrated "that even for losing or recovering the realm he would not have been able to attend to any business." He made another disclosure. He had been suffering from hemorrhoids for twenty years, during which time he had ig-

nored his doctors and refused all remedies "except certain gentle bath-
ings."

The next morning, late, Louis set forth from Chartres; he had had
word that the Earl of Warwick was on the way. As he moved painfully
toward Normandy he dispatched a circular to his good towns. After announcing that he was attempting "to make final peace with the English,
our ancient enemies," in order that "our subjects might live in surety,
commerce be more safely carried on and developed by land and sea,
and that each one could prosper according to his state and vocation,"
he bluntly declared that his coming negotiations with the Earl of Warwick were especially designed to forestall the dangerous machinations of
the Count of Charolais, who, contrary to his allegiance, was seeking to
ally himself with England and marry Edward's sister Margaret.

Louis XI had reason to believe that he had a firm friend in the Earl
of Warwick. During the perilous months of 1465 the Earl had sent him
heartening messages, though the Anglo-French truce expired in the late
spring of that year; then, in January of 1466, as Louis was regaining
Normandy, he was assured by a secret envoy from Warwick that there
would be no interference from England. On the other hand, after Edward had amiably ratified the Anglo-French truce negotiated in 1466 by
Warwick and Louis's envoys,° the English King had promptly entertained friendly overtures from Brittany and in October had signed a
treaty of amity with the Count of Charolais, now alarmed into swallowing his Lancastrian pride and making an offer for the hand of Edward's
beautiful sister, Margaret of York. Early in 1467 a Burgundian and a
French embassy had done diplomatic battle in London while King Edward listened encouragingly to both parties. Yielding to the Earl of
Warwick's representations, however, he duly commissioned the Earl in
late March to treat with the King of France—and had even written a
letter in his own hand to Louis announcing the mission.

The brilliantly attractive young King of England—twenty-four
years of age, six feet four inches of affability, and one of the handsomest
men of his time—was genuinely fond of the House of Neville, which
had done so much to win him a crown. Richard's brother John had been
given the princely earldom of Northumberland; in 1466 brother George,
Chancellor of England in his twenties, was elevated to the archbishopric
of York. But if Edward IV had married Elizabeth Woodville for love, it

---

° The Earl had also been empowered to treat with the Count of Charolais, but
a confrontation at Boulogne of those two haughty personalities had quickly led to
quarrelsome exchanges and an end of negotiation.

was soon evident, from the offices and titles he showered on her numerous kindred, that he aimed at establishing the ambitious Woodvilles, entirely dependent upon him, as a counterbalance to the might of the Nevilles. Easy-going and inclined to shun unpleasantness, Edward hoped that his cousin the Earl would come to accept his determination to be the master as well as the King of England. Despite his laziness, however, Edward IV possessed a remarkable intelligence and was a born politician. He understood—as Warwick refused to understand—that however much his people grumbled against the House of Burgundy,* it was the French and the "usurping" King of France that they cursed. Edward also perceived that ardent offers from King Louis would help to drive the haughty Count of Charolais into his arms. Warwick, on the other hand, whose control of the realm depended on the gratitude of the King and who felt his greatness diminished and his deserts impugned, had come to identify his concluding a French alliance as the symbolical proof of his supremacy.

If Louis XI had not precisely gauged the mind of Edward IV, he was well aware of the Earl's view of himself. He was not so certain as his friend that the Nevilles could regain their ascendancy over King Edward. He had sent to that impassioned refugee Queen Margaret for a Lancastrian representative to join his retinue.† 2

After seeing to it that Rouen had prepared a proper reception for the visitor, King Louis impatiently moved down the Seine a few miles to the village of La Bouille—like an actor in the wings tautly summoning all his arts for a great scene. Two days later, on June 7, the embassy of the Earl of Warwick, accompanied by the returning French ambassadors, reached La Bouille by ship. It was a princely retinue that Louis XI beheld as the Earl debarked. In addition to his fellow envoys, all Neville adherents, Warwick had brought with him some two hundred attendants—trumpeters, heralds, ushers and grooms, household officers, knights and squires, an honorific guard of archers. After Warwick and his men had been royally feasted, they went on to Rouen by water, Louis following a little later on horse in order not to infringe upon the

* Though the Low Countries were England's best customer, the English had not forgiven Philip the Good for deserting them in 1435 to make peace with France and, more lately, for prohibiting the importation of finished English cloth; and they knew that the Count of Charolais was harboring the refugee Lancastrian Dukes of Somerset and Exeter.

† The fallen Queen, vengeance her only thought, was dwelling with her son and a threadbare little court in her father's Duchy of Bar; dimwitted Henry VI, captured in 1465 while wandering almost unattended in northern England, was now a prisoner in the Tower of London.

special welcome the city had prepared for his friend. At the St. Eloi
wharf the Earl of Warwick was grandly received by the chief citizens of
Rouen and the assembled clergy of the city. In a blaze of tapers and
banners and crosses he was escorted to the Cathedral of Our Lady,
where he made an offering, and was then conducted to the lodgings
which had been prepared for him in the Franciscan convent.

For the next eight days King Louis swathed Richard Neville in all
the splendors that his court could devise. He had brought his Queen
and two small daughters to Rouen to grace the entertainments for the
Earl. The usher who conducted Warwick to the royal festivities was a
Prince of the Blood, the Duke of Bourbon. Louis presented his guest
with a cup of gold crusted with gems. Bourbon gave him a fine diamond. The members of the English embassy not only received pieces of
plate and gold coins minted specially for the occasion, but the King invited them to take what they liked from the famous textile shops of the
city; and the envoys hastened to enrich their wardrobes with silks and
satins. It was good business as well as diplomacy: they thus became
walking advertisements for the splendid wares of France that, Louis
hoped, would soon be attracting English merchants across the Channel.

The royal honors paid Richard Neville and the sessions of the
French and English negotiators provided a façade behind which King
Louis daily made his way along a gallery that connected his quarters
with the Franciscan friary where Warwick lodged. There he closeted
himself with his guest—fortunately the Earl spoke French—so that the
two friends could confer without the encumbrance of formalities or the
fear of eavesdroppers. When Louis ventured to suggest that Richard
might better maintain his hold upon England by restoring the House of
Lancaster to the throne, the Earl quickly made it clear that he, creator
and custodian of the Yorkist triumph, was fully capable of handling
King Edward. Otherwise, all was harmony. What with Richard's pride
so expertly salved by Louis's ministrations and Louis's incorrigible exuberance spurred by Richard's optimism, the two of them worked out an
agreement that went far beyond a mere treaty of peace. In return for a
durable truce and for a joint attack upon Burgundy, the King of France
offered a yearly subsidy of 4,000 marks (£2,666 or about 13,000 crowns),
the spoils of the Low Countries to be shared; entirely at his expense, he
would provide Margaret of York with a fitting bridegroom; he would
grant English merchants greater privileges and greater opportunities
than his own traders enjoyed.*

* Only the English annalist William of Worcester and the French chronicler
Jean de Waurin record these terms, but there is no reason to doubt their general ac-

The King had employed other persuasions besides the spell of personality to fire Warwick's imagination. Once the Duke of Burgundy was eliminated, why should not Richard Neville become a prince in his own right, the ruler, say, of Holland and Zeeland?

The King and the Earl came to the conclusion that, instead of Warwick's signing the treaty and bearing it back for Edward IV's ratification, the French ambassadors should return with him in order to negotiate the terms. If it was Warwick's idea, his friend carefully avoided any indication that King Edward's mentor appeared to be slightly uncertain of his power over King Edward. Louis knew that, come what may, he had won the Earl.

The English embassy, accompanied by the French, departed from Rouen on June 16, perhaps in some haste. It may be that unpleasant tidings had come to them from across the Channel or that word had arrived of the imminent death of Philip the Good. A few days later the French court learned that Philip had expired at Bruges on June 15; Louis's and Warwick's mortal enemy Charles now commanded all the resources of the Burgundian state. The King published to the realm the mission of his ambassadors.

iii

BEFORE THE END OF August (1467) Louis XI learned, first from dispatches and then from his envoys themselves, that he had again overreached himself in his hopes of England. During Warwick's absence Edward IV had made another move, a clumsy maneuver like his marriage announcement but this one of unmistakable significance. The Earl and the French embassy were greeted by the news that the King of England had abruptly dismissed George Neville from the chancellorship; London was still buzzing with talk of the great joust held at Smithfield between Antoine, the Grand Bastard of Burgundy, and Anthony Woodville, Lord Scales, eldest brother of the Queen, over which Edward IV had presided in state; the French envoys were received by Edward with chilly formality and, despite Warwick's efforts, accomplished nothing. Before the French quitted England's shore King Edward had renewed his alliance with Burgundy and signed an agreement for the marriage of Charles, now Duke, and Margaret of York. The Earl of Warwick, after fiercely assuring Louis's envoys that, one way or another, he intended to reassert

---

curacy. To soothe English sensibilities the truce was couched in the form of an arbitration scheme—the Pope to decide, within four years, the rightful ownership of the Duchies of Guienne and Normandy; the papacy could easily be encouraged to prolong its deliberations for a century.

his mastery of the realm, had ridden off to his Yorkshire strongholds.

At the same time, the edifice of royal authority which King Louis had been toilsomely rebuilding was riven by perilous fissures. He learned that his feodality—Armagnac, Nemours, Alençon, Brittany, backed by Savoy and Burgundy—were secretly conspiring to make Louis's brother Charles their puppet-King and divide up the realm.[3] Only after tortuous and humiliating negotiations did he procure brief truces with the Dukes of Burgundy and Brittany. The following April (1468) in an attempt to rally public opinion the King convoked the Three Estates of France—the only time this assembly was to meet during his reign—but their expressions of loyalty and general condemnation of feudatories who made alliances with England provided small comfort. In May, the Anglo-French truce having expired, Edward IV's Chancellor announced to Parliament that their sovereign had secured "amity and confederation" with the two "mightiest princes that holden of the crown of France," the Dukes of Brittany and Burgundy, and intended to overthrow his "great rebel and adversary Louis, usurpant King of the same." The Commons responded by voting Edward IV a generous war subsidy.

Louis XI managed to prolong his truces with Brittany and Burgundy until July 15 (1468).

These environing perils but served to stimulate the King's exploration of his resources, tangible and intangible. Assisted secretly by the Earl of Warwick, he sought to keep Edward IV occupied at home; he disposed his diplomacy and his armies to exploit any carelessness on the part of his princely foes; and he was working for an opportunity to exercise his powers in person upon the mind of Charles of Burgundy.

In England, partisans of Warwick spread unrest and played on anti-Burgundian feeling. A plot among London artisans to cut the thumbs, or throats, of the Flemish weavers of Southwark was discovered only at the last minute. Warwick himself proved to be even more helpful. When in July (1468) news reached London that the King of Denmark, ally of the Hanseatic League, had seized four English ships, the Earl and his adherents in the royal council, backed by his merchant friends, forced Edward IV into a costly sea war with the powerful Easterlings. Louis XI encouraged Queen Margaret to infiltrate agents into England; in June a flurry of arrests in the English capital was precipitated by fears of a Lancastrian conspiracy. The following month Jasper Tudor, Henry VI's half brother, provided by Louis with a few ships and some money, caused further panic by landing in Wales and burning Denbigh. The King of France would have little to fear from the English in 1468 and 1469.

Then, the overconfidence of brother Charles and Francis II opened a crack in the Breton-Burgundian alliance which Louis XI was fully prepared to take advantage of. The Duke of Burgundy grudgingly agreed to extend the truce, including his allies, from July 15 to August 1. Having finally married, "against his heart and nature," the Yorkist princess on July 3, he was enmeshed in the glittering jousts and festivals staged at Bruges—such a spectacle, declared young John Paston, a member of Margaret of York's retinue, as had not been viewed since the days of Camelot. July 15 passed, without the Duke of Brittany's bothering to make notification of his inclusion in the prolongation of the truce.

The following day, three French armies thrust against Brittany. Yelling in vain for help from Edward IV and Duke Charles, Louis's brother and Francis II fell into a panic of fears and rage as the royal squadrons advanced with the speed Louis had counted on. The Duke of Burgundy in high dudgeon ordered his troops to assemble for battle in Picardy; but in response to this news relayed by the Count of St. Pol and the Archbishop of Lyons, the King of France imperturbably ordered his envoys to continue negotiations with Burgundy.

On September 15, Louis received word that his brother and the Duke of Brittany, their forces broken, had accepted a settlement, the Treaty of Ancenis of September 10, by the terms of which his enemies were at last sundered. Swearing to obey the King "for and against all," Francis II renounced his alliances with England and with Burgundy, and brother Charles renounced his claim upon Normandy. While the Duke of Brittany and the Count of St. Pol were deciding on the proper *apanage* for Charles, he was to be paid sixty thousand livres a year. Brother Charles sent word that his and Francis II's going astray had been entirely due to the machinations of the Duke of Burgundy.

When Brittany Herald brought news to the Burgundian camp of the Treaty of Ancenis, along with a brusque renunciation by Francis and Charles of their sworn alliance, the Duke of Burgundy fell into such a rage that "the poor herald was in great danger." It was all a forgery, the Duke persisted in declaring—until the Count of St. Pol appeared with confirmation of the herald's mission. Still in a fury, the Duke fulminated about "low deals made under a cart and other filthy tricks," and belligerently reviewed his troops. The King of France, to the astonishment of his commanders and councilors, persisted in negotiations. Their object was to secure a personal interview with Duke Charles.

He had conceived the idea early in 1468. By midsummer he was bombarding the Count of St. Pol with instructions for persuading the Duke to accede to a meeting. Even after he had loosed his forces upon Brittany, he kept the Constable riding back and forth between the Burgundian battle laager near Péronne and his own headquarters at Compiègne, while his other envoy, the Archbishop of Lyons, talked and talked until the Duke was sick of him. Ignoring harsh rebuffs, the King went on inventing ways to impress upon Charles of Burgundy his ardent wish for an interview. It had become an *idée fixe*, the conviction that, if they were face to face, he could again mold Charles to his will. An alteration in the Duke of Burgundy he apparently minimized or insisted upon ignoring.

That alteration had begun to work on the morning after the battle of Montlhéry. When Charles found himself in possession of the field and thus able to claim a victory, his dark and tortuous being was flooded with an intoxicating ichor. Hitherto, Commynes reveals, he had shown no interest in warfare; now he suddenly saw himself as a triumphant commander, one of the Great Captains of history; and his rigorous nature clinched that vision for its own.

It was the people of Liège who first experienced the heat of his new passion for camps and battles, and it was this same people whose links with France had embittered and were continuing to exacerbate the relations between the Duke and Louis XI.

The city-state of Liège, coveted by its neighbor the Duke of Burgundy, had served both Charles VII and Louis XI as a threat to the Burgundian flank. It was nominally ruled by a prince-bishop, the present incumbent being Louis of Bourbon, brother of the Duke of Bourbon and cousin to Duke Charles, an amiable young man who lacked both religious and administrative talents. He and his supporter, the Duke of Burgundy, were perpetually at odds with this community of hardy miners and metal workers. The men of Liège fiercely cherished the hope of liberty but, lacking discipline and leadership, had increasingly given themselves over to demagogues and mob violence. Always hoping for aid from France, they recklessly provoked Burgundian ire. In the winter of 1465–66 Charles of Burgundy, the new-born warrior, had inflicted a humiliating defeat on the Liègeois; the following spring he had ravaged the town of Dinant, ally of Liège, with such fire, killing, and pillage as sent a thrill of fear through all the townsmen of Europe; and in 1467 the Duke had bloodily crushed the forces of Liège in the field, razed the walls and gates of the city, and imposed a Burgundian governor, the lord of Humbercourt, to prop his cousin the Bishop.

This disorderly and fickle commune Louis XI had unscrupulously used, fanning anti-Burgundian fires but providing no assistance. In this month of September, 1468, the Liège mob, despite the defenselessness of the city, were threatening a new rising; through a papal legate Bishop Louis was attempting to make peace with his subjects and escape the yoke of Burgundy; Duke Charles was assembling an attack force; and agents of Louis XI worked, in the shadow of the legate, to inflame both the Bishop and the people.

The Duke of Burgundy continued to act "bellicose, given to war, ferocious, vindictive, and badly disposed," ° despite the defection of the Duke of Brittany and the King's brother, and despite his precarious military situation. The French forces victorious in Brittany were now moving across Normandy toward the Burgundian western flank. The northern army commanded by the King, disposed in a line of strongly fortified towns, outnumbered the Burgundian troops gathered near Péronne. The Burgundian laager, incompetently sited by Duke Charles against the Somme River, had been so inundated with September rains that the Duke was forced to shift the huge encampment, and Burgundian soldiers were straggling all over Picardy. The King's commanders—his Grand Master of the Household, the tough old Écorcheur Antoine de Chabannes, and his Marshals—clamored for immediate attack; their troops were spoiling for a fight with "that arrogant rebel Charles, cursed traitorous Englishman that he is!"

King Louis, however, playing his lone hand, brought the Duke of Burgundy to agree to a conference of envoys on September 21. After nine days of wrangling, the Count of St. Pol and Jean Balue, now a cardinal and ambitiously injecting himself into the negotiations, returned to royal headquarters with nothing to report save the Duke's harsh demands for guaranteed possession of Picardy and almost sovereign jurisdiction over his French fiefs. This result Louis had probably counted on, as a means of demonstrating the necessity for his personal intervention.

The King's councilors, some for motives of their own, continued to preach against the interview their master so ardently pursued. The Duke of Bourbon opposed it in order that he might exert a paramount

---

° So, a little earlier, a papal legate invited by King Louis to work for peace described the Duke. The legate apparently became so frightened by Charles that he then curried favor with Louis's enemies, until the King, in disgust, packed him off to Italy.

influence on events. The Count of St. Pol, by this time as thoroughly confused in his allegiance as Louis could wish, likewise opposed the interview since it might produce a solution that omitted him. Cardinal Balue did what he could to prevent it because it could deprive him of the chance to make himself indispensable. Others had no motive but their fears for their sovereign. The Receiver of Languedoc wrote with heavy heart to a correspondent, "We are all well lodged here, and would to God the King did not go beyond here, for he is here safely at home."

The King of France—though he had at last neutralized his brother and Francis II, dissipated the English threat, and enjoyed a commanding military advantage—held to his imperious will. At the beginning of October he sent word to the indefatigable Balue, now ingratiating himself with the Duke of Burgundy, "Cardinal, do nothing to prevent the interview for I mean to have it." The King wrote the plainest French in all France, and Balue instantly became a partisan of the encounter. Louis XI now offered to pay 100,000 crowns for Charles's expenses, 50,000 of which, in cash, he forwarded to his envoys.

The much-harassed Duke of Burgundy hesitated. On October 6 he grimly reminded Cardinal Balue that he was probably going to have to chastise the incorrigible Liègeois, who, he suspected, were being egged on by royal agents; and under such circumstances his meeting with the King could do more harm than good. Two days later, however, with his own hand he wrote out an ample guarantee of security for the King, signing it simply, "Your very humble and very obedient subject, Charles."

Louis received the precious document the same day, October 8. He immediately appointed Antoine de Chabannes, Count of Dammartin, the Grand Master, as his lieutenant in the Marches of Picardy, and sent Duke Charles a request for a Burgundian escort to meet him on the road next day. That evening, "as if going hunting"—for many of his court knew nothing of his resolve—he rode from Noyon to the Constable's castle of Ham, and there spent the night.

Why was Louis going to Péronne, against considerations of statecraft, of military tactics, of certain risk measured against uncertain gain, against the dictates of elementary safety and subtle calculation alike, contrary to the advice of his councilors, his lords, and his commanders? The best conjecture that Panigarola could afterward report was that "the reason was known to the King alone." Perhaps not entirely to him.

Doubtless the hunter in the King had been spurred by the difficulties of the long chase; and this elusive game he had been pursuing since May. The larger the obstacles, the more unlikely the profit, the greater the danger—the keener burned his ardor. That which all his world, for reasons good or bad, sought to dissuade him from, seemed but more attractive in his eyes. Doubtless too he was stimulated by previous success: what his enchanter's arts had been able to accomplish for him with Charles of Burgundy at the siege of Paris those arts could do for him again: who knew better than he how to play upon the mind that he had studied for more than a decade? If the actor itched to exercise his craft, the statesman, too, could calculate that a military victory might well do no more than open a long and destructive war and drive Duke Francis and his brother back into Burgundian arms, and that, methods of diplomacy having failed, there remained only a personal encounter as a means of securing his ends. And then perhaps, at bottom, Louis insisted on going to the Duke of Burgundy because he assumed responsibility for the Kingdom of France. The mission, like the power, was his.

The next morning he dismissed his guard and all his train except for some fifty lords and attendants. With this scanty retinue, which on his orders wore no armor and bore no weapons, Louis set forth on the road. It could not have been a gay cavalcade. Not a man jack of them had any relish for the enterprise. Except Louis. He was in his element. Thus leaving behind all the King's horses and all the King's men, the King of France rode jauntily to Péronne to put himself in the hands of his mightiest enemy.

iv

IT WAS A mixed company that rode with the King across the Picard country on this willful enterprise: a small band of household attendants and secretaries, including his barber Olivier le Daim, indispensable for overseeing the luggage, and his Italian secretary, Alberto Magalotti; a half-dozen councilors, among them Cardinal Balue; and an array of great lords headed by the Duke of Burgundy's cousin the Duke of Bourbon, and the Duke of Burgundy's friend the Count of St. Pol. A few minutes after noon, about a mile from Péronne, Louis and his cavalcade came upon a glittering Burgundian train of some two hundred horse— "knights and squires in splendid array," a dozen pages in cloth of gold preceding the Duke of Burgundy, who was accompanied by his bastard brother, Antoine, in a cloak of cloth of gold that trailed the ground. As Louis, apparently in simple hunting garb, rode up, Duke Charles bared his head and bowed low. Louis clapped him in a long embrace, then spoke a few words of greeting to the Duke's party and again embraced the Duke. As the two moved off, horse to horse, Louis placed his hand on the Duke's shoulder. He had jests ready to amuse his hosts: "all in laughing" they made their way to the walled town of Péronne and entered through the St. Nicholas gate.

In a moment King Louis was dismounting to take up his abode in the handsome dwelling of the Receiver of Péronne near the gate. The Duke, who was lodged elsewhere, rode on. Nearby stood the little ramshackle castle of Péronne, not fit for royal quarters since its keep was in ruins and but few chambers remained habitable. As the King was entering his lodgings, a clatter and jangle of armed men announced the defiling of a cavalcade through the St. Nicholas gate. Louis turned—and beheld a sight that shook his nerve. There, wearing the Burgundian cross of St. Andrew, rode as bitter a group of Louis's ill-wishers as could be found: his Savoyard brother-in-law, Philip of Bresse, adept at troublemaking; * Antoine, lord du Lau, his traitorous favorite whom he had cast into prison, from which, months before, du Lau had escaped; Poncet de Rivière, a royal captain cashiered for deserting the King's cause during the War of the Public Weal; the lord d'Urfé, a Breton enemy. They were riding under the banner of the Marshal of Burgundy, another enemy.

Philip of Bresse, catching sight of the King, made a gesture of doing reverence. Louis abruptly entered the house. He made no attempt to conceal his agitation from his intimates. Peering through a window, he could see the newcomers take up quarters in the castle of Péronne. Hastily he sent word to the Duke of Burgundy that because of the presence of these enemies he wished the safety of those walls for his own residence. Duke Charles promptly replied that he was happy to comply with his guest's wish, this accompanied by assurances that the King had nothing to fear. Louis learned that the arrivals commanded a force from the County and Duchy of Burgundy, which Charles was sending against the Liègeois. Louis XI sat down to a troubled dinner. For all the Duke's assurances, the unexpected appearance of Philip of Bresse and company

---

* In 1464 Philip of Bresse, after murdering the Chancellor of Savoy, Louis's friend Iacomo di Valperga, and throwing the Duchy into turmoil, had been arrested, on coming into France, by a royal officer, although he bore a safe-conduct. At the end of the War of the Public Weal the King not only released him but sought to win his loyalty by making him Governor of Guienne and commander of one hundred lances; but like his other brothers Philip was drawn to the martial and resplendent Duke of Burgundy, deserted the King's cause, and was elected a member of the Order of the Golden Fleece.

was a bad omen, and Louis was not one to disregard omens. In the afternoon, however, the castle was vacated. About six in the evening the King and a small group of his household took up residence there.

Next day began Louis's campaign to bend once more the Duke of Burgundy to his ends. Negotiations were carried on secretly and in a maze of conferences, comings and goings, interchanges of messages. At times, Louis talked with the Duke alone; it was on these colloquies that he founded his hope of success. At times these meetings were enlarged to a foursome: Jean Balue was summoned to the King's side and to the Duke's came a favorite of long standing, Guillaume Bische—one of the Burgundians who had proved serviceable to Louis during the siege of Paris (1465). Meanwhile royal and ducal councilors pursued formal talks. In public as in private Louis XI zealously tended the Duke's humor, a difficult plant from which he was striving to elicit blossom. During the morning of the 10th, when the King got word of his host's ceremonious approach, he issued from the castle to greet Charles in the street. But he had difficulty keeping his countenance when he discovered that the Duke—maliciously? tactlessly? optimistically?—brought with him Philip of Bresse. Nonetheless Louis embraced Charles with what enthusiasm he could muster, but Charles then insisted on bringing Philip forward to be presented to the King. Unable to conceal his irritation, Louis at first made a pretense of not knowing Philip in order to remark, with barbed irony, "that he had not recognized his brother-in-law of Savoy, who seemed to him much changed." A day or two later Louis presented the Duke of Burgundy with two horses, recently brought to him as a gift from the Duke of Milan. One of the horses had gone lame during its long journey, but the King covered the defect in fine style by making up a story that the steed had been injured in a feat of arms while being ridden by the great Italian condottiere Roberto of Sanseverino. It was, Louis assured Charles, a horse to do miracles.

By this time Louis himself was in a mood for a miracle. The efforts of his councilors, the good words put in by his Burgundian friends, all his own repertory of charm and persuasion had accomplished nothing. It appears that the King of France had come prepared to make an astonishing sacrifice to Burgundy—at least for the time being—in order to gain a free hand in the rest of his realm without fear of English invasion: he would grant the exorbitant demands the Duke's envoys had put forward in the conference two weeks before, provided that Charles renounced the Yorkist alliance and the tie with Brittany and promised to serve him "for and against all." The Duke of Burgundy, however, not only returned stony refusals; he added a fresh proposition. Since the King's brother in the Treaty of Ancenis had made a sworn renunciation of the Duchy of Normandy, the Duke would recognize this if young Charles was given the County of Champagne, a territory which, Louis needed no telling, bordered Burgundian domains.

King Louis sought to evade this highhanded addendum, continued to ply all his arts, reiterated reminders to the Duke that, after all, the King's brother and Francis II had renounced *him*. By October 12 Louis had secured only three concessions, two of them trifling: though the Duke of Burgundy refused to give up his pact with the English, he undertook never to aid them to invade France; settlement of the *apanage* would not be included in the treaty; the Duke of Brittany and the King's brother would not be named in the clause by which the Duke of Burgundy excepted his allies in promising to serve the King. At this point Louis permitted the treaty and the separate agreement giving Champagne to Charles to be drawn up.

Then, just after he had failed in yet another effort to alter the Duke's mind, there began to arrive in Péronne tidings that shattered the negotiations. Brought by galloping horsemen, each with a different story, these tidings threw the Duke of Burgundy into a violent rage.

A force from Liège had, on the day Louis entered Péronne (October 9), marched to nearby Tongres, where the Bishop of Liège and the Burgundian Governor, the lord of Humbercourt, were quartered, had laid violent hands upon the pair, and haled them to Liège as prisoners the next morning. Some who brought the news declared that the Bishop's retinue had been massacred and the Bishop and Humbercourt murdered; some, that many had been killed but the Bishop and Humbercourt were safe in captivity in Liège. According to one report, a number of episcopal attendants were slain on the homeward journey, including a hated canon whom the Liègeois cut into several pieces that they playfully tossed at each other's heads. Many hours passed before it was finally learned that the Bishop was being well treated and that Humbercourt had been released.

With Péronne in an uproar, it was not long before Louis XI heard the news—including a report that two royal emissaries had been identified among the Liègeois. Soon the King learned that the gates of the town had been closed by ducal order. Charles of Burgundy gave out that a box of jewels had been lost; but Louis had only to look from a window to see Burgundian archers now guarding the castle. He learned too that the enraged Duke had instantly sworn revenge on Liège—"not a house would remain standing nor a cock or hen be left alive to sing, but all would be put to fire and sword!" Charles was also declaring that he had never wanted the King to come to Péronne, that the King's coming was all a plot to betray him—these utterances broken by threats of vengeance.

Instantly Louis went into action. He sent eloquent assurances to his host that, outraged by the actions of the Liègeois, he would be happy to march with the Duke in order to chastise the city. He then combed his mind for the information stored there about the ducal councilors, the men most likely, for whatever motive, to be of good will toward him. Summoning Cardinal Balue, he took fifteen thousand crowns from his coffers and told Balue to discreetly distribute sums to the chivalrous Bastard of Burgundy, Guillaume Bische, the clever Archdeacon Ferry de Clugny, and others who might prove useful.*

The King and his intimates "made very piteous cheer." None understood better than Louis the violent temper of the Duke, the dark and dangerous corners of his mind. It would not add to Louis' comfort to know—as, being a student of history, he probably did—that a Count of Vermandois had shut up one of Louis's predecessors, Charles the Simple, in the castle of Péronne until that King died. As he paced his small chamber, all his mercurial nature manifested in fearful agitation, he kept thinking of the quartet of his ill-wishers now at Péronne who might be able, with a word, to explode the unstable compound of the Duke's emotions. He was receiving secret reports of terrible seesawings in the ducal council.

The majority of the Burgundian advisers, including Antoine the Bastard and some other members of the Toison d'Or, spoke of the dishonor to the Duke if he broke his safe-conduct, and urged that the advantageous peace treaty, now drawn up, be accepted. More hotheaded councilors demanded that the King be at once taken into captivity and disposed of. Still others proposed that their master seize the opportunity by sending for the King's brother and forcing the King to sign a treaty "of great benefit to all the princes of France," the King henceforth to be kept in custody. This opinion appealed to Duke Charles, and a messenger stood booted and spurred to depart, awaiting only letters. After fur-

---

* Some time later, Louis learned that Balue had pocketed half the crowns: two thousand had gone to the Bastard, one or two thousand to Bische, five hundred to de Clugny; three thousand only were returned to the King. It is not known whether any money went to that favorite of the Duke who, as will shortly appear, proved most serviceable.

ther discussions, however, those who held to honoring the safe-conduct and signing the peace treaty appeared to prevail upon the angry, irresolute Charles, torn between a blood impulse to make away with the King he hated and a desire to hold high the standard of his honor without losing his revenge. The news of Liège's taking arms had not come as a surprise and by this time he knew that the Bishop and Humbercourt were safe. He had already dispatched the forces of the Marshal of Burgundy toward the city. His rage against Louis stemmed, partly at least, from inchoate feeling that the King had planned all this and somehow meant to trick him. Frustration and suspicion fanned his fires.

By this time Louis was realizing that to accompany the Duke on a campaign against Liège would not only be profoundly humiliating but could be extremely dangerous. When his secret intelligence from the Burgundian court indicated that the worst proposals had been discarded, he repented so much of his hasty offer that he decided to try to wriggle out of it. Neither he nor his advisers could think of a better expedient than hostages. The Constable, the Duke of Bourbon, and Bourbon's brother Charles, Archbishop of Lyons, all expressed a hearty willingness to serve, which doubtless cost them a good deal of heartburning. Louis sent an offer to the Duke: he would sign the treaty, and then, leaving as hostages the best blood of his retinue, he would briefly go to Compiègne in order to arrange measures against the Liègeois.*

The offer was a miscalculation. The Duke's angers and suspicions flared up. Fiercely he declared to his council that the King had promised to go in person with him to conquer Liège and that he would have no scruple of conscience about forcing him to keep that promise. Once again the majority urged him to remember his safe-conduct and be content with the treaty. The Duke had but one reply: "He has promised me and he will have to make it good to me!"

Such was the parlous situation of King Louis on the evening of Thursday, October 13, a situation rendered no easier by the realization that he had brought it about himself. After supper he dispatched a crimson jacket and a silver buttonhook to the Duke of Burgundy, no doubt with the most amicable message he could devise. His household informed him that the Burgundian guard at his gate had been increased. Courtiers were so terrified that none dared speak to their master except in a loud voice, lest the suspicions of a Burgundian informer be aroused. "The King had great fear of being forcibly incarcerated and so had all

* Commynes, much later, commented: "In truth, I think he would have left them there and not come back."

the company." That night Louis was unable to sleep, feverishly turning over in his mind every scrap of information that might be useful, every device that could possibly serve, every role that might extricate him from peril. At one moment he even donned a disguise in order to attempt escape, then thought better of it.

Had he forgotten, as he so eagerly rushed into the Duke's arms, that two of his envoys were even then stirring up the Liègeois? Commynes so took it for granted. Had a royal order for those emissaries to depart been undelivered or ignored? The only surviving evidence is the events themselves. It may be that somewhere in the folds of the unconscious he had allowed himself to forget. Though openly showing his fear to those in his chamber, unkingly in his alterations of voice and countenance, clutching for expedients and reassurances, he was perhaps—again somewhere in his unconscious—never happier. With the water once more up to his neck, he had only his wits to see him through. Sometime during this terrible day, the 13th, Louis wrote to the Duke of Milan, "We are about to conclude a good peace here." By that time it was somewhat doubtful even if he would be alive the next day.

And then, early in the morning of October 14, the King who lived by intelligence touched minds, across the perils of Péronne, with a man who respected intelligence above all else.

The Duke of Burgundy too had spent a sleepless night, not even undressing but pacing his chamber except once or twice when he threw himself for a few moment onto his couch. By dawn he was uttering black menaces and appeared ready to take some irrevocable step. A chamberlain of the Duke's, who, though still in his early twenties, had won high place as a counselor, had walked up and down that night with his master, doing what he could to assuage Charles's wrath and turn him from violent thoughts. Now, as day lengthened, he finally brought the Duke to saying that, if the King would sign a treaty of peace and go with him to Liège, he would be satisfied. The counselor was Philippe de Commynes, the lord of Renescure.

Somehow he got off a message to the King, perhaps not his first.

It was one of the most important pieces of information Louis ever received. After disclosing the Duke of Burgundy's state of mind, the message concluded tersely: if the King accepted the Duke's two conditions no evil would come to him, but if he refused, "he would put himself in the greatest peril that could possibly come to him."

The inner ear of King Louis, "the most suspicious man alive," instantly detected the true ring of his informant's mettle. Unerringly he followed Commynes's cue. Emissaries of the Duke arrived to signify their master's demands and their master's intentions of confronting the King if he were of a mind to receive such a visit. Louis indicated his joy at the prospect. By mid-morning Charles, Duke of Burgundy, was making his entrance into the modest royal chamber. At first glance the King could see that the Duke was barely in control of himself. He managed to make a due obeisance; but when he spoke, his voice trembled with passion, and his looks, his gestures were those of a man on fire within.

Prepared though he was, Louis could not suppress his anxiety at the spectacle. "My brother, am I not safe in your house and in your lands?"

"My lord, yes!" the Duke answered brusquely, adding conventional phrases of assurance. But Louis's timorous greeting had touched off the powder train—a monstrous question from a man who, Charles felt darkly, was somehow doing him devious wrong. He burst out in savage accusations: the King had come to Péronne only to deceive him—to distract him while the Liègeois were stirred up—and as soon as he set out for Liège the royal army were ready to fall upon his rear—!

The sudden danger acted like a tonic on Louis. Calmly, succinctly, he pointed out that these were manifest lies, that to have plotted thus was obviously contrary to his honor, his interest, his safety.

Charles, regaining control, asked abruptly if the King was willing to swear to the treaty, already drawn up and agreed upon.

Louis said, "Yes."

And would the King, Charles grimly went on, accompany him to Liège in order to avenge the treachery of that city, treachery for which the King's coming to Péronne was in one way or another responsible? Perhaps His Majesty needed to be reminded, he added sarcastically, that Louis of Bourbon, Bishop of Liège, was, after all, of the blood royal, a close relative.

Louis replied that if but the peace was sworn, which he desired, he was happy to accompany his brother to Liège and to bring with him such number of troops, large or small, as Charles wished.

That was well, the Duke told him, somewhat mollified, perhaps even a little uneasy. He was willing, he said, to be the King's servant and serve him well and the King would also do *his* duty and, by St. George, he'd expect from him what he'd promised about going to Liège!

Louis quietly repeated that he was ready to set forth on the expedition. He then motioned to his attendants. From the royal coffers were brought copies of the treaty and of the agreement concerning the *apanage* for Louis's brother, and a holy object, a cross containing a sliver from the True Cross, once worn by Charlemagne and now called the Cross of Victory.

Louis and Charles faced each other, prelates and lords gathered at their shoulders. Between them stood Cardinal Balue holding Charlemagne's cross above the documents. It was first the turn of Charles to swear homage—which he had hitherto not done—as Duke of Burgundy. As the Duke got to his knees and put hand on the cross, the storm within him rumbled. "I will swear," he kept muttering, "I will swear, but what has been promised me had better be performed."

The homage given, Louis then put his hand to the cross also and the King and the Duke swore to uphold the treaty and to aid and defend one another as therein specified. The Duke then stalked off to hear Mass. Louis, who had performed his devotions hours before, went to his dinner. Soon the bells in all the churches of Péronne were pealing and priests were chanting Te Deum. Later in the day, it was agreed that the King could summon his Scots guard and four hundred lances under St. Pol to accompany him to Liège. That same afternoon he cheerfully announced by letter to his good towns that the Duke of Burgundy and he had "sworn a final peace on the True Cross." Since the Duke requested him to join a Burgundian expedition against the Liègeois, who had made captive their Bishop, he had agreed to do so but hoped to return shortly. He would take with him a detachment of the standing army under command of the Constable. The King dispatched the same letter to Antoine de Chabannes, now commanding the royal forces facing the Burgundians, with the added injunction that he should dismiss the nobles of the feudal levy and all the franc archers and "see that they depart with the least possible injury to the poor people of the countryside and appoint men to conduct them through each *baillage* and *seneschausée* so that they cause no trouble."

There was even a moment of comedy. When Louis was in private with only two squires, the barber, and a secretary, Jean De Reilhac, the latter disclosed that faithful Jean Bourré, on learning that His Majesty was going to Liège, had sent him a most perplexed and anxious letter. If needed, Bourré would not fail the King, should he die for it, but he knew that if he came he would be a dead man. Therefore, if it was the King's good pleasure that Bourré await him at Meaux or Paris . . .

Louis replied, with a straight face: Yes, he well perceived that, if summoned, Bourré would come, were it to the ends of the earth—but would die of fear on the road. Therefore Bourré should indeed await him at Meaux.

What resolves Louis XI made for the future before he retired that night he apparently kept to himself; but the services of that sagacious young man Philippe de Commynes were indelibly printed in his memory. Four years later, the King frankly recorded in a deed of gift how "in our extreme need, for the deliverance of our person . . . our councilor and chamberlain, without fear of the danger that could come to him, informed us of all he could for our welfare and so employed himself that by his means and aid we escaped. . . ."

The genie had made a mess of it, but he was again out of the jar—almost.

v

UNDER DARK SKIES, through rain and mud, the King of France rode at the side of Charles of Burgundy in the midst of a Burgundian army moving slowly toward Liège. Meanwhile, the lord of Humbercourt had arrived, along with the other victim of rumor, the Bishop of Liège, who was released by his captors to seek terms of surrender from the Duke. Charles would hear of no terms; nor would he allow the Bishop to return, though he had sworn to do so and begged to be allowed to keep his oath. As delicately as possible the King sought to second the Bishop's efforts for peace, but when the Duke began thundering he quickly averred that "whatever my good brother of Burgundy wishes is what I wish." The Duke was going to have his vengeance. It was Louis's daily, hourly care to see that he remained excluded from it.

Charles, with a good deal of what passion had demanded—a treaty that gave him everything he could think of, and a King haled as a prisoner at his heels—was nonetheless uneasily beginning to perceive that all was not quite well, that the King's ignominy somehow rubbed off on him, that perpetrating indignities was hardly a way of guaranteeing a treaty. He also feared that somehow—such was his feeling about the subtlety of Louis of Valois—the King might have *willed* all this for arcane ends of his own still to be disclosed. Sensitive to these flickerings of the Duke's temper, Louis imperturbably enacted the roles of companion-in-arms and King-at-his-ease. At moments Charles even pressed him to leave the expedition. The King always replied, "I will never depart till you have had Liège." To assuage his host's suspicions he made Balue and his other councilors stay a day's journey off; and, sending ahead his Scots guard and St. Pol's lances, he remained almost alone in the company of the Duke and his guards. Like the Duke, he refused to unarm till Liège was won.

At Namur he wrote a letter of relief and appreciation to Antoine de Chabannes. The tough old Count of Dammartin had at first refused to obey the King's command of October 14 to dismiss his troops, fearing his master might be a prisoner. He then sent word, however, that in response to further messages he had obeyed the King's orders. "You may be sure," Louis wrote to him, "that I am not going on this Liège expedition because of any constraint. . . . My lord the Grand Master, my friend, you have indeed showed me that you love me and have done me the greatest pleasure and service that you could do; for the Duke of Burgundy's people would have believed that I wanted to deceive them and your people would have believed that I'd been made a prisoner; so that as a result of mistrust on both sides I would have been lost. . . . Be sure that the day after Liège is reduced I will depart, for my lord of Burgundy is more eager for me to return than I am. François Aunay [the bearer] will tell you the good cheer we're making."

Louis had some nervous moments in the early hours of October 27 when rumors came flying that the advance guard led by the Marshal of Burgundy had been severely mauled by the Liègeois; but soon the Duke himself arrived to report that, in fact, the enemy sally had been bloodily repulsed and that the forces of the Marshal now stood before two of Liège's ruined gates. "The King was very joyous that all was well, for the contrary could have been bad for him." By nightfall of the 27th the King and the Duke had encamped their army in the suburbs of the city, facing a third gate. The walls were everywhere broken down and there was not even a ditch to impede attackers. It was agreed that the forces of the Marshal and of the Duke would attack Liège simultaneously.[4]

At 8 a.m., Sunday, October 30, a bombard sounded the signal for the assault. Ducal battle flags approached the gate, followed by the Duke and the King, accompanied by their guards and household men of arms. Wearing the Cross of St. Andrew and shouting, "Vive Burgone!" Louis XI passed through the gate.

On all three sides the Burgundians thrust into Liège without meeting resistance. Most of the citizens had already fled the city. As soon as Louis perceived that the day was won, he slowed his pace to allow the warlike Duke of Burgundy to taste alone his vengeful triumph. In a little while the Duke turned back and escorted the King to the episcopal palace, then headed for St. Lambert's, the chief church of the city, in which some Liègeois had sought to barricade themselves. King Louis sat himself down to dinner, taking care to laud his host's martial accomplishments. When the victor himself arrived a little later, Louis found even higher praise for his generalship. Charles glowed, became almost genial. But his revenge was still unslaked. Only a few hundred Liègeois had been killed in the attack. Some hundreds of others were murdered during the pillaging or drowned in the river. The Duke swore to burn the whole city to the ground, except the churches, and lay waste the country for miles around. Louis ventured to suggest that he not destroy a town which had "so many noble edifices." Charles's face darkened. Abruptly he answered that there was no need to say anything—he was determined to see Liège in total ruins, like Dinant.

Louis at once subsided. Already he had begun the most delicate operation of the adventure, extricating himself from the Burgundians without shaking the vials of Charles's unstable temper. Before the day closed he wrote confidently to the Count of Foix in Paris, after reporting the taking of the city, "Because I know that you have great desire for me to return, I certify to you that Tuesday morning next [November 1] I will leave here and will not cease to ride, making no halts, until I am there." The following day Louis pursued his campaign for departure, working on those of the Duke's intimates that he counted his friends and speaking to Charles with a careful lack of urgency in his voice. If the Duke had a further mission for him, he would spare no pains to accomplish it. But, if there was nothing for him to do, it was time that he was on his way to his capital to see to the registration of the Treaty of Péronne in the Parlement. Such was the custom of France, he reminded Charles. Without the registration the treaty would be regarded as invalid. Of course, the King's personal word counted for a great deal in such matters—a hint that the French would never accept the treaty unless the King, at his liberty, insisted on it.

Charles grumbled a little. Louis kept on talking. The Duke still grumbled, murmured this-and-that, hesitated uncomfortably, but in the end, finding nothing else to do, agreed to the King's departure. Then Charles's uneasiness took another form. He insisted that the Treaty of Péronne, a long document, be read in its entirety to the King, so that, if he wished, he could strike out or add any article he pleased—this accompanied by a muttered half apology for having brought his sovereign to Liège. Louis assured his host that he had no desire to alter a word of the treaty; his only wish was to register in the Parlement everything he had sworn at Péronne.

But Louis discovered that the frustrated Duke could not leave it alone. In that case, said Charles, he himself had something to add. He wanted the King's consent to an article restoring to my lord du Lau,

Poncet de Rivière, and the lord d'Urfé whatever lands they had been deprived of. Even at such a moment, this was too much for Louis. He answered at once that he would agree, provided that a like article was inserted for the Count of Nevers and the brothers de Croy (whose estates Charles had confiscated). The Duke of Burgundy fell silent.

The King was free to go.

But it was November 2 before he left Liège, the Duke of Burgundy still with him. They spent the night in a village some miles from Namur. The Duke protested that he must honor his sovereign by accompanying him to the borders of his dominions. Louis successfully insisted, however, that his good brother of Burgundy had already honored him more than sufficiently and had important matters to attend to. Not until after dinner the next day did he finally bid his host farewell. It was the last sight he was ever to have of Charles, Duke of Burgundy.

That night the King slept in a village near Namur. Next morning in bad weather he set off for France with a small escort, including two Burgundian nobles. Through cold downpours Louis pounded southwestward, making forty miles a day and more, halting in villages only to eat and sleep. Skirting the western edge of the Ardennes, he lodged on French soil by the fifth or sixth of November. Onward he drove himself, heading across Champagne, and so came to the shrine of Our Lady of Joy, near Laon. At the Virgin's altar the King swore once more, in the presence of the two Burgundian nobles, to maintain the Treaty of Péronne.

By the 12th he had arrived at Noyon, where he spent the following day in council, beginning to knit up all the loose ends of government. Next day at Compiègne he gave Balue the task of ordering the registration of the Treaty of Péronne and explaining its provisions to the Council of Thirty-Six, the royal council, generals of finances, officers of the Chamber of Accounts, members of the Parlement, whom he had summoned from Paris. He was not slow in learning that his absence had thrown many of his subjects, high and low, into panic—a state of affairs that did not say much for his prudence as a ruler but at least suggested that he had the loyalty of most of his people.[5]

Louis stayed away from Paris, spending some days here and there in the outskirts, getting affairs in his hands. He wanted no embarrassing demonstrations of anti-Burgundian sentiment in his capital, being for the moment more ducal than the Duke; nor did he care to hear any gibes about himself. The Parisians were stalwartly loyal but they were also incurable satirists. Once it was known the King was safe, all manner of mocking libels began circulating; even talking birds had apparently been taught to join in the game.[6]

Louis took the road, once again, to Orléans and the Loire Valley. He requested the new Milanese ambassador, Sforza de Bettinis, to inform his master "how things have worked out perfectly and, being in true peace and tranquility, we think only of living happily and making good cheer."

Thus did the bedraggled fox make his escape from the wolf's den.

Louis XI, a contemporary medallion *(Bibliothèque Nationale, Paris)*

LOCHES

Cliché Valoire—Blois

LOUIS XI, a limestone head from Toul (*The Art Institute of Chicago. Lucy Maud Buckingham Medieval Collection*)

CHARLES VII, by Fouquet *(The Louvre)*

Giraudon

AGNÈS SOREL, from the Fontainebleau School *(Private collection)*

Bulloz

THE COURT OF PHILIP THE GOOD, from an anonymous painting, *Le Jardin d'Amour de Philippe le Bon (Museum at Versailles)*

Archives Photographiques

occis en 1477

PHILIP THE GOOD AND CHARLES THE BOLD, a contemporary (1477) drawing.
Philip is wearing the Order of the Golden Fleece (*Museum of Arras*)

Giraudon

Messire Phelippe de Commines Seigneur Dargenton
historien

PHILIPPE DE COMMYNES (*Museum of Arras*)

Giraudon

CHARLES THE BOLD, by Roger van der Weyden (*Berlin Museum*)   Walter Steinkopf

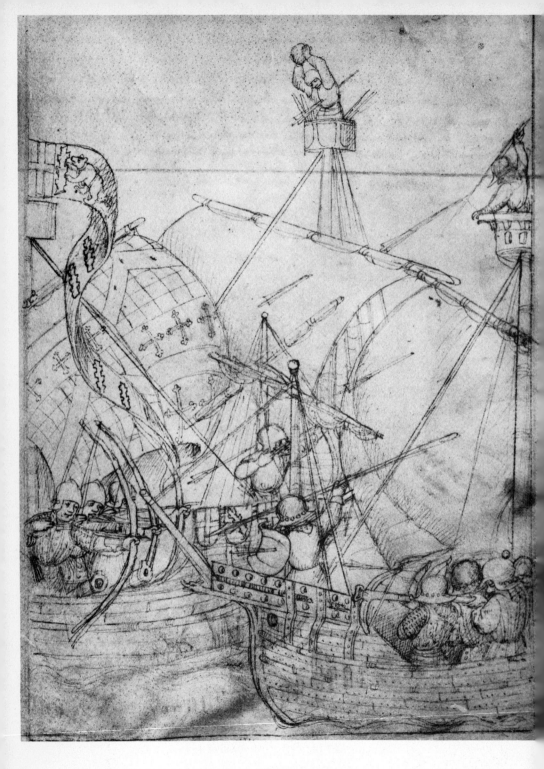

SEA BATTLE AGAINST SHIPS OF WARWICK THE KINGMAKER, identified
by pennant with bear and ragged staff

THE BATTLE OF MORAT, from the *Chronicles* of Diebold Schilling
(Burgerbibliothek Bern)

Schweiz-Landesmuseum

FRANCESCO SFORZA *(National Museum, Florence)*

Viollet

LORENZO DE' MEDICI *(Florence: Maria del Fiore).* Below, LUDOVIC SFORZA *(Museum of Andri)*

Bulloz

JOHN V, COUNT OF ARMAGNAC
(*Bibliothèque Nationale*)

Bulloz

DUNOIS, GRAND BASTARD OF ORLÉANS (*Statue in the chapel of The Château of Châteaudun*)

Viollet

HENRY VI OF ENGLAND

EDWARD IV OF ENGLAND

(National Portrait Gallery)

(Bibliothèque Nationale, Paris)

RENÉ OF ANJOU

JOHN OF CALABRIA

NOTRE DAME OF CLÉRY

THE VIRGIN OF CLÉRY

18. Beauvais

BUT IT WAS NOT the King's way to lose without plucking a few flowers from the nettle of adversity. At the very moment of his parting from the Duke of Burgundy, Louis XI had raised a question, with studied casualness.

"If by chance," Louis remarked, "my brother in Brittany is not satisfied with the *apanage* [i.e., Champagne] I am giving him out of my love for you, what do you want me to do?"

Charles answered carelessly. "If he doesn't want to take it and you can satisfy him some other way, I leave it to you two."

By the beginning of 1470 King Louis was dangling before his brother the province of Guienne, a much richer prize than Champagne but safely distant from Burgundian domains. Young Charles—skittish of mind and assailed by conflicting voices—hesitated, indicated agreement, backed away, hesitated again. Charles's entourage were alternately swayed by fears of the King and by the vision of high offices. The Duke of Brittany was opposed to the settlement, being loathe to lose so profitable a guest. As for the rest of the princes—"Neither the Duke of Burgundy nor Duke John nor any lord of the realm," wrote the Milanese ambassador Sforza de Bettinis, "would like the Duke of Berry [Charles] to be in firm alliance and true fraternity with His Majesty; for it seems to them the King is of such a nature that if he had no cause for fear and could rule the realm as he pleased, he would wrap up all his affairs in one day and make all the lords long for death. . . ." Even in the King's household treachery was at work to undo his efforts.

Optimistically Louis sent for Burgundian ambassadors—so that they could report to their master that the King's brother had freely chosen Guienne—but then, Charles suffering qualms, the King had to think of entertainments to delay them. Finally, however, Louis won over his brother's advisers, particularly the clever Gascon Odet d'Aydie, and on April 3 the Burgundians left the royal court for Brittany. Before the end

of April, Charles signed the treaty by which he accepted Guienne as his
apanage.

About the same time, royal officers searching a suspicious character
found a startling letter sewed in his doublet and soon secured the messenger's confession. That same day at Amboise Louis XI was informed
that Cardinal Balue and the Cardinal's crony, Guillaume de Haraucourt,
Bishop of Verdun, had dispatched a servant to the Duke of Burgundy
with a message urging the Duke to prevent the King's brother from accepting Guienne and to take arms against the King. Summoning the Cardinal and the Bishop from Tours next day, Louis promptly clapped them
under arrest. The miserable ecclesiastics blurted out the incongruous
truth: they had sought to embroil the King in dangers from which only
they could extricate him, in order to rule King and kingdom at their
pleasure. Commissions were appointed to draw up proceedings against
them, but the Pope refused to permit their being tried. They therefore
languished in prison for a decade, being incarcerated part of the time in
iron cages.°

For the next four months the King worked to seal his reconciliation with Charles by means of an interview—having lost no confidence
in his arts and spells. Under the auspices of their genial uncle René, he
devised tournaments and other princely merrymakings to please his
brother, and he entered so enthusiastically into his role that he managed
briefly, Bettinis reported, "to become enamoured of a demoiselle of King
René's queen." But Charles still evaded the fearsome moment of facing
the King. On August first Louis XI indulged in another knightly gesture.
In the style of the English Order of the Garter and the Burgundian
Order of the Golden Fleece, he instituted the Order of St. Michael "because of the special love we have for the state of chivalry," and for the
defense "of our mother Holy Church," and of "the prosperity of the
public weal." Heading the names of the Chevaliers—the King's chief
commanders and councilors—was Charles, Duke of Guienne. The order
bound its members by stringent oaths of loyalty, such as would make it
impossible for the Duke to accept, for example, the Order of the Golden
Fleece. By the end of August, Charles of Guienne, his excuses exhausted,
agreed to a meeting with his royal brother.

To allay the young man's fears, the King ordered a bridge of boats

---

° The use of iron cages was not new. Escapes being not uncommon, important
persons were often placed in such cages at night for greater security. Philippe de
Commynes, after Louis's death, spent five months in an iron cage, as he ruefully but
uncomplainingly discloses.

to be constructed over the Niort branch of the Sèvres River; at the middle point was erected a stout wooden barricade with a barred window. About six-thirty in the evening of September 7, Louis XI walked onto the bridge, followed by a dozen courtiers. The new Duke of Guienne, already waiting with a similar number of attendants, bared his head and knelt, then advanced to the barricade and threw himself on his knees. A hearty greeting from Louis gave him the courage timidly to put his arm through the bars and take the King's hand. In a rush of words the Duke implored his brother for pardon and grace, swearing "with great oaths" that until death he would be a "good son and most deserving servant." As soon as the King motioned the retinues to retire and began a casual conversation, Charles begged hard to be permitted to join his brother. Though Louis gently suggested that it would be better to wait until the morrow, the nervous Duke, miserably embarrassed now by the insulting precautions his timidity had dictated, insisted on making his way around the barrier so that he could fall at his royal brother's feet.

The King raised him, and the two kissed and embraced "more than twenty times." At the sight men burst into tears. From the ranks of lords and gentry in the meadows sounded cries of "Noel! Noel!" It was almost dark by the time Louis bade his brother an affectionate farewell. That night Louis joyfully reported the news to his Chancellor. "During our meeting," he added, "there happened something that the sailors, and others experienced in such matters, declared to be marvelous, for the tide which was today supposed to be the highest of the year was the lowest that has been seen in the memory of man, and it began to ebb four hours sooner than expected, for which God and Our Lady be praised."

After Louis had treated him to days of constant companionship, the Duke of Guienne rode off, about September 18, to his new province. On Christmas Eve (1469) he arrived at Montils-lès-Tours accompanied by a splendid train of lords. After a week of feasting, the brothers rode to Amboise to make merry with the Queen and her ladies. "Wherever the King goes," reported Bettinis, "he walks arm in arm with the Duke or holds him by the hand, and they are together almost continuously, eating, drinking, sleeping in the same chamber. . . ."

Louis had no need to feign a holiday mood. With his brother removed from the grasp of the princes and Francis II making amicable overtures, the King had rid himself of that turbulent southern rebel the Count of Armagnac. Charged with treason by the Parlement of Paris, the Count fled to Spain, and by the beginning of the Christmas season all his territories were in the King's hands.[1] Furthermore, there had been coming from England wild tidings which suggested that the King's long cultivation of the Earl of Warwick might yet bear fruit.

ii

THE RETURN TO the royal fold of the King's brother and heir proved to be the curtain raiser for a more adventurous and ambitious drama of retrieval.

On May 1, 1470, fisher folk of Honfleur were astonished to see an English fleet cast anchor at the mouth of the Seine and then to behold the ceremonious welcome given to the commander of those vessels, who, it turned out, was the famous Englishman Richard Neville, Earl of Warwick.

During the past nine months Louis XI had eagerly followed— through a fog of rumor, false report, messages from Warwick and from his own agents—the bewildering fluctuation of Richard Neville's fortunes. The previous August (1469) he learned that the Earl, after marrying his elder daughter, Isabel, to Edward IV's brother George, Duke of Clarence, had defeated a royal army, taken King Edward prisoner, and evidently meant to put his son-in-law on the throne. Word came in the autumn that Edward had somehow slipped away from custody in Yorkshire and was again ruling in London. By April of 1470 it appeared that the King and the Earl had again taken arms. Then, suddenly, Warwick and Clarence with their womenfolk were fugitives on the sea, their fleet refused entry to Calais. When Louis XI received a request from Warwick for permission to land in Normandy, he hastily sent orders to the Admiral and the Archbishop of Narbonne to pay royal honors to their unexpected guests.[*] Louis's officers informed him that the Englishmen had sailed into the Bay of the Seine flaunting a train of captured Burgundian ships and some Breton prizes. The Earl himself sent word that he was now ready to embrace the enterprise King Louis had proposed in 1467, the restoration of the House of Lancaster to the English throne. He asked for an immediate interview.

But with horrible speed the Duke of Burgundy learned that the "great rebel" of his ally, Edward IV, the pirate who had plundered his shipping, had been warmly received in Normandy with all his booty. Louis was soon being bombarded with accusations of bad faith by the enraged Duke and demands for Warwick's arrest. The King, unprepared

---

[*] For an account of these English events, see P. M. Kendall, *Warwick the Kingmaker*.

for hostilities, could not afford to give the princes grounds for war; he could not even be sure of Warwick's intentions. But Louis was not the man to decline the marvelous gambit which he had long envisaged and which fortune now was offering. To Warwick he dispatched word that he would do all in his power to accomplish the desires of his friend. To the shabby little court of Margaret of Anjou in the Duchy of Bar went a pressing invitation for the fallen Queen to join him at Amboise in order to close with the opportunity offered by Warwick's arrival. He tried to propitiate the Duke of Burgundy with promises that all Burgundian goods would be restored and with the lame excuse that when he had extended Warwick a safe-conduct he did not know that the Earl had plundered the Duke's subjects. But such words, he knew, would never satisfy the violent Duke, and there were Warwick's telltale prizes riding at the mouth of the Seine, and Warwick's seamen hawking their Burgundian booty in Norman ports and villages; and there was the Earl himself, treated like a prince by high royal officers and demanding to make an open appearance at the court of France.

On May 12 Louis hurried off Jean Bourré and William Menypeny [*] with instructions to the Admiral and the Archbishop of Narbonne for negotiating with his very welcome but nerve-racking guest. The instructions fall all over themselves in Louis's anxiety to explain that he could not openly receive the Earl and his Burgundian prizes. Before the King could meet with Warwick, the English fleet must leave the Bay of the Seine. At Honfleur the ships were exposed to the view of the Count of St. Pol, Governor of Normandy, who would relay the information to the Duke of Burgundy. Ports of lower Normandy, or the Channel Islands, or even Bordeaux would do nicely. The Admiral and the Archbishop were to emphasize that Louis XI would help his friend to recover the Kingdom of England, whether through the Lancastrians or by whatever means the Earl chose. But first the ships must be moved. . . . The King would see that the Neville ladies were properly lodged at Carentan or Bayeux or Valognes, or if the Earl preferred to send them to Amboise, they would have no worse a hostess than the Queen.

The Earl of Warwick, however, insisted on speaking with the King; arrangements had been made for the ladies to be sheltered in abbeys near the Seine—so Menypeny and Bourré in nervous haste sent word to their master. On May 19 Louis fired back a vehement answer: "Before concluding any arrangements for a meeting with me, see to it that their

---

[*] This native of Scotland, now the lord of Concressault, Louis XI had many times employed on missions to Warwick.

whole fleet has departed, for I will never receive them until their ships leave that place!

"Also I charge you to dispatch word immediately to the Duke of Burgundy's people that I have sent you there to recover all that you can find of the goods belonging to subjects of my lord of Burgundy, and therefore that if they will get in touch with you, you will see that they receive everything that you can find. . . .

"You enrage me with your allowing the ladies to remain so near the Seine and that region! Therefore, I beg you, see that they go deeper into lower Normandy, even if it costs me twice the expenses, for I will happily pay them. . . . Since those abbeys are not stoutly walled, a night attack could cause trouble to those who would be with the ladies, which would give me the greatest displeasure in the world."

But the efforts of the Admiral, the Archbishop of Narbonne, Bourré, and Menypeny were in vain. The Earl of Warwick knew his value and stood upon his pride: he would not move the ships until he had first arranged personally with the King of France the great enterprise upon which he intended to embark. With aplomb, he dispatched one of his captains to sea to bring in more prizes. While Louis was digesting this troubling information, he received a fiery communication from the Duke of Burgundy. Accusing the King of breaking the Treaty of Péronne, Duke Charles declared that he intended to attack Warwick and Clarence by land and sea, wherever they were. Reports soon reached the King that the Duke was assembling a powerful fleet and encouraging Francis II to unleash his Breton sea rovers.

Yet Louis acceded to the will of the Earl of Warwick. The legend of the kingmaking adventurer he would not diminish. A great design long nurtured, he was not to be frightened from pursuing. Sacrifice imagination to prudence, it was not his style. Bringing his powers to bear on Warwick face to face, the opportunity was irresistible. He invited the Earl and the Duke of Clarence, they leaving their ships at Honfleur, to come openly to the court at Amboise.

On June 8 the King dispatched all of his principal lords, one after another, to give the English refugees a royal welcome as they approached Amboise. He himself then went, on foot, down the hill from the castle and a little way along the road to greet his visitors. He cut short their obeisances by embracing them warmly. When they reached the gate of the castle, there was the Queen, almost nine months big with child, to receive them and be kissed—a good bourgeois welcome which, since it was extended by the most powerful monarch in Europe, was the more flatteringly splendid. No majordomo, but the King himself, conducted the Earl and the Duke to their chambers, then remained with them for a good two hours of private chat.

For the next three days Louis closeted himself with his visitors for long discussions, he in his easy-going way coming to their chambers rather than receiving them in his. At the same time he published to the world his devotion to the Earl by paying him elaborate public honors: courtly receptions, feasts, even a tournament were provided for his guests' delectation. Members of their entourage were well tipped. An acrobat that Warwick had included in his retinue received from Louis—a connoisseur of agility—a reward of twenty crowns. All the while studying his guests, the King had decided that his faith in Warwick's loyalty and Warwick's abilities was not misplaced. When the Earl and the Duke rode away from Amboise on June 12, Louis and Richard Neville had made arrangements for "the enterprise of England." Warwick would restore the House of Lancaster to the English throne; he and Queen Margaret "would put aside all past injuries and enmities," their alliance to be sealed by the marriage of the Earl's younger daughter, Anne, now about ten, to the seventeen-year-old son of Henry VI, Prince Edward; Louis would supply ships and money for the expedition, but as friend and ally of Richard Neville, not of Lancaster; and a treaty between France and Lancastrian England would bring peace between the two countries and destruction to the Duke of Burgundy.

Louis was first confronted with the task of bringing round the imperious Queen Margaret, now on her way with her son, to forgiving and cherishing her bitter enemy. He and Warwick had decided—the latter no doubt with relief—that it would be best for the Earl to absent himself, in moving his ships, and give the King an opportunity "to shape matters a little with her and induce her to agree" to the reconciliation and the marriage alliance. "That done," reported the Milanese ambassador, "Warwick will come back to give the finishing touches to everything, and immediately afterward will return to England with a great fleet, taking with him Prince Edward in order to rally the party of King Henry. . . ."

It did not turn out to be quite that simple.

Queen Margaret proved to be fully as impassioned and balky as Louis could anticipate. From the moment of her arrival at Amboise, two weeks after Warwick's departure, the King set about showing her where her true interests lay. She readily agreed to a thirty years' truce between France and the House of Lancaster, in return for the King's engagement to give Henry VI "all support and favor possible against Edward of March [Edward IV], his aiders and accomplices." But touch the base and bloody hand of Warwick—she never would! Day after day in long discussions, swallowing his distaste for her heroics and his opinion of her pride, King Louis indefatigably cajoled, soothed, flattered, and preached the doctrine of political necessity. The haughty Queen relented so far as to agree to permit the Earl of Warwick to place her husband again on the throne. But the marriage of her son to Anne Neville —that she would never hear of. It was not to her profit and it was even less to her honor, she declared loftily. Louis persevered.

Then, on June 30, occurred the event that he and all loyal Frenchmen had so profoundly longed for: about an hour before daybreak Queen Charlotte gave birth to a healthy son. That same day the infant was baptized by the Archbishop of Lyons and named Charles—perhaps Louis felt he owed that much to his father, or his brother? The jubilant King took the opportunity to show his devotion to the House of Lancaster: Queen Margaret's son, Prince Edward, served as godfather to the child, both of whom had as great-grandfather the mad Charles VI. Whether this amiable gesture or the immediately renewed persuasions of the King moved Queen Margaret, she at last agreed to the marriage of her prince and Richard Neville's daughter. But on the remaining point she was adamant—she would not entrust young Edward to Warwick. Only when he was master of England would she and the Prince of Wales cross the sea. It was good enough for Louis. Doubtless Henry VI's half brother Jasper Tudor, Earl of Pembroke, would suit Warwick as a Lancastrian companion for the enterprise. To provide as congenial an atmosphere as possible, Louis arranged that in a few weeks Margaret should meet Warwick in the city of her childhood, Angers, and promised that her father, King René, and her other cousin, the Duke of Guienne, would be with her.

Meanwhile, an Anglo-Burgundian fleet, after bombarding the Norman coast, had briefly blockaded the Bay of the Seine. French merchants in the Burgundian domain found themselves clapped under arrest. Emissaries Louis had dispatched to the Duke of Burgundy were subjected to a stormy audience. As they began to explain the King's offers of restitution and reparation, the Duke furiously interrupted them. The King had broken the Treaty of Péronne by supporting Burgundy's mortal enemy, Warwick! He wanted to hear no talk of reparations! The interview was brought to an end by an angry outburst—"Among us Portuguese," snarled the Duke [whose mother was a Portuguese princess], "we have an old custom, that when those we have held to be our friends make friends with our enemies, we consign them to all the hundred thousand devils of hell!"

Early in July, King Louis moved down the Loire to the Angevin capital of Angers, where he was joined by his brother. Charles's affections appeared in no way diminished by the fact that he was no longer heir to the throne. Louis took care to associate him in all the arrangements for the reconciliation of Warwick and Margaret of Anjou, which, the King predicted to Bourré, "will very quickly come to effect or come to nothing." On July 22 both the Queen and the Earl made their entrances into Angers, the latter accompanied by that stout Lancastrian John, Earl of Oxford, who had managed to slip across the Channel some days before. Louis spared no charm, but wasted no time and made quite clear whose friend he was. That very evening he took the Earl by the hand and led him into the majestic presence of the Queen whom Warwick had dethroned. Richard Neville had been doubtless well coached by the King, and, zealous cultivator of his own legend, was himself no mean actor. He was well aware that London was worth a genuflection. Humbly he went down on his knees before the haughty Queen and sued to her for her forgiveness. Margaret salved her pride by keeping him there a good quarter of an hour while he begged her pardon for the wrongs he had done her. Finally she brought herself to forgive him with a show of graciousness and he did formal homage to the House of Lancaster. He had already agreed to repeat this act of contrition, once England was won, in a public ceremony at Westminster. The Queen then greeted the Earl of Oxford with genuine warmth, for he and his family had suffered "much thing" for her cause.

Under King Louis's benevolent auspices the Earl of Warwick and Queen Margaret settled the details of their alliance in the course of the next three days. Louis would support in style the Queen, Warwick's wife and Clarence's, Prince Edward and the Prince's bride-to-be, Anne Neville, until Warwick had England firmly in his grip. The Earl did the best he could for his son-in-law the Duke of Clarence, who had prudently stayed away from Angers: in case Prince Edward and Anne had no lawful heir, he was to succeed to the throne. King Louis, clad in a canon's robe, seconded by his brother similarly arrayed, presided over the ceremonious conclusion of the reconciliation in the Cathedral of Angers on July 25. After the betrothal by proxy of Anne Neville to Prince Edward had been solemnized, Queen Margaret promised to treat Warwick as a true and faithful subject and never to reproach him for deeds past, while the Earl swore "to uphold the party and the quarrel of King Henry." The oaths were taken on Louis's favorite cross, the Cross of St. Laud, reputed to bring death within a year to anyone who broke a vow made upon it. Louis and his brother then went surety for Warwick's promises to Queen Margaret, the King "showing the great love that he had unto him, and that he was bound and beholden to the said Earl more than to any other man, and therefore he would do as much and more for him than for any man living." The prime transaction, in Louis's view, was not clothed in ceremony: Warwick's engagement to bind England to a war to the finish against the Duke of Burgundy.

The Neville-Lancaster match shocked that devotee of Burgundian chivalry Georges Chastellain; even Commynes thought it "strange." *
Contemporaries hostile to Louis XI, like Chastellain and Bishop Basin, who had been driven from his Norman See for his enthusiastic support of the King's brother in 1465, regarded the King and the Earl of Warwick as birds of a feather; and in the propaganda war heating up between France and Burgundy, Duke Charles's ballad makers jeered,

Le Roy avait bien rencontré   (*The King had met indeed*
En Warwick proppre compaignon; *In Warwick his true kin.*
Eux deux, leur cas consideré,   *This pair—who runs may read—*
Furent d'une complexion.   *Were brothers under the skin.*)

What Louis's true feeling was for Richard Neville it is impossible to discern, partly because it was so obviously to his advantage to treat the Earl as he did. Once reestablished on the throne, the House of Lancaster might have little compunction in breaking an alliance with France to bolster its position at home; and there was no reason to think that Queen Margaret, with her Angevin prejudices and her vindictive memory, would feel any gratitude to her cousin of France. On the other hand Louis could count on Warwick's loyalty, for the Earl, lacking the unction of kingship, could not do without his support; and if, on the day of success, Queen Margaret's desire for revenge spoke louder than her oath, Warwick's only refuge would be the King of France. But it appears that Louis genuinely felt the kinship with Richard Neville of which his enemies accused him. Like himself and his other great friend, Francesco

---

* Yet the age had been repelled by the marriage of Edward IV and Elizabeth Woodville, "for love." Medieval attitudes still survived in a world they no longer mirrored: naked political cynicism outraged the conventions, not the practices, of the times.

Sforza, the Earl was a political adventurer, a man who dared to leap beyond the customs of the age, who depended on his wits and lived by opportunity. And then, Warwick had proved loyal—out of self-interest, true, but that was the bond Louis respected, as opposed to feudal obligation and chivalric gesture—and Louis, for all his cynical statecraft, was almost always loyal to loyalty. The one surviving expression of his true attitude toward Warwick occurs in a letter to Bourré: "You know the desire I have, and must have, for the return of my lord of Warwick to England: as much for the happiness it would give me to see him come out on top, or, at least, that the realm of England was embroiled in strife—as also to avoid the difficulties that could arise as a result of his longer remaining here."

After the ceremony in the cathedral on the 25th, Louis wrote to Bourré with great satisfaction and a dash of irony, "Today we have made the marriage of the Queen of England and (the Earl of Warwick). . . ."

On the last day of July the Earl set out with Jasper Tudor, Earl of Pembroke, and the Earl of Oxford for his headquarters at Valognes to complete preparations for his expedition. On the same day Queen Margaret and Prince Edward left for Amboise, where they would be joined by Warwick's wife and daughters. Warwick had wanted to witness the marriage of his daughter before he risked his neck in England, but even the King of France could not so quickly produce the papal dispensation necessitated by consanguinity (Anne Neville's great-grandmother Joan Beaufort being half sister to Prince Edward's great-grandfather, Henry IV); and Warwick had accepted Louis's assurance that the ladies would be royally treated at Amboise and the marriage duly performed.

Louis XI swiftly disbursed large sums for victuals, weapons, pay to hearten Warwick's sailors; but before the expedition could sail, a Burgundian fleet had clapped a tight blockade on the Norman ports sheltering the vessels of the Earl and the Admiral of France. On getting word of Burgundian depredations ashore, the King hurried into Normandy to command the defense—"you know what a blow it would be to me," he wrote his Grand Master, "if they [the Burgundians] did not meet with stout resistance." By September 5 he had reached the neighborhood of Bayeux, and it seems likely that he paid an anxious visit to Warwick at Valognes, only forty-two miles distant. The enterprise of England was growing cold with delay and frustration. But the very next day the wheel of fortune turned. A great southeaster smashed the blockade and drove the Burgundian ships through stormy seas northward as far as

Scotland and Holland. The day following, the Admiral of France was able to bring his warships to join Warwick's fleet at St. Vaast-la-Hougue. On September 9, with a fair wind, the Earl of Warwick set sail on his enterprise. On his behalf King Louis offered a great taper, six sacred vessels, and his own image in wax to Our Lady of Deliverance at Caen. He vowed himself to Our Lady of Celles in Poitou. Warwick would need all the help he could get.

Within a week, the King, once more at Tours, had word that after a propitious voyage Warwick had landed his little force at Plymouth and Dartmouth without opposition, and the Admiral's convoying fleet had safely returned to Norman ports. Then, in mid-October, Jasper Tudor arrived from England with triumphant news: Warwick had marched through the kingdom almost unopposed; Edward IV had been forced to flee to Holland; on October 6 the King's Lieutenant of the Realm—such was the title Richard Neville had assumed—had entered London and knelt before poor little Henry VI, whom five years before he had himself delivered to a prison cell. From Jasper Tudor the King of France received an exuberant note written by Warwick on the 8th: "Please to know that by God's help and yours, for which I don't know how to thank you enough, this whole kingdom is now placed under the obedience of the King my sovereign lord, and the usurper Edward driven out of it."

Louis "bathed in roses" (as Chastellain put it). Setting out hastily on the pilgrimage he had vowed to Our Lady of Celles, he dispatched a jubilant circular to his good towns announcing Warwick's reestablishment of the House of Lancaster, "the thing in the world most to be desired for the public weal of both realms," and ordaining "three entire days" of religious thanksgivings. On November 13 he completed the commission for the envoys, all well known to the Earl of Warwick, who were bound for England to put in force the agreements reached at Angers. Meant for the Earl's eye, these instructions were unusually precise, personal, urgent. Louis's emissaries were given orders to conclude the military alliance against Burgundy, arrangements for campaigning to be closely specified. The ambassadors were to suggest that Warwick take for his share of the Burgundian conquest the "countries and lordships" of Holland and Zeeland. In thus fulfilling the dream long ago implanted in Warwick's mind, Louis would, in effect, be keeping the English portion of the spoils in the hands of his own viceroy. As an illustration of the commercial advantages awaiting the entrepreneurs of England, staunchest upholders of the Burgundian alliance, he arranged to send with his embassy two wealthy merchants of Tours with twenty-five thousand crowns' worth of glittering goods—spices, cloth of gold, silks, linens—to sell at bargain rates to London merchants as proof that the marts of France were fully able to supply English wants. It was an entirely novel politico-economic campaign.

On the arrival of the papal dispensation Louis saw to the marriage of Anne Neville and Prince Edward; but he did not yet send off his guests or his embassy. From an assembly of "notables" at Tours, he procured a declaration that Charles of Burgundy had committed double treason, in forcing his sovereign under duress to sign the Treaty of Péronne and then in breaking that treaty by waging war in Normandy the previous summer. In consequence, his title and his domains were confiscated. Publishing this declaration of hostilities on December 3, Louis then dispatched his ambassadors to England: he aimed at confronting Warwick with a war already begun. By mid-December, the Milanese ambassador Bettinis reported, the King received word from the envoys that their welcome in London left nothing to be desired. Louis immediately gave leave to Queen Margaret and her party to begin their journey home, ordering the Parisians to extend them a royal welcome.

The King who despised and distrusted war had not been able to resist the beckoning of fortune. He estimated that with the aid of English forces he could crush the House of Burgundy in the field. He was moving very fast, perhaps because he had doubts that time was on his side.

iii

ALMOST AT ONCE, it looked as if King Louis had unerringly timed his shift from statecraft to arms. The Constable, St. Pol, and the new Duke of Guienne hastened to court with fervent assurances of their services, then rode off to assemble forces; the Duke of Brittany would remain neutral. To give Warwick time, the King had planned a spring campaign, but he suddenly learned, at Orléans on January 13 (1471), that the Constable had persuaded St. Quentin, one of the Somme towns, to open its gates and royal troops were now garrisoned there. Five days later Louis wrote to Bourré, "Go you tomorrow to Paris and you and the President [of the Parlement] find some money in the enchanter's box because I need it, and let there be no slip-up!" He himself soon arrived in his capital, spent but four days there raising funds and ordering up supplies and artillery. After hearing Mass at Notre Dame on the morning of January 26, he paused at a little fort outside the city walls to eat

a meal, then hurried northward to Senlis and Compiègne. His best captains and the crack troops of his standing army were already garrisoned
in towns along the frontiers of Burgundian Picardy. With only his guard
and a small company, Louis moved about the countryside between
Compiègne and Noyon—risking his neck like a pillaging soldier of fortune, Sforza de Bettinis reported, adding that the King's intimates were
most unhappy at this recklessness.

On February 3 King Louis received magnificent news from his best
commander, old Antoine de Chabannes, Grand Master of the Royal
Household: the citizens of Amiens, chief city of Picardy, had welcomed
within their stout walls the Grand Master and his companies of men of
arms. Louis jubilantly wrote to Chabannes the same day, "I praise God
and Our Lady for your letters. I am well aware of the good service you
have done me, and I will forever remember it and the service of those
with you. In regard to the citizens of the town, all that you have promised them I will ratify; and the offers you have made will take effect, as
you will see by the gifts and ratifications I will provide, exactly as you
have promised and without slip-up." Amiens to the west and St. Quentin
to the east now anchored the line of the Somme, with the bulk of the
royal forces established on a line running roughly about fifteen miles behind the river.

Ten days later, Louis received intelligence that the Burgundian
host, beginning to move south, was apparently headed for the Duke's
town of Corbie, ten miles up the Somme from Amiens. Couriers pounded
the roads of northern France to maintain the King's control of his military
machine. In war, as in peace, he required a coordination of services and
a responsiveness to command which were sometimes bewildering to his
servants. When the Grand Master failed to keep in close communication, Louis, on February 14, wrote in a burst of anxiety to his son-in-law
the Admiral, "My son, the route the Duke of Burgundy is taking is for
Corbie. [To my last letters] the Count of Dammartin has made no
reply, and since Monday or Tuesday morning [February 11, 12] I've
had no further news of him. I don't know whether he has laid siege to
Corbie or has decided to await [in Amiens] the power of the Duke of
Burgundy. My son, I've never seen such complete folly as to cross the
river [Somme] with the insufficient troops he has nor a better way of
going hunting for great dishonor or great disaster. I beg you, send some
people there to find out what he's doing and send me news two or three
times a day, for I am in great uneasiness. I'm afraid the Grand Master
has got himself up shit creek [*ait fait du hardi merdoux*]. If God and

Our Lady preserve him and his company from being destroyed by their blunder, I think the Duke of Burgundy is undone." He soon learned, however, that the Grand Master had prudently remained in Amiens.

It was against that city that the Duke of Burgundy, enraged by the loss of his Somme towns, had begun to move. When the northern defenses of Amiens proved too strong for him to attack, he marched downstream to the bridge of Picquigny. Taking the bridge and the town by assault, he boldly crossed the Somme and set up his laager close to the southwestern outskirts of Amiens. His guns began a bombardment, were answered by Chabannes's artillery. Bitter skirmishing developed between royal squadrons sallying from the city and Burgundian attacking parties. While the Duke's raiders moved freely along the south bank between Picquigny and Corbie, Chabannes's patrols harried Burgundian supply trains from the north. King Louis ordered St. Pol and the Admiral to join the garrison at Amiens, then summoned his captains for a council of war. Endorsing the view of that fearless old Écorcheur the Grand Master, they advocated an assault on the Burgundian laager. The King agreed to the attack, but reserved setting a date for it. Again the Duke of Burgundy had put his army in a hazardous situation—the men exposed to the rigors of wintry weather and the laager almost surrounded by royal forces outnumbering his.

Louis XI was awaiting word that the Earl of Warwick had landed at Calais. Once an English army advanced southward from that port, the Burgundians would be caught in a vise.

But the news sent by the King's envoys in London, though always encouraging, remained vague on the subject of the anti-Burgundian alliance. In late February, Louis had received an enthusiastic dispatch— the English Parliament was ready to approve a ten-year truce and a mercantile treaty; Warwick was assembling a powerful fleet and would shortly cross to Calais with an army of some ten thousand men. To this report the Earl had added a postscript in his own hand: "Sire, I promise you that all which is written above will be obeyed and accomplished in every detail, and so I have promised your envoys; and I will see you very shortly, if God pleases, for that is my whole desire. Entirely your humble and loyal servant, R. Warrewyk."

About March 20 there arrived at royal headquarters in Beauvais the envoys themselves, shaken by a harrowing escape from Breton pirates in the Channel. They brought with them only the treaty of truce and intercourse of merchandise, and Warwick's verbal assurance that as soon as Queen Margaret and her son, still lingering mistrustfully at Honfleur, arrived in England to hold the realm in his absence, he would cross to Calais with about eight thousand men. The glittering trade fair provided by Louis had been a fiasco. So indignantly did London merchants inveigh against the French traders for taking bread out of their mouths that Warwick had been forced to forbid further sale of the goods. Indeed, the Kingmaker became so desperately short of funds that he was driven to selling seventeen thousand crowns' worth of the French merchandise in order to pay his troops. The rest of the bales were captured by the Breton pirates and one of the French merchants had lost his life in the sea fight. Worst of all, just as the envoys were departing from London, word had come that, about March 12, a small fleet bearing King Edward and his adherents had attempted a landing on the Norfolk coast, then sailed northward toward Humber.

Even as his envoys finished their tale, the King's vision of an English army closing a trap upon the Burgundians faded into illusion. The Earl of Warwick, surrounded by revengeful Lancastrians and challenged by that peerless warrior Edward IV, must soon be fighting for his life.

Louis XI immediately gave out that his affairs looked so promising he had decided against using the English. He abruptly canceled the attack on the Burgundian laager, informing the commanders at Amiens that he had reason to distrust some of his officers. He opened secret negotiations with the Duke of Burgundy.

The bad news from England had arrived, it appears, just as Louis was getting a whiff of treachery in his princely ranks. It was cooked up by the Count of St. Pol and the Duke of Guienne, who delayed joining his brother until March 27. They had schemed to force the Duke of Burgundy, as the price of their deserting the King, to agree to the marriage of his heiress, Marie, to the King's brother. Such a great marriage would render the Duke of Guienne, shorn of his standing as heir to the throne, once again useful as a figurehead for the French feodality. The Duke of Burgundy for his part, his military situation so precarious that he recognized it and his anger fired by the Constable's attempt to blackmail him, wrote "six lines" to the King, in which he hinted that, if Louis had been informed of what was going on, he would not have begun the war. By the end of the first week in April a three-month truce was proclaimed. The Duke and his army would retire to Péronne, the King to the Constable's castle at Ham, and their representatives would meet at a village somewhere between to negotiate for peace. Thus again ended in failure the labors of the King of France to transform a feudal realm into a national monarchy.

While Louis XI was hearing High Mass in the soaring Cathedral of Amiens on Easter Sunday, April 14, two events were shaping the destiny of England. Queen Margaret of Anjou landed on the southern coast. A few miles north of London, Richard Neville, Earl of Warwick, perished on the fog-shrouded field of Barnet in the crushing defeat of his Neville-Lancastrian forces by the army of Edward IV.

For weeks to come the truth about England eluded the King's anxious quest for information. The Duke of Burgundy, haughty now in negotiation, was acting more and more like a man with the upper hand. With his fleet and Breton corsairs holding the Channel passages, Charles quickly learned what had occurred at Barnet, and what subsequently befell the cause of Lancaster. Three weeks after the defeat and death of the Earl of Warwick, the Yorkist King brought Queen Margaret's Lancastrian army to bay at Tewkesbury (May 5), and disposed of the rest of his enemies. Queen Margaret's son, Edward, was slain in flight, the Queen captured, the chief Lancastrian lords killed in battle or taken and executed; and, on the return of the victorious Yorkists to London, King Henry VI, again a prisoner in the Tower, was put to death on the night of May 21–22. Not until June 1 did Louis finally learn "with extreme sorrow" the dismal end of the grand design he had fashioned with his friend Richard Neville. Meantime, Burgundian ballad-mongers had been chanting:

Entre vous, Franchoix,   (*Frenchmen, one to another,*
Jettez pleurs et larmes: *Rain tears and drip alarms,*
Warwic vostre choix   *For Warwick, your sworn brother,*
Est vaincu par armes . . .   *Is crushed by force of arms.*

Or a-il bien son temps perdu   *Now time his schemes has eaten*
Et son argent qui plus lui touche,   *And his coin—yes, there's the sting:*
Car Warwic est mort et vaincu: *For Warwick's dead and beaten —*
Ha! que Loys est fine mouche!   *Ha! What a sly dog is the King!*)

Louis XI had been accompanied to the Constable's castle and town of Ham by his brother and his host, by his Scots guard, his baggage wagons, and the greyhounds of his chamber. Throughout his journeyings he paused to hear Masses, make offerings, hold infants at the font, distribute alms. At St. Quentin, where he spent a day to encourage the new

loyalty of the inhabitants and give orders for the refortification of the
town, he had the prisoners delivered, and then, crossing the Somme in
the rain, halted to give money to a poor man bitten by a mad wolf. In
the castle of Ham the usual small repairs were effected on his chamber
to make it snug; the collapsible bed he always carried with him was set
up, a special chair installed; braziers of coals were lighted, tapestries
unpacked from the baggage and hung. Among the King's personal effects was an unguent for his hemorrhoids which an apothecary of Tours
had prepared for him as he was leaving for the campaign. For exercise
he galloped the fields outside the town, or, with the aid of the inhabitants, hunted fox and badger. Meanwhile, in a village between Ham and
Péronne the King's commissioners—Marshal Lohéac, the lord of Craon,
and a few other lords—were negotiating with representatives of the increasingly obdurate Duke of Burgundy.

On May 4, as the King was riding in the countryside "for pleasure"
with his brother and the Count of St. Pol, he learned that the Burgundian envoys had returned to Péronne to consult with their master,
his own commissioners remaining in the village. An idea struck him and
he impulsively put it into execution. He ordered a hundred horsemen to
don Burgundian insignia, badges of the Cross of St. Andrew, and ride to
the village like a raiding party. His men, he soon learned, carried out
the mission with zest. Thundering into the village with yells of "Burgundy! Burgundy!" they quickly rounded up most of the commissioners
and made a show of pillaging their baggage. The few envoys who had
by chance escaped capture leaped on horses and galloped for Ham,
crying all along the way the terrible news of the raid. By the time they
came foaming into the town, they were yelling that not only the commissioners but the King himself had been captured. In the next hour,
some dozen messengers spurred into Ham with the same tidings. The
Milanese ambassador, Sforza de Bettinis, was beginning to have "strange
thoughts." By the time Louis arrived on the scene the town was in an
uproar.

The King humbly endured a severe lecture from the lords of his entourage on the foolhardiness of his conduct and agreed that letters must
be sent at once to scotch damaging rumors. On dismounting he found
himself face to face with Bettinis. Solemnly he endured another lecture
from the Italian: the prank was a terrible mistake—it would be no marvel if the news reached Italy and terribly upset the Duke of Milan—a
courier should be sent off at once. The King listened to Bettinis and to
his lords and penitently agreed and agreed. Off went the courier to

Italy. Off went a courier to Paris, and the chief towns between, with a message not to believe rumors that the King and his envoys had been captured. Louis himself dictated a note to the Grand Master at Amiens to contradict the tale. He added in his own hand, "It's only a joke which was played by some of my people who were returning from the conferences with the Burgundian envoys." No use crediting himself with a comedy which even his devoted Grand Master could not be expected to appreciate!

However, if the practical joke showed him to be unregally frivolous, as well as somewhat insensitive to the feelings of others, it was not entirely lacking in point. The military men on the commission were, it seems, among the commanders who had loudly urged a bloody assault by his precious soldiers on the Burgundian laager and had grumbled at the truce. Louis was suggesting perhaps that, when their own necks looked to be in danger, they might better appreciate his aversion to pitched battles and all the waste of war. Certainly the humble folk appreciated it. One of the Burgundians had written in the dark days of March, "May God so provide that we can return in peace, for it's a pitiful life, war is."

Patiently the King persisted in his negotiations with the Duke of Burgundy. Finally toward the end of June, after Charles had given agreement, withdrawn it, added impossible conditions, been steadily reduced from them, he accorded a truce, but only until April 30, 1472. He let it be known that, if it came to war, he did not want to lose May's campaigning weather.

Returning once more, after yet another repulse, to the valley of the Loire, Louis again brought something with him, besides experience, from the failure of his plans. He had regained two of the Somme towns and a few other strongholds, an accession that greatly improved his northern defenses and that gave him at last a bargaining card—if he chose to use it—in his dealings with Duke Charles. He needed the encouragement of such thoughts, for none knew better than he that, as a result of his resort to war, he faced a deteriorating political situation. Already Edward IV and Francis of Brittany and the Duke of Burgundy were reweaving their league against the King of France. Furthermore, he knew that the loyalty of his brother was a thing of the past. To these troubles was added the blow of personal grief: the young Prince of Piedmont, eldest son of his sister Duchess Yolande of Savoy, died suddenly at the beginning of July. He was apparently a vigorous, precocious lad, in contrast to his feeble younger brothers. Louis had reared him at the court of France, cherished him like a son, built hopes upon his one day ending the feudal anarchy in Savoy.

On July 6, at Tours, the morning the news arrived of the Prince's death, Louis had a private interview with Sforza de Bettinis. When the Milanese "soberly and feelingly" conveyed his master's deep displeasure at what had happened in England, Louis answered, "sighing, that he could not fight against fortune." A few moments later, as the King took horse to go on pilgrimage to Our Lady of Celles in Poitou, he again summoned Bettinis. He went over the hopes he had had in Warwick— he was amazed that in so short a time these had all been ruined. Then, if nothing else lacked, the Duke of Guienne had refused to marry the daughter of the King of Castile, thus endangering the Spanish alliance. Finally had come the death of the Prince of Piedmont—and here, Bettinis reported, the King uttered such poignant lamentations that "even if Orpheus had been in his place I do not believe he would have been able to do more.

"Sforza," Louis went on, "I am speaking to you as I would to myself." The King hastened to make plain that he was not at all cast down. "What he had uttered he said only by way of expressing an idea. It seemed to him indeed a strange thing that in one moment affairs unrelated to each other had together gone so contrary for him."

iv

LONG BEFORE the year 1471 was out, the disorderly little court of Charles, Duke of Guienne, buzzed with loose talk, conspiracy, schemes for war, against Louis XI. The King kept himself well informed: among other tidbits he learned that he dared not do anything, for the princes and the English "would put so many greyhounds on his tail that he would not know where to flee." By midsummer the Duke was seeking dispensations from the Pope to undo the oaths he had made to the King and to permit his marriage to Marie of Burgundy. His envoys and messengers were constantly on the roads to the Duke of Brittany, the Count of St. Pol, Charles of Burgundy. In November, the King's brother welcomed the fugitive Count of Armagnac and the following month restored him to his estates. Two bickering factions at the ducal court pulled Charles this way and that, one led by the Duke's mistress, Colette de Chambes, who had borne him two children, and the other by the Duke of Brittany's able friend Odet d'Aydie. By December, however, Colette had fallen mortally ill. At the end of the month King Louis learned that she had died on the 14th, apparently of a very unpleasant disease for the blood taken from her by physicians was unusually "bad." Her lover was himself suffering from a severe quartan fever. To rally morale, Odet d'Aydie prompted the Duke to make all his troops swear an oath to serve him against anyone—"namely, against me," as Louis XI reported to his Grand Master, whom he had dispatched to the borders of Guienne with three hundred lances. Earlier, the King had enlisted the Duke of Milan and Lorenzo de' Medici (Lorenzo the Magnificent) to second his ambassadors at Rome in opposing Guienne's request for dispensation. Louis then issued an open warning to the city of Lyons, and probably other towns, to guard their city walls because the Dukes of Guienne, Brittany, and Burgundy had allied themselves against the monarchy. The lord du Bouchage, whom the King dispatched to inform his brother that he knew all about Charles's perfidies and to require him to abandon his erring ways, had returned with empty answers. In February, 1472, Louis learned that his brother, somewhat recovered in health, had resumed his intrigues to win the heiress of Burgundy and was assembling his troops. This same month there came into the King's hands documents for which he had undoubtedly paid a handsome price —"the original letters and instructions, signed by the hand of our brother and sealed with his seal, which he had sent to the court of Rome in order to be released from his oaths," as Louis wrote on March 3, 1472, to the citizens of Lyons, enclosing a copy of the documents. The originals he carefully consigned to the treasury of the Church of St. Laud, at the gates of Angers, that church housing the dreaded Cross of St. Laud, on which the Duke of Guienne, in 1469, had sworn his oath, and which brought death within a year, it was believed, to those who perjured themselves.

Meanwhile, though Charles of Burgundy was urging the feudal coalition toward war and would soon sign an alliance against France with King Ferrante of Naples and John II of Aragon, Louis XI energetically pursued negotiations with his increasingly arrogant adversary. There developed an elaborate diplomatic comedy of deception and masked maneuver—an art at which Louis was somewhat more adroit than the iron-egoed Duke.[2] The King was playing for time, as marked by the thinning bloodstream of the Duke of Guienne, and for such opportunity as the illusions of the Duke of Burgundy might create. It was the old game with two new counters: in return for Burgundy's abandoning its alliances and signing a peace, he offered to return Amiens and St. Quentin. After tortuous negotiations the Duke of Burgundy agreed, provided his relinquishing of allies was relegated to a separate document which was to be kept secret until after the Somme towns were restored. Louis vigorously signified approval of this transparent proposal, but added two conditions of his own—that the Duke's daughter (now in her teens) be affianced to the Dauphin (aged one) and that the King and Duke exchange membership in their honorary orders. It was mid-January of 1472 by the time the King learned that Charles would not sign the proffered treaty, as Louis must have expected. The oath binding the members of the Order of the Golden Fleece, symbol of ducal glory, was the one engagement Louis XI could be sure Charles would not break.

By the beginning of March, Louis's brother had relapsed into a serious, perhaps mortal, illness. The news intensified the diplomatic comedy. The King, ordering a concentration of troops on the borders of Guienne, dispatched yet another embassy to the Duke of Burgundy. This time he proposed that the truce expiring April 30 be prolonged, in case Duke Charles again refused his offer of Amiens and St. Quentin. The Duke of Burgundy kept the French envoys dangling while he awaited tidings from Guienne: regaining the Somme towns at the price of abandoning a dead man would help compensate for the loss of that once useful ally.

The Duke was also playing a game of his own with the princes. For one thing, Charles of Burgundy had no intention of giving his daughter to the King's brother. One of his lords who had the temerity to ask when he intended to bestow Marie in marriage was brusquely informed that it would be when the Duke of Burgundy turned friar. He encouraged all suitors for what he could get out of them, "and I believe," Commynes adds, "that he never wished to have a son nor would have ever married his daughter while he was alive." The Duke of Burgundy, furthermore, no longer considering himself French, privately scorned the patriotic coloring that his friends like to splash upon their schemes. One day after Brittany's envoy, the lord d'Urfé, had been pressing him to take arms in order to join his confederates in working for the good of France—i.e., disposing of Louis XI—Charles called Commynes to a window "and said to me: 'Behold the lord d'Urfé who urges me to assemble the largest army I can and tells me that we will do wonders for the welfare of the realm. Does it seem to you that if I invade with the forces I will lead, I will do much good there?' I replied, laughing, that I thought he would not. Then he said to me, 'I cherish the welfare of the realm of France more than my lord d'Urfé realizes, for in place of one King that it has I would like to give it six!' "

Though Louis XI sent more than a dozen couriers posting to his embassy at the court of Burgundy, not until May 14, two weeks after the expiration of the truce, did he learn that the envoys had succeeded in prolonging it until mid-June. Suddenly, four days later, the King set off southward from Plessis-lès-Tours toward Guienne. Before he took horse he sent a hasty note to the Grand Master: "I have had news that my lord of Guienne is dying and that there is no possible remedy for his case. I have learned this from one of his special intimates, by express messenger. This man does not believe, so he says, that the Duke will be alive two weeks from now, at the most optimistic calculation. . . . So that you may know the reliability of the one who has made known to me this news: it is the monk [Jordain Faure] who says the Hours with my lord of Guienne—on which account I am very much amazed and I have crossed myself from head to foot." Louis's irony was apparently directed against the monk, who, though supposedly devoted to his brother, was already trying to curry favor with the King.

Louis made better than forty miles that day. After a brief halt for devotions at the shrine of Le Puy Notre Dame, the King was heading southward again at top speed by the 19th or 20th of May, accompanied only by his guard. Sforza de Bettinis reported on May 25, "Though I have ridden five days in a row galloping always directly toward His Majesty, I could not reach him until yesterday." By that time, the King, having imperiously demanded, and received, entry into his brother's seaport of La Rochelle, was again on the road.

On May 27, at Saintes, as he was heading for Bordeaux, Louis had sure word that his brother was no more. Charles, age twenty-five, died at Bordeaux on the night of May 24, succumbing to the inroads of tuberculosis probably aggravated by venereal disease.

Two or three days earlier, the Duke of Burgundy's favorite, Simon de Quingey, had arrived in a gallop with a treaty of peace, on Louis's terms, sealed by Duke Charles and needing but the King's signature. Louis XI has politely temporized, then on receiving news of his brother's death dismissed Simon "with very thin words." Not many months later Louis would learn the truth about the somewhat heavy-handed dénouement the Duke had devised for their diplomatic comedy. An equerry with Simon de Quingey bore a secret commission, which ordered Simon to inform Francis II of Brittany that once the Duke of Burgundy had the two Somme towns he would repudiate the peace and join the Bretons in war upon the King.

In a mere four days at Saintes, Louis established the royal government of Guienne, gave orders for besieging the Count of Armagnac in his strong town of Lectoure—a siege which forced the Count to yield within two weeks—and directed the movement of his troops and artillery northward to the Angevin borders of Brittany. Within a few weeks, in some cases within a few days, the King took under his wing, on his usual generous terms, almost all the dead Duke's chief councilors and commanders, a large number of his men of arms, even some of his household attendants. The captain of his brother's guard soon became the captain of the King's. Louis too keenly appreciated good service to have time for grudges. Besides, there would be no peace in France unless bygones were permitted to be bygones.

The ill-wishers of the King of France were quick to make what capital they could out of the unfortunate disappearance of their puppet. Odet d'Aydie seized Jourdain Faure, the Duke of Guienne's confessor, and Henri de La Roche, an equerry of the ducal kitchens, and bore them off to Brittany. Francis II at once declared that on the instigation of the King they had poisoned their master, and then set the Breton army in motion. The Duke of Burgundy, breaking the truce, took the field on June 4 in a fierce rage. At the head of his invading columns was borne the violet-and-black banner of Burgundy, on which was inscribed "Revenge! Revenge!" The Duke reinforced the terror of his arms by two violent manifestoes, in which he declared that the Duke of Guienne had been done to death on the King's orders "by poisons, evil spells, sorceries, and diabolic invocations." [3]

v

By JUNE 24 Louis XI and his forces were driving down the Loire toward the Breton seaport of Nantes. On July 6 the King set siege to Ancenis. It yielded the next morning. In three weeks Louis had opened the way to overrunning Brittany. Instead, he moved slowly northward along the Breton frontier, so obviously inviting negotiation that Francis II, aware that the Burgundian host was thrusting southward, assumed martial airs and taunted the King with cowardice. Louis's answer was to establish his army in a defensive position and withdraw to the Loire, at Ponts-de-Cé near Angers. For the first, and only, time in his reign he had chosen to face the weaker of two foes attacking France. This dangerous decision, incomprehensible to his officers, had been dictated by a vision of the future probably not yet very clear to Louis himself.

All the while, he had been forwarding troops, munitions, and military orders to Picardy, where a very different kind of warfare was being waged. The Duke of Burgundy had taken the field with a reorganized and enlarged army under his command and fire in his mind. Burning villages and crops as he advanced, Duke Charles on June 11 demanded the surrender of the little town of Nesle, held only by some five hundred franc archers. During a truce, taken to arrange surrender terms, the Burgundians burst into the town and massacred the garrison, slaughtering many of the archers in the Church of Our Lady, where they had sought refuge. According to one report, the mail-clad Duke of Burgundy, spurring his charger into the blood-spattered nave and beholding the heaps of bodies, cried to his troops, "Saint George! Children, you've made a fine butchery!" The news sent a thrill of horror through all France. On June 20, the day after Louis XI was apprised of it, he received an alarming letter from the Constable informing him that the town of Roye, stoutly provisioned and garrisoned, had surrendered, on June 16, after a resistance of only two days. The Constable's loyalties at the moment remained, as usual, very doubtful, but his state of apprehension was unmistakable. "I don't find a town," he wrote, "that is not badly shaken here, nor any troops who desire to fight. I warn you, Sire, that if you don't remedy the situation with all speed, I consider that nothing will stand before him. Therefore it seems to me that you should abandon everything there in order to come here."

The King returned a sharp and military answer. "My opinion has always been that you should not hold either Montdidier or Roye, nor put troops in any place that cannot be held; and it is no marvel if the Duke of Burgundy's successes at Nesle and Roye have swelled his pride and frightened our men. . . . If you but conserve your forces and don't leave them in weak places, they will break his army. I am astonished that you have not put most of the troops garrisoning Amiens and St. Quentin in the field to harass the Burgundian flanks. . . . As for the weak places, he gains nothing when he gains them and enfeebles himself, for he has to leave garrisons there. . . . Above all, keep as many troops in the field as you can to harass the enemy flanks . . . and provide well for Compiègne." Louis then added a prophecy: *"The first place that can resist him—that will be sufficient to undo him."*

On the morning of June 27, two weeks after the fall of Roye, the advance guard of the Burgundian army unexpectedly appeared before the walls of the great town of Beauvais. Though well fortified, it lacked artillery and was defended at the moment only by the citizens themselves and a handful of nobles of the feudal levy. When a demand for surrender was summarily rejected, the lord of Crèvecoeur, ablest of Duke

Charles's commanders, ordered a simultaneous attack against two of the town's gates. The enemy quickly smashed through the suburbs. Their artillery blew a huge hole in one of the gates. The Burgundians rushed to the assault. But the citizen-defenders fought like demons, blocking the shattered gate with their swords and their bodies, pouring down a hail of archery and crossbow fire, stones and lead from the walls. None worked more valiantly than the women and children. Streams of them bore fresh munitions to the men. Some women threw themselves into the bitter hand-to-hand fighting. Others brought lighted torches to fling into the faces of their foes and soon the whole gate was ablaze. Still, the Duke of Burgundy, arriving in the afternoon, considered that the town was all but his once the fire was out.

Then, about eight in the evening, as twilight was coming on, two hundred lances of the standing army, garrisoned at Noyon, came riding through the south gate of the city. Leaving their horses to the care of the women, they ran to the gates and walls to throw themselves into the fighting. Darkness soon put an end to the assaults. Next day the full force of Duke Charles's magnificent artillery began to play upon the city; but in the afternoon Marshal Roualt arrived with one hundred lances and immediately set men to work repairing the breaches in the walls. The following day Antoine de Chabannes, the Grand Master, and another celebrated Écorcheur and companion-of-arms of Louis Dauphin, John of Salazar, entered the city with some two hundred lances. Not long after came the lord of Crussol and Gaston du Lyon and the lord of Torcy, each with stout contingents, and Robert d'Estouteville, Provost of Paris, leading the nobles of the capital. From Paris and Rouen arrived trains of wagons bearing food, munitions, engineering equipment. Additional detachments of troops were sent by the King, along with his heartfelt thanks to the citizens and soldiers of the town.

Day and night Beauvais was hammered by Burgundian artillery, which, planted on high ground, smashed streets and houses as well as fortifications. Within two weeks, Louis learned, Burgundian cannon had destroyed a quarter of the city wall. Against the advice of his commanders, the Duke ordered assault after assault. Each was bloodily repulsed; a night sally by the defenders accounted for additional Burgundians; and the garrisons of Amiens and St. Quentin, raiding the Duke's communications, were cutting off supplies and foragers. Finally, at three o'clock on the morning of July 22, an infuriated Duke of Burgundy raised the siege of Beauvais and led his army westward toward Normandy, burning villages and laying waste fields for miles around the city.

King Louis expressed his gratitude by giving the citizens the right to establish their own municipal corporation, and he exempted them from taxes. He honored the heroic efforts of the women and children, who, "without sparing themselves, even to the point of giving up their lives," had withstood the Burgundian fury. For her brave deeds he bestowed a special favor on one Jeanne Laisné (who has since come to be known as Jeanne Hachette, the heroine of Beauvais). In memory of what the women of the town had done, each of them could henceforth, regardless of her rank, wear what clothing she pleased—a suspension of the sumptuary laws common at the time—and in the yearly municipal procession commemorating the victory they were to precede the men.

The Duke of Burgundy moved into the Pays de Caux, the northeastern coast of Normandy, burning and pillaging. The Grand Master, the Constable, and the chief royal captains were always ahead of him. When he showed signs of besieging Dieppe, the Grand Master was there before him to provision the town and strengthen the garrison. When he moved instead toward Rouen, the Grand Master and the Constable established themselves on the flanks of his army. French garrisons in Picardy continued their attacks on Burgundian supply lines.

Charles of Burgundy found the road to Brittany blocked, and he had nowhere else to go. It was a hungry, battered, and depleted force that the frustrated Duke, unable to besiege Rouen or cross the Seine elsewhere, slowly led back across Picardy, leaving a broad trail of destruction. The King's prediction, that as soon as a single town withstood him the Duke would be undone, had proved to be precisely true. On November 3 Charles of Burgundy grudgingly agreed to a truce lasting until April 1, 1473.

By this time Louis XI was gathering other fruits from his apparently sterile campaign against Brittany. Spinning intricate negotiations with Francis II and Francis' chief councilors—for Louis unfailingly enjoyed the miniatures of diplomacy as well as the grand canvases—he had moved restlessly from the Loire into the region of Chartres and from there back to the Loire and on south to Poitou. There was plague about, enough to prompt him to pay some heed to where he sojourned, but not enough to curtail his activity. On September 13 at Le Mans a new Milanese ambassador, peering from an inn window, had failed to recognize the monarch to whom he was accredited. "He passed by with but about twelve horse, and his manner was such that I did not take him for the King, or even for a great lord." The ambassador added plaintively, "Truly it is death to follow His Majesty, because he travels from village to village where there are no lodgings, and there's plague on every side and nobody takes precaution against it. And the King rides like a courier, not like a King. . . . There is war and death everywhere, and great scarcity. If you want me alive, get me back from here soon."

Despite reports of Breton perfidy, King Louis pressed negotiations. On eliciting tentative proposals for a year's truce, he wrote on November 13 to Tanneguy du Chastel, "You will understand that if these offers are really in earnest, they would mean the breaking of the English invasion plans for the whole coming summer. I think I can go as far as Hermenault and thereabouts to meet them [the Breton envoys], and I must have my whole council with me and labor every day in order to make provision on all sides, as if I were quite sure that they intended to deceive me; for if they appoint in good earnest, I will not have lost my time, and if they are unwilling to appoint, at least I will have made preparations and found a remedy for everything that can be provided against." At Hermenault ten days later Louis XI signed a year's truce with the Breton envoys. Though Francis II insisted on naming as his allies the Duke of Burgundy and Edward IV, he undertook not to support any prince or foreign lord seeking to injure the King. In addition, Louis at last won to his service Odet d'Aydie, lord of Lescun. Apparently weary of laboring for masters of limited intelligence, he was refreshed by King Louis with high offices, eighty thousand crowns in cash, the County of Comminges, and membership in the Order of St. Michael. The King, explains Commynes, knew that "there was neither intelligence nor strength of purpose in Brittany which did not proceed from him."

But Louis XI had won this year a far greater prize. The wisest councilor, and, as it would turn out, the author of the greatest prose work of the age, quit the lover of war to take service with the master of statecraft. Sometime during the night of August 7–8, when the Duke of Burgundy was ravaging the Pays de Caux, Philippe de Commynes slipped away from the Burgundian camp. Within three weeks he had joined the King at Ponts-de-Ce. The outraged Duke, informed at 6 A.M. on August 8 of his departure, immediately ordered the confiscation of his property.[4] To King Louis the acquisition of Commynes was a triumph greater than a victory in the field. He signaled both his appreciation of Commynes's service at Péronne and his estimate of Commynes's future value in the magnificence of the grants he quickly bestowed. Commynes was immediately made a royal chamberlain and councilor and given two thousand livres. Shortly after, he received a pension of six thousand livres, the great principality of Talmont in Poitou, and the hand of an heiress,

Helène de Chambes (sister of the Duke of Guienne's mistress, Colette), whose father, on being paid three thousand crowns by the King, bestowed upon Commynes the rich barony of Argenton. It is as the lord of Argenton that Philippe de Commynes is henceforth known to his contemporaries.

There began between Louis and his new counselor an intimate relationship lasting till the King's death, an adventure in statecraft to be recounted later in the *Mémoires*, which the Emperor Charles V called "a textbook for Kings." Within this work Philippe de Commynes—a man, in Montaigne's famous phrase, who was "void of all manner of vanity or ostentation speaking of himself, and free from all partiality or envy speaking of others"—would create the first, and greatest, biography of Louis XI. It was not a collaboration of equals, for the King always remained the master of his policy; but much of the King's achievement in the eleven years of life left him was engendered in the interplay of their minds.

The gains of King Louis this year were not limited to acquiring the best servitors of his dead brother, of the Duke of Brittany, and of the Duke of Burgundy. Duke Charles had been made to see that there was no glory to be won in attacking France. True, his ally Edward IV was beginning to make preparations for invasion. But what might not be accomplished in the meanwhile? There was beginning to come clear in Louis's mind a vision of how the Duke of Burgundy's grandiose ambitions might be used against him. In the truce he had signed on November 3 Duke Charles had trumpeted as his allies the Emperor of Germany; the Kings of England, Scotland, Portugal, Castile, Aragon, Naples, Hungary, Poland; the Republic of Venice; the Dukes of Brittany, Calabria, Lorraine, Guelders, and Austria; the House of Savoy; and the Count Palatine of the Rhine. Perhaps it might be possible to entrap the Duke of Burgundy in his imperial dreams.

A ballad-monger, commenting on the situation in France at the end of 1472, chanted:

> Berry * est mort,   (*Berry's no more,*
> Bretaigne dort,   *The Bretons snore,*
> Bourgogne hongue, *Burgundy lowers,*
> Le Roy besogne.   *The King works at all hours.*)

* The King's brother, formerly the Duke of Berry.

THE WEAVING OF
THE WEB

19. The Germans

OUTWARDLY, the year 1473 appears
to be a comparatively undistinguished time in the life of Louis XI, almost routine, a fabric of commonplaces. To the casual onlooker of that
life choosing to single out the least eventful of all the years of the King's
reign, the year 1473 would quickly recommend itself.

Louis's daily existence was flecked with illness and with grief, but
both he had known before and would know again. The long days of
hunting, rain or shine, the long hours of talk with his intimates, the hard
riding of the roads of France, the coarsely clad King peering into the
opacity of the future as he munched a bit of bread and meat in a village
hut—all this is familiar. In his administration of the realm—the flood of
decisions flowing from his mind in decrees, letters, notes to his Chancellor, orders to his captains, demands upon Parlement and the Chamber
of Accounts, reports to his good towns—there is to be found no remarkable revelation of his statecraft. His dealing with foreign powers produced no treaties of import, and, constantly negotiating as always, he
seemingly accomplished so little that Philippe de Commynes hardly ac-
cords two pages to the year. If the King's position in Roussillon suddenly deteriorated, his relations with his German neighbors to the east
were never better. With the Duchy of Savoy and the Italian states—on
which powers, as usual, he spent large amounts of his time—the *status
quo* was, in general, maintained. His troublesome brother-in-law Philip
of Bresse had now entered his service, but his clever sister, Duchess Yolande, was more Burgundian than ever. He enjoyed referring to the

chief herald of Burgundy, Golden Fleece, as Golden Fleecer (*Trahison d'Or*, literally Golden Treachery, punning on *Toison d'Or*, Golden Fleece); he kept in communication with an adversary, King Ferrante of Naples; he continued to characterize the Venetians by sizzling epithets; and if his relations with his ally Galeazzo-Maria Sforza of Milan worsened, they had been worsening for years.

Yet the year 1473, despite appearances, marks a decisive turn in the King's hopes, designs, fortunes. There now begins to be discernible a new pattern of statecraft which the fortuity of event, the ambitions of his enemy, his own acuteness of mind have enabled him to lay down. In this seminal season, the daily life of the King, no less than the construction of his enterprises, weaves intermingling significances of character and circumstance.

Always there remained dogs at his side, in the wilds or within his chamber. Smart in their collars of Lombardy leather with gilt studs, the greyhounds were much pampered—their feet washed in warm wine, their ailments tended by apothecaries, their welfare safeguarded by offerings to St. Hubert. The current favorite, Mistodin, wore robes and slept in a bed. It was now well known to many European princes that there was no better way to please Louis XI than to make him a present of hunting dogs. The passage of years had but refined his exacting standards.

So did Christopher da Bollate discover when, in June of 1473, he informed the King that the Duke of Milan's dog keeper, Antonio, had arrived with two hunting dogs, a bitch and a castrated male, for His Majesty. The King at once "had Antonio and the dogs conducted to his own chamber. With what kindness and pleasure His Majesty asked about the qualities and points of the dogs—he always speaking Lombard—I will let Antonio report on his return. But I inform Your Excellency that the bitch pleased him, he told us, and would have pleased him much more if it had been younger and a male. I replied that Your Excellency had not been able to find male dogs so obedient and affectionate and with the kind of coat His Majesty prefers and so absolutely perfect at hawking as this bitch—her sagacity and skill, if one has not seen her hunt, cannot be appreciated. . . . As for the castrated male, His Majesty told me that he did not wish a castrated animal but a big handsome young male with a coat like Stella's [the bitch] and passionate about hawking. I replied that His Majesty had not previously explained to me the particular qualities he liked in dogs and that, in fact, Your Excellency had sent this dogkeeper in order to understand more fully the King's desires so that another time he could better satisfy them. The King then questioned Antonio at length about the kind of greyhounds Your Excellency likes best. Antonio answered—the biggest and handsomest.

"The following day His Majesty told me that Antonio had been here once before and that he had given him about a dozen good dogs to take to Your Excellency, but that Antonio had let some of them die on the road. The King added that this time Antonio had brought the two dogs all the way from Milan with iron collars around their necks. His Majesty then had two most handsome greyhounds brought in, telling me that if Your Excellency wished, he would like to have a servant of his bring them to you—and without collars so that their necks would not be injured. . . ." Having rubbed in his point, Louis went on to say "that he was taking good care of the two dogs [brought by Antonio] and that one day he would go hawking with them." A few days later, the King told Bollate that he had tried out the dogs and found them good, the bitch much better than the castrated male, "but that, since he does not care for castrated dogs [or bitches], perhaps Your Excellency would wish to have them returned to him. . . . In then thanking Your Excellency for the dogs, His Majesty said that if possible he would like a male of Stella's breed, of the sort I described in my last dispatch, a dog that was expressly trained for hawking and, above all, affectionate." Doggedly upholding the honor of the Duke of Milan, Bollate replied that the Duke would be most unhappy that the greyhounds were not to His Majesty's liking, that he would do everything to satisfy the King's desires; as for sending the two dogs back, Bollate had no doubt that the Duke would be very glad to have them again since they were the best and most attractive dogs that he had!

The Milanese ambassador was very much a part of the King's life. That position had grown thorny as the King, always well informed about Italian affairs, began to realize the shortcomings of Francesco Sforza's successor. Handsome, profligate, learned, capricious—the very model of a Renaissance tyrant—Galeazzo-Maria Sforza nervously shifted sails with every wind, and the winds of 1466–72 did not seem to be blowing in the direction of France, all the while that he bombarded Louis XI with protestations of devotion and masses of advice. Young Jean Pierre Panigarola, eloquent reporter of Montlhéry and the siege of Paris, had given way in 1468 to the soldierly Sforza de Bettinis, who in turn was replaced, toward the end of 1472, by Christopher da Bollate, each change reflecting the waning of the Duke's loyalty and the King's increasingly acrid attitude toward his ally. Bollate, entirely his master's man, had, on previous special missions across the Alps, displayed in his letters little enthusiasm for the French or their King. He was of a suspicious and prying turn of mind, but sinuous and quick-witted, inclined to dramatize his difficulties and his adroitness in surmounting them. Some rough treatment by Philip of Breese, of which he was the victim on his journey to the French court in November of 1472, perhaps exacerbated his tendency to waspishness.[1] Louis soon became aware that Bollate's dispatches interpreted darkly his words, actions, prospects.

On a morning early in January, 1474, when King Louis was talking informally in his council chamber, he suddenly unleashed some angry remarks on the subject of the Duke of Milan's failure to support French interests, declaring that the Duke had thus perjured himself in breaking the alliance by which Milan had become ruler of Genoa under the overlordship of the King of France. It would seem that he did not notice the presence of Christopher da Bollate, to whom, a little before, he had graciously given access to the council. Bollate pretended not to have heard and slipped away. That afternoon Louis sent for the Milanese envoy, greeted him with smiling face, "God keep you, Messire Christopher," and, taking him by the arm, led him to the privacy of the King's bedchamber, where there were but two chamberlains. Throwing himself casually on the bed, Louis began chatting sympathetically about the Duke of Milan's difficulties in preventing Genoese conspiracies. Indeed it might be that Genoa would rise against him by June. "I would no more want the Duke of Milan to lose Genoa than I to lose . . . Perpignan," Louis observed blandly. Then, slightly changing tone: "I marvel much, however, that though many times I have sent to request aid from the Duke, never has he been willing to help me. . . ." Suddenly: "Tell me, Christopher, has it been reported to you what I said this morning in council? Tell me the truth—was it not Boffile [de Juge] who told you?" When Bollate replied that he himself, with great unhappiness, had heard the words, and protested that the Duke of Milan regarded himself as a loyal son of the King and was no fairweather friend, Louis merely observed, "Well, did I not give to Milan free and peaceful possession of Savona and Genoa [in 1463]?" True, the King went on, it was no wellwisher of the Duke of Milan who had declared the Duke to be faithless, but if he told the truth, "certainly I would have reason to be angry." Immediately resuming his geniality, Louis ended the interview in casual chat.

The King did not let the matter rest, however. In the course of that day and the next, he sent three different men to sound out Christopher. They asked him if he was content with His Majesty and with the way His Majesty treated his master, and if he was quite satisfied with his lodgings. The last, Jean d'Amboise, a royal councilor, asked him not to write to the Duke what the King had said in council. When Bollate replied that he had not made up his mind what to do, d'Amboise said, "The King reputes you as his own servant when you are here. Both in his chamber and in council the King acts and speaks frankly and familiarly with you, and thus he purges his heart of all the anger that he has had against the Duke in these matters; and much better it is that he do so than to keep it in his throat. We here always take in good part these ways of his. Indeed, are you not well aware that he's always thus talking off the top of his head [an observation that Bollate discreetly put in cipher]?" In the end, Bollate could not be sure—nor can we—whether the King had committed an awkward imprudence or produced a charade designed to warn the Duke of Milan, and the Duke's envoy, that he was not deceived by Milanese wiles.

King Louis was now (in 1473) fifty years old, fast growing bald, often troubled by hemorrhoids. Though he had apparently lost none of his zest for comedy, of his exuberance of mind and his physical endurance, the erosion of years had begun to show traces. His suspiciousness —too often confirmed—had deepened. He was more readily provoked to irritability, more impatient of inefficiency, harsh in some of the means he employed. In short he had perhaps grown less tolerant of adversity, through no less confident in his capacity to overcome it. His game—in the wildwood or in the council chamber—he pursued with undimished tenacity. The erosion of years was also marked in the men about the King. The Duke of Bourbon, who for so long remained, in the words of a Milanese envoy, "at the King's side like a dog on a chain," had now, out of weariness or pique, retired to his estates. Like many others, the King's former favorite, Antoine du Lau, had been forgiven his infidelity and held a command in Roussillon. In September of this year (1473) Louis de Crussol died of pestilence while on service in that country—he the most cherished of the remaining companions of Louis's youth. The stationing of Jean Bourré at Amboise to watch over the Dauphin left only Ymbert de Batarnay, the lord du Bouchage,[2] and the lord du Lude, "John Cleverness [Jehan des habilitez]," as Louis nicknamed this bluff opportunist. These two, along with Philippe de Commynes, Tanneguy du Chastel, and the Bastard of Bourbon, Admiral, were the men closest to the King. Three others were rising to prominence: the soldier Jean Blosset, lord of St. Pierre, Captain of the King's new French Guard; an accomplished Neapolitan, Boffile de Juge, formerly in the service of King René; and the younger brother of the Duke of Bourbon, Pierre de Beaujeu, soon to marry the King's elder daughter, Anne, who had inherited much of her father's intelligence and whom Louis enjoyed calling "the least stupid woman in France."

When the *compères* of the King were absent on special services Louis, as of old, watched over their welfare and sought their counsel by streams of messages. In August of this year he wrote to Tanneguy du Chastel, on a military mission and ailing, "I have received your letter. You speak to the point about your fortifications but you say nothing at all about your coming. I assure you that I have the greatest desire to talk with you. . . . I am still keeping my son [-in-law the Admiral] here with me; but if you see that it would be good for him to go there for a time, write to him and he will make the trip. Get yourself cured as soon as you can and let me know how you are and if you want anything that I can provide, and I assure you that I'll be happy to provide it. . . . I'm sending you some advices; look them over; I'd very much like to have your good opinion on the subject. . . ."

The style of his religious life had not changed. He even spoke exuberantly of going by sea to the next Jubilee at Rome—"with such indulgences as he'd gain by doing so, he did not believe that he would ever have bad fortune!" A vow Louis had sworn to accomplish by the end of March, 1473, at the shrine of the Hospital of Holy Christ in Bayonne, Guienne, a ten days' journey from Tours, caused his advisers much unhappiness; for at this moment of his negotiating for a prolongation of the Burgundian truce the Constable had sent word that the Duke of Burgundy was secretly assembling an army. In such dangerously uncertain circumstances, the royal officers affirmed, the King could put off his pilgrimage without damage to his soul. In the end, however, Louis undertook the journey, observing to his court that he could not very well expect additional credit from God unless he fulfilled previous obligations.

About mid-March, the King, accompanied only by his guard and a few intimates, set forth at six o'clock in the morning from Plessis-lès-Tours, his new country house on the outskirts of Tours, and headed for Bayonne, "riding hard." To insure that he was followed by no presumptuous suitor or ambassador, he ordered the gates of Tours kept closed until 10 A.M., had a bridge on his road broken, and stationed the captain of his household gentlemen there to see that no one passed. In ten days or less, it appears, Louis reached Bayonne and fulfilled his vow.

The strains on mind and body this time took their toll. In early April on the return journey he experienced a severe attack of hemorrhoids. Attempting to make light of his suffering, he casually informed Christopher da Bollate that it was usual at that time of year for his hemorrhoids to come down but that they were giving him more pain than customarily. At least, he observed to Bollate, "anyone with the infirmity cannot be accused of sexual immorality or of leprosy and, in addition, such a sufferer has a long life." But on Maundy Thursday, April 15, he was in such distress that he had to order the holy office of the day deferred until past midday because he could not come sooner to the chapel. "He is indeed afflicted," Bollate concluded, "and quite cast down."

Ordinarily the King was able quickly to throw off his affliction or endure it cheerfully. Later in the year, he wrote to his Grand Master, the Count of Dammartin, that, if negotiations with Burgundy demanded it, he was ready to ride from Tours to Creil, some 150 miles, then on to Guise, fifty miles further, and would return from Guise to Compiègne overnight—"and who would believe," he added, "that I had hemorrhoids!" This time, however, as six years before, the attack led to serious illness. By the beginning of May, he was suffering the same severe headaches, fever, debility as in the spring of 1467. Bollate gloomily diagnosed his trouble as "epilepsy and apoplexy." It may be indeed that the King suffered a slight stroke. One day he was badly shaken by a fall down a flight of stairs.

For a while he struggled to carry on the business of government as usual, but he was forced more and more to stay withdrawn in his chambers. Finally, to hide the seriousness of his condition and secure the isolation in which to fight for his health, he rode from Tours to Amboise about mid-May. He ordered public proclamations, repeated weekly, that on pain of death no one, unless sent for by the King, was to approach within three leagues of Amboise. He was accompanied only by a few *compères*. Numerous embassies were forced to cool their heels at Tours; some nobles who considered themselves above mere proclamations were firmly turned away from Amboise and came back to Tours "malcontent." Georges de La Trémoille, lord of Craon, long one of the King's chief officers, managed to get through the gates of the castle of Amboise but was then refused admittance.

The news that reached the afflicted King was mostly gloomy: the

English Parliament had given Edward IV a large war grant; affairs in Roussillon were going badly; the Duke of Brittany showed signs of backsliding into his old intrigues with Burgundy. These tidings so harried the helpless, pain-racked King that in an outburst of angry frustration he quarreled with his intimates, then ordered them to leave Amboise. Cared for only by attendants, he fought in silence to recover his health. By the beginning of June he had won his battle; within a week he was dealing with his affairs as vigorously as ever.

A few weeks later he suffered another blow. Queen Charlotte had given birth to an infant son several months before. Christened François,* the child was a precious addition to the royal dynasty because of the frail health of Louis's heir, Charles, now three. When the King was hunting in the forest of Loches in mid-July, tidings were rushed to him that François had died. It is reported that in his agony the King gave order to lay waste the whole region of the forest where he had received the message. Louis's religious instincts drove deeper than his observances of the Catholic faith. The well-informed chronicler who records this moment continues, "Such was his custom: when bad news came to him, never afterward would he mount the horse he had been riding or don the garments he was then wearing. And you must know," adds the chronicler, "that the King was better garnished with intelligence than with fine clothes." It was now that Louis swore never to have relations with any woman except his wife, a vow that, Commynes affirms, he scrupulously kept.

In November Louis's own life was threatened. A poison plot against the King was initiated by a slippery adventurer named Ythier Marchant, a former agent of the Duke of Guienne now serving the Duke of Burgundy, one of the shadowy secondary figures in the princely intrigues of the time. It was Louis's generosity in taking servants of his brother into his household that both prompted and frustrated the scheme. Marchant's tool, one Jean Hardy, delivered a supply of poison and a promise of twenty thousand crowns to the King's sauce cook, who, like himself and the chief cook of the royal kitchens, had been in the Duke of Guienne's service. The sauce cook and his superior hastened to reveal the plot to the King. In the spring of the following year (1474), Jean Hardy was decapitated by sentence of the Parlement of Paris, and the houses he owned in France, and his birthplace, were razed to the ground. Though many Frenchmen, and for a time Louis XI too, believed that the Duke

---

* Apparently in honor of Francesco Sforza. The first son, born in December of 1466, who lived but a few hours, was also named François. See p. 198.

of Burgundy had plotted the assassination, Ythier Marchant probably undertook the operation on his own, hoping to be suitably rewarded by the Duke for ridding him of his mightiest enemy without burdening his conscience.

Within this pattern of his ways and days, Louis XI during 1473 had seemingly ventured little and accomplished less to counter the dangers threatening his realm. On the western European scene the year was eventful. But it was Charles, Duke of Burgundy, who dominated events —who schemed grandly, created opportunities, and dared to reach for their fulfillment.

Yet behind appearances Louis XI throughout 1473 was developing the climactic enterprise of his life. It was, metaphorically, another kind of withdrawal, subtle, perilous, and imaginative. Scholar of his own past errors, fumbling in the misty dawn of innovation, Louis XI was moving toward a new kind of warfare, fashioned out of the illusions of his adversary, invisible realities of power, the malleability of human hopes and fears, a form of hostilities that would one day be known as cold war.

ii

LIKE THE master workman who instinctively lays out the right tools even before he quite understands what the job calls for, the King of France had, for many years, nurtured a close relationship with the Duke of Burgundy's eastern neighbors, the Swiss. He had never forgotten the lesson taught him by the hardy mountaineers in 1444 when he had led the Écorcheurs against Bâle. In the crowded years since becoming King, he had warmly welcomed Swiss envoys, sought to tighten the Franco-Swiss treaty of amity, and always addressed his friends as "The Magnificent Lords of High Germany." There was no irony in the appellation, Louis caring only for the actualities of power and being innocent of seignorial prejudices. By 1468, the ablest and most ambitious of Swiss statesmen, Nicolas Diesbach, Avoyer (Mayor) of Berne, had become honorary "councilor and chamberlain" of the King and was receiving a pension. The eastern cantons, like Zug, Schwyz, Glaris, were but rude farming and herding communities; headed by Zurich, they resisted all foreign entanglements and knew but one enemy in the world, the Hapsburgs. Berne, however, had become a rich and powerful trading city. Astride Alpine routes of commerce from Italy to northern Europe, and pressing upon the Pays de Vaud, country between Morat and Lausanne still possessed by the feeble House of Savoy, the Bernese looked ambitiously to the west and nursed hopes of expanding their territory and influence.

The independence of the Swiss cantons was recognized neither by the Hapsburg Emperor, Frederick III, nor by his sluggish cousin Sigismund, Duke of Austria, who ruled lands from the Tyrol to Alsace that had once included the territory of the cantons. With Sigismund's turbulent Rhenish and Alsatian nobles the city of Berne and its ally Bâle were constantly at loggerheads. This enmity flared into war in 1468, the Swiss proving victorious as usual. Sigismund was forced to sign a peace which required him to pay an indemnity of ten thousand Rhine florins or relinquish the town of Waldshut and adjacent territory on the right bank of the Rhine.

Desperately humiliated, the impecunious and self-indulgent Duke of Austria* sought aid from the King of France. He offered in return for a guarantee of French military protection and a financial subsidy, to resign, in pledge, his Rhenish lands.

To this proposition Louis XI made a response which perhaps more than any other act of his rule set going the course he was to impose upon the history of his times. From the opacity of the future he could have snatched only a glimmer. Men once traced the origins of the Trojan War to Leda's egg, from which was hatched the beautiful Helen. But, outside of myth, human events only become origins after indefatigable tugging and hauling, by someone, upon the slippery ropes of opportunity, in intuitive accord with the permissions of chance. All that Louis, at the moment, could hope to foresee was the reaction of the Duke of Burgundy and a faint image of its consequences. It was enough.

Louis XI sent Duke Sigismund's envoy packing in short order. Though Sigismund himself dispatched message on message begging for an interview, Louis curtly refused to see him. He then informed the Swiss that he had emphatically repulsed the overtures of their herditary enemy. He sensed that Sigismund of Austria must needs turn for aid to the Grand Duke of the West. He was aware that Charles coveted Alsace as a link between the Low Countries and the Burgundies. He calculated that the Duke's aggressive occupation of the upper Rhine was likely to provoke the fears and pinch the ambitions of the Bear of Berne.

The Dukes of Austria and Burgundy promptly fulfilled his expectation. By the Treaty of St. Omer, May 9, 1469, Charles took Sigismund under his protection, contracting to aid the Austrian if he was attacked

---

* His six principal castles were all named after himself: Sigismundsburg, Sigmundseek, Sigmundsfreud, Sigmundskron, Sigmundslust, Sigmundsfried.

by the Swiss, and paid him fifty thousand florins with an additional ten thousand to redeem Waldshut. In return, he acquired Sigismund's rights in the "landgraviat of High Alsace" and territory on the opposite bank of the Rhine. Sigismund retained the privilege of repurchase at the same figure, plus Charles's expenses—which could amount to a great deal, for many of Sigismund's places were already pawned and the Duke of Burgundy intended to redeem them. Charles chose as Landvogt, the High Bailiff of his new territory, Pierre de Hagenbach, a hard-fisted, ambitious Alsatian noble who shared the prejudices of his kind against townsmen and Swiss "boors." He soon annoyed the people of the new Burgundian province by his arrogant mien, then outraged them by imposing a tax on wine, the "mauvais denier" (evil penny). By bellicose utterances he stirred the fears of the powerful cities of lower Alsace, like Strasbourg, and of his other neighbors, the Swiss. He even threatened to lay hands on Bâle and Colmar, and went so far as to boast that he would flay the Bear of Berne in order to make himself a fur.

Louis XI, however much as he was pressed in these years by other affairs, continued to keep warm his relations with the Swiss by frequent embassies and messages, supplemented at one point by a tactful distribution of three thousand livres to certain influential men of Berne.

Such was the unstable compound of politics along the Rhine and King Louis's stake in them, at the beginning of 1473.

iii

EARLY IN THE YEAR (1473) the independent towns of lower Alsace, alarmed by the aggressions of Pierre de Hagenbach, banded together with Bâle, in a league of mutual defense called the Basse Union. A few weeks later, some Swiss merchants trading on the Rhine were seized, body and goods, by Austrian nobles. The enraged cantons, blaming the Duke of Burgundy as the avowed protector of Duke Sigismund and his vassals, hastened to enter into defense consultations with the Basse Union. They also dispatched Nicolas Diesbach to France with news that Charles of Burgundy was recruiting troops in Lombardy, their destination unknown, and with the request that the King, as their good friend, keep them informed of Franco-Burgundian developments. The Basse Union went even further: its envoys brought Louis XI an offer to make war on Burgundy if the King would join them. At this point Louis was again solicited by Sigismund of Austria. That shifty-shallow Duke found himself with the Burgundian money spent, a yearning to repossess his lands, and a fat grudge against the Duke of Burgundy for not subduing the Swiss. He proposed that King Louis lend him repurchase money for Alsace, promising in return to attack Burgundy if the Duke made war on France.

Louis XI held resolutely to his role of promoting this political evolution, without appearing to sponsor it. To the cantons he held out the hope that he might possibly secure from Sigismund a Hapsburg acknowledgment of their independence. To Sigismund he indicated that he might be able to arrange for a profitable reconciliation with the Swiss and the Basse Union. To the latter league he made known Sigismund's need of money for the repurchase of Alsace—discreetly saying nothing about himself making such provision—and pointed out that an Alsace repossessed by the feeble Duke of Austria would cease to be a menace to her neighbors. The additional pressure required to fuse these disparate elements into a united front Louis XI looked to the Duke of Burgundy to supply. That Duke had again thrust into the Empire to the river Rhine, this time along its lower reaches. Louis had seen to it that Charles had nothing to fear from France: early in 1473 the King had secured a prolongation of their truce until April 1, 1474.

Like a bare upland with contours gouged by storms into ever sharper relief, Charles of Burgundy, the Grand Duke of the West, had been, in the passage of years, deeply scored by the passionate weathers of his ambitions, frustrations, illusions. Whatever he accomplished, in council or on the field, he attributed to his own genius. Such failures as had to be recognized he laid to the ineptitude or cowardice of his subjects and the machinations of enemies. His reading now was all histories, particularly histories of the famous conquerors of old, like Caesar and Hannibal, whose reputations he meant to equal, if not eclipse. He expressed his greatness in pomp as elaborate as his father's, and in a haughtiness of demeanor that his father had never used. He took no trouble to disguise his aversion to the bourgeois Flemings, who grudged the military taxes he was laying heavily upon them—"I would rather have you hate me than scorn me," he told them fiercely. This distaste now extended to the soldiery his territories provided. To bolster the lances of his standing army and the band of nobles who faithfully endured his relentless campaigning, he increasingly sought Italian mercenaries; for these troops had a grand reputation, were not corrupted by civilian attitudes, and might prove able to execute his brilliant tactics.

As his dark, imperious nature had hardened, his dreams became the more flexibly grandiose. With the aid of the English he meant to destroy Louis XI, to crush France and turn the ruins of the realm over to his ally; but such revenge no longer fulfilled his ambitions. His gaze was now directed eastward toward the spacious destiny of the Germanies, a hodgepodge of feudal lordships under the feeble suzerainty of the Emperor. He had long hoped, as Philip the Good before him, to join his northern domains of the Low Countries with the County and Duchy of Burgundy in eastern France. Beyond this aim there now glowed the vision of reconstituting the ancient kingdom of Lotharingia, or Burgundy, which briefly after the breakup of Charlemagne's empire had stretched between France and the Germanies from the North Sea to the Mediterranean. Such a territory must have a king—and why should not that king, Charles of Burgundy, became Emperor as well? He ruled extensive imperial territories and enjoyed the title of Marquis of the Holy Roman Empire. He had already been dangling his daughter, the greatest heiress in Europe, before the Emperor's son. The Rhine River had become the bloodstream of his hopes.

In order to free Charles for German adventures, Louis XI intended to maintain as long as he could and at any cost of dignity his truce with Burgundy. The English would invade in two years, he remarked to the Milanese ambassador, "but what might not come to fruition by then?" It was, however, a policy of high risk. In the Germanies, Charles of Burgundy could well achieve a power that would spell ruin to France, unless Louis was able to arrange for him there a mortal rendezvous. Patiently the "universal spider" * had begun to spin a web, insubstantial as thought, on a scale gigantic enough to enclose the gigantesque designs of the Duke of Burgundy.

Charles of Burgundy in February (1473) persuaded the dying Duke of Guelders to will him the Duchy. Invading Guelders in mid-June, he completed an easy conquest of that Rhine territory and its capital Nimwegen in six weeks, an acquisition that, in Commynes's phrase, "sharpened his appetite for German affairs." He began heating up negotiations with the Emperor that had been simmering since 1469. In return for the marriage of his heiress, Marie, to the Emperor's son Maximilian, he proposed that Frederick III create him King of the Romans, i.e., Vice Emperor, it being understood that Charles would succeed to the imperial throne, which, on his death, would go to Maximilian. The Emperor, longing for the bride but not the bargain, paltered and tergiversated. By the late summer of 1473, however, the Duke of Burgundy had pushed the

* So the Burgundian chronicler Molinet called him.

always hungry Frederick into making a tentative commitment. He then arranged an interview with the Emperor designed to display his grandeur and consummate his ambitions.

All Europe awaited with fascination, or fear, the meeting of Frederick III and the Grand Duke of the West. None were more apprehensive than the Swiss and the great Alsatian towns of the Basse Union. The King of France, however, to whom the junction of Burgundy and the Empire, with England closing the circle, apparently posed a mortal threat, preserved his *sang-froid*. All summer the King imperturbably continued peace negotiations with Burgundy even though the Duke's envoys grew daily more difficult and Charles's demands became so enormous "that it was stupefying," as Louis observed to Bollate. In late August, Louis told the Milanese ambassador that there was no use trying to deflect the Emperor from a Burgundian alliance: Duke Charles "had always held Frederick III right by the tail." A few days later he remarked that "he would be happy for the Duke to inject himself so deeply into the Germanies that he would be stuck there all the rest of his life."

Agents of Louis XI would be working behind the scenes of the Burgundian-Imperial conference, primed to stimulate the fears of the German princes and the forebodings of Frederick III. The King also dispatched envoys, laden with rich gifts, to his friends the Swiss in order that he and they might consult regarding "our common enemy."

In the early evening of September 30, Frederick III, who had arrived the day before in the old imperial town of Trèves on the Moselle, went from his palace to the city gates to welcome the Duke of Burgundy. By the light of flaming torches the Duke knelt, kissed the Emperor's hand, and they then rode in ceremonious procession through the city, Charles establishing residence in the abbey of St. Maximin, just outside the walls. It was the Grand Duke of the West who took all eyes. Preceded by a hundred blond pages in white and blue, trumpeters with silver instruments, heralds representing the fourteen Burgundian states, sumptuously equipped archers of the guard, lords of the *Toison d'Or* clad in cloth of gold, the Duke of Burgundy rode a courser armored in gold and was himself encased in shining armor over which he wore a cloak of black velvet starred with diamonds. Behind him came an escort of six thousand horse, batteries of guns, and tens of baggage wagons laden with the treasure of stuff which he had inherited from his father —gold plate, jewels in heaps, chests of coins (to be distributed where they would do the most good), priceless tapestries, which included a set of hangings depicting the exploits of Alexander the Great. In his train the Duke flaunted lordly prelates and the ambassadors of a dozen European states.

On successive days Charles feasted the Emperor at the abbey in a dazzle of princely opulence, was entertained in return at the imperial palace. Privately Charles took a high hand in his negotiations with Frederick III, but soon discovered that, despite all that his heiress would bring to Frederick's son Maximilian, there was no hope of becoming King of the Romans. The Duke then insisted upon the erection of his domains into a kingdom, which would likewise include the bishoprics of Utrecht, Tournai, Liège, and Cambrai, the Duchies of Lorraine and Savoy, and the Swiss cantons. The Emperor hesitated, shifted ground; the more he faltered, the more imperiously demanding became his prospective son-in-law. Meanwhile, Charles triumphantly tied another principality to his domains. On the death of Duke Nicolas, son of the Angevin firebrand Duke John, in July of 1473, Nicolas' cousin René, son of King René's daughter Yolande and the Count of Vaudemont, had succeeded to the Duchy of Lorraine. Pushed by his pro-Burgundian nobles, René II was forced to sign a treaty with the Duke of Burgundy which gave the latter virtual control of the Duchy.

At Trèves the days of November were slipping away in outward ceremony and private haggling. A number of the German princes, encouraged by ducal funds and promises, urged Charles's cause, but many feared the intrusion into the Empire of the arrogant Duke, and some had been cultivated by Louis XI. The Emperor Frederick III, bedeviled by his lords, becoming increasingly queasy at the thought of the Burgundian yoke but increasingly eager for the Burgundian heiress, finally signified in mid-November that he was ready to grant Charles the kingdom of his desires. A coronation ceremony was quickly prepared, for November 25, and garments made ready. Suddenly the Emperor, taking refuge in the discord of his princes, sent word to Duke Charles that unforeseen obstacles made necessary a postponement of the coronation— the notice reaching Charles on November 23. In an attempt to mollify the seething Duke of Burgundy, a ceremonial parting was proposed for November 25. Sometime in the night of November 24–25, the Emperor Frederick III secretly left Trèves by water, thus avoiding the payment of his debts and a final confrontation with his fearsome guest.

Charles of Burgundy, outraged by the collapse of his pretensions, feverishly resolved to forge his kingdom for himself. He at once defied the

Empire by meddling openly in a German quarrel. Months before, the Prince-Archbishop of Cologne, driven from the city by his people, had sought the aid of the Duke of Burgundy. Two weeks after that Duke shook the dust of Trèves from his Alexander tapestries, he announced that he intended to restore the Archbishop to his see. The military occupation of Cologne would give him yet another stretch of Rhine territory. Pending that, he proceeded to offer a demonstration of his might. On December 16 he made a bristling entrance into Nancy, capital of Lorraine, with Duke René II, riding like a conqueror rather than an ally. He then sought to overawe his discontented Alsatian province—reviewed his army at Ensisheim with great pomp, and emphatically confirmed all the decrees of his hated lieutenant, Pierre de Hagenbach. On coming to Dijon, capital of his Duchy of Burgundy, in January, 1474, he fiercely informed an assembly of nobles and prelates, and the world, that he intended to recreate the ancient realm of Burgundy-Lotharingia.

Louis XI had closely traced, in reports forwarded from French army headquarters in Champagne, the belligerent progress of the Duke of Burgundy from Trèves to Dijon. While the Duke and the Emperor were still negotiating, he had received from the magistrates of Berne a communication on the subject, which concluded, "We and our allies hope—with the aid of God, of our arms, and of our friends—to repel any aggression, from whatever direction it comes against us." Louis estimated that Charles of Burgundy had now effectively supplied the pressure required to unite the King's friends along the Rhine.

iv

UNDER delicate guidance from the King of France, the towns of the Basse Union agreed, in January of 1474, to provide Sigismund of Austria with money for the repurchase of Alsace, and they and the Swiss then began negotiating an alliance. The moment had struck for Louis to attempt the seemingly impossible: erasing an indurate enmity of centuries in order to reconcile hardheaded suspicious mountaineers and one softheaded petulant Duke. The King preached to Sigismund that he was relinquishing nothing not already lost, and he and his friends at Berne convinced the rest of the cantons that the true enemy was Burgundy, not Austria. Prickly points of disagreement were left to Louis's arbitration, Sigismund hoping that the King, being a feudal personality like himself, would decide in his favor, and the Bernese having Louis's private assurance that all would go as they wished. Sigismund was to have

French troops and a French pension; the cantons, to enjoy princely subsidies.

Final negotiations took place in a conference held at the end of
March. In the presence of the King's envoys, and after consummate diplomacy by the King's councilor, Nicolas Diesbach, Avoyer of Berne,
the Basse Union and the Swiss concluded a ten-year alliance. Sigismund,
allying himself with the Basse Union, was granted by the latter eighty
thousand florins with which to repurchase High Alsace. The Austrian
Duke recognized the independence of the Cantons in return for a treaty
of amity and assistance. Such were the principal provisions of the celebrated League of Constance. On April 6 (1474) Sigismund dispatched to
the Duke of Burgundy the fateful announcement that he had deposited
eighty thousand Rhine florins at Bâle as the price of repurchase and
meant to take immediate possession of his territory. Charles, busy with
plans to occupy Cologne under guise of succoring the Archbishop,
merely sent Hagenbach a few hundred men and Sigismund a haughty
refusal. Within a month the towns of Alsace threw off the Burgundian
yoke and welcomed Sigismund's forces, the Basse Union declared war
on the Duke of Burgundy, and Pierre de Hagenbach, captured at
Brisach, was condemned to death and executed on May 9.

As Louis XI surveyed this rapid evolution of his designs, he continued to press negotiations with the Duke of Burgundy for a renewal of
the truce expiring April 1 (1474). While the Duke displayed his usual
haughty mien and inflated demands, the majority of the King's
councilors—some, excited by his diplomatic successes on the Rhine; others, fearful of Burgundian conquests to come—urged him to let the truce
expire so that he could wage war on Burgundy before the English invaded. However, his shrewdest adviser, Philippe de Commynes, argued
that the King "should boldly continue the truce and allow the Duke
of Burgundy to hurl himself against the Empire . . . pointing out that
. . . the more the Duke became embroiled in an affair, the more he entangled himself. . . ." Duke Charles finally agreed to prolong the truce
until the first of May, 1475.

The Duke of Burgundy, however, also had good reasons for agreeing
to the prolongation. Even as he was resuming his campaign for the
Rhine, he consummated a menacing counter-challenge to the diplomacy
of King Louis. By the terms of the Anglo-Burgundian Treaty of London
of July 25 Edward IV agreed to cross the Channel in arms in 1475. The
Duke recognized him as the sovereign of a dismembered France.
Charles was given in outright sovereignty great territories in the north

and east to add to his swelling Germanic domains.

By the time the treaty was signed the Duke of Burgundy was marching eastward with the greatest army he had ever assembled. Infuriated though he had been by the presumption of the Basse Union and Sigismund, he was deferring his vengeance upon Alsace. First, he would add Cologne to his domains, then conquer the Alsatians, and thus substantially achieve his frontier on the Rhine from the North Sea to the Alps. On July 30 he laid siege to the insignificant little town of Neuss, an outpost of Cologne some twenty miles down the Rhine from that city.

King Louis soon learned about the Treaty of London: he managed to buy a copy of it from Aragonese ambassadors who had been negotiating with the Duke of Burgundy. His answer: to use the Burgundian aggression against Cologne as a means of finally locking into his design the Swiss cantons. After two months of patient maneuvering by the King and his agents, the Swiss were convinced that, conflict with Burgundy being inevitable, it was better to begin while the Duke was still occupied in besieging Neuss. The resultant treaty, sealed on October 26, stipulated that, if the cantons opened war on the Duke of Burgundy, Louis XI would pay a yearly pension of two thousand crowns to each canton and disburse a further subsidy of twenty thousand crowns. Most important, he was not obliged to join the war himself, except in case of dire emergency, but could, instead, pay eighty thousand Rhine florins as his contribution to the joint cause.

After an immediate declaration of war, the Swiss dispatched a force across the Jura Mountains to attack the county of Burgundy. On November 13 the mountaineers crushed a Burgundian army attempting to relieve their siege of Héricourt. By this time René II, the accomplished young Duke of Lorraine, outraged by the Burgundian occupation of his Duchy, had sworn allegiance to King Louis; Neuss continued to withstand the assaults of the Duke of Burgundy's army; Frederick III had issued a call to arms to the princes and cities of the Empire. At the end of December, Louis XI completed a year of diplomatic triumphs by signing the Treaty of Andernach with the Emperor.

As winter gave way to spring (1475), King Louis was once more working to persuade the Duke of Burgundy to prolong their truce, though he knew that, this time, the English were coming; and he even employed the Constable, though he knew that St. Pol was trying to drive bargains of his own. If the King stumbled, it would not be over stones left unturned. Meanwhile, he was mustering the greatest military power he had ever commanded. With the Burgundian truce due to expire on May 1, he tautly awaited every message from the Rhine. Neuss, horribly battered by the Duke of Burgundy's cannon, somehow still held out.

The Burgundian siege of the town had become one of the wonders of the world. Sir John Paston, serving Lord Hastings, Governor of Calais, thought that he was bound to fall sick unless he could visit it. As the siege lengthened, the Burgundian encampment had been transformed into a bizarre town. Around the Duke's portable house of wood rose some nine hundred tents of his elaborate household, his guard, his chief officers and captains. Streets crisscrossed the camp area; two large markets created the atmosphere of a fair; there were bake houses, forges, wind- and water-mills, edifices of wood ingeniously built in the shape of castles; tennis courts, baths, brothels, taverns provided recreation for the troops; weddings, christenings, and funerals kept the chapels busy. Charles loved music, especially when he was meditating on the exploits of the great conquerors of the past, and "the sound of melodious instruments in the Duke's quarters made the place seem an earthly paradise."

It did not seem so to the desperately pressed defenders of Neuss, or to the besiegers. In long-ago July of 1474 the Duke had brought to Neuss a magnificent army: some twenty-two thousand men, bombards and cannon, an array of huge siege engines. Almost half his force was composed of Italian mercenary troops, and there was a stout contingent of English archers. Day after day—summer, winter, spring—the Duke hurled his men and machines against the stubborn town. By daylight his guns pounded the walls to rubble; by night the defenders somehow managed to block the breaches. Terrible fighting took place below the ground, where, as Burgundian mining was frustrated by countermining, men struggled hand to hand in soggy, smoky tunnels or were blown to bits by charges of gunpowder. Across the river from Neuss, a force provided by Cologne ferried supplies to the defenders, and their artillery sank Burgundian supply vessels sailing up the Rhine from the Low Countries. Death, wounds, sicknesses diminished, week by week, the Burgundian host, despite reinforcements.

And still Neuss held out. And still the Duke of Burgundy refused to raise the siege, even though, in April of 1475, the Emperor, accompanied by numerous German princes, was now marching down the Rhine toward Neuss with an unwieldy army, and Edward IV, almost ready to cross the Channel, multiplied envoys and messages begging his ally to fulfill his treaty obligations. On April 29, the penultimate day of the

Franco-Burgundian truce, there arrived in the Burgundian camp yet another English embassy, headed by Anthony Woodville, Earl Rivers,
brother of the pro-Burgundian Queen of England. Seconded by a Breton
embassy and emissaries from the Constable, Rivers urged the Duke to
break off the siege. In vain. Charles huffed and puffed, declared honor
forbade him to abandon the operation, declared he would have Neuss in
a few days, declared he was fully capable of handling his German campaign and supporting the English invasion as he had promised. Commynes could explain Charles's conduct only by supposing that "God had
troubled the Duke's senses" in order to aid the realm of France.

On April 25, five days before the expiration of the truce, Louis XI
moved from Paris to the Picard frontier with his Scots and French
guards, seven hundred lances, " a great company" of nobles and archers
from Normandy and Île de France, and a large artillery train. Around
him the realm stood to arms, awaiting the ancient adversary, the English.

20. The English

As THE King of France prepared to confront the crisis of his reign, the renewal by Edward IV of the Hundred Years War (as it would one day be called), it appeared that he was master in his realm. The rowdy redheaded Count of Armagnac, father of three children by his sister Isabella, had finally disappeared from the feudal scene in 1473: after surrendering his town of Lectoure on March 5, he was the next day stabbed to death in a street brawl by a royal archer. The Duke of Alençon, condemned to death by Parlement for his treacheries, lay in a royal prison, his life spared by his godson. Upon the death of the Count of Foix, his principality passed into the hands of a child under the King's control. The demise of Charles, Count of Maine, King René's brother, removed yet another intriguer against the Crown. When old King René himself showed unmistakable signs of being drawn into the Burgundian orbit in 1474, Louis had quietly garrisoned the Duchies of Anjou and Bar. The Duke of Brittany had been driven by his intimates into agreeing to aid Edward IV as rightful King of France; but Louis, fully informed, knew that Francis II's heart was not in it. He yearned to continue his undemanding role as mediator between France and Burgundy. Louis divined that even when the English sent him some troops, as they did, he would remain irresolutely neutral. The Count of St. Pol was hopelessly entangled in his duplicities. His too-clever game of deceiving both Duke Charles and the King had now earned him the implacable hatred of each.[1] Since the spring of 1474 St. Pol had feverishly been seeking everywhere, as Louis well knew, to bring into being another League of the Public Weal; but even Jacques d'Armagnac, Duke of Nemours, was immobilized by his fear of the King. And there was now no King's brother to provide a figurehead for seignorial treachery.

Events in the County of Roussillon, won from Aragon by King Louis's diplomatic *tour-de-force* of 1462–63, had suddenly threatened to split his defenses. Wily old John II of Aragon, a leading spirit among the powers leagued against France, had seized Perpignan in 1473 and driven the French from the country. Then promising repayment of the 300,000 crowns for which Roussillon was pledge, the King of Aragon sought to spin out negotiations until his allies took the field. On the expiration of a truce in 1474, however, Louis XI—ignoring black menaces from the Duke of Burgundy, thoroughly occupied in the Germanies—had mounted a powerful expedition against Roussillon. On March 10, 1475, Perpignan had surrendered; Aragon was forced to accept a regime of truces lasting the rest of the reign.[2] The King of France just had time to concentrate his forces against the Burgundians and the English.

Yet King Louis's situation, for all the successes of his statecraft in the Germanies, was perilous enough. The Duke of Burgundy commanded great resources and enjoyed a conqueror's prestige. From every shire of England companies of tough men of arms and seasoned archers were assembling on Barham Downs, near Canterbury. They would be lead by thirty-four-year-old Edward IV, one of the ablest of all the famous warrior kings of England, who had won every engagement he had fought. If once the King of France suffered defeat and his rule faltered, Louis knew that the Duke of Brittany, the House of Anjou, St. Pol, the Duke of Nemours, probably the Duke of Bourbon, and lesser lords would, in all likelihood, join the banner of Burgundy to dismember the realm. He sardonically remarked to Commynes that, if he lost a battle, he could well fear a rebellion against him, "for he thought himself not well loved by all his subjects, especially the great. . . ." In a letter to Edward IV (which Louis later bought for £40 from an English secretary), Francis II's chief intimate, the lord d'Urfé, boasted that "the Duke of Brittany would do more in one month by [his network of seignorial] intelligences than the armies of England and Burgundy would accomplish in six, however powerful they were." Commynes adds, "I believe he was right, if the matter had gone to extremes." Sharing all King Louis's knowledge and himself a master of the statesman's craft, the lord of Argenton considered that the King was facing a mortal challenge.

Others took an even gloomier view. On January 25, 1475, Galeazzo-Maria Sforza, Duke of Milan, out of fear, had deserted the French alliance his great father had so loyally maintained, and signed a treaty with the Duke of Burgundy. All over Europe men were predicting a war of hideous slaughter and, for Louis XI, a fate like that of his great-great-grandfather, King John, captured by the English at the battle of Poitiers, 1356. Some months earlier, Louis himself had, in his mercurial way, re-

vealed the strain for a moment when, learning of final English preparations, he cried, "Ah, Holy Mary, even now when I have given thee
fourteen hundred crowns, thou dost not help me one bit!" Otherwise
the records speak only of the King's cheerfulness and aplomb. He still
had confidence in his wits and he knew the face that the King of France
must show when the English and the Burgundians are coming.

ii

THE MOMENT the truce with Burgundy expired, May 1, Louis XI set
forth from the abbey of La Victoire, near Senlis, on a rapid campaign in
Picardy. By the eleventh, he had captured Montdidier, Roye, and the
Somme crossing at Corbie. After the population had been evacuated
each of these towns was razed: Louis had ordered that any place on the
frontier not strong enough to withstand a siege must be destroyed.
Meanwhile young René II of Lorraine, declaring war on the Duke of
Burgundy, headed a French thrust into the Duchy of Luxembourg.
From Champagne, the lord of Craon moved against Burgundian forces
in Lorraine itself. Farther south, a French army commanded by the
Duke of Bourbon invaded the Duchy of Burgundy, and the Swiss were
preparing once again to cross the Jura and fall upon the County of Burgundy. The English had not yet appeared; Neuss still held out; the Emperor's forces were approaching the Burgundian camp.

In the latter part of May, the King hastened with a strong force to
the Norman coast. He had received urgent advices from the Count of St.
Pol that the English were about to come ashore there. Louis had small
confidence in the word of the gyrating Constable, but Normandy, his
richest province, offered a likely point of invasion for the ancient adversaries, who had used it before. As June passed, the King began receiving
reports of the landing of thousands of English troops at Calais, but Edward IV did not seem to be among them. Before the end of the month,
he got word that his army operating in the Duchy of Burgundy had won
a victory at Guipy on June 20 and captured the Governor of the Duchy,
a son of the Count of St. Pol. He himself had dispatched his son-in-law
the Admiral to lay waste Burgundian-held territory between Abbeville
and Arras. Whatever the English ate—and they were famous over Europe as great eaters—they would have to bring with them. Scarred
countryside and blackened villages would demonstrate the King's determination to offer no pickings in France. The Admiral, carrying fire and
destruction to the very gates of Arras, was attacked on June 27 by a
Burgundian force issuing from the town. The Burgundians were bloodily

routed and their chiefs captured, including Jacques de Richebourg, brother of the Count of St. Pol, and the lord of Contay, one of Duke Charles's best commanders.

Reporting the good news to the Grand Master, Louis indicated his plans at the moment: he was reinforcing and revictualing Dieppe, bringing there all the harvest of the countryside "so that the English find nothing. . . . I am remaining at Neuchâtel [between Dieppe and Beauvais] until I know whether or not the English will march on Normandy. . . . At Calais there are four or five thousand English, but they don't budge: not one has come to show himself before our troops. In your time, you've seen other Englishmen who would have come to show themselves!"

Meanwhile, eastward, on the Rhine, events had taken a turn. The Emperor finally arrived on the scene, establishing a huge fortified camp a short distance below Neuss. On May 24 the Duke of Burgundy marched to attack him. Only a few thousand men, in disorderly waves, issued from the imperial camp to engage the Burgundians. They were soon routed, leaving several hundred killed. The Duke of Burgundy, surveying the dead with satisfaction, remarked to his captains that such was the fruit borne by the tree of war. The next day the Emperor, all passion spent, secured an armistice and with the aid of a papal legate began treating for terms. The Duke, one day showing to Frederick III his famous artillery, took the opportunity to announce, "Sacred Majesty, you see these guns here? These are the keys with which I expect to open the towns of the Realm of France." Le Glorieux, the Duke's fool, immediately piped up, "Sacred Majesty, have my master show you the one he used to open up Beauvais." By mid-June an arrangement had been patched together which the Duke of Burgundy, aware that the English were landing at Calais, was able to find sufficiently face-saving to reconcile with his "honor." Neuss would be handed over to the legate while the Pope investigated the quarrel over the Archbishop; and both the Burgundian and imperial armies would leave the region under a truce. The Duke sent his badly battered forces into Lorraine, "to refresh themselves" by pillaging the Duchy. He then rode, in no hurry, to meet Edward IV at Calais. Now that he knew how feeble the Germans were, he told Jean Pierre Panigarola, the new Milanese ambassador to Burgundy, he would soon be back to smash them; meanwhile, he had devised an Anglo-Burgundian campaign that would put an end to Louis XI.

About this time, the latter half of June, there arrived at Louis XI's Norman headquarters the chief herald of England, Garter King of Arms, bringing with him Edward IV's formal *défi,* the declaration of hostilities. What followed Philippe de Commynes learned directly from the King. Louis took care to be alone when he read Edward's letter. "He then withdrew into an antechamber, still entirely by himself, and had Garter summoned." In his best frank and genial style, the King embarked on his favorite method of diplomacy, pointing out for another's benefit, and his own, the true path of self-interest. He told the herald "he knew well the King of England was not coming of his own will but had been forced to it both by the Duke of Burgundy and the English Commons." Edward IV could see that his campaigning season was about finished, that the Duke of Burgundy was coming back from Neuss a man discomfited and impotent. In regard to the Constable, he knew that St. Pol had had intelligence with the herald's master and that the Count would deceive the English King. Louis finished by arming the herald with "several other very good reasons" to be used in making the King of England come to terms with him. He then gave Garter "three hundred crowns cash in his hand" and promised him one thousand more if a treaty was effected.

Completely thawed by this treatment, Garter disclosed that Edward IV was not very enthusiastic about the invasion. He believed that his master would willingly entertain terms, but there was no use speaking of the matter until the King of England had crossed the Channel. Then, however, a French herald should be sent to request safe-conducts for an embassy. The men to get in touch with, Garter concluded, were my lord Howard or my lord Stanley. The names Howard and Stanley King Louis imprinted in his memory: he knew that they enjoyed the confidence of Edward IV.* At the end of his secret talk with Garter, Louis summoned Commynes, ordered him to give the herald thirty yards of crimson velvet and to keep the Englishman constant company so that no one could speak to him till an escort for his return journey was made ready. The King appeared in his presence chamber, "where many people were waiting in intense curiosity to hear what he would say and what countenance he would display when he issued from the inner chamber." Louis, casually moving through the hall, commented to several people on the English *défi,* then called seven or eight aside and had the letter read to them. He showed a cheerful, assured visage: the indiscretions of the herald, perhaps some of them calculated, had served to confirm

---

* John, Lord Howard, a pillar of the Yorkist cause, had become one of Edward IV's chief advisers; Thomas, Lord Stanley, after cleverly switching sides during the Wars of the Roses, was now Steward of King Edward's household.

Louis's estimate of Edward IV's attitude.

It was past mid-July before Louis XI, keeping his vigil in northeast-ern Normandy, learned with certainty that Edward IV had reached Ca-lais. In fact, the English army, with the aid of hundreds of flat-bottomed boats from the Low Countries, had taken three weeks of June to cross the Channel, King Edward following on July 4. The French fleet offered no opposition. Commynes believed that if the King had understood sea warfare as well as he understood land warfare, "never would King Ed-ward have passed, at least in this season; but the King did not under-stand it, and those to whom he gave command at sea understood it still less." Probably so. It is interesting, however, that Louis was employing his son-in-law the Admiral in his land operations and that no surviving document reveals any discontent on the part of the King with his fleet. It is barely possible that Louis, knowing that the English were bound to invade and that the Duke of Burgundy was still immobilized before Neuss, had preferred to let them come now, and with no losses to avenge.

The Duke of Burgundy, having dawdled along the way from Neuss, perhaps to let the English find out how helpless they were without his guidance, finally appeared at Calais in mid-July, but accompanied only by his household and his guard. What he lacked in manpower he sought to make up for in splendid assurances and an aura of military know-how —hardly the way to impress the first soldier of Europe, who now found himself in a strange land, played false by his ally, with the fate of thou-sands of good Englishmen in his hands. Lavish of praise, the Duke de-clared that the English army, of itself, "was great enough to conquer France and then Italy all the way to Rome." He disclosed that he had mapped out an invincible plan of campaign. He himself would return to his troops in Lorraine in order to lead them on a thrust westward into the heart of Champagne; King Edward and his army were to march southeastward into Champagne; the two armies would meet at Rheims and there Edward would be crowned King of France. Presumably, Louis XI would be disposed of in the course of these operations or soon afterward.

The English King and his war council decided to accept the Duke's plan, at least for the time being. In his own men Edward IV had full confidence; captains and soldiers, they had been seasoned, most of them, in the struggles of the Roses. By means of generous Parliamentary grants and money gifts solicited by the King himself, Edward had crossed the Channel with the greatest English army that had ever appeared in

France—some twelve hundred men of arms, eleven thousand of the world's best archers, a large artillery and siege train. Edward's chief commanders, his younger brother, Richard, Duke of Gloucester (later, Richard III) and William, Lord Hastings, had thoroughly proved themselves.

Once the English left Calais, Louis's intelligence network was so effective that he was able to follow them in his mind every step of their march. In addition, he had somehow learned, or divined, the Anglo-Burgundian plan of campaign. By July 20 the English were slowly moving in the direction of Péronne. On the 23rd, at Fauquembergues, the Duke of Burgundy ceremoniously reviewed the army. For two nights Edward IV and his host camped on the battlefield of Agincourt. Through Doullens the army moved, about July 28, past smoldering villages and blackened countrysides, and a week later reached the Somme at Péronne. The Duke of Burgundy entered his city, then closed the gates behind him, leaving the fields to his ally.

As the English departed from Calais, King Louis, accompanied by his Scots and French guard and a force of about one thousand lances, moved southeastward to conform to their march. On July 28, the day Edward IV was marching through Doullens, Louis dispatched an order for Tanneguy du Chastel to burn that town, "except for the churches," as soon as the English evacuated it. He was sending letter after letter to Rheims, thanking the inhabitants for working day and night on their fortifications, informing them that Edward IV aimed at being crowned King there "contrary to the will of God and Our Lady," and insisting therefore that they must at all costs complete the ditch outside the walls or he would be forced to demolish the city. On August 4 the King left Beauvais for Creil. The next morning he rode into Compiègne and there set up his command post. That same day, less than forty miles to the north, Edward IV and his army crossed the Somme at Péronne, entering French territory, and fortified a camp with its back to the river.

And so the English had come again.

Louis XI had increased his standing army to four thousand lances, some twenty-four thousand men, most of them concentrated in Normandy and Picardy; he probably had at least six thousand men of arms from the feudal levy of the nobles and perhaps twenty thousand franc archers and artillerymen—a total force of something like fifty thousand effectives. His left stretched from Dieppe, held by nine hundred lances under the Admiral, to Amiens, where Tanneguy du Chastel commanded a strong force, this line backed by Rouen and Neufchâtel. The center, facing the Somme, occupied the line Beauvais-Creil-Compiègne-Noyon, based on Paris. The advanced position at Noyon was held by that veteran adversary of the English Antoine de Chabannes, the Grand Master. On the right Robert d'Estouteville, Provost of Paris, commanded at Laon, and a powerful garrison anchored the line at Rheims. The long right flank was protected from the Burgundians by the forces of René II and the lord of Craon in Lorraine and by the southern army that had beaten the Burgundians at Guipy.

It was not a static defense: Louis meant to carry the war to the English, using his fortresses as bases from which to operate against the flank and rear of his enemies. On July 15 he had informed his Chancellor, "I am drawing all my garrisons into the field." The English moved aggressively but fought defensively. In every one of the great victories of the Hundred Years War—Crécy, Poitiers, Agincourt, Verneuil—they had taken a stand on foot, archers and men of arms and their commanders, and let the massed cavalry of France hurl itself to ruin against their arrow fire and their battle axes. Louis XI was hardly likely to be so obliging. Should Edward IV venture to advance between Noyon and Laon toward Rheims, French forces were poised to close upon his flank and rear, cut off supplies, harry the invader night and day.

King Louis waited quietly at Compiègne, at the head of his iron ranks. His Scots guard, ready for fighting, had left their money and trinkets with the canons of the Cathedral of Beauvais. The garrison at Noyon was raiding to the very outskirts of the English camp on the Somme.

iii

ON THE EVENING OF August 12 there was brought before Louis XI a servant of a member of the royal household. Captured by the English, he said, he had been freed that morning and given a message for the King of France. He had much to tell besides.

The day before, an English troop, on assurances from the Duke of Burgundy that the Constable would deliver St. Quentin, had trotted carelessly toward the gates of that city—only to be met suddenly by gunfire and a sally of defenders. The Duke of Burgundy had attempted to gloss over the incident. He then had announced breezily that he must now leave to rejoin his troops and would meet Edward IV at Rheims. At this moment, related the servant who had come to Compiègne, he himself had been brought a prisoner into the English camp. Placed in a tent, he had been interrogated by the English King and the Burgundian Duke. Then Charles had taken leave of his English allies and ridden away. The moment the Duke of Burgundy disappeared, Edward IV ordered the captive Frenchman to be given his freedom, "seeing that he was their first prisoner." As he was setting forth, Lords Howard and Stanley appeared, gave him a gold coin, and making sure that he had learned their names, delivered a message: "Recommend us to the good grace of the King your master, if you can speak with him."

After Louis listened, with considerable suspicion, to this unlikely evangel, he had him put in irons and closely guarded. However, the King sent numerous counselors to interrogate the man, all of whom recommended that their master should hear him again. Rising very early in the morning, Louis quizzed him, then had his irons removed but ordered him kept under guard. The King of France made his way to breakfast, not troubling to conceal his excitement. Before sitting at table, he drew Philippe de Commynes aside, reminded him of the two lords mentioned by Garter King of Arms the previous June as the men to address once Edward IV had crossed the Channel: *Howard* and *Stanley*, the very nobles who had dispatched the captive. Then sitting down, the King animatedly began weighing, aloud, whether or not he should send to the English, wagging his head, gesticulating, muttering, as he ate. Suddenly he whispered in Commynes's ear: Philippe should leave the table and breakfast in his own chamber, at the same time sending for a certain servant of the King's cupbearer, Olivier Merichon. He was to inquire if the servant would dare undertake the mission of going to the English camp in a herald's costume. "I did immediately what the King had commanded me," records Commynes, "but I was stunned when I saw this servant, for he did not seem to me to be at all suitable in appearance or manner for such an office. Nevertheless, he had a good mind, as I was afterward to learn, and could talk with charming courtesy. Never had the King spoken to him but a single time."

Merichon's servant, terrified by Commynes's first words, "cast himself on his two knees, like one who believed himself already dead. I heartened him as best I could and promised him an office in the Isle of Ré (of which he was a native) and some money. To hearten him still more, I told him that it was the English who had set the business in motion. Then I had him eat with me, we two being alone except for a serving man. Little by little I unfolded to him what he had to do. I had scarcely finished when the King sent for me. I told him about our man and named to him others who would be, in my opinion, better fitted;

but he would not hear of any other." Accompanied by a single counselor, King Louis "came to speak to the man himself and heartened him
more with one word than I had done in a hundred. When the King
thought our man was ready to undertake the mission," he carefully re-
hearsed him in his instructions. Then he ordered a coat-of-arms to be
made out of a trumpeter's banner—"for the King cared nothing for ceremony nor was he accompanied by heralds and trumpeters as are most
princes." Riding clothes and a horse were secretly fetched; the herald's
costume was put in a saddle wallet to keep it fresh; the makeshift herald, bearing the long-nourished hopes of Louis XI, set off for the English
camp.

Louis had instructed his man to say to Edward IV that the King of
France had always desired to have close friendship with him so that the
two realms could live in peace. The Duke of Burgundy had called the
English into France because he believed that the invasion would enable
him to get better terms from Louis XI; and if others had likewise encouraged the English—i.e., the Duke of Brittany—it was only to further
their own interests, they caring not at all how Edward IV fared once
they had made use of him. Louis also reminded the English King that
the season for campaigning was about past and winter approaching. He
well knew that Edward IV had spent a great deal of money on the
invasion—a hint of the terms he had in mind. Should the King of England be willing to heed his own interests, Louis XI "would make such
attractive offers that he and his realm would be well satisfied with the
result."

At the end of that same day, the King of France had his answer.
Louis's bizarre envoy returned, and with him came an English herald
who bore safe-conducts for an embassy and the proposal that negotiations be forthwith begun in a village between the lines. The brave
young Frenchman had "good cheer" indeed from the King, immediately
received his office in the Isle of Ré and a sum of money. So passed from
history the youth that Louis had unerringly plucked from nowhere to
bear on his shoulders for a day the fate of two kingdoms.

The next morning, a French delegation headed by the Admiral met
with Lord Howard and other English envoys. Louis's instructions were
simple: rather than offer a foot of land, he would put his Crown and life
in hazard; anything else, he was ready to consider. That same evening,
his representatives returned to report. The English had begun *pro forma*
by demanding the Crown of France, or at least Normandy and Guienne.
After the French refusal, they had quickly come to their real terms: a

sum of cash, a yearly subsidy for a long truce, and a marriage to bind the relationship. "With marvelous great joy" at this news, Louis immediately summoned his councilors. "Some were of the opinion that the offer was only trickery on the part of the English. The King thought the contrary." The French delegation set forth next day, August 15, with orders to accept the English offer and work out the details of a treaty. Louis hastened from Compiègne to Senlis, nearer Paris, to spur the quest for funds with which to pay off Edward IV. On the 18th Lord Howard and his fellows journeyed to Senlis for consultation with King Louis.

Next day there rode into King Edward's camp an infuriated Duke of Burgundy. En route to rejoin his army, he had received a brief statement from his royal English brother-in-law of the turn of events. That day and the next, stormy interviews took place between Charles and Edward. To the Duke's violent protests, Edward replied firmly that he had concluded a truce with France, in which Brittany was included, and Burgundy too, if Charles would accede to it, as Edward hoped he would. When the Duke finally realized that he could not block the treaty, he turned to insult, speaking in English so that all of Edward's councilors could understand him. Scathingly he recalled the great victories that former Kings of England had won in France and the toils they had endured to gain such honors. He declared loftily that he had not sought the invasion for any purposes of his own, but only to aid the English to recover what belonged to them. So that they would realize that he had had no need of their coming, he would not accept a truce with the King of France until three months after they recrossed the Channel. With that, Charles haughtily took himself off, leaving Edward in a state of anger with him that time did not diminish.

By Wednesday, August 23, all details of the treaty were settled and Louis had somehow scraped up most of the enormous amount of money he needed. From Senlis he wrote to his Chancellor: "We must have all our sum at Amiens by Friday evening [August 25], and something in addition to give individuals like my lord Howard and others who have played a part in the settlement. Therefore I beg you, my lord Chancellor, by your love for my welfare and my honor and that of the whole realm, be diligent and do not fail this need; for if there were a slip-up you would do me irreparable harm." On August 25 King Louis rode into Amiens with coffers of gold coins.

By the terms of the treaty, Louis had agreed to pay Edward IV seventy-five thousand crowns in cash to take himself and his army home, Lord Howard and Sir John Cheyney remaining as hostages till most of the English had crossed. During a truce of seven years Louis would pay an annual subsidy of fifty thousand crowns, half at Michaelmas and half at Easter. English and French merchants could trade freely in each other's countries, discriminating tolls imposed in the past dozen years being revoked, and a standard rate of exchange would be worked out at a monetary conference. The Dauphin, aged five, was affianced to Princess Elizabeth, twice his age, eldest daughter of King Edward, the dowry for the match to be furnished by King Louis in the form of an annual revenue of sixty thousand livres when the couple came of age to marry. A secret clause in the treaty established a league of amity between Edward and Louis by which each King agreed to succor the other against rebellious subjects. Arrangements were likewise made to ransom Margaret of Anjou, a prisoner of the English since the battle of Tewkesbury (May, 1471), for fifty thousand crowns.

Louis took good care that the chief men about King Edward shared in the golden harvest. With Edward's blessing, William Hastings, his Lord Chamberlain and companion in amorous escapades, was to receive two thousand crowns a year; Lord Howard and Sir Thomas Mongomery, twelve hundred each; the Chancellor of England, one thousand; with lesser sums to a number of others. The King's baggage wagons were stuffed with presents of plate, jewels, coin, to be distributed high and low. Eager to employ his personal arts on Edward, Louis had likewise arranged for the treaty to be sealed at an interview, scheduled for August 29. The English King had been quite willing to accept only fifty-five thousand crowns in cash and take a note for the remaining twenty thousand.

iv

THE MORNING AFTER his arrival in Amiens, King Louis stationed himself at the northern gate to watch the arrival of the English. In cheerful disorder they moved past the city to encamp a short distance downstream on the right bank of the Somme. Louis immediately dispatched to Edward IV three hundred wagonloads of the choicest wines. The train of carts with its drivers and porters looked, to Commynes, as large as Edward's army. The King also thoughtfully sent word that the English, lords and commons alike, would be very welcome in Amiens. Louis gave order for two huge tables to be set up on either side of the gate. These were loaded "with all the kinds of tasty foods that provoke thirst and with flagons of the best wines that could be found." "Of water," adds Commynes, "there was no sign." Behind the tables the King seated half

a dozen courtiers—high officers like the lord of Craon and the lord of
Bressuire—all of them big, fat men who obviously enjoyed eating and
drinking, this touch to provide an atmosphere of bonhomie and jolly
gormandizing. For three days the English came in droves, armed and
unarmed, singly and in big bands. After their appetites had been whet-
ted at the gates, they wandered into the city, to be courteously directed
to one of some ten taverns where they could munch and guzzle to their
heart's content, all at the expense of the King of France. Drunken Englishmen staggered through the streets; English songs were bellowed at
all hours.

Meanwhile, a wooden bridge was constructed over the Somme at
Picquigny, nine miles downstream from Amiens. In the middle, sheltered by a roof, was erected "a very strong wooden trellis, the kind used
for making a lion cage, the interstices just large enough for a man to put
an arm through easily." On the rainy afternoon of Tuesday, August 29,
Louis XI, with twelve followers, walked onto the bridge and stationed
himself at the trellis. Behind him on a plateau were drawn up eight
hundred men of arms. Even on this occasion the King, as was his wont,
was wearing a nondescript costume. Philippe de Commynes, the lord of
Argenton, had the honor that day of being stationed at his sovereign's
elbow and clothed in identical garb, an arrangement that Louis occasionally employed, probably to diminish the chances of assassination.
The other companions of the King were the Duke of Bourbon and the
Duke's amiable brother Charles, Archbishop of Lyons; the Admiral, the
Grand Master, Marshal Lohéac, and the Master of the Crossbowmen,
the lord of Torcy; the lords of St. Pierre and du Bouchage, Tanneguy du
Chastel, the Bishop of Évreux, and the Mayor of Amiens.

Some distance from the opposite bank the full army of the English
was ranged in battle array. Forth onto the bridge strode the debonair
King of England, beginning now to grow a little corpulent but still a
magnificent figure of a man. He wore a black velvet cap with a jeweled
fleur-de-lys and from his towering shoulders hung a gown of cloth of
gold lined with red satin—this resplendent costume having been made
several months before, apparently for Edward's coronation in Rheims
Cathedral. He too was accompanied by twelve men, including his troublesome brother George, Duke of Clarence, the Earl of Northumberland,
Lords Hastings and Howard, and the English Chancellor, Thomas Roth-
erham.

As the King of England approached the barrier, he removed his cap,
half knelt. King Louis, performing a similar reverence, thrust his arms

through the trellis and heartily embraced Edward. As the English King then made a still more sweeping reverence, Louis quickly opened the conversation: "My lord, my cousin, you are very welcome indeed. There's no man in the world I so much desire to see as you. Praise be to God we have here come together for such a good purpose." After Edward had made a suitable reply "in very good French," the English Chancellor produced the treaty documents. Each King put one hand on a prayer book, the other on a reliquary containing a piece from the True Cross, and swore to uphold every article of the appointments. There followed a general conversation among the two parties. Louis, "who was never at a loss for words," said jokingly to King Edward that he must come to Paris. Plentiful entertainment would be provided and there would be no lack of ladies. And here was the Archbishop of Lyons—Louis would appoint him Edward's confessor, for he would very quickly absolve Edward of any sins he might commit! The King of England thoroughly enjoyed the sally "for he well knew that the [Archbishop] was a *bon compaignon*."

After half an hour or so of this pleasant chat, King Louis, "who showed himself to be the man of authority in this company," motioned for his delegation to retire, saying that he wished to speak privately to the King of England. Edward's men, without waiting to be told, immediately followed the example of the French. It appears that Louis, having established a tone of easy good-fellowship, began the colloquy by alluding to the secret treaty of amity. As one professional to another, he spoke of the difficulties they both had experienced with rebellious lords and malcontent brothers: Edward's brother George—"false, fleeting, perjured Clarence"—had proved just as much a troublemaker as Louis's brother. The English King remarked that Louis would never be secure in his realm until he cut off the heads of certain of his lords in whom he too much trusted. Indeed, Edward had some beautifully incriminating documents, especially from the Constable; he would send them to Louis on the morrow—and so he did. Louis then beckoned to Philippe de Commynes, asking Edward if he recognized him. The English King replied that he did indeed, the lord of Argenton having served him well in 1470–71 when Commynes was in the service of the Duke of Burgundy. Louis casually introduced the matter of that Duke's present attitude. Suppose, he asked, that Charles was unwilling to be included in the truce? Edward answered with indifference that the truce should be offered to him once more, and then, if he refused, Edward would leave the matter up to them. Louis thus arrived at what was really on his mind, the Duke of Brittany. What if the Duke made trouble over being included in the truce? Edward suddenly came alert. He emphatically requested the King of France not to make war on Francis II—in his need, he had never found so good a friend. Louis desisted instantly, turned the conversation to pleasantries, and then, recalling the two escorting parties, took a final farewell of Edward of England, not forgetting "some good word for each of his people."

As the King of France exuberantly rode back to Amiens, he chatted with Commynes. Edward's too-evident willingness to take Louis up on his joking offer to taste the delights of Paris was somewhat on his mind. "He's a very handsome King, that one," Louis observed. "He's crazy about girls, and he might find some too clever sweetheart in Paris who would know how to utter such pretty speeches that she'd make him want to come back there." Edward's predecessors, the King went on, had already been too often in Paris and Normandy. Edward's companionship on this side of the Channel was anything but valuable. But, with Edward remaining in England where he belonged, Louis indeed wanted to have him for a good brother and good friend. The King was also a little uneasy, he disclosed to Commynes, about Edward's rather sharp response when Louis had spoken of Francis II. He would have been more than happy if he'd succeeded in persuading the English King to let him make war on Brittany. This tempting possibility Louis could not quite let go. He sent the lords du Bouchage and St. Pierre to feel out King Edward once more on the subject; but when Edward, seeing that he was being pressed, replied flatly that if anyone attacked Brittany he would repass the Narrow Seas to defend it, Louis dropped the matter once for all.

That evening in Amiens the King entertained at supper a few of the most influential English lords. He apparently snubbed the Duke of Clarence, but he had been careful to invite Edward's other, and very different, brother, young Richard, Duke of Gloucester. Gloucester, opposed to the peacemaking, had pointedly absented himself from the ceremonies at Picquigny, but he accepted the invitation to sup; and Louis succeeded in making him quite content to receive a handsome present of plate and some fine horses. As the company were about to begin the repast, Lord Howard whispered to the King that, if he wished, Howard would find a way of persuading King Edward to come to Amiens, perhaps even to Paris, to enjoy a bit of fun with him. Louis put a good face on the matter, said something or other and busied himself with washing. He murmured ruefully to Commynes that just what he'd expected had come about—Edward's offer to make merry. After supper Lord Howard brought the matter up again. Very delicately the King and his intimates set about disposing of it, finally explaining that the King of France would have to leave at once in order to deal with the Duke of Burgundy.

Next day, Wednesday, August 30, was the Day of the Holy Innocents, "on which day," as Commynes explains, "the King did not speak, or permit others to speak to him, about his affairs. He considered it very bad luck if anybody did so and became especially angry if that person was one of his familiars who knew about this custom." That morning as Louis was saying his Hours in his bedchamber, Commynes, who had been summoned from the room, ventured, on his return, to break his master's rule. "Sire, notwithstanding that it's the Day of the Innocents, I must tell you what has just been reported to me." There were already thousands of English in Amiens (their last opportunity to guzzle, for they were departing for Calais next day), all of them apparently armed; more were still coming; nobody dared turn them away at the gates for fear of displeasing them.

Louis, "not a man to stand blindly on rules, immediately ceased his prayers," telling Commynes that there was no need to keep the ceremony of the Innocents that day. He ordered the lord of Argenton to speak with some of King Edward's captains and to see if he could have the English removed. Soon Louis received a report that "for one soldier the English commanders sent back from the town, there entered twenty." On investigating one of the crowded taverns, however, Commynes had found some Englishmen singing, some snoring, all drunk. He thought, therefore, that there was no real danger. The King summoned his guard and went at once to the northern gate of the city. He secretly sent word for some men of arms to be mustered, stationed a number at the gate, commanded the rest to remain at the ready in their lodgings. Then, ordering his dinner to be brought to the gatehouse, he invited several Englishmen of rank to share the repast. At the same time he saw to it that King Edward was informed of the drunken disorder of the town. To an embarrassed request from Edward that no more English be admitted, Louis dispatched word that never would he perform so inhospitable an act. If, on the other hand, Edward would like to send some royal archers to guard the gates, these could allow or deny entry as they wished. Edward IV sent the archers, and soon numbers of tipsy Englishmen were being herded out of the city by order of their own King.

Before dining, Louis had received another report that disturbed him. Louis de Bretaylle, a Gascon long in the service of King Edward, had remarked in private conversation with Commynes that the French would make great mock of the King of England and the English as soon as they departed. Commynes denied it, quickly changed the subject by asking how many victories the English King had won. On being told nine, he then inquired how many he had lost. The Gascon replied sharply that his King had lost but one, this one that the French had made him lose, by which he had incurred a shame outweighing all the honors he had achieved in winning the other nine battles.

On hearing this from Commynes, Louis exclaimed, "He's a rascal, that one. He must be kept from talking this way." The King immediately invited Bretaylle to the repast in the gatehouse. Then, taking him aside, Louis made all sorts of offers if he would remain in France. On perceiving that he was unwilling to do so, the King gave him one thousand crowns then and there and promised to keep a favorable eye on the interests of Bretaylle's brothers living in France. As the Gascon took his leave, Commynes murmured in his ear the hope that he would work to nourish the friendship that had now been engendered between the two Kings.

On returning to his quarters, Louis closeted himself with three or four intimates so that at last he could relax a little. "There was nothing in the world which the King feared more than that he might let slip some remarks which would lead the English to think that they were being made fun of." Now, supposing himself safe, he let his sense of comedy bubble up and his tongue wag, as he thought about all the food, drink, and presents with which he had stuffed King Edward's warriors. "I have chased the English out of France," he said, chuckling, "more easily than ever my father did; for my father drove them out by force of arms whereas I've driven them out by force of venison pies and good wines."

No sooner were the words out of his mouth than, to his consternation, he spied an intruder in his chamber—a Gascon wine merchant, who had earlier sought permission from him to export wines from Bordeaux to England free of duty. By a freak of fortune the man had inadvertently been permitted to enter the room. Recovering himself, Louis learned from fast questioning that the merchant, a native of Guienne, was now domiciled with a wife in England. The King exerted his charms of persuasion and promises on the man, then ordered Commynes to make good the promises immediately. In return for agreeing not to return to England, the merchant secured his valuable concession, was given a lucrative office in his native town, received one thousand francs in cash with which to send a brother across the Channel to fetch his wife. Louis, to make sure that from that moment he spoke to no English-men, had him escorted all the way to Bordeaux. "Thus," concludes Commynes, "did the King give judgment against himself in this settlement, knowing that he was at fault for talking too much." It was a favorite saying of Louis's that "my tongue has cost me, since I was born, a million in gold."

Next morning, August 31, the English set forth, in haste, for Calais. Numbers of them grumbled and grouched over the unheroic end of their invasion. Sir John Paston, however, probably spoke for the thoughts of most when he wrote to his mother, "Blessed be God, this voyage [i.e., expedition] of the King's is finished for this time"—as doubtless his attitude spoke too for the thousands of French wives whose soldier-husbands King Louis, year after year, sent home safe and whole after another season of bloodless campaigning. Edward IV and his men arrived at Calais on September 4 and most of the army had crossed the Channel within a week. The King of France sent his hostages to Paris for a round of feasting.

"Tribute" the English had insisted on calling the annual payment of fifty thousand crowns. Louis did not care about nomenclature: he knew that the King of England had become his pensioner.

v

HAD LOUIS XI been a kingly king rejoicing in military conquest, he could perhaps have inflicted on the Duke of Burgundy, who had rejected the Anglo-French truce, a catastrophic defeat. To the southeast of the Duke, as he rejoined his army in southern Luxembourg, the towns of Alsace were standing to arms. To the south, the chief places of Lorraine were garrisoned by six thousand troops provided by the Basse Union and a few Swiss and French volunteers. To the west, King Louis had a powerful force under the lord of Craon stationed in Champagne, and, to the southwest, a victorious army operating on the borders of the Duchy of Burgundy. In the neighboring County of Burgundy the Swiss were devastating the country and had just captured Blâmont. On the Somme frontier was poised the great army the King had arrayed against the English.

However, Louis XI moved immediately to come to terms with the Duke of Burgundy. Despite that Duke's scornful vaunt to Edward IV, that he would not sign a truce with France for three months, royal envoys were negotiating with Burgundians before the English army recrossed the Channel. Once the invaders had departed from Amiens, the King rode southward to Senlis to give thanks to Our Lady of Victory and to meet with a Burgundian embassy. The arrival of Duke Charles's envoys gave the King an unexpected bad moment. When one of the English hostages—they had returned from their feastings in Paris and were being treated by Louis as intimates—caught sight of the smartly turned-out archers and men of arms escorting the Burgundian embassy, he beckoned Commynes to a window. If the English had seen numbers of men like that with the Duke of Burgundy, he grumbled, perhaps they would not have made peace. The Viscount of Narbonne, overhearing the Englishman, sneered, "Were you so simple-minded as to suppose the Duke of Burgundy did not have a great array of such troops? He had merely sent them off to refit; but you were so eager to leave France that six hundred pipes of wine and a pension that the King is giving you soon sent you back to England."

Outraged, the Englishman cried, "This is just what everyone told us —that you would make fun of us. Call you the money the King is giving us a pension? It's tribute! And, by St. George, you might just talk so much that we would return!" Hastily Commynes turned the conversation into pleasantries, but the Englishman was not mollified. He muttered a word to the King, and Louis flew into a rage with the stupid Viscount.

It was like walking a sword's edge, this trying to keep the English in a good humor. What tightened Louis's nerves still more was the arrival just this moment of an envoy from Edward IV, Sir Thomas Mongomery, one of Louis's pensioners. Edward's pride had been touched on the raw by the Franco-Burgundian negotiations. On behalf of his master, Sir Thomas requested King Louis not to take any truce with Burgundy except the one that he and Edward had already signed, to which the Duke had been invited to adhere. Indeed, if the King of France would continue in war with Burgundy, Edward engaged himself to cross the Channel as France's ally the following summer, provided Louis paid half the expenses of his army and recompensed him for any damage to the Anglo-Burgundian wool trade!

Louis overwhelmed Mongomery with messages of fervent thanks to his cousin, King Edward; he stuffed Mongomery's luggage with an opulent present of plate. These manifestations of his devotion to England he accompanied by all the excuses he could think of. His truce with the

Duke, Louis explained carefully, was a *fait accompli*; indeed, it was just the same as the Anglo-French one, only the Duke, to salve his pride, had insisted on a separate document; Edward IV need have no fear of Louis's attitude toward Burgundy. With enormous relief the King speeded the departure of Mongomery and the two hostages. Louis had quite other plans for the Duke of Burgundy and he had a hunch that if the English came back to the fields of France they might very soon turn good Burgundians.

With only the Admiral, the lord du Bouchage, and Philippe de Commynes at his side, Louis XI closeted himself with the Burgundian envoys and quickly contracted an accord: a truce of nine years, the public articles of which were qualified by devious secret clauses to which were soon added secret codicils. The Treaty of Soleuvre, taking its name from ducal headquarters in southern Luxembourg, was signed by Charles of Burgundy on September 13. Less then three weeks later (September 29), Francis II of Brittany, now feeling dreadfully exposed, engaged himself to live in perfect friendship with the King and renounce all other alliances. The Treaty of Soleuvre was considerably more complex: the King and the Duke of Burgundy had each agreed, in effect, to sacrifice his allies, and for the same reason though with very different hopes —to give the Duke a free hand in wreaking vengeance on his eastern neighbors and forging his Lotharingian empire. The treaty likewise settled the fate of that inveterate intriguer Louis of Luxembourg, Count of St. Pol, who had succeeded in winning the hatred of the King of France, the King of England, and the Duke of Burgundy.

A few days before the interview between the two Kings on the bridge at Picquigny, Louis XI had received two emissaries from the Count of St. Pol, now twisting feverishly in the meshes he had woven for himself. On discovering that the Constable's men were returning from a mission to the Duke of Burgundy, Louis decided to stage a little comedy, in the hope of whetting the Duke's ire against St. Pol. For audience he had at hand the Burgundian lord of Contay, captured at Arras and promised his freedom by the King if he worked for peace.

Louis proceeded to hide Contay and Commynes behind a big old fire screen in his chamber. He then seated himself before the screen and ordered the lord du Bouchage to bring in the Constable's men. As soon as they arrived, the King encouraged them to talk about their mission to the Duke of Burgundy. Warmed by Louis's geniality, they readily explained that the object had been to detach Duke Charles from his alli-

ance with the English. In fact, they found the Duke so infuriated with
the King of England that they had almost persuaded him not only to
abandon the English but to help destroy them as they marched back to
Calais.

"Thinking to please the King," one of the emissaries then began to
imitate the Duke of Burgundy in rage—"stamping on the floor,
swearing by St. George, calling King Edward the bastard son of an
archer. . . .

"The King laughed heartily. 'Speak louder!' he cried. 'I'm growing a
little deaf. Let's have it again!' "

When the envoys took their leave, the lord of Contay emerged from
behind the screen in a state of indignant amazement. Louis laughed
"and made him good cheer," but Contay could think of nothing but reporting what he had heard to the Duke. Within the hour, he was off at a
gallop.°

One of the secret clauses in the Treaty of Soleuvre provided that
whichever party first laid hands on the Constable was to execute him or
deliver him to the other party in eight days. The Count of St. Pol, "not
knowing which saint to vow himself to," had thought of fleeing into Germany or fighting it out behind the walls of Ham. In the end, he made
use of a safe-conduct he had abjectly begged from the Duke of Burgundy and took refuge at Mons in Hainault. Charles of Burgundy, though
he loathed the Constable, also loathed giving satisfaction to Louis XI;
and then there was the unfortunate involvement of his honor in the
safe-conduct. Weeks passed before Louis, by applying constant pressure
and adding secret concessions, finally maneuvered the Duke into ordering St. Pol turned over to a French escort.[3]

Brought to Paris on November 27, the Count was taken to the Bastille under heavy guard, shielding his face in his black cloak. A black
velvet muff kept his hands warm. Pushed by King Louis, the Parlement
of Paris began its proceedings the same day. Their task was not difficult:
a plenitude of documents attested to St. Pol's treasons and broken oaths.
In the end, he made a rambling, shuffling confession of sorts. On December 19 he was declared guilty of lèse-majesté and a sentence of
death was pronounced. A few hours later he emerged from the town hall
and mounted a scaffold draped in black. The Place de Grève was
thronged with Parisians, eager to see the last of the man in the world
they most hated. They had made a joke out of the fact that St. Pol had

---

° Thus it is Louis XI in his school of statecraft, not Richard Brinsley Sheridan
in The School for Scandal, who first employed a famous screen scene.

been taken in charge by the lord of St. Pierre, saying that "there was war in paradise because St. Peter had captured St. Paul." Miserable Louis of Luxembourg, snuffling and committing himself to God and kissing a cross, laid his head on the block. He made an edifying perhaps but hardly gallant end.

The report of the execution was brought by envoys to the Duke of Burgundy on Christmas Day. He gave a noncommittal answer to the news, but then, "as he sat down to his dinner, he began to laugh, and he laughed all the way through the meal. There's a fine example, he said, of the confidence that can be placed in the King and of the way the King treats those who wish to be his friends."

Except for the head of the Constable, Louis XI had apparently gained nothing from the Treaty of Soleuvre; and in ruthlessly abandoning his German allies he had assumed enormous risks. By the end of 1475 the Duke of Burgundy had overrun Lorraine and established an important base at Nancy. If he brushed aside the Swiss and occupied the hapless Duchy of Savoy, he would find himself enthroned upon the seat of Lotharingian grandeur, the passes of the Alps—at his feet on either side the iron crown of Lombardy and the golden circlet of the Germanies. The city of Berne and her allies, meanwhile, had overwhelmed the Savoyard Pays de Vaud, the lovely region of grapes and grain and pasture lands extending from Morat westward to Lake Geneva. The Swiss, accepting a month's truce to expire January 1, 1476, had then shown their indignant suspicions of King Louis by opening negotiations with the Duke of Burgundy—which, however, the Duke's humiliating demands quickly ended. Louis XI, withdrawn to Plessis-lès-Tours, kept his counsel. There were other forces working for him besides the hidden dynamics of the Treaty of Soleuvre and of Charles of Burgundy's character.

During these last years King Louis had waged against his enemy a financial, economic, and propaganda campaign.

The treasure which the Duke of Burgundy inherited from his father made him the richest prince of the West. In the Low Countries he ruled a highly industrialized people who exchanged all over Europe their expensive cloths and hardwares for cheaper bulk goods, raw materials, and food. Traders of many states thronged the four great seasonal fairs of Flanders. The principal cities of the region, a European crossroads, enjoyed not only a thriving commerce and industry but were financial centers also, harboring branches of the chief banking houses of Italy. When, by the beginning of the 1470's, Charles of Burgundy had spent most of his father's fortune on his wars and was reduced, like everyone else, to borrowing, King Louis, who understood the rising power of the time, bourgeois money power, and had studied international financial operations when he was the refugee of Genappe, set about undermining Charles's credit. A friend of Florence and the Medici, he brought increasing pressure on Piero de' Medici and his successor Lorenzo the Magnificent to cease lending money to his enemies, the King of England and the Duke of Burgundy. So successful was he that by 1473 Charles, no longer able to borrow large sums from the Medici bank in Bruges, was forced to seek lenders all over Italy. By the time the Treaty of Soleuvre was signed, Lorenzo de' Medici was preparing to cut off credit entirely.

Louis XI had also worked to throttle the industry and trade of Duke Charles's subjects in the Low Countries. He had dealt a crushing blow to the great fairs of Geneva by establishing fairs at Lyons, thus crippling the trade of Burgundian merchants and the finances of the pro-Burgundian House of Savoy, overlord of Geneva. In most of the truces with Duke Charles in the seventies, Louis offered no trading concessions. When, as in the truce of March, 1473, he could not avoid granting them, he attenuated their effect by ordering his officers to issue as few safe-conducts to Burgundian merchants as possible. Otherwise, in measure after measure, he gradually shut off Franco-Burgundian commerce and likewise blocked Burgundian trade routes running through France from other lands. In the Channel and off the coasts of Spain his sea rovers plundered the Venetian, Genoese, and Neapolitan merchant vessels bound to or from the Low Countries. By 1475 traffic in the Channel had greatly diminished and ships not venturing to sail clogged Duke Charles's harbors.

King Louis's most damaging attack was concentrated on the food supply of the Low Countries. These industrialized regions, unable to feed themselves, depended on the fish procured by their herring fleets and on imported cereals from France, the Baltic, and even from Spain and Italy. In the early seventies the King clamped an embargo on the sale or transport of wheat and wine to the Burgundians. This interdiction and that on commerce were strictly renewed in February of 1475. French corsairs, meanwhile, wrought such havoc in the herring fleets that the food supply of the Low Countries was drastically reduced. The King had frankly explained his motive to an assembly of town delegations in 1470. When some of these asked to be exempted from the regulations prohibiting the export of food, Louis replied, "The King is not willing for his subjects to sell or take for sale into the territories of the Duke of Burgundy wheat or wine, for this reason: the inhabitants of Holland, Zeeland, and Flanders, being in great need of wheat, will have the better cause to rise against the lord of Burgundy."

By the end of 1475, this pervasive policy was taking sharp effect. Hard-pressed for cash to pay his mercenaries, the Duke of Burgundy was saddled with the deteriorating morale of troops unpaid, which was exacerbated by his haughty refusal to acknowledge it. The Duke's subjects, their interests scorned, their trade and their resources dwindling, their food supply endangered, were becoming sullen and recalcitrant, voting subsidies only under increasingly harsh pressure. When the Duke of Burgundy, in 1475, scorchingly accused the Estates of Flanders, in answer to their complaints, of cowardice and base ill-will, they dared reply, "They were, all of them, merchants and traders and industrialists, seamen, laborers" and that "war is incompatible with commerce."

Louis had likewise employed the less obvious weapon of propaganda. The cruelties of the Duke at Dinant and Liège, his avowed contempt for his own townsmen and brutal measures against captured cities enabled the King to depict him as the enemy of the middle class, the intransigent foe of peace, peace that nurtures trade and agriculture and all the arts that make this life good. It was a theme that the King and the King's able agents industriously spread throughout Europe and among the Duke's own subjects.

By December of 1475, Louis XI had completed his diplomatic-economic web designed to envelop the Duke of Burgundy. In the course of weaving it, he had invented what today is known as cold war, a far-flung, intricate, subtle attack, by all means short of military hostilities, upon the enemy. Louis meant to play out his game to the end, at any sacrifice, including honor. As 1475 gave way to 1476, he waited at Plessis-lès-Tours for tidings from regions to the east.

21. The Swiss

In the second week of January, 1477, the Duke of Burgundy pulled his army out of Lorraine and headed southward for the County of Burgundy. He arrived at Besançon on January 22. Berne and her confederates were hastily assembling their tough mountaineers. Western Europe held its breath.

At Plessis, Louis XI explored his network of intelligences. "He had many spies and many couriers abroad," notes Commynes, "most of them dispatched by my hand." For messengers to the Swiss he used "beggars and pilgrims, that sort of people." He was sending constantly to his sister Yolande, Duchess of Savoy, but she and her state were entirely the Duke's. He was sending, too, to King René, seeking to detach him from Burgundy, but old René "hardly listened to the royal messengers, which he promptly dispatched to Duke Charles."

Suddenly the Duke of Burgundy was thrusting his columns southeastward across the Jura Mountains, defying weather. The chastisement of an outrageous world could not wait. He was marching for the Pays de Vaud, to settle accounts, at last, with the Swiss.

For several days, at the head of the pass of Jougne, the Duke stationed himself in the snow to watch his legions struggle across the Jura —rising around him the Alpine ghosts of Hannibal and his Carthaginian elephants. The weather was wretched. "I've campaigned in worse than this," Charles casually observed to the Milanese ambassador, Jean Pierre Panigarola. By February 12 the army had passed the mountains and the Duke's headquarters lay at Orbe in the Pays de Vaud. Burgundian advance guards had already cleared much of that region. A dozen miles to the north stood the fortified outposts of the Swiss, Yverdon at the western foot of Lake Neuchâtel and Grandson a little way up the northern side.

As the forces of the Duke moved northward, the garrison at Yverdon burned the town and withdrew by the lake to Grandson, whose walls

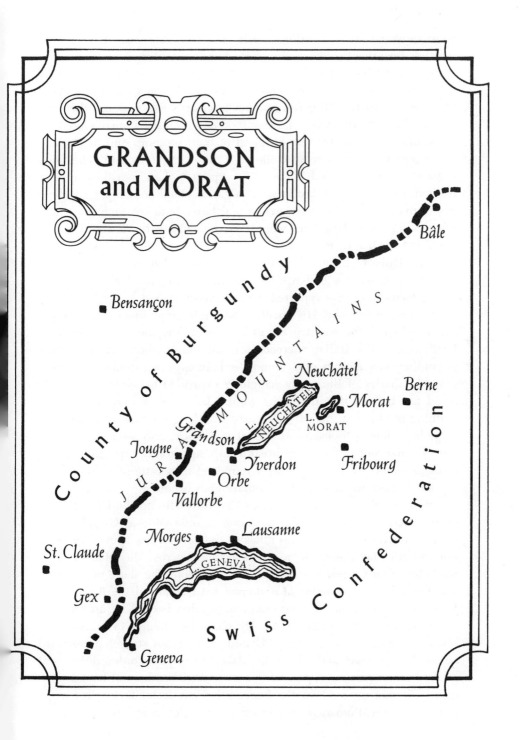

GRANDSON and MORAT

Bâle

Bensançon

County of Burgundy

JURA MOUNTAINS

Neuchâtel

Berne

Morat

Grandson

L. NEUCHÂTEL

L. MORAT

Jougne

Yverdon

Fribourg

Orbe

Vallorbe

Morges

Lausanne

St. Claude

L. GENEVA

Gex

Swiss Confederation

Geneva

were crowned by a bristling castle. On February 19, "in the worst weather imaginable," the Duke of Burgundy established his camp on a plateau above the town. Three days later his forces took Grandson by assault, the Swiss garrison of some five hundred men barricading themselves in the castle. After Burgundian bombards had battered the walls for five days, the defenders, lacking food and munitions, surrendered unconditionally (February 28). Stripped of their weapons and belongings, the conquered were forced to file past the conqueror's tent. The Duke ordered them dispatched at once. "In a quarter of an hour they were all hanged on trees, to the last boy." Panigarola could not keep his feelings out of his dispatch: "It was terrible and horrible to see such hangings." Charles announced that he would do the same with all the Swiss he could get his hands on.

The Duke of Burgundy was now determined to advance eastward and bring the enemy to battle. Several of his commanders objected. A strong Swiss force was reported concentrating around Neuchâtel at the eastern end of the lake. His fortified camp offered an ideal defensive position, whereas the country ahead did not allow room for maneuver. Furthermore, the Italian mercenaries, and other troops as well, were grumbling over arrears of pay and the hardships of camping on frozen ground. Charles of Burgundy haughtily overruled his commanders. He could not believe that the Swiss would dare to seek him out. On the morning of March 2, he set forth eastward along the lake with his army of perhaps fifteen thousand men, foot and horse, and some of his artillery. He had not bothered to break camp, apparently expecting an immediate victory. Within his laager remained a treasure of plate, jewels, tapestries, destined to deck the Lotharingian conquest.

Between the Jura Mountains on Charles's left and the lake of Neuchâtel stretched a rolling plateau, about a mile wide at Grandson but soon narrowing. Less than two miles to the north a low spur of the Jura ran into the lake, forming a wooded hump across the plateau. Two roads led from Grandson to Neuchâtel, one along the shore of the lake, and the other, the remains of a Roman road, followed the flank of the Jura. Charles sent an advance guard of cavalry, backed by archers and pikemen, along the Roman road. He made no attempt to marshal the rest of his army in battle array. Disorderly columns straggled eastward across the plateau and along the lake. The Duke ordered his tent pitched on an eminence, paused to survey the movement of his advance guard. At that moment, as the Burgundian cavalry rode into a narrow pass where the Roman road crossed the wooded ridge, they suddenly collided with Swiss foot in massed battle formation.

Then for the first time the Duke of Burgundy heard the terrible bellow of Swiss battle horns. The Burgundian horse recoiled, were thrust back upon the main body of the army. Down the pass tramped the phalanx of the mountaineers, thousands strong, supported by a few hundred horsemen. Huge pikes thrust out a deadly wall of points at the front of the phalanx; at the flanks and rear marched halberdiers, swinging their spiked battle axes. Arms bared, the Swiss wore steel caps and corselets. "More than thirty green banners" streamed about a high white standard. A cloaked horseman with a long beard, the hunchbacked chieftain of Lucerne, directed the phalanx—Panigarola, close by the Duke of Burgundy, could see him clearly.

As the Swiss debouched onto the plateau, the Duke ordered a cavalry attack on their right flank, while he himself directed infantry columns against their left. Burgundian artillery, hastily ranged, peppered the woods above the mountaineers' heads. Mounted men of arms, swinging down a slope of the Jura, charged upon the phalanx. The Burgundian commander, the valiant lord of Châteaugyon, leaped his steed into the iron ranks—horse and man were instantly spitted on pikes. The cavalry attack faltered, was soon beaten off. On the other flank, sporadic infantry assaults improvised by the Duke were easily repelled by the fearsome halberdiers. The Swiss machine ground onward. Then, as the Duke of Burgundy was finally managing to swing the bulk of his frontline forces toward the enemy on the left, green banners appeared through the trees of the ridge, this time on the Burgundian right near the lake. Again Swiss warhorns bellowed. With roars of "Berne! Berne!" another massive Swiss phalanx rolled down from the woods onto the plateau.

By a flurry of orders to his captains, the Duke of Burgundy tried to bring off a parade-ground maneuver—commanded artillery to be turned upon the newcomers, commanded cavalry masking the guns to pull aside, commanded the mass of Burgundian footmen in the path of the phalanx to fall back in order to gain room for maneuver. With the Swiss machine to the left chopping aside all resistance and the Swiss machine to the right now pounding across the plateau, this attempt at complicated movements threw the Burgundian front into wild confusion. The disorderly masses to the rear thought that their comrades were breaking in flight. A wave of panic rode through the Burgundian host. The dreaded cry of "Sauve qui peut!" began to sound. The Burgundian columns dissolved into streams and clots of fleeing men. In vain the Duke

sought to halt the tide. He was borne back to the camp, again tried use-
lessly to rally his men. With the mountaineers almost upon him, he was
forced to take to ignominious flight. Lack of cavalry in the Swiss host
and a superabundance of booty in the Burgundian laager saved the
Duke's army from destruction.

As the Burgundians fled pell-mell toward Geneva or toward the
crossings of the Jura, the mountaineers joyously set about pillaging.
Most of the Duke's magnificent artillery was taken, some five hundred
pieces, weapons and armor, food stores, richly adorned pavilions, cloth
of gold, arrays of plate, money chests, and jewels that were the pride of
Burgundy.* The rude mountaineers knew so little of such luxuries that
some of them, it was said, sold fabulous stones for a franc or two. Booty
rounded up, the Swiss promptly went home.

The Duke of Burgundy rode headlong back across the Jura to No-
zeroy in the County of Burgundy. On the flight, his mordant fool, Le Glorieux, thinking on the Duke's passion for the great conquerors of the
past, cried, "My Lord, we've been well Hannibal-ed today!"

Once the King of France knew that the Burgundians had crossed
the Jura, he had begun to move southward toward Lyons, his gateway
to Savoy, ordering a concentration of troops at that city. On his journey he turned aside to pay his devotions to the shrine of Our Lady of
Puy. Here, about March 9, he received first word of the Duke of Burgundy's overthrow. Upon reaching Lyons, he sent a glowing letter of
congratulations to the Avoyer and the Council of Berne, addressing them
as "Very illustrious lords, our very dear and special friends, invincible
by the grace of God." Unimpressed, the Swiss dispatched reiterated demands that, since Burgundy had broken the truce, the King join the
struggle and share the burden of the war. By this time Louis knew that
the Duke of Burgundy, breathing fire and vengeance, had recrossed the
Jura to establish a camp at Lausanne. To the Council of Berne the King
addressed a vibrant, if at best but half-truthful reply, in which after a re-
proachful hint, very gentle, that the failure of the Swiss to press farther
into Savoy had prevented his joining forces with them, he gave assurance that, if they persevered in the struggle, he was likewise prepared to
act. To Swiss emissaries with further representations the King gave the
warmest welcomes, promised—and afterward paid—additional money

---

* These included the ducal coronet, crusted with precious stones; a superbly
jeweled sword; the Duke's prodigious diamond, Le Sancy; two great pearls, "each
the size of a nut"; five rubies, "the most beautiful in the world."

to the cantons, with special pensions to their chiefs, "sent the envoys back, their purses full and their bodies clothed in silk, and thus brought the Swiss to accept his failure to declare for them." Commynes believed that by the time of his death Louis had spent one million Rhine florins on the cantons.

Already the rout of the Burgundian army at Grandson was making a new world. Towns and principalities in the Empire began to declare themselves against the Duke of Burgundy. Yolande of Savoy, by means of a secret envoy to the King, proposed Franco-Burgundian reconciliation, thus hoping to find a way back to her brother's grace in case her Burgundian ally came to grief. Galeazzo-Maria Sforza, Duke of Milan, perceiving that he had jumped in the wrong direction, hastily sent an envoy to Lyons to explain away his perfidy. Louis disdainfully rejected the offer of money brought by Giovanni Bianchi, telling the ambassador, "If your master repents of having deserted his alliance with me to ally himself with the Duke of Burgundy, I am content to return as we were." At this time, early April, old King René too came hurrying fearfully to Lyons to make his peace. Louis gave him a cheerful welcome.° In a few days King René agreed to leave Provence to his childless nephew the Count of Maine, and on Maine's death the province would be united with the domain of France. René likewise renounced all ties with the Duke of Burgundy. In return the King of France granted him a handsome pension of sixty thousand francs a year, rewarded his chief officers, and provided court entertainments adorned by lovely ladies galore. Uncle and nephew parted the best of friends.

Meanwhile, the King had come to quite different terms with another peer of France. Revelations by the Constable of treasonable practices with the Duke of Nemours had finally snapped Louis's patience. Besieged in his rocky stronghold of Carlat by a band of royal troops, the feckless Jacques d'Armagnac surrendered on March 9, a few hours after his wife died in childbirth. She had spent her last days feverishly burn-

---

° René's faithful Neapolitan adherent Jean Cossa, Seneschal of Provence, who had long experience of dealing with the King of France, managed René's excuses adroitly. "Sire," he declared at the moment of greeting, "don't marvel that my master, the King your uncle, offered to make the Duke of Burgundy his heir; for so was he counseled to do, especially by me, seeing that you, the son of his sister and his own nephew, had done him such great wrong in taking over the castles of Angers and Bar and had so badly treated him in all his other affairs. We wished to push this bargaining with the Duke of Burgundy so that you had news of it, in order to prompt you to do us right and recognize that the King my master is your uncle; but we never had any intention of bringing matters to a conclusion." A connoisseur of loyal service, Louis appreciated Cossa's bold defense of his master and "very well and wisely" accepted the statement.

ing incriminating documents that Jacques was apparently too helpless to destroy for himself. While the King and his uncle feasted, the Duke of Nemours thought long melancholy thoughts in the Lyons bastille of Pierre-Scise, enclosed, nights, in a cage of wood and iron and watched round the clock by citizen guards. Taken to Paris, he was incarcerated in the Bastille on August 4 and trial procedure was begun. That he was guilty of capital crimes against the King was abundantly proved, even in his own inept attempts at defense. Yet it was a year to a day after his entry into the capital that he received his sentence. On August 4, 1477, in open Parlement, he was pronounced guilty of *lèse-majesté* and condemned to death. Taken to Les Halles, the great covered market, he was given time to confess and was then led to a scaffold and quickly decapitated. The execution took place in a fish warehouse, its walls draped in black, its floors scrubbed and the air sweetened with herbs to conceal the reek.°

The new world wrought by the battle of Grandson was likewise reflected in the Duke of Burgundy's communications with the King. The lord of Contay arrived in Lyons bringing "humble and gracious words from the Duke, which were clean contrary to his custom and nature." Louis gave Contay a hearty reception, but the Burgundian lord had to listen to much mockery in the town. Songs were being sung in the streets in praise of the conquering Swiss and in scorn of the vanquished. Before Contay departed he was able to observe the festive reunion of Louis XI and King René.

Commanding an army of two thousand lances, eight thousand franc archers, and some two hundred guns, the King of France waited at Lyons, exploring, along the threads of his intelligence network, the situation of the Duke of Burgundy on the banks of Lake Geneva.

ii

ONLY TWELVE DAYS after being routed at Grandson, Charles of Burgundy had recrossed the Jura and begun establishing a camp on a plateau above Lausanne. His lieutenants scoured the countryside to round up

---

° The evident reluctance of the Chancellor and certain members of the Parlement to condemn Nemours, despite his obvious guilt, reveals the enormous prestige which still surrounded princely personalities in King Louis's France and also the uneasiness and fear inspired by the newfangled kingship of King Louis. Louis, for his part, discharged from office three of the Parlement officials who had most obstructed the proceedings against Nemours. When their colleagues attempted a plea in their favor, the King wrote back tartly, "I thought that, since you are subjects of the Crown and owe your loyalty to it, you would not be willing to approve anybody's making so good a bargain with my skin."

the fugitives from the battle, while the Duke sent urgently into his domains for supplies, artillery, troops. As the army reassembled, he lashed out bitterly against his men, "calling them all traitors, who had fled in order to inflict a shameful defeat upon him and put him in the power of the King of France or have him killed." In surly mood the troops built themselves rude wooden huts. Soon the camp sheltered a motley force of some fifteen thousand men, approximately the size of the Duke's former army. Consumed by his angers and suffering from exhaustion, Charles became so ill at the end of April that he had to be moved into lodgings in Lausanne. His ill-paid and hungry troops fell to fighting among themselves. In early May a bloody brawl between the English and the Italian mercenaries was halted only by the intervention of the convalescent Duke himself.

Nevertheless, vowing vengeance on the "bestial Swiss," the Duke of Burgundy burned his camp on May 27 and marched through the Pays de Vaud toward the little walled town of Morat, near the eastern end of the lake of the same name, which guarded the road to Berne. On June 9 he arrived before Morat, garrisoned by some two thousand Swiss. Its walls and castle still standing, the town is sited on a small eminence between the water and irregularly rising terrain that sweeps up to wooded summits. In the valley behind these ridges flows the river Saane, bridged by the two roads that run from Berne to Morat. Planting his camp on the high ground to the south and southeast of the town, the Duke of Burgundy established siege works and set his artillery to battering the walls of Morat. A breach having been opened, Charles ordered an assault on June 18. It was bloodily repulsed. By this time an army of some eighteen thousand foot and two thousand horse was advancing from Berne.

Informed of the approach of the enemy, the Duke of Burgundy withdrew the bulk of his forces from the siege and fortified a strong position, facing the heights, on a plateau above the camp. On Friday afternoon, June 21, after the Duke had spent most of the day establishing the battle stations of his troops on the plateau, he was shown an enemy force encamped behind the high woods. Since they appeared few in number and made no move except to fire hand guns, Charles instantly decided that the Swiss were merely trying to make him abandon his siege and would not offer battle. Leaving only a guard at his defense positions, he ordered his troops into camp. In the early hours of June 22 it began to rain. At the entreaties of his captains, Charles consented to draw up the greater part of his forces on the plateau. Most of the morning they stood to arms in the rain, but the Swiss did not appear. The Duke, now utterly fixed in his idea that the enemy would not attack, sent his troops back to the camp for shelter and food, leaving only his artillery, about one thousand foot, including the English archers, and some eighteen hundred horse, to guard the plateau.

About noon the rain stopped. At almost the same moment, the terrible battle horns of the Swiss sounded on the heights. Out from the trees they moved, two bristling phalanxes of pikemen with a strong cavalry force between. At the head of three hundred horse there rode young René II, Duke of Lorraine, who had reached the Swiss army but a few hours before: King Louis had supplied him with money and a strong escort to bring him safely to the field. The smaller phalanx, on the Burgundian left, moved downward against the besiegers of Morat. The larger body, of some ten thousand men, "many banners" flying above their heads, advanced upon the Duke's fortified position, preceded by a screen of hand gunners. From behind a defense work the English archers and Burgundian artillery opened a fire so hot that the Swiss ranks were momentarily checked. Soon, however, a body of enemy infantry swung down a ravine and with roars of "Grandson! Grandson!" burst onto the flank of the Burgundian position.

Only after several frantic messages from his captains was the obdurate Duke of Burgundy persuaded that the enemy was upon him. Shouting orders for his forces to gain the plateau, he armed himself with the aid of his physician and Panigarola, the Milanese ambassador. Even then, he refused to be hurried in mounting horse. By the time he reached the plateau, a disordered mass of infantry were already running from the Swiss gunfire and the fearsome hedge of Swiss pikes. As the enemy closed upon his troops, the Duke of Burgundy was wildly yelling incomprehensible commands. "Never before," reported Panigarola, "had I seen the Duke confused and not knowing what to do." Some squadrons of men of arms attempted a stand, were overwhelmed by the wave of Swiss pikes. Cavalry and infantry broke for the slopes. As troops from the camp below struggled haphazardly onto the plateau, they were swept up in the rout. Torrents of fugitives were streaming toward the lake. "It all happened," Panigarola wrote, "in less time than it takes to say a *Miserere*," i.e., in about two minutes.

At this moment a third phalanx thrust down the hill past the Burgundian right to cut the escape route westward along the lake. The Swiss within Morat sallied from the western gate to help close the trap. As the Duke of Burgundy and broken squadrons of men of arms galloped headlong down the road to Lausanne, Swiss were slitting the throats of Burgundians still arming themselves in the camp. The Grand Bastard of Burgundy, Antoine, momentarily surrounded by mountaineers, got away. The Count of Marle, caught, offered twenty-five thousand ducats for his life—was instantly killed. As Swiss cavalry cut down fugitives, the phalanx thrust the hapless Burgundian infantry to the lake shore. Hundreds flung themselves into the water and drowned. The rest were butchered. Some ten thousand men perished, about half the Burgundian host. With but three hundred horse Charles rode all the way to Morges, on Lake Geneva, without halting, then made his way across the Jura to Gex near St. Claude in the County of Burgundy.[1]

Only two days after the battle, on Monday, June 24, Philippe de Commynes and the lord du Bouchage hurried into Louis XI's chamber with a dispatch which contained the news of Morat.* However exuberantly the King expressed his joy at the Duke of Burgundy's undoing— this moment of triumph is unreported—he had no thought of exploiting by resort to arms the overthrow of his mortal enemy. That same day he ordered forces to the Savoyard borders in order to demonstrate his support for the government of the Duchy; and he sent a letter to the Grand Master on the Picard frontier, commanding him to maintain the Burgundian truce at all cost. Next morning, he set off on a pilgrimage of thanksgiving to Our Lady of Puy. In a letter of congratulations to the Avoyer and council of Berne, his "very special friends, by the grace of God most invincible," he laid chief emphasis on the return of peace which their victory had made possible. A new Milanese ambassador reported simply, "The King is totally dedicated to peace." Louis resolutely held to the script of the drama of statecraft he had created; there yet remained one act to be played. By the end of July, with Duke Charles immobilized in the County of Burgundy, the King was returning to the Loire Valley.

The new Milanese ambassador was Francesco Pietrasanta, whom the Duke of Milan had hastily dispatched to France as soon as he received the news of Morat. Galeazzo-Maria Sforza, like others in western Europe, had now but one thought—to scramble out of his ill-timed alliance with Burgundy and humbly return to the fold of France. Fortu-

---

* The speed with which the tidings reached King Louis reveals the amazing efficiency of his courier service—Morat being distant about 175 miles from Lyons. Louis was fond of saying, "I will give such and such to the one who brings me such and such news." Commynes and Ymbert de Batarnay, for alertly intercepting the messenger, received each a handsome reward of two hundred marcs of silver.

nately, he had chosen for his envoy a man of wit and learning, whom Louis XI knew how to value.[2] The Milanese alliance was renewed, and Francesco Pietrasanta became one of the King's intimates. He it is who makes clear that the success of the King's Burgundian policy was a triumph also for Philippe de Commynes. "The lord of Argenton," wrote Pietrasanta, "has been the beginning, the middle, and the end of our business. He alone manages the King's affairs and sleeps in the King's chamber. He is the all in all and for all matters."

Meanwhile, as the summer passed, Charles of Burgundy's emissary, the lord of Contay, came and went and came again, bringing words, words, words. Louis XI, however, had better sources of information about the Duke of Burgundy. That Duke's first act after his defeat at Morat had been a reflex of black fury. Needing someone to blame for his ruin, and his ally Yolande, Duchess-Regent of Savoy being at hand, he instantly decided that she must have contrived a secret league with her brother, the King of France. After she took leave of him at Gex, to go with her four children to Geneva, the Duke ordered the captain of his guard, Olivier de La Marche, to waylay her at night and carry her and her young ones off to the County of Burgundy. In his *Mémoires* poor Olivier records simply, "What I did, I did to save my life." Olivier swung the Duchess up on his saddle; three of her children were likewise secured; but in the dark one of Olivier's Italian officers allowed eleven-year-old Philibert, Duke of Savoy, to slip away, and he was hidden in a wheatfield by servants of the Duchess. So furious was the Duke of Burgundy at Philibert's escape that Olivier de La Marche almost lost his life in any case. Yolande and the three children were consigned under an English guard—the Duke mistrusted his own subjects—first to a fortress near Dole and then to the castle of Rouvre, outside Dijon. In his terrible rage, Charles called her whore, swore that he would "make her pay for her sins."

The Duke himself remained at Salins until the latter part of July, then moved to La Rivière, likewise in the County of Burgundy, to scramble together an army. From his Estates of the Burgundies and those in the Low Countries he demanded money, supplies, troops. He had already lost, however, the hearts of many of his subjects and now he could no longer command their obedience. By the end of the summer he managed to assemble a scratch force of some eleven hundred lances, badly mounted and armed, low in morale. Ravaged in mind and body, their commander hardly inspired confidence. Some time previously Charles had lost his upper teeth in a fall; he now let his beard grow, until his physicians persuaded him to shave it off because it engendered melancholy; his fingernails were like claws, "longer than had ever been seen"; he alternated fits of despair, seizures of solitary rage, with moments of laughter—during one of which he assured the Milanese ambassador, Panigarola, that he would reappear on the European scene with an army of 150,000 men.° His ire was now directed against the man who had fought with the Swiss at Morat, René II, Duke of Lorraine. René's subjects had rallied to his cause; by September the young Duke had recaptured several towns of his Duchy, which had been held by Burgundian garrisons.

The King of France, surveying the Duke of Burgundy from afar, listened amiably to the lord of Contay, who had come again in early August with vague proposals obviously designed to tranquilize an enemy, who needed no tranquilizing. Before the Burgundian lord departed, Louis could not resist some rather rough humor at his expense. He ordered the proclamation of his renewed alliance with Milan to be made, "with a great blaring of trumpets," directly under the window of Contay's lodging. On occasion in the middle of the night Contay was awakened by a clamor of noise makers and drums outside his door accompanied by cries of "The Swiss are coming!" Louis himself treated the envoy to mocking ironies. Before mid-September, Contay had returned once more, this time with the proposition that the Duchy of Savoy be partitioned between France and Burgundy. To this notion Louis dryly made answer in a parable: Once upon a time a lion commanded his neighbors to join him in a great hunt, promising to give each a fair share of the game. At once a hare spoke up, "Lord, what will my winnings be if I go on the hunt, since I don't eat meat?" The lion replied, "We will capture all manner of furred beasts and give you some pelts." The hare replied, "Lord, there's no need of troubling yourself to offer me such a share, for I have sufficient pelt of my own."

To Pietrasanta the King expressed himself more forcefully on the subject of Duke Charles: "The Duke of Burgundy is so changeable that he never stays fixed in one idea. Now, he sends word to tell me one thing; now, another; and he so continually vacillates that I don't know what he's telling me. In truth, by my faith, he is mad. Though I do ill to use the word, he indeed is so. The fact is, he once had good luck; but

° It was after the King had somehow eluded the Duke's clutch at Péronne and Liège that Chastellain signals the onset of melancholy, moments of strange despair. Perhaps even then, generated by a hidden weariness of imperfection, had begun to unfold within him the dark flower of a death wish.

what went well for him in the past came not through the workings of his own intelligence but by chance and the power of money and because the men of the world were willing to accept it."

By the time Contay departed in late September, Louis had decided to undertake to free the Duchess of Savoy. He was able to find just the adroit man for the mission, his Governor of Champagne, Charles d'Amboise. At the head of two hundred lances, the Governor swiftly rode to the castle of Rouvre, immobilized the guard, and as swiftly bore Yolande and her children to French territory "without doing or receiving the least harm." Louis wrote her a delightful note: "Come as quickly as you can, for I promise you on my word that I have never desired to see pretty girls as much as I desire to see you. . . . ." Hearing of her approach on October 29, the King sent all his chief courtiers to provide her an honorific escort and himself awaited her at the gates of Montils, his small lodge near the palace of Plessis just outside Tours.

When she dismounted, he went to her, his face beaming. "Madame of Burgundy," he said, heartily embracing her, "you are very welcome indeed."

In the midst of "loving demonstrations and claspings," she managed to reply that she was not Burgundian but a good Frenchwoman and happy to obey the King in whatever he wished to command her. Holding her close about the waist, Louis conducted her into the dwelling, both of them talking at a great rate. After they had supped, he summoned her to his bedchamber, and she ceremoniously supervised his undressing and being put to bed. For the next ten days they were constantly together. The lord of Argenton was given the task of finding a goodly sum of money for her and providing four thousand crowns' worth of cloth for her household. On November 8, after they had sworn a pact of friendship and Louis had engaged himself to defend her and her House, they parted with expressions of affection that moved all onlookers. The truth was, Commynes explains, Louis "was eager to get her off his hands. She was a wise woman—the two of them understood each other perfectly—and she was even more eager for her departure than the King. . . . At their parting both were very joyous to see the last of each other; and they lived as good brother and good sister until death."

Despite uncertainties over the next move to be made by the Duke of Burgundy, it had been a good summer for Louis, a moment of golden quiet in the Loire Valley, the like of which the King of France would never know again. True, he had a little trouble with his old affliction, about which he held some curious ideas. After a brief excursion in the valley, he arrived on Friday night, August 9, at Montils-lès-Tours. Sending for the Queen, who had not accompanied him to Lyons, he slept with her that night—a state occasion which the Milanese ambassador matter-of-factly reported. The following morning the King, still in his dressing gown, had Pietrasanta admitted privately to his chamber. Seating himself at a window, he explained that he was feeling ill. When he learned that Pietrasanta had brought with him Master Pantaleone, an Italian physician formerly in Louis's service, the King had him summoned. He told the two of them, speaking in Latin, "I am suffering from hemorrhoids. I have had them before but they were never so painful as now. I believe the cause has been the labor of mind and body I have endured on this expedition [to Lyons in the first half of 1476] and also the lack of sexual intercourse, I having been so long a time absent from my wife." The King shifted to Italian. "This affliction has sent certain vapors to my head and caused a palpitation of the heart that troubles me a great deal." He then extended his hand for Pantaleone to take his pulse, explaining to Pietrasanta that he had known the physician for thirty years and considered him so able that he had made him a royal councilor.

Apparently, Pantaleone's treatment proved successful, for Louis spent a happy August and September. He made a pilgrimage to Our Lady of Béhuard, on her island in the Loire near Angers. During her feast of mid-August he transacted no business for three days. On the day of the week of the Holy Innocents he followed his custom of secluding himself with a few choice spirits to read and discuss intellectual matters. A favorite companion of these days was the Neapolitan Boffile de Juge, who had risen rapidly in Louis's service during the past two years, "a man of most delectable conversation who knows much of history, ancient and modern." As usual, he engaged in some benevolent matchmaking. At Lyons he had been struck by the sterling qualities of two *bourgeoises* of the town, both widows of merchants. He brought them with him to the Loire, chose two able young Parisians as husbands for them, and provided handsome dowries in the form of good offices for the husbands.

The King enjoyed walking in the park at Plessis to look at his aviaries and warrens, to inspect the cows he had had imported from Flanders, and to watch a Flemish dairymaid, imported with the cows, making fresh butter. According to a tale told in Tours, he one day, poking about the kitchens, came upon a little scullion turning a spit. The scullion, who did not recognize the King, energetically continued his labors. "What do you earn?" Louis asked him. "As much as the King," the child replied cheerfully. "He and I both gain our livelihood. God nourishes him and he nourishes me." Charmed, Louis at once took the boy into his personal service as a page. The tale is no doubt apocryphal but it reveals how Louis XI was looked upon by the people of Tours, over whom he clucked and fussed so much. Even when preoccupied at Lyons in the critical days of the previous spring, he had sent orders to the town, on hearing that foodstuffs were too dear there, that the cost of wheat must come down so that the bakers could bake larger loaves at the same price.

In late August, Louis went north of the Loire, in the region of Vendôme, for a session of hunting, quartering himself in a village so small that even most of his household servants were obliged to find lodgings in the hamlets round about. "It was wild country, beautiful, and very good for hunting," and the King, having escaped from his court and his affairs, was in his element. On the first of September he spent nine hours tracking a stag, thought he had lost the animal, and then suddenly bagged it. He was so pleased with himself that in his thick tones he jauntily sang all the way home—a ballad satirizing the defeats of the Duke of Burgundy.

iii

BY THE beginning of October the King of France had returned to Tours. Events were impending in Lorraine: the Duke of Burgundy, heedless of everything except the clamor of his passions, was taking the field with his ragged forces. King Louis soon had word that René II, with an army of Swiss and Alsatians of the Basse Union, had laid siege to Nancy and, on October 6, forced the surrender of the Burgundian garrison. The Duke of Burgundy was already advancing into Lorraine to win back the capital of the Duchy. René II, lacking the forces to oppose Duke Charles in the field, established a strong garrison in Nancy and hastened to his grateful friends the Swiss to beg aid. On October 22 the Duke of Burgundy laid siege to the city, despite entreaties by his captains that his army was too weak to undertake the operation.

The Swiss and the Alsatians and other Germans were more than ready to supply René with troops but there was no money to pay them. Envoys of King Louis were preaching René's cause among the cantons and keeping their master informed of developments. Louis promptly supplied the money. By the first of January, 1477, the Duke of Lorraine was approaching Nancy with an army of ten thousand Swiss, numerous

Germans, and a mounted force of French volunteers. The captains of the Duke of Burgundy begged him to withdraw to Luxembourg to secure reinforcements and supplies. The Duke raged at them, called them cowards. He drew up his army on a plateau southeast of Nancy, blocking the road by which his enemies were advancing. In bitter cold Duke Charles mustered his force of fewer than three thousand men, dispirited, unpaid, badly armed, many of them sick. . . .

At dawn on Thursday, January 9, a great knocking sounded at the door of King Louis's chamber in the palace of Plessis. In strode my lord du Lude with a dispatch in his hand from the lord of Craon, royal lieutenant on the border of Lorraine.

The previous Sunday, January 5, the army of René II, advancing in two phalanxes against the flanks of the Burgundian position, had crushed the feeble force of the Duke of Burgundy at the first onslaught, killed fleeing Burgundians by the hundreds, taken captive the Bastard of Burgundy and other great lords. Of the Duke himself there was yet no news.

"At first," records Commynes, "the King was so overcome with joy that he hardly knew how to react." Talking to himself as much as to those in the chamber, Louis excitedly pushed the news this way and that—so much depended on what had happened to the Duke of Burgundy. He summoned his captains and councilors who happened to be in Tours, showed the dispatch around, made some comments, then went to Mass. Emerging from the chapel, he ordered a table set up in his chamber, invited all the company to dinner.

What an ironic comedy!—Commynes, recording the scene a dozen years later, still savors it, just a little maliciously. For all the King's intense absorption in the great tidings, it would be surprising if he missed the by-play. Perhaps he laid on the repast in order to prolong it.

On hearing the news of the battle of Nancy from their sovereign, all the guests had produced expressions and gestures of great joy—but the demonstration had cost most of them an effort. At dinner, while Louis volubly explored the significance of the Burgundian disaster, his officers struggled to put down food with a show of relish. "Not one of them, apparently, ate half of what was set before him—yet they could not have been embarrassed by the honor of dining with the King, for there wasn't a one who had not often done so!" They were a glum lot, these powers of the realm, hollowly feigning to exult in the triumph of the master who had made them powerful. Unshakable states collapse, amazing dreams are realized; and men of limited vision, the obedient agents of these high enterprises, suddenly feel the air strike cold along their skins. Who should count himself safe, if so great an object in the feudal firmament as the Duke of Burgundy could be destroyed? And what might their incomprehensible sovereign do, now that he had removed the only check upon his will? In the moment of his success, Louis remained as solitary as he had been in his many hours of failure.

Next morning the King received positive word that his mighty adversary had indeed perished in the field. Two days after the battle an Italian page pointed out the Duke's corpse. The furious devotee of Mars, who had shown all the qualities of a great general except generalship and all the trappings of a conqueror except victories, lay face down on a frozen pond, stripped naked. His head had been cloven from top to chin by a Swiss halberd; his body was pierced through by Swiss pikes; the bloody ruin of his face was unrecognizable. Captured servants of his made positive identification by the long nails, the missing upper teeth and several scars on the body.[3]

Through harsh January weather Louis rode to Our Lady of Béhuard to give thanks. The airy strands woven by the universal spider turned out to be perdurable cables. He had not lost a man, nor his kingdom suffered so much as a burned village. That kingdom now stood unchallenged as the great power of the West and its King, the best obeyed of monarchs. Louis was fifty-three, had ruled for fifteen years. He could not know that he had won a triumph in statecraft—whose success is almost always limited, its shape rarely perceptible in sharp outline—that perhaps has never been bettered in the Western world. How the King-entrepreneur would exploit what the artist in cold war had achieved remained to be seen.

THE GATHERING IN

22. The Burgundian Inheritance

ON JANUARY 18, 1477, the aging King
of France swung into the saddle and headed, in bitter weather, for the
great northern territories which had so long been alienated in the grip
of Burgundy.[1] The lean regimen of adversity was broken; the need for
indomitable patience and sensitive maneuver and spartan restraint, suddenly ended. His bizarrely complex being, which, under fearful pressure, had achieved a harmoniously articulated grace, was no longer
chastened by the spare discipline of risk. And, at fifty-three, he could
feel the rush of time buffeting his frail mortality. As if all the world, and
he, were new, he must see to everything himself, do everything out of
his own head. Couriers were riding the roads to summon his troops and
captains. Ahead of him he had sent men to places in Picardy, Artois,
Flanders, Hainault, men with local connections in these territories,
whom he had authorized to promise much and who had answered him
that they would do wonders. To win the Flemings of Ghent he had dispatched as his envoy his Flemish barber, the famous Olivier le Daim.
To his towns went letters demanding supplies, munitions, horses, construction workers, money.

By the time the King entered Péronne, at the beginning of February,
almost all the lands bordering the Channel and the towns of Picardy had
yielded to his representatives. The Estates of the Duchy of Burgundy accepted reunion with the Crown; the County of Burgundy submitted
shortly after, but grudgingly; and the greed of the lord of Craon, in
charge of negotiating the submission of the Burgundies, would soon
cause trouble there. At the moment, Louis had no means but irony by
which to check Craon's clumsy avidity: "I thank you for being willing to

do me honor by sharing the booty with me. . . . As for the Duke of Burgundy's wines which are in his cellars, I am content for you to have them."

Even before the disappearance of the Duke of Burgundy, Louis had spoken of absorbing the Burgundian inheritance by effecting the marriage of the Duke's heiress, Marie, and the Dauphin, Charles. Now, however, with good news arriving daily and better promised, it seemed to the exuberant King that he might possibly win the whole inheritance without having to resort to the uncertainties of such a union. On February 2, the day before Louis entered Péronne, Philippe de Commynes arrived to report that the County of Artois, gateway to Flanders, was in a state of panic for lack of defenders and that Philippe de Crèvecoeur, lord d'Esquerdes, commanding in its capital, Arras, might be willing to enter the King's service.

But at dinner that day Louis perceived that the lord of Argenton did not share his heady optimism or the glowing hopes expressed at table by his other intimates. After the meal the King attempted to convince the sagacious counselor whose views had long supported his own. But it was clear that Commynes, favoring the marriage plan and the way of conciliation, regarded these projects for swooping upon the whole Burgundian domain as overhasty and ill advised. That evening the King conferred on Commynes, Seneschal of Poitou, the captainship of its capital, Poitiers. Next morning, as he took horse to enter Pèronne, he ordered the lord of Argenton to go to Poitou in order to keep an eye on the Bretons. Louis was in no mood to be haunted by the cool calculations of his old self.[2]

Before the end of February the feverishly impatient King had taken to the road again. Having dispatched his old faithful, the Grand Master, to begin military operations on the borders of Hainault, he turned northwestward, to try his luck in Artois. At Péronne he had been attempting to sort out a confusion of reports reaching him from Flanders.

"Mademoiselle [Marie, heiress of Burgundy] was then in Ghent in great tribulation"—so, with eloquent simplicity, records the Burgundian chronicler Jean Molinet, successor to Chastellain. Buffeted by clamorous voices and disastrous tidings, Marie found herself, on the death of her father, to be without troops, without money, without power. Indeed she found herself to be a prisoner of the people of Ghent. The moment news arrived of the death of Duke Charles, the citizens promptly put to death their chief magistrates and a number of wealthy merchants for having favored the Duke's oppressive rule. They required Marie to summon an assembly of the Three Estates of Flanders, then forced her to grant the Estates the right to convene whenever they pleased and the power to veto any declaration of war. On February 11 the Ghentois made her restore all the municipal liberties and privileges that Duke Charles and his father had deprived them of. And still the city remained in ferment. The infection spread rapidly to other great towns—Bruges and Ypres and places in Brabant and Hainault. In these terrifying circumstances Marie had about her but a small group of wrangling advisers: her father's Chancellor, Guillaume Hugonet; the able lord of Humbercourt, one of the dead Duke's best diplomats and soldiers; Louis, Bishop of Liège, her Bourbon uncle; Margaret of York, the childless Dowager Duchess who had cherished Marie like a daughter. The mob masters of Ghent had no use for any of them. Intent only on maintaining their new liberties, they cared nothing for the Burgundian state, but they also had no wish to be governed by their nominal overlord, the King of France.

Marie's councilors were united in one view, that this twenty-year-old girl, the greatest heiress in Europe, needed a husband, and needed him at once. Hugonet and Humbercourt were favorably inclined to the French Dauphin, as was the Bishop of Liège. Marie's stepmother, too, had a candidate, one she dearly loved, her restless, ambitious brother George, Duke of Clarence, who had, providentially, become a widower just this preceding December. Marie, however, had no desire to marry a penniless English Duke, nor the English Earl, a brother of the Queen of England, whom Edward IV had hastily sought to substitute for untrustworthy George. It appears that Marie herself had already set her heart on the dashing young man her father had provided, nineteen-year-old Maximilian, son of Frederick III, to whom the Duke, the previous year, had finally contracted her in the vain hope of securing military aid from the Emperor.

Arras, famous for its textiles, fortress guarding the entry to Flanders, was then divided into two towns: the smaller part, the *cité*, under the jurisdiction of the Bishop, was dominated by the fortifications of the *ville*, the city proper. On March 4 King Louis had entered the *cité*, delivered to him by Philippe de Crèvecoeur, who had become the King's man on receiving high offices and a handsome pension. The best Louis could do with the *ville*, for the moment, was to accept a fragile truce, by which he was acknowledged overlord of Arras but was not to enter it with troops.

By this time the King had learned of the fiasco of Barber Olivier's mission—Marie's court scorning his vulgar ostentation and the folk of Ghent, whom he had secretly tried to win to his master's cause, becoming so threatening that he had fled the city. It was a double miscalculation on the King's part, both his choice of ambassador and his hopes of gaining the Flemings. But when an embassy from the Estates of Flanders, dominated by Ghent, now arrived in the *cité* of Arras, Louis XI persisted in his campaign. His offer to contract the Dauphin at once to heiress Marie provided she placed herself under his protection was regarded by the envoys as "unthinkable." He then sought to exploit the ill will between Marie's court and the Flemings in order to secure his terms from whichever party turned to him. When his councilors produced a letter partly in Marie's handwriting avowing that she intended to have all her affairs managed by Hugonet and Humbercourt and two others, the Flemish ambassadors, who had declared their Three Estates to hold supreme power, went off on March 9 in high outrage, bearing the letter with them. They promptly produced the missive against the Duchess. The leaders of Ghent cast Hugonet and Humbercourt into prison, gave them a drumhead trial, and, despite Marie's humble pleas, had the pair put to death like criminals in the marketplace of the city. Louis XI immediately issued letters-patent to their heirs, ensuring their property and fiercely denouncing the executions. Part of the mob resentment against Hugonet and Humbercourt had been generated by their known support of French interests. It was a second lugubrious miscalculation by the King.

In a fury of frustration, acutely conscious of the slipping by of time and of broad French lands still unredeemed, Louis put soldiers at his back and took to the field. Sweeping unopposed through Artois, he set siege to Hesdin, took the town in forty-eight hours. Within ten days he entered the great seaport-fortress of Boulogne, famous for its Church of the Virgin. To her the King conveyed the city, doing homage on his knees as her vassal and offering a "heart of pure gold worth two thousand crowns." Meanwhile the *ville* of Arras, repenting its truce, dispatched a delegation of envoys to ask aid of Marie. They were arrested at Lens, taken to Hesdin, and promptly beheaded. The King arrived from Boulogne the following day. In a letter of April 20, Louis revealed his grimly sardonic mood. "Among the delegates was Master Oudart de Bussy, to whom I had given a high office in the Parlement of Paris [which Bussy had refused]. So that everybody would recognize his head, I had it covered with a fine furred hood [such as Parlementarians wear] and it is now presiding over the marketplace of Hesdin." The inhabitants of the *ville* responded by displaying gibbets on their walls on which were hanged white crosses, symbol of France, and they pelted the King with rhymes.*

Louis set rigorous siege to the town. "The King," reported a Milanese envoy, "tends to the smallest details, oversees the planting of bombards, the erection of redoubts, and everything else. At his side a son of the lord of Contay has been killed." Directing operations, Louis was himself wounded. The town soon requested, and was granted, an honorable capitulation. On May 4, from the *citè*, he made his entry into the *ville*, riding through a breach his cannon had made in the walls. In the marketplace he addressed these stiffnecked townsfolk: "You have been extremely rude to me. I pardon you for it. If you are my good subjects, I will be your good lord." He demanded a loan of fifty thousand crowns, which the inhabitants somehow scraped together; Louis repaid the money as promised. In the course of time more than a hundred intransigent citizens were executed, "as an example to other towns."

On May 7 Louis wrote to the Grand Master, commanding in Hainault: "Thanks to God and Our Lady, I have taken this town, and I am going off to Our Lady of Victory [near Senlis]. On my return, I am coming to your quarter and will bring you a fine company. Therefore think only of giving me good guidance, for I hope that we will do as well there as I have done here. As for my wound, it's the Duke of Brittany who caused it because of his calling me 'the coward King.' But you know my way of old, for you have seen me throughout the years."

By this time the Duchess Marie had finally chosen a husband. Emissaries from the Emperor appeared in Ghent on April 19, bearing with them a letter and a diamond dispatched the previous November by Marie to Maximilian in token of their engagement. She immediately blurted out that she had indeed consented to the marriage arranged by her father. Two days later it was performed by proxy. On August 18 Maximilian made his entry into Ghent and the wedding ceremony took place the same day.[3]

Meanwhile, by May 21 the King of France had again furiously taken

---

* Quant les ras mangeront les cas
Le roy sera seigneur d'Arras.

(*Only when rats on cats will dine
Can the King say "Arras is mine."*)

Quant la mer qui est grand et lee
Sera à la Saint-Jehan gelée
On verra, par-dessus la glace
Sortir ceulx d'Arras de leur place.

(*When in June the enormous sea
Is frozen to immobility,
The folk of Arras, through ice and snow,
Will leave their city—watch them go!*)

the field, having joined the Grand Master on the borders of Hainault. Setting siege to Bouchain, he directed operations in the front line, risking his life as if he were a youthful man of arms with his fortune to make. At his side Tanneguy du Chastel fell mortally wounded. Bitterly lamenting the death of his Breton *compère*, Louis had Tanneguy interred in the Church of Our Lady of Cléry, where he himself intended to be buried. After a fierce bombardment of sixteen hours Bouchain capitulated. Then it was on to Quesnoy-le-Comte, which next day, May 23, opened its gates. The garrison and the citizens of Avesnes, however, refused to yield. The King took the town by bloody assault. The defenders, Louis wrote laconically on June 12 to the inhabitants of Abbeville, were put to the sword, the city pillaged and then destroyed "to give example to others."

In an attempt to force the capitulation of the great fortresses of Douai and Valenciennes, the King of France relinquished the sword for the scythe. On June 25 he wrote to the Grand Master: "I am sending you three or four thousand reapers to lay waste the countryside, as you know. I beg you, put them to work, and don't grudge five or six hogsheads of wine to let them drink and get drunk. Then, next morning early, set them to their task, and so efficiently that I hear the result spoken of. My lord the Grand Master, my friend, I assure you that it will be the thing in the world which will soonest make the people of Valenciennes come to terms." After Chabannes, the same day, sent word that he lacked sufficient troops to guard the enterprise, the King, perhaps suspecting that his Grand Master had no stomach for the mission, fired back a tart reply: "I beg you, do not fail to return another time to carry out this destruction, for you are an officer of the Crown as well as I am; and if I am King, you are Grand Master." In a few days, Chabannes loosed his thousands of reapers to "make war on the ripening grain." Protected by four hundred lances and four thousand franc archers, they laid waste several miles of flourishing crops between Valenciennes and Douai. The towns, however, refused to yield.

By the end of June, King Louis had returned to Arras to renew his campaigning in that quarter. On learning in early August that the Flemings were assembling an army behind the Neuf-Fosse, the canal running from Aire to St. Omer which marked the Artois-Flanders border, the King once again rode forth to battle. The enemy force was quickly routed; the town of Cassel in Flanders, which belonged to the Dowager Duchess Margaret, fell to the royal army. At the end of September,

Louis established garrisons and winter quarters in the towns he had won in Artois and Hainault.

By the beginning of October he was on his way southward, to winter on the Loire. It was time to withdraw, and think.

In primitive days a conqueror physically consumed his beaten enemy, in order to appropriate his rival's strength. Seemingly, Louis XI had invested himself with the rashness and ruthlessness of Charles, Duke of Burgundy. Perhaps, in the arcane regions of the psyche, Louis was visiting revenge upon his statesman self—which, in triumphing, had ended the desperate testing of his genius, the grand experience of his life—by adopting the headstrong *persona* of the man whom that self had destroyed.

At any rate, Louis XI was still supple enough, at fifty-four, to ask unpleasant questions of himself and return uncompromising answers. During the winter months of 1477-78, he came to recognize that he had jettisoned artistry for action and the long view for immediate advantage, that the intoxication of success had weakened his grasp upon realities, relaxed the discipline of his true style. What now went on within him was a realignment of the *me*, regained, and the *not-me*, restudied—a profoundly difficult process when accomplished within the hardening restraints of age and power. His true ministry, he realized, lay in seeking no foreign conquests but only the return of French lands to the realm. He faced, too, the facts of his own mortality and the tender age of his heir, Charles, but seven and a half years old. He must secure a peaceful settlement with Maximilian and Marie which would ensure the incorporation of the Burgundies, Artois, and the region of northern France which he had long ago repurchased. The King's long thoughts, as he coursed a wintry countryside or, warming himself before a fire in a small chamber, conned his dispatches and listened to his *compères*, left no outward mark, save in the events to come. With the arrival of the spring of 1478, he had fought his way back to himself.

When, in April, he led his army into the field, he was employing it as a weapon of diplomacy. After penetrating deep into Hainault, he withdrew to Arras, as an invitation to negotiate. By early June, Maximilian and Marie had requested a truce as preliminary to treating for peace. Louis promptly granted it and rode to Cambrai to discuss terms with a Burgundian embassy. To the general astonishment, King Louis agreed, even before anything was decided, to withdraw his garrisons from the imperial city of Cambrai, and from Quesnoy and Bouchain. "People were amazed," explains Commynes, "seeing that he sought nothing in return . . . but . . . he said it seemed to him that a King has greater power and authority in his realm, where he is the anointed and sacredly crowned King, than he has outside it, and these [towns] were outside of France. . . ."

On June 10 after dinner the King prepared to leave Cambrai. He bestowed twelve hundred gold crowns on the Church of Our Lady, commanded the garrison to depart, and ordered Messire Louis Maraffin, lord of La Charité, "who had committed terrible extortions," to restore to the churches the chalices, relics, silver plate and jewels, "from which he had made chains and collars to adorn his body." On first taking possession of the town, Louis had had the "very holy Imperial eagle" removed from the gates and the arms of France erected instead. Now, upon leaving, he told the citizens: "We wish you to be neutral and remain as you've always been. . . . In regard to our arms, you will take them down some evening and lodge there your bird, and you will say that he had gone off to play for a little while and has come back to his place as the swallows do when they return in the spring." During the winter he had also regained his sense of humor.

At Arras in early July the King signed a year's truce to begin on July 11, which provided for a diet to meet at Cambrai on September 1 in order to treat for a final peace. At the end of July the King rode slowly southward to the Loire. He would go no more to the wars. Such strength as remained to him he must husband for statecraft.

ii

THROUGHOUT his campaigning of 1477-78, Louis XI had been looking over his shoulder, at England. The disappearance of the Duke of Burgundy had stirred, across the Channel, a storm of anxieties—the Low Countries, ally and best customer of the English, threatened; Calais now enveloped by French lands; the French King no longer held in check by defiant vassals.[4] Louis knew, however, that in England he had several friends, the royal councilors who enjoyed his yearly bounty, and one powerful ally, the King himself. Edward IV, happy in the impish charms of Jane Shore, more than ever now enjoyed his ease. Intent on strengthening the Crown by amassing treasure, he prized his French pension. And he fondly looked forward to the day when his beautiful eldest daughter, Elizabeth, would become the Queen of France.

Could King Edward be kept quiescent long enough, despite the clamor of his subjects, for Maximilian and Marie to be reduced to terms? This grand game of statecraft Louis undertook to play with the gusto of old.

Less than two months after the death of the Duke of Burgundy, King Edward made his opening move—a little innocent blackmail. Two English envoys, all friendliness, brought a proposal that the Truce of Picquigny (1475) be prolonged for the lifetime of the two kings, plus a year after whichever monarch died first—the annual payment of fifty thousand crowns to continue, of course, throughout the period. Quite gratuitously, the envoys gave hearty assurances that if the Duke of Brittany caused any trouble to his sovereign the English would join Louis in forcing him to obedience, and that Edward IV's current negotiations with Spain did not have, and never would have, an anti-French bias. But Louis possessed documentary evidence that England and Brittany were in close communication about the French menace; he likewise had proof that the Spanish were offering Edward a marriage in return for English subsidy to help finance a war against France.[5] With King Edward wasting time on such empty deceptions as these, King Louis cheerfully applied himself to somewhat more artful deceptions of his own, as he continued to gather Burgundian territories into the realm of France.

He had readily agreed to the requested prolongation of the truce. After keeping Edward waiting a few months he dispatched an embassy to London with the duly amended treaty. Louis could not resist the opportunity of proving his friendship to Edward at the same time that he made him thoroughly miserable. Through the mouth of an envoy the King of France sent word that, according to reliable information, one of the reasons Edward's treacherous brother George of Clarence, aided by his sister Margaret, had hoped to secure the hand of Marie of Burgundy was in order to make himself King of England.[*] Shortly after this representation, Edward IV himself placed the Duke of Clarence under arrest and consigned him to the Tower, from which he did not emerge alive.[6]

To keep warm his liaison with Edward, Louis then decided to take a leaf out of the Italian book of statecraft and establish a resident ambassador.[†] For this post he chose a somewhat nervous but very articulate and quick-thinking prelate, Charles Martigny, Bishop of Elne. The Bishop was instructed to keep King Edward entertained by all means

---

[*] The Lancastrian Parliament of Henry VI's brief "Re-adeption," 1470–71, had confirmed the engagement between Warwick and Margaret of Anjou that if the marriage of the latter's son, Prince Edward, to Warwick's daughter Anne produced no son—as it did not—then Clarence would become next heir to the throne.

[†] See note 6, p. 417.

possible and to foil the designs of emissaries from hostile powers. Taking up his onerous mission at the end of October (1477), Martigny applied himself with such zeal that he was soon incurring dark looks and muttered threats from frustrated Englishmen, who blamed him for their King's strange refusal to aid Maximilian against that usurper of English rights, Louis, Prince of Darkness.

In order to provide a fresh distraction, Louis XI now trotted out a warhorse which had proved very serviceable in his relations with the Earl of Warwick. His embassy made the proposal that Edward IV join the attack upon the Burgundian domain and take as his share of the spoils Holland and Zeeland, Brabant, and other imperial territories. English envoys soon crossed the Channel to explore this enticing possibility, which, after much haggling, came to nothing. For ten precious months, however, it occupied the attention of the English—while Louis occupied northern and eastern France and established powerful garrisons on the borders of Flanders and Hainault. By the time the English envoys departed in mid-April of 1478, their saddlebags lined with handsome gifts, Edward IV himself was providing another distraction. His Almoner, Thomas Danet, arrived at French headquarters to report that the King of England was increasingly concerned about the rights of Margaret of York, who was asking him for troops, asserting that the French were overrunning her lands. Louis sent Danet on his way with a soothing letter to King Edward, followed in June by an envoy new to the negotiations, Master Yves de la Tillage, an officer of the Parlement ("Master Yves, my friend, I have been aware that you are a scholar and a clever man, and I have been told that you will know just how to carry out this mission"—Louis to Tillage, June 24). Yves and the resident ambassador, Charles Martigny, assured King Edward that his sister's possessions would be safeguarded and that, indeed, if she put herself under French protection, their master would grant her a pension! Such was the situation when King Louis forced Maximilian to sign a year's truce beginning July 11, 1478.

Edward IV, now hard pressed by his people to aid Maximilian and discontented with the small winnings he had extracted for himself from Louis's prosperity, was soon raising the price of his benevolence. Louis XI found himself confronted by demands from an English embassy that the betrothal of Princess Elizabeth and the Dauphin be immediately solemnized, upon which ceremony the French must begin paying the annual installment of sixty thousand crowns on the Princess' dowry, as provided in the Treaty of Picquigny. Patiently Louis's jurists and his councilors, then Louis himself, and finally an embassy he dispatched to London explained that, according to the treaty, the payments were to begin at the time of the marriage and that since the Dauphin was but eight years old there could as yet be no question of matrimony in the dowry sense. Meanwhile, Edward IV had mounted a tough diplomatic campaign against Charles Martigny, Bishop of Elne. In order to mitigate Edward's money hunger, King Louis had proposed that the Treaty of Picquigny be further prolonged, this time for a century, the annual "tribute" of fifty thousand crowns continuing. King Edward, as a sop to his subjects, now demanded that the Duke of Burgundy, i.e., Maximilian, and the Duke of Brittany be included in the emended treaty as allies of England.

Frantically sending message after message to his master, Charles Martigny used every device he could think of to spin out negotiations. He fervently demonstrated that the only Duke of Burgundy alive was the King of France himself and that the inclusion of Maximilian in the treaty under any name would deprive his master of just claims on the Burgundian dominions. But King Edward's councilors ever more harshly insisted that the Bishop sign the treaty as they had emended it. The English populace added its own pressures. Whenever the Bishop or one of his household ventured from their lodgings, a crowd collected to yell "French dogs!" and jeer them on their way. The Bishop later averred that he went every day in fear of his life. In mid-February, 1479, Martigny was confronted with the choice of signing the agreement immediately or causing a rupture of Anglo-French relations. He signed, scratching in a proviso that the document must be ratified by his master. He had the satisfaction of knowing that he had gained precious time.

Louis XI, quite satisfied with the Bishop's performance, casually told the English ambassadors bringing the treaty for his signature that he was delighted with the new prolongation—he would send an embassy to discuss one or two matters that needed revising before he ratified. A reiterated dun for the first payment of sixty thousand crowns on Princess Elizabeth's dowry Louis had his council solemnly debate for a month, and then gently reject "with a thousand good words." Fortunately, Edward IV had made several other requests to which Louis was graciously able to accede—that a monetary conference fix the Anglo-French rate of exchange, that the French King use his good offices to promote a marriage between the Prince of Wales and a daughter of the Duke of Milan, and that Louis associate King Edward with him in offering to mediate between two warring leagues in the Italian peninsula.[7] In Louis's judgment, apparently, such proposals by Edward IV indicated that, despite the mounting anxieties of the English, the King of France could afford, for the present, to let matters drift.

At the same time, discovering that Maximilian and Marie would not accept his peace terms, King Louis refused to extend the truce. On its expiration in July (1479), he moved to recover the County of Burgundy, which had been lost by the end of 1477 through the stupidity and greed of the lord of Craon, now replaced by the able Governor of Champagne, Charles d'Amboise. Skillful negotiations by Louis d'Amboise, Bishop of Albi—you are "as valiant as ever was Bishop Turpin," Louis wrote him —and skillful military operations by the Bishop's brother, Charles, had won much of the county by the end of summer. In the north, the King ordered his captains to stand on the defensive, hoping to bring Maximilian to terms by a war of harassment and attrition. In early August of 1479 Louis XI received a shock. Philippe de Crèvecoeur, discovering that Maximilian had advanced with an army into Artois, assembled a strong force from French garrisons and attacked the Burgundians on August 7 near the village of Guinegate (now Enquinegatte). His mounted squadrons of men of arms quickly drove the enemy cavalry from the field; but instead of then turning on the mass of Flemish pikemen, Crèvecoeur led his captains in a wild pursuit. Firmly standing their ground, the Burgundian foot inflicted heavy casualties on Crèvecoeur's franc archers. Chassant—galloping headlong in pursuit of glory and ransoms—had deprived the French of an opportunity for a decisive victory.

First news reaching the King made him fear that on one day he might have lost all the fruits of two years of military and diplomatic campaigning. Further tidings were a little more reassuring, but Louis remained deeply troubled, because, as Commynes says, "he was not accustomed to lose." When one messenger attempted to reassure him by saying, "Sire, the field is yours," Louis replied: "Go tell my lieutenants, since they have won the field for me, to have 'crazy beans' [i.e. the eating of which caused lunacy] planted there; for I'm sure that the night of the combat they were too tired . . . to do this." On reading a further message that arrived as he was going to bed, the King remarked to the lord du Lude, "I'm informed that if I wish to have some fine, fast horses, I should send to Picardy for them, for some of my captains have given them a good tryout, in returning to their lodgings." The King added grimly, "I have no doubt that they have very badly guarded my profit and their honor." But Louis soon learned that Guinegate was a defeat only in the sense that it was not a victory. His forces were now so powerful, his border towns so strongly fortified, that Maximilian could do nothing in the field.

Meanwhile, Louis XI continued agilely to turn aside English demands and to send to London envoys armed with eloquent instructions for the Bishop of Elne. "When Edward IV's ambassadors came to France," Commynes explains, "they enjoyed such good cheer and were given such handsome gifts that they departed well satisfied. . . . I am sure that in less than two years the King gave to my lord [John] Howard, in addition to his pension, twenty four thousand crowns in silver and in plate. Then, three weeks or a month—sometimes more and sometimes less—after the English envoys had left, the King dispatched a delegation composed of persons not associated with his previous embassy, so that if the latter had made some promises which remained unfulfilled, these latest ambassadors could plead ignorance. . . . Thus a month or two gained in these comings and goings meant that the enemy had lost a campaigning season in which to do the King harm." Every half year, usually several months late, one of Louis's agents appeared in London with the Easter or Michaelmas payment of twenty five thousand crowns to Edward IV and thousands of crowns more to his chief councilors.[8]

In the spring of 1480 Louis XI learned that his blandishments would no longer suffice: public opinion in England was pushing Edward IV to put muscle into his demands and threats. Louis received a letter from him insisting upon an immediate halt to the war with Maximilian and upon King Edward's being appointed arbiter. This grotesque proposal the King of France rejected without ceremony. "You could not make a decision that would uphold my rights without incurring the discontent of your people, which would profoundly displease me. On the other hand, to avoid that discontent, you would, quite clearly, be forced to deprive me of my just due, an act which I know you would be entirely unwilling to commit." Louis then recalled from London his resident ambassador, the Bishop of Elne. In June, Lord Howard arrived in Paris with an unmistakable ultimatum: if the French King persisted in refusing English arbitration, Edward IV would consider himself free to take sides with Maximilian and Marie. Louis XI bluntly informed Howard that, at any cost, he meant to force Maximilian to accept his peace terms; he then amiably bestowed on the embassy a rich gift of plate and gold coin, and left the English lord "to pound the pavements of Paris" (as a Breton spy put it).

He was soon informed that Edward IV was indeed taking action. Louis's *bête noire*, the Dowager Duchess Margaret—playing wrathful Juno to his storm-tossed Aeneas—arrived in London to negotiate with her brother a resumption of the Anglo-Burgundian alliance that had spelled such peril for France.

In anticipation of these pressures, Louis XI had already taken some action of his own. Turning to France's traditional ally, and England's traditional foe, Scotland, he had easily persuaded James III, with promises of a little aid, that the time was ripe to attack the hated Sassenachs below the border. With the Scots now preparing to give King Edward something to think about at home—and Edward would have no difficulty realizing who had prompted them—King Louis arranged a demonstration at Paris to make clear that he would never allow Burgundy to be mentioned in the Treaty of Picquigny. For the benefit of a herald of Edward IV, Louis ranted against his able diplomat the Bishop of Elne for signing the hundred years' prolongation that included Maximilian. In public he told Martigny, "I was assured that you were a better deceiver than any of the English. I believed it and I am the one deceived!" At the end of July the Parlement of Paris charged the Bishop with having gravely compromised the interests of France. The prosecution roared and thundered. Martigny related in eloquent detail the indignities and coercions to which the English had subjected him. The King's point made, the comedy was quietly abandoned. Charles Martigny returned peacefully to his diocese, perhaps with a goodly number of the King's gold pieces clinking in his saddlebags.

At the same time King Louis was bending all his efforts to achieve yet another demonstration for the benefit of Edward IV. By campaigns of destruction on land and sea, by financial and economic warfare, Louis for month after month had tightened his pressure upon the Low Countries. French raiding parties laid waste crops. Vice-Admiral Colombe destroyed hundreds of craft of the herring fleets, preyed on vessels from the Baltic and from Italy bringing grain. French merchants were forbidden to go to the great fairs of Flanders. Severe restrictions were maintained on the export of food from France. The grumbling of hungry artisans in Ghent and Bruges and Ypres grew louder. At King Louis's request, his good friend Lorenzo de' Medici prohibited his bank at Bruges from making loans to Maximilian and Marie, then closed down the establishment altogether; Lorenzo likewise liquidated his banking interests in England. Despite such pressures, however, King Louis could hardly have hoped to force Maximilian to accept a truce—with Duchess

Margaret urgently negotiating in London the all-important alliance—had the King's information service not provided him with an insight into the young man's character. Years later, after Maximilian had succeeded his father, Frederick III, as Emperor, all Europe would mock foibles of Maximilian that Louis had, evidently, already divined. The Hapsburg's plans were always larger than his means, his enthusiasms greater than his sincerity. He had a hankering for ruses and wiles which, rashly conceived and sloppily executed, were quickly exposed. And he continually shifted proposals, changed sides, generated new schemes.

By the latter part of August (1480), Edward IV had allied himself with Marie and Maximilian. In return for a pension as large as the French one, Edward confirmed the old amity and league with Burgundy; agreed to a match between his daughter Anne and Maximilian's baby son, Philip; made an immediate loan of ten thousand crowns for four months; provided a contingent, paid by Maximilian, of fifteen hundred archers; and secretly engaged himself to declare openly for Burgundy if Louis refused to come to terms, by English arbitration or otherwise. The King of England had moved at last.

But Louis managed to move first. Unsteady Maximilian found French pressure too great, despite the good news from London that Duchess Margaret kept forwarding to him. On August 21 his representative, the Count of Romont, signed a truce with the lord du Lude. It was to last for three months, with a peace conference to be held on October 15. If the conference failed, the truce was to continue until the end of March, 1481. Such was the news that reached Edward IV but a few days after his sister had quitted England's shore with Edward's commitments and promises. And such was the news with which Louis XI greeted Edward's ambassadors when they arrived, about the beginning of September, in the Loire Valley.

Louis now proceeded to pile demonstration on demonstration for his dear cousin Edward. He allowed his court to disclose to the envoys, by mocking jibes, that the Michaelmas term of the pensions would not be paid. He informed them himself that he knew about the archers that were being sent to Maximilian—an act of outright hostility to France. After the English expressed disbelief in statements by the French court that the King enjoyed very good relations with Maximilian's chief advisers, Louis treated Edward's emissaries to a final interview. They doubted that he was on intimate terms with the Burgundians?—let them look at the correspondence which had been given him. With that he displayed for the ambassadors' inspection a sheaf of letters—the originals, of course—that Edward IV had written to Marie and Maximilian. By this time, he had provided another lesson for Edward closer home. The Scots had just swept across the border in force, burning the great Northumberland castle of Bamburgh.

In the circumstances, Edward IV had no recourse but to accept Maximilian's excuses about signing the truce. He also accepted Maximilian's optimistic invitation to take part in the October peace conference. The King of France maintained his pressure by refusing to send representatives to any such conference—not with the English intruding under the guise of mediators and with his vengeful Juno there to make trouble.[9] What Louis did do in the course of October, unable to restrain his sense of comedy, was to dispatch a gift for his cousin's natural-history collection—a boar's tusk, "the largest ever seen," and the dried head of a mysterious animal, somewhat like a roebuck. If Edward did not understand the precise symbolism (nor have any good guesses since been made) the mocking drift was clear enough.

The crisis had arrived. The ailing, nervous King of France, risking all on his reading of the situation, had called King Edward's bluff. Imperturbably he waited for the King of England to make the next move.

Five months later, on March 2, 1481, Louis XI accorded a private interview to a lone emissary of Edward IV. It appears that Thomas Langton indicated his master's desire to reestablish the Treaty of Picquigny on a firm basis. It appears that Louis suggested a simple solution: a return to the revision of 1478, whereby the treaty was prolonged until a year after the demise of the King who dies first. After Langton took his departure, Louis quietly let it be known that the truce with the English was to continue. Negotiations went on, but underground. Edward had no desire to publicize the possibility of his yielding, nor Louis to give any impression of eager bidding. As another demonstration for Edward's benefit, Louis took a hard line with Maximilian on the subject of further prolonging the Franco-Burgundian truce, which had been extended from the end of March to June.

Meanwhile the Hapsburg Duke was bombarding King Edward with appeals to invade France this coming summer or at least send him thousands of troops. Edward glibly indicated that he would do one or the other, if the King of France did not grant satisfactory terms.* But Louis

---

* When Maximilian sent Edward the hopeful tidings that some envoys of German princes, reporting on an interview with King Louis, related that throughout their audience the King had remained seated in a chair and looked very ill, Edward seized the opportunity to advise Maximilian to seek a long truce—and perhaps their adversary might soon die.

XI had taught King Edward to put little confidence in Maximilian. Edward knew, furthermore, that King Louis's friends the Scots were preparing for full-scale war that summer. The loss of fifty thousand gold crowns a year was thus an exceedingly unpleasant prospect. Furthermore, though Edward promised to join his brother Richard, Duke of Gloucester, on the coming campaign against the Scots, he was aware that his health was beginning to fail.

Back and forth went the secret messengers between London and the Loire Valley. The King of France, well informed about affairs in England and the Low Countries, remained courteously immovable.

By June of 1481 Louis had reduced Edward IV to terms.[10] The English King agreed to reconfirm the prolongation of the truce of 1478, in which neither the Duke of Brittany nor of Burgundy was named as ally of England. Nothing more was to be said, it appears, of Princess Elizabeth's dowry or about English mediation of the Franco-Burgundian war. In return, Louis offered hearty assurances for the continued disbursement of the pensions and for the fulfillment, at proper time, of the marriage contract; and he also agreed to give no further encouragement to his Scots friend James III. On August 14 Pierre le Roy made a welcome appearance in London with the Easter term (1481) of the pensions. King Louis, taking his time, signed the reconfirmation of the truce on September 28. The King of England, doubtless with heartburnings, gave his ratification a month later.

By January of 1482 Maximilian got wind—Edward IV had carefully told him nothing—that the English King had confirmed a truce with France which omitted Burgundy and Brittany. His envoys informed King Edward that, if the rumor was true, such a treaty meant his "total ruin and destruction." Frantically he appealed to the King of England to save him from the clutches of Louis XI. Edward merely informed him that the war with the Scots would prevent his offering any aid and advised him to secure another truce. On March 16 Pierre le Roy arrived again in London with the Michaelmas (1481) payment of twenty-five thousand gold crowns to the King and thousands more to his chief officers. There appeared in the English capital at the end of March a ceremonious French embassy, which was "worshipfully received with the mayor and all the crafts" of the city. This time the ambassadors were lodged in a royal dwelling, the Wardrobe. And, however sore the hearts of the Londoners might be, there were no cries of "French dogs!" On May 10 King Edward, trying to assemble funds for yet another year's campaign against the Scots, wrote to King Louis: "Monsieur my cousin, I have given order to my faithful servant, William Laverols, who is at present there, to ask you for the payment which is due for the term of Easter past; and I pray you, Monsieur my cousin, please send it with all diligence possible, letting me know if there is anything I can do for you, for I should do it most willingly. . . ."

He had already done a great deal. But the King kept his cousin waiting until August.

23. The Italian Question

In the midst of the struggle with Maximilian and the delicate duel with Edward IV, Louis XI suddenly found the troubles of the Italian peninsula thrust upon his shoulders.

Italy had to be a sideshow in his international policy, but it was not a sideshow among his concerns. How much he was aware of the ferment of art and learning now called the Renaissance cannot be determined. He was demonstrably interested in the minds of humanist envoys like Alberico Maletta and Tommaso da Rieti. He took into his inner circle cultivated Italians like Boffile de Juge. The special affection he felt for Lorenzo the Magnificent, whom he never met, and his devotion to Lorenzo's Florence suggest that, though he may not have known much about Ficino and the Platonic Academy, Botticelli, Verrocchio, Politian, he recognized the intellectual and artistic preeminence of the golden city on the Arno.

In the world of Italian interstate relations, Louis well knew, everything was magnified. The smallest gesture, subjected to elaborate analysis, became a menace; the slightest fortuity, studied with unrelenting minuteness, was turned into a dangerous portent. The face of Italian politics was scrutinized at claustrophobically close range: the twitch of a cheek, tremor of a lip, a slide of eyeball assumed significance, probably sinister. Excellent communications, the most elaborate network of diplomats and secret agents the world had ever seen, often served to darken rather than to promote understanding. Packed tightly into an intensely competitive political space, the five great powers of the peninsula—Venice, Milan, Florence, the Papacy, and the Kingdom of Naples—to whom were joined in varying degrees of political symbiosis a dozen minor states, constantly shifted policies and alliances in a stylized ballet that was brilliantly energized by the magnetic field of their mutual suspicions. Within this closed space, statecraft had become capable of everything but statesmanship; subtlety of calculation, able to mas-

ter all political mathematics except harmony. The League General of
Italy, encompassing the five chief states, born of the Peace of Lodi of
1454, underwent internal realignments by the laws of its own emulous
nature even as it suffered transformations in shape from outside attrac-
tion.

Throughout the first decade of his reign King Louis, refusing to
countenance Angevin or Orléanist territorial aspirations, maintained in
the peninsula a benevolent authority, which in the main he exerted in
trying to promote a viable Italian balance of power. Then the great
years of Charles, Duke of Burgundy, had brought the Italians flocking to
the Duke's standards. Venice and the Holy See both nursed the delusion
that Charles meant to lead a crusade against the Turk. Ferrante of Naples joined with Burgundy too, for a time. The Duchy of Milan vacil-
lated anxiously, then broke its alliance with Louis XI to climb aboard
Duke Charles's conquering chariot.

As Charles of Burgundy fell upon disaster, Louis XI regained all of
his old prestige in Italy, and more besides. He allowed Milan to scuttle
back to its alliance; he welcomed overtures from King Ferrante for a
marriage bond; he let pass the papacy's devotion to Duke Charles. After
quietly waiting for his old enemy Venice, its commerce damaged by
French raiders, to box the compass of its self-interest, he signed in January of 1478 a treaty firmly re-establishing Franco-Venetian amity.

Meanwhile, in 1477, the Italian League had undergone another political shift. Venice, Milan, and Florence linked themselves in a triple alliance, which, spurned by Ferrante of Naples and the Pope, divided
Italy into two coalitions. It was in Louis XI's anxious spring of 1478 that
smoldering antagonisms between the two burst into sudden flame.

The conflagration was lit by the ambitions of Pope Sixtus IV, who
—setting an example for the notorious Borgia Pope, Alexander VI, two
decades later—was working, by force and intrigue, to carve out a principality for a nephew, Girolamo Riario, or Conte Jérôme, as the French
called him. ° These designs, menacing to Florence, were countered by
Lorenzo de' Medici, who thus became the object of Sixtus' bitter hatred.
Sixtus removed papal finances from the charge of the Medici and gave
them to the Pazzi family, wealthy Florentine bankers and political rivals
of Lorenzo. When the archbishopric of Pisa fell vacant, the Pope, without consulting the Florentines, appointed to the office Francesco Sal-

---

° Another nephew, Cardinal Giuliano della Rovere, would one day become the
warrior-Pope Julius II. A grand nephew, Raphael Riario, had been made Cardinal at
an early age.

viati, of a family likewise hostile to the Medici.

It was in these circumstances that early in 1478 the Pazzi family, the new Archbishop of Pisa, and Conte Jérôme decided on a violent *coup* to overthrow the House of Medici. Sixtus IV gave his approval to the scheme, adding a pious warning against shedding blood. On Sunday, April 26 (1478), Cardinal Riario celebrated Mass in the cathedral of Florence, a ceremony which Lorenzo de' Medici and his younger brother, Giuliano, were bound to attend. At the elevation of the Host, two assassins hurled themselves upon Giuliano and hacked him to death. Two others wounded Lorenzo, but he managed to make his way to safety behind the bronze doors of the sacristy. The citizens rose, not against the Medici but against the Pazzi. The Archbishop of Pisa and a few adherents, trapped in the Palazzo della Signoria in an attempt to take over the government, were promptly hanged from the windows of that edifice, the Archbishop dangling in his sacerdotal robes. The furious Sixtus IV, assured of military support by King Ferrante, hurled an excommunication against Lorenzo and the Florentines and took to arms. Milan and Venice gave full backing to their partner in the Triple Alliance.

Such were the tidings that came flying over the Alps to reach Louis in early May, 1478, when he was on campaign in Artois against Maximilian. They were almost immediately followed by a moving appeal for aid from Lorenzo de' Medici.

The King at once commissioned Philippe de Commynes—"our beloved counselor . . . in whom we have the greatest trust"—to consult with Lorenzo about what was best to be done and on May 12 dispatched to the Florentines warm assurances of support for the House of Medici, "our relatives and friends and allies." A few days later he got off an embassy to Rome with the mission of urging the Pope to abandon hostilities, in the face of the Turkish threat to the western Mediterranean, and offering his aid in the task of peacemaking. After Sixtus IV, encouraged by some early military successes, haughtily rejected the request of the French ambassadors, Louis wrote to him, on August 10, in vehement Latin: "Most Blessed Father, I have received your letters. . . . Would to heaven Your Holiness might realize what you are doing; and, if you are unwilling to resist the Turks, at least cease to give offense to anyone, so that your ministry is not held up to obloquy. For I know that Your Holiness is not unaware that scandals, foretold in the Apocalypse, have come upon the Church or that the authors of these scandals will not survive but rather suffer the most terrible destruction, both in this world and the next. Would to heaven that Your Holiness were unstained by these abominable things." Six days later the King issued an ordinance prohibiting churchmen from going to Rome or exporting money to Rome for benefices, with heavy penalties for offenders—a measure that would inflict a wound in a painful spot, the papal purse.

By the beginning of November (1478) Philippe de Commynes had returned from Florence with first-hand information, the sort Louis prized. Lorenzo had written to the King that "there are in France or in Italy few who are his equal." An impressive embassy from the Triple Alliance now arrived at Tours: G. A. Cagnola (joined in a few days by Carlo Visconti) of Milan; Francesco Gaddi of Florence; Bertucio Gabriel of Venice; and Nicolas de' Roberti representing Ercole d'Este, Duke of Ferrara, the alliance's chief commander. At the same time Lancialoto de Macedonia, shortly reinforced by a second emissary, was at court to uphold the interests of King Ferrante; and papal envoys came and went.

The ambassadors of the Triple Alliance fervidly appealed for immediate military aid. Louis XI, answering "in a mixture of French and Italian," assured them that he would do everything possible for the protection of the Alliance and for the pacification of Italy. Within a week, Commynes and other councilors, working with the Italians, had drawn up instructions for a French embassy to the Pope. If Sixtus IV rejected the envoys' representations that he stop the war, they were then to offer the arbitration of Louis XI. Should this offer be refused, the ambassadors were to announce the summoning of a Church council to reform papal abuses and order all French prelates to quit Rome.

With the embassy dispatched, Louis XI slipped away to Chinon, suggesting, in vain, that the envoys of the Triple Alliance take a holiday in Paris. The King, plagued by bouts of illness and preoccupied with the English, explained to the ambassadors that the lord of Argenton and the Neapolitan Boffile de Juge were fully empowered to deal with their affairs; but though he sought to conserve his energies by taking refuge, as of old, "in wild places," the envoys continually pressed for audience, and sooner or later he had to listen again to their pleas. On a rainy 30th of December (1478) in the countryside near Thouars he received them "affably in a miserable little hut." After they had once more bombarded him with demands for military intervention, he patiently explained, "in Italian, sometimes seasoning his discourse with Latin words," that he wanted first to determine what effect diplomatic pressure would have upon the Pope. Louis XI saw further than his impetuous Italian allies: a cessation of hostilities precariously imposed by French arms could not benefit the Triple Alliance or France, or bring peace to Italy.

While King Louis waited, skeptically, for Sixtus IV's answer to his representations, he was treated, in early February of 1479 to an arrogant lecture by a papal envoy. The burden of his message was that the King of France should favor the Apostolic See rather than Lorenzo de' Medici, a mere merchant, and should defend the Church as his ancestors had done, thus gaining merit from God and glory from the world. Otherwise, the King would incur God's ire and make a wretched end in this world, as had happened to many others hostile to the Apostolic See.

Louis gave the envoy a pungent answer: If France was lending aid and favor to the Triple Alliance, it was only because that league was oppressed by the Pope and King Ferrante, Sixtus IV having unjustly begun hostilities. Therefore, Louis went on, he regarded his attitude as acceptable to God and laudable in the eyes of the world. Indeed it was the Pope who should fear a bad end, especially since in his time he had seen Pope Paul II end badly, because of the vice of flesh that reigned in him (that Pontiff having died on July 28, 1471, after overeating); and since there reigned in Sixtus IV not only such vice of the flesh but also the vice of blood, it was to be thought that his end would be much worse. Indeed, Louis wanted the Pope to know that if he, the King, had been one among the Cardinals when they elected Sixtus IV to the papacy, never would he have assented to the election, because the Pope was Genoese and a man of perfidy, like most Genoese, and, in himself, vicious. Therefore the King reputed himself a much better Christian than Sixtus IV or the Cardinals, especially those that were counseling the Pope. Of Holy Church the King was a humble and faithful servant; of the Pope, not.

When Sixtus IV's envoy ventured two days later to maintain his "brazen front," Louis gave him such a dressing down that "his whole face paled." Then dismissing him, the King summoned the ambassadors of the alliance, recounted the audience in detail, and finished by asking them to ignore the papal emissary. "Leave answering him to a Frenchman!"

The King likewise enjoyed some sharp exchanges with the ambassadors of Ferrante. Indeed on one occasion he went to startling lengths in order to suggest what he thought of the King of Naples. After hearing a complaint by Lancialoto de Macedonia about trouble-making in Italy by the Triple Alliance, the King declared that the real trouble was, King Ferrante spent too much time on other people's business that did not concern him. Louis suddenly launched into an astonishing digression. His own grandfather, Charles VI, had been mad. That King's wife (the notorious Isabeau of Bavaria) was a great whore. He, Louis, was descended from her and therefore he did not really know whose son (i.e., grandson) he was! Louis then turned upon the ambassador: "Your King, such as he is (i.e., the bastard heir of Alfonso V), do you believe that he is the son of King Alfonso?" Lancialoto could think of nothing to say. °

Still, however salty King Louis's language might become, he steadily maintained his intention, not of helping one set of Italian powers to triumph over the other, but of securing the pacification of the peninsula under his benevolent auspices.

Meanwhile, Sixtus IV was spending the first months of 1479 in all manner of vacillations. At one moment, he rejected Louis's offer of arbitration, declaring loftily that "The Vicar of Jesus Christ is not to be judged by anybody" and indicating that he meant to drive Lorenzo de' Medici from Florence. When the French embassy moved to break off relations, the Pope wrote hastily to their master that he would accept arbitration provided that a papal legate was adjoined—and, if necessary, Frederick III and Maximilian in the bargain! On learning that some of his own councilors and the Triple Alliance approved of this grotesque proposal, Louis wearily let himself be persuaded. Evidently he assumed that the Holy Father would renege on his offer, in which case it would be a shame to deprive him of the onus of his duplicity. Before the end of August there arrived a papal envoy to make good Louis's prognostication. Raising all sorts of difficulties, Sixtus IV now proposed that the King of France alone undertake the arbitration, but under conditions laid down by the Holy See. Without even consulting the envoys of the Triple Alliance, Louis ordered the papal emissary from his court. It was now quite clear that negotiations with Sixtus IV would not save Lorenzo de' Medici and secure the pacification of Italy.

But Louis had not lost his flair for nourishing a reserve solution, an alternate possibility.

ii

Louis XI had carefully kept open the way to the other belligerent, King Ferrante. Even in the days when Duke John and his Angevin adherents were clamoring for the King to subsidize their reconquest of the Kingdom of Naples, even when Ferrante aided his uncle, John II of Aragon,

---

° It is quite possible that Ferrante was the son, by Alfonso V's Spanish mistress, of a half-caste Moor of Valencia.

against the French in Roussillon, even when Ferrante leagued with the Duke of Burgundy and sent his second son, Federigo, Prince of Taranto, to take a command in the Burgundian army and to woo the heiress Marie—Louis had maintained diplomatic relations with the King of Naples. The previous year, 1478, much to the distress of the Triple Alliance, Louis had arranged the marriage of Prince Federigo to Anne of Savoy, daughter of his sister Yolande, and had himself provided the attractive dowry, the County of Villefranche and an annual revenue of twelve thousand livres. In early June (1479) the marriage was performed in France; Federigo settled himself at the French court. * The King had been at pains to assure his Italian allies that the marriage of Anne and Federigo posed no threat to them. When dining with the Prince, Louis took occasion to indulge himself in critical observations on Federigo's father, and saw to it that these were repeated to the envoys of the alliance, along with Federigo's prudent conduct at such moments. Under this cover, Federigo kept in touch with his father's ambassadors, still at court. Through them and the Prince, King Louis worked to make good use at last of his long persistence in maintaining relations with Ferrante.

By this time—summer of 1479—Louis calculated that the King of Naples should be ready to heed the counsels of self-interest. His underwriting of the Pope's adventure had brought him no profit; it bade fair to bring him none. Committing himself to a war, he was but playing into the hands of the Turks; for his realm was bound to be the first one attacked in their westward movement through the Mediterranean. Some profit, however, some face-saving gain he hungered for.

In the spring of 1479 Ferrante's envoy Iacomo Dentice had orated at length against the two noxious "weeds" troubling Italy, Lorenzo de' Medici and Cicco Simonetta—the latter, the chief officer of state to Bona, Duchess of Milan and regent for her small son. Dentice had declared that the infant Duke's uncle, Lodovico the Moor (so called because of his swarthy complexion), a protégé of Ferrante's, whom Simonetta had driven from the Duchy, was the rightful governor of Milan until his nephew came of age. King Louis had no reason to love Cicco Simonetta, who had guided Galeazzo-Maria's leap into the Burgundian camp and worked covertly with Venice against France.

The King now got word to Ferrante, that, though he would adamantly defend Lorenzo de' Medici, he would take no hostile action if

* Prince Federigo was the pick of the Neapolitan basket. His elder brother, Alfonso, Duke of Calabria, was as cruel as his father, and stupidly brutal in the bargain.

Ferrante's friend Lodovico succeeded in overthrowing Simonetta at Milan. This modest concession—Louis would undoubtedly have refrained from intervention in any case—gave King Ferrante sufficient motive to be persuaded to make peace.

On September 21, Louis XI, having received a secret affirmative from the King of Naples, dispatched a secretary of his, Pierre Palmier, to arrange for negotiations between Ferrante and the Florentines. With him went the Florentine envoy at the French court, Francesco Gaddi, to explain the situation to Lorenzo de' Medici. Within a day or two Louis learned that Lodovico the Moor had made a triumphant entrance into Milan on September 8. Three days later Cicco Simonetta was consigned to prison (where he was put to death the following year), and Lodovico took over the government in the name of his young nephew. At the beginning of October, King Louis jogged Ferrante, by a message to Pierre Palmier, to fulfill his agreement.[1] Louis then applied strong pressure upon Lodovico the Moor until the new master of Milan gave firm assurances of support for the Triple Alliance.

In December Louis XI got word that Ferrante was "disposed to please the King of France in that King's desire for the peace of Italy." The Pope had agreed to call off his captains; all that was needed was the arrival of an envoy from Florence with full powers to treat. On November 24 a truce was proclaimed to permit such negotiations. The envoy who departed from Florence on December 5 was Lorenzo de' Medici. His countrymen were aghast. He himself fully realized the risk he ran in putting himself in the hands of a man like King Ferrante, but he considered himself responsible for bringing peace to Florence and believed that he could better fulfill the mission than an emissary.

The King of France recognized the uncertainties of the road he had opened for Lorenzo to tread. By mid-February (1480) no tidings had yet come out of the Kingdom of Naples. Louis XI did not hide from the Milanese ambassadors his worry over Lorenzo's prolonged sojourn or his fear that "something bad had happened" to his friend. * Not until late March did a courier from Naples arrive at Plessis. Then Louis learned that Lorenzo de' Medici had won the assent to peace, perhaps even something like the admiration, of King Ferrante. On March 6 they had not only signed an end to the war but sealed a treaty looking to the

---

* Some modern scholars are inclined to pooh-pooh the idea that the head of the House of Medici ran any risk in going to Naples. Perhaps they overlook what almost happened to Louis XI himself at Péronne—and Charles of Burgundy was well-nigh a model of rectitude compared to Ferrante of Naples. Better than latter-day historians, Louis knew the cruel hands into which Lorenzo had given himself.

reestablishment of the League General of Italy. The disgruntled Pope was forced to accept the peace terms, though it was the end of the year before he could bring himself to lift the excommunications against Florence.

Without sending a single soldier beyond the Alps, Louis had saved the political life of Lorenzo de' Medici, extricated his allies from war, yet maintained relations with the adverse coalition, and thus secured the pacification of Italy and confirmed his overlordship of the affairs of the peninsula.

But it was far from a static eminence on which he could repose without care. The feverish political psychology of the Italians saw to that. He was almost immediately having to adjust his position to shifting alignments, to invent new rituals to woo the restless spirit of Italian peace.

Never would Venice accept the Naples-Florence treaty—it gave too much power to King Ferrante! Neither the fervent offers of Milan and Florence to renew, if need be, the Triple Alliance, nor the steadying influence of Louis XI could prevent the suspicious Lion of the Adriatic from withdrawing to its lair. Sixtus IV, now isolated, seized the opportunity to knit up relations with self-isolated Venice. By mid-April (1480) they had signed an alliance to confront the Florence-Naples axis, which in turn left Milan in isolation—until Lodovico the Moor, predictably, completed the evolution by joining Milan with Florence and Naples. Once more the League General was split into two hostile coalitions. Patiently shifting his position to conform to these mutations, Louis XI reestablished cordial relations with the papacy, and thus also signaled his continuing regard for the interest of Venice. The Venetians promptly increased the difficulties of the peacemaker by putting it about that it was Louis XI himself who had brought Venice and the papacy together!

In early August of 1480 the Turk stormed ashore on the heel of Italy and captured the Neapolitan seaport of Otranto.

Tireless shepherd of the flock, Louis XI seized the opportunity to unite the two hostile coalitions into a league for action against the Turk. In the autumn and again in the spring (1481) French embassies made their way across the Alps to preach the cause of unity. Louis himself offered a substantial annual subsidy for concerted action against the Infidel. This time Venice provided the hitch: in January of 1479 she had signed a peace with the Turks, giving her a needed respite from the losing war she had been fighting in the Levant; and for nothing in the world would she abandon the treaty, not even when King Louis promised the full protection of France if her Italian allies afterward abandoned her to face the Turkish fury alone. She had already dispatched Gentile Bellini to paint the portrait of that brilliant strategist Mahomet II, conqueror of Constantinople. Fortunately for Christendom, the death of Mahomet in the spring of 1481 enabled King Ferrante to retake Otranto the following September. Soon Venice was fighting Naples-Florence-Milan in a short-lived war over Ferrara. The Venetians quickly indicated that they would welcome the arbitration which the King of France patiently offered. . . .

All the roads of the Italian peninsula led to the court of France. Until the end of his life Louis XI remained the Protector of Italy. It was a unique, exceedingly difficult, magnificently thankless, but invaluable stewardship, which had been beyond the understanding of his predecessors to aim at and would prove beyond the statesmanship of his successors to maintain—to the ruin of Italy and the plaguing of Europe.* From the first years of his reign—when he had shocked Angevins and Orléanists by asserting the most unmedieval idea that Italy belonged to the Italians—Louis had labored to shield the peninsula against the outward dangers of foreign invasion and the native dangers of destructive interstate rivalries. Machiavelli and Guicciardini, in the melancholy days of foreign conquest that followed, looked back upon the Italy of 1454–94 as a Golden Age, during which, by statesmanship of genius, the Italian principalities had maintained a balance of power among themselves. The two Florentines gave no credit, nor have subsequent historians, to the man beyond the Alps, Louis XI of France, who did so much to keep the Golden Age from tarnishing. In this process, in helping to make possible a milieu nourishing learning and the arts, Louis also became for a crucial twenty years the Patron of the Italian Renaissance.†

* See the Epilogue, p. 371.

† Concerning this period Garret Mattingly writes suggestively (*Renaissance Diplomacy*, 1955, p. 96): "Those forty years saw the amazing flowering of the Italian, particularly the Florentine genius. It seems likely that without that mild, genial springtime some of the finest fruits of the Italian Renaissance would never have ripened at all. And it may be that had the separate city-states been unable to preserve their independence . . . some of those fruits might not have ripened either. All we can say with certainty is that the preservation of the balance of power within the peninsula did create one part of the actual environment of the Italian Renaissance."

24. Ruler and Realm

WITHIN HIS REALM Louis XI after two decades of rule had made himself master as no King of France before had been. The three estates of the kingdom—commons, churchmen, nobles—had all been subjected to the authority of the Crown. The moneyed oligarchy of his townsmen Louis treated with flattering familiarity, labored to promote their prosperity, and exercised control, in one way or another, over their municipal governments. In some cities he chose the mayor from a list of three candidates offered. Of Tours he continued to act as virtual Mayor. The Church of France King Louis had brought entirely under his domination. ° The ecclesiastical establishment represented power, and the King did not mean there to be two governments in France. For the Holy Inquisition he had no use whatever. By alternately abolishing and restoring the Pragmatic Sanction, through which his father had established the liberties of the Gallican Church, he used the Pope to check the pretensions of his clergy and he used his clergy to check papal abuses resulting in wholesale exportation of gold to Rome. He also caused a good deal of clerical confusion by such veerings in policy.

And now at last Louis XI had also broken the power of feudalism in France, had fastened the sway of royal law over unhappy lords and princes who could but sigh for the days of old when their turbulent predecessors exercised the High, Middle, and Low Justice and considered themselves sovereign potentates. By good luck and management Louis was likewise able to gather princely fiefdoms to the domain. When old King René—that charming artist-King of another age—died in July of 1480 the Duchies of Anjou and of Bar came, by agreement, to Louis XI, René leaving his independent County of Provence to his

---

° On occasion he could be imperiously rude in his demands, as when, on behalf of his confessor, the Bishop of Avranches, he wrote to the monks of the Abbey of Bec who were about to choose a new Abbot, "Don't be so senseless as to proceed to the election of anyone else [except that Bishop]."

nephew Charles, Count of Maine. But childless Maine had already made a will in the King's favor. On his death the following year, the Counties of Provence and Maine fell to the crown, and Louis possessed the wonderful port of Marseilles and the Loire Valley to the Breton borders.[1] Francis II, Duke of Brittany, after the death of Charles the Rash, had sworn on the fearsome True Cross of St. Laud to abandon all his alliances and serve only the King; and though in 1480 he signed treaties with Maximilian and Edward IV, the Duchy of Brittany could no longer defy the sovereignty of France. Within a decade (1491), its heiress, Anne, would give herself and her province to Louis's son, Charles VIII.

Young Louis, Duke of Orléans, possessed a Duchy that was sadly shrunken by the ransom which his father, the poet-Duke Charles, had had to pay his English captors. Nonetheless its land lay athwart the Loire Valley, and the Duke was next heir to the throne after the Dauphin. The King had not scrupled, by an act which is perhaps the one really cruel deed of his career, to sacrifice his younger daughter, the deformed and saintly Jeanne of France, to his desires. In 1476 he forced the Dowager Duchess of Orléans to countenance the marriage of her son and Jeanne. He had written to Antoine de Chabannes, his Grand Master, "I have decided to make the marriage of my little daughter Jeanne and the little Duke of Orléans because it seems to me that the offspring they will produce will cost little to bring up." Later he brutally forced the young couple to consummate the marriage, in order to deprive the Duke of grounds for annulment. Ironically, the King's plan that the Duke remain childless and the Duchy be thus eventually united to the domain came true, but it happened because that Duke succeeded Louis's childless son upon the throne. In the south of France, once swarming with semi-independent lords, there remained no prince to defy royal law. The County of Armagnac had been gathered to the domain; the Sire d' Albret was a devoted adherent of the King; and Louis's sister Madeleine, the Dowager Countess of Foix, managed her young son's affairs in accordance with the King's will. The Duchy of Savoy was now likewise docilely submitted to Louis's influence.

Within the realm there remained but one prince with great territorial power, Jean, Duke of Bourbon, who, after being won over to the King by enormous grants at the end of the War of the Public Weal (1465), had stayed for almost a decade, in camp and court, at Louis's side. By 1475, however, the Duke had withdrawn to his vast estates, apparently wearied in the King's onerous service.

To enforce royal authority against the feudal pretensions of Bourbon, King Louis found exactly the man. He was a person of no rank or standing, Jean Doyat, a native of the Bourbonnais. Like many others of his condition, he found his opportunity in the new world of Louis XI, the world of "la carrière ouverte aux talents" (careers open to men of ability). Doyat proved so successful in establishing, by means of inquiries and legal proceedings, the primacy of royal justice in the Duke of Bourbon's territories that the King first promoted him to high office and honors, then made Doyat one of his intimate circle of advisers, a *compère*.[2]

Under Louis IX the functions and services of royal government had grown far beyond anything hitherto known in France. The expenses of government, despite the simplicity of the King's household, had grown with them. A network of diplomats, special investigators, secret agents, officers of foreign states in his pay—source of his magnificent information services—was spread throughout the territories of his feodality and the rest of Europe.* Not even the Italians understood better than he the value of precise knowledge in the conduct of foreign policy. King Louis had also spent largely on grants which won over enemies to the royal service; and each year a heavy cargo of gold went to pay English pensions—an expense considerably less than defending against invasion or feudal strife.

There were also the munificient liberalities Louis XI accorded his chief officers, against which one chronicler grumbled, not so much because the cost was high as because the beneficiaries were men "of low condition." Many of these men, it is true, feathered their nests at public expense, the extent of which corruption the King was apparently unaware of, though he was quite willing for his men to extract high fees from the rich. Louis's servants were probably no worse, however, than their predecessors or successors, and Louis made them work like dogs for their money. Jean Bourré built lovely castles, like that at Langeais, but had precious few moments to enjoy them; Philippe de Commynes rarely saw the principality of Talmont, which his appreciative sovereign had bestowed on him; Jean Doyat practiced his extortions, too, but he did not practice them upon the poor. The King had likewise spent the money and the energies of his people in refortifying the towns of his realm, which, at his accession, had shown crumbling walls and towers.

* In the late 1470's, Louis XI established a royal postal system to speed his communications, in which relays of horses and riders were stationed at regular intervals along the main roads of France.

He was now creating a new military machine: he had expanded the fifteen hundred mounted lances inherited from his father to forty-five hundred lances; and, in a drastic reorganization of the infantry, he replaced most of the inefficient franc archers with companies of pikemen, native and mercenary Swiss, and developed a corps of engineers and a trained artillery service.

Such expanded services of government required a steep increase in taxes. King Louis initiated some fiscal reforms, mainly in allowing localities to collect the *aides*, sales taxes, as best suited them and in relieving large towns of taxation in return for spot contributions of money and services. The King, however, was not deeply interested in financial administration—it was up to his officers to find the money he needed, if necessary in "the enchanter's box."

Chronicles, town records, reports by royal officers reveal the plaints of the people of France, particularly in rural districts, concerning the burden of taxation. Much the same sort of plaints, however, were being uttered by the subjects of Edward IV. In the fifteenth century it was thought the King should somehow "live on his own," i.e., pay the expenses of the government as well as household out of the revenues of the royal estates and feudal perquisites. Though taxes had long been regularly imposed, they were still considered to be an extraordinary payment, one that should be granted to aid the King in his wars or for other special needs. The connection between increased governmental functions and the necessity for an enlarged, steady revenue had not yet occurred to this age.

Furthermore, in the last years of the reign of Louis XI a series of dreadful winters, followed in consequence by bad harvests, created widespread suffering and in men's minds cast a cloud over his rule. The winter of 1478–79 brought incessant rains and flooding of rivers. The following year bad weather continued until the late spring of 1480. In that December began "the greatest cold ever known," which lasted until February 8, 1481. The Seine and Marne were so solidly frozen that horsemen and wagons went on the ice. After a brief respite, the cold settled in again until late May. Vines and fruit blossoms were frozen; the spring planting was ruined. Coming after two bad years, the failure of the harvest of 1481 created famine in Europe. In such conditions taxation cut to the bone. To the magistrates of Tournai, begging for food, King Louis wrote that he was according the arrangement their representatives had requested for supplies of meat and wine. But as for wheat, he was forced to confess, "You know what the year has been, and we are very unhappy . . . that we can't do more for you." In January of 1482 the municipality of Lyons declared to their sovereign that the city would have little money to invest in an imaginative trading venture he was proposing "because of great charges and also the famine and poverty in the town and all the country round." A year later Louis was giving order "for the consolation and aid of the poor," that royal officers and clergy of Paris make processions and prayers to God to stop the northeast wind "which has made the weather bad for a year."

Taxation in the last part of Louis XI's reign more than doubled that which was in force at the death of Charles VII. * The comparison is misleading, however, for King Louis drew his revenues from a greatly enlarged and unquestionably more prosperous realm—both the enlargement and the prosperity owing much to his efforts. Louis perceived that industry and commerce were not fixed elements in a static society but rather dynamic forces capable of increasing the wealth and the resources of his state. He understood the importance of specialists in government service, frequently convoked assemblies of "gens entendus et expers"—authorities—in the field of economics. The silk industry that the King had planted at Lyons, then moved to Tours, was prospering. He took the new craft of printing under his protection. In order to shake up the mining industry, he decreed in 1471 the establishment of a "master general of mines," required all owners of ore-bearing property either to exploit their resources or, for a percentage of the profits, to lease out the holdings, exempted masters and workers from taxes, encouraged foreign miners, especially Germans, who were the best, to settle in France. Though he strove to maintain a favorable balance of payments he drew merchants from many other lands to trade in France; the commercial accord which was part of the Treaty of Picquigny enabled Bordeaux to develop a thriving commerce with English wine importers and cloth exporters.

The most original, though by no means the most successful, of King Louis's experiments in governmental "planning" was aimed at the transformation of the great clothmaking town of Arras, whose inhabitants remained stubbornly anti-French, into a French city, inhabited by loyal Frenchmen turning out the fine textiles that had made Arras a byword —the town enticingly renamed *Franchise*, i.e., "Freedom" (from taxes).

---

* At the end of the reign of Charles VII the *taille* amounted to 1,200,000 livres, the total revenue to 1,800,000 livres. Toward the end of Louis XI's rule, the *taille* reached 3,900,000 livres, the *aides* and *gabelles* 655,000, and the domain brought in 100,000, for a total of 4,655,000 livres.

With expert advice Louis drew up elaborate arrangements, social and economic, for the colonization; but, like much such "planning" since, the experiment was defeated by the recalcitrance of human nature, and by the end of his reign the former inhabitants had returned to . . . Arras.[3]

And now, with the feodality and outward enemies subdued and age fastened upon him, King Louis was dreaming of far-reaching projects for the well-being and enrichment of his subjects. In the way of trade, it was the great port of Marseilles that loomed in his imagination. In December of 1481 he issued a rousing summons to his towns to send, each of them, two delegates, "expert and thoroughly informed," to meet with Michel Gaillart, one of the King's chief financial agents and "captain and grand patron of the galleys of France," to concert plans for the development of "famous Marseilles." The King envisaged an expanded trade, much of it to be carried in French vessels already built or a-building. "By means of great liberties and franchises that we mean to grant," merchants of all nations, "Christian and Infidel," would "come to Marseilles and there discharge their goods and merchandise." These would then "be transferred through our realm, by Bordeaux, Paris, Rouen, and elsewhere, into England, Scotland, Holland, Zealand, Germany, and other countries of the West," with "innumerable benefits, profits, and advantages" accruing to the merchants frequenting this trade route—to "the growth and augmentation of the commerce of our realm."

A national unity he was dreaming of, too, to be achieved by reforms so radical that they would not, in fact, be accomplished until the nineteenth century. "He desired with all his heart," records Commynes, "to establish *une grant police*"—i.e., a single central authority—"in the realm." He aimed first "to bridle this court of Parlement, not to diminish their numbers or their powers," but to transform their proceedings so as to bring speedier and surer justice to his subjects. He ordered increasing numbers of cases to be transferred from the Parlement of Paris to the Grand Council, the judicial section of the royal council, which thus began to function formally somewhat like the courts of equity and the Star Chamber then developing in England. In 1479 he decreed that appeals from the judgment of Parlement must be heard within two years, noting that the court was clogged with "immortal cases."

His grandest dream was to abolish the irrational and uneconomic tyranny of "customs"—that accretion of local sanctions and punishments from the misty past, differing from province to province and town to town, which governed all aspects of life—and create a national standard of laws, regulations, weights and measures. The King made a beginning on this vast design. In 1480 he ordered all seneschals and *baillis* to send to the chancellery "the customs and styles" of their regions in order that they might be reduced to "one new custom." The following year he wrote to the lord du Bouchage, "You know well the desire that I have to give order to the customs, the business of justice, and the policing of the realm. To do this, it is necessary to have the manner and customs of other countries. I beg you to send for the little Florentine in order to learn the customs of Florence and Venice, and have him swear to hold the matter secret so that he gives you the fuller revelation, and let him put it in writing." As Commynes understood it, the King wanted "all these customs codified in French in one handsome book. . . . And if God had given him the grace of living five or six years longer than he did live, without being too much afflicted with illness, he would thus have accomplished much good for this realm."

ii

THE DEVOTIONS, the pilgrimages, continued, the offerings to shrines, early-morning Mass, weekly confession, meditation and "pleasant conversation" on the Day of the Holy Innocents, tens of special Masses said monthly. The King's heavenly precautions, expressed in donations to shrines and churches, reached such sums that even this pious age grumbled at the expenditure, climaxed by a gift to the soldier-missionary saint, Martin of Tours, Patron of France, of a shining metal trellis to enclose his tomb, wrought from 11,000 pounds of fine silver, costing 200,-000 livres.

And Louis was still hunting, in all weathers. He continued restlessly to move about the forests and fields of France, halting at a peasant's hut or a humble village.° The complaints of the Italian envoys about having to "lodge like a dog," of the "savage places" into which the King disappeared, sound precisely like the laments of Alberico Maletta in 1464. As a concession to age and ailments, he traveled more often by water now, sailing on boats of his own design, great barges with wooden houses on

---

° "I forgot to ask you to purchase me a hat," he wrote to one of his Generals of Finance, "like the one the Bishop of Valence gave me [at least fifteen years before]. He told me he had brought it from Rome. It seems to me that it was of some skin other than beaver. . . . It covered the shoulders completely and the back, indeed even the horse's rump . . . so that there was no need of a cloak against the rain; and in hot weather it was as good as a little house. Please try to secure one for me and send it soon, so that I have it before the hot weather arrives."

them furnished with chimneys, glass windows, and other comforts.

But it was hard to escape into the open air and his own thoughts—so many people needed instructions or wanted favors or were convinced that they had pressing business, like foreign ambassadors, whose noses were quickly put out of joint unless they could gain instant admittance to report the latest from their masters. In the miserable November of 1479, the King, feeling ill, decided to slip away from the damps of Tours to the airier region of Chinon. As he was about to depart, word came that the envoys of the Triple Alliance were demanding to see him. He let Commynes tell them that they could catch him for a moment at St. Martin's, where, as was his custom on leaving Tours, he was going to hear Mass. Commynes warned them not to attempt to say a word to the King until after the ceremony, such was his rule. Down the aisle of the packed, noisy church strode Louis XI, booted and spurred, clad in his usual plain gray gown, furred with white lambskins, a fur-lined monk's hood shrouding his head atop which he wore a large hat. Eyes on the ground, heedless of the crowd, he walked to the altar, disappeared into a small loge with a grill, where he could practice his devotions unseen. After Mass, he beckoned the Italians to the altar, said to them at once, "My lord ambassadors, I have decided to journey to a warmer place than this town, so that I can get rid of this cold I've contracted. If you have anything to discuss, tell it to my lord of Argenton, who will report it to me. I recommend myself to you." With that, Louis turned away from the bewildered envoys and strode from the church. Across the marketplace he made his way to a nearby tavern, The Sign of St. Martin, where he unceremoniously munched his breakfast, then mounted horse to ride for Chinon. The rag-taggle of courtiers and attendants crowded after him out of the church in such disorder that the diminutive Francesco Gaddi, Florentine ambassador, was borne to the middle of the nave without his feet touching the ground.

As King Louis's life began to close in upon him, the juices of his ebullience flowing more sluggishly, his bones turning brittle with pain and weariness, and as he sought increasingly to shut out the noisy world, the clamor of court, the whispers of disillusion, the warnings of mortality, he turned more and more for solace to the affection and grace and the uncomplicated wonder of his animals, his birds. He had warrens and cages and pens in all his retreats in the valley of the Loire; and in the forest of Amboise he lodged his menagerie—an elephant, dromedaries, leopards, ostriches, and other fierce and exotic beasts. From many parts came precious cargoes of living things to delight his heart—

"certain red pigs," "several black beasts," "two little otters of Spain," and always horses and dogs; turtledoves, pigeons, peacocks, magpies, canaries by the hundreds, goldfinches, chaffinches, egrets, herons, linnets, quail, partridges, gulls, even crows and owls, Turkey birds, white birds of Tunis, and every variety of hawk. Greyhounds remained the favorites, in chamber and out, smart in their collars of red Lombardy leather and leashes of dyed wools. Apothecaries were constantly supplying ointments, washes, powders, plasters for their cure. One greyhound bitch and her five puppies the King kept at his side in journeyings up and down the Loire and to Paris and back again. His favorite males were called Paris, Plessis, and Artus, and there was a new one, Beauvoisien. There was also a goat named Mignonne (Darling), with six little kids.

In his hard-won solitude the King enjoyed reading, mostly books of devotion, medicine, law, and history. Louis liked to say, "Je ne suis pas grant clerc"—I'm no scholar—and, of Latin, "je n'en scay point"—I don't know a word of it—but in fact he read Latin with ease and could both speak and read Italian. Chastellain, as well as Commynes, calls him a "prince lettré." The Milanese envoy, Carlo Visconti, reported, in a philosophical vein, in 1479, "The King, having long been harassed with toils and illnesses, likes to spend the time left to him in his devotions and in pleasures of the chase. He loves solitude and flees the multitude, which is always odious to good men, although in a prince this is hard to do. He also studies at times, according to what I understand, and I believe it; for in his speaking he demonstrates it, citing the best authorities." [4] Louis was no Maecenas or dilettante of the arts—France, in any case, had not yet been illuminated by the Italian Renaissance—but he knew how to choose the best musicians, sculptors, and painters of his time; and his benefactions to churches, if overlavish, supported the endeavors of many workers in gold and silver and jewelry. Jean Fouquet received the title of "King's Painter"; and Louis had a number of works executed by a young artist of Tours, Jean Bourdichon, who would one day win immortal fame in illuminating the *Hours* of Anne of Brittany. Nor did the King overlook the services of ordinary people: "to Jacob Loys, child of the kitchen, for his pains in watching an entire night to continue the coal fire in the King's chamber," a gift of three crowns.

In the circle of the King's intimates passing years continued to change faces and fortunes. Chief of his chamber favorites were the new man Jean Doyat and "The Barber," Olivier le Daim, now become a lord who entertained cardinals—and would one day be hanged by the princes for his presumption. Of the three men who were Louis's most trusted *compères*—the Burgundian Commynes, the Neapolitan Boffile de Juge, and Imbert de Batarnay, lord du Bouchage—only de Batarnay went back to the days when Louis was the provincial emperor of Dauphiné. That tough Breton Tanneguy du Chastel had been killed by cannon fire at the siege of Bouchain in 1477 while the King was leaning on his shoulder; the companion of his youth, Houaste de Montespédon, lost his life at the battle of Guinegate in 1479; and "John Cleverness," the coarse and witty lord du Lude, would die in 1482. After the death of Charles of Burgundy, Louis had taken into his service, among others, Philippe de Crèvecoeur, now chief commander of the kingdom; Antoine, the Grand Bastard of Burgundy; Guillaume de Rochefort, soon to become Chancellor of France—indeed the King had so many wearers of the Burgundian Toison d'Or, the Golden Fleece, that he talked of holding a meeting of the Order. Some Burgundians he had at first imprisoned but then released and endowed with grants and offices. His old antagonist Simon de Quingey was for a time enclosed in an iron cage and fettered in leg irons (the famous "fillettes du roi," the lady-loves provided by the King that clung to a man's flesh day and night), but Simon emerged to enjoy the King's bounty. Louis did not bear grudges long, and appreciated good service, even when it had been performed for somebody else.

The end of service came, at last, for that toughest of warriors the old Écorcheur Antoine de Chabannes, Grand Master of the Royal Household, who was fighting the English before Louis XI was born. At the end of 1477, the Count of Dammartin, then over seventy, wrote sadly to an acquaintance, "I am not among those in favor for the present." He feared that the lord du Lude and Crèvecoeur were undermining his position. He was still too vigorous to realize that he had grown old. The following month Louis addressed him a charming letter: "I assure you, by the faith of my body, that I am very happy that you have so well managed matters at Quesnoy . . . for [otherwise] it would have been said that you old ones no longer understand the business of warmaking, and we young ones would have to take on the honor. I have always said that you don't have to ask permission of me to go take care of your affairs, for I am sure that you will never abandon mine without seeing that all is secure. Therefore I leave the matter up to you, and you can go at any time." But the good old warrior could not take the hint that time had surprised him. In 1479 the King gently removed him from command of his lances: "Because I know the toils and hardships of service you have continually performed both for my father and for me, I have decided, in order to give you relief and comfort, that you should no longer be a warrior, notwithstanding that I know well I do not have in my realm a man who better understands the business of war than you or in whom I have greater trust if some crisis comes upon me. . . . As for your offices and pension you have from me, I would never remove them from you, but rather add to them; and I will never forget the great services you have done me, no matter what anybody says." It was an almost elegiac farewell—how much of the changed history of France, of the strange checkered life of Louis himself, were bound up in the career of the aged fighter, who, rich in honors, would outlive his sovereign.

One figure is missing from the scene of King Louis's life, the most important figure of all, the Dauphin Charles, born in June of 1470 and now approaching puberty. It was not for lack of feeling that Louis saw almost nothing of the heir of France, so long and ardently desired and now so carefully watched over. Charles was a sickly lad, slightly misshapen in the shoulders, not very intelligent, given to bouts of illness that kept his father in a state of alarm. He was reared in the household of his mother, kindly and self-effacing Charlotte, in the great fortress of Amboise in which Louis himself had found happiness after his early years at gloomy Loches. In charge of the precious Dauphin, Louis put his old faithful Jean Bourré. Madame de Tournel was for a time his governess. His earliest teachers are unknown, but as he grew into boyhood he received instruction from Robert Gauguin and Guiot Pot, one of the King's intimates, and aging Guillaume Cousinot, the man of law and diplomacy.

Louis demanded constant reports on the Dauphin's state of health, his activities and interests, bombarded Bourré with adjurations and inquiries, to which Bourré replied patiently—"My lord, the Dauphin is, thanks to God and Our Lady, in excellent shape and enjoys himself very much." But the King was always anxious—how is Charles sleeping, eating, and does he sleep well-covered at night, and what about his overdoing? Bourré: "He sleeps well; he eats well; he reposes under his gray covers; he busies himself with his birds, but without getting overheated." Louis closely watched the weather, writing in November of 1480, "Don't take the Dauphin into the fields any more until February and send me word tomorrow morning how he has been tonight as a result of having been in the fields." A report that the Dauphin coughed set the King off immediately. Bourré: "Sire, we have received your letters ordering us not to let the Dauphin go out until his cough has disappeared and we see that he is quite cured, also that we let you know where he was taken the cough and how." Bourré could not be sure. Some said Charles had caught cold in the fields on Thursday; Madame Tournel said she had noticed nothing until the past Monday, but what had caused the cough she did not know, unless it was a change in the weather. Such a governess was too casual for Louis. Some time after, he wrote to the lord du Bouchage, "Since Madame de Tournel can no longer exert herself in the Dauphin's service, I beg you, the moment you see this letter, come to me to help me decide what I will have to do." But always there was the danger of Charles's overtiring himself! Bourré: "Sire, there is no need to be uneasy, for be assured the Dauphin is in good health. . . . In regard to his casting little birds to his falcons, and his not fatiguing himself in feeding them, sire, he most assuredly does not do so, for all his birds are now in the mews. He does sometimes go there to watch them feed but he does not become overheated." Poor Bourré. His was a close imprisonment indeed, for rarely would the King let him get away. When he wrote, rather pitifully, on one occasion to beg just eight days' leave to tend to household affairs, promising not to ask again, Louis replied tersely, "My lord du Plessis, I have seen what you have written me. You will under no circumstances go to your house."

Overlooking the Loire with its high walls, at the foot of which straggled a village so small there were no lodgings for transients in it, the castle of Amboise and its park were kept isolated from the world. Strangers were forbidden to enter the locality. Nobody was permitted access to the castle. Men of arms and archers guarded the environs. The villagers kept watch day and night, for which good service they were excused from paying *taille* and *aides*. To see the Dauphin required special permission from the King, and it was seldom granted. On according such leave to his son-in-law Aymar de Poitiers, lord of St. Vallier, husband of his natural daughter Marie, the King carefully delimited the visit: "My lord du Plessis, I am sending tomorrow my lord of St. Vallier to Amboise. I beg you go down into the town to give him dinner. After dinner, take him to visit the Dauphin, but see to it that he then leaves at once."

It was from fear that Louis kept his son out of his life and thus sequestered—fear of Charles's becoming overexcited or being infected with disease or falling victim to the plague; fear, too, that, if the boy were accessible, he might be spirited away and used as a figurehead to countenance some rising against the regime, as he himself had been used by the Duke of Bourbon in the Praguerie (see pp. 47–51)—so he gave Commynes to understand. And perhaps there was something more, a deeper fear, nameless. Charles was the future. Charles was France belonging to someone else. Charles was the yesterday of his own accession —who then gave thought to the dead father?—and thus the tomorrow when he would lie bereft of his realm and his teeming mind and his life.

25. The Last Withdrawal

WHEN PHILIPPE DE COMMYNES returned from Italy in October of 1478, "I found the King our master somewhat aged and beginning to be subject to illness. However, this did not appear quite yet, and he managed all his matters with great intelligence." During the following year the envoys of the Triple Alliance reported that Louis XI was "every day more secluded," and inclined to moods of contrariness or irascibility, "as is the nature of the aged who are touching their decline." He suffered from fevers and colds; he apparently had attacks of gout; and he was beginning to be troubled by a skin disease, perhaps a nervous inflammation akin to shingles.

At the end of February, 1481, the King secluded himself in a favorite little castle at Les Forges, near Chinon. One morning in early March he rode north to the parish church of St. Benoît to hear Mass, then made his way to a dwelling to eat his dinner. In the course of the meal he was stricken by what appears to have been a cerebral hemorrhage. He collapsed, could neither speak nor understand what was said to him, but remained conscious. Fortunately, his Neapolitan physician-astrologer, Angelo Cato,° appeared at that moment and under his ministrations the King began to recover his senses. Battling his illness, he insisted on mounting horseback and returning to Les Forges. Commynes arrived shortly after: "He was hardly able to form words." While the attack lasted "we made few decisions [regarding matters of state] . . . for he was a master for whom one had to plow a straight furrow." At the end of two weeks the King had mostly recovered his powers, but remained feeble.

During the month of September (1481), in his gallery at Plessis, he was again stricken, was laid upon a straw mattress, "and for two hours it

---

° It was at Cato's request that Commynes undertook the writing of his *Mémoires;* the physician was soon to be made Archbishop of Vienne in Dauphiné. For the dating of Louis XI's illness, see Appendix III.

was believed that he was dead." The lords of Argenton and du Bouchage sought the aid of heaven: "We vowed him to St. Claude; and all the others who were there also made the vow. Immediately his speech returned, and soon he was moving about the dwelling, very weak." In November–December he spent a month with Commynes at Argenton, where "he was very ill"; he then settled at Thouars until the latter part of February, 1482, "where he was likewise ill." On December 19 he had written to the prior of the monastery of Salles in Bourges, "I beg you to pray incessantly to God and Our Lady of Salles for me, that they may send me a quartan fever; for I have a malady that the doctors say I can't be cured of without it. When I contract the fever, I'll let you know at once. . . ." *

In mid-March of 1482, Louis XI, in fulfillment of the vow de Bouchage and Commynes had made, set out on his long journey to the shrine of St. Claude in the mountainous region of the County of Burgundy. Evidently he thought he might not return alive: he appointed his son-in-law Pierre de Beaujeu, younger brother of the Duke of Bourbon, as Lieutenant-General of the realm in his absence; and he halted at Amboise to pay a visit to his son and heir, Charles. About April 10 at Beaujeu in the Beaujolais he was rejoined by Philippe de Commynes, who had been sent on a mission to Savoy. "I was astonished at the sight of him," records his faithful councilor, "so thin was he and wasted, and I was amazed that he could ride about the country; but his great heart bore him up."

About April 20 the King reached the church of St. Claude. His intimates had well understood the mind of their master in vowing him to this saint. Here Louis had paused on his headlong flight from Dauphiné in 1456; to this shrine he had since made numerous offerings. In the days of his father there had dwelt here a holy hermit, Jean of Ghent, who had predicted to the Dauphin Charles, when the English armies were overrunning the realm, that Charles would have a male heir who would rule as King of France.

After fulfilling his vow, the King moved by slow stages to the upper reaches of the Loire, there apparently took boat to ease his journey. By June 8 (1482) he had arrived at Cléry. Here he remained until mid-September, shut away from the world in his favorite retreat. He had de

---

* Evidently the King's physicians mistook apoplexy for epilepsy, a common confusion in that day. Fever was regarded as a remedy for epilepsy. Interestingly enough, a Nobel prize in medicine was won in the twentieth century for the treating of certain forms of paralysis by inducing a fever.

cided to be buried in the church. It had been transformed by him into a high-vaulted edifice, a charming and airy shrine in stone to house Our Lady of Cléry, the ancient wooden image that had been found in a neighboring field. On this ground, in the former church sacked by the English, Joan of Arc had knelt in prayer. Louis had purchased the lordship from the Count of Dunois, had built for himself a modest dwelling, partly of wood and partly of stone, with a small garden where he could take his exercise. Even now he busied his mind with ways of making church and dwelling still more attractive. On September 9 he sent orders to Bourré for four pillars to be added to the church. In addition, he wanted a gallery constructed to run the whole length of the house on the garden side, more chambers for the household offices, and "a little stable for my mules. . . . Also see that grape vines are planted all round the garden to make an arbor."

Amidst his pains, his thoughts turned to his son, Charles, now twelve, and to the dangers facing the realm under the rule of a regency government. He gave order for a ceremony of state, a formal meeting between King and heir, so that the former might counsel the latter in the ways of kingship. On September 21, Louis XI came to Amboise to bestow upon his son his testament of statecraft, having braced his spirit to acknowledge the mortality that attends kings as other men. They faced each other—the King accompanied by the Count of Beaujeu, Marshal Gié, the lord du Bouchage, Jean Doyat, and other councilors; Charles, surrounded by the officers of his little household headed by Jean Bourré. Louis painted a grim picture of the bitter "conspiracies and treasons" perpetrated by the feodality of France, which had endured "almost from our accession to the Crown up to the present," and which "after the end of our days could begin again and last long," if careful provision was not made.

For this reason he had come to the Dauphin to enjoin upon him, "as a father can do to his son," that he should be guided by the advice of the captains and councilors who had proved loyal to the Crown. He then frankly acknowledged the capital error he himself had committed in discharging his father's officers and thus bringing upon himself and the realm "great evils and irreparable damage," which evils, "or worse," could come upon his son if he made the same mistake.

The wasted monarch then bade his son withdraw to discuss with his advisers his father's representations—Louis thus emphasizing that he spoke as a formal ambassador of Kingship itself. Young Charles on his return swore a solemn oath to obey all his father's injunctions. The entire proceeding was recorded by a secretary and dispatched, in the form of a royal ordinance, to all the judicial institutions and chief officers of the realm.

There is no record that Louis, either before or after the ceremony, took the Dauphin aside to try to make friends with him, or try to find words by which a father seeks to reveal himself to his son. Perhaps the King was too enfeebled to make the attempt, or unable to think of what might be said; or, perhaps, the bare possibility of walking in the garden of Amboise, just the two of them, the son's hand in his, did not occur to him. The only gift he could leave his son, and to the realm soon to be his son's, the only expression of himself and his feelings, was the gift of peace. Toward this he was now pressing with all the energy and acumen that remained to him.

When Louis XI had paused on his pilgrimage at Beaujeu in April (1482), news had reached him that Marie of Burgundy had died on March 27 as a result of injuries sustained in a fall from a horse three weeks before. Even with the shadow of mortality upon him, the King "had great joy of the news." Instantly the tidings signified to him that the time had come when, at last, he might insure his recovery of Burgundian lands and leave the realm in peace. He knew that Ghent and the other towns of Flanders and Brabant would have small regard for Maximilian, since the Duchess Marie, their sovereign, was dead. The succession now passed to her two children, Philip, born, in June of 1478, and Margaret, born in February, 1480. Louis immediately decided that the surest way to peace would be by the marriage of little Margaret and the Dauphin—whom he had never intended as a match for Princess Elizabeth of England.

Spinning a web of negotiations with the demagogues who controlled Ghent, Louis XI had soon discovered the cities of Flanders to be receptive to his proposals. A delegation of Flemings, arriving at Cléry in July, signified that they desired peace, whether Maximilian wanted it or not, and approved of the marriage of little Margaret and the Dauphin. Late in the month, the great fortress of Aire in Artois, one of the keys to Flanders, surrendered to its French besiegers. Frantically Maximilian implored aid of Edward IV; he was apparently still unaware that the English King had prolonged the Anglo-French truce. Edward, however, could now do nothing. His resources were committed to an invasion of Scotland, which his precarious health prevented him from leading. In misery of spirit the King of England, scales beginning to drop from his eyes, could but hope against hope that Maximilian would somehow escape the net being drawn about him. On August 25 (1482), like a soothing breeze, the Easter payment of the pension arrived in London.

Carefully timing the blow, Louis, in late September—shortly after his interview with the Dauphin—knocked the last prop from under Maximilian: he published the prolongation of the Anglo-French truce. The Duke of Austria, his abandonment by England known to the world, could offer no more resistance. In early November, at the rude insistence of the Three Estates of his dominions, he empowered emissaries to come to terms with representatives of Louis XI at Arras.

On December 23 the Treaty of Arras was formally signed: final peace was established, no mention being made of the Duchy of Burgundy, Picardy, the counties of Ponthieu and Boulogne, concerning whose rightful return to the French domain Louis refused to negotiate; jurisdiction of the Parlement of Paris over appeals from the County of Flanders was reaffirmed; and Margaret of Austria would be delivered into France to become the bride of the Dauphin, bringing as her dowry the Counties of Artois and Burgundy. To all the good towns of his realm Louis XI sent the glorious news, with orders for Te Deums and processions and the lighting of "bonfires of rejoicing" in the streets. He saw to it that the provisions of the treaty were spread far and wide by a recent invention, printing. In France, as in the Low Countries, the rejoicing was heartfelt.

In January, Flemish ambassadors arrived to witness the Dauphin's and the King's swearing of the treaty. Louis, "very low," made vain efforts to avoid the ceremony—he did so "only in order not to be seen." When he finally underwent the ordeal, he had to take the oath with his left hand, his right being "in a sling."

Edward IV was overwhelmed with impotent anger and humiliation. Never would his beautiful daughter become the Queen of France; never, he realized, would he receive another payment of his pension; and it was too late now to think of attacking France with the aid of the Low Countries. His military preparations had to be limited to his war with the Scots. At the beginning of April (1483) he suddenly collapsed, perhaps a victim of apoplexy or acute indigestion. The ninth of the month he was dead. Commynes believed that the Treaty of Arras had killed him. It is certainly true that he had lost his ebullience, perhaps his will to live.

The news of Edward's death brought no pleasure to the shadowed

King of France.* In July he received a bid for friendship from Edward's brother Richard, the former Duke of Gloucester. Richard had suddenly displaced his nephew, little Edward V—who, along with his younger brother, was never seen again—and ascended the throne as Richard III. Louis returned a coolly polite answer; so shaky a government could not trouble France. And Maximilian too, his frontier fortresses gone and his authority flouted by the Flemings, would be unable to threaten the tranquillity of the realm.

Meanwhile, on Sunday, June 22 (1483), tiny Princess Margaret arrived at the gaily bedecked village of Amboise. There to greet her, along with the Dauphin and magnates of the realm, were pairs of delegates from all the chief towns, at the special invitation of the King of France. Louis had thoughtfully ordered the construction of an enclosure, within which, protected from the press of people by barriers and royal archers, these townsmen witnessed the betrothal of their Dauphin to three-year-old Margaret of Austria, and then made their way to the castle chapel for the wedding ceremony. Afterward, the townsmen were invited to nearby Tours in order to discuss measures for the reform of justice and the promotion of trade. On Friday, June 26, Chancellor Rochefort set forth far-reaching proposals devised by their sovereign.

But so much did Louis have this great enterprise at heart that for all his pitiable condition he could not refrain from a last word to his people on the subject. On the Tuesday following, July 1, he invited the delegates to Plessis. The King sought to hide the ravages of illness under the sort of royal raiment he had scorned in the past. He showed himself in a calf-length gown of scarlet satin furred with marten, while on his head he wore a scarlet hood and a scarlet bonnet. After the delegates had swept off their hats and knelt to him, Louis took off his bonnet and hood, revealing that he was now bald save for a short fringe of gray hair. "Messieurs," he told them, "you are welcome. Thank you for having come to see me. And now all of you put on your hats." They did so, but "the good lord remained with his head all bare." To their surprise, he himself began to talk to them—not the Chancellor, as they had expected. Earnestly he sought to impress on them his vision of a united prosperous France offering equal opportunity of enterprise to all. He wanted, he told them, "three principal things for the profit of the whole

---

* The careers of the two Kings were closely intertwined by time as well as circumstance. Louis came to the throne 140 days after Edward became King; he would die 143 days after Edward's demise.

realm": that each might engage in trade as he pleased, without hindrance; that justice be reformed to eliminate intolerable delays and corruption; and that the kingdom be united under one law and enjoy one weight, one measure, and one coinage. He admitted that "his realm was so large, it would only be with great difficulty that this could be achieved." He invited each of the towns to send him a representative within six weeks for further consultation. As Louis took leave of them, he said "he knew well that they preferred to see him an old man rather than a dead one."

The comedian was still able to manage a joke. It was the last time that he and his subjects would ever see each other.

ii

MONTHS BEFORE, after his exhortation to the Dauphin in September of 1482, Louis had immured himself at Plessis-du-Parc-Lès-Tours. It was the last of his many withdrawals, one from which, he knew, there could be no return for him—he who had so often in his life retrieved himself. Against death not all the acumen of his still ardent brain could avail anything. But he would fight as long as he could, and by all possible means. So the life which had opened out from the secret boyhood in the gloomy castle of Loches now closed in again, shrunk to a wasted body in a chair.

Outwardly, Louis had made of Plessis a fortress into which few entered. Along the lanes leading to it he had caltrops scattered, to bring down the horse of anyone seeking to approach by a devious route. The manor was surrounded by a ditch and a wall, the latter with many-pronged iron spits masoned into it. Within the wall a high iron grill served as a second line of defense. The dwelling itself, two stories of brick, was built around three sides of a court. At the four corners stood movable iron watchtowers—"amazing and wonderful things costing more than twenty thousand livres." Within them were stationed forty crossbowmen day and night, with orders to fire on anything that moved, once the outer gate had been closed and the drawbridge raised. Some four hundred archers of the royal household guarded Plessis around the clock, patrolling the grounds and walls. When the gate was opened and the drawbridge lowered at eight in the morning, officers entered to set the watch for the day, "as in a frontier place strictly guarded."

Within Plessis itself, however, Louis had made himself a comfortable and charming dwelling, spacious, simple, gay with color.* Paintings by the celebrated Jean Bourdichon, and doubtless some by Jean Fouquet, "Painter to the King," brightened the walls. Throughout the chambers glowed fifty "great rolls," each one supported by three angels about three feet high, splendid in gold and azure, on which was inscribed in azure *Misericordias Domini in Eternum Cantabo* (I will forever sing the mercy of God).

Louis spent his days in the great windowed gallery looking over the court and the open countryside beyond. For companions, he had his favorite greyhounds and his birds, shifting galaxies of color in great cages or flying free about his head. To keep himself from dozing, perhaps at the injunction of his physicians, there were stationed outside his windows, but unable to see him, a band of rustic musicians, "among whom were several shepherds from Poitou," who played folk melodies on their humble instruments—a reminder of the days when he had coursed the beloved woods and fields of France.

He had become a prisoner of his illness, of his fears. His overriding fear was that an attempt might be made, with the excuse of his feebleness, to take his authority from him "and make him live like a man who had lost his reason." No lords or magnates were lodged at Plessis, or permitted to enter with a train of followers. Of the great nobles, only his son-in-law Pierre, Count of Beaujeu, was permitted to see him. It was to Pierre, steady and loyal, and to his daughter Anne that he had decided to confide the Dauphin and the regency. Those who knew the royal family regarded her, in intelligence and firmness of will, as "the image of her father."

A prey to suspicions, Louis had dismissed from his household many of his intimate attendants, engaged strangers in their places. He constantly changed servants and guards. "Nature," he said, "enjoyed novelties." Too weak to attend to state business except of pressing importance, he developed the fear that his subjects, and neighboring peoples, might think him dead; and he adopted strange means of letting it be known that he was still the master of France. Promoting and demoting officials, paring or increasing pensions, "he passed the time"—as he wearily confided to Commynes—"in making and unmaking people." To im-

---

* The lurid, gloomy, grotesque habitation of popular fancy, with dead men swinging from trees and the King sliding about like a diabolic monk, springs from the romancing of Sir Walter Scott (*Quentin Durward*) and from numerous nineteenth-century "historical" dramas.

pose his presence upon his neighbors, the impassioned lover of animals sent far and wide to secure beasts of all sorts, insisting upon paying such high prices that "he bought dearer than people wanted to sell." Dogs he solicited from all parts. "Into Sicily he sent to seek out a certain variety of mule; if such an animal were owned by an official of the country, he paid double." From Naples he secured horses; from Barbary, a rare sort of small wolf called *adive;* from Denmark and Sweden he sought reindeer and another species of deer, "for six of each kind paying forty-five hundred German florins." But, when the animals arrived at Plessis, he was too ill to pay any attention to them and for the most part did not even speak to those who brought them.

He who had all his life held small regard for doctors and their remedies had now let himself become the frightened victim of a doctor, one Jacques Coitier, a bold, coarse, intelligent man with an insatiable itch for money and power. Become *clerc ordinaire* in the Chamber of Accounts in 1476, Coitier soon pushed his way to Vice-President; and then Louis, fallen into the fear of death and hope in medicine, made him First President of the Chamber in the autumn of 1482, dispensing him from fulfilling the functions of the office. The King's unhappy dependence upon this ruthless opportunist can be traced in grants of lands and offices. By the beginning of 1483 Coitier had extorted the bishopric of Amiens for his nephew and was receiving from the King, merely as wages, ten thousand gold crowns a month cash."This physician became so grossly rude to his master," records Commynes, "as to say to him such crude, outrageous words as one would not address to a servant; but so much did the King fear him that he did not dare send him away."

Daily the juices of Louis's life ran thinner. This King, "who had seemed better made to rule a world than a realm," was now so meager and wasted that he could hardly put his hand to his mouth. He still refused to stretch himself upon his deathbed, keeping to his pleasant gallery, and sought to beguile his mortal illness by dressing in gay garments, silks and satins richly furred. Louis had confided to intimates his belief that he would not reach sixty years—for centuries, he said, no King of France had passed that age. He would turn sixty on July 23. "Never man feared death so much as he nor tried so hard to find remedy against it. At all times of his life," Commynes discloses, "he had begged his servants, me and others, that if we saw him under this necessity of dying we should 'Say little' and only suggest that he have himself shriven, without pronouncing this cruel word *death;* for it seemed to him that he lacked the heart to hear a doom so cruel." To his Chancellor the King wrote on May 25, after acknowledging receipt of communications, "I beg you, never again send me letters by the one who brought me these; for I have found his visage terribly altered since last I saw him, and I promise you on my word that he put me in great fear."

The King neglected no resource, heavenly or otherwise, by which he might prolong his life. In his last year he spent several hundred thousand livres on offerings, not only to his favorite shrines and churches in France but to the Three Kings of Cologne, Our Lady of Aachen, St. Servais of Utrecht, St. Bernadino of Aquila, various saints in the Kingdom of Naples, St. James of Compostella in Spain, St. John Lateran in Rome. For relics and remedies he combed the West. From the Pope he borrowed the "corporal," the altar linen, over which St. Peter himself supposedly had sung Mass. One of his best sea captains, George Bissipat, "George the Greek," he dispatched with three ships all the way to that outpost of the known world, the Cape Verde Islands off the west coast of Africa, "to seek out some things that were important to the health of his person." These "things" were undoubtedly great sea tortoises; bathing in the blood of such beasts was regarded, in medicinal lore, as a remedy for leprosy. And it may be that the last months of Louis's life were darkened, and his seclusion partly explained, by his fear, apparently groundless, that the skin inflammation from which he suffered signified that dread disease.° Laboring under this fear, Louis besought the aid of his friend Lorenzo the Magnificent. He asked to borrow a most precious relic associated with the patron saint of Florence, the fifth-century Bishop Zenobius—that saint's pastoral ring which supposedly could cure leprosy. This revered circlet, it turned out, was owned by a Florentine family, but after many months Lorenzo managed to win their acquiescence and dispatched the ring, along with numerous other holy objects, to the King. Louis had the consolation of wearing it for a little while. The relic came back to Florence enclosed in a gold box crusted with gems.

Another remedy that the King longed for was the holy oil which consecrated the Kings of France at their crowning. The vial of chrism had supposedly been brought by a white dove to St. Remy of Rheims for the coronation, in 496, of Clovis, the skull-splitting Christian King of the Franks. As early as April, 1482, King Louis had written to the Abbot of St. Remy to beg "a tiny drop from the Holy Vial . . . if it can be removed without sin or danger." But it was more than a year later

---

° His use of this remedy may possibly indicate the origin of the story, put about by the princes after his death, that he drank infants' blood.

and only after securing a dispensation from the Pope that the King was
able to dispatch a delegation of lords and prelates to convey the sacred
oil to Tours. On August 1 the Holy Vial, covered in cloth of gold, arrived at Plessis, along with Charlemagne's Cross of Victory and the
Rods of Aaron and Moses from the Sainte Chapelle in Paris. These objects reposed on a buffet in the royal chamber for the remainder of the
King's life. It appears that Louis never ventured to extract "a tiny drop"
of the oil to anoint himself.

From all sides the King sought also for the aid of holy men and
women. He asked neither for grace nor for salvation, merely for the prolongation of his life, a modest enough request for a good Christian—but
then Louis, perhaps, was hardly a Christian at all. "In humility surpass-
ing all the other princes of the world, the King sought some religious or
man of good life . . . who might be a mean between God and him to
lengthen his days"; for "to God and to the saints he remitted his hope of
life, knowing he could scarcely last without a miracle." Many such holy
men from all parts were named to him. "He sent to several of them.
Some came to talk with him, to whom he spoke only of this prolongation
of life. Most of them replied wisely, saying they had no such power."

Above all, the King longed for the ministrations of one especially renowned holy man, Francis of Paola, a hermit who lived in a small cav-
ern under a rock in Calabria in the Kingdom of Naples. Later the
founder of the Order of Friars Minims (*Minimi,* the least of the servants
of God), Francis dwelt in perpetual meditation, eating no meat nor fish
nor milk, cheese, butter, eggs, but subsisting on roots and a little fruit.
In the latter months of 1482, Louis had dispatched a knight of his household on the mission of persuading "The Holy Man," as he was always
called, to take the journey to Plessis. Before Francis would quit his cave,
however, Prince Federigo of Naples had to beg him to go and Pope Sixtus twice sent to him on behalf of the King of France. On finally setting
forth, the sixty-six-year-old hermit, accompanied by three disciples,
halted first at Rome, where the worldly Pope, fascinated by such a life,
gave him three long interviews. By ship he then made his way to Marseilles, took boat up the Rhône for Lyons. Louis had written the magistrates of the town, on February 24, (1483), to have a carriage and litter
constructed "so that The Holy Man may travel more comfortably." On
March 27 he anxiously enjoined on them, "When The Holy Man arrives
there, receive him and celebrate his coming as if he were our Holy Father,
for thus we wish it for the honor of his person and of the holy life that
he leads." After a brief stay in Lyons, where he arrived on April 24, the

hermit was brought to the upper reaches of the Loire, and thence went by water to Tours.

When Francis of Paola appeared at Plessis, Louis went down on his knees before him "as if he had been the Pope"—no easy accomplishment for a man so ill. The King implored Francis "to pray to God for him that the Lord might be willing to prolong his days." Francis replied that he should think of his soul and put his trust in heaven. With all honor the saintly guest was then ushered to the hermitage which Louis had built for him near the chapel of St. Matthew in the lower court of Plessis.* Commynes considered that he had "never seen a living man of so saintly a life nor one from whose mouth the Holy Spirit seemed so truly to speak." On June 29 Louis was writing anxiously to his General of Finances of Languedoc, "I beg you to send me lemons and sweet oranges and pears and parsnips . . . for the Holy Man." Though Francis would not attempt to intercede with heaven for the King's earthly existence, his presence at Plessis greatly comforted Louis, and he often hearkened to The Holy Man's words.

As the King gazed upon his sacred objects, upon the summer green beyond the gallery; as he listened to the flutterings of his birds, the soft sounds of shepherd pipes outside his windows, the scratching of a greyhound, what long thoughts he now had time for. Doubtless his mind cast back, over the years, over the ranging designs, the comedies, the anxieties, the hunting and hawking, to that sulphurous particle Charles of Burgundy who had once been his companion of the chase in the woods around Genappe, and the sympathetic English Earl Warwick, maker of kings, and Francesco Sforza, and the gentlemen of Dauphiné closing round him in the blood and dust of Montlhéry, and his father, who once, like him, had lain in the shadow while a son waited for his death, and, still further back to the Dauphin who became Prince of Cutthroats, and, perhaps, to the six-year-old boy who had looked upon the face of Joan of Arc. . . . What he thought of his strange and wonderful life he told no one, as he had told no one while he was living it. For a single act he expressed regret, the execution of "poor Jacques," the Duke of Nemours.

One clue he would leave to his contemporaries, and to posterity, though he did not intend it as such. His tomb. He could not lie in pompous state with his predecessors in the royal necropolis of St. Denis,

---

* Francis of Paola remained at Plessis, later occupying a church that Charles VIII erected for him on the grounds, for the rest of his life. Born in 1416, he lived until 1507, was canonized by Leo X in 1519.

or take his stance for eternity supine in the panoply of kingship. He was none of those—being, as he was apparently delighted to recall, the grandson of a whore—and royal robes did not denote him truly. He would keep apart, in his own beautiful church, the edifice of Our Lady of Cléry. His image, life-size, upon the tomb, in gilded copper with scarlet and azure enamel, awaited him there. The first sketch had been made by Colin of Amiens, then corrected as a result of injunctions from the King passed on by Jean Bourré; and the casting and gilding were executed by two German masters, "Conrad of Cologne, metal-worker," and "Lawrence Wrine of Tours, caster of cannon for the King," at a cost of one thousand gold crowns. In effigy Louis knelt at the end of the tomb facing his patroness, Our Lady of Cléry. He was clad as a simple huntsman, and appeared as in his youth with long black hair falling almost to his shoulders. He wore a plain jacket, hose, and knee-length boots with spurs, his hat clasped in both hands at his waist, long sword in its hanger at his side, hunting horn slung at his back, the collar of the Order of St. Michael around his neck. Beside him crouched a little greyhound with studded leather collar. A huntsman . . . Only so did he choose to show himself, forever worshiping, to Our Lady of Cléry. Nothing perhaps in the life of Louis is more enigmatic than this effigy; and yet it may have sprung, as much in his complex being did, from that utter simplicity which puzzled men more than all his subtleties. In searching, under the eye of heaven, for the self that was truly he, it was apparently the hunter whom he found.

On Monday, August 25, Louis suffered another cerebral hemorrhage. Until four o'clock Tuesday afternoon he lay "almost like a dead man." He rallied. But, knowing finally that the inescapable was near, he brought himself to perform the official acknowledgment of his approaching end. To his son, Charles, at Amboise—whom he now insisted upon calling "the King"—he dispatched Pierre de Beaujeu, the Chancellor, much of the royal guard, and—what perhaps most painfully symbolized his abandonment of life—his entire staff of huntsmen and falcon keepers.

Even then, however, indefatigable optimist that he was, he still dared to cherish hope, especially in the prayers of Francis of Paola, whom he often summoned to his bedside. Suddenly he was confronted by his theologian, Jean d'Arly, Olivier the Barber, and Jacques Coitier. "Sire," they told him brusquely, "have no more hope in The Holy Man nor in anything else, for, without fail, you are done for, and therefore think of your conscience, for remedy there is none." Each of them added a word or two in the same callous vein.

The King managed to reply: "I have hope that God will help me, for, perchance, I am not so ill as you think." It was, perhaps, the last faint assertion of the comedian. He bore the blow bravely and all the other indignities of man's last hours—"better than any man I have seen die," records Commynes.

By Saturday morning, August 30, Louis XI was dying. He himself called for the final sacraments, "made a good confession," said prayers appropriate to each of the ceremonies. He remained in "full soundness of mind and understanding, his memory good, suffering no pain that anyone could perceive. . . . He continued to talk until the length of a paternoster before his death." To Our Lady of Embrun he addressed his last words, his mind thus returning to Dauphiné, which had once been his whole world. "O Lady of Embrun," he prayed, "my good mistress, aid me." He then repeated the words of the Psalmist: "*In te, Domine, speravi; non confundar in eternum, misericordias Domini in eternum cantabo*" (I have hoped on thee, Lord; may I not be eternally destroyed; the mercy of the Lord I will sing forever).

He died between eight and ten on Saturday evening.

It had been a brilliant summer, warm and dry, good growing weather for the vines. The vintage that year "was the best anyone could remember."

On September 2 clerics bore the body of Louis XI to St. Martin's for solemn obsequies. Four days later, on Saturday, as he had wished, he was interred at Our Lady of Cléry, beneath his effigy. His wife, Charlotte of Savoy, followed him to the grave on December 1. The next year at an assembly of the Three Estates, where the princes of France rejoiced in their deliverance from the man who had mastered them, the orator of the Estates nonetheless proclaimed of Louis XI, "He left us the testament of peace." Louis would probably have asked for no better epitaph.

During the religious wars of the sixteenth century his tomb was destroyed. The church of Cléry remains, a song in stone. Within it remains the massive skull of Louis XI, awesome in its jutting brow, great eye sockets, slab of jaw.

He had the audacity to trust to wits rather than weapons and the grace to exercise a sense of humor that made him an alien in his age. Though he transformed a great realm and left to posterity a lesson in statecraft, he is perhaps no more important for what he did than for what he was—one of the formidable personalities of the human race.

EPILOGUE

NEWS OF THE DEATH OF Louis XI
sent a thrill of expectation through France. What pickings and opportunities were offered by the minority reign of thirteen-year-old Charles
VIII! The commons dreamed of taxes "beaten down"; the clergy hoped
to manage their own affairs as in the palmy days of the Gallican
Church; the nobles, happiest of all, envisioned the return of the good
old feudal universe. Revenges came swiftly. Olivier le Daim, Louis XI's
upstart barber, was seized, sentenced to death, and hanged by the
Parlement of Paris. At the instigation of the Duke of Bourbon, Louis's
favorite Jean Doyat had his tongue pierced by a hot iron, lost an ear,
and was flogged almost to death (see note 2, p. 445). Intimate counselors of the dead king, like Philippe de Commynes, found their situation
suddenly precarious.[1]

From January to March of 1484 the Estates General of the realm—
at which for the first time the words *Tiers État*, Third Estate, were used
in a document to describe the representatives of the commoners—
deliberated upon the making of a new world. In their sessions orators
thundered against the "despotism" of Louis XI and the depredations of
his officers. The lords delighted in retailing gruesome stories about the
ruler who had mastered them. Special interest fought special interest in
a scramble for spoils. The Third Estate got rid of most of the *taille*, but
only temporarily; and they were too enmeshed in their local preoccupations to give heed to the governing of France. The nobles, avidly intriguing to regain their privileges and secure control of the boy-King,
only showed their political ineptitude. The shrewd couple to whom
Louis XI had entrusted the regency, his iron-willed daughter Anne and

her husband, Pierre de Beaujeu, succeeded in riding out the storm and maintaining the strong government Charles VIII had inherited. In 1485 Louis, Duke of Orléans, the heir to the throne (his grandfather having been the younger brother of Charles VI) and leader of the malcontent princes, attempted a new War of the Public Weal. The realm remained indifferent; Louis was unable to gain access even to the town of Orléans. A fiasco, the feeble uprising was soon dubbed the Guerre Folle, the silly war. The weakness of the feodality, "the profound incapacity of its representatives," observes B. de Mandrot, editor of the *Mémoires* of Commynes, had attached the middle classes to the royal power, "the yoke of which, however heavy it was, they preferred to the caprices and exactions of the princes." Even when endangered by a minority reign, the national monarchy created by Louis XI proved to be unshakable.

It turned out ill for France, however, and for Italy, that the new King failed to follow the sagacious policy of his father in maintaining by diplomacy a benevolent protectorship over the Italian peninsula. When Charles VIII, an inoffensive, pleasure-loving ninny, assumed the reins of government in 1491 at the age of twenty, his shallow favorites easily persuaded him to assert the glory of his arms by claiming, as heir to the House of Anjou, the Kingdom of Naples. In vain Philippe de Commynes, again a royal councilor but no longer much heeded, sought to deter his ineffectual sovereign from a military invasion. With a French army Charles VIII crossed the Alps in September of 1494. After what turned out to be a triumphant parade through the disunited peninsula, he occupied unopposed the Kingdom of Naples in February, 1495. Five months later, however, the French had to fight their way home against a coalition of Italian powers, Spain, and the Empire. By the time they had beaten off an Italian army at Fornovo, July 5, the Kingdom of Naples was already lost.

Thus were begun the disastrous campaigns which were to wrack Italy for almost half a century. Childless Charles's successor, Louis of Orléans, Louis XII (1498–1515) and Louis's successor, his cousin Francis I (1515–47) mounted costly expedition after expedition to win Naples and Milan—in which battles Pierre Bayard, the knight "without fear and without stain" gained his renown. In the end the French were driven from Italy by the Imperial-Spanish power of the famous Emperor Charles V; and the Italian states, except for Venice, lost their independence. Louis XI's statesmanship was all too bitterly vindicated.

France was then torn by the religious wars of the last half of the sixteenth century, emerging from them with renewed vigor under the kingship of dashing Henry IV, one-time Huguenot ("Paris is worth a Mass") and first of the Bourbon dynasty. The national monarchy had survived both foreign and domestic catastrophes. It shortly after reached its height in the reign of Louis XIV (1643–1715) and would endure until the French Revolution.

By that time the life of Louis XI was about to become a spectacle in a waxworks of horrors—his accomplishment hidden beneath romantic novelizing and his character transformed into a gothic monstrosity. This zealous distortion by the nineteenth century the researches of the twentieth have made it possible to correct. "The universal spider" still remains, however, something of a figure of controversy—in part perhaps because he is a precursor and one of the shapers of the modern world; and with the modern world we have grown somewhat disenchanted.

APPENDICES

GENEALOGICAL TABLE

RULERS AND
PRINCIPAL LORDS

APPENDIX I

The Reliability of Philippe de Commynes

OVER THE CENTURIES the *Mémoires* of Philippe de Commynes have received a full measure of appreciation. In earlier days they were most admired for their political sagacity (though Montaigne finds subtler qualities to praise); more recently, for their brilliant portrayal of men and events, their merits as a work of biographical literature. In the nineteenth century, however, Commynes himself came under personal attack, and from the mid-twentieth he has been subjected to a more damaging form of criticism. Belgian pride in the Burgundian inheritance, speaking fervently in the voice of Baron Kervyn de Lettenhove, denounced the memorialist as a man who had betrayed his country, the Burgundian domain, and was therefore worthy neither of credence nor respect. Though Kervyn de Lettenhove conscientiously amassed source materials, which are still useful though not set forth with scrupulous accuracy, his three-volume work, *Lettres et négociations de Philippe de Comines*, Brussels, 1867–74, is patently vitiated by passionate prejudice. Three twentieth-century successors, however, have mounted an assault on the reliability of Commynes, which, less obviously biased, lengthy of analysis, and couched in a scholarly argot, seeks to deny the historical validity of much of the *Mémoires*.

A French tome, of 710 pages, Jean Dufournet, *La Destruction des Mythes dans les Mémoires de Ph. de Commynes*, Geneva, 1966, not only is the longest study of Commynes ever undertaken—it is but the first, the author indicates, of five volumes. Merely by disinterring the Belgian charges of treachery—and by distorting or misusing evidences from contemporary chronicles—Dufournet tiresomely purports to show that Commynes, neurotically on the defensive as a renegade and guilty of bad faith at every turn, has intricately falsified history in order to justify himself. Apparently Dufournet did not bother to consult many documentary materials or to face up to the Teutonic rigors of his immediate precursor, Karl Bittman (*Ludwig XI und Karl der Kuhne: die Memoiren des Philippe de Commynes als historische Quelle*, I, Göttingen, 1964). This work falls but a few pages short of Dufournet's, and the author likewise indicates that further tomes are to come. Bittman's admirable diligence has brought to bear upon three of the principal crises in Louis XI's struggle with Charles of Burgundy the testimony of a host of relevant contemporary materials. Unfortunately, Bittman is not content to offer his researches for their true value—that of supplying a convenient assemblage of contemporary sources against which Commynes's narrative can be checked and the scholar's use of it guided. Instead, the German rigidly exploits his researches by using them to support the thesis—not entirely dissimilar from Dufournet's—that Commynes, consciously or unconsciously, employed deceptive stratagems in order to find satisfactory explanations for himself and his world. Painstaking though Bittman is, to accumulate all is not to understand all. He fails to allow for the erosion of memory by the passage of time; he fails to allow for the possibility of error or distortion in some of the source materials by which he measures Commynes's work; and, ridden by his thesis, he is too ready to find Commynes at fault and insufficiently aware, or willing to be aware, of how often Commynes is both right and indispensable.

Of the richest materials which Bittman marshals in order to condemn the memorialist's narrative, most have been printed or cited in previous editions of the *Mémoires* and in special studies, and few therefore are new to the historian of the period. Such a historian is likely to conclude that Bittman is guiltier of distortion than Commynes and that the laborious demonstration of Commynes's omissions and occasional confusions serves to confirm the general reliability, detachment, and judiciousness of a man recollecting, two decades later, a complexity of events and passions in which he was profoundly involved. It seems somewhat gratuitous, not to say bizarre, to examine the *Mémoires* as if they claimed to be an almanac and to find grounds for suspicion in the fact that Commynes does not behave like a scholar with electronic retrieval of documents at one elbow and Karl Bittman at the other. Measured by such loaded tests, which of us—as Hamlet asks—"shall 'scape whipping?"

The third work, American, is much more to be lamented than the previous two, because such a work is genuinely needed. This is a rendition into English of the *Mémoires* by Isabelle Cazeaux under the editorship of Samuel Kinser (*The Memoirs of Philippe de Commynes*, I, University of South Carolina Press, 1969). The editorial apparatus presents some insights of value into Commynes's quality of mind, but on the whole remains naïve, insufficiently informed, addicted to scholarly jargon, and limited of view. The translation is usually stiff or toneless, not infrequently inept, and on occasion embarrassingly inaccurate.* The editor, in an introduction and notes marred by misapprehensions, shows little acquaintance with contemporary documents or indeed with the fifteenth-century world, relying very heavily and uncritically upon Karl Bittman's work and other recent studies.† The

---

* For example, Commynes is made to assert that Henry V "died in the woods of Vincennes"—reminding one of Stonewall Jackson propped beneath a tree after Chancellorsville—instead of "in the castle of Bois de Vincennes." The captive Burgundian lord of Contay, who, Commynes explains, "being given his parole went back and forth between [Louis XI] and the Duke [of Burgundy]" is transformed by Cazeaux into a lord who "wavered in his allegiance to the Duke" ["alloit et venoit sur sa foy devers ledict duc"].

† For example, blindly following Bittman, the editor cites, as an instance of Commynes's deliberate deception, by omission, the fact that the memorialist fails to, mention an attempt by Louis XI to escape from the Castle of Péronne during the night of October 13—this attempt occasioning, contrary to Commynes's version of events, the third outburst of the Duke of Burgundy's anger. This omission by Commynes, we are assured, "cannot be explained as faulty memory." It does not occur to Professor Kinser that if Commynes, and even the Duke of Burgundy, knew about the escape venture, this sensational development must have become a burning topic of discussion at the Burgundian court and could hardly have been overlooked by those observers who in chronicle or letter have left accounts of what happened at Péronne. One reason, evidently, that this does not occur to Professor Kinser is that he is unfamiliar with unpublished dispatches of Milanese ambassadors at the court of France, documents that are indispensable for a study of Commynes. As evidence for the attempted escape, Bittman quotes a bit of a dispatch of October 18 by G. P. Panigarola (whom Louis had declared *persona non grata* and who was lingering in Paris hoping to regain the King's grace): ". . . ultra che una nocte havesse vestita una veste dissimulata per fugire in quello habito, ma vedendo el designo non reuscire resto li in la terra. . . ."—i.e., "one evening he put on garments not his own in order to flee in this disguise, but perceiving that the scheme would not succeed, he remained there in the town." The passage itself indicates that King Louis gave up the attempt before he was detected, gave it up because of his realization that it would fail. An earlier portion of the dispatch, which Bittman does not quote, supports this interpretation and clarifies the whole situation: Panigarola had got his information, in confidence, "per el Conte de Foix che ha suo figliolo che dorme in la guardacamera del Re, et de gente che de la sono venute. . . ."—i.e., "from the Count of Foix [then heading the royal council at Paris which was attempting to keep the wheels of government turning] whose younger son [the Viscount of Narbonne] sleeps in the King's guardchamber and from people who had arrived in Paris from Péronne [probably attendants in the royal household whom Louis XI did not take with him on the expedition to Liège]. . . ." In sum, the only people who knew of the King's impulse to attempt escape in disguise were the intimates of his chamber, like the Viscount of Narbonne, who saw him don garments to mask his identity, and then, wisely, give over the project before making a move to

translator likewise appears unfamiliar with commonplaces of the age. °

Even the editor's biographical notice, a rather simple assignment, fails to pass muster. Commynes is characterized as lacking "even a touch of Latin" (a statement for which there is neither proof nor—considering Commynes's position—likelihood), as a "minor Burgundian nobleman" pursuing, as his "furtive profession," a "scrambling parvenu career." This *tour de force* of misrepresentation manages to overlook the fact that Philippe de Commynes had no less of a godfather than Philip, Duke of Burgundy, that his father (who was indeed of bourgeois origin and died heavily in debt—like many lords of the age) was Sovereign Bailiff of Flanders and received the highest chivalric distinction of the Burgundian state, membership in the Order of the Golden Fleece, that Commynes entered upon his career as a squire to the heir of Burgundy, a position coveted by sons of the greatest Burgundian lords, that in the service of the Duke of Burgundy he rose to eminent and secure estate and would doubtless have continued to win splendid honors, that after he transferred his allegiance to Louis XI he enjoyed high rank as the powerful lord of Argenton and even higher status as one of the most intimate and trusted counselors of his King, lauded by Lorenzo de' Medici for his accomplishments and declared by a Milanese ambassador to be the "all in all" with Louis XI. In a review of Dufournet's work (*Renaissance Quarterly*, XXI [1968], no. 4, pp. 464–69) Kinser justly took that volume to task for its "invidious, impressionistic psychologizing" but he is himself not above making such observations as that the "fragmented quality, which one senses in the personality behind the writing, is probably rooted in the loss of his parents as a very young child." Editorial preoccupation with Commynes's "not very subtle notion of human nature," "rudimentary notions of historical causation," and "insensitivity to institutional factors" does little more than suggest Professor Kinser's pleasure in scoring off the man it is his mission to illuminate. What the *Memoirs* are is almost completely obscured by insistence upon demonstrating what they are not.

Kinser's flat statement that "the *Memoirs* are not a work of literature" reveals in eight words the most painful limitation in his approach to Commynes. Securely enshrined in the European literary tradition of the past four centuries, the *Memoirs* need no defense against so eccentric an assertion. Whether Commynes is edited by a historian or a man of letters, the editor must sufficiently enlarge his horizons to examine the *Memoirs* as both a historical document and a work of art. One of Commynes's greatest, and most obvious, literary accomplishments lies in his magnificent use of irony, an irony no less exuberant but subtler than More's in *Richard III*, which stamps him as a man ahead of his time and as a conscious artist. Yet of this most notable quality of the *Memoirs* the edition offers no discussion. Kinser's onesid-

---

execute it. Kinser is quite right that Commynes's omission "cannot be explained by faulty memory"—but the editor is quite wrong in asserting that Commynes and the Duke learned of a escape by Louis XI which had been thwarted and that this knowledge fired the Duke's third violent rage. This "omission" of Commynes, supposedly calculated, is to be explained, like others, by the fact that he could not record what was unknown to him and what, in this case, never took place.

° Not only is "Conte de Warvic" translated "Count of Warwick," a title that would have surprised the Kingmaker, but in the scholarly apparatus the Earl likewise appears as a "count," as for good measure does Earl Rivers. Editor and translator sometimes collaborate in misunderstanding a straightforward fifteenth-century situation. What Commynes describes as "the captainship [of Calais], the best office of its kind in the world," is reduced to "the nicest frontier post in the world" ["la plus belle cappitainerie du monde"]. After John, Lord Wenlock, deputy at Calais for its Captain, the Earl of Warwick, had refused the Earl and his fleet entry to that port in April of 1470, King Edward IV was so grateful to Wenlock, Commynes narrates, that he sent him letters "elevating him to the captainship ("pour tenu l'office en chief"). The translation and an accompanying note mangle this into a high transaction of feudal vassalage, by having King Edward make Wenlock "holder of his office as tenant-in-chief"—thus depriving the English crown of one of its prized domains and grotesquely transforming Wenlock from an appointed official into the lord of Calais.

edness is directly signaled in an earlier observation—"memoirs are something between the private diary and the town or dynastic chronicle"—which relegates the
form to historical source materials. The editor is evidently unaware that memoirs are
a branch of life-writing between the diary and the autobiography—unlike the former,
designed to be read, and usually less artfully structured and less personal than the
latter. Autobiographies generally concentrate upon the response of the individual to
his experience, memoirs upon the experience itself (as do Commynes's). Commynes's
work joins with two others of its time, the *Commentaries*, i.e., Memoirs, of Pope
Pius II and Thomas More's incomplete *History of Richard III*, as the first great ex-
emplars of life-writing in the modern world.

The *Mémoires* of Philippe de Commynes have riches a-plenty to offer, but a
satisfactory modern English translation is, at this date, still to seek.

APPENDIX II

The Speed of Transmission of News to Louis XI

IT HAS SEEMED TO historians that on occasion important tidings took, even by fifteenth-century standards, a puzzlingly long time to reach Louis XI. However, dispatches of Milanese ambassadors at the French court, published and unpublished, sometimes demonstrate that the appearance results from faulty ascription of date. For example, on the basis of six letters of Louis XI, French scholars have assumed that the King did not learn of the fall of Perpignan, on February 1, 1473, until some time after March 9. An unpublished dispatch of February 18 by Christopher da Bollate, the Milanese ambassador, states, however, that Louis received the news on February 13. The six letters in question, three dated March 9, three undated, have been ascribed by the editors of the *Lettres* to March, 1473. They all concern a threat to Roussillon posed by John II. One requests the Aragonese Bernard d'Oms, Louis's Seneschal of Roussillon, to appear before the King to clear himself of suspicious behavior; two others order du Lau to take all necessary steps to counter subversion. Fortunately, another unpublished Milanese dispatch of a year earlier, March 8, 1472, clears up the mystery. That dispatch reports that "recently King René sent an [intercepted] letter to His Majesty [Louis XI] which King John of Aragon wrote to a bastard son of his." In one of his missives to du Lau ascribed to March 9, 1473, Louis writes that he is dispatching du Lau "a letter that the King of Aragon wrote to his bastard." In addition, a communication of King Louis to King René of March 7, 1472 (cited in J. Calmette, *Louis XI, Jean II, et la Revolution Catalane*, 327) states that Louis is charging du Lau to take precautionary measures and is sending there three hundred lances and two thousand franc archers—the precise number of troops the King mentions in five of the six letters ascribed to March, 1473. Thus it becomes clear that these letters belong not to 1473 but to 1472. There is no reason to question the statement by the Milanese ambassador that Louis XI received the news of the fall of Perpignan in less than two weeks, i.e., on February 13.

This problem in dating briefly illuminates a side of Louis's character. What apparently confirmed French scholars in relating the letters to 1473 is a statement in five of the six that the King has achieved an accord with the Duke of Burgundy and can therefore reinforce his troops in Roussillon. The statement fits the situation in 1473 fairly well: in mid-March of that year the Franco-Burgundian truce was prolonged for a year. At the same time in 1472, Louis's attempts to secure a treaty with Burgundy had completely failed. The Milanese dispatch of March 8, 1472, mentioned above, reveals, however, that the King was still persisting in negotiation. Louis's inaccurate statement, then, in five of the six letters represents yet another example of his predilection for working in an atmosphere of things-going-well—and of his willingness to stretch the truth in order to hearten his men.

APPENDIX III

The Dating of Louis XI's First Attack of Apoplexy

THE ONLY TWO direct pieces of evidence for dating the first cerebral hemorrhage suffered by Louis XI are furnished by Commynes (ed. Mandrot, II, 39) and by the Parisian chronicler Jean de Roye (*Cronique Scandaleuse*, II, 104). The latter places this attack in March, 1481 (though at Plessis-lès-Tours). Commynes, who is sometimes inaccurate in dating, first states that the illness struck the King in March, 1480, when he was at Les Forges near Chinon; then, but three sentences later, he declares it occurred in March of 1481. Though earlier scholars accepted the date 1481, twentieth-century French historians like B. de Mandrot (ed. Commynes, II, 39, note 3) and G. Dodu ("Louis XI," *Revue Historique*, CLXVIII [1931], 55–57) have rejected this evidence, to date the attack in March of 1479, for which there is no support whatsoever except that Louis XI was at Les Forges in March of that year; or, like Charles Petit-Dutaillis (in Lavisse, *Histoire de France*, IV, 2nd part, 418) and Pierre Champion (Louis XI, II, 309–10) they assign the year as 1480, for which there is no evidence save Commynes's first statement. As for March of 1479, there exists proof that this date is incorrect. Among those present during this first attack, according to Commynes (II, 40, 42), were the Bishop of Albi and the royal physician Adam Fumée. But in March of 1479 the Bishop was somewhere in the Burgundies or in Savoy: Louis XI addressed a letter to him on February 17, and two others on March 24 and 26 (*Lettres*, VII, 259–61; 277–78; 281–82), which place the Bishop on his mission of winning over the County of Burgundy (see p. 326). Furthermore, in the letter of February 17 Louis XI writes that he is sending Adam Fumée at once to Savoy to treat Duke Philibert. Finally, Commynes states that during the King's illness royal councilors had sought to cancel an increase in the *taille* which had been levied to pay for the King's new "army of the camp," but this did not come into existence until well after the battle of Guinegate, fought in August of 1479. March of 1480 can also be ruled out because the King, according to his "Itinerary" (*Lettres*, XI), could not have been at Les Forges at any time during that March, because Commynes's reference to the tax for the "army of the camp" does not suit this date, and because Commynes states that the attack took place during a time of truce betwen Louis XI and Maximilian and in March of 1480 they were at open war.

As for the date here adopted, March of 1481, in addition to the statement by Jean de Roye and the (second) statement by Commynes, there exist other indications that this is the right year. The King's "Itinerary" shows that he was at Les Forges in late February–early March of 1481. By this date the "army of the camp" had come into being, and there was a truce between Louis XI and Maximilian. Furthermore, in the late spring of 1481 Maximilian sent word to Edward IV that, according to some German ambassadors, Louis had received them sitting in a chair and looking very ill (see p. 330). Finally, the King's sharp refusal in April of 1481 to receive envoys from Maximilian (*Lettres*, IX, 24–26) and his vowing to St. James of Compostella, the following month, a sum of money so large that the payment of certain pensions had to be deferred (*Lettres*, IX, 37), seem to offer some support for March of 1481. There appears, then, little reason to doubt that this is the correct date.

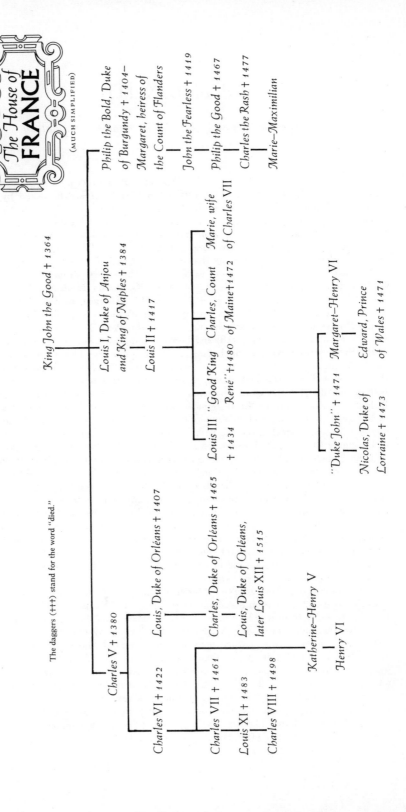

The House of
FRANCE

(MUCH SIMPLIFIED)

The daggers (†††) stand for the word "died."

King John the Good † 1364

Louis I, Duke of Anjou
and King of Naples † 1384

Louis II † 1417

Louis III   Charles, Count   Marie, wife
"Good King   of Maine † 1472   of Charles VII
René" † 1480

"Duke John" † 1471   Margaret—Henry VI

Nicolas, Duke of   Edward, Prince
Lorraine † 1473   of Wales † 1471

Philip the Bold, Duke
of Burgundy † 1404—
Margaret, heiress of
the Count of Flanders

John the Fearless † 1419

Philip the Good † 1467

Charles the Rash † 1477

Marie—Maximilian

Charles V † 1380

Louis, Duke of Orléans † 1407

Charles, Duke of Orléans † 1465

Louis, Duke of Orléans,
later Louis XII † 1515

Katherine—Henry V

Henry VI

Charles VI † 1422

Charles VII † 1461

Louis XI † 1483

Charles VIII † 1498

RULERS AND
PRINCIPAL LORDS

Rulers

HOUSE OF VALOIS

Louis Dauphin; later Louis XI (1423–83)

His father: Charles VII, Joan of Arc's "gentil Dauphin" (reigned 1422–61)

His mother: Marie of Anjou, sister of "Good King René"

His first wife: Margaret (died 1445), daughter of the poet-King, James I of Scotland

His second wife: Charlotte, daugher of Louis, Duke of Savoy

His son and heir: Charles; later Charles VIII (1470–98)

His daughters: Anne, married to Pierre de Beaujeu of the House of Bourbon; Jeanne, married to Louis, Duke of Orléans (later Louis XII)

His bastard daughters: Jeanne, married to Louis, Bastard of Bourbon, Admiral; Marie, married to Aymar, Lord of St. Vallier

His brother: Charles, Duke of Berry; later Duke of Normandy, and then Duke of Guienne (1446–72)

His sisters: Jeanne, married to Jean, Duke of Bourbon; Yolande, married to Amedée, Prince, later Duke, of Savoy; Madeleine, married to Jean, heir of the Count of Foix; also other sisters

HOUSE OF LANCASTER

Henry VI (1421–71); reigned 1422–61; 1470–71

His father: Henry V, victor of Agincourt and conqueror of northern France (died 1422)

His mother: Katherine of France, daughter of the mad Charles VI and sister of Charles VII

His wife: Margaret of Anjou, daughter of "Good King René"

His son: Edward, Prince of Wales (killed at the battle of Tewkesbury, 1471)

His half-brother: Jasper Tudor, Earl of Pembroke, son of widowed Katherine of France and Owen Tudor

HOUSE OF YORK

Edward, Earl of March; later Edward IV (1442–83); reigned 1461–70; 1471–83

His father: Richard, Duke of York, killed at the battle of Wakefield, 1460

His mother: Cicely Neville, aunt of Richard Neville, Earl of Warwick ("The King-maker")

His wife: Elizabeth Woodville, daughter of Richard, Lord, later Earl, Rivers, and of Jacquetta, formerly Dowager Duchess of Bedford, sister to Louis of Luxembourg, Count of St. Pol

His sons: Edward (Edward V) and Richard, Duke of York, murdered (?, 1483?) fol-

lowing the seizure of the throne by their uncle Richard, Duke of Gloucester
(Richard III) in June of 1483

His daughter: Elizabeth, betrothed to Charles, Dauphin of France (also other daughters)

His brothers: Edmund, Earl of Rutland, killed at Wakefield, 1460; George, Duke of
Clarence, executed 1478; Richard, Duke of Gloucester, later Richard III
(1452–85)

His sister: Margaret, married in 1468 to Charles the Rash, Duke of Burgundy

HOUSE OF ARAGON

Alfonso V, King of Aragon and of Naples (1385?–1458)

His bastard son: Ferrante, King of Naples (1423?–1494); Ferrante's sons Alfonso, Duke of Calabria, married to Ypollita Sforza; Federigo, Prince of
Taranto, married to Louis XI's sister-in-law, Anne of Savoy

His brother: John, King of Navarre; later John II, King of Aragon (reigned 1458–79);
John's sons Don Carlos (died 1461); Ferdinand, married to Isabella of
Castile and, with her, joint ruler of Spain; John's third daughter Eleanor,
heiress of Navarre, married to Gaston, Count of Foix

HOUSE OF HAPSBURG

Frederick III, Emperor of Germany (1415–93)

His son: Maximilian (later the Emperor Maximilian), married to Marie, heiress of
Charles the Rash, Duke of Burgundy; their children: Philip, married to
Juana the Mad, heiress of Spain; Margaret, married to Louis XI's heir, the
Dauphin Charles (the marriage later dissolved)

His cousin: Sigismund, Duke of Austria, ruler of the Tyrol and portions of Alsace

THE POPES

Nicholas V (1447–55)
Calixtus III (1455–58)
Pius II—Aeneas Sylvius Piccolomini (1458–64)
Paul II (1464–71)
Sixtus IV (1471–84)

Lords

HOUSE OF BURGUNDY

Philip the Good, Duke of Burgundy

His third wife: Isabella of Portugal (descendant of John of Gaunt, Duke of Lancaster)

His son and heir: Charles, Count of Charolais; later, Charles, Duke of Burgundy (duke,
1467–77); Charles's heiress, Marie, married to Maximilian of Hapsburg;
Charles's second wife, Margaret of York, sister of Edward IV

His most famous illegitimate son: Antoine, the Grand Bastard of Burgundy

HOUSE OF ANJOU

"Good King René" (died 1480), Duke of Anjou, of Bar, and of Lorraine, Count of
Provence, titular King of Naples

His first wife: Isabella of Lorraine

His son: John, Duke of Calabria (Duke John); John's son Nicolas, Marquess of Pont-à-

Mousson and later Duke of Lorraine (died 1473, Nicolas's cousin René
becoming René II, Duke of Lorraine)
His daughter: Margaret of Anjou, wife of Henry VI of England
His brother: Charles, Count of Maine
His sister: Marie, wife of Charles VII

HOUSE OF ORLÉANS

Charles, Duke of Orléans, poet (captured at the battle of Agincourt and 25 years a
prisoner in England)
His son: Louis; later Duke of Orléans and then King Louis XII
His half-brother: Jean, Bastard, Count of Dunois (companion-in-arms of Joan of Arc)

HOUSE OF BOURBON

Jean, Duke of Bourbon
His father: Charles, Duke of Bourbon (leader of the "Praguerie," 1440)
His mother: Agnes, sister of Philip the Good, Duke of Burgundy
His wife: Jeanne, sister of Louis XI
His brothers: Charles, Archbishop of Lyons; Pierre de Beaujeu, married to Louis XI's
daughter Anne and later Duke of Bourbon; Louis, Prince-Bishop of
Liège
His half-brother: Louis, Bastard of Bourbon, Admiral, married to Louis XI's illegitimate
daughter Jeanne

HOUSE OF ARMAGNAC

Jean, Count of Armagnac (killed, 1473)
His sister and "wife": Isabel
His uncle: Bernard, Count of Pardiac, governor of the Dauphin
His cousin: Bernard's son Jacques d'Armagnac, Count of La Marche, and later Duke
of Nemours, executed 1477

HOUSE OF BRITTANY

Francis II, Duke of Brittany
His daughter and heiress: Anne, married first to Louis XI's son Charles VIII, and
then to Louis XII

HOUSE OF SAVOY

Amedée, Duke of Savoy
His father: Louis, Duke of Savoy
His mother: Anne of Cyprus
His wife: Yolande, sister of Louis XI, Duchess and then Regent of Savoy
His son and successor: Philibert, Duke of Savoy
His brother: Philip, Count of Bresse; numerous other brothers

HOUSE OF SFORZA

Francesco Sforza, Count of Pavia, Duke of Milan (1450–66)
His wife: Bianca, illegitimate daughter of the last Visconti Duke of Milan, Filippo-
Maria (died 1447), whose sister Valentina was the mother of Charles, Duke
of Orléans
His son and heir: Galeazzo-Maria, Duke of Milan (assassinated 1476); Galeazzo's wife
Bona of Savoy, sister-in-law of Louis XI, later Regent of Milan for her
son Giangaleazzo

His daughter: Ypollita, married to Alfonso, Duke of Calabria, son of King Ferrante of
     Naples
His brother: Lodovico ("The Moor"), usurper of the Duchy from his nephew Giangale-
     azzo; numerous other brothers

HOUSE OF NEVILLE

Richard Neville, Earl of Warwick ("The Kingmaker"), killed at the battle of Barnet,
     1471
His father: Richard, Earl of Salisbury, brother of Cicely, Duchess of York
His wife: Isabel, heiress of Richard Beauchamp, Earl of Warwick
His daughters: Isabel, married to George, Duke of Clarence; Anne, married first
          to Edward, Lancastrian Prince of Wales, and then to Richard, Duke of
          Gloucester, later Richard III
His brothers: John, Lord Montagu; later Earl of Northumberland and then Marquess
          Montagu, killed at Barnet, 1471; George, Bishop of Exeter, then Chancellor
          of England and Archbishop of York (deprived of his chancellorship,
          1467)

NOTES

BIBLIOGRAPHY

INDEX

NOTES

1. THE CHILD OF SHAME

(1) The first of these favorites was the Sire of Giac, a blustering, brutal fellow of no capacity. After he had poisoned his pregnant wife, Giac wooed the widowed Countess of Tonnère, Louis's godmother; as a condition of marriage, the ambitious Countess made him disinherit his children and turn over to her all his goods. With the King and the King's purse firmly in his grip, the arrogant favorite rode roughshod over everybody, until he made the mistake of giving the lie direct to Georges de La Trémoille, a lord who had powerful connections and insatiable appetites. Giac's wife, tiring of her empty-headed husband and attracted by a climber even more unscrupulous than Giac, had begun an affair with him. La Trémoille allied himself with the Breton Constable, who had likewise had his fill of the favorite. In February of 1427, Giac was wrenched from his marital bed by a band of armed men—his wife leaping naked from the sheets to save her silver—and quickly condemned to death by a drumhead court. While he begged desperately that the hand he had vowed to the Devil be chopped off before he died, he was trussed up and cast into a river, Georges de La Trémoille riding his horse on the bank to see him drown. Then La Trémoille posted off to join Giac's widow, who delivered up a great quantity of Giac's treasure and shortly after married him.

The little King was roused to a bout of bad temper over this high-handed disposal of Giac, but quickly found another favorite to soothe his ruffled feelings. This one was a simple guardsman, called Le Camus of Beaulieu. He was even stupider and more insufferable than Giac, keeping everybody away from the King while he extracted lands and money. When the Constable rejoined the court at Poitiers in early June of 1427, after another fruitless military expedition, he gave orders for Le Camus to be got rid of. As the favorite was riding in a field near the castle, two men hurled themselves upon him with such force that his head was broken, a hand was cut off, and he fell instantly dead. The King beheld Le Camus's mule being brought home, and then Le Camus himself, in a basket. Charles indulged in another bout of temper.

The Constable now decided that while he conducted military operations La Trémoille was the man to govern the King. Charles disliked La Trémoille, an overbearing hulk of flesh, even more than he disliked the brusque Breton; but when the Constable insisted, he contented himself with remarking, "Fair cousin, you are the one who is delivering him to me and you are the one who will repent of it, for I know him better than you." In a few weeks Charles was clinging to La Trémoille in utter dependence. The new favorite, for his part, quickly proved the King a good prophet. He turned against his ally and took over the entire government for himself.

2. THE UNFILIAL SON

(1) When Louis and his father entered Limoges on March 2 (1439), the King lodged in the castle, the Dauphin in the Abbey of St. Martial. One of the monks complained to the Dauphin's physician that he had been unjustly deprived by the Abbot of an office which he had received from the Pope. Louis promptly investigated, then requested the Abbot to restore the monk to his office. The Abbot wrapped himself in his ecclesiastical dignity with much talk of maintaining discipline and of being unable to change his mind without charging his conscience. Louis informed him dryly that he need not worry about his conscience; he need only worry about accomplishing the will of the Dauphin. Louis had with him a little lioness, eight months old, which he kept in one of the cells of the monastery. One night, the lithe, powerful beast made a leap for freedom through a window. The next morning it was found hanged in its halter. Louis, deeply grieved, ordered the skin, fat, and tail to be stored in his baggage. The applicable moral he apparently failed to store in his mind.

3. THE PRINCE OF CUTTHROATS

(1) At Ruffec, where the royal court kept Easter, the eighteen-year-old Dauphin almost lost his life. On Good Friday while he and Charles, Count of Maine, and another lord were walking in the burgeoning fields outside the town, they came to the banks of the river Charente and found a boat drawn up. Pushing off into the stream, they soon discovered, as the current quickened, that they were being swept toward a mill race. Buffeted by rapids, the boat overturned; the Dauphin and his companions were tumbled about like chips in the foaming water. As Louis struggled to get free of his heavy Easter gown, he vowed himself to the Virgin Mary if she would save him. A swirl of current cast the three men up on a small sandbank, from which, after slipping off their sodden robes, they were able to make their way to shore.

(2) At seven o'clock in the morning, the Swiss, drunk on victory, had reached the east bank of the Birse. Heedless of their chiefs, they roared their insistence on crossing the stream to attack a force five times their number. A messenger sent from Bâle to warn them against so foolish an advance they tore to pieces. Then in a solid phalanx they splashed through the river and, indifferent to heavy archer fire, advanced up the slope of the plateau. Clad in iron hats and mail coats, their front ranks thrust out a terrible hedge of pikes while those behind swung massive halberds and "morningstars" (spike-studded clubs).

When they reached the edge of the plateau, Bueil's heavily armed horsemen charged upon them. A wild, bloody battle followed. Tirelessly the Swiss chopped and thrust at the horsemen smashing into their phalanx. Like wolves tearing at a hedgehog, Écorcheurs drove against the iron ranks from all sides. Finally, even the Swiss saw that they had overreached themselves. Under ceaseless attack from plunging cavalry, they somehow managed to turn their phalanx and head back for the Birse. But a violent assault wrenched, then sundered, the column. Grimly the bulk of the Swiss fought their way along the Birse toward a leper hospital, leaving six hundred of their fellows trapped against the stream. Despite all that the maddened Écorcheurs could do, the Swiss succeeded in taking shelter behind the stout walls of the hospital of St. Jacques.

Jean de Bueil brought up his artillery. When stretches of wall had been pounded to rubble, the Écorcheurs, on foot now, hurled themselves into the breaches. Hand-to-hand struggles followed, the bitterest fighting of the day. Infuriated by their losses, the French stormed into the hospital precincts, to be met by an enemy who gave no ground until he dropped. The chiefs of Bueil's army did not spare themselves: Burckhard Munch, leader of the Austrian chivalry, perished in the breach, along with Robert de Brezé, brother of the King's minister, Pierre. Late in the afternoon, the last of the Swiss were cut down in the vineyard close, or perished in a flaming tower where they had barricaded themselves. Hours earlier, their six hundred companions trapped on the riverbank had died to the last man. Of the twenty-five hundred Swiss, there were about two hundred survivors, all of them badly wounded, who had been sent off from the leper hospital to make their way to Bâle. The mountaineers had kept the faith which they had pledged the night before: "We commit our souls to God and our bodies to the Écorcheurs." As Bueil's battered forces made their way back to their cantonments that night, a band of them stopped before an Austrian castle to announce their victory. When asked how many men they had lost, they answered—"Four thousand."

4. THE MALCONTENT

(1) His grandfather, Louis I, Duke of Anjou and younger son of the prisoner-King, John, had been adopted by the Queen of Naples as the heir to that kingdom and to the County of Provence (then a fief of the Empire); the adoption likewise included the now empty title of King of Jerusalem and even a claim upon the Kingdom of Hungary. René himself, by marrying Isabelle, the heir of Lorraine, had come into the possession of the duchies of Bar and of Lorraine. Thus, when his elder brother, Louis III, died in Italy in 1434, René could call himself King of Naples (and Jerusalem), Count of Provence, and, within France, Duke of Anjou, Bar, and Lorraine.

Unfortunately, he was then a prisoner of the Duke of Burgundy. Addicted to chivalric display, he had led a cavalry charge against murderous cannon and archer fire at the battle of Bulgnéville, 1431, and promptly got himself captured. He whiled away his prison hours painting on glass, reading, writing poetry, until, in 1437, the Duke of Burgundy set his ransom at 400,000 gold crowns and allowed him to sail for the Kingdom of Naples, which was under attack from Alfonso V, King of Aragon, another claimant to that realm.

Though he was supported by the Pope, Florence, and Genoa, King René misunderstood his Italian lords, mishandled potential allies, and mismanaged his campaigns. As if he were a paladin of the thirteenth century, he sent gauntlets of defiance and offered set time and place of battle to Alfonso of Aragon, who had half René's resources but was twice the soldier and politician. By 1442, René had been driven back to France, penniless and still owing most of his ransom to the Duke of Burgundy.

(2) One night during the Christmas season, while the Dauphin was at Montbéliard, Jamet de Tillay, a Breton soldier high in the favor of the King, together with the Master of the Dauphin's Household had entered Margaret's "retreat" to find her reclining on her couch with young poet-lords close about her and no light in the room save a good fire. Jamet had impudently thrust his candle close to the Dauphine in order to take in the tableau, and on withdrawing from the chamber he dressed down the Master of the Household for permitting such imprudent behavior. He did not scruple to drop a comment upon princesses who were wantons. To others he made similar remarks. Whether he was simply a malicious busybody or whether he was trying to further some devious court intrigue there is no knowing.

Some of his loose language was reported to the Dauphine. After the return of her husband, she attributed Louis's coldness to the work of Jamet, and she believed that the Breton was also poisoning the mind of the King against her. Worst of all, terrible and insupportable to her, were the insinuations he had dropped, words that befouled innocent evenings of poetry. Jamet and his gossip swelled to horrible proportions in her mind. When she entered a room and found him present, she precipitately turned and fled. In her chamber she burst out with bitter accusations against him. Her ladies, more hardened to the ways of the court, did not feel the same outrage, although they adored their mistress. When Jamet, apparently becoming a little frightened at his success, showed signs of wanting to make amends to the Dauphine, her ladies urged her to hear him but she violently refused.

In her last illness, burning with fever and shaken with bouts of coughing, Margaret lay upon her couch, engulfed in the nightmare of Jamet de Tillay. Her chief lady-in-waiting tried to cheer her, saying that she should not be so melancholy. The suffering girl replied bitterly that she had a perfect right to be melancholy, for the words that had been said about her were false. Agitatedly, she swore on the damnation of her soul that she had never done a thing that was imputed to her nor had she ever thought of it.

Her fever worsened. Noises so oppressed her that the bells in the churches of Châlons were silenced. By Wednesday, August 11, she was at moments half delirious. "Ah, Jamet! Jamet!" she cried out. "You've succeeded! If I die, it's on account of you and the fine words that you've spoken of me without cause or motive!" Then the girl thrashed her arms in anguish and beat upon her chest: "I swear by God and by my soul and by my baptism at the font—may God strike me dead if I speak false! —I have not deserved this nor done wrong to my lord!" Pierre de Brezé left the chamber much moved, murmuring, "It is pitiful, the suffering of this lady."

The Dauphine grew steadily worse. She said no more of Jamet. On Monday, the 16th, as summer twilight came down, Margaret was dying. A little before Vespers, she roused, cried out, "And I swear upon my soul—by the pangs of death—I did no wrong to my lord!"

By the time it was dark, the Dauphine had made her confession and received the last rites. One of her women, coming into the chamber, said loudly, "Madame la Dauphine must pardon Jamet."

Robert Poitevin, her priest as well as her doctor, replied that the Dauphine had already done so, she had pardoned everyone.

The girl found strength enough to assert that she had not.

"Save your Grace, madame," said Master Robert, "You have pardoned him as you should do."

"No," the Dauphine gasped. "No!"

The Dame de St. Michel and other ladies insisted: "Madame, you must pardon everyone, as you wish God to pardon you, and with good heart."

She was silent. Then, straining her voice so that all might hear, she managed to say, "I pardon him then and with good heart."

She sighed: "Except that it would have meant breaking faith, I could be sorry for having ever come into France."

A little later, her lips moved for the last time, hardly more than a murmur: "Fie on this life—speak of it no more—I am utterly weary of it."

The Dauphin Louis, determined to expose the man who had maliciously injured his wife, pressed the case so strongly that six weeks later the royal council was brought to order an inquiry. Confronted by the testimony of numerous witnesses, ranging from the Dauphine's ladies-in-waiting to some of the great lords of court, Jamet de Tillay denied or tried to explain away or could not remember the scurrilities he had dropped. Mysteriously, the inquiry was permitted to lapse. The Dauphin forced a resumption of it the following June (1446) by producing as a witness the Queen herself. She had nothing to offer on the subject of Jamet and the Dauphine, but her testimony showed that Jamet had tried to make trouble over Agnès Sorel. He had informed the Queen that King Charles wanted her to leave Châlons before he did because of scarcity of lodging on the road; Jamet intimated, however, that the King's real motive was a desire to avoid her company. But by this summer the Dauphin's credit was far from high and any matter which thus touched la Dame de Beauté was hardly welcomed. The inquiry was dropped. Jamet de Tillay retained his high offices and the favor of the king.

Pierre Champion, in his biography of Louis, writes that Jamet de Tillay was an intimate of the Dauphin and that the Dauphin set him as a spy to watch his wife. This black view of the Dauphin results from a misinterpretation of the only piece of evidence linking Louis and Jamet de Tillay and from a failure to take into account several pieces of evidence that prove Louis's hostility to the man.

The documentary source on which Champion builds his account of Jamet de Tillay as an intimate of the Dauphin offers the following facts: On June 8, 1442, Louis gave three thousand florins to certain officials of his province of Dauphiné. Half the money went to eleven men specified by the Dauphin. These men in turn decided that four others had done such good service in Dauphiné that the remainder of the money should be shared among them. One of these four men was Jamet de Tillay, titled "Councilor and Chamberlain of the Dauphin." Louis, then, had no hand in the rewarding of Jamet, and Jamet was a member of the council of Dauphiné, an entirely different matter from being a member of the Dauphin's personal council, the advisers constantly with him in his household. The office of Chamberlain was purely honorary. It was the King, not the Dauphin, who had appointed Jamet de Tillay to his post in Dauphiné.

There is, in fact, no connection between Louis and Jamet de Tillay, either before, during, or after 1445. Jamet had taken an active part against the Dauphin in the Praguerie—the office in Dauphiné being his reward. By 1443 he had risen so high in Charles VII's favor that according to one chronicler he, along with Brezé and another lord, had become a ruling figure at court. Jamet was soon made Bailli of Vermandois, a position of importance. In the summer of 1444 he did not accompany the Dauphin on his Swiss expedition but went with Charles VII and Brezé into Lorraine. During the Dauphine's illness, Jamet was so intimate with King Charles that, when the doctors came to report upon the condition of the princess, Charles cleared the chamber of all courtiers except Jamet de Tillay. Though the testimony of the inquiry clearly showed that Jamet was a scandalmonger, he was so firmly entrenched in the King's favor that he was able to ride out the storm and retain his high offices.

Furthermore, the transcript of the inquiry demonstrates that Louis, far from employing Jamet as a spy upon his wife, was the man who tried to make Jamet pay for his malice. The record of the testimony begins thus: "Jeanne de Tuce, Dame de St. Michel, aged about 45, produced by the high and puissant Prince, My Lord the Dauphin against Jamet de Tillay, October 11, 1445 . . ." Further evidence is hardly needed, but it is worth mentioning that some of the most damaging testimony against Jamet was offered by intimates of the Dauphin, such as Louis de Laval, the lord of Châtillon; and that, when the inquiry was resumed, it was Louis who persuaded the Queen to testify against Jamet.

Louis was not a very affectionate husband but he did his best to bring to book the man who had injured his wife.

(3) One day during the Easter season, Louis dismissed everyone from his chamber in the castle of Chinon but his close follower Antoine de Chabannes, Count

of Dammartin. He then took Chabannes by the arm and drew him to a window.
After talking casually for a few moments, the Dauphin pointed below.

"There are the ones who hold the Realm of France in subjection," he remarked.

Chabannes saw that the Dauphin was indicating the King's guards. He asked
prudently, "Whom do you mean?"

"The Scots." Louis added, "But they could be got round."

"How, my lord?"

"Oh, it wouldn't take much to do it."

Chabannes sheered off this risky talk, saying that the Scots guard was necessary for the King's safety. Chabannes's curiosity had been aroused, however, and he
soon brought up what he knew was a sore subject with the Dauphin. People had
thought, he said, when the court was at Châlons, that the King was going to give
his son great authority and employ him grandly, for he had achieved an immense
reputation.

"Would that it had been so," Louis replied. "If I had played the game cleverly, I would have done well. But, as it is, I was duped; the King has not done for
me what I was given reason to believe he would."

With that the Dauphin turned the talk to the affairs of Savoy and gave Chabannes a mission to that Duke, promising to reward him well for his good services.

For some weeks after Chabannes had returned from Savoy, Louis made no
move to renew their conversation; but one day, probably in late May, as the Dauphin was riding back to Chinon from Razilly, where the King had ensconced himself
with Agnès Sorel, he had the word passed down the column that he wanted to
speak with the Count of Dammartin. As soon as the Count came up, the Dauphin
spurred his horse abruptly into the fields, and when the two men were out of earshot, he put his arm around Chabannes's shoulder and said to him, "Look, there will
be no difficulty about getting rid of these people."

"What do you mean?" asked Chabannes.

"Why, there's nothing to it. I have fifteen or twenty crossbowmen and thirty
archers, or thereabouts. You, you have some archers, don't you? You must lend me
five or six."

They chatted for a little about the prowess of the Count's archers, and then
the Dauphin said suddenly, "Send for them."

"But, my lord, this affair is not to be managed so easily, for the King has men
of arms at his beck and call and they are all stationed close by."

"Oh, I have enough men."

"But how do you propose to handle the business?"

The castle of Razilly was unguarded, Louis pointed out. Anyone who wished
might enter it. The Dauphin and his archers and the gentlemen of his household
would have no difficulty slipping in one after the other. Charles, Count of Maine,
was on his side and had promised to win over the captain of the royal household
troops. "I also have the support of the House of Laval and of other lords."

Chabannes interjected, "I can well believe that the Laval people are urging
you to do this, but it is only for their own ends."

The Dauphin ignored this comment. "Since I have all those whom I've named,
I cannot fail to be the strongest once we are inside the castle. True, there are one or
two little situations where we will have to watch our step, but we'll have nothing to
worry about."

Chabannes did not care for this precarious scheme. He pointed out that the
moment the Dauphin had control of Razilly the royal men of arms would trap him
there with the greatest of ease.

Louis told him not to worry, the thing would be well handled, and Chabannes would have a handsome reward. "I will treat you more generously than you have ever been treated before, and I'll see that you have authority enough. For I intend to have you so intimate with the King that you sleep in his chamber. As for the royal 'mignons,' we'll see that they too are well satisfied."

The Dauphin added, "I know that you love the Seneschal [Pierre de Brezé]."

"As I do myself."

"So do I, and I am content that he govern as he has been accustomed to do; but it will be under me. Believe me, this business offers no difficulty. Nothing could be easier."

Nothing could be more unlikely—the Dauphin gently to sequester the King from the business of state and, without disturbing the government, insert himself at the head of it. Louis soon abandoned the idea, which he could hardly have taken very seriously at any time.

The Dauphin's conversations with Chabannes have no doubt been touched up; they are derived from a deposition made by Chabannes—after he had changed sides.

(4) One of the cleverest members of his household, Jean de Daillon, began conferring at length with the King, after which he made mysterious reports to his master. Daillon and other intimates like Louis de Laval, lord of Châtillon, and Jean de Bueil, who had taken service with the Dauphin following the Swiss expedition, and Bueil's brother, Louis, constantly had their heads together. Soon Dauphin Louis's servants, and their servants, were outdistancing their master in reckless talk and bizarre scheming. In midsummer Louis, wearying of the game or perceiving that matters were getting out of hand, temporarily dismissed de Daillon and de Bueil from his household. By this time Antoine de Chabannes, deciding that the Dauphin was heading for disaster, had thrown in his lot with the King and Brezé.

While the Dauphin ground chaff, King Charles was enjoying the chivalresque ingenuity of the Angevins, now returned to court though not to the council chamber. In the fine June weather there was created at a crossroads between Razilly and Chinon a passage of arms out of Arthurian romance. Presided over by the King, with Agnès to admire, "The Challenge of the Rock Perilous" or "The Emprise of the Dragon's Mouth" was guarded by four lords magnificently accoutred, and no lady could pass unless accompanied by a valiant knight or squire prepared to break two lances for the love of her. King René, the poet of his misfortunes, was armored all in black, bearing on his left arm a sable shield sewn with pearls (tears), holding a black lance in his fist and bestriding a charger caparisoned in black. Pierre de Brezé took part in the tourney along with a number of royal *mignons*. The prize went to the woeful chevalier of night. René then treated King Charles and his lords to a second *pas* at Saumur, in which Ferry of Lorraine, René's son-in-law, was proclaimed the winner. Meanwhile, the English still held Normandy and Guienne; and smashed churches, wasted fields, and towns with rotting houses and shrunken populations scarred the land of France.

5. THE EMPEROR OF DAUPHINÉ

(1) Ever since his father had given him partial control of Dauphiné, in 1440, Louis had taken his power seriously, and wherever he was or whatever he was doing, he kept in constant touch with the officers of the province, generating a stream of orders and decrees. He tried to stimulate the economies of his towns, he investigated tax assessments, he reorganized the coinage, he inaugurated a program of judicial reform. He had administered his province from "the host before Pontoise" (summer of 1441); "at the siege before Ax" (August of 1442); from Isle-Jourdain, where he was besieging the Count of Armagnac (January 1444); from Langres in July of the same year, while he was pressed with the thousand duties of getting his Écorcheurs moving toward Bâle; from Altkirch, three days after the defeat of the Swiss; from Alsace, from Montbéliard, from his enforced idleness at his father's court.

(2) Two weeks later he confirmed the liberties of Montélimar, exempted the town from imposts and subsidies accorded by the Three Estates, gave the citizens the right to elect their own judicial officers, and promised that the town would never be transferred to any other authority than the Dauphin's. As a further stimulus to prosperity, he offered to all who would come to dwell there an exemption from imposts for ten years. Minor patterns of public order were regulated as well: women of evil life were to be driven from inns and taverns and made to lodge in the *maison publique* and to wear a red shoulder knot on their gowns, "which is the distinctive sign of debauched girls." Two years later, Louis accorded the town two fairs, the right to have a court of appeal, the privilege of being the seat of a salt warehouse, and exemption for its traders from all provincial tolls.

(3) Finding the town of Cremieu depopulated and impoverished, Louis discovered that, as with other towns, its once-flourishing commerce had been mainly carried on by Jews. But the Jews had left Dauphiné because of the crushing taxes imposed upon them. Louis set about reviving Cremieu: aliens settling there would be exempt from all taxes voted by the Three Estates for twenty years; Jews and Jewesses who remained, or who would come to dwell there, need pay only an ounce of silver instead of the half marc previously demanded. Jews were likewise encouraged to settle in other towns of the province. Louis found it difficult to persuade his subjects, however, to relinquish their prejudices in favor of their prosperity. An assembly of the Three Estates petitioned the Dauphin to expel Jews, for they were ruining the country by their usury (the usual medieval complaint). The Dauphin and his council not only refused this petition but emphasized that Jews were to be allowed to live wherever they wished in Dauphiné.

(4) Louis's most spectacular struggle was with the Bishop of Gap. This embattled prelate stirred up the people of his diocese to attack French troops passing through to Italy, forcibly resisted the Dauphin's officers come to make inquiry, refused to let Delphinal money circulate in his dominions, laid what taxes he pleased, and in general acknowledged no sovereignty but his own. He was a lusty throwback to that earlier Bishop of Gap, Sagittarius, of the sixth century, who went into battle swinging a leaden maul so that, beating his foes to death, he could not be accused of shedding Christian blood. Louis kept up the pressure of his commissions until the people of Gap themselves requested his intervention. Then he took into his hands, as the Bishop continued obdurate, the temporalities of the diocese and fined the town three thousand crowns. The Bishop, Gaucherde Forcalquier, fulminating an interdict and excommunicating the Dauphin's officers left and right, indignantly fled to Rome. But Louis soon succeeded in negotiating a settlement with the Pope: the Bishop had to come humbly and ask the Dauphin's pardon, acknowledge the Dauphin's sovereignty, and take off the excommunication; then Louis released the Bishop's men he had imprisoned and remitted the fine of three thousand crowns.

6. THE UNCHASTENED REBEL

(1) The underground currents flowing between Dauphiné and the royal court were embittered by the hangers-on of the great—bold, clever, greedy men living by

their wits, ready to betray for gain, sometimes becoming hopelessly entangled in their own webs. Such a man was Guillaume Mariette, a secretary of the Dauphin, a notary of the King. Accompanying Louis into Dauphiné at the beginning of 1447, Mariette was soon given a mission to the royal court which enabled him to try his hand at double-dealing on a grand scale. He poured into the ear of Pierre de Brezé a vivid tale of the Dauphin's machinations; then, on his return to Dauphiné, he reported that Brezé was poisoning the King's mind against the Dauphin. Again he was sent back to the French court, and this time—June of 1447—he secured an audience with the King. The Dauphin he declared, was conspiring to return to court and take over the government. He and his supporters were saying that the King governed so badly he could not do worse and that once Charles and his follies were put aside all would go well. Charles VII, who was an excellent judge of all men except his son, received these revelations coldly. What he did not know was that Brezé had coached Mariette in his story, or at least listened to it.

Four months later (October, 1447), some of Mariette's lesser manipulations caught up with him. Charged with forging documents, he was imprisoned in the castle of Loches, then transferred to Lyons and put in irons. He managed to escape, was recaptured by the Dauphin's friend Jacques Coeur, but again escaped. Though he had flagrantly plotted against his master, he headed for Dauphiné nonetheless, hoping that somehow his "revelations" to Brezé and the King could be redeemed by even better revelations to the Dauphin.

As soon as he reached the soil of Dauphiné, Mariette was picked up and clapped into prison. Louis immediately sent men to examine him, being careful to adjoin them to an officer of the King; he did not intend to let himself be accused of collusion in whatever Mariette could be made to say. When Delphinal and royal officers put Mariette to the torture (March 3, 1448), he declared that it was all Brezé's doing. Brezé had got him to create the story about the Dauphin's plotting in order that it might be dished up to the King.

With the Dauphin's permission, Mariette was taken to Paris to be tried. At one point he was confronted with Brezé himself but still stuck to his story. Sentenced to death, he was removed to Tours and beheaded.

Once Mariette was condemned, the Dauphin moved quickly against Pierre de Brezé. Louis's friends in the royal council, on the basis of Mariette's confession, accused Brezé of poisoning the King's mind. Brezé asked Charles VII for an immediate trial, which was granted, and the affair was turned over to the Parlement of Paris. It is perhaps no coincidence that Agnès Sorel, Brezé's partner in ruling the King, appeared at Paris at this same time. Brezé quickly secured his exoneration by the Parlement. It appears from the pardon Charles VII accorded him that he admitted to secret interviews with Mariette before the latter approached the King. Charles handled the affair neatly. He declared that the Seneschal of Poitou in concealing his relations with the traitor had committed only a venial mistake, excused by his service to the realm; besides, Mariette had been proved a liar in his charges against Brezé, and the King's mind therefore had in no way been affected by anything that Mariette said about the Dauphin. But Charles never indicated that he considered his son innocent of plotting.

(2) While at Chambéry, Louis persuaded the Duke of Savoy that his sister Yolande of France, affianced to the Duke's heir, Prince Amedée, and living in the ducal household, should be married at once to Amedée. A fresh treaty of alliance was concluded between the Dauphin and the Duke, and young Amedée signed a declaration acknowledging the Dauphin as his "good and especial lord and master" and promised to serve him with body and goods against anyone, including the King of France. Louis then returned to Dauphiné, soon followed by his little bride, who entered his household to grow up into a wife. In honor of her "joyous arrival," several towns offered handsome gifts of money—and when some of them forgot the offer, the Dauphin sent his officers to collect. Louis was always short of funds, for he believed in paying well for work well done. He dispatched one thousand florins to Yolande's "demoiselle of honor" and the next year, one thousand livres to her governess. He gave five thousand crowns to two of his councilors for their good services in forwarding his marriage. The Chancellor of Savoy pocketed no less than ten thousand of the Dauphin's gold crowns.

8. THE GRATEFUL NEPHEW

(1) On the cold, rainy afternoon of January 17 (1457) Louis Dauphin, at ease in his "retreat," was startled by the appearance of the Duchess of Burgundy and her son Charles, both of them violently agitated. As soon as Louis had cleared the chamber, the Duchess rushed into a woeful tale:

It was the wretched business of the vacant chamberlainship in the household of the Count of Charolais. With permission from his father, Charles had bestowed the office upon the son of the Chancellor Rolin. But the de Croys then went to work, on behalf of Jean de Croy's son, the lord of Sempy. Just now, in the chapel below, after the Duke had heard Mass, he had asked the young Count to show him his household registers. He was disturbed, he explained, by all this fuss over the chamberlainship. "Charles," he said pleasantly, "I wish you to put an end to this strife . . . and I want the lord of Sempy to obtain the vacant place."

"My lord," said Charolais, "you have already given me your promise in the matter. No mention at all was made of the lord of Sempy, and I beg you, my lord, to keep your promise."

"Déa!" exclaimed the Duke. "Let us have no more talk of promises. It is my privilege to give and to take away. And it is my will that the lord of Sempy be settled in the office."

"My lord," Charles exclaimed angrily, "I beg you, pardon me. I am unable to do that. I hold by what you have promised me. I see it well—it is the lord of Croy who has cooked up this plot."

"What? You will disobey me? You refuse to do my bidding?"

"My lord, I will happily obey you, but this I will not do."

"Ha! You dare to cross my will, boy? Get out of my sight!" With that, he cast his son's household registers in the fire.

Philip had turned deadly pale. Then the veins on his forehead swelled with blood and his face flamed a horrible color and he bent on the Count of Charolais so terrible a look that the Duchess of Burgundy feared for her son's life. She seized Charles by the hand and, not daring to say a word to the Duke, thrust him up the aisle. Frantically begging the priest to unlock the chapel door, the Duchess fled with her son to the only refuge they could think of, the chamber of the Dauphin.

Louis had more than one reason to listen to the Duchess's recital with apprehension. Only five or six days before, one of his servants, an astrologer, had whispered in his ear that very soon, he feared, there would be some great, strange mutation in the household of the Duke. Louis had asked if the matter would bring trouble to him. He was told that he was not directly concerned but would suffer a good deal nonetheless. Would it not now be said that everything he touched was blasted? Would not the dangerous guest be blamed for the rift in the household?

Hastily comforting the Duchess and her son, Louis ran down the stairs, knocked on the chapel door and entered. Though he found the old Duke forbiddingly iron-faced, the Dauphin bravely took the plunge, painting a picture of the mother's tearful misery, of the son's fearful penitence, and begging that they be forgiven.

But this disclosure that the family quarrel had been promptly retailed to the heir of France served only to fire the Duke's wrath. Struggling for control, he panted out, "Enough, my lord—pardon me—I beg you to make no such request—I will show Charles that I am his father—that I can appoint a little valet if I please! And better would it have been for his mother, instead of burdening you with her woes, to have slept a long sleep!"

Sinking onto a prayer cushion, Louis clasped his uncle and pleaded with him to pardon the Count of Charolais. "For, if you do not, the mischief will redound on me, and it will be said throughout the world that this is my doing, and in the household of the King they will make much of it, saying that I am only a troublemaker. I am at your mercy; I am in your hands; I have come here to find in you a father and my all in this world. I beg you then, do something for me. . . ." Tears were rolling down his cheeks.

But the old Duke was not to be moved: "My lord, I will not say you nay and your prayers are my commands. If you have this business of Charles so much at heart and want me to pardon him, I will do it then. And you can watch over him and take care of him. But as long as you live and as long as I live, you will never again behold me with your eyes."

Without a word, Louis got to his feet and, still weeping, made his way out of the chapel.

It is Georges Chastellain, that "pearl of historiographers," who reports this scene and the ones to follow. He well knew that princes (especially princes of the House of Burgundy) are grander-passioned than ordinary mortals and must project their greatness in a rhetoric of gesture as well as of pomp. The dialogue is no doubt pitched too high and the Dauphin's responses are given a Burgundian coloring; but if Chastellain soars above the fact, he achieves a psychological realism, mirroring the quarrel as it was seen by the court of Burgundy.

It is a scenario for opera.

Casting his cloak over his face, Louis hastened back to his chamber. His look was enough to tell the Duchess and her son that he had failed. The Duchess withdrew to bewail her lot. Charolais stamped out, flung himself on horseback and rode away to Tendermonde. Rumors were soon running that Philip meant to disinherit his son in favor of his nephew. "Anyone who takes a foot of my land," Charolais muttered sulphurously to his intimates, "will bring an evil hour upon himself."

As Louis was pondering the grotesque behavior of the House of Burgundy, servants of the Duke frantically brought word that their master had disappeared. The bitter January day was drawing to a close. The castle rocked with wailing. Louis hastily summoned a few of his followers, took horse, and set off in search of his uncle. He canvassed townfolk in the streets of Brussels—had anyone seen an elderly man riding toward one of the city gates? Nobody had seen such a man; people recognized the Dauphin and were amazed that he should inquire about a person without naming him. In desperation, Louis sallied out into the countryside, cast along byways, inquired at villages, stopped travelers on the highway—in vain. Night was now coming down, rainy and foggy. Louis, unfamiliar with the land, was forced to turn back.

Spying in the distance a little church dedicated to the Virgin, he made his way there to beg tearfully for her intercession. His men afterward declared that never in the world had so dolorous a lament been heard. When the Dauphin returned to the castle in Brussels, reporting failure in his dejected appearance, the entire establishment from the Duchess to the lowliest groom burst into *roulades* of woe. Louis himself, pacing his chamber, sounded the changes—in a baritone recitative preserved by Chastellain—on the theme that he was the most unfortunate King's son ever born.

Then came the first rift in the mystery: the Duke's valet revealed that after secretly procuring a horse for his master he had carried a message to the de Croys that they should meet the Duke at Hal. Louis arranged for two of his lords, along with the Marshal of Burgundy and a valet, to set out for Hal at four in the morning.

The Dauphin himself was up early, to await news. He invited to breakfast a young knight, Philippe Pot, amusing and ready of tongue, whom he had picked as the man most likely to conjure the Duke's rage. While Louis was coaching Pot in his role, the search party returned from Hal. The Duke was not there but they had word of him: a peasant had brought the de Croys a message "from a gentleman of means" that they were to go about their business.

By this time, the Dauphin's men were beginning to wonder if the whole episode, extravagant and unseemly though it was, had not been arranged by Philip the Good, as one beats the dog before the lion, to let the Dauphin see how his quarrel with his father was really regarded at the Court of Burgundy.

Setting out on his mission, Philippe Pot ran his master to earth next morning at the castle of Genappe. The Duke had had an adventure out of a story book. Riding out of Brussels in a fury, old Philip had taken to the fields and byways in order to confuse his trail and had gradually confused himself. As the night descended, he was wandering like a knight errant of romance through the "great thick trackless forest" of La Soigne. The ways were icy. Four times his horse fell. Philip, gashing his leg on his sword, finally pulled the animal after him. Providentially, he came upon the hut of a peasant who gave him a bite to eat and directed him to the village of Halsenberge, where he spent the night in the lodging of one of his huntsmen.

At Genappe, Philippe Pot found the Duke having his injured leg rubbed. "Good day, my lord, good day," he began cheerfully. "What is all this? Are you acting King Arthur now or Messire Lancelot? What does this mean? Did you think there were not enough Tristans wandering the ways? As I can see, you have not been without adventures."

Pot hit the mark. The Duke laughed and they fell into a joking vein. On returning to Brussels, the Dauphin's envoy was able to report that, provided he was not plagued with entreaties to forgive his son, the Duke of Burgundy would come back in a few days. The Dauphin drew up formal documents, signed by himself and the Countess of Charolais, promising to abide by this condition. Olivier de La Marche, then in the Count of Charolais's household, records the many journeys he made between Brussels and Tendermonde, as the Dauphin carefully assured himself that the Count was properly repentant.

One evening soon after, Louis welcomed an amiable Duke back to Brussels. Not long after that, Philip signified that he was willing to hear what the Dauphin had to say about his son. Taking by the hand the Countess of Charolais, big with child and a favorite of the Duke, Louis presented himself to his host. Philip put himself on his knees. The Countess huddled herself at her father-in-law's feet and burst into tears. Louis vividly enlarged on Charolais's humble penitence until the Duke at last agreed to relent. The Countess covered his feet with kisses.

At once Louis sent for Charolais and brought him into his father's presence. After a little comedy of protests on the part of Duke Philip that the Dauphin should not demean himself to take a hand in the affairs of such humble folk, he let himself be persuaded to forgive his son. "My lord, your prayers are my commands. I will do what it pleases you to order."

"Very well, then," said Louis, "since you wish it that way, I command you."

Thus was the great quarrel appeased, momentarily at least. But the Duke, in his way, attached a condition: two men of his son's household, Guiot d'Usie and an unconventional, adroit personality named Guillaume Bische, whom the Duke regarded as troublemakers, had to be discharged by the Count.

9. THE SQUIRE OF GENAPPE

(1) In April of 1458, Philip of Burgundy was brusquely summoned by his overlord, the King of France, to attend a royal "Bed of Justice" which was to try the Duke of Alençon on a charge of treasonably conspiring with the English. After Louis's feckless godfather had received an English agent while lying naked on a bed and caressing two Barbary goats, he sent an incriminating message by a drunken laborer who betrayed him in a fit of qualms. Philip the Good's bellicose refusal to attend the trial provoked on both sides a flurry of calling up troops; but King Charles then mildly requested that the Duke be represented by an embassy, and the Dauphin, hurrying up to Brussels, was able to persuade his tetchy uncle to take this pacific course. The trial was delayed while royal inquisitors applied torture to Alençon's servants in the hope of implicating the Duke of Burgundy and the Dauphin in the English plot. When no such admissions were forthcoming, the Duke of Alençon, condemned to death, was remitted indefinitely to prison.

(2) Little or no notice has been paid to this seemingly strange name that the Dauphin chose for the infant that, he hoped, would one day become King—a name entirely unknown in the line of the rulers of France. Ardent devotee of the Virgin Mary, Louis apparently named his son for the father of the Virgin, St. Joachim. Information about Joachim derives from an early apocryphal writing, the *Protevange-lium* of James. The veneration of St. Joachim was widespread in the fifteenth century and continues in Catholic tradition (for example, in *The Divine Office* for August 16: Matins, Lesson IV).

10. CREATURE OF CIRCUMSTANCE

(1) Iacomo di Valperga belonged to a prolific and adventurous family which possessed holdings in Savoyard Piedmont. Valpergas, making their various ways, served the Dauphin, the King of France, the Duke of Milan, the House of Savoy. Iacomo had chosen to follow Charles VII, and in 1452, after Charles reduced the Dauphin's father-in-law to submission, the King imposed Iacomo di Valperga as Chancellor of the Duchy of Savoy, much to the discontent of the Savoyards. It did not take the Dauphin long, however, to win the adherence of Iacomo; and the new Chancellor of Savoy soon signed with the Duke of Milan a treaty designed to keep Savoy from completely falling into the French orbit. Consequently, after the Dauphin fled to the Duke of Burgundy, King Charles abandoned Valperga to the wrath of the Savoyards, and Iacomo promptly took refuge with the refugee of Genappe. When, in the late spring of 1460, the Duke of Savoy began a campaign to seize the Valperga lands, Louis mingled his treaty negotiations with ardent demands upon Sforza for military aid on behalf of their mutual friend; but Sforza, threatened by King Charles because of his anti-French policy, felt able to do no more than make representations to the Duke of Savoy and provide in secret a little armed resistance, both of which were useless.

11. HASTY HEART

(1) One day when de Croy and St. Pol happened to appear before the King, Louis took one by the right hand, the other by the left hand, and putting himself between them, joined their hands together willy-nilly. Leading them to an empty chamber, he said, "Now you are going to stay here, and make peace or war just as you please; fight out your causes and your questions as best you can and exchange some blows if you want to; but never are you going to leave until I see you emerge good friends and in accord." Louis then shut the door and stationed two squires before it in order not to let the lords out unless they came forth amicably. After a while, St. Pol and de Croy sheepishly reappeared, arm in arm like two brothers, laughing and thanking the King, and nobody laughed more than Louis. Antoine de Croy then reconciled St. Pol with the Duke of Burgundy so successfully that a few days later the Count and the Duke were bathing together.

(2) Before the end of July (1462) a French army of seven hundred lances and four thousand franc archers under the command of the Count of Foix had crossed the Pyrenees and was pressing southward toward Barcelona. Louis well knew that Spain, a century before, had proved a graveyard for foreign troops; he wanted a quick campaign, Roussillon and Cerdagne in his hands, and his men safely home—as he anxiously reiterated in letters to his captains. By autumn, however, as the King returned to the Loire to pass the winter, he received tidings that the Catalan campaign had suddenly gone awry. Just as the Count of Foix and John II were laying siege to the city of Barcelona, they learned that the hard-pressed Catalans had bestowed their state upon Henry IV of Castile. Then, getting word that a Spanish army was on the march, Foix and his father-in-law hastily withdrew their now-outnumbered troops from Catalonia. At the end of the year, French forces came face to face with the Castilians, but since neither side wished to open hostilities a truce was signed.

Louis realized that, if he were to draw any profit from the expedition, he must close his grip on Roussillon and Cerdagne. By late autumn he had dispatched a fresh army of five thousand men to secure Perpignan, capital of Roussillon. At the same time, he was beginning to work upon the mind of the King of Castile—known to his contemporaries, for more than one reason, as Henry the Impotent. Louis had already taken the precaution of winning the loyalties of Don Juan Pacheco, Marquess of Villena, and the Archbishop of Toledo, who between them controlled the feeble King of Castile. Though a Catalan embassy was urging Henry IV to declare himself King of Aragon and make an end of John II, the Archbishop and the Marquess dissuaded him from this bold step and talked him round to receiving an ambassador from the King of France. Louis, riding rapidly south to keep in close touch with affairs, learned that Perpignan had surrendered on the eve of St. Martin (January 8, 1463). His envoy to Spain and his Spanish friends began pushing Henry IV toward an interview with the King of France.

By the end of January (1463), however, the headlong campaign of King Louis had alarmed the European powers, and the enemies of France were in full cry. An embassy from the Yorkists arrived at the Spanish court to propose an alliance against Louis XI. A legate sent by Pope Pius II, who was bitterly opposed to the Angevin invasion of Naples, worked on Henry IV to accept the English alliance and held out the prospect of bringing in the Italian League. The Catalans exerted pressure on King Henry to ignore the blandishments of the King of France and openly declare himself the King of Aragon. At the same time, conspirators in Roussillon sent secret word that they were ready to massacre all the French in their province.

Louis was well aware of disaffection. Despite the complexities of his diplomacy at this moment, he concerned himself with every detail of the Roussillon occupation. In March he wrote to his Governor of Roussillon, the young Duke of Nemours: ". . . I am sending you a copy of a letter I have just received from the Admiral . . . by which you will see clearly that there is treason being conspired in the town of Perpignan. Therefore, the moment you have read these letters, if you are not at Perpignan go there at once. If the matter is so disposed that you can find out the truth and get to the bottom of this treason . . . see that you immediately put under arrest those who are suspected, and if you find that there is indeed treason, have justice done on all concerned, from the greatest to the least. . . . It seems to me that, to begin with, insufficient provision has been made for safeguarding this place; and therefore give good thought to it, for you are right there and will know what to do. I'm displeased that greater diligence has not been exerted to put all the artillery inside the castle; and therefore, if indeed it is not all within, see to it that you have it put within, without overlooking a single piece—except for the two bombards of the town, which, if they are not already within the castle, I want you to send to Narbonne. Take care that there is no slip-up, and don't delay a day nor an hour.

"I'm sending you Regnault du Chastelet so that you will better believe that I have this matter at heart. Therefore give credence to what he will tell you. Although I have accorded you leave to go home for a while, nevertheless I beg you not to fail me in this need but to remain until the situation is out of danger and until you have everywhere ordered matters so well that no trouble can arise; for, if all things are secure, you can stay at home so much the longer and with the greater ease of heart."

(3) As Louis rode northward in the spring of 1463, he had not given up hopes of drawing a still greater profit from his Spanish triumph. During the arbitral negotiations he had reestablished contact with the leaders of the Catalan revolution; and he knew that his insistence on the Catalans' being confirmed in their privileges if they submitted themselves to the King of Aragon was bound to stimulate those leaders to further communication with him. Abandoned by Henry IV and implacably opposed to John II, Catalonia, just possibly, might now turn to Louis XI.

Not long afterward, a Catalan embassy was besieging him to grant trading privileges and military aid. Though Louis was informed that Catalonia "would rather take the Infidel Turk for lord" than submit to the King of Aragon, he likewise soon became aware that the envoys were sending panicky warnings to their government about French designs on Catalonia. Louis then summoned the embassy to him to make a last play for the prize. He amiably pointed out that it was no marvel if, on receiving a request for military aid, "he wanted to know what language was spoken at Barcelona, for he had been informed that several were spoken. Some people spoke Castilian . . . still other, Aragonese. As for him, he intended to know, whenever he did anything, for whom he was doing it. If in the Principat and the city . . . any language other than Catalan was spoken, he was resolved to hold aloof, since his aid would not benefit the Catalans but the one whose language they used. On the other hand . . . if they spoke only Catalan, then he, who was, on his grandmother's side, truly Catalan [his mother's mother, Yolande of Sicily, was Aragonese], would do what he could for the welfare of Catalonia." This would be very easy, Louis added, "for between the Catalans and him, as everybody knew, *there were no mountains.*" Finally, he urged them to send one of their number home to secure a speedy answer to his interesting question. By the time this envoy arrived in Barcelona in late January (1464), however, he found that the Catalans had already chosen Dom Pedro, Constable of Portugal, as their lord.

This proud people did not realize that, in insisting upon a sovereign who would assure them their liberties, they had elected one who could assure them of little else. When Dom Pedro, hard pressed by the King of Aragon, sent ambassadors to seek aid at the court of France, Louis ordered his Chancellor to answer in pleasant generalities unless the envoys indulged in complaints; in which case, Louis concluded, "You will tell them that I have not impinged on his cause but he has impinged on mine." Louis was still a candidate.

(4) The secular states of Italy had, centuries before, cut themselves loose from the feudal claims of Pope and Emperor. They possessed only what power, what territory, they were able to win by their wits. Venice, Milan, Florence, the Kingdom of Naples jostled each other in the peninsula, their interrelations complicated by that ambiguous spiritual-temporal entity the papal states, and by congeries of minor lordships and quasi-independent towns. In 1454 they had achieved, by the Peace of Lodi, a League General of Italy, headed by the Pope, which brought an uneasy quiet to the peninsula but no lessening of mutual suspicions and perfervid intrigues. This tight competitive network of powers had developed a realism of political activity, a finesse at negotiation, an intensity of diplomacy unknown north of the Alps— but highly congenial to the instincts and the talents of Louis XI.

At some period during his years as Dauphin, Louis had learned to read and speak Italian—an astonishing accomplishment for a King of France and one that signals his abiding interest in Italian affairs. If there is no indication that he read Boccaccio and Petrarch there is abundant evidence provided by foreign envoys that he was a close student of Italian history and Italian statecraft and aware of the intellectual ferment beyond the Alps. Though the French monarchy was traditionally the friend of Florence ° and, briefly at the beginning of the fifteenth century, had enjoyed the sovereignty of Genoa, French intervention in Italy had usually been undertaken by individual princes seeking to augment, with royal aid, their own fortunes. The House of Orléans held the County of Asti in northern Italy and claimed the Duchy of Milan; the House of Anjou had been struggling for more than half a century to make good its title to the Kingdom of Naples.

During the summer of 1461 Louis XI had sent an embassy to Francesco Sforza, Duke of Milan, with whom as Dauphin he had linked himself in the Treaty of Genappe, and to whom he had often expressed his scorn of the Angevins. Now he demanded that the Duke of Milan break his alliance with King Ferrante of Naples, give Duke John his daughter Yppolita, already the fiancée of Ferrante's son, and aid France to regain Genoa, which had driven out the French some months previously.† By the time Louis XI was established at Tours in the autumn of 1461, his embassy had returned with Sforza's refusal of all demands, the Duke explaining with regret that compliance would contravene his obligations to the League of Italy.

During Louis XI's first Christmas season as King, December of 1461, the town of Tours displayed an array of Italian embassies such as had never before been seen in France, or perhaps anywhere else beyond the Alps. Elaborate cavalcades arrived from Venice and Florence and Milan. The Pope was represented by his legate, Jean Jouffroy, Bishop of Arras and soon to be Cardinal. Emissaries had been sent by the

---

° For a vivid account of this traditional friendship, see the instructions given to Angelo Acciaioli, Florentine envoy to France in 1451, in *Dispatches, with Related Documents, of Milanese Ambassadors in France and Burgundy, 1450–83,* ed. by Paul Murray Kendall and Vincent Ilardi, 1970, I.

† Having taken possession of Genoa in 1458, in the name of Charles VII, Duke John had used it as a base to launch his invasion of Naples the following year. Early in 1461 the Genoese, with the covert help of Francesco Sforza, had driven out the French except for the garrison besieged in the citadel. A relief expedition led by King René had failed ingloriously to recover the city.

Neapolitan Prince of Taranto, by two famous *condottieri*, Bartholomeo Colleoni and Jacopo Piccinino, by Sigismund Malatesta, the diabolical and cultured lord of Rimini, even by Count Everso of Anguillaria, a minor baron of the Papal States. Ostensibly dispatched to congratulate the King of France upon his accession, these missions represented the anxiety of Italy regarding the intentions of a trans-Alpine ruler who appreciated both the intellectual accomplishments and political instability of the peninsula and who had announced his support of Angevin ambitions.

The embassy from Florence Louis treated as though they represented a power of the first rank. In private talks he warmly reiterated his admiration for this town-of-all-the-talents, ruled by sagacious old Cosimo de' Medici, at the same time that he urged the Florentines to preach the cause of Anjou to the Duke of Milan. The ambassadors of the mighty Republic of Venice did not fare so well. They pressed the King to support a crusade against the Turks, now threatening the Venetian domination of the eastern Mediterranean, but they had nothing to offer in return. Venice, they announced coolly, preferred to remain neutral as regards the struggle for the possession of the Kingdom of Naples. In response to Louis's increasing irritation, the ambassadors, with typical Venetian *sang-froid*, cut short their sojourn and made for home. After they had departed Louis made no secret of the fact that, as far as he was concerned, *Venetian* was synonymous with *villain*.

Louis lived a life of maneuver, and it was impossible to maneuver against monolithic self-interest backed by an utter conviction of superiority. The Venetian merchant-aristocracy, eschewing the political factions that shook other states, like Genoa, was implacably devoted to the advancement of the Republic. An admirer of Italian civilization, the King of France shared that general Italian prejudice toward Venice which is nowhere more vividly expressed than in the memoirs (*Commentaries*) of Pius II: "As among brute beasts aquatic creatures have the least intelligence, so among human beings Venetians are the least just and the least capable of humanity. . . . They please only themselves and while they talk they listen to and admire themselves. When they speak they think themselves Sirens. . . . They wish to appear Christian before the world but in reality they never think of God and, except for the state, which they regard as a deity, they hold nothing sacred. . . . The Venetians aim at the dominion of Italy and all but dare aspire to the mastery of the world."

At the end of 1463, Louis received another ambassador from Venice, likewise commissioned to spur the King of France to support a crusade. Nicolò Canale turned out to be a nonpareil of arrogance and brashness—qualities which, some years later when he commanded a Venetian fleet, caused him and his countrymen to lose a sea battle to the Turks. Though Louis on one occasion administered him such a dressing-down on the subject of Venetian insolence that, on emerging from the royal chamber, "he looked like a dead man," and though he was soon given his *congé*, he lingered in France for weeks, prying into the affairs of the kingdom without bothering to conceal such undiplomatic activity.

In May of 1464, King Louis, then at Paris, interrupted a conversation with the Milanese envoy, Alberico Maletta, to exclaim—"Look, Dom Alberico, what manner of men these Venetians are! This ambassador was twice given leave to depart three months ago, and yet he still insists on remaining in my kingdom despite me, though he has no business here. I fear me, to tell you a secret, that he may have some thought of having me poisoned. You know that every evening I go out for dinner in the town with my people, and he has been to dine in the home of Messire Jean Arnoulfin of Lucca, my Receiver General of Normandy, where I am going to dine this coming Sunday. I have no fear, you understand, of Dom Jean, but this ambassador might conspire with some of his servants and pop me something in my soup or have me killed in another way; for I am of the firm opinion that the greatest treason would seem a small matter to the Venetians. . . ." When Maletta "tried to excuse Dom Nicolò a little," Louis cut him short with "Say no more!"

Canale departed a few days later, much to the relief of Maletta, who feared that he might provoke a "scandal" that would compromise all Italians. When Alberico reported to His Majesty that, according to advices reaching Milan, the Turk was preparing a new attack upon the Venetian empire, Louis merely commented, "Would it be a catastrophe if the Turks gave them a good beating?" The Duke of Milan was apprehensive, Maletta answered, that unless the Venetians had help they would perhaps make peace with the Ottomans. Louis broke into a laugh: "This I believe, indeed!" More than a decade would pass before he was willing to come to terms with Venice.

It was upon the Milanese ambassadors Pietro de Pusterla and Tommaso da Rieti—both of whom he had met when Dauphin—that Louis XI in this Christmas season of 1461 concentrated his diplomatic campaign in favor of the House of Anjou. Brushing aside Sforza's excuse for not aiding the French, Louis vividly threatened and cajoled the Duke of Milan's envoys. He roundly declared that if Sforza persisted in his refusal the King of France would repute him an enemy, for "*si quis mecum non est, contra me est*" (he who is not for me is against me). A moment later he was earnestly assuring Pusterla, "Petro, I love the Duke of Milan as myself . . . and I want nothing else from him—in Italy I seek no lands nor castles nor even a clod of earth—except my lady Yppolita for my cousin [Duke John]." One day, using the familiar *tu*, he regretfully informed Pietro de Pusterla, "If the Duke of Milan refuses my friendship, I must make war upon him . . . but only to force him to withdraw his aid from King Ferrante." Then suddenly Louis made a startling observation: "I tell you this—when I obtain Genoa, I intend to leave the government of the city to the Duke of Milan, keeping for myself only the overlordship." The King knew that Sforza had long coveted possession of Genoa, which was as inept at governing itself as it was brilliant in its seamanship and commerce. He also knew that the Duke would recognize a genuine hint.

When Louis XI rode south from Tours in early January (1462), he was accompanied by the Milanese embassy, who were awaiting fresh instructions. It was March 19 and he was at Bordeaux when the ambassadors informed him that they had at last had a reply from their master. Louis received them in state, surrounded by Angevins—Duke John's uncle, the Count of Maine; Duke John's son, the Marquess of Pont; and Jean Cossa, King René's Seneschal of Provence. They reported that the Duke of Milan was forced by his obligation to the Italian League to support King Ferrante. As for Genoa, though the Treaty of Genappe did not apply to that situation, he would do there what he could for the King. Louis replied coldly that he had already learned of Sforza's intransigence from his ambassador to Rome. He summarily rejected Sforza's reasons for not breaking with King Ferrante. Though the Duke of Milan's offers regarding Genoa amounted to little or nothing, the King of France accepted and appreciated them, especially since they were made by such a prince as the Duke of Milan, a far greater lord than he himself, who was but a poor man. [The ambassadors thought it best to inform their master that this was said ironically.] Shifting to a casual tone, Louis remarked that though the Duke was not willing to give him a place in paradise, nonetheless he believed that he would find himself a place in hell. Things being thus, the ambassadors might as well go home.

Louis then indulged himself by creating a small comedy. He had not failed to note that Pietro de Pusterla and Tommaso da Rieti were mutually jealous.

At the conclusion of the same interview, Louis strolled to a window and beckoned Tommaso da Rieti to him. He had already perceived the pompous Rieti's jealousy of Pietro de Pusterla and he could not resist creating a little comedy out of the materials which had been thrown in his way. Two days before, when Rieti had paid his respects to the King upon his return from a journey to the court of Burgundy, Louis indicated that the embassy had not done at all well without him. In a confidential tone he revealed that the royal council had even decided to license the departure of the Milanese, and he allowed Rieti to assume that any signs of irritation on the part of the King had been the fault of Rieti's colleagues. Now, with the other ambassadors looking on—but out of earshot—Louis proceeded to develop his little drama. "Even though I know you are not a friend of the House of France," he began, "you are more pleasing to me than any other Italian I have ever known." If Louis had made much of Pusterla in Rieti's absence, "I did it in order not to seem ungrateful for the welcome given my envoys at Milan." He then murmured to the ambassador that—so he understood—Rieti was disliked by the Duchess of Milan because he was not a native Lombard. Why not accept a good pension, then, and high office from the King of France? If Rieti preferred to live in Italy, Duke John would provide him with an estate in the Kingdom of Naples. Rieti had the prudence, as probably the King expected, to decline this kind offer.

Next day Louis finished off his comedy. Summoning Pietro alone, he once again urged the marriage of Yppolita and Duke John. Then he became very confidential. "I will speak to you as a gentleman most faithful to your lord and dear to me. I beg you to keep this secret. You saw the attentions I paid yesterday to Messer Tommaso. . . . The Angevins have asked me to make much of him because he has . . . reconciled himself with King René and has offered to induce the Duke of Milan to do my will since he understands just where the Duke holds his feet." The Milanese embassy, confused and divided, busied itself with false trails. While Pietro and the other ambassadors were writing to their master that they suspected Tommaso of holding secret negotiations with the Angevins, Rieti was reporting that difficulties with the King of France were entirely due to the ineptitude of his colleagues.

Having thus quite shamelessly amused himself by demonstrating to Francesco Sforza that even Sforza-trained diplomats are not immune to leg-pulling, the King finally opened his mind, through Pietro, to the Duke of Milan. The Duke, he declared, "has not his peer among Christians nor Saracens, and so, believe me, it will displease me if I am driven to doing anything he may not like—nor will I come to this if he does not offend me in the matter of Genoa." Thus Louis let Francesco Sforza know that he was prepared to accept the defeat of the Angevins in the Kingdom of Naples.

(5) On Christmas morning after Mass, Louis knighted the two sons of Sforza's envoy; and then with an indifference to protocol which embarrassed the Milanese—and which was soon reported in princely circles—Louis twice beckoned Alberico to pass in front of his brother, Charles, Duke of Berry, and the Count of Foix's son the Prince of Navarre, and drew him into the royal chamber ahead of the others so that they could converse apart. "There by the fire," Louis discussed Anglo-Burgundian affairs with Alberico, questioned him about the latest movements of the Turk—"for he wanted the complete picture"—explored King Ferrante's situation in the Kingdom of Naples so knowingly that, Maletta reported, "you would think, from his thorough understanding of Italian affairs, this King had been reared in Italy." Finally, dismissing the lords in his chamber, Louis insisted that Alberico remain while he held council with three of his intimate advisers.

By the conclusion of this session, the King had hit on a little stratagem, of no utility but offering excellent prospects of comedy. He proposed that, that afternoon when Georges Havart and Admiral Montauban were consulting with envoys from the King of Castile, Dom Alberico should break into the meeting, and, under pretense of demanding the infeudation papers, underline the opportunities accruing to the King of France by his alliance with the Duke of Milan. Maletta replied, "Say no more, Sacred Majesty! Leave the business to me!" Alberico played his part to the hilt. Forcing his way into the chamber, he declared before the startled Spanish ambassadors that, by Heaven, he must have the papers signed that very evening. "And I began to talk about the advantages which the King had won through this enfeoffment, and I said that he had secured the support of Naples. The Admiral broke in, laughing, 'We do not want to know anything of this.' An amazed Spaniard cried, 'King Ferrante is our great friend!'" Maletta replied that he was equally a friend of the Duke of Milan and what the Duke would do for the King, King Ferrante would also do. Maletta's fellow conspirator afterward told him that he had been a great success. It would not be surprising if Louis had been listening at the door.

(6) Francesco Sforza's tie with Florence not only brought together the most astute statesmen of the Italian peninsula, himself and Cosimo de' Medici, but united two states harboring that efflorescence of civilization which a little later would be called the Renaissance. Though Cosimo's grandson Lorenzo was but a boy (later, Lorenzo the Magnificent), Leonardo da Vinci only ten years old (in 1462), and Michelangelo and Machiavelli yet unborn, the fire of the New Learning was already at full blaze; and if old Cosimo, emperor of patrons, had gathered around him an unrivaled array of scholars and writers, Francesco Sforza brilliantly represented that new ideal, the cultured prince—*l'uomo universale* as ruler.

Sforza's precocious and handsome children, tutored by famous humanists, were reared to fulfill the high expectations of the age. His eldest son, Galeazzo-Maria (who would later reveal that the best of educations cannot redeem a flawed nature), at the age of fifteen was praised by the humanist who sat on St. Peter's Throne, Pius II, as showing in "his character, eloquence, and ability . . . a wisdom greater than that of a grown man. . . . His extemporaneous speeches could hardly have been equaled by another after long preparation." Sforza's beautiful daughter Yppolita, affianced to Ferrante's son, delivered before Pius "a speech . . . in such elegant Latin that all present were lost in wonder and admiration." (It appears that the speech was not the work of her tutors but of her own composition; it was sufficiently admired to be written down for preservation and it is extant.)

Pius II treats Francesco Sforza, in his *Commentaries*, with a respect he yields to no other contemporary ruler (except himself). He describes the arrival at the papal Congress of Mantua (1459) of this "prince celebrated alike in peace and war. He sat his horse like a young man (he was then sixty); he was very tall and bore himself with great dignity; his expression was serious, his way of speaking quiet, his manner gracious, his character in general such as became a prince. He appeared the only man of our time whom Fortune loved. He had great physical and intellectual gifts. There was nothing he greatly desired which he did not obtain. . . . A crowd came out of the city to see this famous Duke. . . . When he entered . . . men everywhere were heard saying, 'See how . . . exalted is the . . . majesty of the Bishop of Rome when so great a prince has come to kiss his feet!'" (In stating that Fortune loved the Duke, the Pope is not denigrating Sforza's abilities but admiring his felicity. Pius himself had respect for luck: when, fallen ill of the pest at Bâle, he discovered "that there were two celebrated doctors in the city, one . . . learned but unlucky, the other lucky but ignorant, [he] preferred luck to learning—reflecting that no one really knew the proper treatment for the plague.")

(7) At the conference George Neville and his fellow envoys had proved stubborn, demanding that before talks proceeded the King of France must agree to abandon the cause of Lancaster.

The backs of the English ambassadors had been stiffened by an unfortunate intrusion, which, the Duke of Burgundy wrote to the King, he had done everything he could to prevent.

Like one of the fierce goddesses who descended to the ringing plains of Troy to disrupt the affairs of men, the indomitable Margaret of Anjou had sailed from Scotland to Sluys in order to break up the St. Omer conference, which spelled the doom of her cause. Penniless, depending on Pierre de Brezé for the bread she ate, she ignored Philip of Burgundy's attempts to head her off; and, playing her romantic role to the hilt, she costumed herself like "a village woman" and jolted in a humble cart to meet the Duke, accompanied by the faithful Brezé.

When Philip intercepted her at St. Pol, she cast herself into his arms and overwhelmed him with her woes and her pleas. The chivalric Duke honored her at a banquet that night and did his best to smooth her feathers; but he let it be known that he would do nothing to disturb the conference. Hastily departing early the next morning, he sent back, when at a safe distance, presents of money and jewels; and Margaret of Anjou's enterprise fizzled out at Bruges a few days later in an intricate debate with the Count of Charolais as to whether she or he should wash first before dinner.

Now ensconced at Hesdin, the King counted on dealing with the English in person, but they brusquely refused to present themselves to the man calling himself king of their Continental domain.

Louis was not to be put off. With the aid of his uncle Philip, always a prince of hosts, a little stratagem was arranged. On Monday morning, October 3 (1463), when the English appeared at Hesdin on a courtesy call, the amicable Duke of Burgundy, remarking that only a door separated them from the King and mere politeness dictated a greeting, took Chancellor George Neville firmly by the hand and led the party into an adjoining chamber, where Louis was waiting. The King stood on his dignity, momentarily. He gravely informed his uncle that he was pleased to participate in these Anglo-Burgundian negotiations—at the Duke's request; he wanted people throughout history to know that he was under obligation to do whatever the Duke asked. Then, however, Louis quickly advanced among the envoys, took them by the hand, greeted them like old acquaintances. Warwick's brother, the Chancellor, improvised a little speech in Latin. Louis praised his rhetoric and fell into an easy, familiar chat with Neville's colleagues. He particularly wanted to know about young Edward IV, throwing out many questions and listening with absorbed interest to the answers. He said frankly that he wished their King nothing but good, even though Edward was enemy to Louis's own cousin Henry VI. Before King Edward— who was indeed a "gentil prince"—had climbed to his present height, the two of them, Edward and he, had been comrades in the same cause. Now that Edward's fortune had changed, Louis was not at all sure if the King of England wished to continue their friendship. For his own part, he wanted nothing more than a good understanding with the English. He let his tongue wag so far as to offer to help chastise the turbulent Scots (a statement which much disturbed the traditional allies of France when the English reported it). As for his support of the House of Lancaster, with a smile and a wave of his hand Louis suggested that there would be no trouble about that. Warwick's brother and followers departed from Hesdin in high good humor and ready to resume negotiations.

(8) Louis informed his treasurer, Étienne Chevalier, that he and the King's confidential secretary, Jean Bourré, and Admiral Montauban must raise 200,000 crowns forthwith and deliver them to the Duke of Burgundy as first payment on the recovery of Picardy and the Somme towns. Chevalier, staggered by this casual command, protested that the thing was impossible. Louis merely repeated his instructions.

"It seems to me," the Treasurer wrote hastily to Bourré, who was at the moment on holiday, "that the recovery of these pledged lands and the business of the truce [with the English] are the two greatest matters of this realm, and matters which most concern the King's hopes. Nevertheless, he has dispatched my Lord the Admiral and me so offhandedly and with such little deliberation that we have hardly had time to snatch up our riding leggings; and he has told me that since there is plenty of money about, he knows well that you will not fail him and that you will lend him what you have and also that we will find people in Paris who will lend to us; and, to be brief, this is all that I have been able to draw from him." Chevalier added, "We will have to use our five natural senses because we must be in Paris as soon as we can."

(9) Though the Duke of Burgundy promised to remain at Hesdin, as the King had requested, Louis decided that he would do well to keep his uncle supplied with entertainment. Therefore about mid-July he sent Queen Charlotte and all her household to visit the Duke. He gave further *éclat* to the occasion by putting the expedition in the charge of Charles, Count of Eu, Peer of France, assisted by Louis, lord of Crussol, who, having shared the Dauphin's five years of exile at Genappe, was well versed in all the ways of the Court of Burgundy. Louis gave strict instructions to the party to spend but two nights with the Duke and without fail to set forth on the morning of the third day. Doubtless he calculated that such a limitation would give Philip further opportunity to indulge his chivalresque humor.

The Queen and her train of lords and ladies entered Hesdin after Vespers on a Sunday. From then until late Tuesday Duke Philip's wonderful castle burgeoned in all the entertainments that the ingenious court of Burgundy could devise. In the evening there was dancing until midnight in the great hall, presided over by the Queen "to adorn the feast." The Duke sat at her right hand and at her left, the Dowager Duchess of Bourbon, his gay sister. At the Queen's feet King Louis's lovely sister Yolande, Princess of Piedmont, reclined on a pillow draped in cloth of gold. Below her sat Charles VII's bastard daughter by Agnès Sorel, Charlotte, now married to Pierre de Brezé's son Jacques. Between the Queen and the Duke of Burgundy kneeled that witty gentleman Philippe Pot, who kept a lively conversation going between his master and the Queen. Queen Charlotte's two sisters, Bona and Marie, lent their beauty to the dance, and the Duke of Burgundy had no end of courtiers to appreciate them. The ladies and gentlemen enjoyed themselves so much they danced themselves out of breath, and a wife of one of the Queen's Masters of the Household wounded at least a dozen Burgundians in the heart by her grace and charm. The Queen herself declared that never in her life had she had such a good time but it would cost her very dear for she would be remembering it seven years after. The Princess of Piedmont did not hesitate to say that the thought of leaving such hospitality made her die of annoyance, and the other ladies loudly sang the same tune.

Doubtless Louis would have enjoyed the conversation which occurred late Monday, the last night. When the Queen explained that she must depart in the morning, the Duke of Burgundy smiled and said, "Madam, it's much too late to talk about leaving in the morning. Departing is simply too dull to talk about, and this is the time for festivity. If God pleases you will rise tomorrow morning and dine, and then we will see what the time brings us."

"By my faith, good uncle," the Queen answered in alarm, "you must pardon me. Our departure is all arranged. The King has given his commands and for nothing in the world would I dare disobey his order."

"Madam, my Lord has sent you here and has done me this honor. It is my hope that he trusts me to see to your welfare. A day more or less, between him and me, will not get you into trouble with your lord." Though the Count of Eu and the lord of Crussol—the latter trembling with fear as he fell on his knees before his host —protested that they must without fail leave in the morning, the smiling Duke merely repeated that after the Queen had dined on the morrow then would be time to talk about departing.

Needless to say, after dinner on Tuesday Philip refused to bid his guests farewell. With mock severity he commissioned his nephew Adolf de Clèves as gatekeeper to see that nobody left without his permission.

The Princess of Piedmont and the other ladies laughed with joy but the anxious lord of Crussol pointed out that if the Queen did not leave that day, Tuesday, she could not set out until Thursday, for Wednesday was the unlucky Day of the Innocents. Philip replied casually that in the morning they would talk about it. As for not setting out because of the Innocents, that didn't apply to ladies for they were a law unto themselves. In the end, the Queen and her ladies did not depart until Thursday after dinner, conveyed out of the town by the triumphant Duke.

Next King Louis dispatched a son of the Duke of Savoy, who happened to be titular King of Cyprus, and this modest young man was so awed by the splendor of his uncle, the Grand Duke of the West, that his alarmed efforts to prevent Philip the Good from treating him like a king provided a pleasant interlude for the whole court.

Finally, at the end of the first week in August there appeared at Hesdin, likewise sent by the King of France, a figure curious enough to provide Duke Philip and his court with gossip for a month. This was King Louis's father-in-law, Louis, Duke of Savoy. His mode of travel was so unusual that crowds of people lined the streets of Hesdin to watch him pass as he was conducted to the castle by the Duke and a great train of Burgundian lords. Borne aloft on sweating shoulders, the Duke of Savoy sat in a chair of blue velvet covered by a canopy of blue velvet fringed with gold and silk. His helpless mound of flesh was clad in a long robe furred with marten and he wore around his neck a great collar of gold garnished with precious stones. He looked, Chastellain reports, like somebody who was coming from a country long lost. Afflicted with gout and other diseases which were the result of a long dissolute life, he retained vestiges of his youthful good looks and was considered to be an entertaining talker. Chastellain thought that if Boccaccio were still living he would certainly have made a place for the Duke of Savoy among his circle of story tellers.

A full twenty-five days Duke Louis remained at Hesdin, all his expenses paid by the Duke of Burgundy. He spent the entire time on his couch or in his chair. He dined at eight or nine o'clock in the morning and then went back to sleep, "entirely naked"; he woke again in the mid-afternoon to eat and drink and once more went back to sleep; and after he had roused himself to sup, he again returned to his couch. This mode of life furnished the Burgundian court with endless topics of conversation. By the time he departed from Hesdin, autumn was in the air. Thus did King Louis make sure that his uncle remained contentedly at Hesdin to await the arrival of the Earl of Warwick.

12. A PRIDE OF PRINCES

(1) King Louis would probably have got little profit from meeting Aeneas Sylvius Piccolomini, who took the title of Pius II in honor of the pagan Vergil's "pius Aeneas," but the collision of these two intricate and imperious personalities could hardly have failed to edify posterity. With his jutting features and bold eyes, Aeneas Sylvius, university-trained humanist, rose in the world on the wings of his eloquent voice and facile pen. By the time he ascended the Chair of St. Peter in 1458, he was famous all over Europe as poet, novelist, historian, propagandist, diplomat. Pius II enacted simultaneously the roles of an adroit politician, an illustrious Pope condemned to struggle with a Christendom unworthy of its pastor, and a sophisticated sensibility which went so far, it would seem, as to create cultivated experiences, like a picnic against the Roman ruins of Tivoli or an archeological expedition, in order to leave posterity a record of them in the Pope's memoirs.

He had backed King Ferrante against the House of Anjou because, like Francesco Sforza, he wanted to keep the French out of Italy. He had perpetuated the old papal abuses, sale of offices and even of expectation of offices, in order to finance his wars against rebellious barons. Finally, when, true to his sense of himself as a master propagandist, he sought to reassert the ancient supremacy of the papacy by heading a crusade against the Turk, he discovered that he lacked the moral authority to shake the self-interest of the princes of the West.

Though he fell mortally ill in the early summer of 1464, that magnificent old actor played out his scenario to the end. He had himself borne to the Adriatic port of Ancona, where thousands of humble crusaders—and no princes—awaited him. He died there on August 14 (1464). The citizens of the town had so little enthusiasm for the crusade that they carried through the streets biers with corpses of straw so that Ancona would look like a plague-stricken city to be avoided.

(2) Louis thought it a good idea to stage a little scene for the benefit of the Duke of Burgundy. On Friday, the last day of August, after he had returned from hunting and eaten his dinner in the usual mean lodging in a village, he sent for his brother, Charles, and Jean de Croy and Alberico Maletta. Louis began weightily, "You, my Lord of Berry, are my brother, and you, my Lord of Croy, are my companion and true friend, and you, Dom Alberico, are the ambassador of the Duke of Milan, whom I hold to be my good father and good brother, and also you are a faithful counselor to me. I have something to tell you of great import, but first I want to give audience to an English envoy in your presence."

It turned out that this man had come only to make a complaint about French piracy, which Louis promised to attend to himself. What he wanted to convey to his listeners was the style of the ambassador's letter of credence, which had been made out by the Earl of Warwick's brother George, Chancellor of England. It ran: "To the Most Serene King of the French"; and as he read it out, Louis remarked, "The English write me King of the French, but never were they willing to give that title to my father."

Louis then outlined the whole course of his quarrel with the Duke of Brittany and defended the position he had taken. Touching on the scandalous letters which the Duke had disseminated, he answered all of Francis' accusations and brought the subject around to the Duke of Burgundy, who had likewise received a missive from Brittany. He said that he was more obligated to his uncle than to his own father; if he did not have confidence in him, he would not have gone to Hesdin so many times and put himself in the Duke's power. Indeed, here he was now, lodged in this village, no more than six leagues distant from the Duke of Burgundy, who, if he wished, could come very easily and take him in his bed. "And if he had thought of giving Normady or Guienne to the English, the Duke would have reason indeed to do him every injury and shame; but the Duke knew very well that he had no desire to allow the title of the Crown of France to be lost as some of his predecessors had lost it. . . ." As for his alleged hostility to the other princes, for example the Duke of Bourbon, Bourbon was his brother-in-law, and one of Bourbon's sisters had married into the blood royal of the House of Orléans; therefore he would never seek the ruin of the Bourbons. After elaborating this point, Louis concluded, "I have wanted you, my brother, and you, my *compère* [de Croy], and you, Dom Alberico, to understand the evil attitude of this neighbor of mine [the Duke of Brittany] and also my own justification, which I am every day more intent upon making clear." De Croy then rode back to report to the Duke of Burgundy.

(3) It seems probable that Louis was telling the truth. Even Chastellain goes no further than to insinuate that the Bastard's actions were "suspicious." Alberico Maletta believed the King's story; and, rash though Louis could be, it is hardly conceivable that he would send the Bastard on a mission which could at once discredit him and plunge him into immediate war. The fact that the Count of Charolais, in all the propaganda he spread later against the King, never declared that Rubempré had sought to kill or capture him, can be taken as an indication of the King's innocence. Louis's error, it appears, lay in choosing an overbold adventurer who perhaps had in mind attempting some sensational *coup* of his own.

(4) Neville found King Louis's Provost-Marshal, Tristan l'Hermite, "the most driving, lively, and subtle intelligence in the kingdom"; and before Warwick's secretary quite realized what was happening, he had poured into Tristan's ear everything he knew about the difficulties in England between King Edward and the Earl of Warwick. Then a secret friend of the English bade Neville be on his guard against the Provost-Marshal. Shaken by this warning, Warwick's secretary sent an urgent dispatch to Richard Whetehill at Calais: if Tristan l'Hermite came to the port, he should be carefully watched, for his eyes missed nothing, he could even read people's minds, and everything he learned he immediately reported to King Louis. To tell the truth, concluded Neville, "he is a terrible man." Yet Louis and his Provost-Marshal had cast such a spell that, even after being put on his guard, Warwick's secretary saw no reason to alter his estimate of the might of the King of France.

(5) As if all the world perceived that the arrival of the King's embassy at the Burgundian court marked an ominous new stage in the growing rivalry between the House of Burgundy and the House of France, the event was intensively reported: a *procès-verbal* of the ducal audience was drawn up; Chastellain recounted the affair in his lofty prose; the Burgundian du Clercq and other chroniclers gave every detail they could come by. There was yet another witness, one whose very presence on the scene creates a special glow of interest. Only three or four days before the ambassadors arrived, there came riding to the Burgundian court at Lille a young man of about eighteen—"at the age of being able to handle a horse"—with long flat cheeks and steady eyes. His father, who had died when the boy was about seven, had made himself one of the great figures at the ducal court, being a member of the Toison d'Or and holding the office of Bailli of Flanders; and the Duke of Burgundy himself had served as godfather to the child. Trained in arms and knightly courtesy, rather than—to his regret—in the liberal arts, the young lord of Renescure, Philippe de Commynes, appeared at Lille to begin his courtly career as an equerry in the household of the Count of Charolais. It is no wonder that, writing his memoirs many years later, he vividly remembered this first great scene of state which unfolded before his eyes.

On Tuesday, November 5, the Duke of Burgundy and the Count of Charolais, surrounded by their chief courtiers and councilors, gave ear to the royal embassy in a large hall overflowing with spectators. The Chancellor of France opened the proceedings with a blunt attack upon the conduct of the House of Burgundy. After explaining the true mission of the Bastard of Rubempré, Morvilliers asserted that the Count of Charolais had had no cause to arrest this royal servant. The so-called suspicions of the Count could not be justified. Perhaps, the Chancellor suggested sarcastically, he had acted in this way because the King had taken away his pension—

Old Philip of Burgundy interrupted, in a somewhat frivolous vein. The Bastard had been arrested, the Duke declared, because of his very strange movements. Now, if the Count of Charolais was suspicious by nature, he certainly did not inherit that quality from his father, for he had never been suspicious; but he must have got it from his mother, "who was the most suspicious lady that he had ever known. . . ." Notwithstanding, then, that the Duke himself was of quite a different temperament, he would certainly in the circumstances have arrested the Bastard.

The Chancellor took up the cudgels again and this time belabored the Duke himself. Philip of Burgundy had promised not to leave Hesdin without sending word to the King. "Yet you hurriedly set off next morning and thus you acted just like my Lord of Charolais, for you gave all the appearance of being afraid that the King might have you seized if you remained there another minute, which conduct sounds very strange to His Majesty, who never thought of such a thing and who was amazed that you could have such suspicions of him when he has honored you before all living men—"

Again the Duke interrupted, "looking a little troubled." He said loudly, "I want everyone to know that I have never made a promise to a living man that I have not kept to the best of my ability." Then he began to laugh. "I never break my word—except to the ladies." He added that he had left Hesdin, in broad daylight and without haste, simply because he had pressing business elsewhere and knew that the Earl of Warwick was not coming.

After the Chancellor had resumed with a scathing denunciation of the Duke of Brittany, he turned his attention to the Count of Charolais, accusing him of leaguing himself with Francis II and made the charge "so enormous, so criminal that there was nothing shameful and vituperative that he failed to say against the Count." In a fury Charolais tried to interrupt, but the Chancellor pointed a finger at him and cried, "My Lord of Charolais, I have not come to speak to you but to your father!" Though Charolais begged the Duke to let him reply then and there, Philip remarked calmly, "I have replied for you as I think a father should answer for his son; but since you are so hot about it, take thought today and tomorrow say what you will."

It was, in fact, two days later, on Thursday, November 8, that the Count of Charolais, sinking his knee upon a square of black velvet, declared passionately that he knew nothing of Rouville's mission. He had arrested the Bastard only because of his suspicious behavior, and had never disseminated slander against the King. His alliance with the Duke of Brittany was the innocuous friendship of two lords who had sworn to be brothers-in-arms. The King of France, he asserted in a tone of injured righteousness, should desire such concord among the princes, for then he would not have to seek foreign alliances. As for the stoppage of his pension, he had not asked for it in the first place, did not need it, and was untroubled by the King's withdrawal of it. Finally, though King Louis had said publicly he regarded the Count of Charolais as an enemy and had supported Charolais's foe, the Count of Nevers, against him, Charolais solemnly averred that he would never be hostile to the King of France and begged his father not to believe any of these unjust charges.

On the following day, Friday, November 9, the prolonged audience was brought to a close. The weather of the Duke's humor had shifted slightly to the northeast. When one of the Burgundian courtiers began proudly naming all the lands that the Duke held outside the realm of France, the belligerent Chancellor snapped that he might be lord of these territories but he was not a king. Duke Philip suddenly spoke up—"I want everybody to know," he declared with great formality, "that if I had wished it, I would have been a king." Philip then went on with some complaints of his own: during the negotiations for the repurchase of the Somme towns, the King had certainly suggested that Philip was to enjoy these lordships during his lifetime, but the moment the money was paid and the quittance given, the Duke found himself bereft of all authority; and whereas he had carried out so scrupulously the provisions of the Treaty of Arras, his nephew had not fulfilled all the articles to the letter. He then declared that he hoped King Louis would believe no evil of him or his son. Since the King had sent three ambassadors, he himself would reply through the mouths of three ambassadors. With that he motioned for wine and spices to be brought, ceremonial of dismissal.

When the embassy had returned to Nogent-le-Roi, the Archbishop of Narbonne had a special message for the King, and it was one that Louis did not forget. Of those who recorded the audience, only that acute young squire Philippe de Commynes noticed a bitter by-play which took place as the envoys were departing from the hall. It is he who preserved for posterity the acrid threat uttered by the Count of Charolais.

(6) Only the Italian states, warily competing for power and combining and recombining in uneasy alliances, as yet employed the system of resident embassies which would become the dominant feature of international statecraft in succeeding centuries. During the first years of his reign King Louis had no opportunity to make formal trial of the new diplomacy. Though Francesco Sforza offered (in 1464) to accredit a permanent representative at the French court, Louis knew that the House of Orléans and the House of Anjou, both enemies of Sforza, would regard the arrangement as a mortal affront. He hastened to tell Maletta, "I want you to write to your lord and explain that the custom of France is not like that of Italy. Here, to maintain a resident ambassador is not a sign of affection but a matter of suspicion. In Italy, of course, it is the reverse. Write your lord that there is no need for him to send another ambassador now. When something happens, let him dispatch Manuel [Emanuel de Iacoppo] or another, as he prefers, just so that his embassies come and go and do not remain here permanently." Yet, King Louis was to keep Milanese envoys at his court for two decades: at bottom, they were his own kind, professional men of state, and he enjoyed sharpening his mind against their agile, wary intellects.

If at this moment Louis could not accept a resident embassy, he saw no reason why he should not send one. He informed Maletta that he had decided to commission my lord of Gaucourt to remain in Milan "so that all the world might understand the union between the House of France" and Francesco Sforza. But, on receiving this news, the Duke of Milan in alarm ordered his ambassador to see "that the King abandons this idea. We say that we do not care for this because it will give umbrage to the Pope, to the Venetians, and to others. . . ." Even the Italians were suspicious of their new diplomatic techniques, except when used among themselves.

13. THE LEAGUE OF THE PUBLIC WEAL

(1) Giovanni Pietro Panigarola, a member of an old Milan family—the Panigarola house is still standing—had come into France in 1464 on private business. He was well known to his Duke, for whom apparently he had done some services; and he had appeared at court and several times spoken with the King of France. Maletta seized on him in mid-March for a post that had now become highly dangerous—what would happen to a Milanese ambassador if Duke John got his hands on him?—and would require stamina as well as ability. Panigarola, Maletta reported to his master, was "young, intelligent, and vigorous," a man of some diplomatic experience and entirely acceptable to the King. Jean Pierre embraced his mission with zeal: "If I should lose my life, I will remain here," he assured Dom Alberico. At Saumur, he quickly got a taste of Angevin prejudices—"when the Angevins see me, they act as if they were looking at the enemy of the human race."

(2) "When we arrived . . . His Majesty immediately led me into the bastions where stood the bombards and other artillery loaded to fire; and in truth to one who did not see it, the operation would seem incredible—here they are fighting more with military engines than with manpower. The King, overseeing all, corrected with admirable reasons some errors which had been made in laying the siege, such as the planting of bombards and other matters. . . ." Observing the impression made on Jean Pierre, Louis remarked that "he had been reared in war."

He pushed his way forward to another Bourbon fortress, which at once surrendered. "When the King had seen to everything, posted a castellan and garrison, he went to the church to render thanks to the omnipotent God. In the evening we returned to Montluçon, and on the way His Majesty made numerous dispositions of his forces in which he used wonderful diligence." Panigarola concluded: "His person is very apt for hard work, a trait which helps him a great deal."

14. MONTLHÉRY

(1) That same day, the Count of Charolais had received three urgent messages from the Duke of Berry, begging him to advance quickly so that the Bretons and the Burgundians, united, could more easily deal with the forces of the King—"such as he had the leisure to assemble," Charolais added contemptuously in a letter to his father. The reason the Bretons themselves did not move, however, is suggested by an anecdote, worth little as evidence but a good deal as symbol, which pictures the Duke of Brittany at Châteaudun on July 16.

"The Duke's tailor, who generally spoke to him with great familiarity, said to him in trying on a gown, 'My Lord, it is owing to you that my lord the Duke of Berry is not today the King of France,'

" 'How do you know this?' asked the Duke.

" 'My Lord, it is certain that the King is today going to attack the Burgundian army and if you had been willing to be there with your army the King would be forever defeated and by this means My Lord would be King.' "

Whatever veteran commanders like Lohéac and de Bueil and Dunois thought, the Dukes of Berry and Brittany preferred to leave the fighting to the Count of Charolais.

(2) The fact was, the Count of St. Pol had been permitted to go forward to Montlhéry only as a defensive measure: it was agreed that if the royal army continued its advance he would retire on Longjumeau, where the "main battle" and rearguard of the Burgundians, forming their laager of baggage wagons and artillery carts, had constructed a strong position atop a slope. When, sometime in the night, St. Pol sent word to Longjumeau that his scouts had come on advance units of the royal army less than four miles from Montlhéry, Charolais therefore ordered him to fall back. But the Count of St. Pol, enacting a high chivalric role, declared that he would not retreat "if he died for it." He pulled his men down from the ridge and village and took up a position in the plain to the north, staying east of the Paris-Orléans road in order to leave room for the rest of the army. What Charolais thought about St. Pol's bravery is not on record. As morning approached, he sent Antoine the Grand Bastard of Burgundy with the rearguard to reinforce the Count, and then "after he had debated with himself whether he should go or not, in the end he followed the others. . . ."

15. THE SIEGE OF PARIS

(1) Thousands of Parisians had also issued from the gates, each intent on capturing wealthy prisoners or getting hands on booty; and the people in all the vil-

lages south of the Seine, armed with makeshift weapons, were beating the woods and thickets for Burgundians. That day, or the previous one, the lord of Mouy had ridden with the garrison at Compiègne to Pont-Ste.-Maxence on the Oise and wrested the bridge from the Burgundian garrison, so that those who had managed to pass St. Cloud fell into Mouy's hands. The bridge over the Marne at Lagny was likewise seized by the French.

Not one of the Burgundians who fled from the battlefield as far as the vicinity of the Seine escaped capture. The Parisian chronicler Maupoint records that many thousands of prisoners (no doubt an exaggeration) and more than two thousand horses with valuable saddles were led back to Paris that evening. Those who could not guarantee a ransom were trussed up and unceremoniously pushed into the river. Panigarola reported that more than seven hundred were drowned or otherwise disposed of. Booty won on the battlefield or taken from fugitives amounted to hundreds of thousands of crowns in coin, plate, jewels, and precious furnishings, including Charolais's portable chapel, "a rich and impressive object."

(2) All the while, Louis was working to break the coalition of rebel lords by raising up enemies in their rear and playing a game of offer and counter-offer in order to divide them. He promised money and troops to the Liègeois if they would take the field against the Duke of Burgundy. He even snatched at the possibility of using an agent of King Ferrante at the English court to try to persuade the Earl of Warwick to mount an attack upon the Low Countries. Juggling with the juggling Angevins, he made use of King René, virtuously preaching pacification to both sides, to try for a separate agreement with Duke John. He was also urging the Duke of Milan to induce King Ferrante to send a fleet against René's port of Marseilles, which would oblige René and his son to abandon the rebel cause in order to defend Provence. Word came back from Duke John that if the King would make war on King Ferrante and Francesco Sforza, the Angevin Duke would persuade the other princes to accept terms, price unspecified. Several royal advisers pressed Louis to throw over the Duke of Milan—the Milanese alliance, they pointed, out had been one of the chief causes of princely discontents—but the King declared that he would never abandon Francesco Sforza, in whom "he had found more love and loyalty than in any lords of this realm. . . ." As for the "offers" of the other princes—"Those lords," he informed Panigarola, "demand control of the revenues of the realm, of the army, of clerical benefices. I would rather suffer death than consent. . . ."

(3) While the princes were still at Étampes, Charles de Melun sent a secret message to a distant relative of his, a man named Paviot who was Master of the Duke of Berry's household, that he was eager to work for a pacification. In a feverish attempt to sound virtuous at the same time that he was trying to solicit the Duke of Berry's favor, he declared to Paviot that "he wanted no other goods but his shirt and nothing else but to become a monk, that reconciling the King and his brother was a laudable object, and that, after the King, he would do all pleasure and service to my Lord of Berry." Though Commynes declares positively that Melun did his sovereign "good service all that year," the evidence that on the day of Monthéry Melun had discouraged an attack from Paris, that he was in secret touch with the princes, and that, in consequence, the King had good reason to proceed against him for disloyalty, is quite convincing. Commynes is not often wrong, but he is not infallible. The fact that he is at such pains to commend Melun's loyalty—he makes the point more than once—suggests that in after years he perhaps nursed a secret hostility for the man who was most to profit from Melun's downfall, Antoine de Chabannes, Count of Dammartin, who became a rival of Commynes for the King's ear and favor.

(4) After Duke John and the Marshal of Burgundy (on August 10) and Bourbon, Nemours, and Armagnac (on August 12) had joined the Burgundians and Bretons, the combined armies—probably between thirty and forty thousand men—moved slowly down the right bank of the Seine, making halts of several days. The two fire-eaters, the Count of Charolais and Duke John, became, despite the old enmity of their Houses, inseparable comrades-in-arms. Fully armored, they cantered up and down the line of march giving orders; while the Dukes of Berry and Brittany rode on quiet little hobbies and were armed only in very light brigandines, which, some said, were no more than satin cloth spotted with gilded nails. When the princes reached the prosperous lands of Brie, the pillaging thousands of Armagnac and Nemours were left behind to ravish to their hearts' content that province and Champagne; and the rest of the army continued westward toward Paris.

(5) On Friday, August 30, the King ordered the Oriflamme, sacred symbol of the French monarchy, to be fetched from the Abbey of St. Denis. After he had held it aloft before the altar of the church of Ste. Catherine-du-Val and "prayed long and well," he returned to his Hôtel des Tournelles with the Oriflamme borne behind him by his chaplain. The Parisians this day received mundane encouragement also. Two horseloads of eels arrived to be sold; and the artillery fire from the walls was so accurate that the Burgundians were forced to withdraw from Grange aux Merciers, a country manor between the lines. On Sunday, September 1, a troop of four hundred crossbowmen and pikemen from Anjou entered the city, and immediately sallied out to skirmish to show their mettle. A few days later during an interval of truce some two thousand Bretons and Burgundians, dressed in their best, "came in great pomp to show themselves to the Parisians," parading up and down the bank of a ditch which extended from the convent of St. Antoine des Champs to the river. Many people came out of Paris to look at them and speak to them, though the King had forbidden it. Louis was so displeased with this dangerous mingling that he ordered his captains to fire warning shots from cannon on the walls. "And, when the Parisians returned to the town, he had the names of several of them taken down in writing."

(6) There had been a few preliminaries. Cannon fire had twice holed the lodging of the Count of Charolais at Conflans, killing a trumpeter as he was bearing a platter of meat upstairs to his master. The Count of Maine—not by the King's order—had thoughtfully dispatched to the Duke of Berry two hogsheads of red wine, four half-barrels of claret, and a horseload of cabbages and radishes. The King had received, under surety, a visitor: Edmund Beaufort, Duke of Somerset—brother of Charolais's friend and Queen Margaret's favorite, Henry, killed in 1464—who had found refuge at the court of Burgundy and now held a command in the Burgundian army. Louis and he had talked "for a long time" at the Bastille of St. Antoine. "And then he was offered drink and took leave of the King, who, because it was raining, gave him his cape, which was of black velvet."

(7) On the preceding evening Jean Balue, Bishop of Évreux—returning from who knows what nocturnal pleasure—was ambushed in the rue de la Barre du Bec by a party of armed men. The Bishop's attendants took to their heels, and Jean Balue, bleeding from a sword cut in his crown and in his hand, owed his life to the speed of his mule, which, outgalloping his pursuers, brought the Bishop safely to his lodging in the cloister of Notre Dame. The guilty parties were never found. People suspected that Charles de Melun had thus thought to dispose of a rival in love. He and the Bishop were carrying on a rancorous competition for the favors of Jeanne du Bois, wife of a royal officer. According to the testimony of an enemy, Melun—"a second Sardanapalus"—was also having his way with wives and daughters of citizens and "did no more service to the King than if he had been in a bath, which to him was terrestrial paradise."

(8) On Friday morning, October 11, the Count of Charolais had held a formal muster of his army in order to establish payrolls, having received from his father a convoy of gold. The King did not neglect this opportunity to honor his new-found friend. After being rowed up river, with but a few companions, to Charolais' lodgings in Conflans, Louis rode off with the Count of St. Pol to view the might of Burgundy on parade. The lord of Haynin found himself close beside the King of France that day. "I saw His Majesty arrive on a small gray horse, clad in a black gown without any armor that one could see; he had very few people with him. . . . As he moved along the ranks, he queried St. Pol—whose is that standard? and that one? what company is this? and that? He continued asking questions as he rode from end to end of the muster and then up to the Count of Charolais. . . ." After the review, the King had a long conversation with St. Pol, Duke John, and Charolais, most of the talk being about Duke John's affairs. On the morrow, Saturday, October 12, King Louis received St. Pol's oath of loyalty, presented him with the sword of the Constable of France, and "kissed him on the mouth."

(9) Within the gorgeous expanse of stained glass that is Sainte Chapelle, the Court of Armagnac and the Duke of Nemours swore on the Gospels to serve the King of France for and against everybody, particularly his brother, Charles, to renounce all their previous alliances, and to inform the King of any stirrings of disloyalty that came to their attention. Louis, in turn, pardoned them their rebellion and had the pleasure of promising to protect them against any attempts at revenge on the part of their former confederates. When Duke John still imperiously demanded that the resources of France be devoted to creating an Angevin kingship at Naples, Louis suggested dryly that he present his case to the Parlement of Paris, or, if he preferred, to the Council of the Thirty-Six which his confederates had "ordained for the welfare of the realm. . . ."

The dressing-down administered by Louis took the form of a spontaneous little drama. As the King was talking with the Milanese envoys in a chamber crowded with lords, Duke John strode into the room. Louis immediately beckoned him to his side. Indicating Panigarola and Bollate, he remarked provocatively that Angevins and Milanese were all part of one affair and that peace must be made between Duke John and the Duke of Milan.

Bristling, Duke John answered that though at one time Sforza and the Angevins had been allies, "they were now so far asunder that there was no longer any hope of reconciliation—and this was the fault of the Duke of Milan!"

Louis reminded his cousin that in 1454 King René had suddenly returned to France when he and Sforza were attacking the Venetians. The Milanese ambassadors promptly added that if there was any enmity on the part of the Duke of Milan toward the House of Anjou—which indeed they had no knowledge of—it had been originated by Duke John and his father. Louis teased the fire by observing that the Duke of Milan had the kindiest of natures. Despite any unfortunate occurrences in the past, the King could assure his cousin that Francesco Sforza would lend him ten thousand ducats if he needed it. He could speak so because he regarded himself as Sforza's lieutenant in the realm of France and whatever he promised in behalf of the Duke was as good as done! As an afterthought, Louis remarked that Duke John was, of course, "somewhat bizarre and hotheaded."

With a violent gesture the Duke cried that he was of the Duchy of Lorraine, which was not subject to the Pope or the Emperor or the King or to anybody else and that he had no superior to fear but was his own master. With this, the Cardinal,

Jean Jouffroy, joined the King in demonstrating that "what he said about the Duchy of Lorraine was not true because it duly holds from the Crown"; whereupon Duke John began furiously raking over his own version of past history, declaring that the Pope had only confirmed King Ferrante as the ruler of Naples because of what the King of France had written to him. Louis with the help of the Cardinal had no difficulty showing that this was completely false, as indeed it was.

Duke John snarled at the Cardinal that there was no need for him to bandy words and that in the Roman Curia he was well known as a man who tried to deceive everybody. Jean Jouffroy retorted that it was not he who was the deceiver. If the King in this bitter war had followed his advice and not believed in the treacherous wiles of the lords, all of them would have crept away from the campaign and gone home.

Duke John give him the lie—they would have done no such thing! None of them was willing to be considered a breaker-of-faith and they had all determined to pursue the enterprise to the end!

Louis remarked judiciously that if any were judged guilty by the Council of the Thirty-Six, the Duke should be one, and one of the first, for reasons that he well knew. The Cardinal added piously that it was to be hoped God would prosper the Thirty-Six; after all, when the Athenians created the Thirty, that body reduced the state to greater confusion than it had ever been in before.

Duke John, "scorching, asked the Cardinal if it were true that when he dwelt at Bruges he was known for the sins of the flesh which he committed." With that, "the King and those standing about began to laugh."

Toward the end of this heady wrangle, which "lasted about two hours," Louis put on the brakes and began to get down to cases. He informed his cousin that he would do his best to make the Angevins and the Duke of Milan friends. Though he would help Duke John against Ferrante, "the time and the effort and the cleverness which the Duke had used to try to make his sovereign break the league with the Duke of Milan were wasted because he would die before he broke it." After all, he ended, Francesco Sforza had served him far better than had the House of Anjou.

The Duke sarcastically thanked the King for his offer but declared that he had no wish for the friendship of the Duke of Milan, who had caused him to lose a million of gold in income from the realm of Naples, a loss directly due to the hostility of the Sforzas. Louis answered blandly that he did not think the Sforzas had anything to do with it. The good folk in the Kingdom of Naples had waked up and decided to look at their situation quite differently from the way the Duke looked at it. In fact, his cousin had lost the Kingdom of Naples because after his victory at Sarno in 1460 he had followed the bad advice of the Prince of Taranto and ruined his chances.

Duke John spat out that if the King had been there he would have shown him!

Louis laughed. God had provided well for him, he said, because he had now given him yet another thing to be amused at!

Shifting from comedy to statesmanship, he spent a little time soothing the Duke, then announced that he was ready to give effect to the offers he had made. The King turned to his Treasurer, commanded him to count out the three thousand crowns for the Duke; turned to one of his secretaries and ordered him straightway to draw up the papers for the donation of the royal lands.

But the King had something to say, something that struck to the heart of that indomitable conviction which had carried him through so many dangers. The First President of the Parlement, Louis told the Duke, had declared that these royal lands could not in law be alienated from the Crown. Nobody ever seized from the Crown anything truly belonging to it that was not later restored. Nevertheless, he finished cheerfully, let the Duke remain of good will since he had what he asked for.

Apparently a little shaken, Duke John said that he had five thousand Swiss and five hundred lances to put at the King's command. Louis answered cooly that the cantons were already on his side and were furthermore linked in friendship with the Duke of Milan. "Here making an end, His Majesty, in excuse for what had been said against Duke John, remarked that he had done as the Evangelist says, 'I have spoken openly to the world.'"

After the Duke had stalked away, Louis, pointing to two Angevin lords in the chamber, told the Milanese ambassadors that the pair represented all the politic counsel that the Duke possessed and that the Duke himself "was not clever enough to harm the King as things stood now, nor was he even on the road to it." Panigarola, looking around the room, noticed a number of Angevin adherents who "seemed to be bleeding at the nose."

(10) On Wednesday, October 30, a dreary day of wind and rain, the King of France left Paris about ten o'clock in the morning for the castle of Bois de Vincennes, where the assembled princes awaited him. Louis had meant to take only the lords and gentlemen of his household and a reinforced guard, but his subjects in the capital had other ideas. "The people of Paris remained in good union, love, and reverence with the King and the King in great love with them, to the confusion of all the Bretons and Burgundians and their allies"; and they did not intend to allow their sovereign to risk his life by putting himself in the hands of his enemies.

Henri de Livres and four aldermen secretly mustered in their best array twenty-two thousand men of the Paris militia, ten thousand of whom were told off to guard the walls. So, when the King rode through the rain to Bois de Vincennes, he was followed by a guard of two hundred lances and three hundred archers, and after them came twelve thousand militia-men, "the best equipped and youngest and strongest." When the King had entered the gates of the castle, these forces deployed themselves about the Bois de Vincennes in order to remind the Princes that the King of France did not lack defenders.

About eleven o'clock in the morning, in the presence of the lords assembled in the great hall, young Charles of France did homage to his brother for Normandy. After the ceremony Charles, desperately nervous, stammered out to the King that the war had made him very unhappy—it should be remembered how young he was and how harshly his royal brother had treated him—he was extremely grateful for the share of the realm he had received and would ever faithfully serve his sovereign—

Louis answered dryly that if Charles conducted himself properly the King would treat him as a good brother should.

Instead of dining together—did they fear poison?—King Louis and each of the lords withdrew to a private repast. After dinner they reassembled for an informal session of leave taking; and then about ten o'clock at night the King of France, followed by the faithful thousands who had stood for hours in the rain, rode back to Paris.

16. "A SNAPPER-UP OF UNCONSIDERED TRIFLES"

(1) When Louis learned, on the afternoon of January 16, that an embassy from Rouen had duly returned, he decided it would be well to remind them of the majesty of the Crown. The envoys entered "a hall curtained all round with lustrous silk stuff." Surrounded by councilors and high officers and lords, the King sat "in a chair on an eminence covered with cloth of gold . . . a gold canopy stretching above."

The ambassadors "with their knees on the floor, their heads uncovered, very humbly declared that . . . they were returned with full power from the city to acknowledge His Majesty for their natural sovereign lord . . . begging him to accept benignly his people into his former affection. . . .

"The King comforted them and urged them to persevere in this good intention and said that he would live and die with them. Then the Chancellor, kneeling at His Majesty's feet, from rank to rank received the pledge of obedience of the ambassadors. And," continued Panigarola to his master, "if Your Highness had heard the King reeling off points, clauses, confirmations—all the niceties of legal ceremony— you would have judged him not only a jurisconsult but one of those emperors who found and establish laws. . . ."

(2) At Honfleur there had been played a little comedy of disillusion as Francis and Charles, each in his own way, began to realize what a fool he had been. Talks on the subject of the *apanage* came to nothing; Charles was so frightened that he could think only of flight; Francis II, as his anger against the King's brother vanished and his accustomed fears of the King returned, was beginning to wonder how the devil he had got himself in that galley. Finally Charles, in a fit of nerves, embarked in a ship which had been readied by one of his servants and sent word to Francis that he was taking refuge with the Count of Charolais. As the vessel was about to sail, Francis frantically entreated Charles to give him one last interview. Charles reluctantly complied, the two Dukes began talking, and the tide ran out to leave the ship stranded. It was at this moment apparently that rumor, transforming Louis's outriders into an army, reached Francis and Charles that the King of France was swooping upon Honfleur to capture them. Leaping to horse, they fled in terror for Caen.

17. PÉRONNE

(1) To the citizens of Lyons the King wrote in December of 1466: "We understand that cloth of gold and silk has to be imported and that each year 400,000 or 500,000 gold crowns or thereabouts are drained from the realm, a situation very prejudicial to us and the public welfare. We have been informed that it would be easy to establish the manufacture of cloth of gold and silk in our kingdom, especially at Lyons, where certain ones, it is said, already exercise that craft. Therefore to prevent this yearly drain of gold and silver from the realm and considering the very great good that could accrue to the public welfare, and especially to the city of Lyons and the whole surrounding region, we have ordered . . . that the industry be established at Lyons and that men and women skilled in the craft come there. We are informed that this industry . . . can offer honorable and profitable occupation for ten thousand persons—men and women of Lyons and the vicinity, churchmen, nobles, nuns, as well as others who are at present idle. But this enterprise cannot be undertaken without expense. We have therefore decreed . . . that a tax be imposed on Lyons, beginning January 1, 1467, of two thousand livres to pay the wages of the imported workers and those making the required tools. . . ." The citizens of Lyons, however, were not as ready as their sovereign to embrace new ways, and a few years later Louis would have to take steps to save his experiment.

(2) At least as early as February of 1467, Louis XI had been thinking of the possibility of reconciling Warwick and the dethroned House of Lancaster. In the first days of that month, he set forth on a pilgrimage with his cousin Duke John. On the road they paused for a meal. Louis began the table conversation casually, with some talk about his favorite pastime, hunting. Then, after he had deliberately provoked his companion's ire by commending at length the Marshal of Burgundy, a capital enemy of the Duke, he suddenly turned the conversation to Richard Neville, Earl of Warwick, "the King of England's first lord." As he embarked on a eulogy of the Kingmaker, Duke John angrily interrupted—

Warwick was nothing but a low traitor! He could not allow anything good to be said of him—the Earl had spent his whole life in double dealing! He it was, the malign enemy of Anjou, who had caused the downfall of King Henry and the Duke's sister Margaret, Queen of England. The King would do better, John went on hotly, to help his sister recover her kingdom than to squander favors on such as Warwick! With this, the Duke let loose a violent diatribe on Warwick's villainies.

Imperturbably Louis replied that he had more reason to praise the Earl of Warwick than many others, even some of his own relatives, because the Earl had always been a true friend to the Crown of France. Whereas Duke John's brother-in-law, King Henry, had inflicted many wars on the realm, Warwick had opposed English aggression. For that reason, Warwick's was a friendship worth preserving. As the King continued to laud the Earl, Duke John broke in again—

If His Majesty was so fond of Warwick, all the more reason for him to work to restore the Duke's sister to the English throne—with both Warwick and the Lancastrians on his side, he'd be surer than ever of English friendship!

Louis immediately pounced on the subject. What security for their friendship, he inquired sardonically, would Queen Margaret's people offer him—the same kind as when they had secretly pledged themselves to the League of the Public Weal? Or would they offer as security Queen Margaret's son, Prince Edward—the thirteen-year-old boy who already spoke of nothing else but cutting off heads and making war, as if he had everything in his hands or was the god of battle or enjoyed the untroubled possession of England? Even if security was given, would it be observed?

In a fury Duke John declared violently that if Margaret's son gave his word at the Duke's request, and then failed to keep it, Duke John would fly at his face and tear out his eyes!

"Throughout the meal the two of them continued, as if half in joke, to make many pungent retorts to each other." In addition to giving himself the pleasure of baiting his hotheaded cousin, Louis XI apparently was testing the Duke's attitude toward an alliance of Warwick and the Lancastrians.

(3) Jacques d'Armagnac, Duke of Nemours, had become so terrified by the King's show of power in regaining Normandy that he thought about going on pilgrimage to Jerusalem. Instead, in return for a pardon, he agreed to confess his perfidies during the War of the Public Weal—he had no reason to withhold anything for he knew that his intimate, the lord of Bregons, had sold all his secrets to the King. The charming but feckless Jacques then scuttled back to his stronghold of Carlat, an almost impregnable castle perched on an outcropping of rocks. He could not resist conspiring once again, however. As soon as Louis's brother, Charles, opened secret communications with him, he promised Charles that if he could do nothing else "he would paw the earth before him like a bull." In the summer of 1467 Nemours received the exciting intelligence, brought from Charles and Francis II by the Breton lord of Villeret, that the new Duke of Burgundy would furnish full military aid to get rid of Louis XI. According to the Breton, Charles had said that "when it came to sharing the spoils, the Duke could take at his pleasure and parcel out the rest." Overjoyed, Jacques d'Armagnac urged immediate action on Villeret, for he had learned from his astrologers that the first one to take the field would prove victorious. Jacques was still so frightened by the King, however, that he had made the Breton agent meet him in a village mill and at the end of the interview asked Vil-

leret to tell Charles of his hope that "if some misfortune comes upon me and I have to flee, he will keep some little corner of his territories for me to hole up in." After Villeret returned to Brittany, he began to feel so unsure of his skin that he rode to the King of France and told the whole story.

(4) The King lodged the evening of the 27th in a stout farmhouse about a quarter of a mile from the ruined walls, with St. Pol and his troops close by, while the Duke took up quarters near the gate. About midnight Louis was roused by sounds of wild alarm in the suburbs. Hastily he summoned St. Pol, took horse and galloped through heavy rain to the Duke's quarters. He found Charles in the street vainly shouting questions and commands while all around Burgundians were crying in panic that the enemy were upon them. There was no man braver than the Duke of Burgundy, but he stood impotently in the rain, unable to think what to do and manifestly confused. "He did not hold so good a countenance," reports Commynes, "as a great many of his men, the King being there, would have wished."

Louis instantly took over command and began issuing orders that soon brought the tumult under control. "He told the Constable, 'Go to such-and-such a spot with whatever men you have. If the enemy should attack, that's the route they'll take.' To those who heard his words and saw his countenance, the King appeared a man of commanding personality and great good sense, and one who had much experience in such matters." It turned out to be a false alarm, and Louis withdrew to his quarters, doubtless with immense relief. Had the Liègeois attacked and won even a small success, the suspicious Duke of Burgundy would have known where to find the culprit. As they had approached Liège that day, they could see royal coats of arms and French banners on the gates and hear cries of "Vive le Roi!"

Probably thinking that he had better be close at hand in case of further trouble, Louis the next morning shifted his lodging to a small dwelling in the suburbs close to the Duke's quarters. The hundred archers of his Scots guard and some of St. Pol's men of arms were placed in a nearby village. He was not long in learning that he had again fired his host's suspicions—suspicions that the King might enter the city to defend it, or flee with his guard before the town was won, or even do some outrage on the Duke himself, being now so close. Into a huge barn between the royal and ducal lodgings Charles of Burgundy stuffed three hundred men of arms, "the flower of his household." Louis could see that, having broken holes in the barn walls, they were keeping watch on his dwelling.

Except for minor skirmishing, all was quiet on the day and night of Friday, October 28, but neither the King nor the Duke disarmed. On Saturday, under cover of martial demonstrations, most of the men, women, and children of Liège fled the city through the eastern gates, to seek refuge in Germany or in the wilds of the Ardennes. It had turned cold; freezing rain continued to fall. Many of the people died of exposure or hunger or exhaustion. Others were killed by nobles of the region or captured and drowned in the Meuse. That evening the Duke ordered his men, including the three hundred in the barn, to remove their armor in order to refresh themselves before the assault. The Duke followed suit, but Louis, apparently, kept on his brigandines.

A little before ten that night the King was roused by shouts, sounds of fighting. A band of armed men was storming his dwelling. At windows and doors Louis's Scots were valiantly struggling with the invaders in hand-to-hand combat. Through the black night torches began to flare. Everywhere men were yelling "Burgundy!" "Vive le Roi!" "Kill!" The Scots won enough room to unsling their bows and a storm of arrows hissed through the night. In a few minutes the King was able to emerge from the house into torchlit confusion. The Scots and some of the royal men of arms had put the invaders to flight; men lay stretched on the ground; the three hundred Burgundians in the barn were issuing in all directions. With his guard about him Louis made his way to the Duke. Charles's quarters, too, had been attacked. Assailants had broken into the kitchen and reached the stairs before the ducal archers succeeded in driving them back. It turned out that two bands of some seven hundred men of Liège wearing Burgundian insignia had undertaken this suicidal mission in order to kill or capture the King and the Duke. Had some of the raiders not paused to thrust pikes through holes in the barn and kill a servant or two in the small building nearby, no alarm would have been raised. It had been a near thing.

(5) The news the King had dispatched of the signing of the treaty had produced outbursts of joy in Paris and Amiens and elsewhere. Church bells rang, priests marched in procession and sang Te Deum. Bonfires were lighted in the streets and the well-to-do set out tables of refreshments for neighbors to eat and drink their fill. Immediately after, however, rumors had coursed the kingdom that Louis XI was killed or a prisoner. Some of his captains in Picardy had come to the Council of Thirty-Six at Paris, bewilderedly asking what to do. Headed by Foix and Dunois, that council, meeting twice daily, had sought as best it could to keep the wheels of government turning. In Paris there were even reports of trouble-making by Louis's brother and these, mingled with news of an English naval expedition at sea, intensified fears. Fortunately, the English fleet soon returned to its harbors, and Louis's brother lacked the inclination, even if he had had the resources, to seize the moment.

In the town of Aurillac, where the Duke of Nemours counted some supporters, a merchant had capered in the street crying, "Go look for your King! He's dead, or a prisoner!" Nemours himself, hearing that the King was at Burgundy's mercy, sent messengers to Péronne to secure his share of the good things. When they came back with tidings that the King, free, was returning to France, the astounded Jacques d'Armagnac cried, "What's that? The Great Devil keeps the man alive? Will we never have an end to trouble?"

(6) On Saturday, November 19, royal heralds cried in the squares of the capital the peace signed by the King and the Duke. On the same day proclamation was made that no one was to utter anything opprobrious about the Duke of Burgundy by "word of mouth, writings, scrawlings on walls, posters, rondeaux, ballads, virelais, defamatory libels, heroic lays, or other means." Also on the 19th royal commissioners went through Paris collecting "all magpies, jays, and other talking birds, caged and uncaged" in order to transport them to the King, first registering their owners and what they could say, as "Thief! Scum! Son of a whore! Beat it! Perette, give me something to wet my whistle."

Perhaps the King was hoping to secure a magpie that could squawk "Burgundian son of a whore!"

18. BEAUVAIS

(1) Louis had been aided in his campaign against the Count of Armagnac by his friend the Earl of Warwick—at least according to a story, convincing in its detail, which was related several years after the King's death by an Englishman named John Boon, then imprisoned in France. Toward the end of 1468 Edward IV chose this tough adventurer from Dartmouth to deliver to the Count of Armagnac an invitation to support the English when they invaded Guienne. As soon as Boon received the packet of letters, however, he disclosed his mission to the Earl of Warwick. When Louis was informed of the plot by a herald of the Earl, he sent back word that Boon should undertake his journey and then report its results to Louis himself.

One evening in the spring of 1469 word was brought to the King that Warwick's man had now arrived in Amboise. Inclined to be suspicious, as usual, Louis ordered his wiliest intimate, Jean de Daillon, lord du Lude—"John Cleverness" (Jean des habilitez) Louis called him—to impersonate him. Du Lude, wearing crimson velvet with a black hat pulled down over his face, seated himself on a bench in a small bedchamber, lit by a single candle. Louis stationed himself in the next room. John Boon, admitted to the bedchamber, reported that the Count of Armagnac had refused to take the letters or even talk with the bearer. Satisfied that the man was what he claimed to be, Louis himself, the next night, interviewed Boon in the same chamber. Taking the Englishman familiarly by the hand, the King bade him repeat the story—he had been slightly ill the previous evening and could not remember the details. When Boon finished, Louis said, "On your life, you will tell no one that you have already been on your mission to the Count of Armagnac. You must do me a service." The service was for Boon to pretend that he had not yet visited Armagnac but had come directly from England to Amboise with Edward IV's letters. The following night in the same chamber, Louis had with him du Lude, Tanneguy du Chastel, and two other intimates when he received Boon. While these four sat on the bed to read King Edward's letters, Louis familiarly pulled Boon down beside him on the bench. "Here are the knights in all the world in whom I have the greatest trust," the King whispered. He then remarked aloud, "This is the man who brought the letters. I want them to be resealed and delivered by him to the Count of Armagnac, and I wish a copy of them made." *Sotto voce* he told Boon that he should absent himself for a period under pretense of carrying the letters to the Count—Louis thus flattering Boon with the suggestion that only the two of them were in on the secret.

But next day when Louis entered the gallery of the castle of Amboise, a favorite walking place of his, he saw Boon in some sort of argument with the courtier who had conducted him to Louis's chamber. Inquiring what the matter was, he learned that Boon was displeased because he felt himself tricked—the man in the black hat who had interviewed him the first night, he had told the courtier, was not the King, for he knew the King's face and voice. Louis gave Boon a winning smile, said he was delighted that the emissary of his cousin, the Earl of Warwick,* had been clever enough to see through his little stratagem. The truth was, he had doubts about Boon's identity and had therefore concealed himself in an adjoining chamber that first evening while my lord du Lude played his part. Boon, pleased with the King's flattering bonhomie and with the King's coins jingling in his purse, rode off to simulate a journey to Armagnac.

When Boon returned to court in August, as the King was moving to meet his brother, Louis sent du Lude to him with a packet of forged papers, Armagnac's supposed treasonable reply to Edward IV, and with orders for Boon to deliver the papers when asked for them by the King. While hunting near Niort, Louis caught sight of Boon, called, "Art thou come then, John Boon," but said no more at that moment. The next evening as he was supping, Louis had Boon brought before him and commanded the lord of Craon to undo the packet of forgeries, remarking, "You can attest that you had the letters before I ever saw them!" A few days later, as he was on the road after the interview with his brother, the King summoned Boon to his side in order to instruct him in his story. He was to say that on delivering King Edward's letters to the Count of Armagnac he had been sent off to Bordeaux while the Count conferred with the Duke of Nemours—"who is even worse than Armagnac,"

---

* "His cousin" many times removed. They were both descended from St. Louis, Warwick through his grandmother Joan, bastard daughter, later legitimated, of John of Gaunt, son of Edward III, whose mother Isabel was the daughter of King Philip the Fair of France.

Louis added. On Boon's return to Armagnac's town of Lectoure, the Count gave him letters (those provided by "John Cleverness") for the King of England and swore to help Edward IV conquer Guienne with fifteen thousand men.

Boon nervously muttered that he did not know whether he could play the part to the King's satisfaction. "Oh, act it boldly," Louis told him cheerfully. Louis then sent his councilor Guillaume de Cerisay to take down Boon's deposition, and shortly after the King assembled an array of lords and notables to hear Boon's story, the letters of Edward IV, and Armagnac's "reply." A little later Louis remarked to Boon that if the Count of Armagnac swore that he had written no letters to the King of England Boon must of course offer to meet him in single combat. Boon answered in fright that this went far beyond his daring. Louis laughed and explained that he would only have to offer. In fact, Louis had proof a-plenty of the Count of Armagnac's treachery, but, as in waging war, he always liked to have a much larger force than needed; besides, he had doubtless enjoyed the comic rascality for its own sake.

The King gave Boon a handsome pension and the hand of a well-to-do lady of Nantes. Apparently, however, the Englishman was unable to resist the lures of perilous intrigue. Seven years later he confessed to having conspired, "with the encouragement of the Duke of Burgundy," to poison the King's heir (Charles, born 1470) and was condemned to be beheaded. Instead, however, he was given the alternative of blinding or execution. On his choosing the former, the hangman so bungled the operation, apparently by royal order, that, years later, Boon was still able to see "especially when the weather was clear." Despite the terrible accusation, it appears that King Louis could not resist showing some mercy to an adroit rogue who had amused him. The King delivered Boon to the care of his wife and gave her Boon's pension.

(2) Louis had prepared the way by sending to the Burgundian court an equerry to express his earnest desire for a settlement and to request the dispatch of a Burgundian embassy to that end. The equerry, on his return to the King, dispatched a memorandum to the Duke which bears every sign of having been dictated by Louis himself—in its mingling of flattery, rueful comment on the embittered past, a reminder of the separate peace the Dukes of Guienne and Brittany had made in 1468, and a warning that the King was fully informed about their latest intrigues with Burgundy. What adds pungency to the document is the revealing marginal commentary of Duke Charles himself.

"First," wrote the equerry, "when I arrived here, I found my master [i.e., Louis XI] determined to do for you, my lord, all that he possibly can and in the best will toward you that ever I saw him." Here Duke Charles jotted, "Without the restitution of the towns [Amiens and St. Quentin] . . . matters cannot be shaped to any good purpose."

"Item," continues the memorandum. "I have assured my master he may be certain that you prefer his friendship to that of those who have deceived you [i.e., Guienne and Brittany], on which account my master is more joyous than I have ever seen him. He replied to me that he knows well that you are trusty and that those to whom you give your word you never go back on, and he says that he desires nothing else for his part, for he knows well that there is neither fidelity nor trust in all the rest of them, neither for you nor for him. He also says that both you and he have not done as wisely as if you had begun earlier to realize these things, for you would not have had the troubles that you both have had." The Duke commented: "You have assured your master of the truth. It doesn't depend on mere belief whether he is joyous about it or not, for the event will demonstrate it, and 'who is sage will receive no damage.' "

"Item. [The King] would have sent my lord du Bouchage [dispatched to Guienne on August 18] if it were not for the news that my lord of Guienne sent him which he is forwarding to you." The Duke: "Small causes are not permitted to upset great plans."

"Item . . . The Duke [of Brittany] and my lord of Lescun [Odet d'Aydie] have informed my master that that Duke is sending to you Poncet [de Rivière], partly regarding the marriage of my lord [the Duke of Guienne] and also to offer himself to you, declaring that he will assemble his forces by Michaelmas Day [September 29]; but the Duke [of Brittany] also informs my master . . . that he sends to Burgundy only to keep you amused as is his custom; and that my master should have no fear that the Duke wishes to do anything against him. . . ." Charles of Burgundy's comment: "The words of this article mean nothing, for the deed will make proof of everything; but we will act in such a way that the goslings will lead the geese to pasture."

"Item. My master knows the comings and goings of Gaudete and Master Ythier Marchant [envoys of the Duke of Guienne] at the court of Burgundy and all that they have done." The Duke: "If you know all these things and a great many others, you should make provision for them."

(3) After Louis's death, these accusations were given fresh currency in princely circles. It is now well established, however, that the King was a victim of the political propaganda and wishful thinking of his enemies. He himself later pressed the Duke of Brittany to bring the two accused men to trial, but though they languished in the Duke's prisons never to be seen again, Francis II was not able to find any proof of their guilt—for he would certainly have used whatever he could find. Furthermore, the surviving medical evidence regarding the Duke of Guienne's last illness is quite convincing. For a year the King's brother had been in visibly declining health, afflicted by sweats and fevers, which indicate that he was suffering from tuberculosis. Then that disease was complicated by another, and very unpleasant one, and the combination soon carried him off. In his last weeks, his hair, nails, and teeth fell out. These symptoms, taken with the "bad blood" which had brought his mistress, Colette de Chambes, to her deathbed six months before his own demise, suggest that both of them were suffering the effects of venereal disease.

(4) Commynes had been preparing for this change of sides at least as early as the summer of 1471. Dispatched by the Duke of Burgundy on a mission to Brittany and Spain, which was disguised as a pilgrimage to St. James of Compostella, Commynes had also managed to secure instructions to call upon the King of France. He made his way toward Tours and there he deposited six thousand livres with a merchant of the city, Jean de Beaune, who was likewise a royal financial agent. He probably had had a secret interview with the King, in the course of which he agreed to enter Louis's service. Apparently in an attempt to prevent suspicion from arising in the mind of the Duke of Burgundy, a royal envoy after returning from a mission to the Duke sent a memorandum to the latter (see note 2, p. 429) in which, among other things, he noted that, contrary to what had been told him, Philippe de Commynes had not visited the King. Beside this item the Duke jotted, "Commynes was seen at Orléans and therefore he must have gone by way of the French court." As far as is known, however, this mischance caused Commynes no trouble. When war broke out in 1472, Louis ordered Beaune to confiscate Commynes's deposit, probably as another ruse, and also as an added inducement to Commynes not to break his agreement. The sum was later refunded to the lord of Argenton.

19. THE GERMANS

(1) King Louis himself had created some of the stresses of the Franco-Milanese alliance. When, in the summer of 1466, he broke with the King of Aragon in order to support the House of Anjou in Catalonia (see p. 197), he repeatedly urged Galeazzo-Maria to aid the Angevins. At the same time, however, King Ferrante of Naples, nephew and ally of John II of Aragon, was threatening the Duke that to provide any such aid would contravene the articles of the League of Italy. A little later, Louis made Galeazzo-Maria unhappy by another shift in policy. After encouraging the Duke to make war on Savoy, when hostilities with Burgundy were imminent, he then, on coming to terms with Duke Charles, quickly requested Galeazzo-Maria to abandon any such action. But the King knew full well that Galeazzo-Maria had no intention, in the first place, of complying with his wishes. Fearful of being isolated in Italy by his French alliance—Venice and Naples being both allied with Burgundy —the Duke of Milan intrigued with Duchess Yolande of Savoy in order to open a line of communication with the Duke of Burgundy, and even, it appears, was not above putting himself in touch with the Duke of Guienne. He had retained his father's chief minister, Cicco Simonetta, but either Cicco was obliged to carry out his master's wavering policy or else, an able servant to greatness, he proved to be an inferior statesman in his own right. Between the Duke of Milan's not so artful dodges and the increasingly open scorn of them that Louis displayed, the Milanese ambassador led a strained existence.

By the latter part of 1472, the Duke of Milan had felt his position becoming so untenable that, to display his fidelity, he offered King Louis a gift of fifty thousand ducats, provided that the King did not ask further aid for three years and—to avoid angering King Ferrante—that the money not be spent for military action against Aragon. King Louis happily accepted the offer, and the blatant sophistry of the second proviso, for what they were worth. Louis urged that the sum not be transported to his court, but only to Lyons, to which city it was destined in any case—to pay for the forces that Philip of Bresse was assembling to lead into Roussillon. The Duke of Milan, however, clinging to the feeble pretense, instructed Christopher da Bollate, coming to France to succeed Sforza de Bettinis, to convey the ducats to the King. On leaving Lyons, November 2, Christopher was suddenly confronted by an emissary from Philip of Bresse, a bitter enemy of the Duke of Milan, who demanded that he hand over the money to Prince Philip or return to Lyons—or "he would be cut to pieces on the road!" (An extant letter from the King to Philip authenticates the latter's claim that he was authorized to receive the money at Lyons.) Christopher da Bollate sought refuge for himself and his ducats in a small town in Forez, some dozen miles north of Lyons, which was soon surrounded by Philip's troops. And thus began what might be called the Case of the Ambushed Ambassador. Though he painted a picture of himself in mortal danger, alone amidst ravening foes, with only his fidelity to the Duke and his brain to guide him, he had no difficulty sending daily appeals to his master, protests to the French court, letters to Lionetto de Rossi, head of Lorenzo de' Medici's bank at Lyons and an agent of the King. The townsfolk took good care of him; he was never molested—except for some nocturnal threats shouted outside the walls and "insufferable language" to which he was subjected by one of Philip's squires. Aided, apparently, by the King's friend Lionetto de Rossi, he managed—with consummate adroitness, as he reported to the Duke—to have the ducats secretly conveyed back to Lyons. The King finally sent two men to escort Christopher to that city, where he arrived the evening of November 26. Shortly after, the fifty thousand ducats were duly delivered to Louis's representatives, for conveyance to Philip of Bresse. Finally reaching court, Christopher was careful to send to the Duke an itemized list of extra expenses he had incurred in thus guarding the ducats with his life. King Louis gave him a hearty welcome.

(2) When a group of Paris doctors and surgeons represented to the King that a unique opportunity had arisen for investigating, in a living man, the disease of kidney stone, "from which many people suffered severely," Louis at once thought of the lord du Bouchage, "who was very ill of that malady," and granted the doctors permission to make their experiment. A franc archer, condemned to die that day, was a victim of the disease. Now, given the choice between certain hanging and the uncertainties of his being opened up alive, he chose the latter. The incision was duly made, "the seat of the disease sought out and studied," and then, apparently after the removal of kidney stones, "he was sewn up again. By order of the King, the archer was very well cared for, such that, within fifteen days after, he was entirely cured, was granted a pardon and given money." There is no record whether this operation, perhaps one of the first of its kind in France, aided the cure of my lord du Bouchage; but he recovered, to outlive his sovereign by many years.

20. THE ENGLISH

(1) Louis and all those loyal to him hated the Constable for his intrigues in time of peace and his dodges in time of war. "The Duke of Burgundy," recounts Commynes, "hated him still more, and had better cause, for I know the truth from both sides. The Duke had not forgotten that the Constable had been the cause of his losing St. Quentin . . . and regarded him as the true engenderer of the war between the King and himself; for in time of truce the Constable was all promises and assurances but, as soon as war began, he was the Burgundian's capital enemy; and then he had tried to force the Duke to marry his daughter [to the King's brother]."

During the French-Burgundian negotiations of 1473 and early 1474, both sides had things to say against the Constable, "and thus was begun a negotiation to undo him," the King's men addressing themselves to Burgundians who were particular enemies of St. Pol, and each party revealing the Constable's intrigues against the other. Sensing his danger, St. Pol, at the end of 1473, entered St. Quentin with his troops and forced the King's garrison to vacate the town. He thus gained, he thought, a forceful counter with which to play off the King and the Duke against each other. He then wrote blandly to Louis XI that he had taken St. Quentin only to secure better lodging for his troops and that the King should have no doubts about his loyalty. Dissembling his anger, Louis sent messages and envoys to the Constable, who multiplied protestations of loyalty. At the same time the King increased his offers to the Duke of Burgundy in order to prompt a joint move against St. Pol. In turn, the Constable made handsome overtures to Burgundy. Despite suspicions on both sides aroused by St. Pol's maneuvering, the negotiations to undo him continued. To a Neapolitan ambassador the Duke of Burgundy explained expansively—though it was late April (1474) and Hagenbach lay trussed in a Brisach prison—that the King of France and the Constable were bidding high against each other for his favor, the former offering St. Quentin and the Constable's head, the latter offering St. Quentin and his invaluable services. He would take whatever offer was confirmed first, "adding that he had no faith in either party. The King had kept none of his promises, and the Constable was a man who could not endure an overlord and cared for nothing but his own interests. . . ."

A few days later, in early May, 1474, French and Burgundian envoys sealed an agreement, whereby St. Pol, declared a criminal enemy of both princes, was to be put to death in eight days by the first to take him or delivered to the other for execution. Louis had not hesitated to pay dear for this cooperation: he would aid the Duke with troops, would give him St. Quentin and all the Constable's domains and all the Constable's goods within the realm. St. Pol, however, now aware of his peril and making frantic offers to both princes, succeeded in convincing the ever-suspicious Louis that Duke Charles was intending to betray the King and draw the Constable to his side. As a result of Louis's hasty message to his commissioners, the agreement against the Constable was canceled. "And great good sense the King showed in so doing," observes Commynes, "for I believe that the Constable, in return for delivering St. Quentin, would have been received into the service of the Duke of Burgundy, whatever promise the Duke had made to the contrary."

Two weeks later, on May 14, Louis had an interview with the Count of St. Pol at the village of Fargniers, between Noyon and St. Pol's stronghold of Ham. The apprehensive Count made elaborate arrangements for his safety. On a causeway over a marshy stream had been erected not one but two barriers, about twelve feet apart. The King kept St. Pol waiting a good while. After sending Commynes ahead to make his excuses, he rode into the village accompanied by his chief officers, the Scots guard and some six hundred men of arms led by the Constable's bitterest enemy, Antoine de Chabannes, Count of Dammartin and Grand Master of the Royal Household. Beyond the farther barrier appeared the Constable, mounted, surrounded by half a dozen followers with a force of some three hundred men of arms stationed behind the causeway. St. Pol's household men wore no armor but both Commynes and Christopher da Bollate, the Milanese ambassador, could plainly see that beneath his silken gown the Count was wearing a cuirass. With a few counselors Louis rode up to the nearer barrier. In a loud voice, "because of the distance between them," Louis of Luxembourg, bowing low but not dismounting, greeted the King: "Sire, I have come here to you to show all that world that I am not, nor have been, what you have been given to understand, namely Burgundian, but I am your servant and a good Frenchman, and so I will always be if you will permit me; and I wish to make known that those false ones who have imputed me to be otherwise are the true Burgundians." Louis answered easily, "My brother [i.e., brother-in-law, the Count being married to Louis's sister-in-law, Marie of Savoy], I truly have always reputed you as loyal and so have been of good will. Let us forget these past things and come to others that are more useful for you and me." Louis then motioned his counselors to retire; St. Pol did the same with his; and secretaries of each made out safe-conducts and promises of amity. Then St. Pol had his barrier opened, and rode to the King's barrier. Still mounted, they embraced, and after they had delivered the secretaries' documents to each other, they talked "in very intimate and friendly manner" for more than half an hour. Louis saw—Commynes, farther away, did not miss it—the Constable suddenly lose countenance. He hastily requested the King's barrier to be opened and he moved to the King's side. Volubly he excused himself for the armed men and the precautions. Burgundian territory was nearby, and besides, he dreaded what that fearsome old Écorcheur, Dammartin, might attempt against him. Humbly he sought to accompany the King partly on his way. Louis would not hear of it, adding that he knew the Count would prove loyal. Louis returned alone, to the dark looks and angry murmurs of his intimates. Since they were so enraged by the Constable's presumption, Louis gave them the satisfaction of letting them see that the meeting had but deepened his own antipathy.

"That day," adds Commynes tersely, "the Constable was in great danger." A few days later, St. Pol, in humble guise, met the King and Dammartin in the countryside. In a driving rain Louis made a show of reconciling the two enemies. It was the last time he ever saw the Constable of France.

(2) During the autumn of 1472 John II, King of Aragon, finally crushed the rebellion of his province of Catalonia, which had been doomed since the death of Duke John in December, 1471. In the early hours of February 1, 1473, old John II appeared with a small force before the gates of Perpignan; the citizens joyfully welcomed him into the town; the French garrison under Antoine, lord du Lau, had to take refuge in the citadel. Louis XI immediately dispatched troops and supplies southward and before the end of April received word that his forces were besieging Perpignan. But French attacks on the city failed, du Lau himself being taken captive; heat, illness, lack of food thinned the morale and the numbers of the besiegers; and in mid-July the French were forced to withdraw. A truce to last until October 1 was patched up in order to permit peace negotiations.

Meanwhile, the Duke of Burgundy's threats of war if Louis persisted in attacking his ally, Aragon, the King took very coolly. On June 26 he had written to Antoine de Chabannes: "My lord the Grand Master, two Burgundian heralds, namely Golden Fleecer and Luxembourg have come to tell me the following: Golden Fleecer to summon me to keep the truce in regard to the King of Aragon, and Luxembourg to go to the King of Aragon and tell him I have been so summoned. I have replied to them that, as far as I'm concerned, I am willing to maintain the truce if the King of Aragon maintains it, but it is he who has broken it and taken places from me; and if he is willing to return them to me, I will keep the truce. Further to this matter, I am having Luxembourg conducted to Dauphiné and am sending word to my officers there that they should hold him until [the Governor of Dauphiné has departed on a relief expedition to Roussillon] and then they should send him back to me. In the meanwhile, the Duke of Burgundy will believe that his herald is doing the best job in the world."

With Duke Charles launching himself into the Germanies by taking over the Duchy of Guelders, Louis moved quickly to extricate himself from the mess in Roussillon. To secure reasonable terms he pitched upon a prisoner of his, Pere de Rocaberti, an Aragonese "of great authority with John II." Louis agreed to exchange him for Antoine du Lau, had him dine at the royal table and sleep in the royal antechamber, flattered his ambitions and then—despite the murmurs of his counselors—sent him off with a French envoy to negotiate with King John.[*] By mid-September [1473] Pere de Rocaberti had won him a breathing space: a neutralized Roussillon would be governed by Rocaberti and if within a year John II did not repay the 300,000 crowns owing since 1462, the French were to reoccupy the province. The following spring Louis played an exuberant comedy of the deceiver deceived with Argonese envoys come to forestall French action at the expiration of the year's grace.

John II's splendid embassy, which arrived in Paris in March (1474) had already been delayed in its mission by a "mistake" King Louis made in the wording of their safe-conducts. The ambassadors promptly announced that they had come to confirm the treaty, seek an extension of the repayment date, and offer Prince Ferdinand's daughter in marriage to the Dauphin Charles. Louis had no difficulty divining that repayment would never be made, that crafty old John II was simply trying to delay French military preparations while some of the envoys extended their journey to seek aid from John's allies, Brittany, Burgundy, and England. While the King kept the ambassadors dangling at Paris, he was hastening a build-up of forces on the Roussillon border. On April 9, from Senlis, King Louis wrote to Tanneguy du Chas-

---

[*] As not infrequently happened, many of the King's advisers, and the Milanese ambassador too, believed he was doing the wrong thing: Rocaberti, they thought, had been full of promises only in order to revenge himself as soon as he regained his liberty; Bollate noted that he was "a very practiced courtier, quick with sage remarks in every conversation, but his foxy look and the scars on his face" suggested he was not to be trusted.

tel, then in Dauphiné preparing to reinforce the growing French army at Narbonne, that two men he sent to Paris to "feel out" the envoys' true purposes reported that the latter "brought no news worth anything and their intention is only to amuse me with words until the grain [in Roussillon] has been harvested. Therefore I must play "Master Louis" [i.e., Old Slyboots] and you, "Master John" [i.e., a simpleton], and, instead of their deceiving us, we will show ourselves cleverer than they. As for me, I will entertain them here until the first week of May, and in the meanwhile you set out for [for Roussillon] as soon as you can. . . ." With the troops being forwarded to join the expedition, "you will have enough men to burn the harvest and devastate the whole countryside." It was the first time Louis had ordered such harsh tactics. In dealing with Roussillon, which lay on the periphery of his coronation oath —it was partly French by language, wholly so by geography, and had once belonged to the realm—he was not quite in his element; and he was now sacrificing everything to the weaving of his web.

Five days after dictating the letter to Tanneguy, Louis summoned the Aragonese envoys to a village near Senlis to afford them, at last, an audience. The King meant to make an impressive ceremony of it and himself saw to the arrangements. Standing with prelates and princes on his left and captains and councilors on his right, he gravely listened to the formal exposition of the embassy by the Count of Prades. He was glad to welcome them, he then remarked, provided they had not come to plot anything against him or his interests. To Prades' protestations that the King of Aragon desired only to live in peace with France, Louis replied that the King of Aragon had already broken articles of their treaty; however, he was content to appoint representatives to treat with them. He then added affably that he would shortly join them in Paris and make them good cheer. Louis had appeared in glittering silk and satin with the collar of the Order of St. Michael about his shoulders, "a costume more magnificent than any he had worn in a decade," reported Bollate, who thought the King "looked twenty years younger."

Sure enough, Louis treated the Aragonese embassy to a round of Parisian feasts and entertainments, including a review of the city militia, while the envoys fretfully reiterated that, since nothing was to be concluded, they must and would depart. The Count of Prades fell ill—he is feigning, Louis told Bollate, in order to find an excuse for leaving. Finally Louis let them go, writing with something approaching urchin glee to Tanneguy and his other captains on the Roussillon border, "I held the Catalan ambassadors the whole time that I promised you and longer yet; it was Tuesday [May 5] when they left Paris." The envoys moved at a slow pace homeward, under honorable but strict escort. Ordering them to be most carefully safeguarded but delayed at Lyons and Montpellier, Louis saw to it that they did not reach Aragon until August. By that time his forces were beginning to devastate the Roussillon harvest in order to starve Perpignan into submission.

(3) Upon signing the Treaty of Soleuvre, the Duke of Burgundy, with his army, had moved southward into Lorraine. After attacking and forcing the surrender of Vaudemont, then Épinal, he swung round and, on October 24, laid siege to Nancy, the capital of the Duchy, which two years before he had entered in triumph and since lost to young René II. All the while Louis was sending envoy after envoy to demand the delivering up of the Constable and was being answered by a variety of excuses. As the Duke of Burgundy set siege to Nancy—an evident violation of the Treaty of Soleuvre, in which René II of Lorraine was included—he was assailed by conflicting anxieties. The King's forces in Champagne posed a threat to his flank. His failure to deliver St. Pol, increasing that menace, posed a threat to his sworn word. The existence of St. Pol's safe-conduct posed a threat to his honor. Duke Charles, however, hit upon an expedient by which to conjure these threats and perhaps also to cheat Louis of the Constable. The expedient took the form of two statements to the King: one, that their treaty dealt too vaguely with the Constable's possessions and he now demanded all of them; two, that in peacefully moving through Lorraine, as the treaty permitted (Épinal and Vaudemont apparently falling quite by accident into his hands), he happened to be passing by Nancy when soldiers suddenly issued from the city and fell upon his innocent troops, killing and wounding some, and therefore—the Duke of Lorraine having clearly forfeited by this brutal act his right to inclusion in the truce—the Duke was besieging Nancy. The King made answer by two documents both dated November 12, which indicate either that he perceived an intended connection, or obligingly devised an attractive one, between Charles's statements. In the first document Louis provisionally accepted the Duke's explanation of the siege of Nancy; in the second, he gave Charles a choice—the Constable's entire estate or the right to retain the towns he had won in Lorraine. The Duke of Burgundy, promptly choosing the Lorraine towns, was driven to making a commitment regarding the Count of St. Pol. He ordered the Constable to be taken prisoner at Mons, conveyed to Péronne, and, on November 26, handed over to representatives of the King. It appears that he hoped to win Nancy before that time, and then retain the Constable as well. But the capital of Lorraine managed to hold out until that very date, and St. Pol was duly delivered to the French. On hearing the news, Louis purportedly remarked that "his cousin of Burgundy had done with the Constable as one does with a fox: like a wise man, he kept the skin and he, the King, had only the flesh, which was worth little."

21. THE SWISS

(1) Though it has long been known that on June 25, from St. Claude, at the foot of the Jura in the County of Burgundy, the Milanese ambassador to Duke Charles, Jean Pierre Panigarola, sent a detailed account of the battle of Morat to his master—both refer to the document in later extant communications—the dispatch came to light only in 1892, discovered, undated and unsigned, in the Milanese archives by P. Ghinzoni, who published it in the *Archivio Storico Lombardo*, 2nd series, IX, Milan, 1892. Since this celebrated dispatch offers by far the best eyewitness account of the battle and also a vivid personal narrative by a man at the Duke of Burgundy's side, it is here set forth in translation:

"After I signified to Your Excellency, from Orbe, the defeat inflicted by the Swiss on this lord [the Duke of Burgundy] and his army on Saturday last, the 22nd of this month, I took the route of Jougne into [the County of] Burgundy, where I learned that the aforesaid lord had traveled the road of Geneva the previous night and gone to Gex to Madame [Yolande, Duchess of savoy, who on parting from the Duke at Lausanne had withdrawn to Gex for safety's sake]. . . . I rode, day and night, to St. Claude here at the foot of the mountain and five leagues from Gex, where, on learning that the aforesaid lord was to come here today, I have remained, indeed have had to remain, my horses being unable to go farther because of the great distance they have been ridden. In this place I met with my lord [Antoine], the Bastard [of Burgundy, half brother of Duke Charles], who had ridden from Gex. He says he is indebted to you because the steed you gave him has saved his life— were it not for that horse he would never have escaped from the perilous situation in which I myself saw him, he surrounded by Swiss. It was certainly a miracle, but he attributes his escape to the strength of the steed. . . .

"So that Your Excellency may be fully informed about the defeat, which I can certainly describe for I was right in the midst of it all, I will explain how the thing happened—now that I can breathe a little more easily, for on the day itself I experienced such fear in being pursued by the Swiss that that night my heart and soul were still trembling within me and the more I considered the danger I had undergone the more incomprehensible my escape seemed.

"On Friday the 21st the enemy crossed a bridge . . . and quartered themselves near a village about half a mile from the bridge in a countryside so full of marshes, woods, and the customary thick hedges made of interwoven branches, that their forces could not be attacked. The aforesaid lord, in full armor, had spent the day with his whole army [i.e., except those troops remaining at the siege] in a fine high open place above his camp, where he had arranged the battle stations of his squadrons and battalions. On learning of the arrival of the enemy, he decided to go see where they were lodging. I went also, saw the camp and the enemy, who merely made motions of skirmishing, not issuing from the woods, and fired some handguns. Forming his judgment by the size of their encampment, which could not clearly be seen because it was spread out on low-lying ground, the aforesaid lord conceived the idea that but few troops were there and that they had come in order to encourage the Swiss besieged within Morat to hold out and to cause his lordship to raise the siege and reassemble his forces, and had not come to give battle since they were insufficient in numbers.

"With this opinion he returned to his army. He then signified that [Antoine] the Bastard, my lord of Clessy, Antoine d'Orlier, my lord of Neufchâtel, [Francesco] Troylo [one of the Duke's chief Italian captains], and some others should dismount, and invited me also, in order to consult about what should be done. After the case was put by his lordship, it was decided that that night about two thousand foot and three hundred lances should be left on the plateau where we were, with some horsemen stationed on the perimeter to keep guard. The remainder of the army would retire to the camp to rest, for the men had spent the whole day armed and mounted. After dinner we were to meet again with the aforesaid lord in order to discuss whether or not it would be good to raise the siege altogether, unite the Duke's forces, and go seek out the enemy. At this council of war [i.e., the one held on the return from scouting the enemy] everyone gave his opinion, and I had the great satisfaction of saying, as your representative, what seemed best to me—namely, that a strong force on watch was good but it was necessary to guard against the possibility that the enemy's apparent desire to avoid combat was only a trick and that since they were so near, less than a mile from our forces, an attack could be expected from hour to hour because they were seeking to catch the troops unprepared for battle—as indeed they did—through the advantage they possessed of being able to approach [unseen] through woods. I therefore proposed that even before daybreak the whole army, in battle array, should take position on the plateau to await the enemy, and even lodge there if necessary. Everyone commended my remarks, and the aforesaid lord postponed decision until after dinner.

"After dinner the aforesaid lord remitted the matter to the morning, being firmly convinced that the enemy were only making a demonstration, as explained above. That night after midnight it began to rain and it continued raining the next morning [Saturday, June 22] until almost midday. That morning the aforesaid lord, seeing that the enemy had not attacked in the night not only concluded that his estimate of the situation was sound but took it as an absolute truth, being obstinately set in his opinion that the enemy would not come. The idea became all the more firmly fixed in his head when it was reported that the Swiss were discharging their guns and cannon, which they were doing because their powder was damp from the rain and slow to burn—but they recharged their guns, as the event would prove. From midnight onward the Swiss had begun to advance through the woods toward us, step by step, remaining out of sight and making no noise. The more reports of enemy movements the aforesaid lord received, the less he believed them. He was willing to stake all that they would not come, saying that these reports were made so that he would raise the siege, which he would never do, and that those who made them were French traitors, etc.

"However, the Bastard and the others were now sending so many messages that the enemy were advancing that his lordship began to give some credence to them and commanded that all his men should stand to arms in their quarters, the time being about midday. At this moment the rain ceased. Immediately there began to emerge from the woods above the plateau the front of a battalion of Swiss with long slender pikes, all of them on foot and handgunners ahead of them. Then [on the Burgundian left], farther down toward the flat land appeared a second battalion, with fewer men. Between the two battalions were around four hundred horsemen, who, after they had moved forward a little, halted to await the advance of the foot battalions, which displayed many banners. From the moment the Swiss issued from the woods, our men fired guns and mortars; but the Swiss, in their close-packed phalanx, continued to move forward foot by foot if not yard by yard. In my opinion these two battalions—as others say also—could number from eight to ten thousand persons, twelve thousand at the most, they being the advance guard according to what has since been said. [In fact, the first phalanx to appear, with its "many banners" represented the "main battle," or center, of the Swiss army.]

"The appearance of the enemy was immediately reported to the aforesaid lord, who ordered 'boots and saddles' sounded and began to arm himself. Having already been on the plateau and seen the enemy, I came to his lordship [and urged him] to take horse at once in order to see what was to be done, because there above were no more than two hundred lances and around one thousand foot. He then ordered everyone to the plateau, and Master Matteo [de Clarici, the Duke's physician] and I stayed behind to arm him—but there was no way of persuading him that the enemy were as close as they were and he took so long in mounting horse that by the time he arrived on the plateau our forces were already turning their backs. The Swiss, seeing our forces arriving in drops and driblets on the plateau and struggling to form a battle line, and seeing [on the Burgundian left] toward the town that Troylo had already assembled some three thousand men on a small hill, began at a distance of more than three arrow flights to fire their handguns; and thus it was that the Burgundian foot were beginning to turn in flight, because they realized themselves to be so few in the face of such ferocity. Taking positions behind a small hedge, some Burgundian [mounted] men of arms made a stand to bar the enemy's advance. The Swiss, though helmetless [i.e., wearing only steel caps] cast themselves on the reins of the horses, their arms shielding their faces from the lances of the men of arms. The Swiss cavalry immediately charged and with the Burgundian foot breaking into flight, the men of arms also turned their backs on the enemy. Seeing this, the companies arriving on the plateau, who had no heart for battle in any case, likewise turned and fled. In such manner was it that the whole army was broken in less time than it takes to say a *Miserere*, and it happened with most of the Burgundians neither fighting nor even showing face to the enemy. Had the Burgundian army been assembled on the plateau and stood fast, it would have taken at least three days, they letting themselves be killed, to cut their throats. In sum, because of being taken unprepared, the army has been defeated and crushed. Never did I see this lord confused of mind and not knowing what to do except at the time he was arming himself and afterward when mounted. Since he is usually acute in his thinking and vigilant, I attribute his state to divine judgment or else to the decree of the fates. If the enemy had attacked the day before, when the army was drawn up on the plateau in battle order, there would have ensued a most cruel spectacle, such would have been the bloodshed on both sides.

"The Swiss within Morat had sallied forth and been repulsed. Then when they saw that all the Duke's troops were fleeing, even those maintaining the siege, they sallied forth again. This time they took the Burgundians in the rear by a dreadfully effective maneuver: they ran to a bridge half a league off [to the west, on the escape route along the lake] which it was necessary [for those fleeing] to cross. They captured it after a most cruel combat, for every Burgundian knew that unless he got across he would be trapped. It was thereabouts that the Swiss gave chase to me. When I left the field the enemy were already in the Burgundian camp cutting throats. All the ¡ootmen were trapped—it could not be otherwise—and also the archers: I saw many who, casting away their steel caps, stretched themselves flat on the ground, and with their hands made the sign of the cross. What with the infantry and those who victualed the camp, there must have remained on the field ten thousand men; and also perished many of the cavalry, about whose fate there are differing stories, especially concerning the one who bore the standard of the aforesaid lord, whom they say to be dead—but within two or three days we will know for certain. All the artillery is lost, so that between this defeat and the previous one [at Grandson] the enemy have taken, what with bombards, mortars, and guns, around two hundred pieces, sufficient ordnance to accomplish great things. Of pavilions, tents, wagons, money, garments, I need say nothing; for, because of being caught unprepared, as I said, and of not believing the enemy to be so near, each one has had enough to do to escape with his life. In sum, everything has fallen into enemy hands, and it is no small honor for the Swiss to have gained such renown at the expense of this lord who was accustomed to harry kings and emperors and destroy great cities. What his lordship will now decide to do, I will inform you when I am with him. I know well that his helmet, most richly encrusted with jewels, and his other precious objects are safe. Some of his coffers and money chests have been lost. Without any comparison, this defeat is greater than the previous one, as will soon appear, in the loss both of *matériel* and foot soldiers—that of men of arms being small by comparison.

"Two hours after the battle, I found myself with two Swiss—prisoners of two friends of mine—who seemed to be gentlemen. They affirmed on their word of honor that the entire country of Swiss was empty of men: they had all come to the field, determined to die for their country's salvation. The two Swiss said that the army had a good thirty thousand footmen and sixteen hundred horsemen, among whom was Duke René of Lorraine in person and at least three hundred cavalrymen of the Duke [Sigismund] of Austria, and the whole force had determined at any cost to come to grips with us. Don Federigo [Prince of Taranto, younger son of Ferrante of Naples] had left the Burgundian camp the day before, the 21st, in order to go to Madame [Yolande, Duchess of Savoy], and then, embarking at Nice, to sail to Rome, and he took all his people with him. The Bishop of Sebencio [*nuncio*] of the Pope, also left that day to go into Burgundy [and, a few days earlier, another wise departure was made by Anthony Woodville, Earl Rivers, brother of Queen Elizabeth of England, whom the Duke of Burgundy scornfully called a coward]. [Of foreign ambassadors] there remained only myself and the Prothonotary, [Doctor de] Lucena, emissary of the King of Castile, who was soliciting this lord [i.e., the Duke of Burgundy] to send an envoy to the King of France in order to divert His Majesty from favoring the King of Portugal. Lucena, who was in flight close by me, received two sword blows on the head and the horse on which he was fleeing was wounded. I fear he may be killed—as for me, I put spurs to my horse and, by the grace of God, escaped with my life. But never will I forget such perils."

(2) It was to Philippe de Commynes that Louis gave the mission of discovering what the Milanese ambassador wanted; and only after several reports from Commynes did the King, alone in a chamber, receive the ambassador, accompanied by the lord of Argenton. When Pietrasanta had gracefully explained his master's heartfelt wish to renew the alliance, Louis observed abruptly, "The Duke of Milan has deceived me in the past; and he has done me great damage, which, through an envoy who came to Lyons a little while ago, he offered to make good. What assurance do I have that he will keep his promise and disburse the money which he is obliged to give me because of the harm caused by his leaguing himself with my enemy?"

Pietrasanta recalled the past services of the Duke and the Duke's father which warranted his master's good faith, besides which he was "naturally French" in his feelings. Further, instead of damaging the King, the league with Burgundy had actually been of benefit—since the Duke of Milan, in refusing to supply troops against the Swiss, had precipitated the ruin of the Duke of Burgundy, who thus was deprived of those wings which, he thought, would help him soar to the heavens! As for payment of money, surely the King would not wish to put the Duke in the shameful position of appearing crassly to purchase the renewal of the alliance or to tarnish his own glory by seeming to indulge in vulgar haggling!

Louis thoroughly appreciated the performance. At once changing tone, he inquired the ambassador's name, which he well knew, and then went on, "Francesco, I can tell you that I know you by reputation and know you to be of good lineage and your house to be an old one in Milan and the Pietrasanta family to have produced many men of great ability, valor, and reputation. Furthermore, after your arrival, I investigated your character as thoroughly as I could and asked some Savoyard ambassadors about you. Everyone reported so well of you, and your speech and manner now have so pleased me, that, without your having mandate or credentials [which documents a courier had lost] I will trust what you say and do as you request—but had your master sent that charlatan now in Savoy, [the feckless Giovanni Bianchi] or some other of that ilk, I would have hidden away and never have been willing to hear him."

On receiving Pietrasanta's solemn promise that the Duke would renounce his connection with Burgundy and keep his obligations, Louis agreed to the renewal of the alliance, saying that he wanted the Duke of Milan for his "good brother" and that all past troubles would be consigned to oblivion. Request the Duke, the King went on, to work for the conservation of the state of Savoy. When Pietrasanta replied that Milan was happy to support young Duke Philibert's government, Louis said, "What did you say his name was?—Philibert? Truly we have not yet learned his name." Perhaps it was a private joke between the King and Commynes.

There developed one hitch in the drawing up of the treaty. Louis insisted on removing from the preamble a mention of his league with Francesco Sforza in 1461 when he was Dauphin, "in order not to give this obvious bad example to his son of the things he himself had done against his father."

(3) Not many days before, Louis had received word that Galeazzo-Maria Sforza had been assassinated in Milan on the day after Christmas in the church of St. Stephen, a church the Duke much favored for ogling pretty girls. Like the rest of the world, Louis did not much mourn the demise of the weak and lecherous Duke—his Duchess, Bona, Louis's sister-in-law, wrote to a Roman prelate to inquire if there was hope that her spouse might possibly have slipped into Purgatory. The King's first thoughts on the subject—his response as a ruler to a fellow ruler's murder—were expressed in a letter to the citizens of Poitiers: "We have recently learned of the detestable and cruel death of our brother-in-law the late Duke of Milan."

But, on January 12, the King wrote to these same citizens of Poitiers, "We expressly command you that instantly, without delay, you order a general procession, as you are accustomed to do on religious holidays, to celebrate the good news our couriers have brought us of the death of the Duke of Milan and the Duke of Burgundy, our old enemies." The disappearance within a fortnight of two such princes, one of whom had played false the interests, and the other of whom had long sought the destruction, of the realm of France, offered too vivid a symbolism for Louis to resist.

22. THE BURGUNDIAN INHERITANCE

(1) The lordships making up the Burgundian state were either fiefs of France or territories nominally under the suzerainty of the Emperor. Even the former represented a variety of tenures. The Duchy of Burgundy, a princely *apanage*, would supposedly return to the Crown if the Duke had no male heir (though it has been argued that, in this case, Marie could inherit the Duchy—see A. De Ridder, *Les Droits de Charles-Quint au Duché de Bourgogne*, Travaux . . . de Louvain, III, 1890). The Counties of Artois and Flanders, held in simple homage, rather like Brittany, were subject to the jurisdiction of the Parlement of Paris. Picardy, repurchased by Louis XI in 1463, had been wrested from him by the treaties of Conflans (1465) and Péronne (1468). For the principal imperial lordships—the County of Burgundy, Luxembourg, Hainault, Brabant, Holland, and Zealand—Duke Charles had never done homage or sought imperial investiture. The division of fiefs did not correspond to the division of peoples: the imperial County of Burgundy and most of Hainault are French-speaking, whereas the great towns of Flanders—Ghent, Bruges, Ypres— are inhabited by Flemings.

(2) Commynes's account of this revealing moment is inevitably colored by the wisdom of hindsight and the convenience of memory, recording it as he did a dozen years later. Ignoring the dangers inherent in the marriage of the Dauphin to Marie (see note 3, p. 434) and the very real possibility that a policy of friendship and conciliation might have simply allowed the Burgundian state to recover its strength, Commynes nonetheless presents his case modestly. "I do not intend in any way to blame our King by saying that he had erred in this matter, for others who knew and understood it better than I might perchance be—and some then were—of the same mind as he." What troubled Commynes was that "nothing was discussed, either then or at any other time, regarding the policy." "Nevertheless," he emphasizes, "the intelligence of our King was so great that neither I nor any other of his advisers could have seen so clearly into his affairs as he did." Convinced, however, that his view was correct, Commynes concludes that God, to chastise an unworthy world, had prevented the King from achieving the peaceful absorption of the Burgundian domains.

As the lord of Argenton was about to depart for Poitiers, Jean Daillon, lord du Lude, came up to him. "He was," as Commynes sketches him, "a man very agreeable to the King in some things; he was always avid to feather his own nest; he never feared to deceive anyone and was himself very credulous and often deceived. He knew how to amuse his master and was indeed very good company.

" 'Here you are going off,' " said du Lude mockingly, " 'at the very hour that, if ever, you should be making your fortune—think of the great things that are falling into the King's hand, by means of which he can bestow bounties on those he loves. As far as I'm concerned, I expect to be Governor of Flanders and turn myself into gold there!' And with that he gave a great guffaw." Commynes confesses, "I had no desire to laugh, for I feared that what du Lude said might have been at the King's prompting. I replied that I would be very happy if thus it happened and that I had hope that the King would not forget me. And so I left."

(3) The judgment of Commynes, echoed by some modern French historians, that King Louis gravely erred in failing to bring about the marriage of Marie and the Dauphin is open to considerable question. That Marie would have accepted the offer appears doubtful. That she and the Flemings would have agreed to her putting herself and her domains under the King's protection is denied by the available evidence; yet only under such terms could the marriage probably have been worth the risk. Curiously enough, Commynes leaves out of calculation the decisive fact that the Dauphin was already contracted to the English Princess Elizabeth. Five years later, it is true, Louis did not hesitate to abrogate that engagement, but the situation in England in 1482 was very different from that in 1477, as will be seen. That he carefully refrained from making any public offer for her hand in the Dauphin's behalf suggests that he well realized, as Commynes evidently did not, that a contract uniting Marie and the Dauphin, perhaps even the proffer of such a contract, might embroil him in war with the English. It is Commynes himself who reveals, concerning the situation in early 1477, that the King "was determined to employ all his powers in order that the English peace might be maintained." Such an accomplishment was hardly compatible with openly flouting Edward IV's eldest daughter.

(4) On February 14, 1477, Sir John Paston wrote from London to one of his brothers: ". . . yesterday began the great council to which all the estates [i.e., lords and prelates] of the land shall come to [sic], but if it be for great and reasonable excuses; and I suppose the chief cause of this assembly is, to common [confer about] what is best to do, now upon the great change by the death of the Duke of Burgundy, and for the keeping of Calais and the Marches, and for the preservation of the amities taken late, as well with France as now with the Members [Estates] of Flanders; whereto I doubt not there shall be in all haste both the Dukes of Clarence and Gloucester. . . . It is so that this day I hear great likelihood, that my lord Hastings shall hastily go to Calais with great company. . . . It seemeth that the world is all quavering; it will reboil somewhere, so that I deem young men shall be cherished. . . ."

The heartburnings of the English as King Louis overran Burgundian lands near Calais can be gathered from a letter written April 14, 1477, in that town by Sir John Paston, who had gone there in the household of Lord Hastings, the Governor: "As for tidings here, the French King hath gotten many of the towns of the Duke of Burgundy, as St. Quentin, Abbeville, Montreuil; and now of late he hath gotten Bethune and Hesdin with the castle there, which is one of the royalest castles of the world; and on Sunday at evening [April 13] the Admiral of France laid siege at Boulogne; and this day it is said, that the French King shall come thither; and this night it is said, that there was a vision seen about the walls of Boulogne, as [if] it had been a woman with a marvelous light; men deem that Our Lady there will show herself a lover to that town. God forfend [i.e., forbid] that it were French; it were worth £40,000 that it were English."

(5) A Breton messenger, Maurice Gourmel, copied all the letters that he bore between Edward IV and Francis II of Brittany, delivered the copies, and sold the originals to Louis XI for one hundred crowns apiece. In answer to protestations of complete devotion from Francis, Louis dispatched him some of these letters with the terse message that he wished to hear no more such declarations until the Duke of Brittany broke all ties with England, as he had sworn to do. As for Edward IV's Spanish negotiations, the Castilian envoy to England, Dr. de Lucena, copied out his instructions from King Ferdinand and promptly sold the original to the King of France.

(6) According to the interpolator of Jean de Roye's Parisian chronicle, usually reliable and here quite circumstantial, Edward IV, on receiving Louis's report, immediately dispatched an envoy to France to ask what, in the King's opinion, he should do about Clarence. Louis asked one question: "Do you know for certain that my brother the King of England has the Duke of Clarence in his power?" "Sire, yes," was the reply. The King then quoted a line of Lucan: "*Tolle moras, sepe no-*

cuit differre paratas." (Avoid delay—postponement of a planned course of action often causes harm.) The ambassador asked for an explanation, "but he was unable to get anything more out of the King." The following February, 1478, a Parliament condemned Clarence to death on a charge of treason. Shortly after, he was secretly executed in the Tower, apparently—according to a variety of contemporary accounts —by being plunged into a butt of Malmsey wine.

(7) In Italy war was beginning between two rival alliances of powers, at the same time that Turkish advances in the Mediterranean were threatening Christendom. Knowing that the King of France was deeply involved in efforts to achieve the pacification of Italy, Edward gave to John Doget, treasurer of Chichester Cathedral, the mission of consulting with King Louis as to what might be done, and of then proceeding, if the King so indicated, to Rome to support French efforts. Louis magnanimously informed Doget that, though he himself had already offered his mediation, he would now be delighted to have his brother Edward IV join him in that mission. By March 16 the King had chosen one of his secretaries, Louis Toustain, to accompany Doget to Rome. Toustain was instructed not only to make this new offer of joint mediation, but, wherever he went, to inform all the powers of Italy "in what love, benevolence, and league, the Kings of England and France were linked," so much so that "what one wished, the other wished." Before the end of March, Doget and Toustain had taken the road to Italy.

By this means, not only did the King of France prove his devotion to the King of England but, by courtesy of that King, did himself a service as well. As he probably foresaw, Maximilian's father, the Emperor Frederick III, huffed and puffed in impotent anger that he, the head of Christendom, had not been cast in the role of mediator. Maximilian himself, desperately seeking Edward IV's aid, was lacerated by this demonstration of Anglo-French solidarity, and tired Edward's patience with vain laments and vain proposals for some kind of Anglo-imperial counter-demonstration in Italy. Within a year, Edward's interest in the Milanese match and his desire to cut a figure in Italy had faded away, but not before Louis had drawn considerable profit from this curious impulse of his ally.

(8) Lord Hastings had, at first, made a little trouble. Refusing to sign a receipt, he declared to the French paymaster— "If you wish, put the money in my sleeve, but no acquittance showing I was a pensioner of France will ever be found in the French treasury." Louis was somewhat irritated, but ordered his agents not to ask Hastings for a receipt; and in a little while Edward IV's genial Lord Chamberlain was dispatching dogs and horses to the King of France and assuring him that he would do everything in his power to be of service.

(9) Instead, King Louis sent the lord du Bouchage and two other negotiators to Arras to see what they could accomplish indirectly by winning over some of Maximilian's people and creating "divisions." In letter after letter, answering frequent communications from this diplomatic front, Louis encouraged, advised, warned, his men. October 9: Refuse to hear any more arguments about the right of females to inherit; they'll never make any reasonable proposals till you do so. October 29 [addressing du Bouchage as "the rich Count," a joke about his love of money]: You are doing well; "if you can't accomplish great things, do not scorn little ones. Do as you will see with your eyes." And keep away from the English. November 3: Don't neglect little things; give safe-conducts to people making promises, "bad lot though they may be." Find out what ones are willing to make a reasonable treaty and what their powers are—Maximilian shows himself to be against peace. November 8: Don't go to a town where you might be surprised by the English. Make no agreements merely to avoid a rupture. "You are beasts indeed if you believe that at this great assembly to consider peace terms they intend anything reasonable; for the Dowager [Margaret of York] is there, and she is there only to make trouble. Also, where there are a great many people, one acts very formal and makes stiff demands, and one is ashamed to confess before so many people that it's a matter of sheer necessity. . . . I would not send first to Maximilian, unless there is a special reason. If his intention is good, as mine is, let him dispatch a man or two, and you and the lord of Souliers [Palamède Forbin] work with them to find a way to a good end, with neither party's demanding that the other speak first—rather, all work together, as if the four of you served one master, for peace and amity." November 10: "You have but to let this [Burgundian] assembly break up of itself; certain prelates and lords have come there to Lille only to see that nothing is done, so have no regrets if they do nothing. But when these great ones have departed, you can then negotiate, if there is a desire for peace, with those of Ghent or with the Chancellor. . . . November 13: Maximilian's people never make the same demands twice—always new proposals. "You see well, bloody beasts that you are, that he keeps no faith, so trust only what you see. They are, without question, lying to you; you do a good job of lying in return." December 11: "You have taken too much trouble for me; but I am amazed that they are such almighty liars. . . . If any of them is willing to do something, accept the offer, so that you do not lose your labors. If nothing—go off on your pilgrimages."

By this time Louis's passion for dogs had intruded itself into these intricate maneuverings. For a brief space the French had held a castle of the Burgundian lord of Bossu, during which time someone had apparently noticed, and reported to the King, the magnificent greyhounds Bossu owned. This lord was a friend of one of Maximilian's chief favorites, Wolfgang Polheim, captured at Guinegate, whom the King had treated well and given a temporary release in order to seek his ransom, and also, the King hoped, to influence Maximilian to come to terms. It now occurred to Louis, very eager for Bossu's animals, that he might secure the greyhounds and at the same time strengthen the bonds of gratitude with Polheim. The King had instructed du Bouchage, in the first of two letters of November 13, "If [Polheim] can't be of use to you, at least I want the two or three finest greyhound bitches of the lord of Bossu, and two young male greyhounds, or whatever good ones he has— and investigate carefully what he does have. . . . I know well that Bossu will not deliver them unless he receives one hundred or two hundred marcs of silver. Make no complaint about it, for I will pay." A month later, the King wrote anxiously, "My lord du Bouchage, you have complete authority concerning Polheim, but take care that he does not deceive you and deliver you spayed bitches, and small ones. Take none unless they are very large and unspayed; and as for the males, take none unless they are very large; and be careful how you send them to me so that they are not injured on the road." Four days later, the King tried to clarify, and perhaps rationalize, his preoccupation with the dogs: they provided a cover, he explained to du Bouchage, for working on Polheim in order to make him friendly to the French cause. But Louis's anxiety over the greyhounds remained very much in the foreground: "Get me some of them," he pleaded with du Bouchage, "and I will give you the thing which you love best, which is money." By the first weeks of 1481, however, Bossu was hinting that he would require a special recompense for his incomparable dogs, Polheim had somehow failed to be useful, and the negotiations faded away.

(10) King Louis's victory is signaled in a letter he wrote sometime in June to Lord Hastings: "My good cousin, I have been informed by some Norman merchants coming from England of a rumor running there that I was at Boulogne and was going to put siege to Calais. My good cousin, since this matter closely concerns me and my honor, I beg you kindly to tell my lord my cousin [Edward IV] that I have not thought of such a thing at all nor would do so nor would allow the smallest village in the Calais pale to be touched; and if anyone would undertake an attack on

Calais, I would defend if to the best of my ability. I did not move from Plessis du Parc until May 26, and I am going off to see my military camp near Pont de l'Arche, which I have not yet seen, and I have ordered my lord d'Esquerdes [Philippe de Crèvecoeur] and the Picards to be there at the end of this month. I assure you that this is the truth of the matter, *and never will my lord my cousin find me remiss in what I have promised him* [italics added]." The last sentence indicates that Louis had brought Edward to terms.

23. THE ITALIAN QUESTION

(1) On October 3 Commynes dispatched to Palmier a letter which he first gave the Milanese envoys a chance to copy surreptitiously. "Following your departure there has occurred at Milan what you will have since learned. It is necessary that you proceed with all diligence to King Ferrante, because everything depends on him, and that you learn what his intention is as regards the matter that the Prince his son has made known to him. One of the points was to eject Messer Cicco from the government . . . and to establish in power those who are there today. This point is accomplished. But for nothing in the world would the King be willing to allow the destruction of the Florentines nor the person of Lorenzo; and if at Milan there is any idea of making war on Florence, the King is resolved to aid by all means the Florentines and Lorenzo. . . ." With this missive went one from the Prince of Taranto in the same vein.

24. RULER AND REALM

(1) The last leaf fell from the Angevin tree in 1482 with the death of that Princess of passions and misfortunes Margaret of Anjou, ransomed by Louis XI for fifty thousand crowns and living in heartbroken retirement on a pension he had provided in exchange for her renunciation of her claims upon the Angevin inheritance. To her chief lady-in-waiting he wrote, on hearing of her death, "Madame, I am sending you an equerry to bring me all the dogs you have had from the late Queen of England. You know that she has made me her heir, and that the dogs are the only goods I will have from her—also they are what I prefer to have. I beg you, hold back none of them, for you would terribly displease me in doing so; and if you know of anybody else who has any, tell [my equerry]."

(2) Perhaps because his father had been a petty royal official, at a time when such officers often found life difficult for them in princely domains, Jean Doyat was from youth a devoted partisan of Louis XI. During the King's campaign in the Bourbonnais in the spring of 1465 he had done notable service with the royal artillery. Louis did not forget it. When Doyat was driven from Cusset, his native place, the following year because of his marked devotion to the King's interests, Louis took him into service as a valet of the wardrobe. By 1477 his ability and his fidelity had marked him out, in the King's mind, as the man to reduce the Duke of Bourbon to the rule of royal law. Louis appointed him *Bailli* and Captain of Cusset; he was, in fact, the King's deputy for the Bourbonnais. So successfully did he undertake the task of enforcing the royal law against the Duke of Bourbon's legal and police officers that the King made him "councilor and chamberlain," Baron of Montréal, and Governor of Auvergne. As a result of Doyat's legal battles and investigations, the chief officers of the Duke were summoned before the Parlement of Paris in 1480 to answer to an imposing array of violations—judging of privileged cases, issuing letters of grace, creating fairs, coining money, forcing people to renounce letters of safeguard signed by the King, conducting litigation regarding the property of cathedral churches. Louis XI addressed a sharp warning to the Parlement: "We have no desire whatsoever to remove any of the rights in their territories enjoyed by the late Duke Charles of Bourbon and by our very dear and beloved brother, the present Duke, at the time of the death of our late lord and father. We are unwilling, however, to be prevented from enjoying the rights in those territories held by our father at his death as we are also unwilling to allow the present Duke to enjoy additional rights. Therefore see to it that you act in this sense, and let there be no slip-up. If you do otherwise, we will undo it, for we have decided that the matter remain thus." After a trial lasting a year, the ducal officers were freed, but Parlement decreed that their enterprises had clearly infringed upon royal authority and reaffirmed the principle that all justice emanates from the King. Louis appointed special hearings, "Grands Jours," to be held in the Duke's territories. Parlement also brought charges against Geoffrey Hébert, the learned Bishop of Coutances, Bourbon's intimate adviser, who was accused of practicing necromancy to forward ducal schemes. Consigned to prison by the Parlement, the Bishop was freed five months later by King Louis. When the Archbishop of Tours protested against such treatment of a prelate, Louis returned the terse answer: "In regard to my lord of Coutances who was arrested at Paris, say to my lord of Tours that it was done in accordance with justice, and, if it had not been that I ordered him freed, it would have gone hard with him. He is an invoker of devils in Latin, Greek, and the vernacular, he has served my lord of Bourbon in so being, and he has done more for him than he should." Doubtless the devils Louis had in mind were those of intransigent feudalism. Louis enjoyed consulting astrologers too, no less than did Bourbon, Brittany, and the late Duke of Nemours.

Doyat returned to the charge with undiminished zeal, this time establishing himself at Clermont in the Duke of Bourbon's territory of Auvergne. For centuries the citizens had been fighting for their rights against their bishop, who at this moment was Bourbon's brother Charles, Archbishop of Lyons. Having persuaded the townspeople to seek from the King a charter of incorporation, which was promptly granted, Jean Doyat vigorously set about improving law enforcement and developing trade, and was soon attempting to found a university. When famine and plague struck the town in the winter of 1480–81, Doyat hurried from the court to risk his life in helping the city—enlarging hospitals, distributing alms, securing shipments of grain. This son of his own spirit Louis then wanted near him; Doyat returned to court as one of the King's chief advisers. After the death of Louis XI, Doyat paid for his service of the future against the past. The Duke of Bourbon had him arrested, shipped from prison to prison, and finally condemned to condign punishment: he was banished from the realm with the loss of all his goods, but not until he was whipped through the Duke's territories, had an ear cut off, and his tongue pierced with a red-hot iron. He survived, to serve Louis XI's son, this time in the old trade of artilleryman, when Charles VIII invaded Italy. Over the Alps, Doyat shepherded the French ordnance, without loss of a single gun. He died as he was negotiating the surrender of a little town in the Kingdom of Naples.

(3) The intransigence of the inhabitants of Arras, exacerbated by the extortions of the lord du Lude and his officers, had produced a series of acts of disobedience, plottings, petty revolts. It was early in 1479 that the King decided to expel the troublemakers and institute a plan of municipal colonization. The general idea was not entirely new. The English in the preceding century had turned Calais into an English town, and had made gestures of colonization in Normandy after Henry V's conquest; but no such thorough social-economic undertaking as Louis now envisaged had ever been tried. After thrashing out the principal design with his financial advisers, representative merchants, a number of municipal officers, Louis appointed commissioners to convoke at Tours an assembly of delegates from the main cities of the realm. Here the plan was explained, amended, developed in full detail. Louis had been careful to consult the experts and to secure in advance the approval, if not the enthusiasm, of the bourgeois community of the realm; but the conception, the working out of ways and means, most of the regulations and provisos, were clearly his. In mid-May (1479) the inhabitants of Arras began to take their departure; before the end of June almost all of them had left of their own volition or been expelled. Some were given shelter and a modicum of assistance in French towns; others withdrew to Burgundian territory. The name of the city was now changed to "Franchise": the new colonists were to be freed of all manner of taxes and tariffs, as an inducement for them to create a model city and carry on with zeal the great tradition of cloth-making. Throughout June regional assemblies all over France spelled out the final details of the King's experiment to representatives from the surrounding towns.

Franchise was to be colonized by three thousand households, artisans and shopkeepers, and by a certain number of well-to-do merchants. Each of the chief towns of the realm was awarded its quota of households and merchants—Orléans, seventy heads of households; Tours, fifty; Troyes in Champagne, forty-eight; Évreux, twenty-five; and so it went. Eight provinces of southern France were to furnish each twenty merchants and two hundred workers. Emphasis was placed on wool workers and cloth producers. In addition to a number of the latter and four merchants, Orléans contributed, among its householders, two barbers, three bakers, two candle-makers, one haberdasher, two carpenters, three masons, two millers, a tavern keeper. At the expense of their respective towns, the new colonists received carefully specified indemnities according to the value of the property they left behind, their traveling costs, the number in the family. They were also given two months' wages, fixed at six livres the household. Between July 5 and 14 all municipal contingents were inspected by royal commissioners at Senlis or at the bridge of Meulan, west of Paris. They were then organized into convoys and dispatched northward. Between Amiens and Arras a military escort guarded them from Burgundian raiders.

The trouble was that the objects of this solicitude, the new colonists, persisted in acting like human beings, overlooking benefits and opportunities and exhibiting a flagrant disregard of the whole concept. Although a few of the artisans and merchants were happy to respond to the call of adventure and profit, most of the colonists had not wanted to uproot themselves from their homes and seek a new life. A Milanese ambassador reported from Paris that he had seen fifteen hundred men going to Franchise "with tears in their eyes." Nicolas de' Roberti, the envoy of Ferrara, wrote that "the greater part of the [colonists] are going only because they are forced to, and the King has much embittered the minds of his people over this." The towns had of course taken advantage of the situation to get rid of the less desirable members of the community. The officers of the city of Orléans, fearing that twelve of their party would be turned back by the royal commissioners at Meulan, offered a present of wine and one hundred gold crowns. Only six were refused, but their replacements had to be provided at once, to whom were joined a number of wives with children who had somehow evaded accompanying their husbands. It was a miserable cavalcade that wound its way across Picardy, men on horseback, women and children jolting along in straw-filled carts, wagons piled high with household goods and tools of the trade following behind. At Franchise, houses were refilled with families, shops with artisans. But nothing happened. The city did not start into life. The colonists, most of them, were not interested in work; no goods were produced for trade; people preferred to go hungry and lament their lot.

King Louis, refusing to be beaten, called in his experts and came up with a new plan. Deciding that there had been insufficient attention to cloth making, the historic industry, the King ordered a fresh recruitment limited to merchants and textile workers. Franchise began to produce some cloth but it was too often of poor quality and there was not enough of it. In 1481 Louis generated still another plan. To remedy lack of capitalization, he decreed the formation of cloth-producing companies, each with a capital of five thousand crowns. But the realm refused to buy the cloth because it was too high-priced and still deficient in quality. The King then gave the town a municipal organization, added still more privileges and exemptions, and ordained that the towns of the realm must absorb the products of the textile workers of Franchise. Each piece of cloth was sealed with a lead seal, stamped with an F. This measure inspired all sorts of evasions and failed to inspire the colonists. In the end, Louis sadly allowed the new inhabitants of Franchise to drift away to their old homes and the former inhabitants to return to their town, Arras.

(4) Louis's mind did not cease its questing after all manner of knowledge. An unusual death reported to him prompted the King to call for a careful autopsy. One February Saturday in 1480 he ordered a different kind of scientific inquiry. In the presence of the Mayor and four aldermen of Tours, a number of royal officials, and priests of the town, "there was performed an experiment with certain poisons, which they made a dog swallow in fried mutton and an omelet." The Mayor and aldermen solemnly signed a certificate of death. Next day, with a roaring fire in the chamber and a large meal to hearten them "in case they missed dinner," seven surgeons then performed an autopsy on the dog, in the presence of officialdom, and the animal was afterward interred by the banks of the Loire. The report sent to the King has not survived.

EPILOGUE

(1) Philippe de Commynes fared badly after the death of Louis XI. The powerful La Trémoille family sued to regain the great principality of Talmont, which Louis XI had bestowed upon Commynes with more regard for his services than for the true title of the property, and which Commynes fought to keep by means not always scrupulous—pointing out to the Parlement of Paris, with some justice, that it was not his doing but the late King's which had put him in possession of the estate. Evidently in the hope of protecting himself, the lord of Argenton became a partisan of Louis, Duke of Orléans, leader of the princes seeking to restore the feudal regime of old (see the Epilogue). As a result, after the Guerre Folle he "tasted" an iron cage in the castle of Loches for five months, was then transferred to prison in Paris. In 1489 the Parlement adjudged Talmont to the La Trémoille family and sentenced Commynes to pay heavy costs and to sequester himself on his estates. It was in this year and the next that he composed the first part of his *Mémoires,* the biography of Louis XI. By 1491, regaining favor at court, he had become a royal councilor. After he crossed the Alps with Charles VIII in 1494, the King's favorites got rid of him and his judicious counsels by sending him to soothe the Venetians while the King pursued his journey to Naples. Given almost no instructions and little news, he helplessly watched the formation of the coalition against France in the spring of 1495. After rejoining Charles VIII on the homeward march, he fought in the battle of Fornovo, which he brilliantly describes in the *Mémoires,* and played a statesmanly role, though enjoying small favor, in the temporary settlement that allowed King Charles to return to France. His talents unused, he employed his time in 1497—98 in completing his *Mémoires,* which afterward received some revision. At the accession of Louix XII in 1498 he once more took part in the royal councils and accompanied the King on an expedition to subdue Genoa in 1507. Four years later, as the result of a "sudden accident," he died at Argenton, on October 18, 1511, at about the age of sixty-five.

BIBLIOGRAPHY

A LISTING OF WORKS useful for a study of the life of Louis XI—encompassing, as it must, not only sources and treatises which illuminate the whole European political scene in the fifteenth century but also materials dealing with the social, economic, administrative aspects of the reign—would well-nigh require a book in itself. I have limited the bibliography to identifying the chief manuscripts, printed sources, and scholarly books and articles on which the biography is directly based. In short, it is intended as a convenient substitute for a cumbersome scholarly apparatus of notes. I have thus, after giving those works covering the life of Louis XI in general, divided the bibliography into sections, corresponding to the principal sections of the book, in which I list additional materials on which I have drawn for those respective sections. Unlike the pertinent Italian diplomatic documents (see Preface), the manuscript sources in French archives, especially the great collection in the Bibliothèque Nationale, Paris, have been well worked over; and the most important papers have been printed as appendices to a variety of scholarly editions of other source material, notably in the four-volume eighteenth-century edition of Commynes' *Mémoires,* edited by N. Lenglet du Fresnoy. Those historical works in the bibliography which reproduce such important primary sources have been marked with an asterisk.

In "outdoor research" I have followed King Louis's journeys and campaigns along the roads of France and viewed the principal localities, in the Loire Valley and elsewhere, associated with him; and for the main battles described—Montlhéry (July 1465), south of Paris; Grandson (March, 1476), on the shores of Lake Neufchâtel; and Morat (June, 1476), likewise in modern Switzerland—I have studied the terrain in the light of the contemporary accounts of these engagements. Montlhéry is probably reported in fuller detail and from a greater variety of viewpoints than any battle of the Western world fought up to that time. For all three of these fields the eyewitness accounts of Giovanni Pietro (Jean Pierre) Panigarola, Milanese ambassador to the court of France, 1465–68, and to the court of Burgundy, 1475–76, are invaluable.

GENERAL

I. MANUSCRIPT SOURCES

Bibliothèque Nationale, Paris: Le Grand Mss., B.N. fonds français 6963–6990. B.N. fonds italiens 1585–88; 1593–95, 1649 (Italian diplomatic documents).

Archivio di Stato, Milan: Archivio Sforzesco, Potenzi Estere: *Borgogna,* cart. 514–521 (1450–81); *Savoya,* cart. 491–497 (1474–76); *Francia,* cart. 524–525 (1450–61), cart. 532–545 and 1312 (1466–82).

II. PRINTED SOURCES, BOOKS, AND ARTICLES

Arnaud, Eugène. "Louis XI et les Vaudois du Dauphiné," (document inédit de 1479), Paris, Impr. Nat., 1896. (Extr. du Bulletin historique et philologique, 1895.)

Asse, E. *Louis XI et Charles le Téméraire*. Paris, 1889.

Barante, (de). *Histoire des ducs de Bourgogne*. 12 vols. Paris, 1824–26.

Barbé, Louis A. *Margaret of Scotland and the Dauphin Louis*. London, 1917.

Basin, Thomas. *Histoire des règnes de Charles VII et de Louis XI*, ed. J. Quicherat. 4 vols. Paris, 1855–59.

Bazin, Arthur. *Compiègne sous Louis XI* . . . Compiègne, 1907.

Beaurepaire, Ch. de. *Notes sur six voyages de Louis XI à Rouen*. Rouen, 1458. (Also in *Travaux de l'Académie de Rouen*, 1856–57.)

Bernus, P. *Louis XI et Pierre de Brezé*. Angers, 1912.

Bittman, Karl. *Ludwig XI und Karl der Kühne: die Memoiren des Philippe de Commynes als historische Quelle*, I, Gottingen, 1964.

Bonnafous, M. *Toulouse et Louis XI*. Toulouse, 1927.

Bosseboeuf, L. A. *Dix ans à Tours sous Louis XI* . . . Tours, 1890.

——. "Comptes royaux inédits," *Bulletin de la Société Archéologique de Touraine*, XII, 1900.

Boulieu. "Louis XI à Lyon," *Revue d'histoire de Lyon*, II (1903).

°Bricard, G. *Un serviteur et compère de Louis XI, Jean Bourré*. Paris, 1893.

Brown, Rawdon, ed. *Calendar of State Papers* . . . *Venice*. I. London, 1864.

Bulletin de la Société archéologique du Finistère, X, 100–33. (Correspondence, etc. of Louis XI and Francis II of Brittany.)

Buser, B. *Die Beziehungen der Mediceer zu Frankreich, 1433–94, in ihrem Zusammenhang mit den allgemeinen Verhaltnisse Italiens*. Leipzig, 1879.

Caillet, Louis. *Étude sur les relations de la commune de Lyon avec Charles VII et Louis XI, 1417–1483*. Annales de l'Université de Lyons, fasc. 21. Lyon-Paris, 1909.

°Calmette, Joseph. *Louis XI, Jean II, et la Révolution Catalane*. Toulouse, 1903.

° ——. and G. Périnelle. *Louis XI et l'Angleterre*. Paris, 1930.

Carrière, V. *Nicole Tilhart, secrétaire et général des finances de Louis XI, Le Moyen Age*. Paris, 1905.

Cerioni, Lydia. "La Politica Italiana di Luigi XI," *Archivio Storico Lombardo*, ser. 8, vols. I–II (1949–50), 58–156.

Chabannes, H. de. *Preuves* . . . *Histoire de la Maison de Chabannes*. 4 vols. Dijon, 1890–98.

Champion, Pierre. *Vie de Charles D'Orléans*. Paris, 1911.

——. *François Villon, sa vie et son temps*. 2 vols. Paris, 1913.

——. *Louis XI*, 2 vols. Paris, 1927.

Champollion-Figeac, J. J., ed. *Documents historiques inédits* . . . 4 vols. Paris, 1843–48.

Chantelauze, R. *Portraits historiques: Philippe de Commynes*. 2nd edition, Paris, 1887.

Charavay, E., J. Vaesen, B. de Mandrot, eds. *Lettres de Louis XI*. 11 vols. Paris, 1883–1909.

Chastellain, Georges. *Oeuvres*, ed. Kervyn de Lettenhove. 8 vols. Brussels, 1863–66.

Chevalier, Ulysse. *Répertoire des sources historiques du Moyen Age*. 2 vols. Paris, 1907.

Chmel, Joseph. "Briefe und Actenstücke zur Geschichte der Herzoge von Mailand von 1450 bis 1503," *Notizenblatt*, VI (1856).

Cimber, M. L. and A. Danjou. *Archives curieuses de l'histoire de France*. Ser. 1, I. Paris, 1834.

Combet, J. *Louis XI et le St. Siège*. Paris, 1903.

°Commynes, Philippe de *Mémoires*, ed. N. Lenglet du Fresnoy. 4 vols. Paris, 1747.

°——. *Mémoires*, ed. Mlle. Dupont. 3 vols. Paris, 1840–47.

——. *Mémoires*, ed. B. de Mandrot. 2 vols. Paris, 1901–1903.

——. *Mémoires*, ed. J. Calmette and G. Durville. 3 vols. Paris, 1924–25.

Courteault, H. *Gaston IV, Comte de Foix*. Bibliothèque méridionale, ser. II, vol. III. Toulouse, 1895.

Degert, Antoine. "Louis XI et ses ambassadeurs," *Revue Historique*, 154 (1927), 1–19.

Desjardins, A. and Canestrini. *Negociations diplomatiques de la France avec la Toscane*, I. Paris, 1859.

Diesbach, M. de, trans. *Louis de Diesbach, page de Louis XI*. Paris, 1901.

Dodu, Gaston. "Louis XI," *Revue Historique*, CLXVIII (1931), 55–57.

Doucet, R. "Le Gouvernement de Louis XI," *Revue des Cours et Conférences*, 1922–23 and 1923–24.

Douet d'Arcq, L. *Comptes de l'hôtel des rois de France aux XIVe et XVe siècles*. Paris, 1863.

Du Clercq, Jacques. *Mémoires*, ed. F. A. F. T. de Reiffenberg. 4 vols. 2nd edition, Brussels, 1835–36.

Duclos. *Histoire de Louis XI*. 4 vols. Paris, 1745.

——, ed. *Recueil de pièces pour servir de suite à l'histoire de Louis XI*. Paris, 1746.

Dufournet, Jean. *La destruction des Mythes dans les Mémoires de Ph. de Commynes*, I, Geneva, 1966.

Dupont-Ferrier, G. *Études sur les institutions financières de la France à la fin du moyen âge*. 2 vols. Paris, 1930–32.

Dupuy, A. *Histoire de la réunion de la Bretagne à la France*. 2 vols. Paris, 1880.

Duyse, Prudent van, and Edmund de Busscher. *Inventaire analytique des chartes et documents appartenant aux archives de la ville de Gand*. Gand, 1867.

Fawtier, R. "Organisation de l'artillerie royale au temps de Louis XI," *Essays in Medieval History*. Presented to T. F. Tout. Manchester, 1925.

Florio, Francesco. *Description de Tours*, ed. A. Salmon. *Mémoires de la Société Archéologique de Tours*, VII (1854), 82.

Forgeot, Henri. *Jean Balue, cardinal d'Angers*. Paris, 1895.

Gachard, Louis Prosper. *Collection de documents inédits concernant l'histoire de la Belgique*. 3 vols. Brussels, 1833–35.

——. *Compte rendu des séances de la commission d'histoire de Belgique*. II,2, 269–448; II,3, 193–324 (1852–53).

——. *Notices et extraits des manuscrits qui concernant l'histoire de Belgique*. 2 vols. Brussels, 1875–77.

Gandilhon, A. *Contribution à l'histoire de la vie privée et de la cour de Louis XI*. Bourges, 1906.

Gandilhon, René. "Louis XI Fondateur du Service des Postes en France," *Revue Historique*, 183 (1938), 37–41.

——. *Politique économique de Louis XI*. Paris, 1941.

Ghinzoni, P. "Galeazzo-Maria Sforza e Luigi XI," *Archivio Storico Lombardo*, ser. 2, II (1885), 17–32.

Guerin, P. and L. Celier, eds. *Recueil de documents concernant le Poitou . . .* vols. X–XII, Poitiers, 1906–19.

Guillaume. *Histoire de l'organisation militaire sous le ducs de Bourgogne*. Mémoires couronnés par l'Académie de Bruxelles, XXII (1847–48).

Harcourt, Louis d' and C. Maumené. *Iconographie des rois de France, de Louis XI à Louis XIII*. Paris, 1929.

Haynin, Jean de. *Mémoires*, ed. R. Chalon. Société des bibliophiles de Mons, 2 vols. Mons, 1842.

Hinds, Allen B., ed. *Calendar of State Papers and Manuscripts . . . Milan*. I. London, 1912.

Huizinga, J. "L'Etat bourguignon, ses rapports avec la France et les origines d'une nationalité néerlandaise," *Le Moyen Age*, XL, XLI, Paris 1930–31.

Ilardi, Vincent. "Fifteenth-Century Diplomatic Documents in Western European Archives and Libraries (1450–94)," *Studies in the Renaissance*, IX (1962), 64–112.

Jaurgain, J. *Deux Comtes de Comminges: Jean de Lescun et Odet d'Aydie*. Paris, 1919.

Kendall, P. M. *Richard the Third*. London and New York, 1955.

——. *Warwick the Kingmaker*. London and New York, 1957.

——. *The Yorkist Age*. London and New York, 1962.

——. and Vincent Ilardi, eds. *Dispatches, with Related Documents, of Milanese Ambassadors in France and Burgundy, 1450–83*. (Only Vol. I, 1450–60, has so far been published: Ohio, 1970.)

Kirk, J. F. *History of Charles the Bold, Duke of Burgundy*. 3 vols. London, 1863–68.

°La Marche, Leçoy de. *Le Roi René*. 2 vols. Paris, 1879.

La Marche, Olivier de. *Mémoires*, ed. H. Beaune and J. d'Arbaumont. 4 vols. Paris, 1883–88.

La Mure, J. M. de. *Histoire des ducs de Bourbon*, ed. R. Chantelauze. Paris, 1868. Vol. II.

La Trémoille, Duc de. *Archives d'un serviteur de Louis XI, Louis de La Trémoille, 1451–81*. Nantes, 1888.

Lauer, Philippe. *Les chapeaux de Louis XI*. Paris, 1926.

Lavisse, E. *Histoire de France*. Paris, 1902. Vol. IV, part ii.

Legeay, U. *Histoire de Louis XI*. 2 vols. Paris, 1874.

Lesellier, J. "Une curieuse correspondance inédite entre Louis XI et Sixte IV," *Mélanges d'archéol. et d'hist.*, XLV (1928), École francaise de Rome.

Leseur, Guillaume. *Histoire de Gaston IV, Comte de Foix*, ed., H. Courtenault. 2 vols. Paris, 1893–96.

Lettenhove, Kervyn de. *Lettres et négociations de Philippe de Commynes*. 3 vols. Brussels, 1867–74.

——, ed. *Chroniques relatives à l'histoire de la Belgique sous la domination des ducs de Bourgogne*. 3 vols. Brussels, 1873.

Lincey, Leroux de. *Chants historiques et populaires du temps de Charles VII et de Louis XI*. Paris, 1857.

Lincy, Le Roux de and Tisserand. *Paris et ses historiens*. Paris, 1867. (Contains Antoine Astesan, "Éloge descriptif de la ville de Paris et des principales villes de France.")

Lot, Ferdinand, and Robert Fawtier, eds. *Histoire des institutions françaises au Moyen Âge*. 2 vols. Paris, 1957.

Louandre. *Lettres et bulletins des armées de Louis XI aux officiers municipaux d'Abbeville*. Abbeville, 1837.

Luce, S., ed. *Chronique du Mont-St.-Michel, 1343–1468*. 2 vols. Paris, 1879–83.

Mandrot, Bernard de. *Jacques d'Armagnac, duc de Nemours*. Paris, 1890. (Also in *Revue Historique*, XLIII, XLIV [1890].)

——. *Les relations de Charles VII et de Louis XI avec les cantons suisses, 1444–83*. Zurich, 1881.

——. *Louis XI, Jean V d'Armagnac, et le drame de Lectoure*. Paris, 1888. (Also in *Revue Historique*, XXXVIII [1888].)

Marchegay, P., ed. "Lettres de Marie de Valois à Olivier de Coëtivy, 1458–72," Annuaire départemental de la Société d'émulation de la Vendée, 1874.

Marneffe, E. de. *Itineraire de Charles le Hardi, comte de Charolais, puis duc de Bourgogne. Bulletin de la Commission royale d'histoire*, 4th series, XII (1885).

Mattingly, Garret. *Renaissance Diplomacy.* London, 1955.

Maulde, R. de. *Procédures politiques du règne de Louis XI.* Paris, 1885.

Maupoint, Jean de. *Journal Parisien*, ed. G. Fagniez. *Mémoires* de la Société de l'Histoire de Paris et de l'Île-de-France, IV. Paris, 1878.

Mazzatinti, Giuseppe. *Inventario dei Manoscritti Italiani delle Biblioteche di Francia.* 3 vols. Rome, 1886–88.

Menabrea, L., ed. *Chroniques de Yolande de France.* Chambéry, 1859.

Meschinot, Jean. "Satires contre Louis XI," ed. A. La Borderie, in *Jean Meschinot, sa vie et ses oeuvres.* Bibliothèque de l'École des Chartes, 1895.

Michelet, Jules. *Louis XI et Charles le Téméraire.* Paris, 1853.

Molinet, Jean. *Chroniques*, ed. J. Buchon. 2 vols. Paris, 1827–28.

Molinier, A. *Les Sources de l'histoire de France des origines aux guerres d'Italie* (1494), V. Paris, 1901–1906.

°Morice, P. H. *Mémoires pour servir de preuves à l'histoire de Bretagne.* 3 vols. Paris, 1742–46.

Natale, A. R. "I diari di Cicco Simonetta," *Archivio Storico Lombardo.* ser. 8 (vol. 1 [1949], 80–114;) vol. 2 (1950), 157–80.

Oeuvres Complètes de Duclos, IV (Preuves). Paris, 1806.

Ordonnances des Rois de France de la troisième race. Vols. XV–XIX. Paris, 1811–35.

Pasquier, F. "Un Favori de Louis XI, Boffile de Juge," *Documents inédits du Chartier de Léran* (Archives historiques de l'Albigeois X). Albi, 1914.

Perret, P. M. *Histoire de relations de la France avec Venise du XIIIe siècle à l'avènement de Charles VIII.* 2 vols. Paris, 1892.

Phabrey, G. *L'Ami du Téméraire.* (Chronique du règne de Louis XI.) Paris, 1956.

Pirenne, H., A. Renaudet, E. Perroy, M. Handelsmann, L. Halphen. *La Fin du Moyen Age.* 2 vols. Paris, 1931.

Pius II (Aeneas Sylvius Piccolomini). *The Commentaries of Pius II*, trans. Florence A. Gragg, ed. Leona C. Gabel. *Smith College Studies in History*, XXII (1936–37), XXV (1939–40).

Plancher, D. *Histoire de . . . Bourgogne.* 7 vols. Dijon, 1773–85.

Pocquet du Haut-Jussé, B. A. *François II, duc de Bretagne, et l'Angleterre* (1458–88). Paris, 1929.

Prarond, E. *Abbeville aux temps de Charles VII, des ducs de Bourgogne, maîtres du Ponthieu, de Louis XI* (1426–83). Paris, 1899.

Reilhac, A. de. *Jean de Reilhac, secrétaire, maître des comptes, general des finances et ambassadeur des rois Charles VII, Louis XI, et Charles VIII.* 3 vols. Paris, 1886–89.

Roye, Jean de. *Journal, connu sous le nom de "Chronique Scandaleuse,"* ed. B. de Mandrot. 2 vols. Paris, 1894–96.

°Samaran, Charles. *La maison d'Armagnac au XVe siècle . . .* Paris, 1908.

Scofield, Cora L. *The Life and Reign of Edward the Fourth.* 2 vols. London, 1923.

See, H. *Louis XI et les villes.* Paris, 1891.

Sorbelli, A. *Francesco Sforza à Genova* (1458–66). Bologne, 1901.

°Stein, Henri. *Charles de France, frère de Louix XI.* Paris, 1921.

Wavrin, Jean de. *Anchiennes chroniques d'Engleterre*, ed. Mlle. Dupont. 3 vols. Paris, 1859–63.

Zeller, Gaston. "Un Faux du XVIIe Siècle: Édit de Louis XI sur la Poste," *Revue Historique*, 180 (1937), 286–92.

Book I: THE DAUPHIN

Ardant, Maurice. "Relation des passages de Charles VII à Limoges," *Bulletin de la Société historique et archéologique du Limousin*, V.

Basin, Thomas. *Histoire de Charles VII*, ed. and trans., Charles Samaran. Paris, 1933.

°Beaucourt, G. Du Fresne de, ed. *Chronique de Mathieu d'Escouchy*. 3 vols. Paris, 1863.

°——. *Histoire de Charles VII*. 6 vols. Paris, 1881–91.

Boudet, M. "Charles VII à St. Flour et le prélude de la Praguerie (1437)," *Annales du Midi*, VI (1894), 301–26.

Breuils, A. "La Campagne de Charles VII en Gascogne, une conspiration du dauphin en 1446 . . . ," *Revue des Questions Historiques*, B—XIII (1895), 104–39.

°Bueil, Jean de. *Le Jouvencel*, ed., C. Favre and L. Lecestre. 2 vols. Paris, 1877.

But, Adrien de. *Chronique*, ed., Kervyn de Lettenhove. Brussels, 1870.

Champion, P., ed. *Chronique Martiniane*. Paris, 1907.

——. *La Dauphine mélancolique*. Paris, 1921.

——. *Agnès Sorel, la dame de Beauté*. Paris, 1931.

Charavay, Étienne. *Louis XI en Dauphiné*. (Positions des Thèses de l'École des Chartes.)

Chartier, Jean. *Chronique de Charles VII*, ed., Vallet de Viriville. 2 vols. Paris, 1858.

Chevalier, Ulysse. *Itinéraire de Louis XI dauphin*. Voiron, n.d.

Colville, A. "La Jeunesse et la vie privée de Louis XI," *Journal des Savants*, May–June, 1908.

Cousinot, Guillaume. *Chronique*, ed., Vallet de Viriville. 2nd edition, Paris, 1892.

Devie, C. (Dom), and (Dom) J. Vaissete. *Histoire Générale de Languedoc*, IX. Toulouse, 1885.

Dodu, Gaston. "Le Roi de Bourges," *Revue Historique*, 159 (1928), 38–78.

Douet-d'Arcq, L., ed. *Chronique d'Enguerran de Monstrelet*. Paris, 1860. vols IV, V.

Dusevel, H. *Instructions de Louis Dauphin à l'archevêque d'Embrun et autre ses envoyés vers le roi* (14 Oct. 1452). ed. Champollion-Figeac, Documents historiques inédits, II, ii, 189, 1843.

Dussert, A. *Les États du Dauphiné, de la guerre de Cent Ans aux guerres de religion*. Grenoble, 1923.

Freminville (de). *Les écorcheurs en Bourgogne* (1435–45). Dijon, 1888.

Godefroy, D. "Berry l'Heraut, Les Chroniques du feu roi Charles Septiesme de ce nom," *Histoire de Charles VI*. Paris, 1661. 411–44 and *Histoire de Charles VII*. Paris, 1661. 369–424.

Gruel, Guillaume. *Chronique d'Arthur de Richemont*, ed., A. Le Vavasseur. Paris, 1890.

Ilardi, Vincent. "The Italian League, Francesco Sforza, and Charles VII (1454–61)," *Studies in the Renaissance*, VI (1959), 129–66.

Leroux, Alfred. "Passages de Charles VII et du dauphin Louis à Limoges en 1439 . . . ," *Bibliothèque de l'École des Chartes*, XLVI (1885), 303–14.

Mandrot, B. de. "Un projet de partage du milanais en 1446," *Bibliothèque de l'École des Chartes*, XLIV (1883), 179–91.

Mandrot, B. de. "Jean de Bourgogne, duc de Brabant et le procès de sa succession," *Revue Historique*, XCIII (1907).

Max, J. *L'Inquisition en Dauphiné*. (Bibliothèque de l'École des Hautes Études 206.) Paris, 1914.

Moranville, H., ed. *Chroniques de Perceval de Cagny.* Paris, 1902.

"Naissance de Louis XI," *Bibliothèque de l'École des Chartes,* XXXIX (1878), 586.

Pasquier, Felix. *Louis Dauphin et les routiers en Languedoc.* Foix, 1895.

Péchenard, P. L. *Jean Juvénal des Ursins . . .* Paris, 1876.

Peyronnet, Georges. "La Politica Italiana di Luigi Delfino di Francia (1444–61)," *Rivista Storica Italiana,* 1952, 19–44.

Poitiers, Alienor de. "Les honneurs de la cour," *Mémoires sur l'ancienne chevalerie,* Lacurne de Sainte-Palaye. II, prem. ed., 183–267.

Quicherat, Jules. *Rodrigue de Villandrando.* Paris, 1879.

Reiffenberg, F. A. F. T. de. *Mémoire sur le séjour que Louis Dauphin . . . fit aux Pays-Bas.* Brussels, 1829.

Thibault, Marcel. *La Jeunesse de Louis XI.* Paris, 1907.

Thorey, E. Pilot de. *Catalogue des actes du Dauphin Louis II, devenu le roi de France Louis XI, relatifs à l'administration du Dauphiné.* Vols. I, II (Société de statistique de l'Isère). Grenoble, 1899. Vol. III, supplt., ed. G. Vellein. Grenoble, 1911.

°Tuetey, A. *Les écorcheurs sous Charles VII.* 2 vols. Montbéliard, 1874.

Tuetey, A., ed. *Journal d'un bourgeois de Paris, 1405–49.* Paris, 1881.

Vaissette, (Dom). *Histoire générale du Languedoc,* ed. Molinier. n.d. Vol. IX.

Book II: THE KING

FALSE START

Anchier, C. *Charles I de Melun . . . , Le Moyen Âge.* Paris, 1892.

°Bittman, Karl. *Die Ursprunge der französisch-mailandischen Allianz von 1463.* Wiesbaden, 1952.

Borgnet, A. *Sac de Dinant par Charles le Téméraire (1466). Annales de la Société archéologique de Namur,* III (1853).

Champollion-Figeac, J. J., ed. *Lettres, mémoires, et autres documents relatifs à la guerre du Bien Public en 1465,* in *Documents historiques inédits . . . ,* vol. II.

Chazaud, M. A. *Une campagne de Louis XI . . . Bulletin de la Société d'émulation de l'Allier.* Moulins, 1872.

Couderc, C. *L'Entrée solennelle de Louis XI à Paris.* Nogent-le-Poitou, 1896.

Dupont, Gustave. "Louis XI et la Basse-Normandie de 1461 à 1464," *Mémoires de l'Académie des sciences, arts, et belles lettres de Caen,* XXXV (1880), 330–64.

Finot, J. *L'artillerie bourguignonne à la bataille de Montlhéry. Mémoires des sciences de Lille,* 5 ᵉ ser., fasc. V, 1896.

Ghinzoni, P. "Spedizione Sforzescane in Francia, 1465," *Archivio Storico Lombardo,* XVII (1890).

Lucius, C. *Pius II und Ludwig XI von Frankreich, 1461–62.* Heidelberger Abhandlungen zur mittleren und neuern Geschichte, Heft 41. Heidelberg, 1913.

°Mandrot, B. de, and C. Samaran, eds. *Dépêches des ambassadeurs milanais en France sous Louis XI et François Sforza.* 4 vols. Paris, 1916–23.

Milanesi, M. "Viaggio a Parigi degli Ambasciatori Fiorentini nel 1461," *Archivio Storico Italiano,* 3rd ser., first part, 1865.

Pelissier, L. G. "Una relazione dell'entrata de Luigi XI a Parigi," *Archivio Storico Italiano,* XXI (1898), 5th ser., 123–31.

Perroy, Edouard. "L'artillerie royale à la bataille de Montlhéry," *Revue Historique,* CXLIX (1925), 187–89.

Wratislaw, A. H. *Diary of an Embassy From King George of Bohemia to King Louis XI of France in . . . 1464 . . .* London, 1871.

THE SPINNING OF THE STRANDS

Adigard, Pierre. *Le voyage de Louis XI en Normandie et dans le Maine aux mois d'* *août et de Septembre 1470.* Alençon, 1902.

Champion, P. *Calendrier royal pour l'an 1471.* Abbeville and Paris, 1928.

Cust, Mrs. Henry. *Gentlemen Errant.* New York, 1909. (Bohemian ambassadors at court of Louis XI in spring of 1466.)

THE WEAVING OF THE WEB

Chabeuf, Henri. *L'entrée de Charles le Téméraire etc. en janvier et fevrier 1474.* Dijon, 1903.

Gingins la Sarraz, F., ed. *Dépêches des ambassadeurs milanais sur les campagnes de Charles le Hardi.* 2 vols. Geneva and Paris, 1858.

Marchal, (l'Abbé). *Recueil de documents sur l'histoire de Lorraine,* V. Nancy, 1859.

Panigarola, J. P. Dispatch recounting the battle of Morat [June 25, 1476, from St. Claude] published by P. Ghinzoni in *Archivio Storico Lombardo,* ser. 2, vol. IX (1892), 103–109.

Samaran, C. "Les Frais du Procès et de l'Exécution de Jacques d'Armagnac, Duc de Nemours," *Mémoires de la Société de l'Histoire de Paris,* XLIX (1927), 142–54.

Toutey, E. *Charles le Téméraire et la Ligue de Constance.* Paris, 1902.

THE GATHERING IN

Bardoux, Agénor. "Les Grands Baillis au Quinzième Siècle," *Revue Historique de Droit Français,* IX (1863), 5–44.

Boutiot. "Louis XI et la ville d'Arras," *Mémoires* de l'Académie d'Arras, XXXIX (1867).

Brachet, Dr. Auguste. *Pathologie mentale des rois de France: Louis XI et ses ascendants.* Paris, 1903.

Champion, Pierre. *Louis XI et ses physiciens.* Lyons, 1935.

Choisnet, Pierre. *Le livre des trois eages et le rosier des guerres,* ed. C. Samaran. Bibliothèque de l'École des Chartes, 1926.

Foisset, Th. *Causes secrètes de la chute de Charles le Téméraire. Mémoires* de l'Académie de Dijon. 1851–52. 109–35.

Giraudet. "Documents inédits sur les prisonniers du roi Louis XI à Tours," *Bulletin de la Société Archéologique de Touraine,* III (1877), Tours.

Héricourt, A. de. *Les sièges d'Arras.* Paris, 1844.

Jarry, E. "Conditions d'Etablissement d'un Marchand d'Orléans à Franchise en 1479," *Bulletin de la Société Archéologique et Historique de l'Orléanais,* XX (1929), 224–31.

Laroche, A. *Une Vengeance de Louis XI. Mémoires de l'Académie d'Arras,* XXXVII (1865), 237–384.

Périnelle, G. "Dépêches de Nicolas de' Roberti," *Mélanges d'Archéologie et d'Histoire,* XXIII (1903), Paris, 139–203.

Petit-Dutaillis, Ch. (Louis XI's skin disease.) *Revue Historique,* 157 (1928), 85.

Pompadour, M. de. "A Letter from M. de Pompadour to Alain d'Albret, of Saturday morning, August 30, 1483," in *Archives Historiques du Département de la Gironde,* VI (1864), 3–4.

Salmon, A. "Essai de poison sur un chien fait par l'ordre de Louis XI," *Mémoires de la Société Archéologique de Touraine,* VII (1854–55), 109–11.

Stein, Henri. "Les Habitants d'Évreux et le Repeuplement d'Arras en 1479," *Bibliothèque de l'École des Chartes,* 84 (1923), 284–97.

"Une Ambassade de Lucerne," *Bulletin de la Société Archéologique de Touraine,* XVIII (1911–12), 366–80.

INDEX

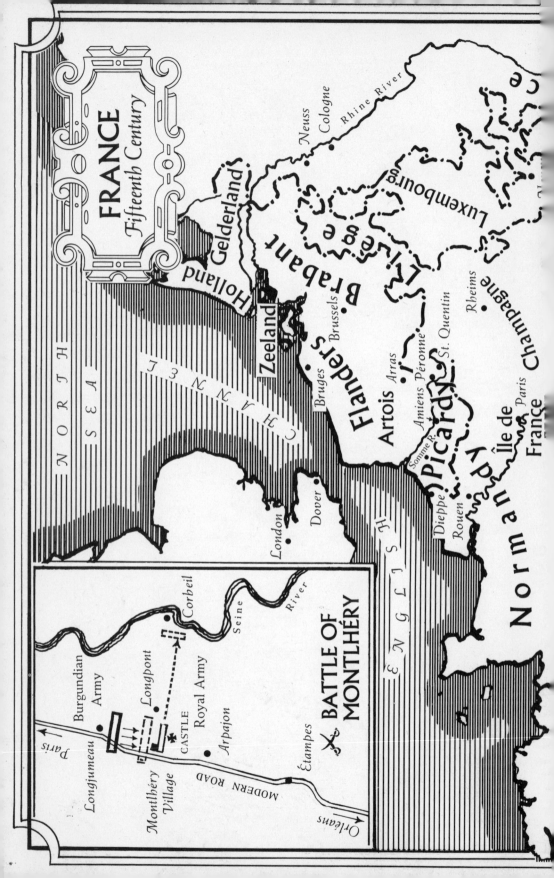

FRANCE
Fifteenth Century

Gelderland
Holland
Zeeland
Neuss
Cologne
Rhine River

Brabant
Liège
Luxembourg

NORTH
SEA

Bruges
Brussels

Flanders
Artois
Arras

Amiens
Péronne
Somme R.
St. Quentin

Rheims

CHANNEL

London
Dover

Dieppe
Rouen

Picardy

Paris
Île de
France
Chaumagne

Normandy

ENGLISH

BATTLE OF
MONTLHÉRY

Corbeil

Seine River

Burgundian
Army

Longpont
Royal Army

CASTLE

Longjumeau

Paris

Monthéry Village

Arpajon

Étampes

MODERN ROAD

Orléans

CHAPTER NINE

The Revised Organization Assessment Framework and Instruments

The preceding chapters have gone into considerable depth to describe and evaluate the third version of the Organization Assessment framework and instruments. Now we attempt to extend upon and put to use what has been learned by (1) introducing the fourth version of the Organization Assessment Instruments (OAI) recommended for future assessments of organizations, (2) suggesting a set of guidelines for using the revised OAI appropriately, and (3) placing into a larger perspective the principal results obtained in the previous chapters and their implications for measuring and assessing organizations.

The actual measurement instruments and documentation for the revised OAI are presented in the appendices. Appendix A contains a glossary of definitions and measurement procedures for all the dimensions measured in the revised OAI, whereas the actual questionnaires for conducting an OAI survey are presented in Appendices B to E. Based upon the evaluations of the 1975 OAI in Chapters 4 to 8, Appendix A also discusses any changes that have been made in the measurement of each dimension in the new version of the OAI, as well as caveats for using these indices in future organization assessments. Thus, the reader is referred to these appendices for technical descriptions and uses of the revised OAI.

The purposes of this concluding chapter are to provide a broader conceptual perspective on the revised Organization Assessment Framework and Instruments and to draw out some of their implications for theory and practice. To do this, it is useful to look back briefly at the evolution of the OA research program and the progress that has been achieved thus far, and to extrapolate from this the future directions necessary for realizing the practical and basic research goals for OA.

EVOLUTION OF THE OA FRAMEWORK AND INSTRUMENTS

In response to the practical problems that managers and analysts have in explaining, managing, and improving the performance of complex organizations, in 1972 we embarked upon an ambitious program of applied longitudinal research called Organizational Assessment. OA consists of an evolving conceptual framework, a process, and a set of measurement instruments developed to predict and explain the performance of complex organizations on the bases of how they are organized and the environment in which they operate. Using the OA framework as the conceptual guide, we set out to describe and evaluate the measurement properties of the Organization Assessment Instruments (OAI). However, as the evaluations and revisions of the OAI progressed over the years, it quickly became clear that we were simultaneously revising and expanding the OA framework and assessment process.

These revisions did not emerge from a single source or through a neat orderly process. Instead, they emerged as the composite result of many diverse learning experiences obtained from: (1) reviewing the literature, and either incorporating or often reacting to ideas of others while developing a conceptual scheme for assessing organizations, (2) operationalizing the framework with a set of measurement instruments, (3) working closely with practitioners in organizations to collect data and feedback survey results pertaining to specific managerial problems, (4) using the data to empirically evaluate the OA framework and instruments, and (5) repeating each step in the process three times in the same set of organizations. Although such a setting limits the generalizability of the OA evaluation, it provides the opportunity for multiple trials that are very necessary in theory and instrument construction. As a consequence, the revised OA framework and instruments have expanded (and we believe improved) considerably over the last published version (Van de Ven, 1976a).

The OA framework and instruments have been expanded to include what we believe is necessary to conduct a comprehensive and systematic assessment of a complex organization. Namely, *a framework and a set of measurement instruments are needed which (1) identify the properties of context, design, and performance at the macroorganization, work unit, and job levels of analyses, (2) examine the different design patterns of units and jobs that exist within the complex organization, and (3) determine how these different organizational units and jobs are integrated and how they contribute to overall performance.* This premise was operationalized by proposing that a thorough assessment of a complex organization focus on the four different levels of analyses shown in Figure 9-1 in terms of the dimensions outlined in Figure 9-2.

OA Perspective on Macroorganization Context and Structure

At the macroorganizational level, the OA framework and instruments were extended to examine more carefully the currently held view that organizations are designed by choices and not simply by natural or deterministic conditions outside the organization. Our starting premise in Chapter 4 was that decision makers have varying degrees of control over choices regarding *organization domain, the production function* and *organization design* and that over time they must live with the consequences of past choices while making adjustments in these choices for the future.

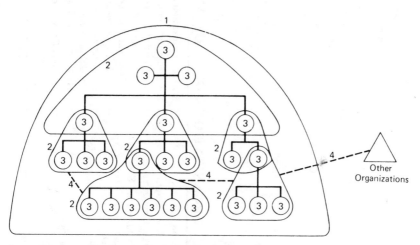

Key to Numbers: 1 = Overall Organization Focus of Analysis
                    2 = Organizational Unit Focus of Analysis
                    3 = Individual Job or Position Focus of Analysis
                    4 = Relations within and between Units Focus of Analysis

Figure 9-1 Levels of analyses involved in conducting an in-depth organization assessment.

1. OVERALL ORGANIZATION FOCUS OF ANALYSIS

Macroorganization Context	Macroorganization Design	Macroorganization Outcomes
1. Organization Demographics —History, Age, Growth Stage 2. Organizational Domain (Strategy) —Type, Uncertainty, Complexity, Restrictiveness 3. Projected Demand and Supply for Period —Production/Service Quota —Resources (budget, personnel) Available	1. Structural Configuration —Vertical, Horizontal, & Spacial Differentiation —Forms of Departmentation (by function, program, geography, matrix) —Administrative Intensity 2. Distribution of Power and Authority among Corporate Decision Makers	—Value judgments on criteria used to evaluate the overall effectiveness of the organization. For example: 1. Attainment of Goals in Organization's Domain 2. Market Share in Product Lines 3. Profitability, Return on Investment 4. Impact on Society

2. ORGANIZATIONAL UNIT FOCUS OF ANALYSIS

Organizational Unit (Department) Context

1. Macroorganization Context and Design
   —Functional Contribution of Unit to Organization (institutional, managerial, technical)
   —Vertical & Horizontal Location of Unit in Organization Chart
2. Nature of Work Performed by Unit
   —Task Difficulty and Variability
3. Size of Unit (number of personnel)

Design of Organizational Units (Work Groups)

1. Unit Specialization
   —# Different Tasks Assigned Unit
   —# Different Job Titles in Unit
2. Personnel Composition
   —Heterogeneity of Personnel Skills
   —Interchangeability of Roles
3. Unit Standardization
   —Automation of Work Methods
   —# & Detail of Unit Rules, Procedures
4. Unit Decision Making
   —Centralization of Decisions in Spv.
   —Decision Strategies Used (computational, judgmental, bargaining, heuristic)
5. Unit Performance Norms & Standards
   —Quality/Quantity-Control Emphasis
   —Group/Individual-Based Incentives
   —Group Pressures to Conform (Soldiering)

Organizational Unit Outcomes

—Value judgments on criteria used to evaluate effectiveness of organizational unit. For example:
1. Percentage of Unit Performance Goals Attained (MBO)
2. Quantity of Unit Output
3. Quality of Unit Output
4. Unit Efficiency: cost per unit of output
5. Unit Morale: cohesiveness of work group, turnover rate
6. Unit Adaptiveness: responsiveness to changing demands

Figure 9-2 Dimensions examined in framework for organization assessment.

3. INDIVIDUAL JOB OR POSITION FOCUS OF ANALYSIS

Individual Jobs or Positions Context

1. Organization & Unit Context & Design
   —Functional Role or Contribution of Job to Unit and Organization
2. Characteristics of Person in Job
   —Education and Job-Related Skills
   —Job Tenure and Job Career History
   —Growth Need Strength

Design of Individual Jobs or Positions

1. Job Specialization
   —# Different Tasks Performed
   —Scope of Tasks Performed
2. Job Expertise
   —Education
   —Length of Job-Entry Orientation
   —Time in On-the-Job Training
3. Job Standardization
   —Detail of Job Description
   —# & Detail of Job Rules, Procedures
4. Job Discretion
   —Latitude in Making Job-Related Decisions
   —Closeness of Supervision
5. Job Incentives
   —Feedback from Work, Supervisor, Peers
   —Job Contingent Rewards & Sanctions

Individual Job or Position Outcomes

—Value judgments on criteria used to evaluate effectiveness of individual jobs or positions. For example:

1. Percentage of Job Performance Goals Attained (MBO)
2. Quantity of Individual Output
3. Quality of Individual Output
4. Individual Productivity: cost per unit of output
5. Job Satisfaction
6. Work Motivation

4. RELATIONS WITHIN AND BETWEEN UNITS FOCUS OF ANALYSIS

Resource Flows (Work, Personnel, Money)	Information Flows (Impersonal, Personal, Group Communication Mechanisms)	Coordination and Control Outcomes
1. Resource Dependence Pattern —Directions and Amounts of Resource Flows within and between Organizational Units, Levels, and with other Organizations. 2. Routinization of Resource Flows —Number of Exceptions Encountered in Resource Flows 3. Perceived Dependence among Organizational units, levels, and positions.	1. Integration Pattern —Direction and Frequency of Information Flows within and between Organizational Units, Levels, and with other Organizations 2. Distribution of Influence in Relations —Amounts of Say on Relations by Parties —Impact of Parties in Relationships 3. Conflict & Quality of Communications —Frequency of Conflict —Modes of Conflict Resolution	—Value judgments on criteria used to evaluate effectiveness of coordination and control between jobs, units, levels and with other organizations. For example: 1. At interposition level, the perceived effectiveness of interpersonal relationships. 2. At interunit level, the degrees of suboptimization and competition among organizational units. 3. At macroorganizational level, the costs of managing transactions across units within organization relative to across organizations or the market.

Figure 9-2 Dimensions examined in framework for organization assessment.

Although these three choices have long been recognized in the literature, they have been examined largely in isolation from each other: Domain choice has tended to be the major focus of strategic management writers, the production function problem of microeconomic theorists, and the organization design problem of organizational sociologists and psychologists. Incorporating these three decisions in the OA framework forces one to question how these different bodies of theory and research can be integrated to obtain a more complete appreciation of how and why an organization is structured and managed the way it is at the overall corporate level. Furthermore, the different bodies of literature highlight what dimensions are critical for assessing each decision and provide a systematic guide for determining how the domain choice, production function, and organization design problems are interrelated. In Chapter 4 we argued and presented some empirical evidence that the processes by which these choices are made are a function of domain uncertainty, complexity, and restrictiveness, as well as of the distribution of power and authority among corporate decision makers. Through such analyses, hopefully, one can come to learn what alternative methods for decision making tend to work and tend not to work in various organizational settings.

Chapter 4 also described and evaluated the indicators used for measuring most of these factors in Employment Security offices. For the ES offices included in the 1975 OAI survey, the correlations among the macroorganization context and structure dimensions were substantial and largely consistent with the underlying theory. In addition, significant proportions of the variations in overall ES office effectiveness, efficiency, and job satisfaction were accounted for by the organization context and structural dimensions. These results suggest good overall concurrent validity for the OAI macroorganizational dimensions. In addition, these OAI indices were found to be useful for addressing practical strategic managerial decisions on the size and structural configuration of local ES offices.

In the revised OAI presented in Appendix A, we outline a specific set of procedures for measuring the macroorganization structure dimensions from organization charts. Although the table of organization is commonly used in practice, relatively little systematic attention has been given to understanding its underlying dimensions and to using it for comparative assessments of organizations. Chapter 4 and Appendix A propose to broaden the use of the organization chart by suggesting specific standards and conventions for constructing organization charts and for obtaining eight generally applicable measures of the structural configuration of organizations from these charts.

However, in keeping with our conclusion in Chapter 4, we do not propose to offer in the revised OAI a set of indicators that are generally applicable for measuring the macroorganizational context factors listed in Figure 9-2. Operational indicators of these contextual dimensions are necessarily idiosyncratic to the types of organizations under investigation. This is not to suggest that the contextual factors have different conceptual meanings across organizations—only that they should be adapted to fit the types of organizations being assessed. Because of the great diversity in organizational domains, we believe that measures broad enough to fit all organizations are too general to be reliable and valid for assessing any particular set of organizations. At this early stage of research on macroorganization contexts, we believe that these dimensions are best measured by indicators specific to the type of organization being assessed and that inferences from these studies should be limited to the specific organizations being examined.

OA Perspective on Organizational Units and Individual Jobs

Once an analyst understands the choices made regarding the overall context and structural configuration of an organization at the macro level, then he or she can begin to examine the various subunits and jobs within it. As Figure 9-1 illustrates, Likert's (1967) concept of "linking pins" is used to operationally identify work units at all supervisory levels in an organization. An organizational unit, in turn, is composed of a set of identifiable jobs or positions.

The basic perspective taken in OA is that a focus on organization units is needed to examine the different subsystems that exist within organizations. By definition, a complex organization consists of many differently structured units each dealing with a different environment and making a different contribution to the total organization. As a result, these units adopt different structural designs to perform their unique tasks and functions. Chapter 5 demonstrated that in attempting to examine different units from a macroorganizational perspective, one obtains a distorted assessment; whereas some organizational units may be highly structured, others may be very organic, and any overall average profile is an inaccurate summary of both. Furthermore, the unique and significant relationships that exist between the design and performance of these different kinds of units wash out if one attempts to explain performance across all organizational units.

By the same token, an assessment of individual behavior within organizations requires a focus on the individual's job or position. Just as variations in the design and performance of organizational units are not detected at the macro level, the designs of different jobs and employees' reactions to them are glossed over when they are examined at the work unit level. Therefore, in Chapter 6 we expanded OA to examine the context and design of jobs because the ways in which jobs are organized and individuals are selected are critical concerns in any in-depth assessment of organizations.

The job design dimensions included in the revised OA framework lean heavily on the major conceptual and empirical contributions of Hackman and Oldham (1975) and their foretrekkers. While measures of the job characteristics by Hackman and Oldham in their Job Diagnostic Survey (JDS) focus quite heavily on the attitudinal aspects of jobs, the OA job design measures emphasize their behavioral aspects. The reason we lean toward a behavioral description of jobs is that behaviors are more objective and easier for analysts and practitioners to observe, control and change than the more subjective attitudes of people regarding their jobs. Specific operational distinctions between the JDS and OAI job design characteristics were discussed in Chapter 6, and Appendix A presents the proposed measures of job design in the revised OAI.

After the OA framework was expanded to include individual jobs, it became clear that some conceptual revisions were needed in the structural dimensions of organization units (Chapter 5) because they confounded with the properties of jobs (specifically, unit expertise, standardization, and employee discretion). Following Lazarsfeld and Menzel's (1969) guidelines, distinctions were made between global properties of work groups and analytical properties of jobs. The OA job design characteristics outlined in Figure 9-2 are *analytical* properties of unit members which are defined and measured without reference to the organizational unit to which they belong. The organizational unit dimensions are *global* characteristics of the group itself which have no meaning in terms of unit members individually. Specifically, as the operational definitions and measures in Appendix A show, the following pairs of unit and job design characteristics in the revised OAI tap similar construct domains from different levels of analyses: (1) unit and job specialization (2) unit personnel composition and job expertise, (3) unit and job standardization, (4) distribution of unit authority and job discretion, and (5) unit and job incentives. The unit design dimensions are not simply the summation or average of the jobs of all unit personnel; they clearly have different reference points and require different measurement procedures.

However, just as important as these distinctions are their parallel meanings at the unit and job levels of analyses. By examining counterpart dimensions of units and jobs, one is stimulated to search for alternative options and tradeoffs that may exist between the ways organizational units and individual jobs can be organized effectively. For example, Hackman (1976) indicates that one important option in the design of autonomous work groups is to determine under what conditions heterogeneous skills should be structured within a job (by decreasing job specialization) or between jobs in a unit (by staffing a unit with experts from different disciplines; i.e., increasing skill heterogeneity). Out of such an investigation we may come to appreciate that a far broader and richer repertoire of options exists for designing jobs, organizational units, and personnel recruitment programs than is in current use. There remains a great deal of work to be done in analyzing the relationships between global units and individual jobs. However, the first major step in such an investigation has been completed by developing a framework and proposing a parallel set of measures for units and jobs in the revised OAI.

The results from the 1975 OAI unit and job design indices were quite encouraging. Overall, tests of the unit and job design indices in Chapters 5 and 6 showed that the internal consistency reliabilities and the convergent and discriminant validities for most of the measures were quite good. In addition, the evaluation identified specific items that require revision to improve the measurement properties of selected OAI dimensions. As described in Appendix A, these findings were used as a basis for making refinements in the revised OAI.

An impressive body of evidence was obtained to substantiate the extrinsic validity of the OAI context and design indices for both organizational units and individual jobs. Relationships among the context and design indices were highly consistent with the theories on which they are based. The OAI indices detected systematic differences in the contexts and designs of different types of organizational units and jobs in ES offices. These empirical differences were consistent with the authors' on-site observations over the years of the qualitative differences between the various types of units and jobs in ES offices. Finally, the OAI unit and job indices have high concurrent validity. When regressing performance on the unit task, structure, and process dimensions for each of the different types of units in ES offices, on the average it was found that the OAI unit dimensions accounted for 52, 55, and 57 percent of the variances in unit efficiency, effectiveness, and job satisfaction, respectively. These percentages of explained variance in unit performance are far higher than those reported in other research reports reviewed by the authors.

Concurrent validity estimates for the job design indices were not as impressive. Although eight or nine of the ten OAI job design indices were significantly correlated with work motivation and job satisfaction in a statistical sense, only three or four of the correlations were large enough to be practically meaningful for predicting or explaining employee affective responses to their jobs. However, the sizes and directions of the correlations obtained were quite similar to those obtained on similar job characteristics in other studies. Furthermore, the 1975 OAI did not measure a number of individual difference factors and job characteristics (later added to the revised OA framework) that were found in other research to be important in explaining job satisfaction, motivation, and productivity. Appendix A proposes a new set of indices to measure these new job context and design dimensions and also describes the changes that have been made in the revised OAI to correct specific limitations identified in the 1975 OAI job indices. Hopefully, future evaluations of the measurement properties of these new and revised indices will show improvement in their intrinsic and extrinsic validity.

OA Perspective on Interunit Relations

After organization, unit, and job structure become clear, then one can examine patterns of interdependence, coordination, and control. In addition, an assessment of the linkages between organizational units is needed to determine how they cluster together as subsystems and are integrated into the macroorganizational system. Chapters 7 and 8 evaluated two initial attempts to conceptualize and measure interunit relations by examining the external relationships of ES units (Chapter 7) and pairwise relationships between child care organizations (Chapter 8). Although different levels of analyses apply, the evaluations in Chapters 7 and 8 suggest that a social network perspective is fruitful for assessing relationships both between organizational units and between organizations themselves.

In Chapter 7 the initial ideas for a social network approach were developed by arguing that the external relationships of organizational units can be assessed systematically in terms of work and information flows that each organizational unit receives from and sends to other units, levels, and organizations. The reasons presented for why the OA framework focuses on work and information flows are that they: (1) appear to be the basic elements of process in organizations, (2) behaviorally indicate the task-instrumental and pattern-maintenance functions necessary for any organization to survive, (3) provide a way to operationalize sociotechnical theory, and (4) provide ways to link micro- and macro levels of organizational analyses.

Operationally, the external relationships of ES units with different sectors of their environments were measured in terms of work flow amount, variability, and dependence; and communication mode, frequency, and standardization. The psychometric evaluation of these measures found that work flow variability and communication standardization were not adequate and require substantial revision. However, the other measures of work and information flows were found to have satisfactory indications of internal consistency reliability as well as convergent and discriminant validity. Good indications of the extrinsic validity of these measures were also obtained. The correlations among the work and information flow indices were found largely consistent with the theory. The OAI dimensions detected significantly different patterns in the external relationships maintained by different ES local office units and explained large proportions of the variations in their performance. On the average it was found that these OAI dimensions accounted for 49, 53, and 45 percent of the variances in unit efficiency, effectiveness, and job satisfaction, respectively.

The OAI external unit relations factors were also found to be useful for answering practical questions pertaining to the reorganization of employment security offices. However, the OAI data could have been even more useful had the frame of reference been made more specific for respondents. In the 1975 OAI, informants were asked to describe the external relationships of their units with other units, levels, and organizations without clearly specifying the names of these other units. With the exception of a shift in the level of analysis, this data collection strategy is the same as that taken by many open-systems researchers who examine how the internal design of an organization is associated with its external environment. Although this strategy was found to provide sufficient information to make a general assessment of a unit's external environments, a more specific assessment could have been made had the focus of observation been on the pairwise relationships each ES unit maintained with other units within and outside of their offices.

The study of coordination among early childhood organizations discussed in Chapter 8 overcame this deficiency by measuring the pairwise relationships each of the child care organizations maintained with other organizations in their communities. The dyad is the basic building block for examining linkages among organizational units from a social network perspective. One can examine relationships among clusters and networks of organizational units by constructing sociograms of pairwise relationships. Chapter 8 went on to suggest how information on interunit networks can be analyzed from multiple perspectives to obtain an understanding of the emergent social structure in organizations as distinct from formal structures displayed in organizational charts. Although the discussion in Chapter 8 focused on interorganizational networks, the theory and approach are directly transferable to networks of relationships among organizational units.

Chapter 8 also expanded the conceptual framework presented in Chapter 7 in two important ways. First, the concept of work flow was expanded to include other forms of resources that are frequently transacted between organizational units, including money, personnel, technical services, and work. If a systematic assessment of interunit relations is desired, then these other prevalent forms of resource flows should also be examined. Furthermore, it was found that the patterns of coordination vary significantly according to the form of resource transaction.

Second, Chapter 8 expanded upon the relevant set of dimensions for assessing interunit relations by developing a theory on how and why relationships among organizational units are created and maintained over time. The theory argued that organizational units do not communicate and transact resources for coordination's sake. Instead, interunit relationships are primarily a social–psychological consequence of (1) the perceived need by unit personnel for resources to achieve their goals or self-interests, (2) an awareness of other units where these resources can be obtained, and (3) consensus or conflict on the terms of a relationship by the parties involved. Once an interunit relationship is established, it is maintained over time by adopting a structure that is commensurate with the amounts of resources that are transacted among the parties. Over time, then, the functioning of interunit relationships is viewed as a result of a need for: resources or support, interunit communications to spread awareness and consensus, resource transactions, and structural adaptation and pattern maintenance. What may start out as an interim solution to a problem or as an attempt to obtain a specific resource may eventually become a long-term set of commitments and resource transactions *if* previous cycles in the process are perceived by the parties involved to have been successful or effective encounters.

A test of this theory on the formation and maintenance of relationships among organizational units requires longitudinal data, and our longitudinal study of coordination among child care organizations in Texas is still in progress. However, the psychometric evaluation of the OAI indices in Chapter 8 represents the first major step in testing the theory. Overall, satisfactory indications of internal consistency as well as convergent and discriminant validity were obtained for eight of the ten dimensions in the theory, whereas improvements were found necessary in two of them. In terms of the practical usefulness of these measures for assessing interunit coordination, it was found that the OAI indices represent a good compromise between being: (1) general enough to apply to a variety of different types of contractual and voluntary relationships, and (2) specific enough to significantly account for 35 to 65 percent of the variations in different kinds of resource transactions between organizations.

Appendix A proposes a specific set of strategies and measures for assessing relationships between units both within an organization and also in other organizations. The revised OAI measure the dimensions of interunit relationships outlined in Figure 9-2. These indices integrate the key dimensions examined in Chapters 7 and 8 and are central to the expanded framework for assessing the formation and maintenance of interunit relations over time.

The indices focus on interunit rather than interorganizational relations. As used in Chapter 7, an assessment of relations between specific organizational units rather than between entire organizations provides more concrete and systematic information about patterns of interdependence, coordination, and control in social networks. This is because in large organizations, different units perform specialized functions and are each involved in many different relationships. The study of coordination among child care organizations in Chapter 8 did not encounter this problem because these organizations are very small, indeed often the size and structure of an organizational unit.

DESIGN VARIATIONS WITHIN ORGANIZATIONS

The preceding section has provided an overview of the revised OA framework and instruments. In a sentence, we propose that a systematic assessment of complex organizations should focus on the four different levels of analyses shown in Figure 9-1 (organization, work unit, job, and interunit relationships) by examining the dimensions of context, design, and performance outlined in Figure 9-2.

The OA framework is admittedly complex, but so too are complex organizations. Indeed the complexity of organizations has been demonstrated consistently and dramatically in Chapters 4–8 at each level for assessing organizations.

- At the macroorganizational level (Chapter 4), it was found that personnel in different vertical and horizontal positions in the organizational hierarchy have significantly different views of the structure of authority within the organization.

- At the unit level (Chapter 5), large differences were found to exist between ES units in terms of task, structure, and process and in terms of patterns of correlations between these factors and the efficiency, effectiveness, and job satisfaction of ES units.

- In Chapter 6 the contexts and designs of individual jobs were found to differ systematically and affect employee responses to their jobs in different ways depending upon the kinds of tasks performed in those jobs.

- Chapter 7 found that the various ES units dealt with different relevant environments, and that different OAI external unit factors accounted for significant proportions of the variations in unit performance.

- Finally, in Chapter 8 significantly different patterns of coordination were found to exist according to the types of resources transacted between organizations.

Methodologically, these results provide substantial evidence of the practical usefulness of the OAI for organization research and diagnosis. The OAI detect systematic differences in the designs of organizations, work units, jobs, and linkages among them and also explain large proportions of their variations in performance.

Substantively, these findings have important implications for research and practice because they suggest that an assessment of organizations may require a greater level of conceptual and methodological sophistication than previously recognized. Although simple approaches are obviously preferred to complex ones, the findings obtained here indicate that simple, quick, and neat approaches may not be adequate. These results also emphasize the need for a conceptual perspective that can help one make sense of these complexities in organizations.

This section attempts to provide such a perspective by classifying and explaining the different types of subsystems that tend to exist within most complex organizations. We find the classification of design variations within organizations useful for (1) explaining why and how organizations are complex, (2) motivating an appreciation of the broader set of issues and implications involved in assessing organizations, and (3) reducing the complexity of the OA framework by focusing on the most salient dimensions for each organizational subsystem.

The classification is illustrated in Figure 9-3. It is obtained by distinguishing between technical, managerial, and institutional functions that tend to be performed at lower, middle, and upper levels of an organization; and between systematized, discretionary, and developmental modes of structure that organizational units and positions tend to adopt when they perform tasks low, medium, or high in difficulty and variability. (These different functions and structural modes are defined below.) Cross-hatching the three functions with the three modes of structure produces nine design variations within complex organizations. This nine-cell classification of unit designs is superimposed on an organization chart in order to illustrate the relative locations where these structural variations tend to exist.

In practice, of course, there is considerable overlapping of functions and tasks among organizational units and positions. Seldom are they as clearly distinguished as Figure 9-3 and the following discussion imply. In addition, a given organizational unit or position may often operate in a number of different cells in Figure 9-3 at different points in time. This is particularly true when the unit or position performs a variety of functions in the organization or encounters tasks, problems or issues that vary substantially in difficulty or variability.

The important point to recognize is that the nine cells in Figure 9-3 represent qualitatively different kinds of subsystems found in many complex organizations. As the definition of a subsystem suggests, organizational units or positions operating in the nine subsystems: (1) strive to achieve different subgoals, (2) respond to different relevant environments to perform their unique tasks and functions, (3) adopt different structural programs for organizing their activities into predictable patterns of behavior, (4) tend to be evaluated on different criteria of performance, and (5) approach problems and organizational issues from different perspectives and value orientations. These qualitative differences between subsystems are elaborated in the following text.

What makes organizations complex to manage and assess is not the sheer number of organizational units or positions, but rather the problem of determining *what kinds of designs are appropriate and feasible for organizing each subsystem and for integrating these qualitatively different subsystems into the overall organization.* Those organizations that do not contain all nine subsystems in Figure 9-3 tend to be easier to manage than those that do. Indeed, a count of the number of different cells in Figure 9-3 that are represented in a given organization

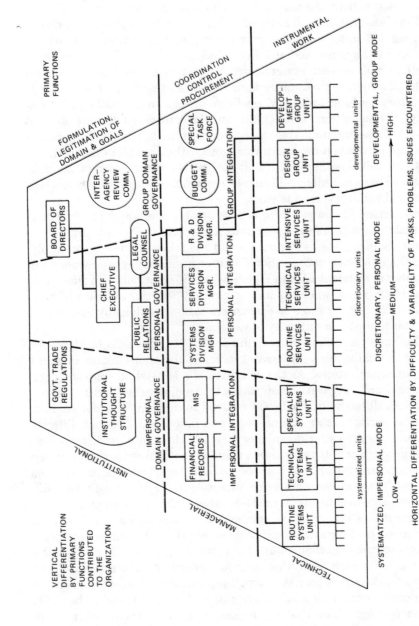

Figure 9-3   A classification of design variations within complex organizations.

provides a good measure of the structural complexity of that organization.

Differentiation of Functions in Complex Organizations

Talcott Parsons (1960) warned against undertaking an analysis of complex social systems without adequately clarifying the structural reference points that identify the functional subsystems and the applicable situations or contexts within which behavior takes place. If organizations are to survive, Parsons and Smelser (1956) as well as Katz and Kahn (1978) argue that they must perform: (1) *technical* functions of production to achieve task-instrumental goals; (2) *managerial* functions of coordinating, controlling, and procuring resources for the performance of technical functions; and (3) *institutional* functions, which include formulating, legitimating, and governing the domain and charter of the organization in relation to the larger social system of which the organization is a part. In small organizations participants will necessarily have to perform all these functions simultaneously. Given sufficient size, however, organizations will attempt to achieve the benefits of process specialization by dividing the primary performance of these functions to different hierarchical levels in the organization. Obviously, personnel at all levels in the hierarchy will perform all these functions to varying degrees; the point is that personnel and units at lower, middle, and upper levels in the hierarchy tend to be responsible for primarily technical, managerial, and institutional functions, respectively, as a consequence of the division of labor in an organization. Moreover, when certain personnel or units in an organization shift between technical, managerial, or institutional functions, different dimensions of context, design, and performance (listed in Figure 9-2) become salient for assessing how these functions are performed.

1. Technical Functions. Because technical functions concern task-instrumental production, the appropriate referent for assessing the performance of technical functions is the nature of the work and the ways in which units and positions are organized to do their work. Most of our understanding of technical functions in organizations has been contributed by the literature on the design of jobs (see reviews by Hulin and Blood, 1968; Pierce and Dunham, 1976; and Steers and Mowday, 1977), work groups or units (Grimes et al., 1972; Hrebiniak, 1974; Van de Ven and Delbecq, 1974; Hackman and Suttle, 1977), and more generally sociotechnical theory (Emery and Trist, 1960; Trist, 1970).

Most of the context and design dimensions of organizational units and jobs evaluated in Chapters 5 and 6 are derived from this literature. Although these dimensions have been used extensively for examining technical operations at the lowest levels of organizations, we argue that they are also very relevant for understanding how technical functions are organized at all supervisory levels of an organization.

   2.   Managerial Functions.   Stimulated by the Weberian model of bureaucracy, most organization theories and research to date have focused upon structural configurations for coordination and control by examining differentiation, departmentation, and administrative overhead (Crozier, 1964; Blau and Schoenherr, 1971; Pugh et al., 1968; Galbraith, 1977). Recently, however, an increasing number of researchers are focusing on processes of resource and information flows and social network analysis to study coordination and control (Tichy, 1973; Roberts and O'Reilly, 1974; Aldrich, 1979; Van de Ven et al., 1976; Tushman, 1977; Tichy and Fombrun, 1978). Our evaluation of this literature (Chapters 4, 7, and 8) leads to the inclusion of the structure and process dimensions outlined in Figure 9-2. Clearly, these dimensions have been found to be highly relevant in assessing managerial structures and processes. However, they are less appropriate for assessing technical and institutional functions in organizations, because the major spheres of activities in performing these other functions do not focus on managerial coordination, control, and procurement of resources.

   3.   Institutional Functions.   As suggested by our discussion of the domain choice problem (Chapter 4), institutional functions are principally concerned with (1) developing and choosing the charter of the organization in terms of its role in the community or society, the products or services it delivers, and the target populations and markets it services, and (2) legitimating this corporate domain and the contributions of the organization to the larger social system of which it is a part. Generally, the unit of analysis for assessing institutional functions includes the board of directors or trustees, the top management unit, and also influential stakeholders and external interest groups who have control over critical organizational contingencies and resources.

   The dimensions in the OA framework that are particularly relevant for assessing institutional functions are: domain uncertainty, complexity, and restrictiveness; organizational age and history; the distribution of power and authority among corporate decision makers; and group decision-making strategies and conflict. We admit, however, that much further work in OA is needed to understand the institutional subsystem in organizations. Fortunately, the institutional function is receiving increasing attention in the recent literature on strategic choice (Child, 1972; Miles and Snow, 1978), corporate planning (Hofer and Schendel, 1978; Steiner and Miner, 1977; Mintzberg, 1977), and political behavior (Pfeffer, 1978; MacMillan, 1978). This "policy" literature appears particularly promising for coming to understand the institutional function in organizations.

Design Modes within Complex Organizations

As illustrated in Figure 9-3, systematic differences in structures and processes for performing technical, managerial, and institutional functions should also be expected to the extent that organizational units and positions performing these functions encounter tasks, problems, or issues that differ in difficulty and variability. Our previous research found that organizational units that undertake work at low, medium, and high levels of difficulty and variability adopt systematized, discretionary, and developmental programs or modes of structure, respectively (Van de Ven and Delbecq, 1974; Van de Ven, 1976b). As March and Simon (1958) suggest, differences between the systematized, discretionary, and developmental modes are not simply variations on a theme; instead, they are qualitatively different logics for organizing patterns of behavior.

To make these qualitative differences clear, Table 9-1 hypothesizes the specific differences expected between the three design modes in terms of the dimensions most salient for assessing institutional, managerial, and technical functions in a complex organization. In other words, the dimensions in Table 9-1 operationalize the classification in Figure 9-3, which focuses specifically on explaining design variations within an organization. These design variations are now discussed.

1. The Systematized Mode. The logic of a systematized mode is to create a program for efficiently organizing and managing tasks, problems, or issues that occur repetitively, are generally well understood, and exhibit the same basic characteristics each time they are encountered. A systematized program generally specifies: (1) a detailed blueprint of the sequence of steps and procedures to be followed in advance of their execution, (2) the standards to be attained at each step in terms of quantity (timing and pacing rules) and quality (specifications on tolerable ranges of behavior and output), and (3) built-in monitoring and control devices to detect departures from the blueprint so that corrections can be made. Once implemented, departures from the blueprint are immediately detected, and human discretion does not enter into the determination of what, where, when, and how roles are to

Table 9-1 **Hypothesized Patterns of Systematized, Discretionary, Developmental Modes of Institutional, Managerial, and Technical Subsystems within Organizations**

Difficulty & Variability of Tasks, Problems, Issues Encountered by Subsystem—	Systematized Impersonal Mode Low	Discretionary Personal Mode Medium	Developmental Group Mode High
Salient Dimensions of Institutional Subsystem			
1. Organizational Referent	Institutional thought structure	Top management unit	Board and stakeholders
2. Domain Restrictiveness	High	Medium	Low
3. Domain Formalization (Codification)	High	Medium	Low
4. Conflict on Domain Ends (goals)	Low	Medium	High
5. Uncertainty of Domain Means to Ends	Low	Medium	High
6. Domain Decision Process	Computational	Judgmental	Bargaining
7. Locus of Power and Influence	Diffuse	Hierarchy	Interest groups
Salient Dimensions of Managerial Subsystem			
1. Organizational Referent	Central information systems	Hierarchy & staff	Coordination committees
2. Coordination and Control by:	Rules, plans schedules	Exceptions to hierarchy	Mutual group adjustments
3. Resource & Information Flows among Organizational Levels, Units, & Positions:			
a. Direction	Diffuse	Vertical	Horizontal
b. Amount	High	Medium	Low
c. Standardization & Codification	High	Medium	Low
4. Perceived Interdependence among Components	Low	Medium	High
5. Frequency of Conflict among Components	Low	Medium	High

	Capital-intensive operations	Labor-intensive services	Team-intensive R&D projects
Salient Dimensions of Technical Subsystem			
1. Organizational Referent			
2. Unit Specialization	High	Low	Medium–High
3. Heterogeneity of Personnel Skills	Medium	Low–Medium	Medium–High
4. Interchangeability of Roles	Low–Medium	High	Low–Medium
5. Standardization of Work Procedures	High	Medium	Low
6. Centralization of Decision Making	High	Medium	Low
7. Incentives Based on Performance of:	Individual or work system	Individual	Group
Typical Design of Jobs in All Subsystems			
1. Job Specialization	High	Low	Medium–High
2. Required Job Expertise	Low–Medium	Low–High	Medium–High
3. Job Standardization	High	Medium	Low
4. Job Discretion	Low–Medium	Medium–High	High
5. Major Source of Feedback	Supervisor or controller	Supervisor & work	Peers & work
Outcomes in All Subsystems			
1. Uniformity of Product, Service, or Program	High	Medium	Low
2. Adaptability of Product, Service, Program	Low	Medium	High
3. Quantity of Outputs or Services	High	Medium	Low
4. Cost per Unit of Output or Service	Low	Medium	High
5. Personnel Orientations	Universalistic	In between	Particularistic
	Neutral	In between	Affective
	Specific	In between	Diffuse

be articulated to deal with the problem, task, or issue; rather, roles and their articulation are formally prescribed in the impersonal blueprint for action. Since the coordination and control procedures are impersonally codified, their use requires minimal verbal communication between role occupants (Van de Ven et al., 1976:323).

As Figure 9-3 illustrates, there are many examples of technical, managerial, and institutional functions in organizations that are structured according to the impersonal systematized mode. Mechanical or clerical assembly lines, technicians operating capital intensive systems, and intensive-care nursing units exemplify routine, technical, and intensive variations of the systematized mode for performing technical functions (Van de Ven and Delbecq, 1974:186).

Impersonal integration of managerial functions is often accomplished by manualized or computerized management information systems and financial, bookkeeping, payroll, and purchasing units. From this perspective, we view the functional contributions of the disciplines of operations research, computer science, managerial finance, and accounting largely as that of developing systems for impersonally coordinating and controlling organizations. Indeed, the rapid growth and demand for personnel trained in these disciplines is a reflection of the current trend in most complex organizations to increasingly systematize those managerial functions that are repetitive, simple, and nonvarying.

The systematized mode for institutional domain governance often is not supported or maintained with full-time personnel positions. Instead, it is exhibited in organizational records and documents, verbal agreements, and "between the ears" of organizational members and its constituents. *The Wall Street Journal* and other practitioners' newsletters provide daily examples of the growth and concerns over impersonalized and systematized ways that the domains of organizations are governed and legitimated. They include: trade, legal, and governmental regulations; contracts and agreements that organizations enter into with labor unions, governments, and other organizations; and also ethical values, standards, and norms regarding acceptable practices for personnel within the organization and in the larger trade, profession, or craft.

Although these examples have long been recognized as having significant influence on the structure and the behavior of organizations, they have not been incorporated into a systematic framework of organization design. Instead, they have been viewed as largely exogenous to the organization and existing somewhere in its environment. Yet the fact remains that organizational decision makers either create many of these impersonal mechanisms for domain governance themselves, or choose to accept them as constraints and as consequences of the type of domain they chose for the organization. Furthermore, in this post-Watergate era, there is ample evidence that decision makers have the option to either abide by or violate regulations, contracts, and ethical standards governing organizational domains, and to suffer the personal and organizational consequences when violations are detected. Therefore, we view organizations as having significant control over the institutional regulations, contracts, and standards of fair practice by which they choose to govern themselves.

When internalized and codified, these controls become a systematized mode for organizing what Roland Warren identified and labeled as the "institutionalized thought structure" of an organization. The institutionalized thought structure consists of the aggregate set of values, norms, and expectations of an organization in relation to its members and to other organizations. It "serves to reduce uncertainty to controllable dimensions, to minimize contest, to resist change, and to insure organizational viability. . . . This institutionalized thought structure is reflected in the technological and administrative rationales of organizations, the source of their legitimation, and their relation to power configurations" in the industry or community (Warren, 1971: 67–68).

2. The Discretionary Mode. The logic of a discretionary mode is to create a program for organizing and managing tasks, problems, or issues that recur periodically but exhibit a sufficient number of exceptions or variations each time they are encountered that different methods, procedures, and adjustments are required to handle them. A discretionary mode generally consists of: (1) a repertoire of alternative means or strategies for handling various tasks, problems, or issues, (2) guidelines for using discretion to diagnose situations and to respond by selecting an appropriate strategy from the repertoire, and (3) standards on expected levels of output quantity and quality for which personnel are held accountable. Once trained and indoctrinated in the discretionary program through formal academic or craft schools, job-entry, and continuing on-the-job training programs (which themselves represent examples of discretionary modes), personnel are basically independent actors, and the output of one group member often does not affect the output of others. Increases in group output are achieved by increasing the number of personnel or the skills of individuals. Thus, the discretionary mode is a labor-intensive structural design because the number of exceptions encountered in the work renders systematization either impractical or impossible to completely program in advance. Finally, the discretionary mode is a relatively flexible structure.

Frequent alterations and substantial changes of strategies in the repertoire are less costly and time-consuming than in the systematized mode (Van de Ven and Delbecq, 1974).

Examples of routine, technical, and intensive discretionary modes of structure for the performance of task-instrumental functions include: watch guards, janitors, and secretaries; salesmen, butchers, bakers, and candlestick makers; and medical, legal, and professional consulting units. As predicted by the more difficult tasks performed by these three groups of discretionary units, they will have personnel with progressively higher levels of skills and expertise and will exercise increasing levels of discretion in task performance (Van de Ven and Delbecq, 1974:187).

The discretionary mode for managerial coordination and control is exhibited in the forms of departmentation and in the flows of vertical and horizontal communications among departments and positions. Organizations will divide labor and resources into functional, geographic, program, and matrix arrangements to respond to critical contingencies in their product and factor markets and to minimize problems of coordination and control (Galbraith, 1977; Davis and Lawrence, 1977). Within and between these departmental arrangements, hierarchy serves as the basic mechanism for vertical integration (Thompson, 1967), and its basic function is to deal with exceptions (Dale, 1965). That is, repetitive and predictable integration issues are systematized through rules, plans, and schedules, whereas exceptions are referred to higher levels of authority.

As the number of exceptions and the interdependence among organizational units increase, more information exchange is required to make the necessary mutual adjustments. Two ways to "extend the arms of a manager" are to appoint assistant managers and add support staff to handle technical and administrative matters. In addition, horizontal channels of communications will emerge, in which the integration function is assumed by organizational members who communicate directly with others on a one-to-one basis in a nonhierarchical relationship. If there is a continuing need for mutual adjustments through horizontal communications, these nonhierarchical mechanisms are often formalized by designating individuals to the roles of project expeditor, integrator, or coordinator (Lawrence and Lorsch, 1967). Ultimately, the personal, discretionary mode of coordination at the managerial level may expand to the point where coordination departments are established, as is frequently observed in matrix or program management organizations (Galbraith, 1971; Delbecq and Filley, 1974).

The positions and units that operate in a discretionary mode to perform institutional functions generally include the chief executive officer, vice-presidents, and headquarters staff (e.g., legal counsel, public relations, and corporate affairs). Although considerable variations in the design of these discretionary mode units and positions may exist, the common element is that their principal functions are to deal with the exceptions and problems encountered in formulating, legitimating, and governing the domain of an organization in relation to its members and external constituents.

3. The Developmental Mode. The logic of a developmental mode is to create a program for handling tasks, problems, or issues that have not been encountered before and/or are sufficiently difficult and complex that they require group search, evaluation, and judgment. In varying degrees a developmental program consists of: (1) general goals or ends to be achieved in a specified amount of time, leaving unspecified the precise means to achieve them, and (2) a set of norms and expectations regarding the nature of behavior and interactions among group members. There is an important distinction between the adaptive processes in discretionary and developmental programs. A discretionary program is adaptive insofar as it has procedures for selecting from a repertoire of strategies appropriate to the various tasks or problems encountered. With a developmental program, the repertoire of strategies does not exist, and the unit is adaptive insofar as trial and error processes are followed in the design of a strategy. As a result, adaptation through problem-solving and learning processes during the period of task performance is a distinctive feature of the developmental program (March and Simon, 1958). Typically, tasks and issues undertaken by developmental-mode units are temporary and center on the solution to specific problems through a creative problem-solving process (Delbecq and Van de Ven, 1971; Van de Ven and Koenig, 1976). Developmental modes are team intensive, and group members are highly interdependent because they contribute their complementary skills to group problem-solving. Depending upon the degree of agreement among members on means or ends, decisions tend to follow either judgmental or bargaining strategies (Thompson and Tuden, 1959), and an individual's discretion is subject to guidelines set forth by the team (Van de Ven and Delbecq, 1974).

Two variations in technical functions of developmental mode units in organizations are illustrated in Figure 9-3. In the *design group*, tasks center on analysis, revision, and modification of existing products or services; in the *development groups*, the tasks require conceptual reorientations (Normann, 1971). For example, industrial design groups may perform yearly product revisions, whereas development groups explore the creation of new products or services traditionally not considered germane to the organization's technology. Thus, the distinction between design and development units is that the latter undertakes more difficult and open-ended tasks and problems (Van de Ven and Delbecq, 1974).

As Figure 9-3 illustrates, a variety of temporary and standing committees, task forces, and study groups are commonly used to perform managerial and institutional functions. Classically, the developmental mode with its group decision-making processes and committee structures has been viewed as an aberration of formal organization. For example, Weber (1947:402) states, "Collegiality unavoidably obstructs the promptness of decision, the consistency of policy, the clear reponsibility of the individual, and the ruthlessness to outsiders in combination with the maintenance of discipline within the group." Weber did recognize, however, that collegial bodies may be necessary where thoroughness in weighing of the institutional and managerial decisions is more important than efficiency (Weber, 1947:399). We should add that these developmental modes of structure and group decision processes for managerial and institutional functions provide a necessary and important forum for: (1) making strategic corporate decisions, (2) addressing conflicts and power contests among competing participants, and (3) creating and periodically reorganizing the discretionary and systematized modes of structures used by various organizational units and levels. An indication of the criticalness of these functions is that an entire industry of management consulting firms and professionals has grown up largely to assist organizations in creating temporary developmental modes and group processes to deal with these problems.

The institutional role of the board of directors is a subject that has received far too little attention in practice and management theory (Drucker, 1978). By law, the "managing organ" of every United States corporation is its board of directors, and currently the composition and responsibilities of corporate boards are being scrutinized and debated in the courts and federal regulatory agencies. For example, the Securities and Exchange Commission has recently proposed that the composition of corporate boards become totally independent of top management personnel, and the courts are increasingly demanding more responsibility and higher standards of accountability for boards of directors in stockholder suits. Clearly, there is a need to systematically include an examination of the structure and process of the board of directors as an institutional decision-making and governing unit in an assessment of organizations.

Summary

This section has presented a classification of nine different types of subsystems that often exist in complex organizations. The structural configurations that these subsystems are likely to adopt can largely be predicted from the different kinds of functions and tasks they perform. The classification helps to explain the significant design variations within organizations that were observed in previous chapters. The classification also brings out the reality of our starting definition of a complex organization by highlighting that at least nine qualitatively different subsystems may need to be taken into account when managing and assessing organizations.

Of course, any particular organization may not have all nine subsystems in the classification. From the view of a discretionary mode, Figure 9-3 represents a repertoire of nine key design strategies, and the analyst must use discretion, first in terms of determining which particular subsystems exist in the specific organization being assessed, and second in terms of judging what dimensions of context, design, and performance are relevant for evaluating and understanding each subsystem.

Hopefully, the descriptions and examples of each subsystem are useful to the analyst in exercising this discretion. The classification reduces the complexity of the OA framework to manageable proportions by (1) providing the analyst nine key reference points from which to diagnose a complex organization, (2) suggesting what specific dimensions in the OA framework are most relevant to focus upon when assessing each subsystem, and (3) hypothesizing the particular structural arrangement each subsystem is likely to have.

CONCLUDING DISCUSSION

This chapter has (1) summarized the evolution of the OA framework and instruments over the years, (2) presented a conceptual introduction to the revised OAI presented in the appendices, and (3) proposed a classification scheme for explaining design variations within complex organizations. The revised OA framework has expanded considerably over the years as a result of learning experiences obtained from our ongoing research on OA (much of which has been presented in this book) and also in response to the wealth of new theories and research in the literature during the intervening period. Expansions in the OA framework and instruments were made to more nearly achieve a systematic measurement and assessment of organizations. The analyst should (1) examine a complex organization at macro and micro levels of analyses, (2) identify and assess the unique design patterns of units and jobs, and (3) determine how the different units and jobs are linked together and contribute to the overall performance of the organization.

In developing and revising the OA framework we have relied extensively upon several bodies of theory and research, including economics, industrial psychology, sociometry, organizational sociology, management policy, systems theory, and mainstream organization theory. In doing so we were able to suggest a number of new directions for studying organizations; this was made possible by moving beyond the confines of a particular theoretical paradigm. However, there is the danger of using concepts incorrectly because they were abstracted from their parent disciplines, which provided the concepts with their original meaning and purpose. Furthermore, by borrowing ideas from several disciplines, one may lose sight of the paradigm origin or base in which the OA framework is grounded. As a result, we may be developing an eclectic conceptual model that is without "roots."

To guard against these dangers, we have made efforts to define our concepts and dimensions as clearly as possible and to cite the literature from which they originated. In addition, we have gone to considerable lengths to evaluate the constructs in the OA framework for logical validity and consistency from theoretical and empirical perspectives. Clearly, however, much further conceptual work lies ahead to evaluate the nature and interrelations of constructs in the OA framework.

These problems are not unique to the OA framework; they represent a significant challenge to the entire field of organization theory, which itself is interdisciplinary. The value in taking these risks lies in the potential for conceptual advances that are present when concepts from different paradigm origins are juxtaposed to create a new paradigm. Indeed, as Kaplan (1964:297) observes,

> A new theory requires its own terms and generates its own laws; the old concepts are not merely reorganized, but reconstituted, the old laws not just corrected, but given new meaning.

Thus, we believe that a continued program of theory building and research along the lines suggested here constitutes a promising and important direction for the scientific assessment of organizations and the application of its findings to help managers and analysts address practical organizational problems.

Caveats in Using the Organization Assessment Instruments

While clarifying and extending the OA framework, this chapter also presented a conceptual introduction to the revised OAI (see Appendices). The revised OAI incorporate the conceptual revisions made in the OA framework as well as the changes that were found necessary to improve the measurement properties of various indices in the previous version of the OAI. With the revisions made here, we believe the OAI have reached a design stage that warrant their use by other researchers to conduct their organizational studies and to further develop and test the generality of the OAI. In addition, the OAI can have important practical uses for diagnosing the strengths and weaknesses in the design and performance of organizations, particularly when OAI surveys are conducted regularly and used as part of an ongoing program of organizational development. However, to use the OA framework and instruments for basic and applied purposes, it is important to conclude by restating three basic caveats on the appropriate uses of the OAI.

First, it is critical that users conduct a pilot study and evaluate the measurement properties of the OAI in the organizations under investigation before they are used for assessing those organizations. As Appendix A details, the revised OAI contain a number of new or modified indices, and future evaluations are necessary to determine their measurement properties. In addition, as stated in Chapter 1, one of our goals could not be achieved here—that is, to test the generality of the OAI. Although attempts have been made to develop a framework and set of measurement instruments for assessing a wide variety of organizations, the data used here to evaluate the OAI are limited to a sample of employment security and child care organizations. Much further work in testing the OAI in other types of organizations is needed before we can confidently address the generality of the OAI.

Second, any practical uses of the OAI require serious attention to the process by which organizations are assessed. Although the OAI can be used to obtain a cross-sectional snapshot of organizational context, design, and performance, the practical usefulness of the OAI is greatly enhanced when they are used longitudinally and incorporated as part of an ongoing program of data-based feedback, learning, and organizational development. In this regard, our experiences suggest that the *processes* followed in designing and conducting an organization assessment will largely determine the degrees of relevance, learning, and use of the survey data by organizational participants *and* evaluators.

Chapter 2 presented our normative position on this matter by suggesting an overall process model for conducting assessments of organizations and for using the OAI properly in such assessments. In essence, the OA process model departs from conventional evaluation research approaches by emphasizing the importance of establishing a clear understanding of the nature, purposes, and intended uses of the assessment at the outset, and of performing three preparatory tasks when initiating any organization assessment effort. First, identify the people who will use the findings from an OA. Second, through a series of meetings ask each user group what goals, criteria, and standards they consider relevant for judging the effectiveness of the organizational components that will be assessed. Third, obtain the involvement of users in developing and reviewing specific design components of the OA to be conducted within their organizations. These design components include a review of: the specific organizational and performance characteristics to be examined, the measurement instruments to be used, the data-collection procedures to be followed, and the methods and information to be used in providing survey feedback. When used properly within the context of such an overall process of assessment that is tailored to the needs of a specific set of organizations being assessed, we believe that the OAI can provide substantial opportunities for learning to diagnose and improve the design and performance of organizations, work groups, and individual jobs.

Useful elaborations and extensions of the assumptions underlying the OA process model have been presented by Argyris (1968). He offers a penetrating discussion of the intended and unintended consequences of the ways organizational studies are traditionally designed and conducted. Readers are also referred to Nadler (1977) and Dunham and Smith (1979) for useful practical advice on developing ways to plan organizational surveys, collect data, and provide feedback to organizational participants.

Tailoring the OAI to the specific needs of an organization may imply decisions to use only parts of the OAI and to make various other changes in the OAI. In this regard, it must be understood that the more one makes changes in the format or content of the OAI, the less the results of our evaluation of the OAI apply to the resulting modified OAI. This is because making changes in the OAI in effect constitutes the creation of a new and untested measurement instrument. Therefore, we recommend that only those changes in the OAI that are absolutely necessary be made, and that expert technical advice be obtained in making these changes. It is impossible to predict or discuss here the various modifications that may be necessary to use the OAI in a particular set of organizations.

Finally, data obtained with the OAI are most useful when analyzed and interpreted by individuals with a qualitative understanding of the organization being assessed. In each chapter we exemplified how data from an OAI survey can be used for practical managerial purposes by addressing specific applied problems and decisions on the organization and performance of employment security offices and units. In addressing these practical problems and issues, we relied heavily upon our qualitative understanding of ES offices to organize and analyze the quantitative OAI data. This type of in-depth understanding of the functioning of an organization is critical for making sense of the numbers produced by the OAI. For analysts and managers familiar with the nature and operating problems of their organizations, the OA framework and instruments provide a powerful set of analytic tools to systematically assess the context, design, and performance of organizations.

APPENDIX A

Glossary for the Revised Organization Assessment Instruments

TABLE OF CONTENTS OF ALL INDICES IN REVISED
ORGANIZATION ASSESSMENT INSTRUMENTS (OAI)

This appendix contains a glossary of all the dimensions measured in the revised Organization Assessment Instruments (OAI). The dimensions are measured from organizational records (which are described within this glossary) as well as four OAI questionnaires: (1) a Unit Supervisor Questionnaire, presented in Appendix B, (2) a Unit Member Questionnaire, shown in Appendix C, (3) a Focal Unit Questionnaire in Appendix D, and (4) an Other Unit Questionnaire in Appendix E. This glossary includes a brief definition and explanation of each OA dimension, the names of the items that are used to measure each dimension, and the question numbers in the OAI questionnaires presented in Appendices B to E. In addition, based upon the evaluations of the 1975 OAI in Chapters 4 to 8, this glossary discusses any changes that have been made in the measurement of each construct in the new version of the OAI. The Table of Contents provides a ready reference of the pages in this glossary where each OA index is described.

To remain clear on the different levels of an organization that are examined with the OAI, the glossary and revised OAI are divided into four component parts or modules: (1) individual job design, (2) work unit design, (3) interunit relations, and (4) macroorganization design. The reader is referred to Chapters 4 through 8 for a detailed discussion and evaluation of the development of these four OAI components or modules. Only very brief descriptions of these modules can be presented in this glossary.

A fifth component of an OAI survey requires obtaining measures of performance of the organizations, work units, and jobs that are included in an organization assessment. As argued in Chapter 2, these measures require decision makers to make value judgments on the goals, criteria, and standards desired from the organizational components being assessed. These value judgments are necessarily unique to the organizations, units, and jobs being assessed and are often not generalizable to other organizations. Therefore, objective measures of effectiveness are not included in the revised OAI. Instead, they are uniquely defined and operationalized for the sample of organizations included in an OAI survey according to a process as suggested in Chapter 2.

Since this glossary refers often to the four OAI questionnaires presented in Appendices B to E, it is appropriate at this point to clarify briefly the overall contents and intended applications of these instruments.

The OAI Unit Supervisor and Member Questionnaires are designed as two complementary instruments that measure all the job and work unit design factors listed in the Table of Contents. The two questionnaires contain two parts. The first part of the Unit Supervisor and Member Questionnaires is the same and measures the context, design, and outcomes of jobs held by the respondents. Part II of both questionnaires focuses on characteristics of the work unit but differs in two ways. First, the wording of questions is different to reflect the different positions of unit supervisors and members. Second, some relatively objective characteristics of organizational units are measured only in the Unit Supervisor Questionnaire to minimize the time requirements of organizational participants in an OA survey. These specific differences are pointed out in this appendix.

The OAI Unit Supervisor and Member Questionnaires are intended to be administered to all personnel in all units and supervisory levels of the organizations included in an OA survey. If not all personnel can participate in an OA survey, then at a minimum, it is expected that *all supervisory personnel* at all levels complete the Unit Supervisor Questionnaire and *at least two* or more *nonsupervisory employees* be sampled at random *from each unit* and asked to complete the Unit Member Questionnaire. The critical importance of an adequate sample of respondents from each organizational unit was clearly brought out in Chapter 3.

To examine job design, the data obtained from Part I of the Unit Supervisor and Member Questionnaires are not aggregated but examined at the individual respondent level. An assessment of the design of organizational units, however, requires that data obtained from Part II of the Unit Supervisor and Member Questionnaires be aggregated to the work group level. The reliability of work group scores is greatly enhanced by obtaining responses of many individuals occupying different positions in each organizational unit. Thus, it is important to recognize that the *Unit Supervisor Questionnaire does not substitute for the Unit Member Questionnaire, and vice versa.* Data obtained with both questionnaires are necessary to assess work unit design.

Appendices D and E contain the OAI Focal Unit and Other Unit Questionnaires, which measure all the dimensions of interunit relationships outlined in the Table of Contents from the perceptions of both parties involved in each pairwise relationship. The Focal Unit Questionnaire asks respondents to select the five most important other units from inside or outside the organization that they had to develop or maintain a relationship with during the past six months. Then the respondents answer questions about their unit's relationships with each of the other units they selected. The Focal Unit Questionnaire only provides a one-sided perspective on each interunit relationship. A follow-up survey with the OAI Other Unit Questionnaire overcomes this limitation. This questionnaire is intended to be completed by informants in the other units that were selected as the most important units to each focal unit. Responses to matching questions in the Focal and Other Unit Questionnaires are averaged to obtain a balanced two-sided perspective of each interunit relationship.

As discussed in this appendix, the OAI Focal and Other Unit Questionnaires are constructed so that they are adaptable to a variety of data collection strategies. They can be appended to either the Unit Supervisor or Member Questionnaires or administered separately as an interunit coordination survey. Furthermore, respondents to the Focal Unit Questionnaire can be asked to self-select the other units that they coordinate with (as described previously), or the investigator can specify the particular other units in the organization to be focused upon in an interunit coordination survey.

OAI JOB DESIGN MODULE

As discussed in Chapter 8, the job design module is a recent addition to the OA framework and measurement instruments. It measures the way in which individual jobs or positions within the organization are structured, the background characteristics of job incumbents, the organization's technical and functional requirements of jobs, and employees' affective responses to their jobs. These job characteristics are measured in Part I of the OAI Unit Supervisor and Member Questionnaires; in fact, the first part in the two questionnaires is precisely the same. It is important to keep in mind that the job or position is the focus of analysis in all these measures, and individuals occupying jobs at all levels in the organization act as respondents (rather than as informants) in answering questions about their own jobs. Specific definitions and measures of the job characteristics in Part I of the Unit Supervisor and Member Questionnaires (in Appendices B and C) are presented as follows.

A. Job Specialization. Job specialization refers to the number of different tasks performed in a job and the scope or breadth of these tasks. Individuals are generalists when their jobs involve a large number of broadly defined tasks, problems, or issues, whereas they are specialists when a small number of rather narrow tasks and problems occupies most of their working time.

Two basic approaches can be taken to measure job specialization. One approach is to ask respondents two questions:

a. Describe your job by listing the *different kinds of tasks and work activities* you perform in a normal working week. (Respondent writes answer to this open-ended question.)

b. Indicate the number of *hours per week* you normally spend performing each of the tasks you just listed.

Based upon a content analysis of answers to the first question by all respondents, a standardized listing of unique tasks and work activities is developed and then used for judgmentally coding the number of different tasks each respondent performs. The number of unique tasks that occupy five hours or more of the respondents' work time per week is then used as the measure of job specialization.

An alternative approach to measuring job specialization, and the one used in the 1975 OAI, is to develop a standardized list of unique tasks performed by the population of respondents before conducting the OAI survey. This list is developed from prior knowledge and observations of the tasks performed by respondents and is included in the OAI questionnaires. Respondents are then asked to indicate the number of hours per week they normally spend performing each of the different types of tasks listed in the questionnaire. (Spaces are included in the questionnaire to allow respondents to write in tasks that are not included in the list and to indicate the number of hours they spend on these additional tasks.) With this alternative approach, job specialization is then computed by counting the number of different tasks that the respondent recorded as occupying five hours or more of his/her time per week.

An illustration of the second approach for measuring job specialization in ES organizations was shown in Figure 6-3 in Chapter 6. Obviously, this particular index is limited to ES offices, and the user of the OAI will need to develop another listing of unique tasks performed by the population of respondents included in the organizations being assessed if the user desires to adopt this second approach for measuring job specialization.

The first approach for measuring job specialization is shown on the first page of the revised OAI Unit Supervisor and Member Questionnaires in Appendices B and C. This approach is more general since it allows the respondent to describe in an open-ended format what tasks and activities he or she performs. However, the measurement of job specialization from these open-ended responses requires an extensive amount of judgment to determine the number of unique tasks each respondent performs. A listing of the population of unique tasks performed by all respondents needs to be developed after the data are collected to standardize these judgments of the number of different kinds of tasks and work activities each respondent performs.

B. Job Expertise. Job expertise is the skill level of job incumbents in terms of formal education, length of job-entry orientation and training, and the amount of time spent by the job incumbent in on-the-job training and reading necessary for upgrading and remaining current in the knowledge needed to perform the job. Job expertise is measured with the following four items in Part I of the OAI Unit Supervisor and Member Questionnaires:

1. Years of school beyond grade school: Q (Question) 14.

2. Educational degree obtained: Q 15.

3. Length of job-entry training: Q 13.

4. Time in on-the-job training: Q 11.

Items 2 to 4 were included in the previous OAI. Item 1 is added to measure the simple number of years of advanced schooling which a respondent obtained, regardless of whether a degree or diploma was obtained (as measured by Item 2). In the evaluation of the job expertise index in Chapters 5 and 8, it was found that Items 2 to 4 tap different aspects of job expertise and that much information is lost if one averages the items together into one overall composite score. The items are more useful if examined separately for an assessment of jobs.

C. Job Standardization. Job standardization is the degree to which the roles and task assignments that make up a job are written out in a job description. It is also the number and detail of rules and procedures established to guide the job incumbent in work performance. Thus, job standardization focuses on the clarity and detail of guidelines spelled out for a job incumbent regarding the duties and responsibilities of the position.

Job standardization is measured as the average of the following items in the OAI Unit Supervisor and Member Questionnaires:

1. Number of written job rules: Q 19.

2. Detail of job rules: Q 20.

3. Percent time have SOPs: Q 24.

4. Extent follow SOPs: Q 18.

5. Clarity of job performance standards: Q 27.

6. Extent job description specifies performance standards: Q 28.

Items 1 to 4 were included in the previous OAI and were evaluated in Chapter 6. Items 5 and 6 are added in the revised OAI to measure the extent to which employees' job descriptions accurately state the roles they perform and the standards they are expected to achieve in performance appraisals. These two items are becoming increasingly important criteria in preventing job discrimination complaints and legal suits according to Title VII of the Civil Rights Act of 1964 (Peres, 1978).

D. Job Authority. Job authority is defined as the amount of discretion or influence that the job incumbent exercises in making job-related decisions regarding: (a) what tasks, projects, and assignments constitute the roles and responsibilities of the job, (b) how the work is to be done in terms of what procedures and rules to follow, (c) how work exceptions and problems are to be handled, and (d) what performance criteria are established and to be attained in performance appraisals.

Job authority is measured as the average of the following four items in the revised OAI Unit Supervisor and Member Questionnaires:

1. Decide what tasks to perform: Q 25a.

2. Decide work rules and procedures: Q 25c.

3. Decide how to handle exceptions: Q 25d.

4. Decide work quotas and standards: Q 25b.

This job authority index was included in the previous OAI and found to have good indications of convergent and discriminant validity.

E. Job Pressure. Job pressure refers to the amount of work load assigned to a job incumbent, the lead time available to perform it, and the extent to which the job incumbent can control the pace of his/her work. As discussed in Chapter 6, job pressure, along with job authority, is part of the larger concept of job discretion. High amounts of job pressure imply that an employee can exercise little job discretion, because large work loads with little control over the pace or lead time in which to perform them represent externally imposed work demands on a job incumbent who is given little slack time to exercise discretion in deciding how to handle the work load other than to follow previously determined work procedures.

Four indicators of job pressure are included in the revised OAI Unit Supervisor and Member Questionnaires. The first three items were found to load together as a unique factor in the 1975 OAI (see Chapter 8). The fourth item is added to tap the job-related pressure that comes with setting difficult performance standards.

1. Heaviness of work load: Q 21.

2. Control over work pace (reverse scale): Q 23.

3. Work lead time (reverse scale): Q 22.

4. Difficulty achieving performance standards: Q 30.

Job pressure is the average of these four items after reversing the scaled responses to items 2 and 3 for each respondent.

F. Job Accountability. Job accountability is the degree to which a job incumbent *feels responsible* and is *asked to answer for his or her work* decisions and behavior. Job accountability is also part of the larger concept of job discretion. We argue in Chapter 6 that even if an employee is authorized to exercise a high degree of job authority and is given sufficient slack time to do so, the employee in fact exercises little discretion if he or she is not held accountable for work decisions and behavior.

The extent to which a job incumbent is held accountable is measured as the average of items 1 and 2 below, whereas felt accountability is the average of items 3 to 6 below.

1. Held accountable for work decisions: Q 26.

2. Held accountable for achieving standards: Q 32.

3. Fairness of job appraisal standards: Q 31.

4. Take credit or blame for work results: Q 40i.

5. Feel responsible for work: Q 40e.

6. Don't care if work done right (reverse scale): Q 40a.

An evaluation of these indices is required to determine their reliability and validity since they are new to the OAI.

G.   *Job Feedback.* Job feedback is the degree to which the job incumbent receives information about the procedures and results of his/her work efforts. There are two parts to this construct, feedback from others (the supervisor and peers) and feedback from the job itself (simply by assessing the procedures and results of one's own work). Job feedback is used as one indicator of job incentives because feedback provides the job incumbent the positive and negative internal or external cues necessary for error detection, learning, and conformance to expected job performance standards and procedures.

In the OAI Unit Supervisor and Member Questionnaires, feedback from the job is measured by item 1, feedback from peers by the average of items 2 and 3, and feedback from the supervisor as the average of items 4 to 7.

Feedback from the job:

1.   Job lets me know how well doing: Q 9.

Feedback from peers:

2.   Frequency of feedback from peers: Q 10.

3.   Never get feedback from co-workers (reverse scale): Q 40h.

Feedback from supervisor:

4.   Frequency of feedback from supervisor: Q 33.

5.   Degree supervisor discussed performance standards: Q 29.

6.   Frequency receive practical suggestions: Q 34.

7.   Supervisor often provides feedback: Q 40c.

Items 1, 3, and 7 are adopted from the Job Diagnostic Survey developed and evaluated by Hackman and Oldham (1975). Items 4 and 6 remain unchanged from the 1975 OAI, whereas items 2 and 5 are new.

H.   *Expectation of Rewards and Sanctions.* Expectation of rewards and sanctions are two separate constructs that refer to the degree to which the respondent anticipates that good job performance will result in some reward (be it formal promotion or informal recognition) and that poor job performance will result in some punishment (either informal reprimand or formal demotion). Expectations of rewards and sanctions are measured in the revised OAI Unit Supervisor and Member Questionnaires with the same items as used in the 1975 OAI (evaluated in Chapter 6), plus a new item for each index.

Expectation of rewards is the average of:

1. Chance of recognition for good job: Q 35a.

2. Chance of promotion for good job: Q 35b.

3. Rewarded for extra effort: Q 40k.

Expectation of sanctions is the average of:

4. Chance of reprimand for poor job: Q 36a.

5. Chance of demotion for poor job: Q 36b.

6. Reprimand for inferior work: Q 40l.

Job Outcomes

Job satisfaction, work motivation, and salary are three criteria that are included in the OAI to measure what job incumbents obtain from their jobs. Job satisfaction and work motivation measure an employee's affective response to his or her job. Salary indicates the economic payoff that a person receives from the job. They are defined and measured as follows.

A. Job Satisfaction. Job satisfaction is an affective reaction or feeling by an employee on how happy or satisfied he or she is with the job, supervisor, co-workers, pay, and his/her current and future career progress and potential. This general construct is measured by asking the following questions, which were also included in the 1975 OAI and which represent a modified version of the job satisfaction index in the Survey of Organizations as developed and evaluated by Taylor and Bowers (1972).

1. Satisfied with job: Q 37a.

2. Satisfied with supervisor: Q 37b.

3. Satisfied with pay: Q 37c.

4. Satisfied with co-workers: Q 37d.

5. Satisfied with past career: Q 37e.

6. Satisfied with career potential: Q 37f.

7. Often think of quitting job (reverse scale): Q 40f.

B. Work Motivation. Work motivation is the amount of effort an employee exerts in performing the job and the degree to which she or he is self-motivated to perform effectively on the job. Only effort was measured in the 1974 OAI. In the revised OAI we expand the index to include a measurement of intrinsic self-motivation by incorporating the Job Diagnostic Survey measures of internal motivation, which were developed and evaluated by Hackman and Oldham (1975). The latter are added to the OAI because Hackman and Oldman (1974) report that the measures of internal motivation have been shown to relate directly to the quality of the employee's work.

In the revised OAI Supervisor and Member Questionnaires, work effort is measured as the average of items 1 and 2 below, whereas internal self-motivation is the average of items 3 to 6.

1. Effort put into work: Q 38.

2. Attempts to improve performance: Q 39.

3. Self-opinion in doing job well: Q 40b.

4. Accomplishment felt in doing job well: Q 40d.

5. Feeling when job done poorly: Q 40g.

6. Feeling unaffected by how well job done (reverse scale): Q 40j.

C. Salary. Salary is the amount of pay a job incumbent receives from the organization. It is measured by item 102 in the Unit Supervisor and item 90 in the Unit Member Questionnaires. In some organizational studies it may be important to distinguish between employees' base salaries and additional forms of remuneration obtained through commissions, bonuses, or working overtime. This information can usually be obtained from organizational payroll records.

Job Context and Individual Difference Characteristics

The OAI Job Design Module also includes a set of situational factors that measure the organization's requirements of a job and the background characteristics of individuals who occupy the job. The organization's requirements of a job are indicated by measuring the difficulty and variability of work assigned to a job incumbent and the level in the hierarchy at which the job is located in the organization. Individual difference characteristics are examined in terms of the job incumbent's tenure in the organization, age, sex, number of dependents, and growth need strength. Definitions and measures of these factors are now presented. See Chapter 6 for further descriptions and evaluations of the measures.

A. Task Difficulty. Task difficulty refers to the *analyzability* and *predictability* of the work undertaken by an organization unit. The construct stems from the work of March and Simon (1958) and of Perrow (1967), who refers to it as the ability to understand the characteristics of the raw materials or work objects encountered. The construct focuses on the analyzability and predictability of the search process that individuals undertake when they encounter a task or problem. The analyzability of work (items 3 and 4 following) is the clarity of knowing how to diagnose incoming work and select an appropriate method or strategy for dealing with the incoming work. The ease with which one can determine in advance the outcomes of a particular sequence of task steps is the predictability of the work (items 1 and 2 following). Both task analyzability and predictability indicate the extent to which search processes are trivial and programmed at one extreme or, at the other extreme of the task difficulty continuum, the extent to which they rely upon chance and guesswork.

Task difficulty is computed as the average of the following items in the Unit Supervisor and Member Questionnaires:

1. Difficulty knowing work correct (reverse scale): Q 4.

2. Unsure of work outcomes (reverse scale): Q 5.

3. Frequency problems arise: Q 7.

4. Time spent solving problems: Q 8.

The four items included in this task difficulty index were all part of the 1975 OAI evaluated in Chapter 5. A fifth item (lack of task clarity) was deleted because it confounded with the task variability index.

B. Task Variability. Task variability is defined as the number of exceptions encountered in the characteristics of the work. Perrow (1967) includes in his definition of exceptions the degree to which stimuli are perceived as familiar or unfamiliar. However, we do not include the familiarity of work objects in our definition of task variability because its inclusion would confound our definitions of difficulty and variability. Instead, task variability focuses only on perceived variations of incoming work materials and objects. In this narrow sense, task variability is similar to materials technology (Hickson et al., 1969:380) and the perceived uniformity and stability of raw materials (Perrow, 1967).

Task variability is measured as the average response to the following four items in the Unit Supervisor and Member Questionnaires.

1. Perform different tasks (reverse scale): Q 2.

2. Number of daily tasks different: Q 3.

3. Frequency of exceptions: Q 6.

4. Frequency follow different steps (reverse scale): Q 17.

This index is unchanged from the 1975 OAI.

C. *Level in the Hierarchy.*   Level in the hierarchy is an indicator of the vertical location of the job in the organization. It is measured from organization charts (described in the OAI Macroorganizational Module) as the number of supervisory levels between the job incumbent and the top manager in the organization.

D. *Growth Need Strength of Job Incumbent.*   Growth need strength refers to the degree to which the respondent desires to fulfill self-actualization needs from his or her job. This construct is viewed as an individual difference factor which has been shown by Hackman and Oldham (1974:1975) to moderate the relationships of job design characteristics with job satisfaction and motivation. Individuals high on growth needs have been shown to respond positively (i.e., with high satisfaction and work motivation) to complex, challenging, and "enriched" jobs. Individuals low on this measure tend *not* to find such jobs satisfying or motivating.

In the Job Diagnostic Survey, Hackman and Oldham (1974) developed two growth need strength scales, a "would like" format and a "forced choice" format. The "would like" format consists of six questions pertaining to how much respondents would like stimulating work, independent thought, learning new things, creative work, personal growth in their job, and a sense of accomplishment from their work. Respondents simply rate how much they would like these characteristics in their jobs along a five-point scale from "some" to "extremely much."

Because of its simplicity, most researchers have adopted the "would like" format to measure growth need strength. However, in personal conversations, Richard Hackman, the author of the Job Diagnostic Survey, expressed a concern over the degree of bias in the "would like" format because the questions tend to elicit socially desirable responses. The "forced choice" format tends to elicit less bias because respondents are forced to choose among two alternatives that tend to be approximately equal in social acceptance. However, as is true with most measurement indices, the more reliable "forced choice" format consists of more items (twelve) and takes more time for respondents to complete. Although length and time to complete the OAI Questionnaires are critical concerns to their practical usefulness for assessing organizations, we have chosen to adopt (with permission) the "forced choice" format for measuring growth need strength, particularly since the construct itself is more psychologically complex than most other dimensions included in the OAI.

The "forced choice" growth need strength index consists of the following twelve items in the Unit Supervisor and Member Questionnaires:

1. Prefer creativity over pay: Q 41.

2. Prefer pleasant people over important decisions: Q 42.

3. Prefer loyalty over responsibility: Q 43.

4. Prefer no discretion over financial trouble: Q 44.

5. Prefer unfriendly workers over routine job: Q 45.

6. Prefer no-skill job over critical supervisor: Q 46.

7. Prefer learning over supervisor respect: Q 47.

8. Prefer no challenge over chance of layoff: Q 48.

9. Prefer fringe benefits over job skill development: Q 49.

10. Prefer poor work conditions over little freedom: Q 50.

11. Prefer personal skill use over teamwork: Q 51.

12. Prefer isolated job over no challenge: Q 52.

The responses to items 2, 3, 4, 6, 8, and 9 are reversed, and then the twelve items are averaged to obtain the growth need strength score.

E. Other Individual Difference Characteristics. Finally, the revised OAI Unit Supervisor (S) and Member (M) Questionnaires contain questions to measure the following other individual difference characteristics of job incumbents.

1. Tenure in organizations: SQ 94, MQ 82.

2. Number of previous positions: a count of the number of different job titles in answer to SQ 95 and 96, or MQ 83 and 84.

3. Average time in previous positions: the average time spent in previous positions held by job incumbent in answer to SQ 95 and 96 or MQ 83 and 84.

4. Age of job incumbent: SQ 99, MQ 87.

5. Sex of job incumbent: SQ 98, MQ 86.

6. Number of dependents: SQ 100, MQ 88.

OAI ORGANIZATIONAL UNIT DESIGN MODULE

The OAI Organizational Unit Design Module measures all the global properties of organizational units, as well as relationships among members within organizational units, as described in Chapter 5. An organizational unit is defined as consisting of a supervisor and all employees who report directly to that supervisor. Most of the characteristics of organizational units are measured in Part II of the Unit Supervisor and Member Questionnaires.

Definitions and measures of all the unit structure and process dimensions in the revised OAI are described in this section. Task difficulty and variability, shown in Chapters 5 and 6 to be two important predictors of the designs of individual jobs and organizational units, were presented in the Job Design Module. This is because task difficulty and variability are measured at the individual level and then aggregated to the group level to evaluate unit design characteristics.

A. Number of Job Titles in Unit. The number of job titles in the unit is an indicator of unit specialization. It is measured by counting the number of unique job titles or functions of unit personnel. This construct refers to the degree of functional differentiation within a unit. The greater the number of different jobs or functions performed by a unit, the lower the unit specialization and the greater the functional differentiation.

The number of job titles in a unit is computed by counting the number of unique job titles that appear in the right-hand column of the unit personnel roster beginning Part Two of the Unit Supervisor Questionnaire. This measure was also used in the 1975 OAI. A considerable amount of judgment is involved in determining whether the job titles written by the supervisor on the Unit Personnel Roster are the same or different. In our study of ES units, we developed a standardization listing of all job titles of personnel in the ES agency with the help of internal management analysts. This standardized listing was used to eliminate or standardize much of the subjective judgment involved in counting the number of unique job titles in each organizational unit.

B. Role Interchangeability in Unit. Number of job titles in a unit is a measure of the division of labor within an organizational unit. It does not indicate how specialized unit personnel are in performing these jobs. This latter dimension is measured by role or job interchangeability. In operational terms, interchangeability, or the converse, personnel specialization, means the degree to which A can perform B's job at short notice and B can perform A's job, even when A and B have different job titles or different functional assignments (Beer, 1966; Tyler, 1973). In a unit with high personnel specialization, job rotation is very difficult because personnel roles are not interchangeable in the near-term future. Thus, job interchangeability, or personnel specialization, refers to the bifurcation of skills among unit employees (Blau and Schoenherr, 1971).

It is important to recognize that the level of expertise or professionalism is conceptually independent of job interchangeability. Thus, interchangeability is different from "role variety" (Tyler, 1973), the number of "specialists" (Hage, 1965; Hage and Aiken, 1967), "functionalization" (Samuel and Mannheim, 1970), and "personal specialization" (V. Thompson, 1964; Blau, 1974; Hall, 1972). Each of these terms have been used to refer both to our job interchangeability and to the level of professionalism or expertise of personnel. For purposes of organizational analysis, we find it important to keep unit specialization, job interchangeability, and expertise distinct conceptually and empirically in order to examine their interrelations.

Role interchangeability is measured by averaging the responses to the following items in the Unit Supervisor and Member Questionnaires.

1. Members perform same tasks: Q 53.

2. Members qualified in one anothers' jobs: Q 54.

3. Ease of job rotation: Q 55.

4. Frequency of job rotation: Q 56 in Supervisor Questionnaire only.

This index remains unchanged from the 1975 OAI. However, in Chapter 5 it was shown that although the first three items clearly cluster together as a unique factor, the fourth item does not correlate well with the others in the index. This fourth item is maintained in the revised OAI because, although we do not believe it is a particularly good indicator of role interchangeability in a unit, an investigator may desire a behavioral measure of the frequency with which jobs are rotated in an organizational unit.

C. Unit Skill Heterogeneity. Skill heterogeneity is a new construct introduced in the OA framework in Chapter 6 to examine the extent to which the skills or expertise of personnel within an organizational unit are similar or different. The construct is a unit-level counterpart to the degrees of expertise or professionalism of individual members of a work unit, which is now examined in the job design module of the OAI. That is, whereas job expertise is the skill level of individual employees, skill heterogeneity is the variation in skills among employees within an organizational unit.

Skill heterogeneity is defined as the range of different skills and competencies possessed by people in an organizational unit as a group. If all personnel in a unit have the same amount of schooling in the same disciplines and specialties and spend similar amounts of time in the same job-entry and on-the-job training programs, then the unit is homogeneous in personnel skills. A heterogeneous unit, on the other hand, would consist of people who are hired with different amounts of formal education in different disciplinary specialties and are involved in different job orientation and on-the-job training programs. A unit with heterogeneous skills is more equipped to respond to a greater variety of different tasks, problems, or issues than a homogeneous unit because the former has a greater breadth of skills to apply to the unique problems encountered. However, units with heterogeneous skills tend to be less flexible than units with homogeneous skills in handling cyclical variations in the quantity of the same kinds of work because it is more difficult to interchange roles or shift work loads among unit personnel.

Skill heterogeneity is computed in the OAI Unit Supervisor and Member Questionnaires as the standard deviations of responses to items 1, 3, and 4 following for all personnel within an organizational unit. Items 2 and 5 provide a qualitative understanding of the different skills and training of unit personnel.

1. Years of school beyond grade school: Q 14.

2. Type of major if obtained Bachelor's, vocational, or graduate degree or certification: Q 16.

3. Length of job-entry training: Q 13.

4. Time in on-the-job training: Q 11.

5. Type of on-the-job training or education programs: Q 12.

A qualitative content analysis is necessary to count the number of different responses to items 2 and 5. To standardize the judgements required in coding these open-ended responses, it is necessary to develop a listing of all educational majors, job-orientation programs, and on-the-job training or educational programs of all employees in the organization being assessed. These master listings are then used as a standardized guide to count the number of unique responses made by all personnel in an organizational unit.

D. Unit Automation. Unit automation refers to the degree to which machines, equipment, and other mechanical devices are used to perform and control work activities in an organizational unit. Automation is a new addition to the OAI and taps one aspect of the technological sophistication of an organizational unit and also detects discontinuities in work procedures created by breakdowns or failures in the mechanical devices upon which an organizational unit has become reliant.

The degree of automation of a unit's work methods is measured by items 1 to 3 following, whereas the amount of disruption caused by breakdowns in mechanical devices is measured by items 4 and 5 in the Unit Supervisor (S) Questionnaire only.

1. Extent use mechanical devices: SQ 58.

2. Type of mechanical devices: SQ 59.

3. Reliance on mechanical work appraisal systems: SQ 67a.

4. Frequency of mechanical breakdowns: SQ 60.

5. Down-time due to mechanical failures: SQ 61.

The open-ended responses to item 2 are coded according to the level of sophistication of the mechanical devices reported to be used in the unit.

E. Unit Standardization. Unit standardization is defined as the extent to which rules, standard operating procedures, and performance expectations are formalized and followed to coordinate, control, and evaluate unit activities. Standards are formalized when they are specified in detail (items 1 and 2 following) and codified or written out (items 3 and 4 following). Standards are followed when unit personnel report they use and abide by these rules, policies, and procedures for coordinating their work activities (items 5 and 6). Thus, the unit standardization index consists of the average of the following items in the Supervisor(S) and Member(M) Questionnaires.

1. Clarity of unit performance standards: SQ 68, MQ 60.

2. Preciseness of unit rules, policies, procedures: SQ 75, MQ 65.

3. Degree performance criteria quantified: SQ 65 (only).

4. Percent unit rules, procedures written out: SQ 78 (only).

5. Extent unit rules violated (reverse scale): SQ 76, MQ 66.

6. Strictness of rule enforcement: SQ 77, MQ 67.

This unit standardization index is a new addition to the OAI and represents a unit-level counterpart to job standardization measured in the OAI Job Design Module. As discussed in Chapter 6, the unit standardization index used in the 1975 OAI and evaluated in Chapter 5 taps the properties of individual jobs rather than those of an organizational unit. Therefore, the previous standardization index is used to measure job standardization, whereas the new index described here will be used to measure those rules, policies, and procedures that pertain to the overall functioning of a work unit.

F. Distribution of Unit Authority. Centralization commonly refers to the locus of decision-making authority within an organization. When most decisions are made hierarchically, an organizational unit is considered to be centralized; a decentralized unit generally implies that the major source of decision making has been delegated by line managers to subordinate personnel. In survey research, therefore, centralization has often been measured as the degree of hierarchy of authority on work-related decisions (e.g., Hall, 1962; Hage and Aiken, 1967; Khandwalla, 1977).

However, it has long been recognized that a number of additional sources of decision-making authority exist within organizations and their units. Max Weber (1947:392–402) indicated that in addition to bureaucratic hierarchy, authority can be exercised by "collegial bodies" and by the "separation of powers" (entrusting functional authority to individuals with unique spheres of competence and expertise). Once these alternative sources of decision authority are recognized, then decision authority by nonsupervisory employees must be considered a unique dimension of centralization and not simply the inverse of hierarchical authority (Van de Ven, 1977). The existence of multiple sources of decision making within organizations has also been recognized by Lammers (1967), Duncan (1972), and Wood (1973). In addition, simple observations and experiences in organizational life suggest that these alternative sources of decision-making are not new and that they are exercised often in different task situations.

To keep this broader perspective of centralization clear, we have called it the *distribution of unit authority* among the unit supervisor (hierarchical authority), unit members (personal authority), unit supervisor and members as a group (collegial authority), and staff or line positions outside of the organizational unit (functional authority). Distributions of authority among these postions are measured in the revised OAI in terms of the following unit decisions: (1) what kinds of tasks and work are to be performed in the unit, (2) what criteria are chosen and used to evaluate performance effectiveness, (3) who makes the appraisals regarding how well the unit performs its work, and (4) what operating rules, policies, and procedures are established to coordinate and control unit activities. Specifically, the following indices are included in the revised Unit Supervisor (S) and Member (M) Questionnaires to measure the distributions of unit authority.

Supervisory authority is the average of the following items:

1. Spv. say on unit tasks: SQ 57b, MQ 56b.

2. Spv. say on performance criteria: SQ 63b, MQ 58b.

3. Spv. say on performance appraisal: SQ 67c (only).

4. Spv. say on rules, policies, procedures: SQ 79b, MQ 68b.

Unit employee authority is the average of the following:

5. Member say on unit tasks: SQ 57c, MQ 56c.

6. Member say on performance criteria: SQ 63c, MQ 58c.

7. Member say on performance appraisal: SQ 67d (only).

8. Member say on rules, policies, procedures: SQ 79c, MQ 68c.

Unit collegial authority is the average of:

9. Group say on unit tasks: SQ 57d, MQ 56d.

10. Group say on performance criteria: SQ 63d, MQ 58d.

11. Group say on performance appraisal: SQ 67e (only).

12. Group say on rules, policies, procedures: SQ 79d, MQ 68d.

External authority over unit (functional and higher management) is the average of the following items:

13. External say on unit tasks: SQ 57a, MQ 56a.

14. External say on unit performance criteria: SQ 63a, MQ 58a.

15. External say on unit performance appraisal: SQ 67b (only).

16. External say on unit rules, policies, procedures: SQ 79a, MQ 68a.

These indices of the distribution of unit authority were not included in the 1975 OAI. However, an earlier version of these indices was included in the 1973 OAI and was reported in Van de Ven (1977) to have satisfactory measurement properties. As discussed in Chapter 6, the indices of supervisory and employee discretion used in the 1975 OAI are more appropriately indicators of job authority, since they ask respondents to indicate how much say or influence they have in making job-related decisions. Thus, the 1975 OAI indices tap a property of individual jobs and are now included in the OAI Job Design Module.

 G. Unit Incentives. Unit incentives is a broad construct that includes (a) the degree to which individual or group performance results in rewards for doing good work and sanctions for doing poor work, and (b) the degree to which group pressures on unit members achieve conformity to low output expectations (pretending to work hard, or soldiering) or stimulate excellence and higher levels of output. These two constructs are grouped together because they both tap an important aspect of the way the group provides incentives to members to produce at varying rates. Unit incentives is a new addition to the OAI and respresents a unit level counterpart to job incentives for individuals examined in the OAI Job Design Module.

Group-based incentives are measured as the average of:

1. Extent rewards based on group performance: SQ 71a (only).

2. Extent sanctions based on group performance: SQ 72a (only).

Individual-based incentives are the average of:

3. Extent rewards based on individual performance: SQ 71b (only).

4. Extent sanctions based on individual performance: SQ 72b (only).

Group pressure on individual members to conform is the average of the following measures.

5. Group gangs up on lagger: SQ 73b, MQ 64b.

6. Group gangs up on rate-buster: SQ 73c, MQ 64c.

7. Group encourages higher individual performance: SQ 73d, MQ 64d.

8. Members compete with one another (reverse scale): SQ 73a, MQ 64a.

Since these are new measures in the OAI, no evidence of their reliability or validity is available.

H. Work Flow Interdependence within Unit. *Work flows* are the materials, objects, or clients that are sent or transported between people and/or machines within organizational units. According to Thompson (1967), a hierarchy of work interdependence between unit personnel can be determined by observing the work flows in (1) independent, (2) sequential, (3) reciprocal, or (4) team arrangements among unit personnel. On the assumption that these types of work flows exhibit the characteristics of a Guttman scale, answers to the work flow cases are weighted by multiplying the supervisor's response to independent flow by zero, sequential flow by .33, reciprocal flow by .66, and team flow by one, and then adding the products to obtain the overall work flow interdependence score. (Independent work flow is given zero weighting because it implies no interdependence among unit members).

Work flow interdependence, therefore, is computed by weighting the scores to the work flow items in the Unit Supervisor Questionnaire:

1. Independent work flow (multiply score by 0): SQ 80a.

2. Sequential work flow (multiply score by .33): SQ 80b.

3. Reciprocal work flow (multiply score by .66): SQ 80c.

4. Team work flow (multiply score by 1.00): SQ 80d.

This index is the same as included in the 1975 OAI and evaluated in Chapter 5.

I. Job Dependence among Unit Personnel. The work flow index provides only an indication of the work interconnectedness of unit members. It does not provide an indicator of the intensity of work interdependence among unit personnel or with other organizational units. Work flows may be reciprocal among unit members, and yet each person may perform his or her job as though it were self-contained because of buffering, stockpiling, or the standardized nature of the work (Thompson, 1967). Therefore, there is a need to also examine the tightness of coupling among jobs within the unit and with other units. This is the definition of job dependence. It refers to how much each person's job depends upon the activities performed by the supervisor, other unit members, and people in other units. Job dependence is measured at each cycle of work activity: input, transformation, and output.

Job dependence on the superviror is computed by averaging the following items in the OAI Unit Supervisor (S) and Member (M) Questionnaires:

1. Input job dependence on supervisor: SQ 81a, MQ 69a.

2. Process job dependence on supervisor: SQ 82a, MQ 70a.

3. Output job dependence on supervisor: SQ 83a, MQ 71a.

Job dependence among unit members is computed by averaging the following:

1. Input job dependence among unit members: SQ 81b, MQ 69b.

2. Process job dependence among unit members: SQ 82b, MQ 70b.

3. Output job dependence among unit members: SQ 83b, MQ 71b.

These indices of job dependence among unit personnel were included in the 1975 OAI and were evaluated in Chapter 5.

Job dependence on other units is computed by averaging the following items:

1. Input dependence on other units: SQ 81c, MQ 69c.

2. Process dependence on other units: SQ 82c, MQ 70c.

3. Output dependence on other units: SQ 83c, MQ 71c.

The indices of job dependence on supervisor and among unit members were included in the 1975 OAI and were evaluated in Chapter 5. Although external unit relationships are examined in depth in the OAI Interunit Module, measures of job dependence (and communications, listed below) with other units are included here because the primary assignments of many organizational units require spanning many unit boundaries.

J.   Unit Communications or Information Flows.   Information flows are work-related messages sent among unit personnel through three different modes of communication: *written* memos, reports, and letters; *personal* one-to-one discussions; and *group* or staff meetings among three or more unit personnel. The *frequency* of information flows through each of the three communication modes is measured with the following questions.

Written communications is the average of:

1. Frequency of supervisor–subordinate reports: SQ 85a, MQ 73a.

2. Frequency of reports among members: SQ 85b, MQ 73b.

3. Frequency of reports with other units: SQ 85c, MQ 73c.

Personal communications is the average of:

1. Frequency of supervisor–subordinate discussions: SQ 86a, MQ 74a.

2. Frequency of discussions among members: SQ 86b, MQ 74b.

3. Frequency of discussions with other units: SQ 86c, MQ 74c.

Group communications is the average of:

1. Frequency of scheduled unit meetings: SQ 87, MQ 76.

2. Frequency of unscheduled unit meetings: SQ 88a, MQ 75a.

3. Frequency of unscheduled meetings with other units: SQ 88b, MQ 75b.

A distinction between scheduled and unscheduled group meetings is made because Hage, Aiken, and Marrett (1971) and Van de Ven, Delbecq, and Koenig (1976) found significantly different patterns of coordination on these forms of group meetings. With the exception of unscheduled group meetings, these communication measures are the same ones used in the 1975 OAI. The evaluation in Chapter 5 showed that it is often more meaningful not to average together these different forms of communication but to examine them separately.

K. Unit Conflict. Conflict refers to the frequency of disagreements or disputes among unit personnel and the extent to which unit members hinder the efforts of others in work performance. The OAI index following has been expanded to obtain a more reliable measure of conflict among people within a unit and with people in other units. The index consists of the average of the following items:

1. Frequency of supervisor–subordinate conflict: SQ 89a, MQ 77a.

2. Frequency of conflict among unit members: SQ 89b, MQ 77b.

3. Frequency of conflict with other units: SQ 89c, MQ 77c.

4. Members get ahead at expense of others: SQ 73e, MQ 64e.

5. Agreement on unit performance criteria: SQ 64, MQ 59.

L. Methods of Conflict Resolution. Four basic methods of conflict resolution are examined in the OAI to determine how disagreements and disputes are dealt with by unit personnel. These are based upon Burke's (1970:394) description of the conflict-resolution methods and have been examined extensively by Blake and Mouton (1964), Lawrence and Lorsch (1967), and Filley et al. (1976). (1) Ignoring or avoiding the issues—easier to refrain than to retreat from an argument; silence is golden. See no evil, hear no evil, speak no evil. (2) Smoothing over the issues—play down the differences and emphasize common interests; issues that might cause divisions or hurt feelings are not discussed. (3) Openly confronting the issues—open exchange of information about the conflict or problem as seen by the parties involved and a working through of differences to reach a mutually agreeable solution. (4) Resorting to authority—having the unit supervisor or other person with power or authority over the contesting parties resolve the matter.

The same index used in the 1975 OAI is used to measure the four intraunit conflict resolution methods in the revised OAI Unit Supervisor and Member Questionnaires.

1. CR by avoiding issues: SQ 90a, MQ 78a.

2. CR by smoothing over issues: SQ 90b, MQ 78b.

3. CR by confronting issues: SQ 90c, MQ 78c.

4. CR by hierarchy: SQ 90d, MQ 78d.

M. Perceived Unit Performance. The principal criterion used to measure the performance of an organizational unit is chosen by the users of an organizational assessment; it is often measured with the organization's performance-reporting system. In addition to this criterion (which was used throughout this book to evaluate the measurement properties of the 1975 OAI), an index of perceived performance of an organizational unit has been added to the revised OAI. This has been done to obtain a subjective measure of performance in those organizations that do not regularly measure unit performance and to generalize the findings from future organization assessments.

The perceived unit performance index measures the degree to which the unit has achieved its performance targets (item 1 following) and also measures the relative rating of the unit in comparison to other units on the criteria stated in items 2 to 8 following.

1. Percent of performance targets attained: SQ 70, MQ 63.

2. Unit rating on quantity of output: SQ 93a, MQ 81a.

3. Unit rating on quality of work: SQ 93b, MQ 81b.

4. Unit rating on innovativeness: SQ 93c, MQ 81c.

5. Unit rating on reputation for excellence: SQ 93d, MQ 81d.

6. Unit rating on goal attainment: SQ 93e, MQ 81e.

7. Unit rating on efficiency: SQ 93f, MQ 81f.

8. Unit rating on morale: SQ 93g, MQ 81g.

It should be recognized that this index taps only the subjective perceptions of unit personnel on the performance of their own unit. To increase its validity, it is recommended that managers and other informants who are not members of the unit be asked in interviews to rate the performance of the units with the same questions presented here.

OAI INTERUNIT RELATIONS MODULE

The OAI Interunit Relations Module combines the constructs discussed in Chapters 7 and 8 because the same basic conceptual framework is used to assess relations between units within and among organizations. It focuses on the relationships that an organizational unit maintains with other organizational units which may exist in the same office or plant, in other corporate divisions or levels within the organization (as examined in Chapter 7), or in other organizations (see Chapter 8). Wherever these other units may exist, the key point is that the level of analysis or observation in all cases is the *pairwise* or *dyadic relationship* between a focal (F) organizational unit and one other (O) organizational unit. Whereas the other modules in the OAI measure attributes or properties of organizations, work groups, or jobs, the Interunit Module examines the *relationships* between these organizational components. Relationships between units are measured in terms of *context* (the degrees of dependence, awareness, consensus, and domain similarity among the parties involved), *process* (the transactions of resources and information between the units), *structure* (the formalization and complexity of the relationships, and the distribution of influence among the parties in the dyad), and *outcomes* (the perceived effectiveness of the relationship). Definitions and measures of these dimensions are presented in this section.

The OAI Interunit Module contains two questionnaires to measure these dimensions of dyadic relationships: a *"Focal Unit Questionnaire"* (FQ) and an *"Other Unit Questionnaire"* (OQ). These two questionnaires are presented in Appendices D and E, respectively. They are designed so they can be administered separately or appended to the OAI Unit Supervisor and/or Member Questionnaires, depending upon the specific data collection strategy that is adopted in a particular Organization Assessment study.

Strategies for Assessing Interunit Relations

Three basic strategies could be taken to assess interunit relationships. One strategy is to ask each organizational unit to describe its external relationships with other organizational units, levels, and organizations without clearly specifying the names of these other units. This strategy was taken in Chapter 7. It amounts to a study of an organizational unit's relationship with different sectors of its external environment. With the exception of a shift in the unit of analysis, this strategy is the same as that taken by many open-systems researchers who have examined how the internal design of an organization is associated with its external environment. However, as Van de Ven, Emmett, and Koenig (1974:115) point out, this strategy treats the organization or the unit as the focus of observation. Formally, therefore, it does not constitute an interunit or interorganizational study, because the focus of observation is not on the relationships that connect organizational units. Furthermore, in Chapter 7 we found that this strategy was somewhat limiting in making a clear assessment of the external relationships of ES units because the frame of reference in the 1975 OAI was too general. It did not ask respondents to identify and answer the questions in terms of the specific other units with which the focal units maintained relationships. Thus, although this first strategy has the advantage of simplicity and may provide sufficient information to make a general assessment of a unit's external environments, it does not measure directly the relationships this unit maintains with others.

A second strategy, which does treat the dyadic relationship as the unit of observation, is to ask informants in each organizational unit to describe the relationships they maintain with specifically named other organizational units. This strategy could be implemented by administering the OAI Focal Unit Questionnaire (FQ—see Appendix D) to informants in each organizational unit. Since most units maintain relationships with many other units, informants could be asked to complete the FQ for only the five most important other units that they are involved with. Informants could either self-select these most important other units, or the FQ could be precoded to specify the names of the other units that one desires to have informants answer for in an organization assessment. For example, if a study is conducted specifically for evaluating relationships between intake, adjudication, placement, counseling, and WIN units in local ES offices, then the investigator would specify and write the names of these units into the columns of the FQ before administering it. The informants who complete the FQ could include all personnel in each organizational unit, in which case the FQ would be appended to the OAI Supervisor and Member Questionnaires. However, practical time and cost considerations may necessitate that only one or a few personnel in each organizational unit complete the FQ. In this case, only the unit supervisor (at a minimum) plus one or two unit members could be asked to complete the FQ.

This second strategy satisfies our concluding recommendation made in Chapter 7 for directly measuring the external relationships of an organizational unit. It provides a concrete way to assess the specific linkages that organizational units maintain with others. Since it is usually impossible and often not desirable to assess all the external relationships of an organizational unit, this strategy sacrifices breadth for depth by focusing only on the five most important other units connected with the focal unit. That is, the FQ provides an in-depth assessment of the five most important external relationships of a focal unit by measuring all the dimensions of context, structure, process, and outcomes defined in the following pages. If this strategy had been adopted, our assessment of the external relationships of ES units in Chapter 7 could have been far more specific in addressing practical administrative questions regarding the coordination and control structure in ES offices. However, the basic limitation of this second strategy is that it provides only a one-sided perspective of interunit relationships because it does not include a measurement of how other units view their relationships with the focal unit.

A third strategy for assessing interunit relationships, which overcomes this limitation, is to obtain the perspectives of both parties to a dyad on the nature of their relationship. Specifically, this third strategy consists of three steps: (1) Treat each organizational unit as a focal unit and ask informants in that unit to complete the Focal Unit Questionnaire for the most important five other units that it maintains relations with (as done in strategy 2). (2) Then go to informants within these other units and ask them to complete the OAI Other Unit Questionnaire (OQ—see Appendix E) which obtains the perceptions of the other units on those dimensions that are particularly susceptible to bias if measured from only one side of a pairwise relationship. (3) Finally, average the responses of the focal unit and other unit informants to matching questions in the FQ and OQ to obtain composite pairwise perceptions of each dyadic relationship.

Although this strategy involves much work in conducting an initial survey of focal units with the FQ and a follow-up survey of other units with the OQ, it provides a systematic way of obtaining the combined perceptions of the two parties involved in each dyadic relationship. We believe this combined average perception approximates a balanced "true" score of interunit relations better than would be obtained if perceptions from only one party were obtained or if some other weighting scheme were used.

An important additional advantage of this third strategy is that it provides a way to characterize the clusters and networks of relationships that exist among organizational units. As described in Chapter 8, data obtained on pairwise relationships can be examined from a broader perspective to assess patterns of relations within sets, clusters, and networks of organizational units. Using network theory and matrix algebra, Appendix F describes how one can operationally obtain sociometric indications of the intensity, centrality, and complexity of interunit networks based on data collected according to this third strategy.

Therefore, we recommend that this third strategy be used to conduct a systematic and comprehensive assessment of interunit relationships within and between organizations. The measures and instruments in the OAI Interunit Module are designed with this third strategy in mind and are now described.

Definitions and Measures of Interunit Relationships

A. Basic Identification Variables. When the Focal Unit Questionnaire (FQ) is administered, the investigator can either precode the names of the other units for which one desires the informants in the focal unit to answer or allow informants to self-select the five most important other units with which the focal unit maintains relationships. If it is the former, then the investigator writes the names of the other units into the designated columns of the FQ before administering the questionnaire to F informants. It it is the latter, then it is obviously necessary to ask some basic questions that identify specifically the other units that the F informants have chosen. The introductory section of the FQ includes some basic questions to identify the other units, their organizational location, their perceived importance to F, and the qualitative nature of the relationship. Responses to these items are used for creating an identification code of pairwise relations and for classification purposes in subsequent statistical analysis of the data.

As stated previously, the OAI Other Unit Questionnaire (OQ) survey is conducted after the FQ survey and is completed by informants in all the other units that were either precoded or self-selected by informants in the FQ. Before a follow-up survey can be conducted with the OQ, the names and identification codes of the focal unit are written into the OQ. This is done because the sole purpose of the OQ is to obtain the perspective of the other unit informants regarding the relationship they maintain with the focal unit. Answers to matching questions are subsequently averaged to obtain measures for the dimensions of each pairwise relationship.

The basic identification items in the FQ and OQ, then, are the following:

1. Name of Focal Unit: ID questions in FQ, precoded in OQ.

2. Name of Other Unit: FQ 1, precoded in ID box of OQ.

3. Other unit located within or outside focal unit organization: FQ 4.

4. Qualitative reason for relationship: FQ 2.

5. Types of reasons for relationship:
   a. For work: FQ 5a, OQ 5a.
   b. For resources: FQ 5b, OQ 5b.
   c. For technical assistance: FQ 5c, OQ 5c.
   d. For information: FQ 5d, OQ 5d.

6. Prior effectiveness of relationship: FQ 8, OQ 4.

B. Interunit Resource Dependence. Dependence is defined as the extent to which parties in a relationship perceive they need the other party to attain their self-interest goals or intentions. The index is computed as the average of the following items in the FQ and OQ:

1. Other unit dependence on focal unit: FQ 9, OQ 8.

2. Focal unit dependence on other unit: FQ 10, OQ 7.

3. Importance of other unit to focal unit: FQ 3.

4. Importance of focal unit to other unit: OQ 19.

Items 1 and 2 represent the interunit dependence index used in the 1975 OAI. Items 3 and 4 are added to increase the reliability of the index.

C. Interunit Awareness. Two levels of awareness are of interest in studying interunit relations, unit awareness, and personal acquaintance. In a dyadic relationship, interunit awareness is the extent to which people in the focal and other units are familiar with the services and goals of each other. Interunit personal acquaintance refers to how long and how well the boundary spanners in F and O know each other on a personal basis.

Awareness of other unit is measured as the average of:

1. Years/months relationship in existence: FQ 7 (only).

2. Focal unit informed of other unit goals and services: FQ 11.

3. Other unit informed of focal unit goals and services: OQ 3.

Personal acquaintance is measured as the average of:

4. Years/months of personal acquaintance: FQ 15 (only).

5. Degree of personal acquaintance: FQ 16, OQ 1.

In the 1975 pairwise interagency survey evaluated in Chapter 8, the personal acquaintance index was found to correlate very highly with the consensus index. However, the personal acquaintenance index is maintained in the revised OAI, with slight changes in wording, to determine if this confounding is the result of measurement error or simply a reflection of two highly related "true-score" dimensions.

D. Interunit Consensus/Conflict. Consensus is defined as the degree of agreement or disagreement (i.e., conflict) among the parties in a relationship on their operating goals (ends), specific ways they do their work (means), and the terms of their relationship. Consensus is computed as the average of the following questions in the OAI Focal and Other Unit Questionnaires:

1. Agree on goal priorities: FQ 17a, OQ 2a.

2. Agree on ways work/services are provided: FQ 17b, OQ 2b.

3. Agree on terms of relationship: FQ 17c, OQ 2c.

4. Extent other party hindered performance (reverse scale): FQ 19, OQ 17.

5. Frequency of conflict (reverse scale): FQ 32, OQ 16.

The first four items in this index remain unchanged from the 1975 OAI, with the exception of changing the wording to reflect interunit relations. The fifth item is repeated from the intraunit module to obtain a behavioral indication of the frequency of conflict between parties.

E. Methods of Conflict Resolution. As in the OAI Unit Design Module, four basic methods of conflict resolution are measured in the Focal Unit Questionnaire to determine how disagreements and disputes are dealt with by the parties involved in a dyadic relationship.

1. CR by avoiding issues: FQ 33a.
2. CR by smoothing over issues: FQ 33b.
3. CR by confronting issues: FQ 33c.
4. CR by hierarchy: FQ 33d.

In the 1975 OAI this index was only used to examine the methods of conflict resolution within organizational units. Since it was found to be highly related to unit performance (see Chapter 5), it is now generalized to assess how conflict resolution methods affect interunit relationships.

F. Interunit Domain Similarity. Domain similarity refers to the extent to which units in a relationship obtain their money from the same sources; have the same goals, work, technology, and professional skills; and provide the same kinds of products and services to the same clients or customers. Thus, domain similarity is a very broad construct of the degree of overlap in domains of the units in a relationship.

Domain similarity is computed as the average of the following six items:

1. Same funding source: FQ 18a.
2. Same kind of work: FQ 18b.
3. Same clients or customers: FQ 18c.
4. Same operating goals: FQ 18d.
5. Same employee skills: FQ 18e.
6. Same technology: FQ 18f.

In Chapter 8 the interagency domain similarity index was found to confound with several other indices of pairwise relations. The wording of the questions in the revised OAI has been changed considerably to attempt to decrease this confounding and to make the referent of the questions apply to interunit rather than interorganizational domain similarity.

G. Interunit Communications. Interunit communications is a broad concept which includes the *mode, amount, content, direction,* and *ease* of information flows between parties in a dyadic relationship. The *mode* of interunit communications refers to the frequency with which messages are transmitted between the focal and other unit through written reports or letters, telephone calls, face-to-face discussions, and group meetings. As in the 1975 OAI, these different modes of communications are measured only in the Focal Unit Questionnaire with the four items following. An assessment of the different modes of communications can provide practical and useful guidelines for determining what methods of communication help and hinder the effectiveness of pairwise relationships under varying conditions.

1. Frequency of written reports: FQ 22a.
2. Frequency of face-to-face talks: FQ 22b.
3. Frequency of telephone calls: FQ 22c.
4. Frequency of group meetings: FQ 22d.

In addition, the revised OAI has been expanded to include a measurement of the overall amount, direction, and time spent in communications between the units. As stated in Chapter 8, this information is necessary to develop indices of interunit networks. These dimensions are measured with the following items.

1. Overall frequency of contacts: FQ 21, OQ 13.
2. Percent time spent with other party: FQ 26a, OQ 12.
3. Percent contacts initiated by focal unit: FQ 23 only.

Finally, the *ease* of sending and receiving messages between parties in a pairwise relationship is measured by two items that were included in the quality of communications index in the 1975 OAI. The evaluation in Chapter 8 of the communication quality index found that the two items that refer to the ease of getting in touch and of getting ideas across loaded together as a unique factor. However, the other items intended to measure communication quality confounded with other dimensions of pairwise relationships. We now believe that communication quality is too broad a concept to measure in a concrete and meaningful way when assessing interunit relations. Instead, it is more productive to focus on more operational aspects of the nature of communications among parties, such as the ease of communications, which is measured as the average of the following two items in the OAI Focal and Other Unit Questionnaires:

1. Difficulty getting in touch (reverse scale): FQ 25, OQ 14.

2. Difficulty getting ideas across (reverse scale): FQ 24, OQ 15.

H. Interunit Resource Flows. The operational criterion that we use to define the existence of an interunit relationship is that a transaction of resources occurs between the units involved. A resource is broadly defined to include any valued transaction between the units, including money, work, personnel, supplies and equipment, and technical or functional assistance.

Obviously, the specific kinds of resources that are transacted between units will differ depending upon the kinds of organizational units assessed. This presents a measurement problem in deciding not only what terms or labels to use for the different kinds of resource flows that may be transacted between different kinds of organizational units but also what scale to use to measure these resource flows. As stated in Chapter 8, in the pilot study of interagency relations we found that respondents were unable to specify the amounts of resources transacted in terms of ratio scales (e.g., dollars, number of days of consultation, number of clients referred), even though a ratio scale would be the ideal way to measure resource flows. Therefore, an "extent" scale was used, in which focal unit informants subjectively indicated the relative amounts of resources they received from and sent to the other unit. However, upon reflection, a more appropriate metric to use may be a "percent" scale which provides an indication of the proportion of resources an organizational unit transacts with others. This "percent" scale provides more information than an "extent" scale, because the former is less subject to differing frames of reference of respondents and approaches a ratio scale far more nearly than the latter. Further, in Chapter 7, a "percent" scale of external unit work flows was used and found to be useful in discriminating the different relevant environments of ES units. Therefore, in the revised OAI a "percent" scale has been adopted to measure the proportions of total external resource flows of a focal unit that are transacted with the other unit. The proportions of total external resource flows that a focal unit received from and sent to the other unit are measured with the following items.

Total resource flow from the other unit to the focal unit is the sum of:

1. % Focal unit's work (objects, clients) received from other unit: FQ 26b.

2. % Focal unit's money or budget received from other unit: FQ 26d.

3. % Focal unit's technical/functional assistance received from other unit: FQ 26c.

Total resource flow from the focal unit to the other unit is the sum of:

1. % Focal unit's completed work sent to other unit: FQ 27a.
2. % Focal unit's money or budget allocated to other unit: FQ 27b.
3. % Focal unit's technical/functional assistance provided to other unit: FQ 27c.

Thus, the interunit resource flow index in the revised OAI provides an indication of the proportions of resources of a focal unit that are sent to and received from the other unit. Modifications in the wording of the questions in the FQ may be necessary to clarify their meanings when assessing interunit relations in a specific set of organizations. Furthermore, we strongly recommend that investigators also search for ratio measurements of the *amounts* of resource flows between units when designing an organizational assessment. Such ratio measures are often available from organizational records, particularly for industrial or production-oriented firms.

I. Variability of Resource Flows.   Variability of resource flows refers to the number of exceptions and problems encountered in the flows of resources between the focal and other unit. It is operationalized in terms of the uniformity of resource flows and the frequency of interruptions and problems encountered in transferring work objects and materials between the parties in a pairwise relationship. Variability of resource flows is measured with the following questions in the OAI Focal and Other Unit Questionnaires.

1. Resource flows the same each time transacted: FQ 28.
2. Resource flow problems encountered: FQ 30.
3. Resource flow interruptions: FQ 29.

The variability of resource flows index represents a substantial expansion of the work flow variability index examined in Chapter 7: (1) because the former is intended to measure the more general concept of resources (one aspect of which is work), and (2) because we attempted to correct the measurement deficiencies found in the latter index. Obviously, a future evaluation is necessary to determine the measurement properties of this new index.

J. Formalization of Interunit Relationship. The formalization of a dyadic relationship refers to the degree to which the role behavior and activities of each party are clearly specified, mandated, and standardized. Once an expression has been made between the parties regarding the terms of their relationship, the formalization of this relationship increases the more the agreement is verbalized, written down, organizationally mandated, or contracted. The standardization of this relationship refers to the degree to which official communication channels and standard operating procedures, rules, and policies are used in making transactions between the parties in a dyad. Thus, the formalization of a pairwise relationship is measured in terms of the degree to which the relation is mandated (item 1), clearly specified (items 2 and 3), and standardized (items 4 and 5).

1. Extent relation mandated: the sum of FQ 4a–4d.

2. Relation explicitly verbalized: FQ 6a, OQ 11a.

3. Relation written down in detail: FQ 6b, OQ 11b.

4. Extent SOPs established: FQ 31a.

5. Extent formal channels followed: FQ 31b.

This index has been revised substantially from the one used in the 1975 OAI to measure our broader conceptualization of the concept of formalization.

K. Interunit Influence. Interunit influence is the ability of the focal unit to change or affect the internal operations of the other unit and vice versa. Since both parties in a relationship can influence and be influenced by the other simultaneously, one can consider interunit influence to be the ability of the focal and other units to change or affect one another.

Focal unit influence on the other unit is the average of:

1. Focal unit say over other unit's operations: FQ 13, OQ 9.

2. Extent focal unit changed other unit's goals or services: FQ 40, OQ 26.

Other unit influence on the focal unit is the average of:

3. Other unit say over focal unit operations: FQ 12, OQ 10.

4. Extent other unit changed focal unit goals or services: FQ 41, OQ 25.

The *total amount* of influence in a dyadic relationship is the sum of the four items. The *distribution* of influence among the focal and other units in a dyadic relationship is the difference between the average of items 1 and 2 and the average of items 3 and 4. A positive result indicates the amount of focal unit influence over the other unit. A negative result indicates the amount of other unit influence over the focal unit. A zero result indicates a balanced distribution of influence among the parties in a dyadic relationship. This index of interunit influence is a new addition to the OAI and is included as one important dimension of the structure of an interunit relationship.

L. Perceived Effectiveness of Interunit Relationship. The perceived effectiveness of an interunit relationship is defined as the extent to which the parties involved subjectively (1) believe that each unit carries out its commitment and (2) feel their relationship is equitable, worthwhile, productive, and satisfying. Thus, perceived effectiveness focuses on the subjective attitudes of each unit's boundary spanners. By intention, the construct does not measure effectiveness in an objective way, except to the extent that boundary spanners use objective criteria in formulating their subjective attitudes. The reason attitudes are important here is because the theory argues that boundary spanners act or behave on the basis of their attitudes or perceptions of a relationship rather than some external objective criterion of effectiveness which is generally not known to boundary spanners in practice.

The perceived effectiveness of an interunit relationship is measured as the mean response to the following items in the OAI Focal and Other Unit Questionnaires:

1. Extent other unit carries out commitments: FQ 35, OQ 21.

2. Extent focal unit carries out commitments: FQ 36, OQ 20.

3. Extent relationship is productive: FQ 37, OQ 22.

4. Extent time and effort worthwhile: FQ 38, OQ 23.

5. Extent satisfied with relationship: FQ 39, OQ 24.

6. Equality of transactions: FQ 20, OQ 6.

This index is the same as that used in the 1975 OAI, with the exception of a change in wording to refer to interunit relations rather than interagency relations (see Chapter 8).

OAI MACROORGANIZATION DESIGN MODULE

The OAI macroorganization design module focuses on the overall domain, scale of operations, and structural configuration of the total organization. Chapter 4 described and evaluated the indicators used to measure these macroorganizational factors in our study of employment security offices. In keeping with our conclusion in that chapter, we do not propose to offer indicators that are generally applicable to other organizations of: the history of an organization; the uncertainty, complexity, and restrictiveness of its domain; and economic indicators of demand and supply. Measures of these contextual dimensions are necessarily idiosyncratic to the type of organization under study Although these dimensions are generalizable across organizations at the conceptual level, at an operational level we believe that different indicators of these concepts are necessary to measure them in a reliable and valid way. As argued in Chapter 4, attempts to develop operational indicators of these contextual dimensions which may apply to all types of organizations will yield measures too general to be useful for assessing a specific subset of organizations.

However, we do believe that our state of knowledge has progressed to a stage to develop generalizable measures of the overall structural configuration of an organization. The specific procedures for measuring these characteristics of macroorganization design in the OAI are now described.

Standards for Constructing Organization Charts

Chapter 4 described how all of the operational indicators of the aggregate structural configuration of an organization in the OAI are measured from detailed and up-to-date organization charts. However, for organization charts to be useful for making an organization assessment, it is necessary that they be current and developed in a consistent way. The organization charts maintained by the organizations we studied were not sufficiently precise for our purpose and were also found to be nine months out of date on the average. Therefore, a crucial and time-consuming part of the preparation for an OAI survey was to create up-to-date organization charts for each ES office. It was necessary to develop standards for constructing organization charts and to revise the charts prepared by the agency in accordance with these standards. These standards are described in this section.

The information needed to construct organization charts was obtained through interviews and telephone calls with key informants in each administrative and local office in the organization. Discussions with several informants in each office were needed to develop and verify the accuracy of each table of organization. Map-size organization charts were constructed and hung on display in the rooms where respondents completed the OAI questionnaires. Respondents were asked to write the correct identification code of their work unit in their questionnaires from the unit ID codes written on the organization chart. Even after all the preparatory work and interviews with key informants, it was found in several cases that a respondent indicated that he or she was not properly identified in the organization chart. In these instances corrections were made on the table of organization that hung on a wall before respondents proceeded to answer the OAI questionnaire.

Standards and conventions for constructing organization charts are now described using an employment security office as an example. The reader should have no difficulty applying these standards and conventions for constructing charts of other organizations, even though nuances in terminology may exist.

Figure A-1 presents an exemplary organization chart of a district employment security office. The circled numbers with arrows on the organization chart represent examples of the OAI standards and conventions numbered as follows.

1. Write the complete formal name of the organization represented by the organization chart. Also write the address where the organization is located and the telephone number of the top office manager.

2. Write the date of the table of organization. As indicated previously, several revisions of the charts were made before they were accurate. The last revision date of the organization chart was the date on which the OAI were administered in the organization or office. The correct organization chart on the date of data collection was filed permanently along with other OAI data.

3. A *box* in the organization chart represents a supervisor. A supervisor is defined as an individual who has at least one professional or two or more nonprofessional subordinates reporting directly to him or her in performing their normal work. Lead workers can be supervisors if, and only if, at least one professional, or two or more nonprofessional employees, report directly to this lead worker for work instructions and performance appraisals. The civil service classification was used to determine the professional or nonprofessional status of an individual. A job title or civil service classification of "supervisor," "director," "administrator," or "manager" does not automatically designate that the individual be drawn in a box in the organization chart; he or she must directly supervise the work of at least one professional or two or more nonprofessional

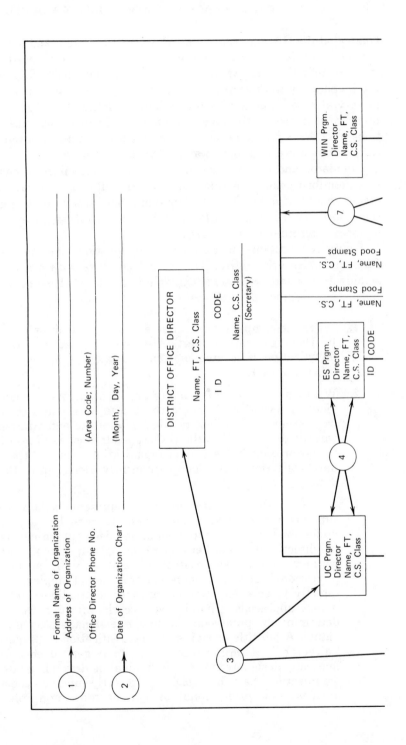

420

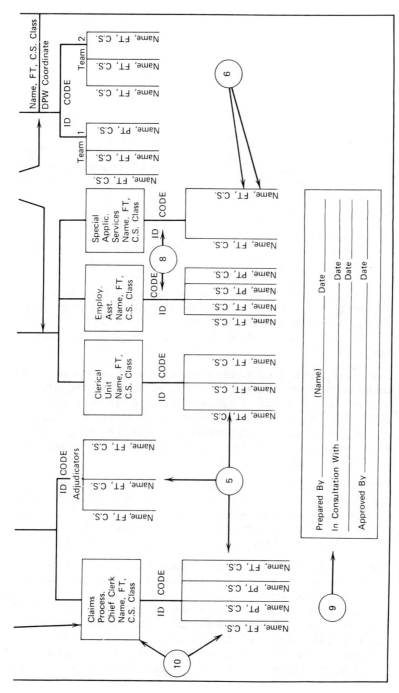

Figure A-1   Example of an organization chart for a district job service office.

421

employees on the date that the OAI are administered in the office or organization.

A box in the organization chart, then, is reserved for the sole purpose of representing a supervisor—one box per supervisor. This convention was also followed by Blau and Schoenherr (1971) in their national survey of 53 employment security agencies.

4. Three vital pieces of information are written into each supervisory box in the organization chart: (a) the name and geographical location (if different from the total organization's location) of the unit or function that the supervisor is in charge of, (b) the last name of the individual who holds the supervisory position, and (c) whether the supervisor is employed full-time (FT) or part-time (PT) by the organization.

5. A *stick* (as we call it) in the organization chart represents a nonsupervisory employee. Nonsupervisory employees are all personnel on the organization's payroll (both full- and part-time) who cannot be classified as supervisors according to the criteria in 3 preceding. One stick represents one nonsupervisory employee. The organization chart must reflect the number of nonsupervisory personnel employed by the agency on the date of the OAI questionnaire survey. A stick may be drawn horizontally or vertically.

6. Two vital pieces of information are written on each stick in the organization chart: (a) the last name of the employee, and (b) whether the individual is employed full-time (FT) or part-time (PT). The name of the employee is necessary for tracking changes in personnel assignments over time. The designation of employees as part- or full-time is necessary to correctly compute organization size.

7. The vertical and horizontal lines connecting supervisory boxes and nonsupervisory sticks represent formal (i.e., officially designated) reporting relationships. Informal (or functional) reporting relationships may be denoted as dashed lines but are not drawn into the OAI organization charts as a general rule.

8. The identification (ID) code of each unit is written on the formal reporting line that connects the unit supervisor with his or her unit members.

An organizational unit consists of a supervisor and all employees (unit members) reporting directly to that supervisor. Likert's (1967) notion of "linking pins" is used to identify and code units above the bottom or first-line level of work units. For example, in Figure A-1 the ES Program Director is coded as supervisor for the unit consisting of the clerical, employment assistance, and special applicant services unit supervisors who report to him/her. At the same time, the ES Program Director is a member of the unit consisting of the District Office Director (as unit supervisor) and the UC, ES, and WIN Program Directors (as unit members).

For consistency, all supervisors are assigned the identification code of the unit that they supervise. The ID code written on the organization chart is the master code. In completing the OAI questionnaires all respondents identify themselves with the ID numbers of their unit listed on the organization chart.

9. The process control box at the bottom of Figure A-1 is completed by research team members at each stage in constructing the organization charts. Key informants who were interviewed or consulted in the preparation or revision of the charts are named, as well as the dates of their involvement. All organization charts are reviewed and approved by the principal OA investigator before the site visit to the office to administer the OAI questionnaires. In spite of these precautions, we have found that minor changes often need to be drawn into the charts during the on-site administration of the OAI. However, without these precautions, *major* changes would have been required.

10. After the OAI questionnaires have been completed, the civil service classifications or job titles and grades (e.g., Clerk Typist III, Manpower Counselor II) are written on the sticks for each employee and in the box for each supervisor. The job title or civil service classification and grade of an employee are often considered confidential information. Therefore, they are not written on the chart before OAI questionnaire administration. However, they are written onto the charts after the OAI survey because civil service classes and grades are used to measure horizontal differentiation and to track personnel promotions over time. Most private sector organizations have standardized employee job classification systems analogous to civil service classifications. Standard 10 would be satisfied by documenting the standardized job title and grade of each employee in private sector organizations.

It cannot be overemphasized that organization charts are a valuable source of data for comparative and longitudinal studies of organizations *if* and only *if* (1) they are consistently constructed according to a precise set of standards such as those defined previously, and (2) they have been explained and verified by informants who are familiar with the current operations of the organization in question. In practice there is such a wide range of styles and degrees of detail that is used to construct organization charts that data can easily be lost or misinterpreted unless a systematic effort is made to record and verify them.

The standards defined previously are similar to those used to construct organization charts for employment security agencies (Blau and Schoenherr, 1971), nine different federal agencies (Beyer and Trice, 1979) and a variety of industrial organizations (Blau et al., 1976). This suggests that the standards are sufficiently general to apply to most public and private, profit and nonprofit organizations.

Measures of Organization Structural Configuration

Once organization charts are constructed according to the standards described, the structural configuration factors defined as follows (and discussed in Chapter 4) can be computed from it. In other types of organizations additional indicators of formal organization structure may become salient. For example, the number of divisions, the form of departmentation (functional, goal, product, or matrix forms) and administrative intensity have been used extensively to describe the division of labor in large industrial and multinational corporations (Chandler, 1962; Williamson, 1975). What is important to recognize is that these and other indicators of formal structure can be obtained directly from organization charts that are constructed according to the standards described in the previous section.

A. Organization Size. Size is defined as the number of equivalent full-time salaried employees in the organization. The most conventional approach to measuring size is to count the number of people in the organization chart (e.g., Blau and Schoenherr, 1971; Hickson et al., 1969; Hall et al., 1967). In this study, size was measured by counting each full-time employee as 1 and each part-time employee as $\frac{1}{2}$.

B. Number of Supervisory Levels. The number of supervisory levels refers to the different strata that are manifest in the reporting relationships between formal positions in an organization. The major indicator of vertical differentiation is the number of hierarchical levels. This indicator refers to the number of links in the chain of command, not to skill gradations or salary grades.

The number of supervisory levels is measured by counting the longest chain of command in the organization chart. In other words, the number of levels is obtained by finding the deepest or longest division in the organization chart and counting the number of supervisory boxes in the chain of command from top manager to the first-line unit supervisor. For example, Figure A-1 illustrates three hierarchical levels of supervision.

C. Number of Job Titles. The number of different job titles is an indicator of the overall division of labor among formal positions in an organization. The number of civil service classifications, not counting different grades within a classification, was used as the measure of the number of job titles in this governmental agency. The official roster of job classifications maintained by the personnel section in the state's Department of Administration describes in detail the duties for all positions as well as the qualifications and entry tests necessary for an individual to obtain a given civil service classification. The employment security agency typically determines the job classes that it needs but must have them authorized by the personnel section. Grades within job classifications (e.g., Manpower Specialist I, II, or III) indicate differences in skill or experience and are counted as one job title in the measure.

D. Number of Sections. "Sections," a generic term synonymous with Blau and Schoenherr's (1971:401) "major subunits," is used as one indicator of the horizontal division of labor in an organization. In employment security district offices the major subunits or sections are most often the employment service, unemployment compensation, and work incentive program sections.

The director of a section always reports directly to the top manager. By definition, a section must have a section supervisor. Nonsupervisory personnel reporting directly to the top manager are not counted as a section. Thus, in the Figure A-1 organization chart, there are three sections (UC, ES, and WIN). The secretary or the individuals in charge of food stamps do not constitute sections. As in the case of the UC and ES sections, section directors are generally middle-level supervisors who have subordinate supervisors reporting to them. As in the case of the WIN program, a section director can also be a bottom (or first) level unit supervisor who reports directly to the top manager. In the very small offices or organizations, there may be no sections because there are no supervisors who report to the top manager. The number of sections will be the same as the number of first-line units only when all section directors have no supervisory staff reporting to them.

E. Number of Geographical Operating Sites. The number of different geographical locations where an organization operates is an indicator of spacial differentiation. From the organization charts, geographical differentiation was measured by counting the number of different locations in communities where the employment security office provided services through satellite offices or outstations. These locations were written into the organization charts according to standard 9 (preceding) for constructing the charts.

F.   Supervisor–Staff Ratio.   One indicator of administrative intensity is the supervisory ratio, computed as the total number of supervisors divided by the total number of nonsupervisory personnel in an organization. The supervisory ratio is an overall indicator of the shape of the pyramid of an organization chart. The higher the supervisory ratio, the taller they pyramid, and the higher the administrative overhead.

G.   Top Manager's Span of Control.   A second indicator of administrative intensity is the span of control of the top manager. Blau and Schoenherr (1971:193) state that the span of control has the advantage over the supervisory ratio of not having a mathematical nexus with the number of levels and sections in an organization.

The span of control of the office manager is computed by counting all personnel reporting directly to the office manager or the deputy office manager. This measure differs from the number of sections in that it includes the nonsupervisory employees (e.g. secretaries) often under the direct supervision of the top manager.

H.   Percentage of Supervisors above Bottom-Level Unit Supervisors.   A supplementary indicator of administrative intensity or overhead is the percentage of all supervisors in an organization who are located hierarchically above bottom-level unit supervisors. This indicator reflects the proportion of supervisors who are middle- and upper-level managers and who are not directly supervising production and line operations of nonsupervisory workers.

The proportion of middle- and upper-level supervisors is obtained from the organization charts by dividing the total number of supervisory positions into the number of supervisors above the first-line unit supervisors. First-line unit supervisors are most easily identified by approaching the organization chart from the bottom and looking upward to the lowest level supervisors. By definition, there will be as many bottom-level supervisors as there are first line units. Figure A-1 illustrates six bottom-level supervisors that are subtracted out of the total number of supervisory positions to obtain the numerator of the number of middle- and upper-level supervisors. In Figure A-1, 25 percent of the supervisors exist above the bottom-level unit supervisors.

I.   Perceived Structure of Authority or Influence.   The structure of authority is defined as the distribution of influence of various groups of people within an organization on various decisions. Influence is defined as the amount of say or control that one has in determining the behavior or affairs of others in an organization. The structure of authority is conceptualized in terms of Tannenbaum's (1968) control graph, which distinguishes (1) the distribution of authority, i.e., the differences in the degrees of influence exercised by people at different hierarchical levels, and (2) the total amount of authority, i.e., how much influence is exercised by all organizational groups of people.

The analysis in Chapter 4 found that the crucial factor to control for in measuring the perceived structure of authority in ES agencies is the level in the organizational hierarchy at which the informants were located. Once hierarchical level of the informant was taken into account, clear distinctions were found in the amounts of influence exercised by different groups on various decisions. However, the slopes of the control graphs (or distributions of influence) remained about the same for informants at different levels in the organization; i.e., a high convergence was obtained between informants at different levels on the relative degrees of influence various groups had in making organizational decisions. This suggests that it is important to obtain the perceptions of informants at all levels in the organization to measure the structure of organizational authority, particularly the amounts of influence various groups exercise.

Chapter 4 presented the specific index used to measure the perceived structure of authority in employment security offices. Obviously, a different index will be necessary for assessments in other organizations because the names of the decision-making groups will differ, as will the key questions or issues on which decisions are made. Therefore, as with the macroorganization context dimensions, we do not propose a general index for measuring the structure of authority in all complex organizations. We believe it is more prudent to develop (and pilot test) an instrument to measure these macroorganizational factors for the specific set of organizations included in the sample. Using the indices presented in Chapter 4 (as well as those published and evaluated elsewhere) as a guide, we believe that an investigator can develop more reliable and valid measures when these are uniquely designed for the particular set of organizations being assessed.

OAI Unit Supervisor Questionnaire

This questionnaire is part of an Organization Assessment (OA) Survey that is being conducted throughout your organization. The purpose of the OA Survey is to learn more about how various jobs, work groups, sections, and levels in your organization are structured and work together. The results of the OA Survey will be used to identify and help solve organizational problems and to determine if and where improvements can be made to increase organizational effectiveness, productivity, and employee morale.

This particular questionnaire focuses on your job and the organizational unit that you supervise. It measures various characteristics about your job and work unit that have been found in other studies to be importantly related to performance and job satisfaction. You are also given opportunities to indicate your feelings about your job and unit and suggest ways they might be improved.

Your answers are strictly confidential. The answers you give will be grouped with the answers of other people, and no individual person will ever be identified in any report. After the questionnaires for the organization have been analyzed, you will receive feedback on the OA Survey in the form of grouped statistical summaries. Hopefully, you will find these feedback sessions valuable for evaluating your job and unit and for identifying where improvements might be appropriate.

If this OA Survey is to be useful, it is important that you answer each question frankly and honestly. There are no hidden meanings behind any questions. This is not a test, and there are no right or wrong answers.

This OA Survey was developed and is being conducted by the Center for Organization Assessment from The Wharton School at the University of Pennsylvania, Philadelphia. The Center has been contracted by your organization to conduct this OA Survey as an independent agent. Your completed questionnaire will be taken to the Center for analysis and safekeeping. It will not be available to anyone in your organization.

Thank you very much for your cooperation.

> Dr. Andrew H. Van de Ven, Director
> Center for Organization Assessment
> The Wharton School
> University of Pennsylvania
> Philadelphia, Pa. 19104

GENERAL INSTRUCTIONS

Definitions: This questionnaire asks many questions about your immediate unit and your unit members.

- *Your immediate unit* includes you (as the supervisor) and all individuals who report *directly* to you. In cases where your immediate subordinates are lower level supervisors, be careful NOT to include individuals reporting to your subordinates when answering questions about your immediate unit.

- *Unit members* are all individuals in your immediate unit except you as the unit supervisor.

Most of the questions ask you to circle one of several numbers that appear on a scale below the item. Corresponding with each number on a scale is a brief description of what the number represents. You are to circle the one number that most accurately reflects your answer to each question.

For example, if your answer to the following question is "very much" (and we believe it should be), circle the number "5" on the answer scale:

> How much is it worth my time to fill out this questionnaire during the next hour?
>
> | NONE | LITTLE | SOME | QUITE A BIT | VERY MUCH |
> |------|--------|------|-------------|-----------|
> | 1 | 2 | 3 | 4 | (5) |

If you do not understand any question, BE SURE TO ASK US FOR HELP. We realize that not all questions are simple, and that is why we are here to answer any questions you have.

INTRODUCTORY QUESTIONS

The following questions are very important for properly coding and analyzing the data. As indicated before, all responses will be kept strictly confidential. When you are finished with this questionnaire, seal it in the accompanying envelope. It will not be opened until all envelopes are received by the Center for Organization Assessment.

1. Name of ORGANIZATION in which you work: _____

2. Name of DIVISION in which you work: _____

3. Name of OFFICE or CITY in which you work: _____

4. Name of UNIT in which you work: _____

5. Write your UNIT CODE NUMBER as it is shown on the organization chart hung on the wall. Unit Code # _____

6. Write YOUR NAME: _____

7. Write your present JOB TITLE or POSITION: _____

For computer coding only:

All
cards: | | | | | | | | | | | | | O | 1 | | | | | | | | | | |
Column: 1 2 3 4 5 6 7 8 9 10 11 12 13 14 15 16 17 18 19 20 21 22 23

THE NATURE OF YOUR WORK AND JOB

WE WOULD LIKE TO KNOW THE SPECIFIC KINDS of tasks and work activities that make up your job. Please describe below the types of tasks or work activities you have been performing regularly during the past three months. Briefly explain what each task is and indicate the numbers of hours each week you spend doing it.

Task 1: _____ hours/week

_____

_____

_____

_____

Task 2: _____ hours/week

_____

_____

_____

_____

Task 3: _____ hours/week

_____

_____

_____

_____

Task 4: _____ hours/week

_____

_____

_____

_____

Task 5: _____ hours/week

_____
_____
_____
_____

Task 6: _____ hours/week

_____
_____
_____
_____

Task 7: _____ hours/week

_____
_____
_____
_____

Task 8: _____ hours/week

_____
_____
_____
_____

1. Indicate the total number of hours per week you normally worked. Hours/week during the past three months: _____

PLEASE ANSWER THE FOLLOWING QUESTIONS BY THINKING ONLY ABOUT THE TYPES OF TASKS THAT OCCUPY MOST OF YOUR WORKING TIME.

2. *To what extent* do you perform the *same tasks* from day to day? (Circle a number below the scale.)

ALMOST ALL MY TASKS ARE THE SAME DAY-TO-DAY	MANY OF MY TASKS ARE THE SAME DAY-TO-DAY	ABOUT HALF MY TASKS ARE THE SAME DAY-TO-DAY	SOME OF MY TASKS ARE THE SAME DAY-TO-DAY	ALMOST NO TASKS ARE THE SAME DAY-TO-DAY
1	2	3	4	5

3. *How much the same* are the day-to-day situations, problems, or issues you encounter in performing your major tasks? (Circle a number below.)

VERY MUCH THE SAME	MOSTLY THE SAME	QUITE A BIT DIFFERENT	VERY MUCH DIFFERENT	COMPLETELY DIFFERENT
1	2	3	4	5

4. *How easy* is it for *you* to *know* whether you do your work correctly?

VERY DIFFICULT	QUITE DIFFICULT	SOMEWHAT EASY	QUITE EASY	VERY EASY
1	2	3	4	5

5. *What percent of the time* are you *generally sure* of what the *outcomes* of your work efforts will be?

40% OR LESS	41–60%	61–75%	76–90%	91% OR MORE
1	2	3	4	5

6. During a normal week, *how frequently* do *exceptions arise* in your work which require *substantially different* methods or procedures for doing it?

VERY RARELY	OCCASIONALLY	QUITE OFTEN	VERY OFTEN	CONSTANTLY
1	2	3	4	5

7. In the past 3 months, *how often* did *difficult problems arise* in your work for which there were no immediate or apparent solutions?

ONCE A WEEK OR LESS	ABOUT 2–4 TIMES A WEEK	ABOUT ONCE A DAY	ABOUT 2–4 TIMES A DAY	5 TIMES OR MORE A DAY
1	2	3	4	5

8. About *how much time* did you spend solving these *work problems*?

LESS THAN 1 HOUR/WEEK	ABOUT 1–4 HOURS/WEEK	ABOUT 1 HOUR/DAY	ABOUT 2–3 HOURS/DAY	4 HOURS OR MORE PER DAY
1	2	3	4	5

9. To what extent does *just your work alone* give you many *clues* to figure out *how well you are doing* your job (without relying on feedback from your supervisor or co-workers)?

MY WORK GIVES ME NO CLUES ON HOW WELL I DO MY JOB	MY WORK GIVES A FEW CLUES ON MY JOB PERFORMANCE	MY WORK GIVES SOME CLUES ON MY JOB PERFORMANCE	MY WORK GIVES MANY CLUES ON MY JOB PERFORMANCE	MY WORK GIVES ALL CLUES NEEDED TO KNOW HOW WELL I DO MY JOB
1	2	3	4	5

10. During the past 3 months, *how often* did you receive *suggestions or feedback* from your *co-workers* on your work?

NOT ONCE	ABOUT ONCE A MONTH	ABOUT ONCE A WEEK	ABOUT EVERY DAY OR SO	SEVERAL TIMES A DAY
1	2	3	4	5

11. *How many hours per week on or off the job* do you spend in some kind of *reading or training* to keep current in the skills needed to do your job?

LESS THAN 1 HR/WK	ABOUT 1–3 HR/WK	ABOUT 4–6 HR/WK	ABOUT 7–9 HR/WK	ABOUT 10 HR/WK OR MORE
1	2	3	4	5

12. Describe the specific kinds of training programs or reading materials you spent this time on to remain current in your job.

_____
_____
_____
_____

13. When you *began* this job, *how long a period of orientation and training* did you receive that was *directly related to your job?*

A FEW HOURS OR LESS	ABOUT A DAY	ABOUT A WEEK	ABOUT A MONTH	MORE THAN A MONTH
1	2	3	4	5

14. How many *years* of academic, vocational, or professional *education* have you obtained *beyond high school?*

YEARS AFTER HIGH SCHOOL

0 1 2 3 4 5 6 7 8 9

15. What is the highest educational degree you obtained in school?

GRADE SCHOOL DIPLOMA	HIGH SCHOOL DIPLOMA	VOCATIONAL OR CRAFT CERTIFICATION	COLLEGE BACHELOR'S DEGREE	MASTER'S DEGREE	DOCTORAL DEGREE
1	2	3	4	5	6

16. Indicate the *specific major* or *field of specialization* in which you obtained this degree.

_____

17. *How often* do you follow about the *same work methods or steps* for *doing* your major tasks from *day to day?*

VERY SELDOM	SOMETIMES	ABOUT HALF THE TIME	QUITE OFTEN	VERY OFTEN
1	2	3	4	5

18. To what *extent* did you follow *standard operating procedures* or practices to do your major tasks the past 3 months?

TO NO EXTENT	LITTLE EXTENT	SOME EXTENT	GREAT EXTENT	VERY GREAT EXTENT
1	2	3	4	5

19. *How many written rules and procedures exist* for doing your major tasks?

VERY FEW IF ANY	A SMALL NUMBER	A MODERATE NUMBER	A LARGE NUMBER	A GREAT NUMBER
1	2	3	4	5

20. *How precisely* do these rules and procedures *specify* how your major tasks are to be done?

VERY GENERAL	MOSTLY GENERAL	SOMEWHAT SPECIFIC	QUITE SPECIFIC	VERY SPECIFIC
1	2	3	4	5

21. *How heavy* was your *work load* during the past 3 months?

OFTEN NOT ENOUGH TO KEEP ME BUSY	SOMETIMES NOT ENOUGH TO KEEP ME BUSY	JUST ABOUT THE RIGHT AMOUNT	HARD TO KEEP UP WITH	ENTIRELY TOO MUCH FOR ME TO HANDLE
1	2	3	4	5

22. *How far in advance* do you generally *know* how much work will be required of you?

ABOUT AN HOUR OR LESS IN ADVANCE	ABOUT A DAY IN ADVANCE	ABOUT A WEEK IN ADVANCE	ABOUT A MONTH IN ADVANCE	ABOUT 6 MONTHS OR MORE IN ADVANCE
1	2	3	4	5

23. During the past 3 months, how much *control* did you have in setting the *pace* of your work?

NONE	VERY LITTLE	SOME	QUITE A BIT	VERY MUCH
1	2	3	4	5

24. When considering the various situations that arise in performing your work, what *percent of the time* do you *have* written or unwritten procedures for dealing with them?

0–20%	21–40%	41–60%	61–80%	81–100%
1	2	3	4	5

25. Listed below are four common decisions about your work. *How much authority* do you have in making each of the following decisions about your work:

	AMOUNT OF AUTHORITY I HAVE IN EACH DECISION				
	NONE	LITTLE	SOME	QUITE A BIT	VERY MUCH
a. Determining *what* tasks I will perform from day to day?	1	2	3	4	5
b. *Setting quotas* on how much work I have to complete?	1	2	3	4	5
c. *Establishing rules and procedures* about *how* my work is to be done?	1	2	3	4	5
d. Determining *how work exceptions* are to be handled?	1	2	3	4	5

26. How *much* does your *supervisor hold you personally accountable* for the *work decisions* you make in your job?

NOT AT ALL	VERY LITTLE	SOME	QUITE A BIT	VERY MUCH
1	2	3	4	5

27. *How clearly* do you *know what level of work performance* is *expected* from you (in terms of amount, quality, and timeliness of output)?

VERY UNCLEAR	QUITE UNCLEAR	SOMEWHAT CLEAR	QUITE CLEAR	VERY CLEAR
1	2	3	4	5

28. How *clearly* does your *job description specify* the *standards of performance* on which your job is evaluated?

THERE IS NO JOB DESCRIPTION FOR MY JOB.	MY JOB DESCRIPTION DOES NOT STATE ANY PERFORMANCE STANDARDS TO BE ACHIEVED IN THIS JOB.	MY JOB DESCRIPTION IS VERY GENERAL IN STATING WHAT PERFORMANCE STANDARDS ARE TO BE ACHIEVED.	MY JOB DESCRIPTION IS QUITE CLEAR IN STATING WHAT PERFORMANCE STANDARDS ARE TO BE ACHIEVED.	MY JOB DESCRIPTION IS VERY CLEAR AND PRECISE IN STATING WHAT PERFORMANCE STANDARDS ARE TO BE ACHIEVED.
1	2	3	4	5

29. To what degree has your *supervisor discussed* with *you* these *performance standards* on which your job is evaluated?

MY SUPERVISOR NEVER DISCUSSED THEM WITH ME.	MY SUPERVISOR ONLY MENTIONED THEM TO ME VERY GENERALLY AND DID NOT CLARIFY THEM.	MY SUPERVISOR DISCUSSED THEM WITH ME QUITE SPECIFICALLY AND CLEARLY.	MY SUPERVISOR DISCUSSED THEM WITH ME IN A VERY DETAILED AND CLEAR WAY.
1	2	3	4

30. *How hard* is it to *attain* the *level of performance* that is *expected* from you?

I DON'T KNOW WHAT'S EXPECTED OF ME.	QUITE EASY	QUITE HARD	VERY HARD BUT ATTAINABLE	EXCESSIVELY HARD AND IMPOSSIBLE TO ATTAIN
1	2	3	4	5

31. To what extent do *you believe* that the *performance standards* upon which your work is evaluated are *fair*?

I DON'T KNOW WHAT STANDARDS ARE USED TO EVALUATE MY WORK.	VERY UNFAIR	SOMEWHAT FAIR	QUITE FAIR	VERY FAIR
1	2	3	4	5

32. *How much* does your *supervisor hold you personally responsible* for achieving these *performance standards* for your job?

NOT AT ALL	VERY LITTLE	SOME	QUITE A BIT	VERY MUCH
1	2	3	4	5

33. During the *past year, how often did* your immediate *supervisor discuss* your *work performance with you?*

NOT ONCE	ABOUT 1–4 TIMES A YEAR	ABOUT ONCE A MONTH	ABOUT ONCE A WEEK	ABOUT EVERY DAY OR SO
1	2	3	4	5

34. When your work performance was discussed with you, how often did you receive *practical suggestions* for improving your work?

NEVER	SELDOM	ABOUT HALF THE TIME	OFTEN	EVERY TIME
1	2	3	4	5

35. *If you attain* the *performance level* that is expected of you, *how likely is it that* each of the following *will happen:*

	NO CHANCE	SMALL CHANCE	50% CHANCE	QUITE LIKELY	ALMOST A CERTAINTY
a. You will be *recognized* for your good work (e.g., given a special word of appreciation or given a pat-on-the-back)?	1	2	3	4	5
b. You will be given a *promotion* in this organization?	1	2	3	4	5

36. *If you do not attain* the *performance level* that is expected of you, *how likely is it that each* of the following *will happen:*

	NO CHANCE	SMALL CHANCE	50% CHANCE	QUITE LIKELY	ALMOST A CERTAINTY
a. You will be reprimanded, or told to improve your work?	1	2	3	4	5
b. You will be demoted in this organization?	1	2	3	4	5

YOUR FEELINGS ABOUT YOUR JOB

NOW WE WOULD LIKE TO ASK YOU SOME QUESTIONS ABOUT HOW YOU PERSONALLY FEEL ABOUT YOUR JOB.

37. *How satisfied* are you with each of the following:

	VERY UNSAT-ISFIED	QUITE UNSAT-ISFIED	SOME-WHAT SATIS-FIED	QUITE SATIS-FIED	VERY SATIS-FIED
a. Your job?	1	2	3	4	5
b. Your supervisor?	1	2	3	4	5

		VERY UNSAT- ISFIED	QUITE UNSAT- ISFIED	SOME- WHAT SATIS- FIED	QUITE SATIS- FIED	VERY SATIS- FIED
c.	Your pay?	1	2	3	4	5
d.	The friendliness and cooperativeness of your *co-workers*?	1	2	3	4	5
e.	The *career progress* you have made in this organization up to now?	1	2	3	4	5
f.	Your chances for *career advancement* in this organization *in the future*?	1	2	3	4	5

		NONE	A LITTLE	SOME	QUITE A BIT	VERY MUCH
38.	*How much effort* do you put into your work?	1	2	3	4	5
39.	*How much* did you try *to improve* your job performance in the past 3 months?	1	2	3	4	5

40. Each of the statements below is something that a person might say about his or her job. Please indicate your own, personal *feelings* about your job by circling a number on the scale to the right of each statement to indicate how much you agree or disagree with each statement.

		DISAGREE STRONGLY	DISAGREE SOMEWHAT	NEUTRAL	AGREE- SOME- WHAT	AGREE STRONGLY
a.	It's hard, on this job, for me to care very much about whether or not the work gets done right.	1	2	3	4	5
b.	My opinion of myself goes up when I do this job well.	1	2	3	4	5
c.	My supervisor often lets me know how well I am performing my job.	1	2	3	4	5
d.	I feel a great sense of personal accomplishment when I do this job well.	1	2	3	4	5

		DISAGREE STRONGLY	DISAGREE SOMEWHAT	NEUTRAL	AGREE-SOME-WHAT	AGREE STRONGLY
e.	I feel a very high degree of *personal responsibility for the work I do on this job.*	1	2	3	4	5
f.	I frequently think of quitting this job.	1	2	3	4	5
g.	I feel bad and unhappy when I discover that I have performed poorly on this job.	1	2	3	4	5
h.	My co-workers on this job almost *never* give me any "feedback" about how well I am doing on my work.	1	2	3	4	5
i.	I feel I should personally take the credit or blame for the results of my work on this job.	1	2	3	4	5
j.	My own feelings generally are *not* affected much one way or the other by how well I do on this job.	1	2	3	4	5
k.	I am recognized and rewarded for putting in additional effort to do superior work in this job.	1	2	3	4	5
l.	I am reprimanded or told to "shape up" when I do inferior work in this job.	1	2	3	4	5

What Kind of Job Do You Prefer?

PEOPLE DIFFER IN THE KINDS OF JOBS THEY WOULD MOST LIKE TO HOLD. THE QUESTIONS IN THIS SECTION GIVE YOU A CHANCE TO SAY JUST WHAT IT IS ABOUT A JOB THAT IS MOST IMPORTANT TO YOU PERSONALLY.

FOR EACH QUESTION BELOW, TWO DIFFERENT KINDS OF JOBS ARE BRIEFLY DESCRIBED. YOU ARE TO INDICATE WHICH OF THE JOBS YOU PERSONALLY WOULD PREFER—IF YOU HAD TO MAKE A CHOICE BETWEEN THEM.

IN ANSWERING EACH QUESTION, ASSUME THAT EVERYTHING ELSE ABOUT THE JOBS IS THE SAME. PAY ATTENTION ONLY TO THE CHARACTERISTICS ACTUALLY LISTED.

ONE EXAMPLE IS GIVEN BELOW:

JOB A	JOB B
A job requiring work with mechanical equipment most of the day.	A job requiring work with other people most of the day.

1— — — — —2— — — —(3)— — — 4— — — — 5

| STRONGLY PREFER A | SLIGHTLY PREFER A | NEUTRAL | SLIGHTLY PREFER B | STRONGLY PREFER B |

IF YOU LIKE WORKING WITH PEOPLE AND WORKING WITH EQUIPMENT EQUALLY WELL, YOU WOULD CIRCLE THE NUMBER 3, AS HAS BEEN DONE IN THIS EXAMPLE.

PLEASE ASK FOR ASSISTANCE IF YOU DO NOT UNDERSTAND EXACTLY HOW TO DO THESE QUESTIONS.

JOB A	JOB B

41. A job where the pay is very good.   A job where there is considerable opportunity to be creative and innovative.

1— — — — —2— — — — —3— — — 4— — — — —5

STRONGLY PREFER A   SLIGHTLY PREFER A   NEUTRAL   SLIGHTLY PREFER B   STRONGLY PREFER B

42. A job where you are often required to make important decisions.   A job with many pleasant people to work with.

1— — — — —2— — — — —3— — — — —4— — — — —5

STRONGLY PREFER A   SLIGHTLY PREFER A   NEUTRAL   SLIGHTLY PREFER B   STRONGLY PREFER B

43. A job in which greater responsibility is given to those who do the best work.   A job in which greater responsibility is given to loyal employees who have the most seniority.

1— — — — —2— — — — —3— — — — 4— — — — —5

STRONGLY PREFER A   SLIGHTLY PREFER A   NEUTRAL   SLIGHTLY PREFER B   STRONGLY PREFER B

44. A job in an organization which is in financial trouble—and might have to close down within the year.   A job in which you are not allowed to have any say whatever in how your work is scheduled or in the procedures to be used in carrying it out.

1— — — — 2— — — — —3— — — — —4— — — — 5

STRONGLY PREFER A   SLIGHTLY PREFER A   NEUTRAL   SLIGHTLY PREFER B   STRONGLY PREFER B

45. A very routine job.   A job where your co-workers are not very friendly.

1— — — — 2— — — — —3— — — — —4— — — — —5

STRONGLY PREFER A   SLIGHTLY PREFER A   NEUTRAL   SLIGHTLY PREFER B   STRONGLY PREFER B

JOB A	JOB B

46. A job with a supervisor who is often very critical of you and your work in front of other people.

1— — — — 2— — — -3— — — -4— — — —5
STRONGLY   SLIGHTLY   NEUTRAL   SLIGHTLY   STRONGLY
PREFER A   PREFER A   PREFER B   PREFER B

A job that prevents you from using a number of skills that you worked hard to develop.

47. A job with a supervisor who respects you and treats you fairly.

1— — — — 2— — — -3— — — -4— — — —5
STRONGLY   SLIGHTLY   NEUTRAL   SLIGHTLY   STRONGLY
PREFER A   PREFER A   PREFER B   PREFER B

A job that provides constant opportunities for you to learn new and interesting things.

48. A job where there is a real chance you could be laid off.

1— — — —2— — — -3— — — -4— — — —5
STRONGLY   SLIGHTLY   NEUTRAL   SLIGHTLY   STRONGLY
PREFER A   PREFER A   PREFER B   PREFER B

A job with very little chance to do challenging work.

49. A job in which there is a real chance for you to develop new skills and advance in the organization.

1— — — — 2— — — -3— — — -4— — — —5
STRONGLY   SLIGHTLY   NEUTRAL   SLIGHTLY   STRONGLY
PREFER A   PREFER A   PREFER B   PREFER B

A job that provides lots of vacation time and an excellent fringe benefits package.

50. A job with little freedom and independence to do your work in the way you think best.

1— — — — 2— — — -3— — — -4— — — —5
STRONGLY   SLIGHTLY   NEUTRAL   SLIGHTLY   STRONGLY
PREFER A   PREFER A   PREFER B   PREFER B

A job where the working conditions are poor.

51. A job with very satisfying teamwork.

1— — — — 2— — — -3— — — -4— — — —5
STRONGLY   SLIGHTLY   NEUTRAL   SLIGHTLY   STRONGLY
PREFER A   PREFER A   PREFER B   PREFER B

A job that allows you to use your skills and abilities to the fullest extent.

52. A job which offers little or no challenge.

1— — — — 2— — — -3— — — -4— — — —5
STRONGLY   SLIGHTLY   NEUTRAL   SLIGHTLY   STRONGLY
PREFER A   PREFER A   PREFER B   PREFER B

A job which requires you to be completely isolated from co-workers.

A SELF-APPRAISAL OF YOUR JOB

NOW MAKE AN ASSESSMENT OF THE WAY YOUR JOB IS ORGANIZED. HOPEFULLY,
THE QUESTIONS YOU HAVE ANSWERED SO FAR HAVE HELPED YOU THINK ABOUT
THINGS YOU WANT TO SAY TO EACH QUESTION BELOW.

A. Describe what *you like* about the way your job is organized.

_____
_____
_____
_____
_____

B. Describe what *specific problems* you experience with the way your
job is organized.

_____
_____
_____
_____
_____

C. Suggest some *specific ways* that the organization of your job could
be *improved*.

_____
_____
_____
_____
_____

THE ORGANIZATION AND WORK OF YOUR UNIT

SO FAR YOU HAVE BEEN ASKED QUESTIONS ABOUT your work and your job. This next part asks how your unit is organized to do its work and achieve its performance goals. Please keep in mind that your unit consists of you, as the unit supervisor, and all individuals who report directly to you.

FIRST, PLEASE FILL OUT THIS PERSONNEL ROSTER OF YOUR IMMEDIATE UNIT AS IT EXISTS TODAY.

LIST NAMES OF ALL UNIT PERSONNEL WHO REPORT DIRECTLY TO YOU (INCLUDE ALL FULL- AND PART-TIME SALARIED STAFF AND VOLUNTEERS)	AVERAGE NUMBER HOURS WORKED PER WEEK IN PAST 3 MONTHS	LIST THE MAJOR JOB FUNCTION OR RESPONSIBILITY PERFORMED BY THIS INDIVIDUAL IN THE PAST 3 MONTHS
1. UNIT SUPERVISOR (YOUR NAME)		
2. UNIT MEMBERS:		
3.		
4.		
5.		
6.		
7.		
8.		

443

9. _____

10. _____

11. _____

12. _____

13. _____

14. _____

15. _____

16. _____

17. _____

18. _____

19. _____

20. _____

21. _____

22. _____

53. During the past 3 months, *how many* of your immediate unit *subordinates performed the same basic tasks*, or did each perform a different task?

NO ONE PERFORMED SAME TASKS	ONLY A FEW PERFORMED SAME TASKS	ABOUT HALF PERFORMED SAME TASKS	MANY PERFORMED SAME TASKS	ALL PERFORMED THE SAME BASIC TASKS
1	2	3	4	5

54. *How many of your immediate subordinates are qualified* to do one anothers' jobs?

NONE	ONLY A FEW	ABOUT HALF	MANY	ALL
1	2	3	4	5

55. *How easy* would it be to rotate the jobs of your *immediate subordinates*, so that each could do a good job performing the others' tasks?

VERY DIFFICULT. MOST MEMBERS WOULD NEED EXTENSIVE RETRAINING	QUITE DIFFICULT. SOME MEMBERS WOULD NEED EXTENSIVE RETRAINING	SOMEWHAT DIFFICULT. A FEW MEMBERS WOULD NEED RETRAINING	QUITE EASY. SOME MEMBERS WOULD NEED MINOR RETRAINING	VERY EASY. NO MEMBERS WOULD NEED RETRAINING
1	2	3	4	5

56. During the past 3 months, *how often* did your immediate subordinates *rotate* their jobs by performing one anothers' work?

NOT ONCE	ABOUT EVERY MONTH	ABOUT EVERY WEEK	ABOUT EVERY DAY	ABOUT EVERY HOUR
1	2	3	4	5

57. *How much say or influence do each of the following have in deciding what kinds of work or tasks are to be performed in your unit:*

AMOUNT OF SAY IN DECIDING UNIT'S WORK

	NONE	LITTLE	SOME	QUITE A BIT	VERY MUCH
a. People in line management or staff positions *outside* of your immediate work unit?	1	2	3	4	5
b. *You,* as the unit supervisor?	1	2	3	4	5
c. Your immediate subordinates, *individually*?	1	2	3	4	5
d. You and your immediate subordinates *as a group* in unit meetings?	1	2	3	4	5

58. To do its work, *how much* does your unit *use automated equipment, machines, or computer devices* (e.g., computer desk monitors, direct data entry, or IBM cards)?

NOT AT ALL	VERY LITTLE	SOMEWHAT	QUITE A BIT	VERY MUCH
1	2	3	4	5

59. Specifically, please indicate the kinds of equipment, machines, or computer devices used by your unit to do its work.

_____

_____

_____

60. *How frequently* did your unit *encounter breakdowns* in these mechanical devices for doing its work *during the past three months*?

NOT ONCE	ONLY ONCE	ABOUT EVERY MONTH	ABOUT EVERY WEEK	ABOUT EVERY DAY
1	2	3	4	5

61. About *how much non-work "down time"* did all people in your unit accumulate *as a result of breakdowns* in these mechnical devices during the past three months?

NO DOWN TIME EXPERIENCED	A FEW HOURS	ABOUT ONE MAN-DAY	2–4 MAN-DAYS	5 MAN-DAYS OR MORE OF DOWN TIME
1	2	3	4	5

Criteria and Methods Used to Evaluate the Performance of Your Unit

62. Consider now the specific criteria or measures that are used to determine how effectively your unit performs its work.

List below the *three most important criteria* that are used to measure how well your unit performs its work.

Rank the importance of these three criteria.

1 = MOST IMPORTANT
2 = SECOND MOST IMPORTANT
3 = THIRD MOST IMPORTANT

1. _____

RANK: _____

2. _____

RANK: _____

3. _____

RANK: _____

63. *How much influence* or say did *each* of the following have in *deciding upon these criteria* for evaluating the performance of your unit:

AMOUNT OF INFLUENCE IN DECIDING CRITERIA

	NONE	LITTLE	SOME	QUITE A BIT	VERY MUCH
a. People in line management or staff positions *outside* of your immediate work unit?	1	2	3	4	5
b. *You*, as the unit supervisor?	1	2	3	4	5
c. Your immediate subordinates, *individually*?	1	2	3	4	5
d. You and your immediate subordinates *as a group* in unit meetings?	1	2	3	4	5

64. *How much* do people in your immediate unit *agree* that these are the three most important criteria for evaluating the performance of your unit?

NOT AT ALL	AGREE A LITTLE	AGREE SOMEWHAT	AGREE QUITE A BIT	AGREE VERY MUCH
1	2	3	4	5

65. To *what degree* are *numerical* or *quantified procedures used* to *measure* these performance criteria of your unit?

NO MEASURE-MENT IS MADE	ONLY SUBJECTIVE NONQUANTIFIED IMPRESSIONS ARE RECORDED	LOOSE BUT QUANTIFIED MEASURES ARE RECORDED	QUITE SPECIFIC QUANTIFIED MEASURES ARE RECORDED	VERY SPECIFIC AND PRECISE QUANTI-FIED MEASURES AND PROCEDURES ARE RECORDED
1	2	3	4	5

66. *How frequently* do you receive *numerical reports* detailing the performance of your unit in terms of these criteria?

NO REPORTS ARE DEVELOPED	ALTHOUGH MEASURED I HAVE NOT RECEIVED ANY REPORT	ONLY AT YEAR-END	EVERY MONTH	EVERY WEEK	EVERY DAY	SEVERAL TIMES DAILY
1	2	3	4	5	6	7

A VARIETY OF APPRAISAL METHODS CAN BE RELIED UPON TO DETERMINE AND EVALUATE HOW WELL AN ORGANIZATIONAL UNIT IS ACHIEVING ITS PERFORMANCE CRITERIA.

67. To *what degree* are *each* of the following methods of appraisal *relied upon* to evaluate how well your unit performs its work:

DEGREE RELIED ON FOR EVALUATING WORK

	NONE	LITTLE	SOME	QUITE A BIT	VERY MUCH
a. Automatic control systems or built-in monitoring devices (e.g., computer rejections, mechanical alerts)?	1	2	3	4	5
b. Appraisals made by line managers or staff specialists *outside* of your immediate work unit?	1	2	3	4	5
c. Appraisals made by *you individually*, as the unit supervisor?	1	2	3	4	5
d. Appraisals made by your *immediate subordinates* who *individually* review and evaluate their own performance?	1	2	3	4	5
e. Appraisals made by you and your immediate subordinates *as a group*, who meet to review and evaluate the work of one or more unit members?	1	2	3	4	5

68. *How clearly* have specific *performance tagets been set* for your unit?

NO TARGETS WERE SET	TARGETS ARE VERY UNCLEAR	TARGETS ARE SOME- WHAT CLEAR	TARGETS ARE QUITE CLEAR	TARGETS ARE VERY CLEAR
1	2	3	4	5

69. *How difficult* is it for your unit to *attain* these *performance targets*?

NO TARGETS WERE SET	TARGETS VERY EASY TO ATTAIN	TARGETS QUITE EASY TO ATTAIN	TARGETS DIFFICULT BUT ATTAINABLE	TARGETS VERY DIFFICULT TO ATTAIN	TARGETS IMPOSSIBLY DIFFICULT TO ATTAIN
1	2	3	4	5	6

70. Overall, what *percent* of these *performance targets were attained* by your unit last year?

NO TARGETS WERE SET	0–20%	21–40%	41–60%	61–80%	81–90%	91–100%	MORE THAN 100%
1	2	3	4	5	6	7	8

HOW OFTEN THIS HAPPENS

71. When *target* performance goals for your unit *are attained or surpassed, how often* do the following things *happen*:

	ALMOST NEVER	SELDOM	ABOUT HALF THE TIME	QUITE OFTEN	ALMOST ALWAYS
a. *All people* in this unit are rewarded or recognized *as a group* for their *team* achievements?	1	2	3	4	5
b. *Specific individuals* in this unit are rewarded or recognized for their *individual* achievements?	1	2	3	4	5

72. When *target* performance goals for your unit are *not attained, how often* do the following things *happen*:

a. *All people* in this unit *as a group* are reprimanded or told to "shape up" to improve unit performance?	1	2	3	4	5
b. *Specific individuals* in your unit are reprimanded or told to "shape up" to improve their individual performances?	1	2	3	4	5

73. How much do members of your unit do the following things:	HOW MUCH THIS HAPPENS				
	NOT AT ALL	A LITTLE	SOME	QUITE A BIT	VERY MUCH
a. *Compete* with each other to achieve performance targets?	1	2	3	4	5
b. "Gang-up" on the *individual* whose work is *far below* that of the others?	1	2	3	4	5
c. "Gang-up" on the *individual* whose work far exceeds that of the others?	1	2	3	4	5
d. *Encourage individuals* to *excel* and strive for increasingly higher levels of work performance?	1	2	3	4	5
e. Try to *get ahead* at the *expense* of other unit members?	1	2	3	4	5

Rules, Policies, and Procedures for the Unit as a Whole

THINK ABOUT THE VARIOUS OPERATING RULES, POLICIES, AND PROCEDURES THAT ALL PERSONNEL IN YOUR UNIT ARE EXPECTED TO FOLLOW TO COORDINATE AND CONTROL ALL THE WORK ACTIVITIES PERFORMED IN YOUR UNIT. THESE RULES AND PROCEDURES MAY BE FORMAL OR INFORMAL, WRITTEN OR UNWRITTEN. HOWEVER, THEY ARE DIFFERENT FROM THOSE USED TO GUIDE EACH INDIVIDUAL IN PERFORMING HIS OR HER OWN JOB, BECAUSE THEY APPLY TO ALL PEOPLE IN YOUR UNIT, REGARDLESS OF THE PARTICULAR JOB EACH PERFORMS.

74. Please *describe* the basic *operating rules, policies, and procedures* used to *coordinate and control* all jobs and activities of your *unit as a whole*.

_____
_____
_____
_____
_____
_____

75. *How precisely* do these rules, policies, and procedures *specify* how work activities are to be coordinated and controlled in your unit?

VERY GENERAL	MOSTLY GENERAL	SOMEWHAT SPECIFIC	QUITE SPECIFIC	VERY SPECIFIC
1	2	3	4	5

76. *How often* did unit members *violate or ignore* these operating rules, policies, and procedures during the past three months?

NOT ONCE	VERY SELDOM	ABOUT HALF THE TIME	QUITE OFTEN	ALL THE TIME
1	2	3	4	5

77. *How strictly* are these operating rules, policies, and procedures *enforced* in your unit?

NOT AT ALL ENFORCED	VERY LOOSELY ENFORCED	SOMEWHAT STRICTLY ENFORCED	QUITE STRICTLY ENFORCED	VERY STRICTLY ENFORCED
1	2	3	4	5

78. What *percent* of these operating rules, policies, and procedures for your unit as a whole *are written out* in memos, reports, or a procedures manual?

0–20%	21–40%	41–60%	61–80%	80–100%
1	2	3	4	5

79. *How much influence* or say did *each of* the following have in *deciding* upon these unit operating rules, policies, and procedures:

	AMOUNT OF INFLUENCE IN DECIDING UNIT PROCEDURES			
	NONE	LITTLE	SOME	QUITE A BIT	VERY MUCH
a. People in line management or staff positions *outside* of your immediate work unit?	1	2	3	4	5
b. *You*, as the unit supervisor?	1	2	3	4	5
c. Your immediate subordinates *individually?*	1	2	3	4	5
d. You and your immediate subordinates *as a group* in unit meetings?	1	2	3	4	5

THE NEXT FOUR QUESTIONS ARE ABOUT THE INTERNAL FLOW OF WORK BETWEEN YOUR IMMEDIATE SUBORDINATES. LISTED AND DIAGRAMMED BELOW ARE FOUR COMMON WAYS THAT THE WORK PERFORMED IN YOUR UNIT CAN FLOW BETWEEN YOUR IMMEDIATE SUBORDINATES. (YOU, AS THE UNIT SUPERVISOR, SHOULD CONSIDER YOURSELF OUTSIDE THE BOXES BELOW.)

80. Please indicate *how much* of the *normal work* in your unit *flows between your immediate subordinates* in a manner as described by *each* of the following cases:

HOW MUCH WORK NORMALLY FLOWS BETWEEN MY IMMEDIATE SUBORDINATES IN THIS MANNER

	ALMOST NONE OF THE WORK	LITTLE	ABOUT 50% OF ALL THE WORK	A LOT	ALMOST ALL OF THE WORK
a. *Independent Work Flow Case*, where work and activities are performed by your immediate subordinates separately and do not flow between them?	1	2	3	4	5

Work Enters Unit

Work Leaves Unit

b. *Sequential Work Flow Case*, where work and activities flow between your immediate subordinates, but mostly in only one direction?	1	2	3	4	5

Work Enters

Work Leaves

c. *Reciprocal Work Flow Case*, where work and activities flow between your immediate subordinates in a back-and-forth manner *over a period of time*?	1	2	3	4	5

Work Enters

Work Leaves

	ALMOST NONE OF THE WORK	LITTLE	ABOUT 50% OF ALL THE WORK	A LOT	ALMOST ALL OF THE WORK
d. *Team Work Flow Case*, where work and activities come into your unit and your immediate subordinates diagnose, problem solve, and collaborate as a group *at the same time* in meetings to deal with the work.	1	2	3	4	5

Work Enters

Work Leaves

		NOT AT ALL	A LITTLE	SOME	QUITE A BIT	VERY MUCH
81. To obtain the information and materials needed to do their work, *how much* do unit members have to *rely* upon each of the following people:						
a.	You, the unit supervisor?	1	2	3	4	5
b.	Other members in your unit?	1	2	3	4	5
c.	People outside of your unit?	1	2	3	4	5
82. *How much* do unit members have to *depend* on each of the following people *while doing their respective jobs*:						
a.	You, the unit supervisor?	1	2	3	4	5
b.	Other members in your unit?	1	2	3	4	5
c.	People outside of your unit?	1	2	3	4	5

83. After unit members finish their part of the task, *how much* do they have to *rely* on each of the following people to *perform the next steps* in the process before the total task or service is completed:

	NOT AT ALL	A LITTLE	SOME	QUITE A BIT	VERY MUCH
a. You, the unit supervisor?	1	2	3	4	5
b. Other members in your unit?	1	2	3	4	5
c. People outside of your unit?	1	2	3	4	5

84. During the past 3 months, to what *extent* did you experience *problems* in coordinating work activities:

	TO NO EXTENT	LITTLE EXTENT	SOME EXTENT	LARGE EXTENT	VERY GREAT EXTENT
a. Between you and unit members?	1	2	3	4	5
b. Among unit members?	1	2	3	4	5
c. With people outside of your unit?	1	2	3	4	5

85. To coordinate the work of your unit during the past 3 months, *how often* were *written reports or memos* sent or received:

HOW OFTEN RECEIVED OR SENT WRITTEN REPORTS OR MEMOS IN PAST 3 MONTHS

	NOT ONCE	ABOUT 1–3 TIMES A MONTH	ABOUT 1–3 TIMES A WEEK	ABOUT 1–3 TIMES A DAY	ABOUT EVERY HOUR
a. Between you and unit members?	1	2	3	4	5
b. Among unit members?	1	2	3	4	5
c. Between you and people outside of your unit?	1	2	3	4	5

86. During the past 3 months, *how often did* work-related *discussions (face-to-face or by telephone)* occur on a one-to-one basis:

HOW OFTEN HAD WORK DISCUSSIONS IN PAST 3 MONTHS

	NOT ONCE	ABOUT 1–3 TIMES A MONTH	ABOUT 1–3 TIMES A WEEK	ABOUT 1–3 TIMES A DAY	ABOUT EVERY HOUR
a. Between your and unit members?	1	2	3	4	5
b. Among unit members?	1	2	3	4	5
c. Between you and people outside your unit?	1	2	3	4	5

87. *How frequently* did you conduct *regularly scheduled staff or unit meetings* with your immediate subordinates during the past 3 months?

HOW OFTEN MEETINGS WERE HELD
IN PAST THREE MONTHS

	NOT ONCE	ABOUT ONCE A MONTH	ABOUT EVERY 2 WEEKS	ABOUT ONCE A WEEK	ABOUT 2–4 TIMES A WEEK	ONCE A DAY OR MORE
	1	2	3	4	5	6

88. During the past 3 months, *how frequently* were you involved in *impromptu, unscheduled meetings to solve specific work problems:*

a. With two or more of your subordinates?

	1	2	3	4	5	6

b. With two or more people from outside of your unit?

	1	2	3	4	5	6

HOW OFTEN DISAGREEMENTS
OR ARGUMENTS OCCURRED

89. During the past 3 months, how often were there disagreements or arguments:

	NOT ONCE	ABOUT ONCE A MONTH	ABOUT EVERY 2 WEEKS	ABOUT ONCE A WEEK	SEVERAL TIMES A WEEK	EVERY DAY
a. Between you and unit members?	1	2	3	4	5	6
b. Among unit members?	1	2	3	4	5	6
c. Between you and people in other units?	1	2	3	4	5	6

90. When these disagreements or disputes occurred, *how often were they handled* in *each* of the following ways during the past three months:

HOW OFTEN DISPUTES
RESOLVED THIS WAY

	ALMOST NEVER	SELDOM	ABOUT HALF THE TIME	OFTEN	VERY OFTEN
a. By ignoring or avoiding the issues?	1	2	3	4	5
b. By smoothing over the issues?	1	2	3	4	5
c. By bringing the issues out in the open and working them out among the parties involved?	1	2	3	4	5
d. By having a higher-level supervisor resolve the issues between units?	1	2	3	4	5

91. Overall, to what *extent* does this *conflict resolution help or hinder* your unit's performance?

HINDERS PERFORMANCE A LOT	HINDERS MORE THAN HELPS	NEITHER HELPS NOR HINDERS	HELPS MORE THAN HINDERS	HELPS PERFORMANCE A LOT
1	2	3	4	5

92. *How much* are unit *members willing to give other members the support* they need to do a good job?

NONE	LITTLE	SOME	QUITE A BIT	VERY MUCH
1	2	3	4	5

93. In *relation* to other *comparable* organizational units, *how did your unit rate* on *each* of the following factors during the past year:

	FAR BELOW AVERAGE	SOME-WHAT BELOW AVERAGE	ABOUT AVERAGE	SOME-WHAT ABOVE AVERAGE	FAR ABOVE AVERAGE
a. The *quantity* or *amount* of work produced?	1	2	3	4	5
b. The *quality* or *accuracy* of work produced?	1	2	3	4	5
c. The number of *innovations* or *new ideas introduced* by the unit?	1	2	3	4	5
d. *Reputation* for work excellence?	1	2	3	4	5
e. Attainment of unit productions or service *goals*?	1	2	3	4	5
f. *Efficiency* of unit operations?	1	2	3	4	5
g. *Morale* of unit personnel?	1	2	3	4	5

A SELF-APPRAISAL OF YOUR UNIT

NOW MAKE A SELF-ASSESSMENT OF THE ORGANIZATION AND EFFECTIVENESS OF YOUR UNIT. HOPEFULLY, THE QUESTIONS YOU HAVE ANSWERED SO FAR STIMULATED YOU TO MAKE SUCH A SELF-ASSESSMENT.

A. Describe the major *strengths* of your work unit.

_____

_____

_____

_____

_____

_____

B. Describe the major *weaknesses* of your work unit.

_____

_____

_____

_____

_____

_____

C. Describe the *specific organizational changes* you think are necessary to *improve* the effectiveness of your unit.

_____

_____

_____

_____

_____

_____

FINALLY, PLEASE ANSWER THE FOLLOWING QUESTIONS ABOUT YOURSELF. YOUR ANSWERS ARE USE-
FUL FOR STATISTICAL ANALYSIS AND ARE STRICTLY CONFIDENTIAL.

94. *How long* have you *worked in this organization?*

LESS THAN 6 MONTHS	6 MONTHS- 2 YEARS	3-5 YEARS	6-10 YEARS	MORE THAN 10 YEARS
1	2	3	4	5

95. List below the *positions* or *job titles* you have held
since you began working for this organization.

Indicate the *months*
and *years* during
which you held each
position.

1. _____ From _____ to _____

2. _____ From _____ to _____

3. _____ From _____ to _____

4. _____ From _____ to _____

5. _____ From _____ to _____

6. _____ From _____ to _____

96. List below the *positions or job titles* you have held
before you began working for this organization (if any).

1. _____ From _____ to _____

2. _____ From _____ to _____

3. _____ From _____ to _____

4. _____ From _____ to _____

5. _____ From _____ to _____

6. _____ From _____ to _____

97. Presently, what is your *monthly gross salary* (before deductions and taxes)?

BELOW $500	$500- $999	$1000- $1499	$1500- $1999	$2000- $2999	$3000- $4000	ABOVE $4000
1	2	3	4	5	6	7

98. Indicate your sex: Female _____ Male _____
                                  1   2

99. How old were you on your last birthday?   _____ Years old.

100. How many dependents do you have? (You and others who depend on your income
for their financial support.)   _____ Number of dependents.

OAI Unit Member Questionnaire

This questionnaire is part of an Organization Assessment (OA) Survey that is being conducted throughout your organization. The purpose of the OA Survey is to learn more about how various jobs, work groups, sections, and levels in your organization are structured and work together. The results of the OA Survey will be used to identify and help solve organizational problems and to determine if and where improvements can be made to increase organizational effectiveness, productivity, and employee morale.

This particular questionnaire focuses on your job and the organizational unit that you work in. It measures various characteristics about your job and work unit that have been found in other studies to be importantly related to performance and job satisfaction. You are also given opportunities to indicate your feelings about your job and unit and suggest ways they might be improved.

Your answers are strictly confidential. The answers you give will be grouped with the answers of other people, and no individual person will ever be identified in any report. After the questionnaires for the organization have been analyzed, you will receive feedback on the OA Survey in the form of grouped statistical summaries. Hopefully, you will find these feedback sessions valuable for evaluating your job and unit and for identifying where improvements might be appropriate.

If this OA Survey is to be useful, it is important that you answer each question frankly and honestly. There are no hidden meanings behind any questions. This is not a test, and there are no right or wrong answers.

This OA Survey was developed and is being conducted by the Center for Organization Assessment from The Wharton School at the

458

University of Pennsylvania, Philadelphia. The Center has been contracted by your organization to conduct this OA Survey as an independent agent. Your completed questionnaire will be taken to the Center for analysis and safekeeping. It will not be available to anyone in your organization.

Thank you very much for your cooperation.

Dr. Andrew H. Van de Ven, Director
Center for Organization Assessment
The Wharton School
University of Pennsylvania
Philadelphia, Pa. 19104

GENERAL INSTRUCTIONS

Definitions: This questionnaire asks many questions about your immediate unit and your unit members.

- *Unit supervisor* means that person whom you report to directly, today.

- *Work unit* means your immediate supervisor and all individuals (your co-workers) who directly report to your immediate supervisor.

- *Unit members* are all the individuals in your immediate unit except your immediate supervisor.

Most of the questions ask you to circle one of several numbers that appear on a scale below the item. Corresponding with each number on a scale is a brief description of what the number represents. You are to circle the one number that most accurately reflects your answer to each question.

For example, if your answer to the following question is "very much" (and we believe it should be), circle the number "5" on the answer scale:

How much is it worth my time to fill out this questionnaire during the next hour?

NONE	LITTLE	SOME	QUITE A BIT	VERY MUCH
1	2	3	4	⑤

If you do not understand any question, BE SURE TO ASK US FOR HELP. We realize that not all questions are simple, and that is why we are here to answer any questions you have.

INTRODUCTORY QUESTIONS

The following questions are very important for properly coding and analyzing the data. As indicated before, all responses will be kept strictly confidential. When you are finished with this questionnaire, seal it in the accompanying envelope. It will not be opened until all envelopes are received by the Center for Organization Assessment.

1. Name of ORGANIZATION in which you work: _____

2. Name of DIVISION in which you work: _____

3. Name of OFFICE or CITY in which you work: _____

4. Name of UNIT in which you work: _____

5. Write your UNIT CODE NUMBER as it is shown on the organization chart hung on the wall. Unit Code # _____

6. Write YOUR NAME: _____

7. Write your present JOB TITLE or POSITION: _____

For computer coding only:

All cards: | | | | | | | | | | | | | | *0* | *1* | | | | | | | | | | | |

Column: 1 2 3 4 5 6 7 8 9 10 11 12 13 14 15 16 17 18 19 20 21 22 23

THE NATURE OF YOUR WORK AND JOB

WE WOULD LIKE TO KNOW THE SPECIFIC KINDS of tasks and work activities that make up your job. Please describe below the types of tasks or work activities you have been performing regularly during the past three months. Briefly explain what each task is and indicate the numbers of hours each week you spend doing it.

Task 1: _____ hours/week

_____
_____
_____
_____

Task 2: _____ hours/week

_____
_____
_____
_____

Task 3: _____ hours/week

_____
_____
_____
_____

Task 4: _____ hours/week

_____
_____
_____
_____

Task 5: _____ hours/week

_____
_____
_____
_____

Task 6: _____ hours/week

_____
_____
_____
_____

Task 7: _____ hours/week

_____
_____
_____
_____

Task 8: _____ hours/week

_____
_____
_____
_____

1. Indicate the total number of hours per week you normally worked. Hours/week during the past three months: ———

PLEASE ANSWER THE FOLLOWING QUESTIONS BY THINKING ONLY ABOUT THE TYPES OF TASKS THAT OCCUPY MOST OF YOUR WORKING TIME.

2. *To what extent* do you perform the *same tasks* from day to day? (Circle a number below the scale.)

ALMOST ALL MY TASKS ARE THE SAME DAY-TO-DAY	MANY OF MY TASKS ARE THE SAME DAY-TO-DAY	ABOUT HALF MY TASKS ARE THE SAME DAY-TO-DAY	SOME OF MY TASKS ARE THE SAME DAY-TO-DAY	ALMOST NO TASKS ARE THE SAME DAY-TO-DAY
1	2	3	4	5

3. *How much the same* are the day-to-day situations, problems, or issues you encounter in performing your major tasks? (Circle a number below.)

VERY MUCH THE SAME	MOSTLY THE SAME	QUITE A BIT DIFFERENT	VERY MUCH DIFFERENT	COMPLETELY DIFFERENT
1	2	3	4	5

4. *How easy* is it for *you* to *know* whether you do your work correctly?

VERY DIFFICULT	QUITE DIFFICULT	SOMEWHAT EASY	QUITE EASY	VERY EASY
1	2	3	4	5

5. *What percent of the time* are you *generally sure* of what the *outcomes* of your work efforts will be?

40% OR LESS	41–60%	61–75%	76–90%	91% OR MORE
1	2	3	4	5

6. During a normal week, *how frequently* do exceptions *arise* in your work which require *substantially different* methods or procedures for doing it?

VERY RARELY	OCCASIONALLY	QUITE OFTEN	VERY OFTEN	CONSTANTLY
1	2	3	4	5

7. In the past 3 months, *how often* did *difficult problems arise* in your work for which there were no immediate or apparent solutions?

ONCE A WEEK OR LESS	ABOUT 2–4 TIMES A WEEK	ABOUT ONCE A DAY	ABOUT 2–4 TIMES A DAY	5 TIMES OR MORE A DAY
1	2	3	4	5

8. About *how much time* did you spend solving these *work problems*?

LESS THAN 1 HOUR/WEEK	ABOUT 1–4 HOURS/WEEK	ABOUT 1 HOUR/DAY	ABOUT 2–3 HOURS/DAY	4 HOURS OR MORE PER DAY
1	2	3	4	5

9. To what extent does *just your work alone* give you many *clues* to figure out *how well you are doing* your job (without relying on feedback from your supervisor or co-workers)?

MY WORK GIVES ME NO CLUES ON HOW WELL I DO MY JOB	MY WORK GIVES A FEW CLUES ON MY JOB PERFORMANCE	MY WORK GIVES SOME CLUES ON MY JOB PERFORMANCE	MY WORK GIVES MANY CLUES ON MY JOB PERFORMANCE	MY WORK GIVES ALL CLUES NEEDED TO KNOW HOW WELL I DO MY JOB
1	2	3	4	5

10. During the past 3 months, *how often* did you receive *suggestions or feedback* from your *co-workers* on your work?

NOT ONCE	ABOUT ONCE A MONTH	ABOUT ONCE A WEEK	ABOUT EVERY DAY OR SO	SEVERAL TIMES A DAY
1	2	3	4	5

11. *How many hours per week on or off the job* do you spend in some kind of *reading or training* to keep current in the skills needed to do your job?

LESS THAN 1 HR/WK	ABOUT 1–3 HR/WK	ABOUT 4–6 HR/WK	ABOUT 7–9 HR/WK	ABOUT 10 HR/WK OR MORE
1	2	3	4	5

12. Describe the specific kinds of training programs or reading materials you spent this time on to remain current in your job.

_____
_____
_____
_____

13. When you *began* this job, *how long a period of orientation and training* did you receive that was *directly related to your tasks* in this job?

A FEW HOURS OR LESS	ABOUT A DAY	ABOUT A WEEK	ABOUT A MONTH	MORE THAN A MONTH
1	2	3	4	5

14. How many *years* of academic, vocational, or professional *education* have you obtained *beyond high school*?

YEARS AFTER HIGH SCHOOL

0 1 2 3 4 5 6 7 8 9

15. What is the highest educational degree you obtained in school?

GRADE SCHOOL DIPLOMA	HIGH SCHOOL DIPLOMA	VOCATIONAL OR CRAFT CERTIFICATION	COLLEGE BACHELOR'S DEGREE	MASTER'S DEGREE	DOCTORAL DEGREE
1	2	3	4	5	6

16. Indicate the *specific major* or *field of specialization* in which you obtained this degree.

_____

17. *How often* do you follow about the *same work methods or steps* for *doing* your major tasks from day to day?

VERY SELDOM	SOMETIMES	ABOUT HALF THE TIME	QUITE OFTEN	VERY OFTEN
1	2	3	4	5

18. To what *extent* did you follow *standard operating procedures* or practices to do your major tasks the past 3 months?

TO NO EXTENT	LITTLE EXTENT	SOME EXTENT	GREAT EXTENT	VERY GREAT EXTENT
1	2	3	4	5

19. *How many written rules and procedures exist* for doing your major tasks?

VERY FEW IF ANY	A SMALL NUMBER	A MODERATE NUMBER	A LARGE NUMBER	A GREAT NUMBER
1	2	3	4	5

20. *How precisely* do these rules and procedures *specify* how your major tasks are to be done?

VERY GENERAL	MOSTLY GENERAL	SOMEWHAT SPECIFIC	QUITE SPECIFIC	VERY SPECIFIC
1	2	3	4	5

21. *How heavy* was your *work load* during the past 3 months?

OFTEN NOT ENOUGH TO KEEP ME BUSY	SOMETIMES NOT ENOUGH TO KEEP ME BUSY	JUST ABOUT THE RIGHT AMOUNT	HARD TO KEEP UP WITH	ENTIRELY TOO MUCH FOR ME TO HANDLE
1	2	3	4	5

22. *How far in advance* do you generally *know* how much work will be required of you?

ABOUT AN HOUR OR LESS IN ADVANCE	ABOUT A DAY IN ADVANCE	ABOUT A WEEK IN ADVANCE	ABOUT A MONTH IN ADVANCE	ABOUT 6 MONTHS OR MORE IN ADVANCE
1	2	3	4	5

23. During the past 3 months, how much *control* did you have in setting the *pace* of your work?

NONE	VERY LITTLE	SOME	QUITE A BIT	VERY MUCH
1	2	3	4	5

24. When considering the various situations that arise in performing your work, what *percent of the time* do you *have* written or unwritten procedures for dealing with them?

0-20%	21-40%	41-60%	61-80%	81-100%
1	2	3	4	5

25. Listed below are four common decisions about your work. *How much authority* do you have in making each of the following decisions about your work:

	AMOUNT OF AUTHORITY I HAVE IN EACH DECISION				
	NONE	LITTLE	SOME	QUITE A BIT	VERY MUCH
a. Determining *what* tasks I will perform from day to day?	1	2	3	4	5
b. *Setting quotas* on how much work I have to complete?	1	2	3	4	5
c. *Establishing rules and procedures* about how my work is to be done?	1	2	3	4	5
d. Determining *how work exceptions* are to be handled?	1	2	3	4	5

26. How *much* does your *supervisor hold you personally accountable* for the *work decisions* you make in your job?

NOT AT ALL	VERY LITTLE	SOME	QUITE A BIT	VERY MUCH
1	2	3	4	5

27. *How clearly* do you *know what level of work performance* is *expected* from you (in terms of amount, quality, and timeliness of output)?

VERY UNCLEAR	QUITE UNCLEAR	SOMEWHAT CLEAR	QUITE CLEAR	VERY CLEAR
1	2	3	4	5

28. How *clearly* does your *job description specify* the *standards of performance* on which your job is evaluated?

THERE IS NO JOB DESCRIPTION FOR MY JOB.	MY JOB DESCRIPTION DOES NOT STATE ANY PERFORMANCE STANDARDS TO BE ACHIEVED IN THIS JOB.	MY JOB DESCRIPTION IS VERY GENERAL IN STATING WHAT PERFORMANCE STANDARDS ARE TO BE ACHIEVED.	MY JOB DESCRIPTION IS QUITE CLEAR IN STATING WHAT PERFORMANCE STANDARDS ARE TO BE ACHIEVED.	MY JOB DESCRIPTION IS VERY CLEAR AND PRECISE IN STATING WHAT PERFORMANCE STANDARDS ARE TO BE ACHIEVED.
1	2	3	4	5

29. To what degree has your *supervisor discussed* with *you* these *performance standards* on which your job is evaluated?

MY SUPERVISOR NEVER DISCUSSED THEM WITH ME.	MY SUPERVISOR ONLY MENTIONED THEM TO ME VERY GENERALLY AND DID NOT CLARIFY THEM.	MY SUPERVISOR DISCUSSED THEM WITH ME QUITE SPECIFICALLY AND CLEARLY.	MY SUPERVISOR DISCUSSED THEM WITH ME IN A VERY DETAILED AND CLEAR WAY.
1	2	3	4

30. *How hard* is it to *attain* the *level of performance* that is *expected* from you?

I DON'T KNOW WHAT'S EXPECTED OF ME.	QUITE EASY	QUITE HARD	VERY HARD BUT ATTAINABLE	EXCESSIVELY HARD AND IMPOSSIBLE TO ATTAIN
1	2	3	4	5

31. To what extent do *you believe* that the *performance standards* upon which your work is evaluated are *fair*?

I DON'T KNOW WHAT STANDARDS ARE USED TO EVALUATE MY WORK.	VERY UNFAIR	SOMEWHAT FAIR	QUITE FAIR	VERY FAIR
1	2	3	4	5

32. *How much* does your *supervisor hold you personally responsible* for achieving these *performance standards* for your job?

NOT AT ALL	VERY LITTLE	SOME	QUITE A BIT	VERY MUCH
1	2	3	4	5

33. During the *past year, how often did* your immediate *supervisor discuss* your *work performance with you*?

NOT ONCE	ABOUT 1–4 TIMES A YEAR	ABOUT ONCE A MONTH	ABOUT ONCE A WEEK	ABOUT EVERY DAY OR SO
1	2	3	4	5

34. When your work performance was discussed with you, how often did you receive *practical suggestions* for improving your work?

NEVER	SELDOM	ABOUT HALF THE TIME	OFTEN	EVERY TIME
1	2	3	4	5

35. *If you attain* the *performance level* that is expected of you, *how likely is it that* each of the following *will happen*:

	NO CHANCE	SMALL CHANCE	50% CHANCE	QUITE LIKELY	ALMOST A CERTAINTY
a. You will be *recognized* for your good work (e.g., given a special word of appreciation or given a pat-on-the-back)?	1	2	3	4	5
b. You will be given a *promotion* in this organization?	1	2	3	4	5

36. *If you do not attain* the *performance level* that is expected of you, *how likely is it that each* of the following *will happen*:

	NO CHANCE	SMALL CHANCE	50% CHANCE	QUITE LIKELY	ALMOST A CERTAINTY
a. You will be reprimanded, or told to improve your work?	1	2	3	4	5
b. You will be demoted in this organization?	1	2	3	4	5

YOUR FEELINGS ABOUT YOUR JOB

NOW WE WOULD LIKE TO ASK YOU SOME QUESTIONS ABOUT HOW YOU PERSONALLY FEEL ABOUT YOUR JOB.

37. *How satisfied* are you with each of the following:

	VERY UNSAT-ISFIED	QUITE UNSAT-ISFIED	SOME-WHAT SATIS-FIED	QUITE SATIS-FIED	VERY SATIS-FIED
a. Your job?	1	2	3	4	5
b. Your supervisor?	1	2	3	4	5
c. Your pay?	1	2	3	4	5

		VERY UNSAT-ISFIED	QUITE UNSAT-ISFIED	SOME-WHAT SATIS-FIED	QUITE SATIS-FIED	VERY SATIS-FIED
d.	The friendliness and cooperativeness of your *co-workers*?	1	2	3	4	5
e.	The *career progress* you have made in this organization up to now?	1	2	3	4	5
f.	Your chances for *career advancement* in this organization *in the future*?	1	2	3	4	5

		NONE	A LITTLE	SOME	QUITE A BIT	VERY MUCH
38.	*How much effort* do you put into your work?	1	2	3	4	5
39.	*How much* did you try *to improve* your job performance in the past 3 months?	1	2	3	4	5

40. Each of the statements below is something that a person might say about his or her job. Please indicate your own, personal *feelings* about your job by circling a number on the scale to the right of each statement to indicate how much you agree or disagree with each statement.

		DISAGREE STRONGLY	DISAGREE SOMEWHAT	NEUTRAL	AGREE-SOME-WHAT	AGREE STRONGLY
a.	It's hard, on this job, for me to care very much about whether or not the work gets done right.	1	2	3	4	5
b.	My opinion of myself goes up when I do this job well.	1	2	3	4	5
c.	My supervisor often lets me know how well I am performing my job.	1	2	3	4	5
d.	I feel a great sense of personal accomplishment when I do this job well.	1	2	3	4	5
e.	I feel a very high degree of *personal responsibility for the work I do on this job*.	1	2	3	4	5
f.	I frequently think of quitting this job.	1	2	3	4	5

	DISAGREE STRONGLY	DISAGREE SOMEWHAT	NEUTRAL	AGREE-SOME-WHAT	AGREE STRONGLY
g. I feel bad and unhappy when I discover that I have performed poorly on this job.	1	2	3	4	5
h. My co-workers on this job almost *never* give me any "feedback" about how well I am doing on my work.	1	2	3	4	5
i. I feel I should personally take the credit or blame for the results of my work on this job.	1	2	3	4	5
j. My own feelings generally are *not* affected much one way or the other by how well I do on this job.	1	2	3	4	5
k. I am recognized and rewarded for putting in additional effort to do superior work in this job.	1	2	3	4	5
l. I am reprimanded or told to "shape up" when I do inferior work in this job.	1	2	3	4	5

What Kind of Job Do You Prefer?

PEOPLE DIFFER IN THE KINDS OF JOBS THEY WOULD MOST LIKE TO HOLD. THE QUESTIONS IN THIS SECTION GIVE YOU A CHANCE TO SAY JUST WHAT IT IS ABOUT A JOB THAT IS MOST IMPORTANT TO YOU PERSONALLY.

FOR EACH QUESTION BELOW, TWO DIFFERENT KINDS OF JOBS ARE BRIEFLY DESCRIBED. YOU ARE TO INDICATE WHICH OF THE JOBS YOU PERSONALLY WOULD PREFER—IF YOU HAD TO MAKE A CHOICE BETWEEN THEM.

IN ANSWERING EACH QUESTION, ASSUME THAT EVERYTHING ELSE ABOUT THE JOBS IS THE SAME. PAY ATTENTION ONLY TO THE CHARACTERISTICS ACTUALLY LISTED.

ONE EXAMPLE IS GIVEN BELOW:

JOB A	JOB B
A job requiring work with mechanical equipment most of the day.	A job requiring work with other people most of the day.

```
1————2————③————4————5
STRONGLY   SLIGHTLY   NEUTRAL   SLIGHTLY   STRONGLY
PREFER A   PREFER A             PREFER B   PREFER B
```

IF YOU LIKE WORKING WITH PEOPLE AND WORKING WITH EQUIPMENT EQUALLY WELL, YOU WOULD CIRCLE THE NUMBER 3, AS HAS BEEN DONE IN THIS EXAMPLE.

PLEASE ASK FOR ASSISTANCE IF YOU DO NOT UNDERSTAND EXACTLY HOW TO DO THESE QUESTIONS.

JOB A	JOB B
41. A job where the pay is very good.	A job where there is considerable opportunity to be creative and innovative.

```
1———— 2—————3—————4————— 5
STRONGLY   SLIGHTLY   NEUTRAL   SLIGHTLY   STRONGLY
PREFER A   PREFER A             PREFER B   PREFER B
```

JOB A	JOB B
42. A job where you are often required to make important decisions.	A job with many pleasant people to work with.

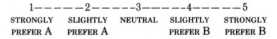

```
1————2—————3—————4————5
STRONGLY   SLIGHTLY   NEUTRAL   SLIGHTLY   STRONGLY
PREFER A   PREFER A             PREFER B   PREFER B
```

JOB A	JOB B
43. A job in which greater responsibility is given to those who do the best work.	A job in which greater responsibility is given to loyal employees who have the most seniority.

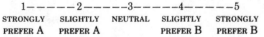

```
1————2—————3—————4————5
STRONGLY   SLIGHTLY   NEUTRAL   SLIGHTLY   STRONGLY
PREFER A   PREFER A             PREFER B   PREFER B
```

JOB A   JOB B

44. A job in an organization   A job in which you are not
which is in financial   allowed to have any say what-
trouble—and might have   ever in how your work is sched-
to close down within the   uled or in the procedures to
year.   be used in carrying it out.

1————2————3————4————5
STRONGLY   SLIGHTLY   NEUTRAL   SLIGHTLY   STRONGLY
PREFER A   PREFER A   PREFER B   PREFER B

45. A very routine job.   A job where your co-workers are
not very friendly.

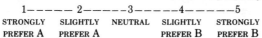

1————2————3————4————5
STRONGLY   SLIGHTLY   NEUTRAL   SLIGHTLY   STRONGLY
PREFER A   PREFER A   PREFER B   PREFER B

46. A job with a supervisor   A job that prevents you from
who is often very critical   using a number of skills that
of you and your work in   you worked hard to develop.
front of other people.

1————2————3————4————5
STRONGLY   SLIGHTLY   NEUTRAL   SLIGHTLY   STRONGLY
PREFER A   PREFER A   PREFER B   PREFER B

47. A job with a supervisor   A job that provides constant
who respects you and   opportunities for you to learn
treats you fairly.   new and interesting things.

1————2————3————4————5
STRONGLY   SLIGHTLY   NEUTRAL   SLIGHTLY   STRONGLY
PREFER A   PREFER A   PREFER B   PREFER B

48. A job where there is a   A job with very little chance
real chance you could be   to do challenging work.
laid off.

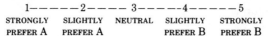

1————2————3————4————5
STRONGLY   SLIGHTLY   NEUTRAL   SLIGHTLY   STRONGLY
PREFER A   PREFER A   PREFER B   PREFER B

49. A job in which there is a   A job that provides lots of
real chance for you to   vacation time and an excellent
develop new skills   fringe benefits package.
and advance in the
organization.

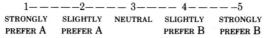

1————2————3————4————5
STRONGLY   SLIGHTLY   NEUTRAL   SLIGHTLY   STRONGLY
PREFER A   PREFER A   PREFER B   PREFER B

50. A job with little freedom   A job where the working con-
and independence to do   ditions are poor.
your work in the way you
think best.

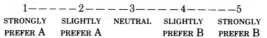

1————2————3————4————5
STRONGLY   SLIGHTLY   NEUTRAL   SLIGHTLY   STRONGLY
PREFER A   PREFER A   PREFER B   PREFER B

JOB A	**JOB B**

51. A job with very satisfying teamwork.

A job that allows you to use your skills and abilities to the fullest extent.

1— — — —2— — — —3— — — — 4— — — —5
STRONGLY   SLIGHTLY   NEUTRAL   SLIGHTLY   STRONGLY
PREFER A   PREFER A   PREFER B   PREFER B

52. A job which offers little or no challenge.

A job which requires you to be completely isolated from co-workers.

1— — — — —2— — — — 3— — — — 4— — — — —5
STRONGLY   SLIGHTLY   NEUTRAL   SLIGHTLY   STRONGLY
PREFER A   PREFER A   PREFER B   PREFER B

A SELF-APPRAISAL OF YOUR JOB

NOW MAKE AN ASSESSMENT OF THE WAY YOUR JOB IS ORGANIZED. HOPEFULLY, THE QUESTIONS YOU HAVE ANSWERED SO FAR HAVE HELPED YOU THINK ABOUT THINGS YOU WANT TO SAY TO EACH QUESTION BELOW.

A. Describe what *you like* about the way your job is organized.

_____
_____
_____
_____
_____

B. Describe what *specific problems* you experience with the way your job is organized. ·

_____
_____
_____
_____
_____

C. Suggest some *specific ways* that the organization of your job could be *improved*.

_____
_____
_____
_____
_____

THE ORGANIZATION
AND WORK OF
YOUR UNIT

SO FAR YOU HAVE BEEN ASKED QUESTIONS ABOUT your work and your job. This next part asks how your unit is organized to do its work and achieve its performance goals. Please keep in mind that your unit consists of your immediate supervisor and all individuals (your co-workers) who report directly to your supervisor.

53. During the past 3 months, *how many other people* in your unit *performed the same basic tasks* as you did?

NONE	ONLY ONE	A FEW OTHERS	MOST OTHERS	ALL OTHERS
1	2	3	4	5

54. *How many other people* in your unit *are qualified* to do your tasks?

NONE	ONLY ONE	A FEW OTHERS	MOST OTHERS	ALL OTHERS
1	2	3	4	5

55. *How easy* would it be to *rotate* the jobs *between unit members*, so that each could do a good job performing someone else's tasks?

VERY DIFFICULT. MOST MEMBERS WOULD NEED EXTENSIVE RETRAINING	QUITE DIFFICULT. SOME MEMBERS WOULD NEED EXTENSIVE RETRAINING	SOMEWHAT DIFFICULT. A FEW MEMBERS WOULD NEED RETRAINING	QUITE EASY. SOME MEMBERS WOULD NEED MINOR RETRAINING	VERY EASY. NO MEMBERS WOULD NEED RETRAINING
1	2	3	4	5

56. *How much say or influence* do *each* of the following have in *deciding what kinds of work or tasks* are to be performed in your unit:

	AMOUNT OF SAY IN DECIDING UNIT'S WORK				
	NONE	LITTLE	SOME	QUITE A BIT	VERY MUCH
a. People in line management or staff positions *outside* of your immediate work unit?	1	2	3	4	5
b. Your *unit supervisor*?	1	2	3	4	5

473

		NONE	LITTLE	SOME	QUITE A BIT	VERY MUCH
c.	Unit members, *individually*?	1	2	3	4	5
d.	The unit supervisor and members *as a group* in unit meetings?	1	2	3	4	5

Criteria for Evaluating Unit Effectiveness.

CONSIDER NOW THE SPECIFIC CRITERIA OR MEASURES THAT ARE USED TO DETERMINE HOW EFFECTIVELY YOUR UNIT PERFORMS ITS WORK AND RESPONSIBILITIES.

57. List below the *three most important criteria* that are used to determine how well your unit performs its work.

Rank the importance of these three effectiveness criteria.
1 = MOST IMPORTANT
2 = SECOND MOST IMPORTANT
3 = THIRD MOST IMPORTANT

1. _____

RANK: _____

2. _____

RANK: _____

3. _____

RANK: _____

58. *How much influence* or say did *each* of the following have in *deciding these performance criteria* for your unit:

AMOUNT OF INFLUENCE IN DECIDING CRITERIA

		NONE	LITTLE	SOME	QUITE A BIT	VERY MUCH
a.	People in line management or staff positions *outside* of your immediate work unit?	1	2	3	4	5
b.	Your *unit supervisor*?	1	2	3	4	5
c.	Unit members, *individually*?	1	2	3	4	5
d.	Your supervisor and unit members *as a group* in unit meetings?	1	2	3	4	5

59. *How much* do people in your unit *agree* that these are the three most important criteria for evaluating the performance of your unit?

NOT AT ALL	AGREE A LITTLE	AGREE SOMEWHAT	AGREE QUITE A BIT	AGREE VERY MUCH
1	2	3	4	5

60. Overall, *how clearly* have specific *performance targets been set* for your unit?

NO TARGETS WERE SET	TARGETS ARE VERY UNCLEAR	TARGETS ARE SOME-WHAT CLEAR	TARGETS ARE QUITE CLEAR	TARGETS ARE VERY CLEAR
1	2	3	4	5

61. *How difficult* is it for your unit to *attain* these *performance targets*?

NO TARGETS WERE SET	TARGETS VERY EASY TO ATTAIN	TARGETS QUITE EASY TO ATTAIN	TARGETS DIFFICULT BUT ATTAINABLE	TARGETS VERY DIFFICULT TO ATTAIN	TARGETS IMPOSSIBLY DIFFICULT TO ATTAIN
1	2	3	4	5	6

62. *How frequently* do you receive information about how well your unit achieves these performance targets?

NO TARGETS WERE SET	NEVER	ONLY AT YEAR-END	EVERY MONTH	EVERY WEEK	EVERY DAY	SEVERAL TIMES DAILY
1	2	3	4	5	6	7

63. Overall, what *percent* of these *performance targets were attained* by your unit last year?

NO TARGETS WERE SET	0–20%	21–40%	41–60%	61–80%	81–90%	91–100%	MORE THAN 100%
0	1	2	3	4	5	6	7

64. *How much* do members of your unit do the following things:

	HOW MUCH THIS HAPPENS				
	NOT AT ALL	A LITTLE	SOME	QUITE A BIT	VERY MUCH
a. *Compete* with each other to achieve performance targets?	1	2	3	4	5
b. "Gang-up" on the *individual* whose work is *far below* that of the others?	1	2	3	4	5
c. "Gang-up" on the *individual* whose work far exceeds that of the others?	1	2	3	4	5
d. *Encourage individuals* to *excel* and strive for increasingly higher levels of work performance?	1	2	3	4	5
e. Try to *get ahead* at the *expense* of other unit members?	1	2	3	4	5

Rules, Policies, and Procedures for the Unit as a Whole

THINK ABOUT THE VARIOUS OPERATING RULES, POLICIES, AND PROCEDURES THAT ALL PERSONNEL IN YOUR UNIT ARE EXPECTED TO FOLLOW TO COORDINATE AND CONTROL ALL THE WORK ACTIVITIES PERFORMED IN YOUR UNIT. THESE RULES AND PROCEDURES MAY BE FORMAL OR INFORMAL, WRITTEN OR UNWRITTEN. HOWEVER, THEY ARE DIFFERENT FROM THOSE USED TO GUIDE EACH INDIVIDUAL IN PERFORMING HIS OR HER OWN JOB, BECAUSE THEY APPLY TO ALL PEOPLE IN YOUR UNIT, REGARD-LESS OF THE PARTICULAR JOB EACH PERFORMS.

65. *How specific or general* are the *rules, policies, and procedures* in your unit for coor-dinating and controlling the work activities of all unit personnel?

THERE ARE NO SET RULES, POLICIES, OR PROCEDURES	VERY GENERAL	SOMEWHAT SPECIFIC	QUITE SPECIFIC	VERY SPECIFIC
1	2	3	4	5

66. *How often* did unit members *violate or ignore* these rules, policies, or procedures during the past three months?

NOT ONCE	VERY SELDOM	ABOUT HALF THE TIME	QUITE OFTEN	ALL THE TIME
1	2	3	4	5

67. *How strictly* are these operating rules, policies, or procedures *enforced* in your unit?

NOT AT ALL ENFORCED	VERY LOOSELY ENFORCED	SOMEWHAT STRICTLY ENFORCED	QUITE STRICTLY ENFORCED	VERY STRICTLY ENFORCED
1	2	3	4	5

68. *How much influence* or say did *each* of the following have in *deciding* upon the rules, policies, and procedures for your unit:

	AMOUNT OF INFLUENCE IN DECIDING UNIT PROCEDURE				
	NONE	LITTLE	SOME	QUITE A BIT	VERY MUCH
a. People in line management or staff positions *outside* of your immediate work unit?	1	2	3	4	5
b. *Your unit supervisor?*	1	2	3	4	5
c. Unit members, *individually?*	1	2	3	4	5
d. The unit supervisor and members *as a group* in unit meetings?	1	2	3	4	5

Coordination of Job and Unit Activities with Others

IN GENERAL, YOUR JOB AND YOUR UNIT DO NOT EXIST IN ISOLATION FROM OTHER PEOPLE IN THIS ORGANIZATION. THE FOLLOWING QUESTIONS ASK HOW MUCH YOU DEPEND UPON AND COORDINATE WITH OTHERS TO DO YOUR WORK.

69. To *obtain* the materials, clients, or information needed to do your job, *how much* do you have to *rely on each* of the following people:

	NOT AT ALL	A LITTLE	SOME	QUITE A BIT	VERY MUCH
a. Your unit supervisor?	1	2	3	4	5
b. Other unit members or co-workers?	1	2	3	4	5
c. People outside of your unit?	1	2	3	4	5

70. *While doing your assigned tasks, how much* do you have to *depend* on *each* of the following people:

a. Your unit supervisor?	1	2	3	4	5
b. Other unit members and co-workers?	1	2	3	4	5
c. People outside of your unit?	1	2	3	4	5

71. After you finish your part of the work, *how much do* you have to *rely* upon *each* of the following people to *perform the next steps* in the process before the total task or service is completed:

a. Your unit supervisor?	1	2	3	4	5
b. Other unit members or co-workers?	1	2	3	4	5
c. People outside of your unit?	1	2	3	4	5

72. During the past 3 months, to what *extent* did you experience *problems* in coordinating these work activities with each of the following people:

	TO NO EXTENT	LITTLE EXTENT	SOME EXTENT	LARGE EXTENT	VERY GREAT EXTENT
a. Your unit supervisor?	1	2	3	4	5
b. Other unit members or co-workers?	1	2	3	4	5
c. People outside of your unit?	1	2	3	4	5

73. During the past 3 months, *how often* did you receive or send *written reports* or *memos* related to your work from or to each of the following people:

	HOW OFTEN RECEIVED OR SENT WRITTEN REPORTS OR MEMOS IN PAST 3 MONTHS				
	NOT ONCE	ABOUT 1–3 TIMES A MONTH	ABOUT 1–3 TIMES A WEEK	ABOUT 1–3 TIMES A DAY	ABOUT EVERY HOUR
a. Your unit supervisor?	1	2	3	4	5
b. Other unit members or co-workers?	1	2	3	4	5
c. People outside of your unit?	1	2	3	4	5

74. During the past 3 months *how often* did you have work-related *discussions* (*face-to-face or by telephone*) with each of the following people:

	HOW OFTEN HAD WORK DISCUSSIONS IN PAST 3 MONTHS				
	NOT ONCE	ABOUT 1–3 TIMES A MONTH	ABOUT 1–3 TIMES A WEEK	ABOUT 1–3 TIMES A DAY	ABOUT EVERY HOUR
a. Your unit supervisor?	1	2	3	4	5
b. Other unit members or co-workers?	1	2	3	4	5
c. People outside of your unit?	1	2	3	4	5

75. During the past 3 months, *how often* were you involved in *special group problem-solving meetings* with:

	HOW OFTEN WERE MEETINGS HELD IN PAST THREE MONTHS					
	NOT ONCE	ABOUT ONCE A MONTH	ABOUT EVERY 2 WEEKS	ABOUT ONCE A WEEK	ABOUT 2–4 TIMES A WEEK	ONCE A DAY OR MORE
a. Two or more people from your unit?	1	2	3	4	5	6
b. Two or more people from outside of your unit?	1	2	3	4	5	6
76. *How often* were regularly scheduled staff meetings held among people in your unit?	1	2	3	4	5	6

	HOW OFTEN DISAGREEMENTS OR ARGUMENTS OCCURRED					
77. During the past 3 months how *often* did *disagreements or arguments* occur:	NOT ONCE	ABOUT ONCE A MONTH	ABOUT EVERY 2 WEEKS	ABOUT ONCE A WEEK	SEVERAL TIMES A WEEK	EVERY DAY
a. Between unit members and your supervisor?	1	2	3	4	5	6
b. Among unit members?	1	2	3	4	5	6
c. Between people in your unit and people outside of your unit?	1	2	3	4	5	6

	HOW OFTEN DISPUTES RESOLVED THIS WAY				
78. In general, when these disagreements or arguments occurred, *how often were they handled* in *each* of the following ways during the past three months:	ALMOST NEVER	SELDOM	ABOUT HALF THE TIME	OFTEN	VERY OFTEN
a. By ignoring or avoiding the issues?	1	2	3	4	5
b. By smoothing over the issues?	1	2	3	4	5
c. By bringing the issues out in the open and working them out among the people involved?	1	2	3	4	5
d. By having a higher-level supervisor resolve the issues between the people involved?	1	2	3	4	5

79. Overall, to what *extent* did this *conflict resolution help or hinder* your unit's performance?

HINDERS PERFORMANCE A LOT	HINDERS MORE THAN HELPS	NEITHER HELPS NOR HINDERS	HELPS MORE THAN HINDERS	HELPS PERFORMANCE A LOT
1	2	3	4	5

80. *How much* are unit *members willing to give other members the support* they need to do a good job?

NONE	LITTLE	SOME	QUITE A BIT	VERY MUCH
1	2	3	4	5

81. In *relation* to other *comparable* organizational units, *how did your unit rate* on *each* of the following factors during the past year:

	FAR BELOW AVERAGE	SOME-WHAT BELOW AVERAGE	ABOUT AVERAGE	SOME-WHAT ABOVE AVERAGE	FAR ABOVE AVERAGE
a. The *quantity* or *amount* of work produced?	1	2	3	4	5
b. The *quality* or *accuracy* of work produced?	1	2	3	4	5
c. The number of *innovations* or *new ideas introduced* by the unit?	1	2	3	4	5
d. *Reputation* for work excellence?	1	2	3	4	5
e. Attainment of unit production or service *goals*?	1	2	3	4	5
f. Efficiency of unit operations?	1	2	3	4	5
g. Morale of unit personnel?	1	2	3	4	5

A SELF-APPRAISAL OF YOUR UNIT

NOW MAKE A SELF-ASSESSMENT OF THE ORGANIZATION AND EFFECTIVENESS OF YOUR UNIT. HOPEFULLY, THE QUESTIONS YOU HAVE ANSWERED SO FAR STIMULATED YOU TO MAKE SUCH A SELF-ASSESSMENT.

A. Describe the major *strengths* of your work unit.

_____

_____

_____

_____

_____

_____

B. Describe the major *weaknesses* of your work unit.

_____

_____

_____

_____

_____

_____

C. Describe the *specific organizational changes* you think are necessary to *improve* the effectiveness of your unit.

_____

_____

_____

_____

_____

_____

FINALLY, PLEASE ANSWER THE FOLLOWING QUESTIONS ABOUT YOURSELF. YOUR ANSWERS ARE USE-
FUL FOR STATISTICAL ANALYSIS AND ARE STRICTLY CONFIDENTIAL.

82. *How long* have you *worked in this organization?*

LESS THAN 6 MONTHS	6 MONTHS- 2 YEARS	3–5 YEARS	6–10 YEARS	MORE THAN 10 YEARS
1	2	3	4	5

83. List below the *positions* or *job titles* you have held since your began working for this organization.

Indicate the *months* and *years* during which you held each position.

1. _____ From _____ to _____

2. _____ From _____ to _____

3. _____ From _____ to _____

4. _____ From _____ to _____

5. _____ From _____ to _____

6. _____ From _____ to _____

84. List below the *positions or job titles* you have held *before* you began working for this organization (if any).

1. _____ From _____ to _____

2. _____ From _____ to _____

3. _____ From _____ to _____

4. _____ From _____ to _____

5. _____ From _____ to _____

6. _____ From _____ to _____

85. Presently, what is your *monthly gross salary* (before deductions and taxes)?

BELOW $500	$500– $999	$1000– $1499	$1500– $1999	$2000– $2999	$3000– $4000	ABOVE $4000
1	2	3	4	5	6	7

86. Indicate your sex: Female _____ Male _____
                                     1   2

87. How old were you on your last birthday?   _____ Years old.

88. How many dependents do you have? (You and others who depend on your income for their financial support.)   _____ Number of dependents.

OAI Focal Unit Questionnaire

This questionnaire is part of an Organization Assessment (OA) Survey that is being conducted throughout your organization. The purpose of the OA Survey is to learn more about how various jobs, work groups, sections, and levels in your organization are structured and work together. The results of the OA Survey will be used to identify and help solve organizational problems and to determine if and where improvements can be made to increase organizational effectiveness, productivity, and employee morale.

This particular questionnaire focuses on how your unit coordinates with others. In varying degrees your unit does not exist in isolation. For a variety of reasons your unit may have to maintain many relationships with other units, departments, and groups both within and outside of your organization. This questionnaire asks you to indicate the most important other units that you had to coordinate with in order to accomplish your unit's goals and responsibilities during the past six months. Each of the questions will get at some aspect of the relationships between your unit and these other units.

Your answers will be especially helpful in understanding how units in this organization are coordinated and in identifying how and where interunit relationships can be improved. Moreover, we hope that your answering the questions will help you step back and evaluate for yourself how your unit coordinates with others.

Your answers are strictly confidential. The answers you give will be grouped with the answers of other people, and no individual person will ever be identified in any report. After the OA survey is completed, you will receive a feedback report on how various clusters of units coordinate in this organization. Hopefully, you will find these feedback

483

sessions valuable for evaluating patterns of coordination between units and for identifying where improvements might be appropriate.

If this OA Survey is to be useful, it is important that you answer each question frankly and honestly. There are no hidden meanings behind any questions. This is not a test, and there are no right or wrong answers.

This OA Survey was developed and is being conducted by the Center for Organization Assessment from the Wharton School at the University of Pennsylvania, Philadelphia. The Center has been contracted by your organization to conduct this OA Survey as an independent agent. Your completed questionnaire will be taken to the Center for analysis and safekeeping. It will not be available to anyone in your organization.

Thank you very much for your cooperation.

> Dr. Andrew H. Van de Ven, Director
> Center for Organizational Assessment
> The Wharton School
> University of Pennsylvania
> Philadelphia, Pa. 19104

General Instructions

Definitions: This questionnaire asks many questions about *your unit* and *other units*.

- *Your unit* includes you (as the supervisor) and all individuals who report *directly* to you. If you are not a supervisor, then your unit includes your immediate supervisor and all individuals (your co-workers) who directly report to your immediate supervisor.

- *Other units* refers to any other groups, departments, levels, or divisions within or outside of your organization that your unit coordinates with.

This questionnaire asks you to answer each question five times, once for each of the five most important other units that your unit coordinates with. These other units are listed in the columns to the right of the questions. For each question there is a five-point answer scale with brief descriptions of what the numbers on the scale represent. You are to choose one number that most accurately reflects your answer to each question for each other unit and write it in the appropriate column.

For example, if you were asked the following question, and your answers were "daily", "monthly", "hourly", "never", and "weekly" for other units 1–5, respectively, then you would write the numbers "4", "2", "5", "1", and "3" in the appropriate columns for the other units like this:

How often were you in contact
with this other unit during the past
six months?

NEVER	MONTHLY	WEEKLY	DAILY	HOURLY	**Unit 1**	**Unit 2**	**Unit 3**	**Unit 4**	**Unit 5**
1	2	3	4	5	_4_	_2_	_5_	_1_	_3_

If you do not understand any question, BE SURE TO ASK FOR HELP. We realize that not all questions are simple. That is why we are here to answer any question you have.

INTRODUCTORY QUESTIONS

The following questions are very important for properly coding and analyzing the data. As indicated before, all responses are kept strictly confidential. When you have completed this questionnaire, seal it in the accompanying envelope. It will not be opened until it is received by the Center for Organization Assessment.

1. Name of ORGANIZATION in which you work:_____

2. Name of DIVISION in which you work:_____

3. Name of OFFICE or CITY in which you work:_____

4. Name of UNIT in which you work:_____

5. Write YOUR NAME:_____

6. Write your present JOB TITLE or POSITION:_____

For Computer Tabulation Purposes

1	2	3	4	5	6	7	8	9

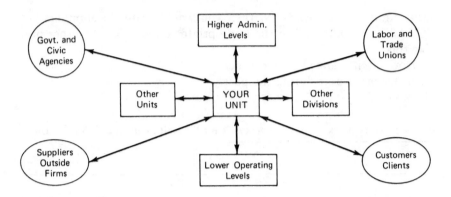

The External Relations of Your Unit

In varying degrees your unit does not exist in isolation. As the figure illustrates, your unit may have to maintain many relationships with other units, levels, and divisions within your organization, as well as with various groups and agencies outside of your organization. These relationships may exist for a variety of purposes, such as: coordinating work flows; obtaining money, personnel, equipment, and technical services; and responding to or initiating administrative directives and rules.

This questionnaire focuses on these external relationships your unit maintained during the past six months. In the space below, *draw a picture* that indicates the *major* units, levels and groups within and outside your organization that your unit had contact with during the past six months. Identify these other units by name. Use the figure above as a guide for drawing your picture below.

PICTURE OF EXTERNAL RELATIONS MAINTAINED BY MY UNIT

My
Unit

WE NOW FOCUS ON THE MOST IMPORTANT "OTHER UNITS" THAT YOUR UNIT MAINTAINED OR DEVELOPED CONTACTS WITH DURING THE PAST SIX MONTHS TO ACCOMPLISH YOUR UNIT'S GOALS AND RESPONSIBILITIES.

IN ALL QUESTIONS, THE TERM "OTHER UNITS" REFERS TO ANY OTHER GROUPS, OFFICES, LEVELS, OR DIVISIONS WITHIN OR OUTSIDE OF YOUR ORGANIZATION THAT YOUR UNIT COORDINATES WITH.

1. NAMES OF KEY OTHER UNITS	2. REASONS FOR RELATIONSHIP WITH OTHER UNIT	3. IMPORTANCE
From the picture you drew, write the *names of the most important other units* that your unit had to coordinate with during the past 6 months. (Select up to five of the most important other units.)	State as clearly as possible the *reasons why* your unit had to coordinate or work with this other unit during the past six months.	*How important* was this other unit in attaining the goals of your unit the past 6 months? (Write a number from scale below) 1 = NOT VERY IMPORTANT 2 = SOMEWHAT IMPORTANT 3 = QUITE IMPORTANT 4 = VERY IMPORTANT 5 = ABSOLUTELY CRUCIAL
Unit 1 [1] 1 2 3 4		
Unit 2 [2] 1 2 3 4		
Unit 3 [3] 1 2 3 4		
Unit 4 [4] 1 2 3 4		
Unit 5 [5] 1 2 3 4		

IN THE COLUMNS ON THE RIGHT, PLEASE WRITE THE NAME OF THE FIVE OTHER UNITS THAT YOU SELECTED ON THE PREVIOUS PAGE. THEN ANSWER THE FOLLOWING QUESTIONS FOR EACH OTHER UNIT INDIVIDUALLY BY WRITING IN THE APPROPRIATE COLUMN THE MOST ACCURATE NUMBER FROM THE ANSWER SCALE FOR EACH QUESTION.

	NAME: UNIT 1		NAME: UNIT 2		NAME: UNIT 3		NAME: UNIT 4		NAME: UNIT 5	
4. Does this other unit exist within your organization? (Circle No or Yes)	No	Yes	No	Yes	No	Yes	No	Yes	No	Yes
If Yes: **a.** Do you supervise this other unit in your organization's hierarchy?	No	Yes	No	Yes	No	Yes	No	Yes	No	Yes
b. Do you formally report to this other unit in your organization's hierarchy?	No	Yes	No	Yes	No	Yes	No	Yes	No	Yes
If No: **c.** Do you have a contractual relationship with this other unit?	No	Yes	No	Yes	No	Yes	No	Yes	No	Yes
d. Is it mandatory by government or trade regulations that you coordinate with this other unit?	No	Yes	No	Yes	No	Yes	No	Yes	No	Yes
5. During the past six months, how much was your unit involved with this other unit for each of the following reasons: (use scale below)										
a. To receive or send work or clients (e.g., customers, raw materials, or work objects)?	——		——		——		——		——	
b. To receive or send resources (money, personnel, equipment, office space)?	——		——		——		——		——	
c. To receive or send technical assistance (e.g., consultation or staff services in functional areas)?	——		——		——		——		——	
d. To receive or send information for purposes of coordination, control, planning, or evaluation?	——		——		——		——		——	

NOT AT ALL	A LITTLE	SOME-WHAT	QUITE A BIT	VERY MUCH
1	2	3	4	5

	UNIT 1	UNIT 2	UNIT 3	UNIT 4	UNIT 5
	Extent: ||	Extent: ||	Extent: ||	Extent: ||	Extent: ||
	_____ Yrs	_____ Yrs	_____ Yrs	_____ Yrs	_____ Yrs.

6. To what *extent* have the *terms of the relationship* between your unit and this other unit:
   a. Been explicitly *verbalized or dicussed?*
   b. Been *written down in detail?*

TO NO EXTENT	LITTLE EXTENT	SOME EXTENT	CONSIDERABLE EXTENT	GREAT EXTENT
1	2	3	4	5

7. For *how many years* has your unit been directly involved in some fashion with this other unit?

8. *Prior to the past six months,* to what extent has your unit had *effective working relationships* with this other unit?
   (Write best scale number in each column)

NO PRIOR CONTACT	TO NO EXTENT	LITTLE EXTENT	SOME EXTENT	CONSIDER-ABLE EXTENT	GREAT EXTENT
0	1	2	3	4	5

9. For this *other unit* to accomplish its goals and responsibilities, *how much does it need the services, resources,* or *support from your unit?*

NOT AT ALL	VERY LITTLE	SOME	QUITE A BIT	VERY MUCH
1	2	3	4	5

10. For *your unit* to accomplish its goals and responsibilities, *how much do you need the services, resources, or support from this other unit?* (Use scale for Question 9.)

	UNIT 1	UNIT 2	UNIT 3	UNIT 4	UNIT 5
	—	—	—	—	—
	—	—	—	—	—

PLEASE CONTINUE TO ANSWER THE FOLLOWING QUESTIONS FOR EACH OF THE OTHER UNITS IN THE RIGHT COLUMNS, REMEMBERING TO USE THE SAME UNIT NUMBER AS THAT ON THE PREVIOUS PAGE.

11. How well *informed* are you about the specific goals and services of this other unit?

NOT IN- AT ALL FORMED	LITTLE IN- FORMED	SOME- WHAT IN- FORMED	QUITE IN- FORMED	VERY WELL IN- FORMED
1	2	3	4	5

12. How much *say or influence* does this *other unit* have on the internal operations of your unit?

NONE	LITTLE	SOME	QUITE A BIT	VERY MUCH
1	2	3	4	5

13. How much *say or influence* does your unit have on the internal operations of this other unit? (Use scale for Question 12.)

14. Write the *name* and *address* of the *primary* individual that you contact or communicate with when dealing with this other unit.

UNIT 1: Name: _____ Address: _____

UNIT 2: Name: _____ Address: _____

UNIT 3: Name: _____ Address: _____

UNIT 4: Name: _____ Address: _____

UNIT 5: Name: _____ Address: _____

490

	UNIT 1	UNIT 2	UNIT 3	UNIT 4	UNIT 5
	___Years	___Years	___Years	___Years	___Years
	___Months	___Months	___Months	___Months	___Months

15. *How many years and months have you personally known the contact person in this other unit?*

16. *How well are you personally acquainted with the contact person in this other unit?*

NO PERSONAL ACQUAINTANCE	NOT VERY WELL	SOMEWHAT WELL	QUITE WELL	VERY WELL
1	2	3	4	5

17. *How much* do you and this contact person *agree* or disagree on:

   a. The *goal priorities* of your unit?

   b. The *specific ways* work is done or services are provided by your unit?

   c. The specific *terms of the relationship* between your unit and this other unit?

DON'T KNOW	DISAGREE MUCH	AGREE A LITTLE	AGREE SOMEWHAT	AGREE QUITE A BIT	AGREE VERY MUCH
0	1	2	3	4	5

18. To what extent does this other unit:

   a. Obtain its *funding from the same source as your unit* does?

   b. Do the *same kind of work* as your unit does?

   c. Have the *same clients or customers as your unit?*

   d. Have *operating goals similar* to your unit's goals?

UNIT 1	UNIT 2	UNIT 3	UNIT 4	UNIT 5
—	—	—	—	—
—		—	—	—
—	—	—	—	—
—			—	
—				

e. Have *employees* with *similar professional or trade skills* as those required of personnel in your unit?

f. Use the *same technology, equipment, or information sources* as your unit in doing its work?

DON'T KNOW	TO NO EXTENT	LITTLE EXTENT	SOME EXTENT	CONSIDERABLE EXTENT	GREAT EXTENT
0	1	2	3	4	5

19. To what extent did individuals in this other unit *hinder* your unit in performing its functions during the past six months?
(Use scale for Question 18 above.)

20. Consider now the *equality* of the give-and-take relationship with each unit. Compared to other units that you are involved with, *how fair* do you feel are the "*payoffs*" *to your unit* from this unit?

WE GET MUCH LESS THAN WE OUGHT	WE GET SOMEWHAT LESS THAN WE OUGHT	BALANCED	WE GET SOMEWHAT MORE THAN WE OUGHT	WE GET MUCH MORE THAN WE OUGHT
1	2	3	4	5

21. During the past six months, *how frequently* have people in your unit *communicated or been in contact* with people in this other unit?

NOT ONCE	1–2 TIMES	ABOUT MONTHLY	ABOUT EVERY 2 WEEKS	ABOUT WEEKLY	ABOUT DAILY	MANY TIMES DAILY
0	1	2	3	4	5	6

492

	UNIT 1	UNIT 2	UNIT 3	UNIT 4	UNIT 5

22. Specifically, *how frequently* did your unit *communicate* with this other unit *through each* of the following ways during the past six months:

   a. Through *written letters, memos, or reports* of any kind?

   b. Through *personal face-to-face discussions?*

   c. Through *telephone* calls?

   d. Through *group or committee meetings* between three or more people from your unit and this other unit?
(Use scale for Question 21.)

23. In general, what *percent* of all these communications with this other unit were *initiated by* people in your unit during the past six months?
(Indicate percent.)

24. Overall, how much *difficulty* do you experience in *getting ideas clearly across* to individuals in this other unit when you communicate with them?

NO CONTACT	NONE	LITTLE	SOME	QUITE A BIT	VERY MUCH
0	1	2	3	4	5

25. When you wanted to communicate with individuals in this unit, how much *difficulty* have you had *getting in touch* with them?
(Use scale for Question 24.)

493

THE NEXT TWO QUESTIONS MAY BE DIFFICULT TO ANSWER. MAKE THE MOST APPROXIMATE ESTIMATE YOU CAN. WRITE "0" IF YOUR ANSWER IS NONE OR NOT APPLICABLE.

26. During the past six months:

a. What *percent of your total working hours* did you spend on matters directly related to the operations, work, or projects of this other unit?

b. What *percent of all the work* done by your unit *came from* this other unit?

c. What *percent of all technical assistance and services* did you *receive from* this other unit?

d. What *percent of your unit's operating budget* (money, personnel, supplies, equipment) was *obtained* from this other unit?

27. During the past six months:

a. What *percent of all the work completed by your unit was sent to* this other unit?

b. What *percent of all resources allocated by your unit was given to* this other unit?

c. What *percent of all person-hours of technical assistance or services* provided by your unit was *given to* this other unit?

28. During the past six months, *how much the same* were these work materials, resources, or services each time they were sent to or received from this other unit?

	UNIT 1	UNIT 2	UNIT 3	UNIT 4	UNIT 5
26a.	__%	__%	__%	__%	__%
26b.	__%	__%	__%	__%	__%
26c.	__%	__%	__%	__%	__%
26d.	__%	__%	__%	__%	__%
27a.	__%	__%	__%	__%	__%
27b.	__%	__%	__%	__%	__%
27c.	__%	__%	__%	__%	__%
28.	___	___	___	___	___

ALMOST ALL THE SAME EACH TIME	MOSTLY THE SAME EACH TIME	ABOUT HALF THE SAME EACH TIME	MOSTLY DIFFERENT EACH TIME	ALMOST ALL DIFFERENT EACH TIME
1	2	3	4	5

494

UNIT 1	UNIT 2	UNIT 3	UNIT 4	UNIT 5
│	│	│	│	│
│	│	│	│	│
│ │	│ │	│ │	│ │	│ │
│	│	│	│	│

29. To what *extent* did your unit *encounter interruptions or delays* to the *normal flows* of work, resources, or services from or to this other unit during the past six months?

TO NO EXTENT	LITTLE EXTENT	SOME EXTENT	MUCH EXTENT	VERY GREAT EXTENT
1	2	3	4	5

30. During the past six months, *how often* did *exceptions or problems arise* in sending or receiving work, resources, or services to or from this other unit?

NOT ONCE	1 OR 2 TIMES	ABOUT MONTHLY	ABOUT WEEKLY	ABOUT DAILY	SEVERAL TIMES A DAY
1	2	3	4	5	6

31. To coordinate activities with this other unit during the past six months, *to what extent*:

a. Have *standard operating procedures been established* (e.g., rules, policies, forms, etc.)?

b. Are *formal communication channels followed*?

TO NO EXTENT	LITTLE EXTENT	SOME EXTENT	CONSIDERABLE EXTENT	GREAT EXTENT
1	2	3	4	5

32. During the past six months, *how often* were there *disagreements or disputes* between people in your unit and this other unit?

NOT ONCE	ABOUT ONCE A MONTH	ABOUT EVERY 2 WEEKS	ABOUT ONCE A WEEK	SEVERAL TIMES A WEEK	EVERY DAY
1	2	3	4	5	6

495

	UNIT 1	UNIT 2	UNIT 3	UNIT 4	UNIT 5

33. When these disagreements or disputes occurred, *how often were they handled* in *each* of the following ways during the past six months?

   a. By ignoring or avoiding the issues?

   b. By smoothing over the issues?

   c. By bringing the issues out in the open and working them out among the parties involved?

   d. By having a higher level manager or authority resolve the issues between the parties involved?

ALMOST NEVER	SELDOM	ABOUT HALF THE TIME	OFTEN	ALMOST ALWAYS
1	2	3	4	5

34. How well are any differences worked out at this time between your unit and this other unit?

VERY POORLY	POORLY	ADEQUATELY	QUITE WELL	VERY WELL
1	2	3	4	5

	UNIT 1	UNIT 2	UNIT 3	UNIT 4	UNIT 5

TO CONCLUDE THIS SECTION, PLEASE ANSWER THE FOLLOWING QUESTIONS USING THE SCALE FOLLOWING QUESTION 41.

35. To what extent has *this unit* carried out its responsibilities and commitments in regard to your unit during the past six months?

36. To what extent has *your unit* carried out your responsibilities and commitments in regard to this other unit during the past six months?

37. To what extent do you feel the *relationship* between your unit and this other unit is *productive?*

38. To what extent is the *time and effort spent* in developing and maintaining the relationship with this other unit *worthwhile?*

39. Overall, to what extent were you *satisfied with the relationship* between your unit and this other unit during the past six months?

40. During the past six months, to what extent has *your unit changed or influenced* the services or operations of *this other unit?*

41. During the past six months, to what extent has *this other unit changed or influenced* the services or operations of *your unit?*

TO NO EXTENT	LITTLE EXTENT	SOME EXTENT	CONSIDERABLE EXTENT	GREAT EXTENT
1	2	3	4	5

497

A SELF-APPRAISAL OF YOUR UNIT'S EXTERNAL RELATIONS

NOW MAKE A SELF-ASSESSMENT OF THE RELATIONSHIPS YOUR UNIT MAINTAINS WITH EACH OF THE OTHER UNITS. HOPEFULLY, THE QUESTIONS YOU HAVE ANSWERED SO FAR HAVE STIMULATED YOU TO MAKE SUCH A SELF-ASSESSMENT.

Describe the major *problems* you have encountered in relating or coordinating with each of the other units during the past six months.

Suggest some specific ways for overcoming these problems with each of the other units.

UNIT 1 Name_____

UNIT 2 Name_____

UNIT 3 Name_____

UNIT 4 Name_____

UNIT 5 Name_____

OAI Other Unit
Questionnaire

This questionnaire is part of an Organization Assessment (OA) Survey that is being conducted to learn how various organizational units are structured and work together. The OA Survey is being conducted by the Center for Organization Assessment from The Wharton School at the University of Pennsylvania, Philadelphia. XYZ Firm has contracted with the Center to conduct this study as an independent agent.

This particular questionnaire focuses on how your organizational unit coordinates with one or more units in XYZ Firm. These units are designated on page 2. In a previous survey, individuals from these units reported they were involved in some way with your organizational unit during the past six months. The purpose of this questionnaire is to obtain your perspective of the relationship your unit has had with each of these other units in the XYZ Firm.

We believe the results of this study will be helpful to you and XYZ Firm and to our knowledge of coordination in general.

1. *For you and your organizational unit,* the results of this study will be reported back and may provide useful information for more effectively coordinating services and activities among organizational units.

2. *For XYZ Firm,* the results of this study will be used to identify and help solve organizational problems and to determine if and where improvements can be made in the ways services and activities are coordinated.

3. *In general,* we believe that a better understanding of effective interunit coordination can only be obtained through objective evaluation and accurate information.

499

To accomplish these purposes, it is important that you answer each question frankly and honestly. There are no hidden meanings behind any questions. This is not a test, and there are no right or wrong answers. Your answers are kept strictly confidential and will only be seen by researchers at the Center for Organization Assessment. Your answers will be grouped with those of other people, and no individual will ever be identified in any report. After the study is completed, you will receive a report on how various patterns of interunit coordination are related to effectiveness.

We would appreciate your completing this questionnaire within a week from the time you receive it. It should take about 30 minutes. When you have finished, please seal your questionnaire in the enclosed self-addressed and stamped envelope and drop it in the mail box.

If you have any questions feel free to call us collect at 215 243-4690. Thank you very much for your cooperation.

Dr. Andrew H. Van de Ven, Director
Center for Organization Assessment
The Wharton School
University of Pennsylvania
Philadelphia, Pa. 19104

General Instructions

This questionnaire focuses on the relationships your organizational unit has had during the past six months with one or more other units from the XYZ Firm. These other units are designated on the next page. You are asked to answer the questions for only the units specified.

For most questions there is a five-point answer scale with brief descriptions of what the numbers on the scale represent. You are to choose one number that most accurately reflects your answer to the question for each designated other unit and write it in the appropriate column.

For example, if you were asked the following question, and your answers were "daily" and "monthly" for units 1 and 2 from the XYZ Firm, then you would write the numbers "4" and "2" in the respective columns, like this:

How often were you in contact with this
other unit during the past six months?

NEVER	MONTHLY	WEEKLY	DAILY	HOURLY	Unit 1	Unit 2	Unit 3	Unit 4	Unit 5
1	2	3	4	5	*4*	*2*	—	—	—

Introductory Questions

The following questions are very important for properly coding and analyzing the data. In addition, they are needed to make sure we have your correct address so that we can mail you a report on the results of this study. As indicated before, all responses are kept strictly confidential.

1. Write YOUR NAME: _____

2. Your ADDRESS: _____

   _____

3. Name of ORGANIZATION in which you work: _____

4. Name of OFFICE or DIVISION in which you work: _____

5. Name of UNIT in which you work: _____

6. Write your present JOB TITLE or POSITION: _____

7. How many years and months have you held this position? _____Years, _____ Months.

8. How many years and months have you worked in your organization? _____Years, _____ Months.

IN A PREVIOUS SURVEY, THE CONTACT PERSONS FROM THE FOLLOWING UNIT[S] IN XYZ FIRM REPORTED THEY COORDINATED IN SOME WAY WITH YOUR ORGANIZATIONAL UNIT DURING THE PAST SIX MONTHS.

UNIT 1. Name _____ Contact person _____

UNIT 2. Name _____ Contact person _____

UNIT 3. Name _____ Contact person _____

UNIT 4. Name _____ Contact person _____

UNIT 5. Name _____ Contact person _____

WE WOULD LIKE YOUR PERSPECTIVE ON THESE INTERUNIT RELATIONSHIPS. PLEASE ANSWER THE QUESTIONS FOR EACH OF THE DESIGNATED OTHER UNITS INDIVIDUALLY. WRITE IN THE APPROPRIATE COLUMNS THE NUMBER FROM THE ANSWER SCALE THAT REFLECTS YOUR MOST ACCURATE ANSWER TO EACH QUESTION FOR EACH OTHER UNIT. BE SURE TO USE THE COLUMN WITH THE SAME UNIT NUMBER AS THAT DESIGNATED ABOVE TO ANSWER THE QUESTIONS FOR EACH OF THE OTHER UNITS. IF NO NAMES ARE WRITTEN ABOVE FOR UNITS 2–5, THEN LEAVE THOSE COLUMNS BLANK.

UNIT 1	UNIT 2	UNIT 3	UNIT 4	UNIT 5
—	—	—	—	—
—	—	—	—	—

1. *How well* are you *personally acquainted* with the *contact person* in this other unit?

NO PERSONAL ACQUAINTANCE	NOT VERY WELL	SOMEWHAT WELL	QUITE WELL	VERY WELL
1	2	3	4	5

2. *How much* do you and this contact person *agree* or disagree on:

a. The *goal priorities* of your unit?

b. The specific *ways* work is done or services are provided by your unit?

502

	UNIT 1	UNIT 2	UNIT 3	UNIT 4	UNIT 5

c. The specific *terms of the relationship* between your unit and this other unit?

DON'T KNOW	DISAGREE MUCH	AGREE A LITTLE	AGREE SOMEWHAT	AGREE QUITE A BIT	AGREE VERY MUCH
0	1	2	3	4	5

3. How well *informed* are you about the specific goals and services of this other unit?

NOT AT ALL INFORMED	LITTLE INFORMED	SOMEWHAT INFORMED	QUITE INFORMED	VERY WELL INFORMED
1	2	3	4	5

4. *Prior to the past six months,* to what *extent* has your unit had *effective working relationships* with this other unit?

NO PRIOR CONTACT	TO NO EXTENT	LITTLE EXTENT	SOME EXTENT	CONSID-ERABLE EXTENT	GREAT EXTENT
0	1	2	3	4	5

5. During the past six months, *how much* was your unit involved with this other unit for *each* of the following *reasons:*

a. To receive or send *work or clients* (e.g., customers, raw materials, or work objects)?

b. To receive or send *resources* (money, personnel, equipment, office space)?

NOT AT ALL	A LITTLE	SOME-WHAT	QUITE A BIT	VERY MUCH
1	2	3	4	5

PLEASE CONTINUE TO ANSWER THE FOLLOWING QUESTIONS FOR EACH OF THE OTHER UNITS IN THE RIGHT COLUMNS, REMEMBERING TO USE THE SAME UNIT NUMBER AS THAT ON THE PREVIOUS PAGE.

	UNIT 1	UNIT 2	UNIT 3	UNIT 4	UNIT 5

c. To receive or send *technical assistance* (e.g., consultation or staff services in functional areas)?

d. To receive or send *information* for purposes of coordination, control, planning, or evaluation?

NOT AT ALL	A LITTLE	SOME-WHAT	QUITE A BIT	VERY MUCH
1	2	3	4	5

6. Consider now the *equality* of the give-and-take relationship with each unit. Compared to other units that you are involved with, *how fair* do you feel are the "*payoffs*" *to your unit* from this unit?

WE GET MUCH LESS THAN WE OUGHT	WE GET SOMEWHAT LESS THAN WE OUGHT	BALANCED	WE GET SOMEWHAT MORE THAN WE OUGHT	WE GET MUCH MORE THAN WE OUGHT
1	2	3	4	5

7. For this *other unit* to accomplish its goals and responsibilities, *how much does it need the services, resources, or support from your unit?*

NOT AT ALL	VERY LITTLE	SOME	QUITE A BIT	VERY MUCH
1	2	3	4	5

8. For *your unit* to accomplish its goals and responsibilities, *how much do you need the services, resources, or support from this other unit?* (Use scale for Question 7.)

	UNIT 1	UNIT 2	UNIT 3	UNIT 4	UNIT 5
9.	—	—	—	—	—
10.	—	—	—	—	—
11a.	—	—	—	—	—
11b.	—	—	—	—	—
12.	____%	____%	____%	____%	____%
13.	—	—	—	—	—

9. How much *say or influence* does this *other unit* have on the internal operations of your unit?

NONE	LITTLE	SOME	QUITE A BIT	VERY MUCH
1	2	3	4	5

10. How much *say or influence* does your unit have on the internal operations of this other unit? (Use scale for Question 9.)

11. To what *extent* have the *terms of the relationship* between your unit and this other unit:
   a. Been explicitly *verbalized or discussed?*
   b. Been *written down in detail?*

TO NO EXTENT	LITTLE EXTENT	SOME EXTENT	CONSIDERABLE EXTENT	GREAT EXTENT
1	2	3	4	5

12. During the past six months, what *percent of your total working hours* did you spend on matters directly related to the operations, work, or activities of this other unit? —Indicate percent.

13. During the past six months, *how frequently* have people in your unit *communicated or been in contact with* people in this other unit?

NOT ONCE	1–2 TIMES	ABOUT MONTHLY	ABOUT EVERY 2 WEEKS	ABOUT WEEKLY	ABOUT DAILY	MANY TIMES DAILY
0	1	2	3	4	5	6

505

	UNIT 1	UNIT 2	UNIT 3	UNIT 4	UNIT 5

14. When you want to communicate with individuals in this unit, how much *difficulty* have you had *getting in touch* with them?

NO CONTACT	NONE	LITTLE	SOME	QUITE A BIT	VERY MUCH
0	1	2	3	4	5

15. Overall, how much *difficulty* do you experience in *getting ideas clearly across* to individuals in this other unit when you communicate with them? (Use scale for Question 14.)

16. During the past six months, *how often* were there *disagreements or disputes* between people in your unit and this other unit?

NOT ONCE	ABOUT ONCE A MONTH	ABOUT EVERY 2 WEEKS	ABOUT ONCE A WEEK	SEVERAL TIMES A WEEK	EVERY DAY
	1	2	3	4	5	6

17. To what extent did individuals in this other unit *hinder* your unit in performing its functions during the past six months?

DON'T KNOW	TO NO EXTENT	LITTLE EXTENT	SOME EXTENT	CONSIDERABLE EXTENT	GREAT EXTENT
0	1	2	3	4	5

18. How well are any differences worked out at this time between your unit and this other unit?

VERY POORLY	POORLY	ADEQUATELY	QUITE WELL	VERY WELL
1	2	3	4	5

	UNIT 1	UNIT 2	UNIT 3	UNIT 4	UNIT 5
19. Overall, *how important* was this other unit *in attaining the goals of your unit* during the past six months?	—	—	—	—	—

NOT VERY   SOMEWHAT   QUITE   VERY   ABSOLUTELY
IMPORTANT   IMPORTANT   IMPORTANT   IMPORTANT   CRUCIAL

   1   2   3   4   5

FINALLY PLEASE ANSWER THE FOLLOWING QUESTIONS USING THE SCALE FOLLOWING QUESTION 26.

	UNIT 1	UNIT 2	UNIT 3	UNIT 4	UNIT 5
20. To what extent has *this unit* carried out its responsibilities and commitments in regard to your unit during the past six months?	—	—	—	—	—
21. To what extent has *your unit* carried out your responsibilities and commitments in regard to this other unit during the past six months?	—	—	—	—	—
22. To what extent do you feel the *relationship* between your unit and this other unit is *productive?*	—	—	—	—	—
23. To what extent is the *time and effort spent* in developing and maintaining the relationship with this other unit *worthwhile?*	—	—	—	—	—
24. Overall, to what extent are you *satisfied with the relationship* between your unit and this other unit during the past six months?	—	—	—	—	—
25. During the past six months, to what extent has *your unit changed or influenced* the services or operations of *this other unit?*	—	—	—	—	—
26. During the past six months, to what extent has *this other unit changed or influenced* the services or operations of *your unit?*	—	—	—	—	—

TO NO   LITTLE   SOME   CONSID-   GREAT
                                    ERABLE
EXTENT   EXTENT   EXTENT   EXTENT   EXTENT

   1   2   3   4   5

Thank you very much for completing this questionnaire.
Please insert this questionnaire in the self-addressed and stamped envelope and drop it in a mail box.

507

Computing
Structural Indices of
Interunit Networks

As discussed in Chapter 9, a social network approach is used in the revised OA Framework to assess interunit relationships both within and between organizations. An interunit network is defined as the total pattern of relationships among a cluster of organizational units that are meshed together as a social system to attain collective and self-interest goals. Chapter 8 suggested that various structural characteristics of networks can be obtained from patterns of resource and information flows between organizational units. This technical appendix describes specific procedures for developing indices of the intensity, centrality, and complexity of an interunit network from data collected with the OAI Focal and Other Unit Questionnaires.

Network analysis has been used extensively as a method to study communication patterns in small groups by social psychologists (Bavelas, 1948; Leavitt, 1951; Glanzer and Glaser, 1959, 1961; Shaw, 1964), to study kinship and community ties by anthropologists (Mitchell, 1969; Boissevain, 1974), and opinion leadership and diffusion of innovations by sociologists (Coleman, 1961; Rogers and Schoemaker, 1971). Only recently has network analysis been suggested as a method for examining emergent social structure in organizations as distinct from formal structures displayed in organization charts (Kadushin, 1975; Tichy and Fombrun, 1978; Aldrich, 1979).

With network analysis a system of pairwise interunit relationships can be represented in the form of a graph consisting of a set of nodes (or circles which represent organizational units) and lines (or arcs which represent some form of linkage between the nodes). In the OAI linkages

508

are primarily examined in terms of various characteristics of resource and information flows between the nodes. Depending upon the values taken on by the lines, the graph is either a diagraph (Figure F-1) or a network (Figure F-2). Both diagraphs and networks can be cast in the form of matrices and the operations of matrix algebra applied to them. Harary et al. (1965) and Barnes (1969) present a good introduction and review of graph theory and matrix algebra as it applies to social network analysis. The basic characteristics of diagraphs and networks are reviewed briefly before actually suggesting how indices of the intensity, centrality, and complexity of networks can be computed from them.

DIAGRAPH REPRESENTATION OF AN INTERUNIT SYSTEM

The graph is generally called a *diagraph* when the presence or absence of a line connecting any two nodes represents the existence or nonexistence of a relationship, respectively, between two units; the arrows represent the directions of the linkages. Corresponding to the diagraph in Figure F-1 is an adjacency matrix with cells a_{ij}, which summarizes the interrelations among organizational units. By convention the subscripts i and j identify the respective row and column of the matrix cell entry. If a given relationship exists between units i and j, then the matrix cell contains a "1," and "0" if no relationship exists. If unit i sends a message to unit j, then the a_{ij} cell contains a "1," and if unit j sends a message to unit i then the a_{ji} cell contains a "1." The treatment of the diagonal a_{kk} depends on the purposes of the investigator. In most cases, zeros will be entered in the diagonal. By following these procedures, one obtains a square nonsymmetrical matrix of 0s and 1s which mathematically summarize the interunit relationships in the diagraph. If directionality between unit links is not measured or specified, then one obtains a symmetric matrix with identical entries below and above the diagonal.

The adjacency matrix obtained from a diagraph simply notes the presence or absence of a link between units and the direction of existing relationships. Although such a socio-matrix is useful for answering some basic questions on the connectedness of a system, it is not an accurate representation of the actual patterns of resource or information flows between units unless all possible channels are used equally. Although most of the work on graph theory has been developed for diagraphs (e.g., Harary et al., 1965), it provides insufficient information for detailed analysis of interunit relations because linkages are presented in all-or-nothing terms. The design of most evaluations of interunit net-

DIAGRAPH COMMUNICATION MATRIX

Receiving Unit

S e n d i n g U n i t		U1	U2	U3	U4	U5	U6	Total Sent
	U1	0	1	1	1	1	0	4
	U2	1	0	0	1	0	0	2
	U3	1	0	0	0	0	0	1
	U4	1	1	0	0	1	1	4
	U5	1	0	0	1	0	1	3
	U6	0	0	0	0	0	0	0
Total Received		4	2	1	3	2	2	14

Whether or not communications were sent or received by units in past six months

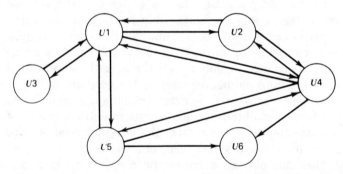

Figure F-1 Diagraph of communication flows in simple inter-unit system.

works clearly calls for constructing and analyzing valued graphs where the valuations of the lines are other than 0 or 1.

NETWORK REPRESENTATION OF INTERUNIT SYSTEM

A graph of an interunit cluster is formally called a *"network"* when numerical values are assigned to the lines of a diagraph and loops on

each unit node are permitted (Harary, Norman, and Cartwright, 1965:362). Loops are not examined here because they are not necessary for developing the indices of network structure following.

Just as for diagraphs, an adjacency matrix of a network can be developed to mathematically summarize the degrees of relationships among units in the system on any given dimension. For example, Figure F-2 presents a simple fictitious network of communication flows. The a_{ij}

NETWORK COMMUNICATION MATRIX (C)

Receiving Unit

		U1	U2	U3	U4	U5	U6	Total Sent
S e n d i n g	U1	0	3	3	5	12	0	23
	U2	2	0	0	10	0	0	12
	U3	2	0	0	0	0	0	2
U n i t	U4	2	6	0	0	2	3	13
	U5	6	0	0	4	0	1	11
	U6	0	0	0	0	0	0	0
Total Received		12	9	3	19	14	4	61

Number of times communications were sent and received by units in past six months

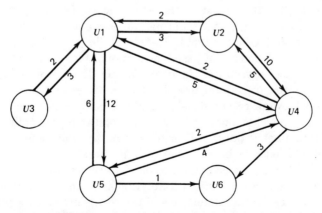

Figure F-2 Fictitious network of communication flows in a simple interunit system.

cells in the communication matrix represent the actual number of times that unit i sent messages to unit j during a six-month period. A summation of the cell values across columns shows the total number of messages each unit directly sent to other units (the far right margin of the communication matrix). The total number of messages each unit received from other units in the network is shown in the bottom margin of the matrix and is obtained by adding the cell values across rows. For the entire network the total number of messages sent and received is equal (61); this number is shown in the bottom row, last column margin of the matrix.

The matrix obtained from a network is the basic unit of observation for evaluating a system of interunit relationships. Because the cells of the matrix summarize all possible interrelations among units, the analyses of matrices provide a means for maintaining and reflecting *systemic* variations present in interunit networks. One can evaluate the data summarized in a matrix at the pairwise, set, or network levels to answer different questions about interunit relations. All the indices of network structure to be developed below can be computed directly from the matrix by relatively simple procedures. In addition, matrices permit many types of complex analyses with multidimensional scaling (Breiger et al., 1975) as well as matrix algebra operations of addition, subtraction, multiplication, and division (see Horst, 1963). For example, equations can be written for describing overall changes in network structure over time, as well as for tracing the long-run effect of each unit upon the others.

One of the major problems in analyzing matrix data is the relatively undeveloped statistical procedures for relating and comparing matrices representing different (1) dimensions, (2) interunit networks, and (3) time periods. To date, most of the available statistical techniques in sociometry for relating and comparing matrices only apply to diagraphs (see Glanzer and Glaser, 1959). Katz and Powell (1953) and Hohn (1953) have developed some basic correlational techniques for network matrices. These procedures involve pairing the corresponding cell entries or the row or column totals in two matrices and correlating the values found. More recent developments of canonical correlation and principal components analyses for metric data (or multidimensional scaling for nonmetric data) appear to hold much promise for examining statistical relationships between network matrices.

Until satisfactory procedures are found to relate complete matrices, our statistical analysis is limited to relating and comparing networks on composite scores for the dimensions of interest. These composite scores are obtained by adding or averaging the matrix cell entries or the row and column totals of the matrix constructed for a given dimension. The problem with such composite scores, of course, is that they are generally not sensitive to systemic variations present within networks. Given the existence of these problems, we now suggest some definitions and procedures for computing interunit network indices of intensity, centrality, and complexity.

NETWORK INTENSITY

Intensity is the strength of the network, as indicated by the total sum frequency of information flows and amount of resource flows in the network divided by the number of organizational units in the network. It could be computed as follows.

Let

C = a communication matrix with cell entries of the total number of times in the past six months that messages were sent and received by units in the network through written reports, telephone calls, face-to-face discussions and committee meetings

and

R = a resource flow matrix with cell entries of the total amount of resources in the past six months that were sent or received by units in the network in terms of money, work, personnel, client referrals, or technical services

Then the

$$\text{Intensity matrix} = C + R$$

A standardized index of network intensity is obtained by adding the marginal row or column totals of the intensity matrix and dividing by the number of units in the intensity matrix.

NETWORK CENTRALITY

Centrality refers to the degree to which information and resource flows in a network are centered on one or a few organizational units. Mackenzie (1966) has developed a centrality index that appears useful for computing network centrality from an incidence matrix of actual communications or resource flows between units.

The procedure begins with the intensity matrix as developed previously to obtain an overall index of network centrality. However, for simplicity we begin with the communication frequency matrix C in Figure F-2 and develop an index of communication centrality for that network. It will be shown that useful measures of unit role, dominance, and centrality can also be obtained as intermediate by-products of developing the network centrality index.

From the matrix C (in Figure F-2) one computes a normalized incidence matrix Q whose cell entries q_{ij} are the total number of messages sent by unit i to unit j divided by the total information flows in the entire network (61). Figure F-3 shows the normalized incidence matrix Q for C. The matrix Q gives dimensionless entries that vary in size with the intensity of communications between the $n(n - 1)$ possible lines (where n is the number of units in the matrix). By virtue of being dimensionless, incidence matrices of the same number of units—but sending different numbers of messages—can be compared.

To develop the centrality index from the incidence matrix, Mackenzie defines a homogeneous matrix and computes an absolute difference matrix by subtracting the homogeneous matrix from the incidence matrix. A *homogenous* matrix is a totally decentralized network with all equal cell entries (except for the diagonal entries, which are zero). A complete network of n units is homogeneous if every q_{ij} cell equals $1/n \, (n - 1)$. The degree of centrality of an actual incidence matrix can be obtained by examining the degree to which it deviates from a totally decentralized or homogeneous matrix. Thus, in Figure F-3 the abolute difference matrix $|\Delta Q|$ is computed by subtracting $1/n \, (n - 1) = .03$ from each q_{ij} entry in the incidence matrix. (Absolute differences are used so that the terms will not cancel each other out under summation.)

In developing the centrality index, Mackenzie also weights the total row and column marginals from the incidence matrix to obtain a ranking of the units by their *communication dominance* in terms of sending and receiving messages. That is, the dominance of a unit D_i equals $(q_r + q_c)/2$.

D_i distinguishes between different network structures of the same number of units, but is not suitable for detecting differences among the matrix entries since each is formed by averaging the corresponding row and column sums of the incidence matrix. On the other hand, the difference matrix ΔQ is very useful in pointing out differences between the incidence matrix and the totally decentralized homogeneous matrix.

However, the sum of all the terms of $|\Delta Q|$ is identical for homogeneous networks of the same number of communication channels.

Therefore, Mackenzie derives the centrality index of a network by weighting the average of the row and column marginals of Q by D_i and

multiplying by a normalizing parameter $a(n) = \dfrac{4n\,(n-1)}{n^2 - 4}$. The result is

a more sensitive measure of the structural centrality of a network $C(N)$. Figure F-3 shows the computations for obtaining the structural centrality of each unit $C(U_i)$

(1) $C(U_i) = a(n)\,D_1\,\dfrac{|\Delta q_r| + |\Delta q_c|}{2}$

as well as the centrality of the network $C(N)$

(2) $C(N) = \displaystyle\sum_{i=1}^{n} C(U_i)$

Mackenzie computed centrality indices for 336 matrices and reports that equations (1) and (2) were found to be sensitive indicators of structural centrality in communication networks. The centrality index ranges from approximately .00 (value for the totally decentralized, homogeneous, all-channel network) to 1.00, which reflects a very centralized wheel communication structure.

A question often raised in the evaluation of interunit networks is what roles different units perform in the system—specifically, which units perform the predominant roles of sending, connecting, or receiving communications or resources among the units. These roles, of course, vary in degrees. However, one can quantify the predominant role performed by each unit by computing the ratio of outflows to inflows from the row and column marginals of the incidence matrix; that is, $r = q_{ri}/q_{ci}$. The result is a directly interpetable index of the extent to which a unit is a sender ($r > 1$), connector (r approximates 1), or receiver ($r < 1$). For example, unit 1 in Figure F-3 ($r = 2$) sends twice as many messages as it receives from network units. On the other hand, unit 3 ($r = .60$) could be classified as a receiver because it receives about 5 messages for every 3 it sends out.

NETWORK COMPLEXITY

Complexity refers to the number of different elements that must be contended with and integrated in order for the network to act as a unit.

Figure F-2 Communication Matrix C

	U1	U2	U3	U4	U5	U6	Total Sent
U1	0	3	3	5	12	0	23
U2	2	0	0	10	0	0	12
U3	2	0	0	0	0	0	2
U4	2	6	0	0	2	3	13
U5	6	0	0	4	0	1	11
U6	0	0	0	0	0	0	0
Total Received	12	9	3	19	14	4	61

Normalized Incidence Matrix Q with cells $a_{ij}/61$

	U1	U2	U3	U4	U5	U6	q_r
U1	0	.05	.05	.08	.20	.00	.38
U2	.03	0	.00	.16	.00	.00	.19
U3	.03	.00	0	.00	.00	.00	.03
U4	.03	.10	.00	0	.03	.05	.21
U5	.10	.00	.00	.07	0	.02	.19
U6	.00	.00	.00	.00	.00	0	.00
q_c	.19	.15	.05	.31	.23	.07	1.00

Absolute Difference Matrix $|\Delta Q|$ with cells $|q_{ij} - 1/n(n-1)| = |q_{ij} - .03|$

	U1	U2	U3	U4	U5	U6	Uq_r
U1	0	.02	.02	.05	.17	.03	.29
U2	.00	0	.03	.13	.03	.03	.22
U3	.00	.03	0	.03	.03	.03	.12
U4	.00	.07	.03	0	.00	.02	.12
U5	.07	.03	.03	.04	0	.01	.18
U6	.03	.03	.03	.03	.03	0	.15
Δq_c	.10	.18	.14	.28	.26	.12	.12

	Unit Role (r) $\dfrac{q_{ri}}{q_{ci}}$ $\begin{cases} >1 \text{ Sender} \\ \approx 1 \text{ Connect.} \\ <1 \text{ Receiver} \end{cases}$	Unit Dominance (Di) $Di = \dfrac{Qr + Qc}{2}$	Unit Centrality $C(Ui)$ $C(Ui) = 3.75\,Di\left(\dfrac{|\Delta Qr| + |\Delta Qc|}{2}\right)$
$U1$	$\dfrac{.38}{.19} = 2.0$ Sender	$\dfrac{.38 + .19}{2} = .29$	$3.75\,(.29)\left(\dfrac{(.10 + .29)}{2}\right) = .21$
$U2$	$\dfrac{.19}{.15} = 1.27$ Sender	$\dfrac{.19 + .15}{2} = .17$	$3.75\,(.17)\left(\dfrac{(.18 + .22)}{2}\right) = .13$
$U3$	$\dfrac{.03}{.05} = .60$ Receiver	$\dfrac{.03 + .05}{2} = .04$	$3.75\,(.04)\left(\dfrac{(.14 + .12)}{2}\right) = .02$
$U4$	$\dfrac{.21}{.31} = .68$ Receiver	$\dfrac{.21 + .31}{2} = .26$	$3.75\,(.04)\left(\dfrac{(.29 + .12)}{2}\right) = .20$
$U5$	$\dfrac{.19}{.31} = .61$ Receiver	$\dfrac{.19 + .23}{2} = .21$	$3.75\,(.04)\left(\dfrac{(.26 + .18)}{2}\right) = .17$
$U6$	$\dfrac{.00}{.07} =$ Receiver	$\dfrac{.00 + .07}{2} = .04$	$3.75\,(.04)\left(\dfrac{(.12 + .15)}{2}\right) = .02$

Centrality of Network $C(N) = n\,C(Ui)$ .75

Figure F-3   Computation of communication centrality index for Figure F-2 network.

517

ADJACENCY MATRIX

	U1	U2	U3	U4	U5	U6	Total Sent
U1	0	1	1	1	1	0	4
U2	1	0	0	1	0	0	2
U3	1	0	0	0	0	0	1
U4	1	1	0	0	1	1	4
U5	1	0	0	1	0	1	3
U6	0	0	0	0	0	0	0
Total Rec'd	4	2	1	3	2	2	14

SUBSYSTEM OR CLIQUE

(Largest set of reciprocally connected units)

Cliques:
(U1, U2, U4)
(U1, U4, U5)
(U1, U3)
Peripheral Units
U6

A. *SEMI-ANNUAL CONTACTS DIAGRAPH*

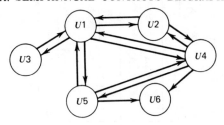

	U1	U2	U3	U4	U5	U6	Total Sent
U1	0	1	1	1	1	0	4
U2	1	0	0	1	0	0	2
U3	0	0	0	0	0	0	0
U4	1	1	0	0	1	0	3
U5	1	0	0	1	0	0	2
U6	0	0	0	0	0	0	0
Total Rec'd	3	2	1	3	2	0	11

Cliques:
(U1, U2, U4)
(U1, U4, U5)
Peripheral Units
U3, U6

B. *QUARTERLY CONTACTS DIAGRAPH*

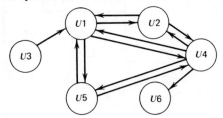

Figure F-4 Decomposition of Figure F-2 communication networks into diagraph levels.

518

	$U1$	$U2$	$U3$	$U4$	$U5$	$U6$	Total Sent
$U1$	0	0	0	1	1	0	2
$U2$	0	0	0	1	0	0	1
$U3$	0	0	0	0	0	0	0
$U4$	0	1	0	0	0	0	1
$U5$	1	0	0	1	0	0	2
$U6$	0	0	0	0	0	0	0
Total Rec'd	1	1	0	3	1	0	6

Cliques:
 ($U1$, $U5$)
 ($U2$, $U4$)
Peripheral Units
 $U4$ is peripheral to
 ($U1$, $U5$)
Isolated Units
 $U3$, $U6$

C. *BI-MONTHLY CONTACTS DIAGRAPH*

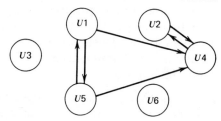

	$U1$	$U2$	$U3$	$U4$	$U5$	$U6$	Total Sent
$U1$	0	0	0	0	1	0	1
$U2$	0	0	0	1	0	0	1
$U3$	0	0	0	0	0	0	0
$U4$	0	1	0	0	0	0	1
$U5$	1	0	0	0	0	0	1
$U6$	0	0	0	0	0	0	0
Total Rec'd	1	1	0	1	1	0	4

Cliques:
 ($U1$, $U5$)
 ($U2$, $U4$)
Isolated Units
 $U3$, $U6$
 ($U1$, $U5$) isolated
 from ($U2$, $U4$)

D. *MONTHLY CONTACTS DIAGRAPH*

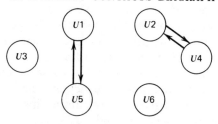

Figure F-4   (Continued)

Two indicators of complexity are (1) the number of different cliques, subgroups, or subsystems (used synonymously) in the network and (2) the number of different kinds of resources that are transacted between units in the network. The latter is computed by creating a matrix, with cell entries a_{ij}, which represents a simple count of the number of kinds of resources sent by unit i to unit j in the network.

A clique or subsystem is defined as the largest cluster of units within the network, each in reciprocal relation to one another. Doreian (1969) has developed a procedure for detecting subsystems within systems from a general theory of connectivity in valued graphs or networks. The procedure becomes somewhat involved, and computerized algorithms are available for detecting cliques within cliques for large networks. Here we are only concerned with demonstrating the basic idea and do so by calculating the number of cliques in the very small communication network shown in Figure F-2.

The procedure begins by decomposing a valued graph of communication frequencies into a set of nonvalued diagraphs representing successively higher levels of communication frequency. For example, the communication frequencies in Figure F-2 can be classified into the following levels:

Semi-annual Contacts = at least 1 or more messages in past 6 months
Quarterly Contacts   = at least 2 or more messages in past 6 months
Bi-Monthly Contacts = at least 4 or more messages in past 6 months
Monthly Contacts   = at least 6 or more messages in past 6 months

For each of these levels of communication intensity, a diagraph and corresponding adjacency matrix can be constructed by including only those lines (arcs) which satisfy the internal restrictions. Such a set of diagraphs and adjacency matrices are shown in Figure F-4.

Harary and Ross (1957) have developed an algorithm for detecting cliques from the adjacency matrix. By applying the computerized algorithm on successive levels of the communication diagraphs, subsystems within systems will be revealed. As higher levels of communication frequency are considered, the lines with low values are eliminated, and as the lines in the graph become fewer, the cliques or subsystems in general become smaller. Thus, what at a low level of communication frequency is a large cluster of reciprocal relationships is gradually reduced by eliminating peripheral units until finally the network core is obtained.

Unit cliques within each of the simple communication diagraphs in Figure F-4 can be visually determined by identifying the largest sets of reciprocally connected units. At the lowest level three cliques exist in the semi-annual contacts diagraph ($U1$, $U2$, $U4$), ($U1$, $U4$, $U5$), and ($U1$, $U3$). $U6$ is peripherally connected because although $U4$ and $U5$ send messages to $U6$, it does not reciprocate by communicating back to $U4$ and $U5$.

At the level of quarterly communications, there are two cliques ($U1$, $U2$, $U4$) and ($U1$, $U4$, $U5$), and $U3$ has become a peripheral unit to the network along with $U6$. $U1$ and $U4$ overlap in the two cliques at this level. If there were a mutual exchange of communications between $U5$ and $U2$, the two cliques would fold into one four-unit subsystem.

When the procedure is repeated at the third level of bi-monthly communications, the two cliques reduce to $(U1, U5)$ and $(U2, U4)$. In addition, $U4$ has become peripheral to the $(U1, U5)$ clique, whereas $U3$ and $U6$ have become isolates.

The significance of $U4$ being peripheral to the $(U1, U5)$ clique is that communications in this subsystem can reach the $(U2, U4)$ clique on a bi-monthly basis. However, at this level messages are not transmitted from the $(U2, U4)$ subsystem to the $(U1, U5)$ clique. Thus, the $(U1, U5)$ subsystem is a sender, whereas the $(U2, U4)$ clique is a receiver, and $U4$ is the pivotal connector.

If one wished to introduce a new idea to as many units in the system as possible by planting it with only one unit, then either $U1$ or $U5$ would be an appropriate unit to contact. Since $U3$ and $U6$ are isolated from bi-monthly communications but peripheral to quarterly communications from other units in the system (level 2), $U3$ and $U6$ will be last to learn of the new idea.

At the most frequent level of monthly contacts between units, $(U1, U5)$ and $(U2, U4)$ cliques remain, but now they are isolated individually. $(U1, U5)$ and $(U2, U4)$ constitute the core subsystems within the network, and on a monthly basis they communicate independently of one another.

Thus, the technique appears useful for clearly revealing subsystems within systems of interunit networks. When the procedure is applied to networks of resource flows as well as information flows, it provides a heuristic procedure for identifying differentiated subgroupings of patterned activities in an interunit network. The complexity of a network, then, is determined by counting the number of subsystems of resource flows and information flows at each level of activity.

Bibliography

Aiken, Michael, and Jerald Hage
1968 "Organizational Interdependence and Intra-Organizational Structure," *American Sociological Review*, 3: 912–30 (December).

Aldrich, Howard
1972 "An Organization-Environment Perspective on Cooperation and Conflict between Organizations in the Manpower Training System," Paper presented at Comparative Administration Research Institute Conference, Kent State University.

1974 "The Environment as a Network of Organizations, "Paper presented at the International Sociological Association Conference, Toronto (August).

1979 *Organizations and Environments*, Englewood Cliffs, N.J.: Prentice Hall.

American Psychological Association
1974 *Standards for Educational and Psychological Tests*, Washington, D.C.: American Psychological Association, Inc.

Argyris, Chris
1957 *Personality and Organization*, New York: Harper and Row.

1964 *Integrating the Individual and the Organization*, New York: Wiley.

1968 "Some Unintended Consequences of Rigorous Research," *Psychological Bulletin*, 70, 3: 185–197.

Bachman, Jerald G., Clagett G. Smith, and Jonathan A. Slesinger
1966 "Control, Performance, and Satisfaction: An Analysis of Structural and Individual Effects," *Journal of Personality and Social Psychology*, 4, 2: 127–36.

Bakke, E. Wight
1950 *Bonds of Organization*, New York: Harper and Row.

1959 "Concept of the Social Organization," in M. Haire, (ed.), *Modern Organization Theory*, New York: Chapman and Hall.

Bales, R. F., and F. L. Strodtbeck
1967 "Phases in Group Problem Solving," in M. Alexis and C. Wilson (eds.), *Organizational Decision Making*, Englewood Cliffs, N.J.: Prentice-Hall, pp. 122–133.

Barnard, Chester R.
1938 *The Functions of the Executive*, Cambridge, Mass.: Harvard University Press.

Barnes, J. A.
1969 "Graph Theory and Social Networks: A Technical Comment on Connectedness and Connectivity," *Sociology*, 3: 215–32 (May).

522

Bass, B.
1971 "When Planning For Others," *Journal of Applied Behavioral Science*, **6**: 151–72 (April/June).

Baumol, William J.
1965 *Economic Theory and Operations Analysis*, 2nd edition, Englewood Cliffs, N.J.: Prentice-Hall.

Bavelas, A.
1948 "Some Problems of Organizational Change," *Journal of Social Issues*, **3**: 48–52.

Beckhard, R.
1969 *Organization Development: Strategies and Models*, Reading, Mass.: Addison-Wesley.

Beer, S.
1966 *Decision and Control: The Meaning of Organizational Research and Management Cybernetics*. New York: Wiley.

Bell, Gerald
1967 "Formality Versus Flexibility in Complex Organizations," in *Organizations and Human Behavior: A Book of Readings*, Englewood Cliffs, N.J.: Prentice-Hall, pp. 97–106.

Bendix, A. W.
1954 "Reliability and the Number of Rating Scale Categories," *Journal of Applied Psychology*, **38**: 38–40.

Bennis, Warren G., K. D. Benne, and R. Chin
1962 *The Planning of Change*, New York: Holt, Rinehart, and Winston.

Berger, Chris J., and L. L. Cummings
1979 "Organizational Structure, Attitudes, and Behaviors," in Barry M. Staw (ed.), *Research in Organizational Behavior*, Volume 1, Greenwich, CT.: JAI Press, pp. 169–208.

Beyer, Janice M. and Harrison M. Trice
1979 "A Reexamination of the Relations Between Size and Various Components of Organizational Complexity," *Administrative Science Quarterly*, **24**, 1: 48–64 (March).

Blake, Richard R., and Jane S. Mouton
1964 *The Managerial Grid*, Houston, Texas: Gulf Publishing Co.
1969 *Building A Dynamic Corporation Through Grid Organization Development*, Reading, Mass.: Addison-Wesley.

Blau, Peter M.
1974 *On the Nature of Organizations*, New York: Wiley.

Blau, Peter M., Cecilia McHugh Falbe, William McKinley and Phelps K. Tracy
1976 "Technology and Organization in Manufacturing," *Administrative Science Quarterly*, **21**, 1: 20–40.

Blau, Peter M., and Richard H. Schoenherr
1971 *The Structure of Organizations*, New York: Basic Books.

Blau, Peter M., and W. Richard Scott
1962 *Formal Organizations: A Comparative Approach*, San Francisco, Calif.: Chandler.

Blood, M. R., and C. L. Hulin
1967 "Alienation, Environmental Characteristics, and Worker Responses," *Journal of Applied Psychology*, **51**: 281–290.

Boissevain, Jeremy
1974 *Friends of Friends*, New York: St. Martin's.

Borgatta, Edgar F., and G. W. Bohrnstedt
1970 *Sociological Methodology*, San Francisco, Calif.: Jossey-Bass.

Bouchard, Thomas J., Jr.
1976 "Field Research Methods: Interviewing, Questionnaires, Participant Observation, Systematic Observation, Unobtrusive Measures[1,2]," in Marvin D. Dunnette (ed.), *Handbook of Industrial and Organizational Psychology*, Chicago, Ill.: Rand-McNally.

Breiger, R. L., S. A. Boorman, and P. Arabie
1975 "An Algorithm For Clustering Relational Data, With Applications to Social Network Analysis and Comparison with Multidimensional Scaling," *Journal of Mathematical Psychology*, **12**: 328–83 (August).

Brief, Arthur P., and Ramon J. Aldag
1975 "Employee Reactions to Job Characteristics: A Constructive Replication," *Journal of Applied Psychology*, **60**, 2: 182–86 (April).

Burke, Edmund M.
1965 "The Road to Planning: An Organizational Analysis," *Social Service Review*, **39**, 3: 261–270.

Burke, Ronald J.
1970 "Method of Resolving Superior–Subordinate Conflict: The Constructive Use of Subordinate Differences and Disagreements," *Organizational Behavior and Human Performance*, **5**, 4:393–411.

Campbell, Donald T., and J. C. Stanley
1963 *Experimental and Quasi-Experimental Designs for Research*, Chicago, Ill.: Rand-McNally.

Campbell, John P.
1976 "Psychometric Theory," in Marvin D. Dunnette (ed.), *Handbook of Industrial and Organizational Psychology*, Chicago, Ill.: Rand-McNally.

1977 "On the Nature of Organizational Effectiveness," in Paul S. Goodman, Johannes M. Pennings, and Associates (eds.), *New Perspectives on Organizational Effectiveness*, San Francisco, Calif.: Jossey-Bass, pp. 13–15.

Caplow, Theodore
1964 *Principles of Organization*, New York: Harcourt, Brace. pp. 201–28.

Champney, Horace
1941 "The Measurement of Parent Behavior," *Child Development*, **12**: 131–66.

Champney, Horace, and Helen Marshall
1939 "Optimal Refinement of the Rating Scale," *Journal of Applied Psychology*, **23**: 323–31 (June).

Chandler, Alfred
1962 *Strategy and Structure*. Garden City, N.Y.: Anchor Books.

Child, John
1972 "Organizational Structure, Environment and Performance: The Role of Strategic Choice," *Sociology*, **6**: 1–22.

1973 "Predicting and Understanding Organization Structure," *Administrative Science Quarterly*, **18**: 168–85 (June).

Clark, A. W. (ed.)
1976 *Experimenting With Organizational Life: The Action Research Approach*, New York: Plenum.

Clark, Burton
1965 "Interorganizational Patterns in Education," *Administrative Science Quarterly*, **10**: 224–37 (September).

Clark, Peter, and James Wilson
1961 "Incentive Systems: A Theory of Organizations," *Administrative Science Quarterly*, **6**: 129–166 (September).

Clark, Terry
1968 "Community Structure, Decision-Making, Budget Expenditures and Urban Renewal in 51 American Communities," *American Sociological Review*, **33**: 576–93 (August).

Coleman, James S.
1961 *The Adolescent Society*, New York: The Free Press.

Conklin, E. S.
1923 "The Scale of Values Method for Studies in Genetic Psychology," University of Oregon Publication 2.

Cronbach, Lee J.
1951 "Coefficient Alpha and the Internal Structure of Tests," *Psychometrika*, **16**: 297–334.

Cronbach, L. J., and G. Gleser
1965 *Psychological Tests and Personnel Decisions*, 2nd edition, Urbana: University of Illinois Press.

Cronbach, L. J., G. Gleser, H. Nanda, and N. Rajaratnam
1972 *The Dependability of Behavioral Measurements: Theory of Generalizability for Scores and Profiles*, New York: Wiley.

Crozier, Michael
1964 *The Bureaucratic Phenomenon*, Chicago, Ill.: University of Chicago Press.

Cummings, L. L., and D. Schwab
1973 *Organizational Effectiveness*, Glenview, Ill.: Scott-Foresman.

Dale, Ernest
1965 *Management: Theory and Practice*, New York: McGraw-Hill.

Dalton, M.
1959 *Men Who Manage*, New York: Wiley.

Davis, Keith
1968 "Success of Chain-of-Command Oral Communication in a Manufacturing Management Group," *Academy of Management Journal*, **11, 4**: 379–87 (December).

Davis, Louis E., and Eric L. Trist
1972 "Improving the Quality of Work Life: Experience of the Socio-Technical Approach," H.E.W. paper (June).

Davis, Stanley M., and Paul R. Lawrence
1977 *Matrix*, Reading, Mass.: Addison-Wesley.

Dearborn, D. C., and Herbert A. Simon
1958 "Selective Perception: A Note on the Departmental Identification of Executives," *Sociometry*, **21**: 140–44.

Delbecq, Andre L., and Alan C. Filley
1974 "Program and Project Management in a Matrix Organization: A Case Study," Madison: Bureau of Business Research, Graduate School of Business, University of Wisconsin.

Delbecq, Andre L., and Andrew H. Van de Ven
1971 "A Group Process Model for Problem Identification and Program Planning," *Journal of Applied Behavioral Sciences*, **7**: 466–92 (September).

Delbecq, Andre L., Andrew H. Van de Ven, and D. H. Gustafson
1975 *Group Techniques for Program Planning*, Glenview, Ill.: Scott-Foresman.

Dill, William R.
1958 "Environment as an Influence on Managerial Autonomy," *Administrative Science Quarterly*, **2**, 4: 409–43 (March).

Doreian, Patrick
1969 "A Note on the Detection of Cliques in Valued Graphs," *Sociometry*, **32**, 2: 237–42 (June).

Drucker, Peter F.
1978 "The Real Duties of a Director," *The Wall Street Journal* (June 1).

Duncan, Robert B.
1972 "Characteristics of Organizational Environments and Perceived Environmental Uncertainty," *Administrative Science Quarterly*, **17**, 3: 313–27 (September).

Dunham, Randall B., Ramon J. Aldag, and Arthur P. Brief
1976 "Dimensionality of Task Design as Measured by the Job Diagnostic Survey," *Proceedings*, Annual Academy of Management Meeting, Kansas City, pp. 89–93.

Dunham, Randall B. and Frank J. Smith
1979 *Organizational Surveys: An Internal Assessment of Organizational Health*, Glenview, Illinois: Scott, Foresman.

Dunnette, Marvin D.
1976 *Handbook of Industrial and Organizational Psychology*, Chicago, Ill.: Rand-McNally.

Durkheim, Emile
1947 *The Division of Labor in Society*, trans. George Simpson, Glencoe, Ill: Free Press.

Emery, F. E., and Eric L. Trist
1960 "Socio-Technical System," in C. W. Churchman and M. Verhulst (eds.), *Management Science, Models, and Techniques*, Vol. 2, Pergamon, pp. 82–97.

Emery, F. E., and Eric L. Trist
1965 "The Causal Texture of Organizational Environments," Paper-presented at the 17th International Congress of Psychology, Washington, D.C. (August).

Etzioni, Amitai
1961 *A Comparative Analysis of Complex Organizations*, New York: Free Press of Glencoe.

Evan, William M.
1963 "Indices of Hierarchical Structure of Industrial Organizations," *Management Science*, **9**, 3: 468–77.
1966 "The Organization Set: Toward a Theory of Inter-Organizational Relations," in James D. Thompson (ed.), *Approaches to Organizational Design*, Pittsburgh, Penn.: University of Pittsburgh Press.

Fayol, Henri
1949 *General and Industrial Management*, Translated by Constance Storrs, London: Pittman.

Feldman, J., and H. E. Kanter
1965 "Organizational Decision Making," in J. G. March (ed.), *Handbook of Organizations*, Chicago, Ill.: Rand-McNally.

Ferguson, L. W.
1941 "A Study of the Likert Technique of Attitude Scale Construction," *Journal of Social Psychology*, **13**: 51–57.

Ferry, Diane L.
1979 *A Test of a Task Contingent Model of Unit Structure and Efficiency*, Philadelphia: The Wharton School, University of Pennsylvania, Unpublished doctoral dissertation.

Filley, Allen C., Robert J. House, and Steven Kerr
1976 *Managerial Process and Organizational Behavior*, 2nd edition, Glenview, Ill.: Scott-Foresman.

French, J. R. P., Jr., and B. Raven
1959 "The Bases of Social Power," in D. Cartwright (ed.), *Studies in Social Power*, Ann Arbor: University of Michigan Institute for Social Research, pp. 150–67.

Friedmann, John
1973 *Retracking America*, Garden City, N.Y.: Doubleday.

Galbraith, Jay R.
1971 "Matrix Organization Designs: How to Combine Functional and Project Forms," *Business Horizons*, **14**: 29–40.
1977 *Organization Design*, Reading, Mass.: Addison-Wesley.

Galbraith, Jay R., and Daniel A. Nathanson
1978 *Strategy Implementation: The Role of Structure and Process*, St. Paul: West Publishing Company.

Galtung, Johan
1967 *Theory and Methods of Social Research*, New York: Columbia University Press.

Georgopoulous, Basil S. and Floyd C. Mann
1962 *The Community General Hospital*. New York: Macmillan.

Ghiselli, E. E.
1973 "The Validity of Aptitude Tests in Personnel Selection," *Personnel Psychology*, **26**: 461–77.

Ghiselli, E. E., and C. W. Brown
1955 *Personnel and Industrial Psychology*, New York: McGraw-Hill.

Gilbert, Neil
1969 "Neighborhood Coordinator: Advocate or Middleman?", *Social Service Review*, **43**, 3: 136–44 (June).

Glanzer, Murray, and Robert Glaser
1959 "Techniques for the Study of Group Structure and Behavior: I. Analysis of a Structure," *Psychological Bulletin*, **56**, 5: 317–31 (September).
1961 "Techniques for the Study of Group Structure and Behavior: II. Empirical Studies of the Effects of Structure in Small Groups," *Psychological Bulletin*, **58**, 1: 1–27 (January).

Gorsuch, Richard L.
1974 *Factor Analysis*, Philadelphia, Penn.: Saunders.

Gouldner, Alvin
1959 "Reciprocity and Autonomy in Functional Theory," in Llewellyn Gross (ed.), *Symposium on Sociological Theory*, pp. 241–70.

Gregson, Robert A. M.
1975 *Psychometrics of Similarity*, New York: Academic.

Grimes, Andrew J., Stuart M. Klein, and Fremont A. Shull, Jr.
1972 "Matrix Model: A Selective Empirical Test," *Academy of Management Journal*, **15**: 9–31.

Guetzkow, Harold
1966 "Relations Among Organizations," in R. V. Bowers (ed.), *Studies in Behavior in Organizations*, pp. 13–44.

Guilford, J. P.
1954 *Psychometric Methods*, 2nd edition, New York: McGraw-Hill.

Guion, Robert M.
1965 *Personnel Testing*, New York: McGraw-Hill.

Haberstroh, C. J.
1965 "Organization Design and Systems Analysis," in J. G. March (ed.), *Handbook of Organizations*, Chicago, Ill.: Rand-McNally.

Hackman, J. Richard
1976 "The Design of Self-Managing Work Groups," Technical Report No. 11, New Haven, Conn.: Yale University School of Organization and Management.

Hackman, J. Richard, and Edward E. Lawler
1971 *Employee Reactions to Job Characteristics, Journal of Applied Psychology* Monograph, **55**: 259–86 (June).

Hackman, J. Richard, and Greg R. Oldham
1974 "The Job Diagnostic Survey: An Instrument for the Diagnosis of Jobs and the Evaluation of Job Redesign Projects," Technical Report No. 4, Department of Administrative Sciences, Yale University (May).
1975 "Development of the Job Diagnostic Survey," *Journal of Applied Psychology*, **60**, 2: 159–70 (April).

Hackman, J. Richard, and J. Lloyd Suttle
1977 *Improving Life at Work: Behavioral Science Approaches to Organizational Change*, Santa Monica, Calif.: Goodyear.

Hage, Jerald
1965 "An Axiomatic Theory of Organizations," *Administrative Science Quarterly*, **10**: 289–320 (December).
1971 *Techniques and Problems of Theory Construction in Sociology*, New York: Wiley-Interscience.

Hage, Jerald, and Michael Aiken
1967 "Relationship of Centralization to Other Structural Properties," *Administrative Science Quarterly*, 12: 72–92 (June).
1969 "Routine Technology, Social Structure, and Organization Goals," *Administrative Science Quarterly*, 14: 366–76 (September).

Hage, Jerald, Michael Aiken, and Cora Bagley Marrett
1971 "Organization Structure and Communications," *American Sociological Review*, 36: 860–67 (October).

Hall, Douglas T., James G. Goodale, Samuel Rabinowitz, and Marilyn A. Morgan
1978 "Effects of Top–Down Departmental and Job Change Upon Perceived Employee Behavior and Attitudes: A Natural Field Experiment," *Journal of Applied Psychology*, 63, 1 (62–72).

Hall, Richard H.
1962 "Intraorganizational Structural Variation: Application of the Bureaucratic Model," *Administrative Science Quarterly*, 7: 295–308 (December).
1963 "The Concept of Bureaucracy: An Empirical Assessment," *American Journal of Sociology*, 69: 32–40 (July), note erratum in 69: 291 (November).
1972 *Organizations, Structure, and Process*, Englewood Cliffs, N.J.: Prentice-Hall.

Hall, Richard H., and John P. Clark
1973 "Problems in the Study of Inter-Organizational Relationship," in Anant R. Negandhi (ed.), *Modern Organizational Theory: Contextual, Environmental, and Socio-Cultural Variables*, Comparative Administration Research Institute, Center for Business and Economic Research, Kent State University, pp. 45–60.

Hall, Richard H., John P. Clark, Peggy C. Giordano, Paul V. Johnson, and Martha Van Roekel
1977 "Patterns of Interorganizational Relationships," *Administrative Science Quarterly*, 22, 3: 457–74 (September).

Hall, Richard H., J. Eugene Haas, and Norman J. Johnson
1967 "Organizational Size, Complexity, and Formalization," *American Sociological Review*, 32, 6: 903–911, (December).

Hannan, Michael T.
1970 "Problems of Aggregation and Disaggregation in Sociological Research," *Working Papers in Methodology, No. 4*, Chapel Hill, N.C.: Institute for Research in Social Science.

Hannan, Michael T., and J. Freeman
1977 "Obstacles to Comparative Studies," in Paul S. Goodman, Johannes M. Pennings, and Associates (eds.), *New Perspectives on Organizational Effectiveness*, San Francisco, Calif.: Jossey-Bass.

Harary, Frank, Robert Norman, and Dorwin Cartwright
1965 *Structural Models: An Introduction to the Theory of Directed Graphs*, New York: Wiley.

Harary, Frank, and I. C. Ross
1957 "A Procedure for Clique Detection Using the Group Matrix," *Sociometry*, **20:** 205-15 (September).

Harman, H.
1967 *Modern Factor Analysis*, 2nd edition, Chicago, Ill. University of Chicago Press.

Havelock, R. G.
1973 *Planning for Innovation Through Dissemination and Utilization of Knowledge*, Ann Arbor: Institute for Social Research, University of Michigan.

Helson, H.
1948 "Adaptation-Level as a Basis for a Quantitative Theory of Frames of Reference," *Psychological Review*, **55:** 297-313.

1964 "Current Trends and Issues in Adaptation-Level Theory," *American Psychologist*, **19:** 26-38.

Hemphill, J. K.
1950 "Relations Between the Size of the Group and the Behavior of 'Superior' Leaders," *Journal of Social Psychology*, **32:** 11-22 (August).

Henderson, James J., and Richard E. Quandt
1958 *Microeconomic Theory: A Mathematical Approach*, New York: McGraw-Hill.

Herzberg, F., B. Mausner, and B. Snyderman
1959 *The Motivation to Work*, New York: Wiley.

Hickson, David J., C. R. Hinings, C. A. Lee, R. E. Schneck, and J. M. Pennings
1971 "Strategic Contingencies Theory of Intraorganizational Power," *Administrative Sciences Quarterly*, **16:** 216-229 (June).

Hickson, David J., D. S. Pugh, and Diana C. Pheysey
1969 "Operations Technology and Organizational Structure: An Empirical Reappraisal," *Administrative Science Quarterly*, **14:** 370-97 (September).

Hofer, Charles W., and Dan Schendel
1978 *Strategy Formulation: Analytical Concepts*, St. Paul, Minn.: West Publishing.

Hohn, F. E.
1953 "Some Methods of Comparing Sociometric Matrices," Technical Report No. 5, Bureau of Research, University of Illinois, Urbana.

Homans, George C.
1950 *The Human Group*, New York: Harcourt, Brace, and World.

1961 *Social Behavior: Its Elementary Forms*, New York: Harcourt, Brace, and World.

Horst, Paul
1963 *Matrix Algebra for Social Scientists*, New York: Holt, Rinehart, and Winston.

House, Robert
1963 *A Predictive Theory of Management Development*, Ann Arbor: University of Michigan, Bureau of Industrial Relations.

Hrebiniak, Lawrence G.
1974 "Job Technology, Supervision, and Work-Group Structure," *Administrative Science Quarterly*, **19,** 3: 295–410 (September).
1978 *Complex Organizations*, St. Paul, Minn.: West Publishing Co.

Hulin, C. L., and M. R. Blood
1968 "Job Enlargement, Individual Differences, and Worker Responses," *Psychological Bulletin*, **69:** 41–55.

Inkson, J., et al.
1970 "A Comparison of Organizational Structure and Managerial Roles," *Journal of Management Studies*, **7:** 347–63.

Jahoda, M., M. Deutsch, and S. W. Cook (eds.)
1951 *Research Methods in Social Relations*, New York: Dryden

Jennings, H.
1960 "Sociometric Choice Processes in Personality and Group Formation," in J. L. Moreno (ed.), *The Sociometric Reader*, New York: The Free Press.

Johns, Ray, and David Demarche
1957 *Community Organization and Agency Responsibility*, New York: Associated Press.

Jurkovich, Ray
1974 "A Core Typology of Organizational Environments," *Administrative Science Quarterly*, **19,** 3: 380–89 (September).

Kadushin, Charles
1975 "A Conceptual Introduction to the Study of Networks," New York: Bureau of Applied Social Research, Columbia University, Unpublished Working Paper.

Kaplan, Abraham
1964 *The Conduct of Inquiry: Methodology for Behavioral Science*, New York: Chandler.

Katz, Daniel, and Robert L. Kahn
1978 *The Social Psychology of Organizations*, 2nd edition, New York: Wiley (first edition published 1966).

Katz, L., and J. H. Powell
1953 "A Proposed Index of the Conformity of One Sociometric Measurement to Another," *Psychometrika*, **18:** 249–56.

Kerlinger, F. N.
1973 *Foundations of Behavior Research*, New York: Holt, Rinehart and Winston.

Khandwalla, Pradip N.
1977 *The Design of Organizations*, New York: Harcourt, Brace, Jovanovich.

Kimberly, John R.
1977 "Organization Size and the Structuralist Perspective: A Review, Critique and Proposal," *Administrative Science Quarterly*, **21:** 571 (December).

Klonglan, Gerald E., Richard D. Warren, and Judy M. Winkelpleck
1973 "Inter-Organizational Measurement Differences Between Hierarchical Levels of Organizations," presented at the Rural Sociological Society Meeting, College Park, Maryland (March 30).

Komorita, S. S.
1963 "Attitude Content, Intensity, and the Neutral Point on a Likert Scale," *Journal of Social Psychology*, **61:** 327–34.

Komorita, S. S., and W. K. Graham
1965 "Number of Scale Points and the Reliability of Scales," *Educational and Psychological Measurement*, **4:** 987–95.

Lammers, C. J.
1968 "Power and Participation in Decision Making in Formal Organizations," *American Journal of Sociology*, **73:** 201–16 (September).

Lawler, Edward E., L. A. Koplin, T. F. Young, and J. A. Fadem
1968 "Inequity Reduction over Time in an Induced Overpayment Situation," *Organizational Behavior and Human Performance*, **3:** 253–68.

Lawrence, Paul R., and Jay W. Lorsch
1967 "Differentiation and Integration in Complex Organizations," *Administrative Science Quarterly*, **12:** 1–47 (June).

Lazarsfeld, Paul F., and H. Menzel
1969 "On the Relation between Individual and Collective Properties," in Amitai Etzioni (ed.), *A Sociological Reader in Complex Organizations*, New York: Holt, Rinehart and Winston.

Leavitt, Harold J.
1951 "Some Effects of Certain Communication Patterns on Group Performance," *Journal of Abnormal and Social Psychology*, **46,** 38–50.

Lessnoff, M. H.
1968 "Parsons' System Problems," *Sociological Review*, **16:** 185–215 (July).

Levine, Sol, and Paul E. White
1961 "Exchange as a Conceptual Framework for the Study of Interorganizational Relationships," *Administrative Science Quarterly*, **5:** 583–601 (March).

Levine, Sol, Paul E. White, and Benjamin D. Paul
1963 "Community Interorganizational Problems in Providing Medical Care and Social Services," *American Journal of Public Health*, **53,** 8: 1183–95.

Lewin, Kurt
1947 "Group Decision and Social Changes," in T. Newcomb and E. Hartley (eds.), *Readings in Social Psychology*, New York: Holt, Rinehart and Winston.

Likert, Rensis
1967 *The Human Organization: Its Management and Value*, New York: McGraw-Hill.

Lissitz, Robert W., and Samuel B. Green
1975 "Effect of the Number of Scale Points on Reliability: A Monte Carlo Approach," *Journal of Applied Psychology*, **60,** 1: 10–13 (February).

Liston, Jennie S., and Andrew H. Van de Ven
1976 *Community-Planned Programs for Children: Do They Work?*, Austin: Texas Department of Community Affairs.

Litwak, Eugene
1961 "Models of Bureaucracy Which Permit Conflict," *American Journal of Sociology*, **67:** 177–84 (September).

Litwak, Eugene, and Lydia F. Hylton
1962   "Interorganizational Analysis: A Hypothesis on Co-ordinating Agencies," *Administrative Science Quarterly*, **6**: 395–420 (March).

Litwak, Eugene and Jerald Rothman
1970   "Towards the Theory and Practice of Coordination Between Formal Organizations," in William Rosengren and Mark Lefton (eds.), *Organization and Clients*, Columbus, Ohio: Charles E. Merrill.

Locke, E. A.
1976   "The Nature and Causes of Job Satisfaction," Chapter 30 in Marvin D. Dunnette (ed.), *Handbook of Industrial and Organizational Psychology*, Chicago, Ill.: Rand-McNally.

Lord, F. M., and M. R. Novick
1968   *Statistical Theories of Mental Test Scores*, Reading, Mass: Addison-Wesley.

Maas, H. S.
1950   "Personal and Group Factors in Leaders' Social Perception," *Journal of Abnormal and Social Psychology*, **45**: 54–63.

Mackenzie, Kenneth D.
1966   "Structural Centrality in Communications Networks," *Psychometrika*, **31**, 1 (March).

MacMillan, Ian C.
1978   *Strategy Formulation: Political Concepts*, St. Paul, Minn.: West Publishing Co.

Madge, J.
1965   *The Tools of Social Science*, New York: Anchor Books.

Maier, N. R. F.
1964   "Maximizing Personal Creativity Through Better Problem-Solving," *Personnel Administration*, **27**: 14–18 (January/February).

March, James G. and Johan P. Olsen
1976   *Ambiguity and Choice in Organizations*, Olso, Norway: Universitetsforlaget.

March, James G., and Herbert A. Simon
1958   *Organizations*, New York: Wiley.

Marrett, Cora Bagley
1971   "On the Specification of Interorganizational Dimensions," *Sociology and Social Research*, **56**: 83–99 (October).

Matell, M. S., and J. Jacoby
1971   "Is There an Optimal Number of Alternatives for Likert Scale Items? Study I: Reliability and Validity," *Educational and Psychological Measurement*, **31**: 657–74.

McGrath, Joseph E.
1976   "Stress and Behavior in Organizations," Chapter 31 in Marvin D. Dunnette (ed.), *Handbook of Industrial and Organizational Psychology*, Chicago, Ill.: Rand-McNally.

Melman, Seymore
1958   *Decision Making and Productivity*, Oxford: Blackwell.

534   BIBLIOGRAPHY

Miles, Raymond E., and Charles C. Snow
1978   *Organizational Strategy, Structure, and Process*, New York: McGraw-Hill.

Miles, Robert H., and Kim S. Cameron
1978   "Coffin Nails and Corporate Strategies: A Quarter-Century View of Organizational Adaptation to Environment in the U.S. Tobacco Industry," New Haven: Yale University, School of Organization and Management, Working Paper No. 3 (summer).

Miller, G. A.
1956   "The Magical Number Seven, Plus or Minus Two: Some Limits on Our Capacity for Processing Information," *Psychological Review*, 63: 81–97.

Miller, S. M.
1952   "The Participant Observer and 'Over-Rapport'," *American Sociological Review*, 17: 97–99 (February).

Miller, Walter B.
1958   "Inter-institutional Conflict as a Major Impediment to Delinquency Prevention," *Human Organization*, 17: 20–23 (fall).

Mintzberg, Henry
1977   "Patterns in Strategy Formation," Montreal: McGill University Faculty of Management, Working Paper (August).

Mitchell, James Clyde (ed.)
1969   *Social Networks in Urban Situations*, Manchester, England: University of Manchester Press.

Mitroff, Ian I. and T. R. Featheringham
1974   "On Systemic Problem Solving and the Error of the Third Kind," *Behavioral Science*, 19, 6: 383–93 (November).

Mohr, Lawrence B.
1971   "Organizational Technology and Organizational Structure," *Administrative Science Quarterly*, 16, 4: 444–59 (December).
1973   "The Concept of Organizational Goal, "*American Political Science Review*, 67: 470–81 (June).

Morgan, Marilyn A.
1977   "The Relative Impact of Job Histories on Career Outcome Variables," Unpublished Doctoral Dissertation, Evanston, Ill.: Northwestern University, Graduate School of Management.

Morris, Robert
1963   "Basic Factors in Planning for the Coordination of Health Services—Part 1, Part 2," *American Journal of Public Health*, 53: 248–59 (February) and 53: 462–72 (March).

Morse, J., and J. Lorsch
1970   "Beyond Theory," *Harvard Business Review*, 61–68 (May/June).

Nadler, David A.
1977   *Feedback and Organization Development: Using Data-Based Methods*, Reading, Mass.: Addison-Wesley.

Nemiroff, Paul M., and David L. Ford, Jr.
1976   "Task Effectiveness and Human Fulfillment in Organizations: A Review and Development of a Conceptual Contingency Model," *Academy of Management Review*, 1, 4: 69–82 (October).

Normann, Richard
1971 "Organizational Innovativeness: Product Variation and Reorientation," *Administrative Science Quarterly*, **16:** 203–25.

Nunnally, Jum C.
1967 *Psychometric Theory*, New York: McGraw-Hill.

Oldham, Greg R., J. Richard Hackman, and Jone L. Pearce
1976 "Conditions Under Which Employees Respond Positively to Enriched Work," *Journal of Applied Psychology*, **61:** 395–403 (August).

O'Reilly, Charles A. III, and Karlene H. Roberts
1975 "Information Filtration in Organizations: Three Experiments," *Organizational Behavior and Human Performance*, **14,** 1: 144–150.

Osborn, Richard N., and James G. Hunt
1974 "Environment and Organizational Effectiveness," *Administrative Science Quarterly*, **19,** 2: 231–46 (June).

O'Toole, R., et al.
1972 *The Cleveland Rehabilitation Complex: A Study of Inter-Agency Coordination*, Cleveland, Ohio: Vocational Guidance and Rehabilitation Services.

Parsons, Talcott
1960 *Structure and Process in Modern Societies*, New York: The Free Press.

1962 *Toward A General Theory of Action*, New York: Harper and Row.

Parsons, Talcott, and Neal J. Smelser
1956 *Economy and Society*, Glencoe, Ill.: Free Press.

Payne, Roy, and Derek S. Pugh
1976 "Organizational Structure and Climate," in Marvin D. Dunnette (ed.), *Handbook of Industrial and Organizational Psychology*, Chicago, Ill.: Rand-McNally College Publishing.

Pennings, Johannes M.
1973 "Measures of Organizational Structure: A Methodological Note," *American Journal of Sociology*, **79,** 3: 686–704 (November).

Peres, Richard
1978 *Dealing with Employment Discrimination*, New York: McGraw-Hill.

Perlman, Robert, and Arnold Gurin
1972 *Community Organization and Social Planning*, New York: Wiley.

Perrow, Charles B.
1967 "A Framework for the Comparative Analysis of Organizations," *American Sociological Review*, **32:** 194–208 (April).

Pfeffer, Jeffrey
1978 *Organizational Design*, Arlington Heights, Ill.: AHM Publishing.

Pfeffer, Jeffrey, and Gerald R. Salancik
1974 "Organizational Decision Making as a Political Process: The Case of a University Budget," *Administrative Science Quarterly*, **19,** 2: 135–51 (June).

1978 *The External Control of Organizations: A Resource Dependence Perspective*, New York: Harper and Row.

Pierce, Jon L.
1978 "Employee Affective Responses to Work Unit Structure and Job Design:

A Test of an Intervening Variable," unpublished paper, Duluth: University of Minnesota, School of Business and Economics.

Pierce, Jon L., and Randall B. Dunham
1976 "Task Design: A Literature Review," *Academy of Management Review*, 1: 83–97 (October).

Porat, A., and J. Haas
1969 "Information Effects on Decision-Making," *Behavioral Science*, 14: 98–104.

Porter, Lyman W.
1958 "Differential Self Perceptions of Management Personnel and Line Workers," *Journal of Applied Psychology*, 42: 105–9.

Porter, Lyman W., and Edward E. Lawler III
1965 "Properties of Organization Structure in Relation to Job Attitudes and Job Behavior," *Psychological Bulletin*, 64: 23–51.

Porter, Lyman W., Edward E. Lawler III, and J. Richard Hackman
1975 *Behavior in Organizations*, New York: McGraw-Hill.

Porter, Lyman W., and Karlene H. Roberts
1976 "Communication in Organizations," in Marvin D. Dunnette (ed.), *Handbook of Industrial and Organizational Psychology*, Chicago, Ill.: Rand-McNally, pp. 1553–90.

Presthus, Robert V.
1962 *The Organizational Society*, New York: Knopf.

Pugh, D. S., D. J. Hickson, C. R. Hinings, K. M. MacDonald, C. Turner, and T. Lupton
1963 "A Conceptual Scheme for Organizational Analysis," *Administrative Science Quarterly*, 8, 3: 289–315 (December).

Pugh, D. S., D. J. Hickson, C. R. Hinings, and C. Turner
1968 "Dimensions of Organization Structure," *Administrative Science Quarterly*, 13: 65–105.

1969 "The Context of Organization Structure," *Administrative Science Quarterly*, 14: 91–114 (March).

Rand, A.
1964 "The Objectivist Ethics," in A. Rand (ed.), *The Virtue of Selfishness*, New York: Signet, pp. 13–35.

Read, William H.
1962 "Upward Communication in Industrial Hierarchies," *Human Relations*, 15: 3–16 (February).

Reid, William J.
1964 "Interagency Coordination in Delinquency Prevention and Control," *Social Service Review*, 38: 418–28 (December).

Rieker, Patricia, Joseph Morrissey, and Patrick Horan
1974 "Interorganizational Relations: A Critique of Theory and Method," Prepared for an Organizations Day Round-Table Presentation at the American Sociological Association, Montreal, Canada (August).

Roberts, Karlene H., and Charles A. O'Reilly III
1974 "Measuring Organizational Communication," *Journal of Applied Psychology*, 59, 3: 321–26 (June).

Rogers, Everett M., and D. K. Bhowmik
1970 "Homophily-Heterophily: Relational Concepts for Communication Research," *Public Opinion Quarterly*, 34: 523-38 (winter, 70-71).

Rogers, Everett M., and F. Floyd Schoemaker
1971 *Communication of Innovations*, New York: The Free Press.

Rosen, S., and A. Tesser
1970 "On Reluctance to Communicate Undesirable Information: The MUM Effect," *Sociometry*, 33: 253-63.

Rossi, Peter
1957 "Community Decision Making," *Administrative Science Quarterly*, 1: 415-43 (March).

Rumelt, Richard
1974 "Strategy, Structure and Economic Performance," Boston, Mass.: Harvard Business School, Division of Research.

Salancik, Gerald R., and Jeffrey Pfeffer
1974 "The Bases and Use of Power in Organizational Decision Making: The Case of a University," *Administrative Science Quarterly*, 19, 4: 453-73 (December).

Samuel, Yitzhak, and Bilha F. Mannheim
1970 "A Multi Dimensional Approach Toward a Typology of Bureaucracy," *Administrative Science Quarterly*, 15, 2: 216-28 (June).

Samuelson, Paul A.
1948 *Economics*. New York: McGraw-Hill.

Scheuch, Erwin K.
1969 "Social Context and Industrial Behavior," in M. Dogan and S. Rokkan (eds.), *Quantitative Ecological Analysis in the Social Sciences*, Cambridge, Mass.: The M.I.T. Press, pp. 133-56.

Schmidt, Stuart M., and Thomas A. Kochan
1977 "Interorganizational Relationships: Patterns and Motivations," *Administrative Science Quarterly*, 22, 2: 220-344 (June).

Scott, W. Richard
1976 "On the Effectiveness of Studies of Organizational Effectiveness," Paper presented at the Symposium on Organizational Effectiveness, Graduate School of Industrial Administration, Carnegie Mellon University, Pittsburg, Penn. (June).

1977 "Effectivenss of Organizational Effectiveness Studies," in Paul S. Goodman, Johannes M. Pennings and Associates (eds.), *New Perspectives on Organizational Effectiveness*, San Francisco, Calif.: Jossey-Bass, pp. 63-95.

Seidler, John
1974 "On Using Informants: A Technique For Collecting Quantitative Data and Controlling Measurement Error in Organization Analysis," *American Sociological Review*, 39: 816-31 (December).

Shaw, Marvin E.
1964 "Communication Networks," in L. Berkowitz (ed.), *Advances in Experimental Social Psychology*, New York: Academic.

Shull, Fremont A., Jr., Andre L. Delbecq, and L. L. Cummings
1970 *Organizational Decision Making*, New York: McGraw-Hill.

Simon, Herbert A.
1946 "The Proverbs of Administration," *Public Administration Review*, **6:** 53–67 (Winter).
1957 "The Compensation of Executives," *Sociometry*, **20:** 32–35.
1961 *Administrative Behavior*, 2nd edition, New York: Macmillan.
1977 *The New Science of Management Decision*, Revised edition, Englewood Cliffs, N.J.: Prentice-Hall.

Smith, Adam
1937 *The Wealth of Nations*, New York: Random House.

Smith, Patricia C., L. M. Kendall, and C. L. Hulin
1969 *The Measurement of Satisfaction in Work and Retirement: A Strategy for the Study of Attitudes*, Chicago, Ill.: Rand-McNally.

Spitalieri, Peter, Marcel Genet, and Andrew H. Van de Ven
1978 "A Comparison of Procedures for Aggregating Individual Responses to the Level of Organizational Units in the 1975 Organization Assessment Instruments," Philadelphia: University of Pennsylvania, The Wharton School, Working Paper.

Stagner, Ross
1969 "Corporate Decision Making: An Empirical Study," *Journal of Applied Psychology*, **53:** 1–13.

Starbuck, William H.
1976 "Organizations and Their Environments," in Marvin D. Dunnette (ed.), *Handbook of Industrial and Organizational Psychology*, Chicago, Ill.: Rand-McNally, pp. 1069–1123.

Steers, Richard M., and R. T. Mowday
1977 "The Motivational Properties of Tasks," *Academy of Management Review*, **2:** 645–58 (October).

Steiner, George A., and John B. Miner
1977 *Management Policy and Strategy: Text, Readings, and Cases*, New York: Macmillan.

Suchman, E.
1967 *Evaluation Research*, New York: Russell Sage.
1971 "Action for What? A Critique of Evaluation Research," in R. O'Toole (ed.), *The Organization, Management, and Tactics of Social Research*, Cambridge, Mass.: Schenkman.

Symonds, P. M.
1924 "On the Loss of Reliability in Ratings Due to Coarseness of the Scale," *Journal of Experimental Psychology*, **7:** 456–61 (December).
1931 *Diagnosing Personality and Conduct*, New York: Appleton-Century-Crofts.

Tannenbaum, Arnold S.
1965 "Unions," in J. March (ed.), *Handbook of Organizations*, Chicago, Ill.: Rand-McNally.
1968 *Control in Organizations*, New York: McGraw-Hill.

Taylor, Frederick W.
1911 *The Principles of Scientific Management*, New York: Harper and Row.

Taylor, James C., and David G. Bowers
1972   *Survey of Organizations: A Machine-Scored Standardized Questionnaire Instrument*, Ann Arbor, Mich.: Malloy Lithographing.

Terreberry, Shirley
1968   "The Evolution of Organizational Environments," *Administrative Science Quarterly*, **12**, 4: 590–613 (March).

Thomas, Kenneth W.
1976   "Conflict and Conflict Management," in Marvin D. Dunnette (ed.), *Handbood of Industrial and Organizational Psychology*, Chicago, Ill.: Rand-McNally.

Thompson, James D.
1967   *Organizations In Action*, New York: McGraw-Hill.

Thompson, James D., and W. J. McEwen
1958   "Organizational Goals and Environment: Goal-Setting as an Interaction Process," *American Sociological Review*, **23**: 23–31 (February).

Thompson, James D., and Arthur Tuden
1959   "Strategies, Structures, and Processes of Organizational Decision," in J. D. Thompson et al. (eds.), *Comparative Studies in Administration*, Pittsburgh, Penn.: University of Pittsburgh Press.

Thompson, Victor
1961   *Modern Organization*, New York: Knopf, pp. 152–77.

Thorndike, Edward L.
1939   "On the Fallacy of Inputting the Correlations Found for Groups to the Individuals or Smaller Groups Composing Them," *American Journal of Psychology*, **52**: 122–24 (January).

Tichy, Noel M.
1973   "An Analysis of Clique Formation and Structure in Organizations," *Administrative Science Quarterly*, **18**: 194–208.

Tichy, Noel M., and Charles Fombrun
1978   "Network Analysis in Organizational Settings," New York: Columbia University, Graduate School of Business, Research Paper No. 102A.

Timasheff, Nicholas
1967   *Sociological Theory: Its Nature and Growth.* New York: Random House.

Trist, Eric L.
1970   "A Socio-Technical Critique of Scientific Management," Paper presented at the Edinburgh Conference on the Impact of Science and Technology, Edinburgh University (May 24–26).

Trist, Eric L., and K. W. Bamforth
1951   "Some Social and Psychological Consequences of the Longwall Method of Coal Mining," *Human Relations*, **4**: 3–38.

Turk, Herman
1973   "Comparative Urban Structure from an Interorganizational Perspective," *Administrative Science Quarterly*, **18**: 37–55 (March).

Turner, A. N., and Paul R. Lawrence
1965   *Industrial Jobs and the Worker: An Investigation of Response to Task Attributes*, Boston, Mass.: Harvard University Press.

Tushman, Michael L.
1977 "Special Boundary Roles in the Innovation Process," *Administrativ* *Science Quarterly*, **22:** 587–605.

Tyler, William B.
1973 "Measuring Organizational Specialization: The Concept of Role Variety," *Administrative Science Quarterly*, **18,** 3: 383–92 (September).

Van de Ven, Andrew H.
1974 *Group Decision Making and Effectiveness*, Kent State, Ohio: Kent State University Press.

1976a "A Framework for Organization Assessment," *Academy of Management Review*, **1,** 1: 64–78 (January).

1976b "Equally Efficient Structural Variations within Organizations," Chapter 6 in R. H. Kilmann, L. R. Pondy, and D. P. Sleven (eds.), *The Management of Organization Design: Research and Methodology*, Vol. 2, New York: North-Holland, Ellsevier, pp. 155–70.

1976c "On the Nature, Formation, and Maintenance of Relations Among Organizations," *Academy of Management Review*, **1,** 4: 24–36 (October).

1977 "A Panel Study on the Effects of Task Uncertainty, Interdependence, and Size on Unit Decision Making," *Organization and Administrative Sciences*, **8,** 2: 237–253.

Van de Ven, Andrew H. and Andre L. Delbecq
1974 "A Task Contingent Model of Work-Unit Structure," *Administrative Science Quarterly*, **19,** 2: 183–97 (June).

Van de Ven, Andrew H., Andre L. Delbecq, and Richard Koenig, Jr.
1976 "Determinants of Coordination Modes within Organizations," *American Sociological Review*, **41:** 322–38 (April).

Van de Ven, Andrew H., Ben E. Dowell, and Diane L. Ferry
1977 "Measurement of Unit Task, Structure and Process in the Organization Assessment Instrument," Paper presented at the National Academy of Management Conference, Orlando, Florida (August).

Van de Ven, Andrew H., Benjamin Dowell, Martin Katz, and Diane Ferry
1975 "A Psychometric Evaluation of the 1973 Organization Assessment Instruments," Working Paper, The Wharton School, University of Pennsylvania.

Van de Ven, Andrew H., Dennis Emmett, and Richard Koenig, Jr.
1974 "Frameworks for Inter-organizational Analysis," *Organization and Administrative Sciences Journal*, **5,** 1: 113–29 (spring).

Van de Ven, Andrew H., and Richard Koenig, Jr.
1976 "A Process Model for Program Planning and Evaluation," *Journal of Economics and Business*, **28,** 3: 161–70.

Van de Ven, Andrew H., Mary Joan Treis, George Esser, and Diane L. Ferry
1976 "1975 Wisconsin Job Service Organization Assessment: Organization and Performance Efficiency of District Offices," Report prepared for Wisconsin Job Service Division of the Department of Industry, Labor and Human Relations, Madison, Wis.

√an de Ven, Andrew H., Gordon Walker, and Jennie Liston
1979 "Coordination Patterns within an Inter-Organizational Network," *Human Relations*, **32**, 1: 19–36.

Von Bertalanffy, Ludwig
1972 "The History and Status of General Systems Theory," *Academy of Management Journal*, **15**, 4: 407–26 (December).

Wanous, John P.
1974 "Individual Differences and Reactions to Job Characteristics," *Journal of Applied Psychology*, **59**: 616–22 (October).

Warren, Roland
1967 "The Interorganizational Field as a Focus for Investigation," *Administrative Science Quarterly*, **12**: 396–419 (December).
1971 *Truth, Love and Social Change*, Chicago, Ill.: Rand-McNally.

Warren, Roland, Ann Bergunder, J. W. Newton, and Stephen Rose
1971 "The Interactions of Community Decision Organizations: Some Conceptual Considerations and Empirical Findings," in Anant R. Negandhi (ed.), *Organization Theory in an Interorganization Perspective*, Kent, Ohio: Comparative Administration Research Institute, Kent State University, pp. 35–52.

Warren, Roland, Stephen M. Rose, and Ann F. Bergunder
1974 *The Structure of Urban Reform*, Toronto: D.C. Heath.

Webb, E. J., D. T. Cambell, R. D. Schwartz, and L. Sechrest
1966 *Unobtrusive Measures: Non-Reactive Research in the Social Sciences*, Chicago, Ill.: Rand-McNally.

Weber, Max
1947 *The Theory of Social and Economic Organizations*, Trans. by A. M. Henderson and Talcott M. Parsons, New York: The Free Press.

Weick, Karl E.
1969 *The Social Psychology of Organizing*, Reading, Mass.: Addison-Wesley.
1976 "On Re-Punctuating the Problem of Organizational Effectiveness," Paper presented at the symposium on Organizational Effectiveness, Graduate School of Industrial Administration, Carnegie-Mellon University, Pittsburgh (June).
1977 "Enactment Processes in Organizations," Chapter 8 in Barry M. Staw and Gerald R. Salancik (eds.), *New Directions in Organizational Behavior*, Chicago, Ill.: St. Clair Press.

Whisler, Thomas L., Harold Meyer, Bernard H. Baum, Peter F. Sorenson, Jr.
1967 "Centralization of Organizational Control: An Empirical Study of Its Meaning and Measurement," *Journal of Business*, **40**, 1: 10–26.

White, Paul, Sol Levine, and George Vlasek
1971 "Exchange as a Conceptual Framework for Understanding Inter-Organizational Relationships: Applications to Non-Profit Organizations," Paper presented at the Comparative Administration Research Institute Conference, Kent State University.

Wilensky, Harold
1967   *Organizational Intelligence: Knowledge and Policy in Industry and Government*, New York: Basic Books.

Williamson, Oliver E.
1975   *Markets and Hierarchies*, New York: The Free Press.

Wood, M. T.
1973   "Power Relationships and Group Decision–Making in Organizations," *Psychological Bulletin*, **79**: 280.

Woodward, Joan
1965   *Industrial Organization: Theory and Practice*, London: Oxford University Press.

Wrigley, Leonard
1970   "Divisional Autonomy and Diversification," Unpublished Doctoral Dissertation, Boston, Mass.: Harvard Business School.

Yuchtman, Ephraim, and Stanley E. Seashore
1967   "A System Resource Approach to Organizational Effectiveness," *American Sociological Review*, **32**: 891–903 (December).

Zelditch, Morris, Jr.
1962   "Some Methodological Problems of Field Studies," *American Journal of Sociology*, **67**: 566–76 (March), note **68**: 250 (September).

Zupanov, Josip, and Arnold S. Tannenbaum
1968   "The Distribution of Control in Some Yugoslav Industrial Organizations as Perceived by Members," in A. S. Tannenbaum (ed.), *Control in Organizations*, New York: McGraw-Hill, pp. 91–109.

Author Index

Subject Index

Note: Page numbers in italics refer to Appendix A citations.